THE
BUSINESS
OF MEDICINE

THE
BUSINESS
OF MEDICINE

THE EXTRAORDINARY HISTORY OF GLAXO,
A BABY FOOD PRODUCER,
WHICH BECAME ONE OF
THE WORLD'S MOST SUCCESSFUL
PHARMACEUTICAL COMPANIES

§

EDGAR JONES

Research assistant
JOHN SAVAGE

P

PROFILE BOOKS

First published in Great Britain in 2001 by
Profile Books Ltd
58A Hatton Garden
London ECIN 8LX
www.profilebooks.co.uk

Designed by Geoff Green Book Design, Cambridge

Typeset in Minion by MacGuru
info@macguru.org.uk

Printed and bound in Great Britain by
St Edmundsbury Press, Bury St Edmunds, Suffolk

A CIP catalogue record for this book is available from the British Library.

ISBN 1 86197 340 3

CONTENTS

LIST OF FIGURES

TABLES

§

LIST OF ABBREVIATIONS

§

A&H	Allen & Hanburys
ABPI	Association of the British Pharmaceutical Industry
AEU	Amalgamated Engineering Union
AHP	American Home Products
APST	Association of Professional Scientists and Technologists
ARP	Air Raid Precautions
ASTMS	Association of Professional Scientific, Technical and Managerial Staffs
AUEW	Amalgamated Union of Engineering Workers
BCG	Bacille Calmette-Guérin
BDH	The British Drug Houses
BMJ	*The British Medical Journal*
BNF	*The British National Formulary*
BP	board paper
CEO	chief executive officer
CNS	central nervous system
CSII	Centre for the Study of Industrial Innovation
CSL	Commonwealth Serum Laboratories
DBB	*Dictionary of Business Biography*
EPI	Edinburgh Pharmaceutical Industries
EPO	European Patent Office
FDA	Food and Drug Administration
FRS	Fellow of the Royal Society
GATT	General Agreement on Tariffs and Trade
GMWU	General and Municipal Workers Union
IFPMA	International Federation of Pharmaceutical Manufacturers Associations
JCNC	Joint Consultative and Negotiating Committees
LNER	London & North Eastern Railway

NEDO	National Economic Development Office
NUGMW	National Union of General and Municipal Workers
OTC	over-the-counter medicine
PAS	para aminosalicylic acid
PPRS	Pharmaceutical Price Regulation Scheme
PRO	Public Record Office
SKF	Smith Kline & French
TGWU	Transport and General Workers' Union
TRC	Therapeutic Research Corporation
TRIP	Trade Related Intellectual Property Rights
VPRS	Voluntary Price Regulation Scheme

FOREWORD

by Sir Richard Sykes

§

WHEN, IN 1873, Joseph Nathan became the sole proprietor of a general merchants business in Wellington, New Zealand, he can have had little inkling of the spectacular development that was to take place over the next hundred and thirty years. However, it was his son, Alec Nathan, who presided over two turning points in the history of the company. First, in charge of the fledgling Glaxo Department, he established its infant dried milk as a brand leader in the UK and the Empire. Secondly, he led the strategic change in direction by which Glaxo Laboratories became a manufacturer of innovative medicines, establishing a reputation in the fields of vitamins and antibiotics. His maxim, prophetically, was 'It can be done!'

One of the key elements of Glaxo's success has been a readiness to get things done while readily embracing change. The company has been consistently associated with dynamic elements of the economy, whether infant foods in the 1900s, penicillin in the 1940s, or respiratory and anti-ulcer medicines in the 1970s and 1980s, and today is playing a full part in the burgeoning genetic revolution. This book deals in depth with the years from 1935 to 1985, a period of intense growth for the company, with a concluding chapter to bring the story of this remarkable company through the '90s to the present day. The mergers with Wellcome in 1995 and SmithKline Beecham in 2000 have reflected the group's determination to remain at the forefront of scientific innovation and at the very top of a rapidly changing international pharmaceutical industry.

Yet despite the increasing tempo of change, Glaxo has retained certain fundamentals that owe much to the founding Nathans, and to Alec in particular. These include a desire to perform in a professional manner, a meritocratic culture, an emphasis on high-quality products and a global reach. These are qualities that should endure into the twenty-first century.

Our thanks go to Edgar Jones for his scholarly study of the company. I hope that the many friends, associates, customers and employees – past and present – of Glaxo, and indeed Glaxo Wellcome, around the world will enjoy reading this history of a company with a distinguished record of achievement.

ACKNOWLEDGEMENTS

❦

M Y THANKS are due to Sir Richard Sykes, chairman of Glaxo Wellcome, for supporting the completion and publication of this history. The study itself has a lengthy and complex history. It was commissioned from Terry Gourvish, director of the Business History Unit at the London School of Economics, by Sir Paul Girolami in 1992, and owes its existence to the dedication and interest of both individuals. Dr Gourvish appointed myself as the author and John Savage as the research assistant. The history was managed at Glaxo by Nicholas Morris, company secretary, and the research guided by a Steering Committee whose members included Stephen Cowden, Donald Derx, Nick Godman, Terry Gourvish, Nicholas Morris and Sir Geoffrey Owen. They are each owed a debt of gratitude for their advice and support. Subsequently, Simon Sargent took responsibility for the management of the project, and thanks are due for his contribution and interest. The study remained under the auspices of the Business History Unit until July 1996 when Glaxo brought the project in-house. Henceforth, much of the practical work of guiding the history to its completion fell to Simon Bicknell, whose dry humour was much appreciated. Geoffrey Potter has been responsible for the book's final form and launch, while David Holmes has managed the latter stages of the project. They have all been supportive and enthusiastic contributors to the project.

Sir Austin Bide and David Smart have carefully read several versions of the text and their combined expertise and experience has proved invaluable. Sir David Jack commented in detail on the research and development chapters and I am grateful to him for his sustained efforts. Dr Tom Walker, Professor Patrick Humphrey and Dr John Wood also helped greatly with the scientific passages. Without Dr John Hunt's careful reading of the entire draft, it would have contained a significant number of errors and omissions. I also thank those former non-executive directors of Glaxo who provided a further perspective on the group. They included Lord Cuckney, Lord Dahrendorf, Lord Fraser, Lord Howe, Jeremy Raisman, and Sir Richard Southwood.

A special note of thanks is owed to John Savage, research assistant on the project for over three years. His consistent interest, enthusiasm and careful attention to detail were invaluable. Not least, he proved an amiable and amusing companion on lengthy flights and journeys to Glaxo's many factories and laboratories.

A debt of gratitude is owed to those individuals who have never worked for Glaxo Wellcome but who nevertheless offered their help. They include Sir Arthur Knight, formerly chairman of Courtaulds, Adrian Towse, director of the Office of Health Economics, Mrs F. J. Wilkins, Dr Joan Skinner, Dr A. W. McKenzie and Dr Dorothy Vollum.

I have received great assistance from the directors and staff of Glaxo Wellcome, past and present; so many that they defy a list. However, those retired members of the company who kindly agreed to be interviewed are recorded in the 'Sources'. The group's records managers and archivists have been a consistent source of help and encouragement. I thank John Davies and Sarah Flynn, based at Greenford, and Glen Burchett, corporate archivist at Research Triangle Park, who was a kind and helpful host. I have also received much assistance and advice from former historians of Glaxo and its subsidiaries, notably Dr Richard Davenport-Hines and Judy Slinn, and from Dr Geoffrey Tweedale, author of a study of Allen & Hanburys.

Most of the manuscript was typed by Alex Hodson, and she is owed much thanks for her care, expertise and perseverance. Other parts have been conscientiously completed by Andrea Grahame and Susan Patterson. I also acknowledge the contribution of the publishers, in particular Penny Daniel and Andrew Franklin, and my copy editor, Trevor Horwood, who between them guided the book from manuscript to launch. I also thank John Murray (Publishers) for permission to quote from John Betjeman's poem 'Middlesex'.

Although many have contributed to this history, the responsibility for any errors or omissions that remain in the final text is mine.

Edgar Jones
London, December 2000

PREFACE

A desire to take medicine is, perhaps, the great feature which
distinguishes man from other animals.

Sir William Osler (1849–1919)[1]

GLAXO WELLCOME was one of the world's largest pharmaceutical
companies with sales of £7,983 million in 1998, generating profits of
£2,683 million, and represented one of Britain's outstanding examples of industrial success.[2] With a truly global organisation, it has been responsible for the discovery of a number of major new medicines for the
treatment of asthma, peptic ulcers, skin disorders and bacterial infections.[3]
However, it has not always been so. Glaxo Laboratories had at one time
been a mere department in the affairs of Joseph Nathan & Co., general
merchants trading between London and New Zealand, set up to manufacture and sell dried milk powder.[4] Under the leadership of Alec Nathan, the
youngest son of the founder, the business flourished. His innate entrepreneurial flair and marketing skills drove up sales of Glaxo milk powder after
an inauspicious launch and eventually the department came to dominate
its parent. A modern factory and offices were built at Greenford in 1935 and
a new subsidiary, Glaxo Laboratories, was created to reflect its new-found
importance. This book is the history of the first fifty years of Glaxo from its
foundation as a private limited liability company until 1985 when, on the
retirement of Sir Austin Bide as chairman, it had become one of the leading pharmaceutical groups in the world.

When Glaxo Laboratories was established in 1935 it was not a science-
driven business, although the new factory at Greenford incorporated
analytical laboratories to test the purity of its food products and to experiment in the field of vitamin supplements. It was in these two areas that

university-trained chemists and pharmacists were recruited and formed the basis of an embryonic team which was later directed to work on antibiotics. The imperative demand for penicillin to treat wounded servicemen during the Second World War drew Glaxo Laboratories into pharmaceuticals proper, though there was no thought of abandoning its infant-food business. Having established a beachhead in science-based medicines, Sir Harry Jephcott, who had succeeded Alec Nathan as chairman in June 1946, continued to license both products and manufacturing processes from US competitors as a way of developing the business in peacetime. As a result, Glaxo Laboratories broadened its focus in the field of antibiotics, producing a range of cephalosphorins – anti-bacterial medicines effective against a variety of infections including septicaemia, pneumonia and peritonitis. Despite Jephcott's reluctance to commit comparatively scarce resources to innovative research, the Greenford scientists entered the field of steroid chemistry and in 1963 their labours bore fruit with the launch of the company's first truly novel compound, betamethasone valerate (Betnovate), a potent topical treatment for skin conditions such as eczema. Not only did it prove to be of significant therapeutic value, it also rapidly became one of the group's most important products in terms of sales. By the time that Glaxo Group was established in December 1961, the organisation could rightly be described as a diversified pharmaceutical business.

Fearful of competition from the United States, where companies were in general far larger and often provided with generous research budgets, Jephcott sought to protect the firm's many small and medium-sized pharmaceutical companies that had grown up in the UK by absorbing them under the Glaxo umbrella. Although they became subsidiaries, Jephcott offered a personal guarantee of autonomy, allowing them to continue to trade much as before. Principal among these were Allen & Hanburys, taken over in 1958, and Evans Medical, taken over in 1961. Their acquisition advanced Glaxo's development as a pharmaceutical company proper, with Allen & Hanburys proving of particular significance as the laboratories at Ware under Dr David Jack went on to discover two of the group's most successful medicines: salbutamol (Ventolin), launched in 1969, and ranitidine (Zantac), introduced in 1981. It was income from these products, in particular from ranitidine, which became the highest selling prescription medicine of all time, that allowed the group to invest in modern research facilities, manufacturing plant and sales organisations beyond the UK and Commonwealth. Without the financial resources these medicines provided, it is doubtful whether Glaxo could have established itself as a major force in the US market without resorting to a merger with an indigenous competitor. Ventolin and Zantac provided the group with the commercial strength to adopt ambitious plans and to broaden its horizons across a world stage.

Once Glaxo Holdings had established its credentials as a significant player in the pharmaceutical industry, Paul Girolami, the group chief executive from 1981, took the strategic decision to focus its many activities within the field of research-based prescription medicines. In 1984, for example, as the first stage in this programme, the group's wholesaling business, Vestric, was sold, followed in 1985 by both Matburn (Holdings), a surgical engineering business, and Farley Health Products, which included the group's traditional portfolio of infant foods. Subsequently, Glaxo withdrew from the manufacture of generic medicines with the disposal of Evans Medical and in 1987 sold its veterinary subsidiary, Harefield Animal Health. The group's first mission statement, devised in 1987, reflected this strategic realignment: 'Glaxo is an integrated research based group of companies whose corporate purpose is the discovery, development, manufacture and marketing of safe, effective medicines of the highest quality.'[5] Curiously, the essential meaning in this statement was not so very different from that expressed by Sir Harry Jephcott in the mid 1950s:

> The policy of this company remains today just what it was at the time when we first entered the field of nutrition and medicine. We will market nothing without the implicit approval, both public and private, of medical authorities. All our goods must be of proven value and they must provide means of curing, better still of preventing, sickness and disease. It is not often that men and women employed to promote sales for the benefit of their company and themselves can do so in the certain knowledge, which we possess, that the outcome of their activities is at the same time to reduce the extent of the world's avoidable suffering and to increase the happiness of men, women and children everywhere.[6]

The goals defined by Jephcott were idealistic and derived from his paternalistic view of management in which a highly qualified executive elite (hence his selection of high-ranking civil servants for senior office) looked after the interests of those less favourably placed. The mission statement of Glaxo Wellcome left society to make its own decisions about the products that the group introduced, an approach more in tune with the market-driven style of the 1980s and 1990s.

Although an unbroken thread of continuity has run through Glaxo over the last thirty years, the group of the early 1960s was fundamentally different from that of the 1990s. Apart from its dramatic growth in size and territorial spread across the world, notably into the US and Japan, the crucial change has been the focusing, to the exclusion of everything else, of its activities into the discovery of novel medicines. As late as the 1970s Glaxo had a diversified range of interests including foods, veterinary products, whole-saling and distribution together with generic pharmaceuticals. In the early 1980s the company began to rationalise its activities, paring them down to the core and leaving only those that were the result of extensive scientific research and represented an incremental gain on existing treatments. This was a significant cultural shift. Under Jephcott, in a context of limited financial resources, the chemists at Greenford had struggled to gain approval for truly innovative projects. He preferred to license existing compounds and concentrate on their development and efficient manufacture rather than seek to discover wholly new molecules. It was not until Sir Alan Wilson, a scientist with an impressive pedigree in academic research, became chairman that resources were consistently committed to this field of endeavour. Henceforth expenditure rose in absolute terms and as a proportion of turnover. During the last two decades, modern large-scale laboratories have been constructed at Stevenage, Research Triangle Park in North Carolina and at Verona, while existing facilities at Greenford and Ware have been substantially rebuilt and expanded.

What, then, are the features that have endured throughout these thirty years of growth and change; ones that Jephcott himself would recognise? First, the name Glaxo remains, though now joined with that of SmithKline. Once the trade name of a product and now the style of a company, its long use and reputation have won the word a familiarity akin to 'tabloid', the term coined by Wellcome to describe many of its preparations. Although the symbols and colours employed on packaging have changed, the marketing names Glaxo Laboratories, Allen & Hanburys and Duncan Flockhart have been preserved because of their established appeal to prescribers. The group has remained a UK holding company with its headquarters in west London. Greenford was in many ways the spiritual home of Glaxo Laboratories with its purpose-built factory, offices and laboratory. It is significant that with the closure of Lansdowne House, the Berkeley Square head office, the group decided to relocate at Greenford.

An important element in the culture of the group was an unsnobbish and meritocratic attitude to all grades of staff. This originated with Alec Nathan, who had been brought to London in 1907 to revitalise the ailing Glaxo department. Born in Wellington, New Zealand, and brought up as a Jew, he was in many ways an outsider, who never adopted the mores of class and background that so bedevilled British society and management. Industrious and clear thinking, Nathan had a touching faith in human nature, writing in September 1923 in an open letter to staff that

the feverish chase for money and power is a brittle shell unless guided by a healthy kernel of wisdom and unselfish goodness ... It is better to be mistaken and deceived a thousand times than underrate once the nobleness of human nature or to miss once the opportunity of helping the other fellow. Without that ethical ideal and its practical everyday application you cannot progress ...[7]

This code of behaviour was adopted by Jephcott, Nathan's chosen successor. The son of a train driver, he, too, took little account of class or birth and both managers and scientists were judged by ability. This enduring characteristic of the group has played a significant, though unquantifiable, role in its success.

Although the history of medicine, and indeed the sub-specialism of pharmacology, have been widely explored, the pharmaceutical industry, and in particular the individual companies of which it is formed, remain neglected areas. In the past, scholars researching these topics were often forced to rely on documents in the public domain, such as annual reports and marketing material. This gap in the literature was partly a result of the secrecy adopted by some businesses during the 1960s and 1970s. Pressurised by governments, who believed them to be earning excessive profits and concerned to protect their vital scientific research from rivals, pharmaceutical companies were understandably reluctant to open their archives to external scrutiny. It may be significant, for instance, that the Wellcome Foundation, though acutely aware of its distinguished historical pedigree, never commissioned an objective study of its evolution as a commercial organisation. Yet with the development of agreed pricing strategies, tougher patent regulations and a need to demonstrate to regulators and doctors alike that their medicines are both efficacious and cost-effective, pharmaceutical companies have increasingly seen the merit in unbiased assessments of their development. In recent years histories have been published of May & Baker,[8] Smith & Nephew,[9] Allen & Hanburys,[10] the Norwegian company, Nycomed[11] and indeed of the foundations and growth of Glaxo to 1962.[12] But, these cover a small proportion of the total industry. This history is, therefore, an attempt to widen understanding and may serve to inspire other companies to open their doors to scholars. There is to date, for example, no objective study of any of the leading US pharmaceutical groups, despite their collective dominance of the global trade.

Birth and death are the defining fundamentals of human existence, and no event can exceed them. Glaxo has been closely involved with both almost from its foundation. Generations of mothers have fed their new-born infants with the group's dried milk products and the name 'Glaxo' became synonymous with nutrition for the very young. Fortified with vitamins during the 1920s and supplemented by other products such as Farex and

Glucose D, the company played a part in improving the health of the nation. That managers such as Alec Nathan and Jephcott took such pains to ensure the purity and quality of these infant foods proved to be of great commercial significance for the future. The name Glaxo was established in the minds of the public and the medical profession as being reliable and beneficial. When the company diversified into pharmaceuticals, doctors and patients alike accepted the transition without demur. A sure marketing foundation had been laid by Nathan with his promotion of infant foods and vitamin products. From encouraging life in newborns, Glaxo Laboratories broadened its focus to include combating death and disease as it entered the field of antibiotics and vaccines. Most, though not all, of the innovative medicines discovered by the group have had the aim of treating disorders that carry a significant mortality rate such as asthma, peptic ulcers, hypertension and resistant bacterial infections. Other medicines have been targeted towards recalcitrant and particularly unpleasant skin conditions, migraine attacks and intense nausea. In recognition of this sustained attack upon human disorders, the first television advertisement commissioned by Glaxo Wellcome, shown in June 1996, concluded with the statement:

> Man has no greater enemy than disease. Disease has no greater enemy than Glaxo Wellcome.

This, then, is the story of how a medium-sized UK manufacturer of infant foods was transformed into one of the world's leading pharmaceutical companies, one with a truly global network of sales, production and research facilities and responsible for the discovery of innovative medicines.

THE NATHANS AND THE
ORIGINS OF GLAXO

§

GLAXOSMITHKLINE, one of the world's largest pharmaceutical companies, began in the 1840s as a general store in Wellington, New Zealand. In January 1861 Jacob Joseph, who had founded the business, was joined in partnership by his brother-in-law, Joseph Edward Nathan. Ultimately, Nathan took command and turned what was little more than a shop into a significant commercial enterprise. Dealing in a wide variety of goods from drapery, clothing, shoes, ironmongery and crockery to wines and spirits, in 1877 Nathan constructed an impressive four-storey warehouse, then the largest building in Wellington. From 1900 onwards, the sale of dried milk from the company's creameries and dairies became an increasingly important element in the business. Exported to the UK as infant food, it was sold under the brand name 'Glaxo'. So profitable was the product that a Glaxo Department was set up. To monitor quality, an analytical laboratory was commissioned, run by Harry Jephcott, Nathan's first scientist. Jephcott was also alert to the possibility of new products emerging from nutritional science and, in 1924, obtained licences to manufacture vitamin D. Marketed as Ostelin, this was the Nathans' first pharmaceutical product, leading not only to a range of fortified foods but also to research in the field of vitamins. Such was the commercial significance of the Glaxo Department under the management of Alec Nathan that in 1935 it was formed into a private limited liability company, Glaxo Laboratories.

Glaxo was not unusual in entering the pharmaceutical industry by diversification; indeed, few of the major drugs companies were originally established as manufacturers of medicines. Amongst the world's leaders, Pfizer began life in 1849 as a supplier of chemicals and ingredients to the food and drink industry, being drawn into penicillin production as pioneers of deep fermentation techniques.[1] Merck, too, had its origins in a fine chemicals business at Darmstadt, which, in turn, could trace a lineage back to the seventeenth century.[2] The synthetic dye industry was also an important route for companies entering pharmaceuticals. Both Ciba and Geigy, independently set up at Basel in 1859, and Hoechst, founded in 1863 near Frankfurt, all began as makers of dyestuffs.[3]

There were, however, significant exceptions as businesses were also founded to take advantage of the advances in the embryonic science of pharmacology. In the UK these included Burroughs Wellcome, set up in 1880 by two Philadephia-trained pharmacists, and in Switzerland, F. Hoffman-La Roche, established in 1894 at Basel to make galenicals and other medicinal agents.[4] However, Allen & Hanburys could trace an even longer history of involvement in pharmaceuticals. In 1715, Sylvanus Bevan opened an apothecary's shop at No. 2 Plough Court, off Lombard Street, London, where he made his own medicinal preparations. The partnership eventually passed into the hands of William Allen and various members of the Hanbury family and diversified into milk and malted foods, vaccines, surgical instruments and operating tables.[5] Astra, too, the largest manufacturer of pharmaceuticals in Sweden, had been established in 1913 as a drugs company and developed its own research programme during the interwar period.[6]

Founding the business: Joseph Nathan & Co.

Glaxo Laboratories was originally a subsidiary of Joseph Nathan & Co., a family-owned firm of general merchants, established in Wellington, New Zealand. The founder, Joseph Edward Nathan, had been born in Houndsditch, east London, on 2 March 1835, the sixth son of a jobbing tailor, Edward Nathan, and his wife Rachel. Tradition has it that Edward was 'a charming old man with very little brains', whilst his partner 'was a very intelligent woman' with little formal education.[7] Edward Nathan earned a living by making up suits and other garments which he then loaded on to a trap and sold in the villages around London. From the age of twelve, Joseph accompanied his father, learning the rudiments of the tailoring trade.[8] At a relatively early age, Joseph appears to have exhibited business acumen, encouraging his father to wear a tail coat and silk hat to impress customers, though he failed to persuade him to export his clothes. Disillusioned by Edward's lack of ambition, Joseph left to work in a Houndsditch furniture store, whilst also enrolling at the Bishopsgate Institute to improve his scant knowledge.

In 1852, when Joseph Nathan was seventeen, his mother Rachel died. The grief he felt, combined with the realisation that his ambitions were unlikely to be realised in the East End, led Joseph to make a key decision. A year earlier gold had been discovered in Australia, at Ballarat near Melbourne, and the newspapers told stories of prospectors who had become rich overnight. An asthmatic, Joseph emigrated to seek a new living and to improve his ailing health. On 19 August 1853, he embarked on the *William Ackers*, a 330-ton bargue, bound for Melbourne. Arriving in December, Joseph set off for the goldfields, but met a fatherly policeman who suggested that he did not have the physique to survive the rigours of prospecting. Rather, he would be better advised returning to the city to open a supply store for prospective diggers.

1. *Edward Nathan (d. 1876), the Houndsditch tailor, photographed c. 1850. Joseph, eighth of his ten children, became exasperated by his father's lack of ambition and decided to seek his fortune abroad.*

Having family connections in Melbourne, Joseph retraced his steps and set up a business in Farmers Place, Little Collins Street. The small shop made money but, reliant upon goods shipped on credit from Houndsditch, earned only modest profits.

In the meantime, Joseph Nathan's eldest sister, Kate, married Jacob Joseph, a merchant. Jacob, despite being blind, had emigrated to New Zealand in 1840 and established a prosperous hardware business at Lambton Quay, Wellington.[9] In 1856 the young Nathan decided to visit his new brother-in-law and sailed in the *Zingari* for Christchurch. New Zealand was then far less developed than Australia and Wellington was a relatively young settlement. Jacob Joseph wished to visit England and, not trusting hired managers, asked Nathan to run the firm in his absence. Nathan agreed on condition that he was given a salary of £300 a year and a share of the profits. His return fare to Melbourne was also paid by Joseph Jacob so that he could marry his fiancée, Dinah Marks. Her family were also recent Jewish immigrants, having arrived in Australia from Stoke Newington a year before Nathan sailed. He closed his Melbourne shop and

2. Joseph Nathan (1835–1912) as a young man. This photograph may have been taken when at the age of 18 he decided to emigrate to Australia.

settled in the Te Aro district of Wellington to concentrate his energies on building up Jacob Joseph's business. Nathan appears to have won the confidence of his suspicious employer, and three years later, on 1 January 1861, his diligence was rewarded with a partnership in the firm.[10]

Joseph, Nathan & Co. described themselves in advertisements as 'Merchants and commission agents: importers of British and foreign merchandise, fancy goods, tobacconists' wares, druggists' sundries, patent medicines &c'. Despite the economic disruption caused to the North Island by the Maori wars, the firm grew steadily during the 1860s, dealing in whatever goods they could sell in Wellington province, while buying wool from local farmers for export to the UK. The partnership lasted for just over twelve years, though it suffered from repeated quarrels over the distribution of profits. However, in June 1873, Joseph Nathan, exhausted by Jacob Joseph's difficult character and having accumulated sufficient capital of his own, acquired his partner's share of the business.

Joseph Nathan chose to develop the reclaimed land the firm had bought from the government in Wellington on the corner of Grey Street and Featherston Street.[11] He had been quick to realise that the 100ft square plot was in a prime position, located opposite the post office and customs house. He built a distinctive, four-storey warehouse and office at a cost of £4,000, totara timber being used for the structure because of fear of earthquakes. When completed, it was one of the largest buildings in Wellington. However, the imposing Italianate façade was simply a timber veneer, concealing sides made from corrugated iron sheeting. Filled with ironmongery, drapery, oils, paints, fancy goods and even wines and spirits, a local reporter commented on the quantity of merchandise: 'in one part of the room there

3. Lambton Quay, Wellington in the 1850s when Joseph Nathan moved there from Melbourne to work for Jacob Joseph. In the centre of the photograph beneath the sign 'Lott' is the empty site at the corner of Grey and Featherston Streets which Nathan bought after the dissolution of their partnership in 1873. (Alexander Turnbull Library, National Library of New Zealand)

are unmentionables enough to supply an army; and in another direction there is a cloud of ostrich feathers'.[12]

In 1876, however, Joseph Nathan decided to sail to London to see his ailing father and entrusted the business to Messrs Watty and Roxburgh, whom he did not know but who came with a recommendation from a local bank. They turned out to be respectively an alcoholic and a rogue and their combined efforts brought the firm to the brink of bankruptcy.[13] On his return, Nathan had to act determinedly to rescue its fortunes. In doing so he was helped by his sons who, as they came of age, joined the business.

Between 1858 and 1877, Joseph and Dinah Nathan had thirteen children, though a daughter died shortly after birth and Edward, their second son, drowned in a fishing accident aged six. The family bond was particularly strong and Joseph encouraged seven of the boys to enter the firm (David, Louis, Maurice, Philip, Frederick, Alec and Charles, the youngest).[14] The Nathans were orthodox Jews and took their religion seriously. Anecdote has it that Joseph, out walking with his children after a Sabbath service,

4. The warehouse and offices built by Joseph Nathan in 1874 at a cost of £4,000. The timber street façade designed by Christian Toxward is in the fashionable palazzo *style. When opened, it was the tallest building in Wellington and had the city's first hydraulic lift. It was filled with ironmongery, drapery, fancy goods, 'unmentionables enough to supply an army'.*

observed through an open window one of his clerks completing some outstanding tasks. He ordered the office closed and threatened the hapless employee with instant dismissal if he were ever again found at work on the Sabbath. Joseph Nathan contributed £100 towards a synagogue in Wellington and later served as the president of its committee, being, in effect, the official representative of the Jewish community there until his retirement to London in 1894.[15] Many of Nathan's religious beliefs could be applied in business. In a letter written to his sons in February 1903, he outlined some of his guiding principles:

> we are only Trustees all is not given us for our own use to be used only for selfish pleasures. All my life I have held these views and have done my best to carry same out sharing with others, seeking where help was wanted and acting according to the judgement vouchsaved to me, do you do likewise you will find happiness in helping others ... I hope each and all of you will at all times feel as I have felt that it is a blessing to have been born a Jew be proud of your Birthright ... I need not tell my sons that Honour, truth & integrity are sure roads to success because they are Thank God all Honourable Men.[16]

5. The rear and one side of Nathan's warehouse were constructed of sheet corrugated iron to save on construction costs.

His sons were brought up as orthodox Jews and Alec Nathan, in particular, allowed his faith to influence the early culture of Glaxo Laboratories.

Expansion to London

When Joseph Nathan travelled to London in March 1876 in the *Zealandia*, it was not solely to visit his father. He sought finance from the City of London, as local banks had limited resources and often charged higher interest rates. An arrangement was concluded with the Royal Bank of Scotland that continued until the winding up of Joseph Nathan & Co. Furthermore, the firm's trade had reached the point where it had become desirable to set up a permanent base in the UK. In October 1876, Nathan rented an office at 98 Leadenhall Street and later at Sugar Loaf Court, Fenchurch Street, appointing a clerk, Thomas Ham, to assist his former agent, Henry Isaacs.[17] Although Joseph Nathan returned to Wellington in the following year and remained as senior partner of the merchanting business, he surrendered much of the daily responsibilities to his sons. As president of the town's Chamber of Commerce, he was instrumental in the promotion of the Wellington & Manawatu Railway, established in 1881. He saw that his farms in Palmerston North could never flourish unless they had efficient

6. Joseph Nathan c. 1875 in his early forties at about the time that he set up on his own account.

communication with the port of Wellington.[18] As chairman, Joseph exhausted himself over the execution of the project[19] and in 1886, the year of its completion, he made an extended visit to London, though as his wife Dinah wrote, 'the doctor says that J.E.N. requires at least two years rest'.[20] Henceforth, Joseph divided his time between London and Wellington, though it was his wife who died first, in 1893 at the age of 53. In the following year, accompanied by his son Maurice, he returned to Wellington to resign from his many directorships. Nathan then made London his permanent home, taking up residence at 23 Pembridge Gardens, near Notting Hill Gate.

Despite its scale, the business remained a sole proprietorship, in which Joseph Nathan contributed the entire capital. Although he rarely visited the office in Sugar Loaf Court, he was, of necessity, consulted on matters of policy involving substantial finance. David, his eldest son, took charge in New Zealand, while Louis ran the City office, where he was assisted by a third brother, Maurice, who supervised the import of butter. By degrees, therefore, the centre of gravity in Joseph Nathan & Co. moved from Wellington to London. In July 1899, partly to resolve the differences that had arisen between the two elements of the business, Joseph Nathan & Co. was established in the UK as a private limited liability company with a capital of £127,000.[21] Joseph served as chairman and his three eldest sons (David, Louis and Maurice) became joint managing directors, joined by Philip in the following year.[22] Jackson, Pixley & Co. were appointed as the auditors and continued in that role long after the Nathan company had been subsumed within Glaxo Laboratories.[23] While this registration introduced certain legal formalities, it made little practical difference to the running of the business: board meetings, for example, remained irregular and were sometimes held at Nathan's home in Pembridge Gardens.[24]

Joseph Nathan died on 2 May 1912 and shortly afterwards Louis agreed that a local New Zealand board (under the chairmanship of David Nathan) should be set up to diffuse continuing difficulties between family members in London and Wellington.[25] Tension had arisen as executive decisions were increasingly taken in the UK, while the farms, factories and principal warehouse were in New Zealand. Meetings of both boards took place every month and their minutes were exchanged to facilitate communication. Under the terms of Joseph Nathan's will, the shareholding remained confined to the family and a small number of senior managers until 1913.[26] Then the need for further capital investment led to the flotation of the company on the London Stock Exchange, and the issue of 20,000 ordinary shares of £1 together with 103 preferred ordinary shares of £1.[27]

From merchanting to manufacture

The introduction of a regular steamer service to New Zealand from the UK in the early 1890s threatened to destroy much of the Nathans' market. Increasingly, manufacturers sold direct to retailers rather than deal with wholesale importers. At first, the Nathans entered the wool trade but found stock and station agents too well established, though this activity was not abandoned until 1908 and they remained in flax for a further five years.[28] David Nathan then suggested that the firm turn to the other great agricultural product of New Zealand, butter. Refrigerated ships made overseas sales possible and the government had consulted Danish experts on the development of an export trade. In the course of their commercial travelling, the Nathans had built up good working relations with the farmers' co-operatives of the North Island. Selling the drapery business to finance the construction of a small butter factory in New Plymouth, they began to trade in the dairy market.[29] To expand, it was necessary to forge closer links with the farmers and David Nathan negotiated an arrangement with the Co-operative Society at Palmerston North whereby the firm would market their entire output of butter on commission in return for guaranteed supplies of milk. Driven by demand in the UK, the business developed rapidly and by 1904 the Nathans owned three central factories served by a large number of creameries (or skimming stations).[30]

Whilst butter provided Joseph Nathan & Co. with an important new commodity, it also left them with a by-product that they had difficulty selling – skimmed milk.[31] Yet chance threw an opportunity into the path of the company that was to offer unparalleled rewards. Maurice Nathan regularly called at Debenhams' wholesale warehouse in St Paul's Churchyard to order stocks of drapery for despatch to Wellington. Calling at the Wigmore

Street office, Ernest Debenham showed Nathan a parcel of skimmed milk powder which he said had been made by a novel machine.[32] The rights to the process were being touted by James Robinson Hatmaker, an American, who had acquired the foreign patents from its inventors, two New York dairymen, John Augustus Just and Roy Bent. In essence, it involved drying milk at high temperature using heated rollers. Milk was poured into the gap between two slowly rotating cylinders (heated internally by steam) so that the water content evaporated to leave a powder free from pathogenic organisms. At first, Joseph and Louis Nathan dismissed the project, but were impressed by the Debenhams' commitment. As a result, the two families joined forces, setting up two companies with patent rights in South America and Australasia, respectively. However, continuing disputes with the greedy Hatmaker led in January 1905 to the formation of a new enterprise, the Imperial Dry Milk Co., to take over the interests of the earlier businesses and acquire the Debenham holding. This company, in turn, was wound up in 1909 following a petition from Hatmaker claiming an infringement of his patents and its assets were granted to Joseph Nathan & Co. in settlement of a £20,000 loan.

Although the implications were not fully appreciated, the Nathans had, by the purchase of rights to the Just–Hatmaker process, moved from merchanting into manufacture. The priority was to open a factory in New Zealand. Frederick and Alec Nathan, then farming at Palmerston North, were asked to take this challenge. They sold their farms and Fred took charge of the creameries and Alec the dried milk operations.[33] John Merrett, Hatmaker's engineer, was sent to New Zealand to supervise the construction of the plant and, after a false start at Makino, a wood and corrugated iron structure was erected at Bunnythorpe. The Defiance Dried Milk Factory with four roller dryers came into production in October 1904. Alec Nathan later recalled that

> certain directors have the idea that they, out of brotherly kindness, found billets in J. N. & Co. for Fred and myself, whereas J. N. & Co.'s manufacturing dairy business had never been satisfactorily managed until Mr Fred was put in charge … At that time it was thought J. N. & Co. had a gold mine in the dried milk business … Had there been no blood tie or sentiment, it would have been more profitable for one or the other, or both of us, to have deserted Nathans and looked after our own business.[34]

His observations were confirmed by Merrett, who wrote that the 'Nathans had not the slightest idea of what they were expected to do nor had they any policy or plans for the new venture'.[35] It was the diligence and perseverance of Fred and Alec Nathan, aided in technical matters by Merrett,

7. The first factory built by the Nathans at Bunnythorpe in 1904 to make milk powder, then marketed under the name 'Defiance'.

that translated a bright idea into commercial reality.

In January 1906 the Bunnythorpe factory was virtually destroyed by fire.[36] Although rebuilding followed immediately, the enterprise received a further setback in July when a discontented workman threw a stick of dynamite into the boiler. The new structure was 94ft by 60ft accommodating eight roller dryers and a packing machine capable of filling 12,000 tins a day, together with a small analytical laboratory.[37] By this time, however, the Nathans' most pressing problems were in marketing and, as Alec recalled, they encountered considerable consumer resistance to the novel product.

> It is a curious and interesting fact that the Nathans thought, when they purchased that patent, that their fortune was made and that dried milk, with its convenience and adaptability, would replace liquid milk, and their disillusionment was very costly. When first dried milk was put on the New Zealand market, there was an enormous rush to purchase supplies, which confirmed the Nathans' idea that a fortune was waiting at their door … However, they were too ignorant … to realise that this was a 'curiosity' demand, and they waited impatiently and fruitlessly for repeat orders to come … They found themselves with a very substantial stock of dried milk that was unsaleable, nor was there any substantial sale for it in England. They did not know how to create a market for it as household milk, so they were forced to try to sell it to biscuit makers and confectioners.[38]

8. *Roller drying machines at Bunnythorpe. Milk was poured between two steam-heated rollers which had the effect of not only drying the liquid but also purifying it.*

Having failed to persuade consumers that 'Defiance' dried milk had a general household use, the Nathans decided to relaunch the product tailored to the needs of a specific market.

The birth of Glaxo

At the turn of the century widespread concerns were expressed in the medical press about the adulterated state of much cows' milk sold to the public.[39] In addition, *The Lancet* identified a need to educate mothers about proper hygiene and nutrition when feeding infants.[40] Hence, a ready market existed for a baby food that was free from infection and yet contained valuable minerals and vitamins. Given that their drying method had bactericidal properties, Louis Nathan considered selling powder milk as an infant food. The problem lay in producing a consistent product. In the past, 'desiccated milk' had been either deficient in protein when made from skimmed milk or turned rancid when reconstituted if made from full-cream. A baby's digestive system is unable to tolerate high levels of protein, so it was important to make a reliable formulation, modified by the addition of either lactose or cream. In 1906, Louis Nathan arranged for feeding trials at the Finsbury Health Centre in London and Lewisham Infirmary to test the response of both babies and physicians.[41] Tests conducted at the Brentwood laboratory of Richard Woosnam, chemist to the Imperial Dry Milk Co., on a sample of Defiance dried milk had shown that it was free from infection and 'composed of those constituents most necessary for the building up ... of the human frame'.[42]

About to relaunch their dried milk, in 1906 the Nathans sought a name to replace 'Defiance'. The idea was that the name should not contain more than

*9. The packing room at Bunnythorpe. These bulk containers of milk powder were then
shipped to the UK for packaging and distribution.*

five letters and, if possible, end with the letter 'o'. They originally chose 'Lacto'
(*lac, lactis* being the Latin for milk) but the Trade Marks Office turned it
down. As Alec Nathan recalled, 'letters were put in front and behind the word
"Lacto" until an ephonious word was arrived at: the result was the word
"Glaxo".'[43] Later it was hypothesised that the choice of the letter 'g' was influenced by the fact that the ancient Greek for milk was *gala, galaktos*, though,
as Nathan explained, no one at the meeting had studied the language and the
word had simply been invented by trial and error.[44] It was by this circuitous
route that one of the world's largest pharmaceutical companies received its
name. One of the employees of E. & C. Barlow, the makers of the tins in
which Glaxo was packed, conceived the slogan 'builds bonnie babies'.[45]

At first, the Nathans faltered in their resolve to promote their renamed
product, as in November 1907 they accepted a bulk order from J. Lyons &
Co. for dried milk. Lyons were to market it as baby food under their own
name. Yet the agreement, if it ever came into force, was short lived. In May
1908, Joseph Nathan & Co. launched the renamed powder themselves. This
may have been influenced by Alec Nathan's decision to emigrate to the UK
in that year to take responsibility for the promotion of Glaxo. Dynamic, energetic and imaginative, he was the ideal candidate for such responsibilities.
Little attention had been paid to the product, as he recollected:

Glaxo as a business in itself did not exist – Mr L. J. N. used to put his spare time

10. Deliveries of milk arrive at Bunnythorpe from local diary farms.

on Saturdays into it. No separate Glaxo books or staff, nobody's sole business, no defined policy or proper business organisation. No literature about Glaxo, though there was a booklet on dried milk.[46]

With a single typist to help, Alec Nathan set out to devise a coherent marketing strategy. He wrote the first promotional literature and contacted physicians treating small children. Two doctors, one at the Chelsea Hospital and the other at the Royal Waterloo, were particularly supportive and recommended the use of dried milk to colleagues.

As the turnover began to grow, the directors believed that Alec Nathan was too inexperienced to be left in sole charge and a committee of management was formed to run the Glaxo Department. Louis Nathan, then chairman, launched a press campaign, having been persuaded by the Imperial Press Agency to take the entire front page of the *Daily Mail* for an advertisement. This was not the first time that a company had adopted this tactic, that honour going to another baby food manufacturer, Mellins, in 1902. The space was booked for 27 May 1908 at a cost of £350 to coincide with the launch of a new decorative tin and the publication of the first *Glaxo Baby Book*.[47] However, E. & C. Barlow could not produce the tins on time and at the last minute Alec Nathan had to arrange for the printing of paper labels. The *Daily Mail* advertisement listed the retailers that had ordered the product, together with the offer of a free sample to all who sent 'seven penny stamps'. Under the banner 'The food that builds bonnie babies', the advertisement listed six qualities: 'Glaxo contains no starch or any farinaceous substance ... is easily and quickly digested ... is prepared with water ... contains 25 per cent of fat ... will keep indefinitely ... is inexpensive and economical'.[48] Having unrealistic expectations of the campaign's impact, Louis and Maurice Nathan were disillusioned when they received only fifty-seven replies.[49] Further advertisements were placed in other national newspapers and in provincial dailies at a cost of £1,061 in 1908. An additional £1,684 was spent in the following year but in 1910 the budget was cut to £604,[50] though Alec Nathan believed that the promotion had not been given a 'fair trial'.[51]

11. Alec Nathan in early middle age when in charge of the Glaxo Department in London. His dynamic leadership and keen interest in marketing rescued an ailing product.

The failure of the press campaign was attributable to two causes. First, the Nathans underestimated consumer resistance since, as Alec later wrote, the idea of selling dried milk as a baby food

> was entirely novel and new – it took years ... to get doctors, nurses and mothers to accept the idea ... in spite of the fact that there was a high infant mortality rate among babies under one year of age and this was mainly due to dirty and contaminated milk.[52]

There had also been the 'want of clearly defined policy and tenacity of purpose'.[53] This Alec Nathan attributed to the absence of a coherent management structure as the dried milk business had been entrusted to a committee composed of Louis, Maurice and Alec Nathan, R. C. C. Potter and Mr Van Allen. While Alec had responsibility for sales and marketing, his elder brothers exercised overall control without themselves being closely involved in the operation. There was 'no settled policy, except one of procrastination'.[54] Having endured this system for two years, Alec presented his colleagues with an ultimatum that they should

12. *The front-page advertisement placed in the* Daily Mail *on 27 May 1908 to herald the launch of Glaxo milk powder. The campaign, in fact, was not a great success and Alec Nathan believed that it had not been given sufficient time to catch the public's imagination.*

give me complete and sole charge of building up the Glaxo business for eighteen months or two years and, if at the end of the time, I had not made a success of it, it should be closed down and I would resign ... They had but little option, since they had to pay the debts that had been incurred ... so in the finality they accepted my offer.[55]

When the Glaxo Department moved into profit in 1912, the three-year marketing arrangement with Brands (the proprietary food manufacturers specialising in beef teas) was ended.[56]

Continued advertising and a judicious policy of re-educating the public and health care professionals progressively expanded the market for Glaxo. In 1908, the first edition of the *Glaxo Baby Book* was launched, written by Charles Brunning, advertising manager of Lewis's of Manchester and later revised by a qualified nurse, Margaret Kennedy. Over a million copies were printed between 1908 and 1922 and distributed free or for the cost of postage. In addition, with only limited funds available, Alec Nathan wrote personally to doctors and potential customers. As he recalled,

> for five long years I depended almost entirely upon the post, and I can pretty well claim that Glaxo is the only baby food in the country that has been built on the principle of a mail order campaign ... Every letter delivered at the Glaxo offices received individual attention and each and every reply emphasised the vital message of service to the mother, the baby and to the trade.[57]

Having decided to target doctors, the campaign was initially focused in specific areas, such as Newcastle, so that its effect could be more easily monitored. In the first round, 662 letters were sent to which 122 received replies.[58] Follow-up letters were devised by Alec Nathan, who undertook a detailed analysis to discover, for example, the best day for posting, the optimum length of letters, the number of follow-ups and enclosures. Care was taken when writing to pharmacists to ensure their preference for being called 'druggists' rather than 'chemists'. Slowly sales of Glaxo improved and a loss of £2,191 for 1910 became a profit of £2,028 in 1912. Louis Nathan congratulated Alec:

> The success is well earned and richly deserved … it means much more than a departmental success – it will be far reaching in a larger direction – it will seriously affect the view of others when looking at the balance sheet.[59]

Alec Nathan did not rest on his laurels. In February 1913, he moved from the small office at St. John's House, The Minories, which had been leased for the Glaxo Department five years earlier, to larger premises within the Idris drinks factory at 47–49 King's Road (now called St Pancras Way), St. Pancras.[60] This enabled the Nathans to undertake their own blending and packing operations, which until then had been entrusted to Brands.

Established in his new premises and concerned by the growth of rival producers, Nathan embarked on a second and more ambitious press campaign in June 1913. He approached the advertising consultant Thomas Russell, who in turn introduced him to the Chancery Lane agents Saward Baker & Co. Saward himself looked after the account together with Miss Woodyard and Alexander Cox, who joined Glaxo as its advertising manager after the First World War.[61] Nathan continued to direct the overall strategy and wrote much of the copy. Over the six months of the 1913 campaign, Glaxo spent £4,270 in newspapers and net profits increased threefold to £3,311 (Table 1, p. 444). The effectiveness of the promotion was acknowledged in the *Advertising World* for November 1915, which commented 'seven years ago Glaxo was known among a very small section of the community – today it is no exaggeration to say that every mother at least knows about Glaxo'.[62] The name became inseparably associated in the public's mind with infant milk, and Virginia Woolf in *Mrs Dalloway* (1925) described a mother, Mrs Coates, standing with her baby in St James's Park as an aeroplane flew overhead tracing out an advertising slogan:

> Whatever it did, wherever it went, out fluttered behind it a thick ruffled bar of white smoke which curled and wreathed upon the sky in letters. But what letters? … 'Blaxo', said Mrs Coates in a strained, awe-stricken voice, gazing straight up, and her baby, lying stiff and white in her arms gazed straight up.[63]

A French adventure: Le Breuil-en-Ange

In 1913 the London directors of Joseph Nathan & Co. set up a roller-drying factory at Le Breuil-en-Ange in the dairy-farm region of Calvados between Pont l'Évêque and Lisieux. Given that sales of Glaxo had reached 'very satisfactory' levels by November 1912,[64] and that the UK packing and sales organisation was totally reliant upon dried milk imports from New Zealand, this was a defensive ploy, designed to offset their dependence on the Wellington board, though it is not known why Normandy, rather than England, was chosen as the site for the factory. In January 1914 Louis Nathan took out a lease on the Breuil creamery from Arthur Blondel and drying plant was installed.[65] Shortly after the outbreak of war, a private company, styled Laiterie du Breuil-en-Ange, was established.[66] Situated well behind the front line, the factory operated throughout the hostilities, though when demand for powder fell it made cheese to consume stocks of milk.

The Wellington board suggested that the Glaxo Department cost operations in Normandy in such a way that profits were, in effect, transferred to the UK. The London directors rejected this tactic, recording that 'great difficulty and financial risk will be experienced in passing such accounts through the French government's income tax department which has powers, if it thinks that profits are not fully shown, to assess the company for tax without reference to its balance sheet'.[67] The accounts prepared by Marwick Mitchell Peat & Co. for 1918 were considered 'satisfactory' and it seemed that a settled future lay ahead.[68] Indeed, in the post-war boom the Nathans decided to sell Glaxo in France rather than ship all the factory's output to London, and in May 1919 a Paris office was opened.[69] To prevent the business being subject to taxation in both France and the UK a further subsidiary, Établissement Joseph Nathan Société Anonyme, was set up in October 1919.[70] Yet the slump of 1921 together with surplus capacity in the New Zealand factories (see p. 126), brought the French operation to a close.[71] The roller dryers were shipped to London, though depressed demand even prevented their sale to a creamery in Waterford.[72] Thus, what had been a promising venture into the Continent came to an ignominious end and deterred the Glaxo Department from further territorial expansion there for over a decade.

The First World War

By 1914, Glaxo dried milk had become an established brand leader in the UK.[73] Glaxo was stocked by over 9,000 pharmacists and purchased by 189 municipal health departments. No salesmen were involved, orders being solicited by post, supplemented by limited advertising in the press and specialist medical and nursing journals. Eight typists were employed to turn out the 50,000 letters that were sent every month.[74] So successful was this strategy that from 1912 onwards sales were determined by the availability of supplies from New Zealand rather than the volume of orders. Turnover continued to rise impressively despite the disruption caused by the outbreak of hostilities (Table 2, p. 444). Continued expansion created pressure on space at the King's Road factory and, in view of the industrial character of the district, new offices were leased at 155–157 Great Portland Street in 1916. Such was the pace of growth that by December 1920 164 staff were employed there, together with a further 25 at 88 Gracechurch Street (the registered office of Joseph Nathan & Co.) and 22 at other London locations.[75]

In September 1914, the London board of Joseph Nathan had debated the wisdom of separating the Glaxo Department from the rest of the business and creating a wholly owned subsidiary.[76] The Wellington directors, under David Nathan, were in favour since they supplied the Department with all its dried milk and this division would have tightened their control over its activities. Alec Nathan did not welcome the proposal as he would have been ever more reliant on the New Zealand board. In the event, Louis Nathan and his fellow London directors did not agree as the creation of a new company would have robbed the core business of its main source of sales and profits. However, in recognition of the importance of the Glaxo Department, Alec Nathan, at the age of 43, was elected to a directorship of the London board in November 1915.

In some respects, the First World War was advantageous to Glaxo. Alec Nathan successfully negotiated a number of contracts with the War Office for milk powder to supplement or replace condensed milk issued to troops in the field. The drying factories at Bunnythorpe and Breuil-en-Ange could not meet the greatly increased demand. As a result, in the summer of 1916, the Nathans opened two new milk-drying factories in New Zealand at Te Aroha in the Waihou valley and at Matamata, while a third at Matangi followed in November 1917 (see p. 125). The imperative need to feed a vast conscript army drove the Nathans to over-extend their operations without any guarantee that this inflated market would be sustained once an armistice had been signed.

A determination to maintain nutritional levels in the face of attacks on shipping and the loss of much of the agricultural workforce to the armed forces led to the setting up of the Ministry of Food in December 1916. This assumed responsibility for supplying infant welfare centres with dried milk powder. Although Nathan had targeted municipal authorities, succeeding in winning orders from Rotherham and Sheffield in 1908, followed by

*13. Outside the King's Road factory and warehouse a car loaded with Red Cross parcels of
'Glaxo' in 1915. In the latter stages of the First World War it was sold in large quantities to
municipal authorities and welfare clinics with only minimal profit as a patriotic gesture but
also as a potential loss leader for the peace.*

Lincoln, Norwich and the Manchester School for Mothers in 1909,[77] sales of
Glaxo to these bodies remained modest, amounting to 10 per cent of the
Department's UK turnover. Such was the scale of the bulk contracts being
offered by the Ministry that the Nathans agreed to a figure of 2⅛d per lb, including packaging and distribution; this price represented 'simply a reimbursement – no profit'.[78] As a result of government contracts, sales to
municipal authorities rose dramatically, from £30,000 for the year to September 1917 to £102,000 in 1918 and to £237,000 in 1919.[79] When the Ministry of Food relinquished control over this business in April 1919, the
Glaxo Department resumed direct trading with the infant welfare centres
at commercial rates and succeeded in building on what had been a valuable
loss leader. Yet these government contracts were a mixed blessing.[80] Rising
sales and the need to advertise widely had created the impression in the
public's mind that Glaxo earned excessive profits, whereas the narrow margins they had been forced to accept and high milk prices combined to tem-
per the company's growth.[81]

14. Staff at the King's Road (now St Pancras Way) factory c. 1919, where dried milk powder was packed into tins.

Post-war growth: Osnaburgh Street

The boost given to the company's fortunes by government orders combined with the post-war boom (Table 3) encouraged the London board of Joseph Nathan & Co. to recruit Major Archie Sandercock, recently demobilised from the Royal Artillery where he had been a gunnery instructor. Sandercock first came to the attention of the Nathans in March 1913, when Joseph Nathan & Co. was floated on the Stock Exchange and he represented the underwriters.[82] Despite opposition from the Wellington board, who saw their influence further eroded, Sandercock was elected a director in November 1919, being given responsibility for the wholesale butter and cheese side of the business.[83] The London board then consisted of Louis Nathan, chairman and joint managing director, Maurice Nathan, joint managing director, Alec Nathan, R. C. C. Potter and Sandercock, while the Wellington company comprised David Nathan, Frederick Nathan and J. M. Muir.

Alec Nathan also set about recruiting a new management team. In 1919, Lieutenant-Colonel Ernest Rose, a graduate of Liverpool University in mechanical engineering, was hired to help with mass production methods.[84] Before the hostilities, Rose had worked in the nascent automobile industry and become general manager of the New Arrol-Johnston Car Co. Wounded when serving in Italy, Rose had been decorated and continued to use his military title in peacetime despite not having been a regular officer. On the marketing side, Hugo Wolff, who had been Alec Nathan's assistant, was promoted to sales manager, reporting to Alexander Cox, 'director of propaganda'.[85]

By 1917, with the continually rising orders for Glaxo, it had become clear that the existing factory and warehouse in King's Road, St Pancras, could no longer cope efficiently with such demand. New premises were sought in the area and in June an agreement was signed with the Crown Estates to lease a substantial plot of land located at the junction of Osnaburgh Street and Longford Street. It was close to the Camden Town, St Pancras, Euston and King's Cross goods depots for bulk distribution by train.[86] Walter J. Fryer was appointed architect and building contractor, and later became factory manager.[87] Manpower shortages and the discovery of a valuable deposit of ballast led to delays, the building not being completed until the end of 1920.[88] Because Fryer had also been responsible for equipping the factory and furnishing its offices, Nathan sought Rose's help in settling what had become complex accounts. With a dignified façade in brick and Portland stone, 'Glaxo House' cost £80,000, financed by a loan from the Norwich Union. The offices, a 'handsome reception room' and, most unusual for the time, a cinema were on the ground floor, while four loading bays provided space for eight lorries at a time. The five upper storeys housed the factory, laboratories and a canteen with seating for 500 workers.[89] Although the blending and packing of milk powder remained labour intensive, a determined attempt had been made to introduce modern machinery and to arrange the process to flow downwards through the building to the loading bays.

To recoup this expenditure, a complex reconstruction was undertaken between 1919 and 1922. Whilst the company had been floated on the Stock Exchange in 1913, the entire issued capital had been provided by the Nathan family. A further 223,000 'A' preference shares of £1 were created in 1919 and sold to an enthusiastic investing public. In May 1921, an extra 300,000 preferred ordinary shares of £1 were issued, followed in June 1922 by the creation of 250,000 'A' preference shares.[90] Although the company increased its capital threefold by these issues, the directors made themselves vulnerable to less propitious economic circumstances. Britain fell into a slump in 1921 and trading conditions remained unfavourable throughout the decade. Sales of Glaxo collapsed as mothers sought cheaper substitutes, and between 1923 and 1926 profits fell to such a level that Joseph Nathan & Co. could only cover their 7 per cent preference dividends.[91] The solution was an enforced capital reconstruction in July 1926 by which preferred ordinary shareholders lost one half of their preferred capital and received in compensation nearly two-thirds of the equity. The share capital of the company was reduced from £1.5 to £1.2 million by writing nine shillings (45p) off each issued £1 preferred ordinary share and eighteen shillings (90p) off each issued £1 ordinary share. These losses left many investors feeling

15. A Glaxo lorry decorated for a carnival possibly shortly after the armistice.

aggrieved and temporarily upset the confidence of the Nathan family and board. The memory of this event seems to have been deeply etched and thirty years later, when Jephcott wrote to staff to inform them of his retirement as managing director, he commented on 'the forbearance' of those investors who 'provided us with capital … whose money, by 1926, we had largely lost'.[92]

In fact, with the exception of 1926, the financial fortunes of Joseph Nathan recovered steadily after the post-war depression and grew in real terms until 1930 when the slump led to a dramatic and sustained fall in profits (Table 3, p. 445). The business expanded from 1933 in real terms and this growth was interrupted only by the Second World War which eroded what were otherwise substantial figures. Although the overall trend was upwards, the company's earnings were characterised by sudden fluctuations during the interwar period with sharp falls in 1923, 1926 and 1932 and peaks in 1919–20, 1930 and 1937.

Having established the Glaxo Department in Osnaburgh Street, Alec Nathan set up an executive committee with himself at the head and the seven principal managers: Fryer (factory), Wolff (sales), Cox (advertising), Randall (financial and staff), Ginger (medical), Miss Kennedy (welfare) and Foster (export). Although the organisation devised by Nathan may

16. Glaxo House in Osnaburgh Street which housed the factory, warehouse, offices and laboratories of the Glaxo Department. The building had been designed by Walter J. Fryer, who was appointed the factory manager on its completion.

seem simplistic by the standards of today, it represented an early attempt to think strategically about the business.

Alec Nathan's business philosophy

During the late 1920s the locus of power within Joseph Nathan moved away from the older members of the family towards Alec Nathan and the talented managers that he had recruited into the Glaxo Department. In 1927, when Louis Nathan retired as chairman, Alec succeeded him and continued in this role until June 1946, though he was to resign as managing director in 1939. Harry Jephcott, who had been appointed general manager of the Osnaburgh factory, joined the board in 1929.[93] Of the old guard, only Maurice Nathan remained, the other London directors being Archie Sandercock, Frederick Randall (formerly the company secretary) and Sydney Jacobs, elected in 1923. Jacobs had originally joined the Nathans just before the First World War, when he succeeded J. J. Reich as the 'confidential manager' in Wellington. When Maurice Nathan retired in 1934, Hugo Wolff, the dynamic sales manager, and Rose, the factory manager, joined

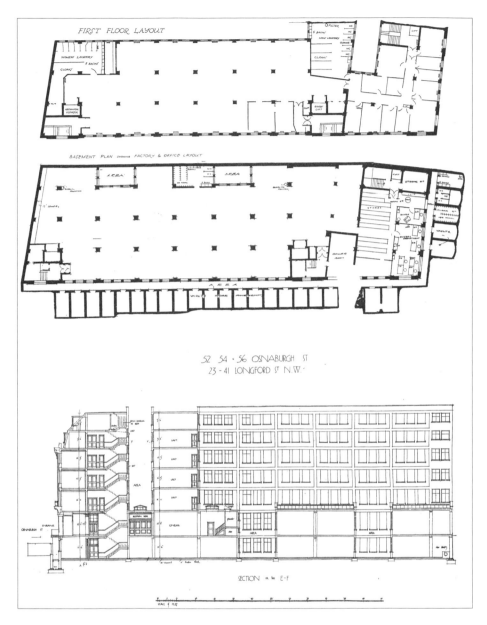

17. The plan and elevation of Glaxo House.

the board of Joseph Nathan, while Jephcott and Randall became joint deputy chairmen. In effect, authority and dynamic inspiration were vested in Alec Nathan and Jephcott, who continued to dominate the company until the former's retirement in 1945. Just as the founder's Jewish faith had influenced the culture of the company, it was not unnatural with the

18. Staff in Eastern fancy dress for the cake and candy fair at Osnaburgh Street in October 1920, photographed on the roof of the factory.

continuing involvement of family members that religious calling still exercised an effect on recruitment; Rose, Jacobs and Wolff were all Jewish. This was not, however, a conscious policy and the predominance of Jewish directors disappeared in the mid 1940s.

Neither Nathan nor Jephcott was radical in his approach to business, both believing in evolutionary change and a benign paternalism towards employees. Alec described his philosophy in a series of letters typed on bright yellow paper and sent to staff between January and September 1923 under the general heading 'It can be done'. Employees were encouraged in the first letter to read them

> with your wife (and if you are a girl with your man) – if you are not married, read them with the girl you hope will be your wife … Read and discuss them together, for the biggest thing in your business life is not the everyday mechanics of business, wages, prices and conditions; they can be adjusted, but attitudes, motives, relationships, emotions and spiritual development.[94]

Nathan debated a range of topics from 'Mental processes' (understanding the minds of customers), 'That Inner I' (developing a determination to succeed), 'Courtesy', 'Clothes' and 'Is business a profession?'. Personal documents, written in a disarming style, they provided Nathan with an opportunity to express his own deeply held views. On the matter of how to behave, he suggested that

> one who is inclined to measure the amount of courtesy he should show to persons by their importance and the position they occupy, does not possess that innate courtesy which reflects good breeding.[95]

Nathan himself was renowned throughout the company for treating all with equal respect. He had a touching faith in his occupation, arguing that

> it is only now that some ... are beginning to realise business is one of the difficult and complex professions. It is your privilege as a business representative ... to represent its ideals of service, its fine traditions ... As missionaries spreading this new gospel, do your work thoroughly, do it cleanly, do it cheerfully.[96]

More than any other individual, Alec Nathan was responsible for setting the tone, or defining the culture, of Glaxo Laboratories. As he himself wrote,

> a business is only a reflection of the man at the top – if he is small, mean and petty – if he is afraid to spend to expand – if he bullies and hectors his staff – this will be reflected and reproduced from the top down to the office boy.[97]

The emphasis he laid on an egalitarian approach served the company well. Differences of class and background were eschewed and individuals judged on their performance. Being an outsider himself (an immigrant from New Zealand, a former student of Lincoln Agricultural College, and a committed orthodox Jew),[98] he had little time for the niceties of the English class system. As he himself commented in a press interview, coming from farming and 'not being used to business, he made many mistakes, but for the same reason, he employed many novel methods, the most unusual of which was to adapt mail order methods to the sale of a proprietary article'.[99] Marketing was his particular forte, such that by 1925 he merited a special feature in the inaugural issue of *Newspaper Advertising* which concluded that Nathan had been 'the creative and dominating force behind the marketing of this food [Glaxo]'.[100] Clifford Turner, an advertising manager who worked for Nathan for thirteen years, later wrote:

> To this great little man with the ready smile, the blunt simplicity, the outdoor

19. A card trick being performed at a staff party in the Osnaburgh factory c. 1920. Alec Nathan stands fourth from the left.

complexion and the inner sadness, all of us who worked with him were genuinely his friends … Those words 'my friend' preceded often a gentle rebuke, a shrewd reminder of some home truth … albeit apologetically offered. 'My friend', he would begin, 'I am going to disagree with you completely'.[101]

During the 1920s, Joseph Nathan & Co. continued to operate in New Zealand and the UK as general merchants, though specialising in agricultural products. Dried milk for infants had become the core business and its principal generator of profits. Interestingly, in March 1921, Alec Nathan considered launching a Glaxo chocolate, though in view of the depressed state of the economy he did not proceed.[102] Had it succeeded, the company might have developed in confectionery rather than pharmaceuticals. By this time, five milk drying factories had been built in New Zealand and, in 1919, a further plant was constructed in Australia at Port Fairy, Victoria.[103] It was, therefore, a vertically integrated organisation that embraced every operation from the purchase of milk from local farm co-operatives to the sale of sealed tins.

Harry Jephcott and quality control

In 1919, Alec Nathan decided that it was necessary to monitor and improve the quality of their milk powder by scientific methods, as both purity and nutritional value were key sales messages. In April of that year, he recruited Harry Jephcott as the department's first chemist. Jephcott, the son of a Redditch train driver, had been educated at King Edward the Sixth Grammar School, Camp Hill, Birmingham.[104] With financial help from his elder brother, Charles Josiah Jephcott, he trained as a pharmacist, being apprenticed in 1906 to John Thornton of Redditch. He followed in the footsteps of Charles, who had worked there ten years earlier.[105] Coming third in the John Bell scholarship examination of the Pharmaceutical Society in 1911, Harry Jephcott narrowly failed to obtain the finance he needed to continue his studies. Finding the work of a retail pharmacist limiting, he joined the Customs and Excise Department in 1912, where he specialised in the analysis of tobacco samples. Two years later, he secured a position in the Department of the Government Chemist that enabled him to read for an external London University degree in chemistry at West Ham Technical College. Graduating in 1915 with a first, Jephcott was encouraged to pursue research and completed an M.Sc. three years later; he was also awarded the Pharmaceutical Society's silver medal in 1917.

No doubt impressed by the younger Jephcott and anxious to recruit experienced professional staff, Alec Nathan wrote in 1920 to Charles offering him an interview. As a result, he was appointed assistant to Hugo Wolff, the sales manager, based at 155 Great Portland Street. His brother Harry later speculated how this orderly and courtly man had coped with

> the congestion and utter lack of organisation existing there … To me the reception office, which was also the telephone exchange and post department, was characteristic of the general confusion.[106]

Subsequently, Charles Jephcott played an important part in recruiting and training the team of medical representatives assembled to promote Glaxo's first pharmaceutical product, Ostelin. In an attempt to build up 'friendly personal yet professional relationships' with retailers, he insisted that all salesmen should also be qualified pharmacists, a policy which endured into the 1960s.[107]

At first, Harry Jephcott did not have a proper laboratory to conduct his quality-control tests but had to work at Glaxo's small warehouse and packing station in Bravington Road, off the Harrow Road, in west London. His windowless room was about twenty feet square and at first had no furniture, so that he had to use packing cases as a desk and chair. Early on,

20. The pilot plant assembled at Osnaburgh Street to extract vitamin D from cod liver oil.

Jephcott was visited by Maurice Nathan. Jephcott introduced himself only to be surprised by the reply, 'Oh! Alec's bloody folly'.[108] For six months his assistant was a boy of seventeen, Edward Farmer, but in the autumn of 1919, they were joined by an experienced chemist, Norman Ratcliffe, and in January 1920 by Alfred Bacharach, a graduate of Clare College, Cambridge, who from 1915 had worked at the Wellcome Chemical Research Laboratories, later moving to the analytical department at their Dartford factory. G. P. Dodds was also recruited from the public analyst's laboratory at Oxford. Farmer, as Jephcott recalled,

had an intimate knowledge of Pepys' Diary and Belloc's *Cautionary Tales*, from which he could always make a quotation appropriate to the occasion, and a less pleasing habit of persistent whistling from a limited repertoire of hymn tunes ... Norman Ratcliffe, a native of Lancashire with a physical handicap, his knees having been damaged when playing cricket, ... had a very practical approach to problems and a typical north-country pawky humour. His comments resulted in a speedy decline in Farmer's whistling.[109]

Bacharach, who remained at Glaxo until his retirement in 1956, became something of a company celebrity and specialised in nutrition research. He was also noted for his writings on music and an insistence on precise English in scientific papers.[110] In years to come, when laboratory staff published their findings, Bacharach, acting as an informal editor before submission, often reduced inexperienced authors to despair with his annotations in green ink. Farmer ultimately became manager of Glaxo's first UK milk-drying factory at Driffield, while Ratcliffe was appointed managing director of Glaxo New Zealand and Dodds was made foods factory manager at Greenford.

Jephcott and his team set about establishing standardised routines for testing the quality of dried milk. In July 1920, he departed for a ten-month visit to Australia and New Zealand to implement controls there. A minute from a board meeting shows that Jephcott was not without a streak of ruthlessness. He argued that the existing laboratory at Palmerston North should be moved to Hamilton, and commented of a chemist there that he was 'a good bench worker, but has no initiative and should be offered a position as a benchman at a reduced salary, or be allowed to send in his resignation'.[111] In the event, the hapless employee left. Under the system devised by Jephcott each vat of milk was analysed to adjust the proportions of fat, lactose and protein by the addition of cream and lactose so that it could be digested by new-born infants.[112] The dried powder was also examined to ensure it was free from bacterial contamination. Laboratory data recorded 'the date of manufacture, the time the milk was received, the temperature of the milk ... and details of the chemical and bacteriological examination of the powder'.[113] Once the dried milk was shipped to London, random samples were collected for analysis to detect any deterioration in transit, and further tests were made of packaged powder. Each tin was given a reference number so that any faulty milk could be traced back to its source.[114]

The first pharmaceutical product: Ostelin

Having established a small analytical department and improved the testing rouines, Jephcott set more ambitious targets for the laboratory. In the immediate post-war years, the medical profession took an increasing interest in nutrition to combat those diseases considered the product of a deficient diet or a lack of what Sir Frederick Gowland Hopkins had called 'accessory factors'. Subsequently termed vitamins, considerable effort was devoted to discovering their chemical nature and physiological effects. The British Medical Research Committee and the Lister Institute of Preventative Medicine jointly set up the Accessory Food Factors Committee in 1918 to publish research on nutrition. Paediatricians took an interest in dried milk in the hope that it might help to prevent scurvy and contain fat-soluble vitamins to promote growth. Jephcott and his team conducted a lengthy series of experiments but showed that it had no more ascorbic acid (later identified as vitamin C) than raw milk. Jephcott then turned his attention to the vitamin necessary for the formation of healthy bones in children, also known as the 'anti-rachitic factor'. The aetiology of rickets, then one of the most common diseases of infancy, had puzzled physicians for years. By 1918 the widely held hypothesis that a deficiency of 'milk, butter or of the fat-soluble A substance' was responsible had been disproved.[115] Rickets had been successfully treated with cod-liver oil and exposure to sunlight or ultra-violet light but no one understood why these diverse treatments worked.[116] Then, in 1922, Professor E. V. McCollum, a biochemist at the School of Hygiene and Public Health at Johns Hopkins University, Baltimore, published results which demonstrated that the anti-rachitic factor in cod-liver oil was relatively stable to heat and aeration, differentiating it from the previously discovered vitamin A.[117] In a second paper, McCollum and his team identified the dietary factor, which they termed vitamin D, necessary for the prevention of rickets.[118] When, in the following year, Jephcott heard that the International Dairy Congress was to be held in Washington DC, he obtained permission to attend with the idea of visiting McCollum. Little novel information emerged at the Congress but a telephone call to Baltimore gained Jephcott the invitation he sought. A meeting with McCollum in his laboratory led to a full and open discussion and Jephcott departed convinced of the efficacy of vitamin D.

Travelling to New York, Jephcott was then told that Dr Theodore F. Zucker at Columbia University claimed to have devised a method for extracting vitamin D from fish oil.[119] Convinced of the commercial advantages that would accrue to the Glaxo Department if dried milk could be fortified in this way, Jephcott visited Zucker's laboratory and later secured a licence for the production process. The original contribution made by the Glaxo Department was to translate Zucker's bench process, which had never produced more than five gallons of oil, into large-scale manufacture. Jephcott and his team working with Rose built an experimental plant (with a capacity of sixty gallons a week) at Osnaburgh Street that successfully made vitamin D in a glycerine suspension. In February 1924, as the product approached its launch, Jephcott asked Nathan to reward him financially for his work in developing Zucker's patent.[120] Louis Nathan, as chairman, agreed that Jephcott should be paid 10 per cent of net profits from sales of vitamin D and this arrangement was confirmed after the former's retirement in 1927.[121] (In general, pharmaceutical companies have not adopted the principle that inventors should have a direct stake in any medicines they discover largely because of the team nature of research and difficulties in apportioning an individual's contribution.)

Marketed as 'Ostelin', vitamin D was sold in small glass phials for drop dosage. Although the first order from a London wholesaler had been received in August 1924, production difficulties delayed a proper launch campaign until October, at which time literature was sent to physicians.[122] In the meantime, the plant had been dismantled and re-erected in an expanded form at the premises of the London & Thames Haven Oil Wharves. However, John Spencer, managing director of Isaac Spencer of Aberdeen, from which Glaxo purchased its cod-liver oil, offered to reduce the price to

£4 per ton if they agreed to move the manufacturing operation to a site he had leased close to his own factory. The transfer was completed in December 1925, when a modified process using salvaged plant came on stream, and in the following year it achieved its maximum economic capacity of 2,400 gallons a month.[123]

At first, sales of Ostelin proved disappointing, largely, as Jephcott observed, because of Glaxo's 'want of experience in marketing a product of this type'.[124] They sent samples to paediatric hospitals for clinical trials to use the results in promotional material. 'More than twelve months were, in effect, wasted in these endeavours which … failed to come to fruition'. Doctors were receptive to vitamin supplements, as an editorial in the *British Medical Journal* for December 1925 commented:

> This concentration of vitamins is of importance in several ways. In the first place, it is of some therapeutic importance because relatively enormous quantities of vitamins can be given in a single dose … Intensive treatment of this kind may prove valuable as an emergency measure in the treatment of deficiency diseases.[125]

In December 1925, Glaxo launched a campaign directed at general practitioners. A series of postcards were sent at weekly intervals, the last with a tear-off stamp for a free phial. The programme was repeated in May with 7,000 responses.[126] Sales rose to 2,864 phials in April 1926.[127] By the autumn, Jephcott concluded that there was likely 'to be comparatively little increase in the present sales of Ostelin', though he predicted 'rapid growth' for other formulations, particularly tablets and a mixture of Ostelin, malt extract and a fortified orange juice known as 'Ostelin OMO'.[128]

The first pharmaceutical product launched by the Glaxo Department had not, therefore, been an outstanding commercial success. It had encountered production problems and revealed gaps in marketing expertise. Although the gross profit margin for Ostelin in 1926–27 was estimated at 70 per cent,[129] the cost of the entire enterprise perturbed Jephcott and he acknowledged that there was 'a risk of other work or Ostelin being neglected'.[130] Of vitamins and pharmaceuticals in general, Jephcott wrote:

> it is believed an industry with great possibilities for commercial success, but withall an industry new and hedged about with many difficulties of a technical nature. At present, we are well ahead of our competitors: to remain so can only be assured by continuous work of investigation both upon product and method of production. An allotment for research purposes … is desirable so that work can be made specific, and not as at present, incidental as time from routine work permits.[131]

21. The first laboratory set up for quality control was in the warehouse at Bravington Road and was under the sole charge of Harry Jephcott. Photographed here in 1959.

Because Jephcott failed to convince the Nathan board of the need for a defined policy on pharmaceutical development until 1935 (see p. 51), the manufacture of Ostelin was improved and new formulations introduced only by diverting scientists from routine work and *ad hoc* funding. In addition to the original glycerine suspension, tablets, an emulsion, a colloidal solution for subcutaneous injection, an ointment and a nasal spray were devised.[132] These new preparations were made possible in 1929 by the adoption of a more efficient manufacturing process using crude, irradiated ergosterol, an unsaturated sterol derived from ergot (the fungus *Claviceps purpurea*), a parasite of rye.[133] Five years earlier, Dr Harry Steenbock at the University of Wisconsin had demonstrated that the anti-rachitic properties were derived from ultra-violet light and could, therefore, be greatly increased by irradiation.[134] Jephcott acquired a licence to use the Steenbock process and Glaxo began to make calciferol (vitamin D_2) from ergosterol obtained from purified yeast. The potency of Ostelin made by irradiation did not, however, immediately render the cod-liver oil method obsolete as the latter yielded a compound that also contained vitamin A and iodine. For the patient, the significant advantage of the ergosterol product was that it eliminated the

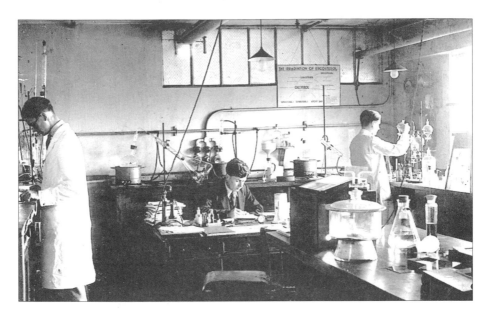

22. A youthful Dr Lester Smith (seated) at work in a laboratory at Osnaburgh Street. The sign on the rear wall describes the Steenbock process of irradiating ergosterol to make vitamin D_2 (calciferol).

unpleasant fishy taste. The continued refinement of the process by Jephcott's team, drawing upon research undertaken at Grottingen and the National Institute of Medical Research at Hampstead, allowed them to remove impurities from crude vitamin D preparations. From 1932, 'Calciferol G.L.', the pure crystalline form, became the ingredient in Ostelin, leading to a more stable chemical preparation and greater accuracy in titrating doses.

Having established a niche in the rapidly developing world of vitamins, Jephcott sought to broaden Glaxo's pharmaceutical base. In 1915, Elmer Mc-Collum, then professor of agricultural chemistry at Wisconsin, together with Marguerite Davis, had shown that butter or egg yolk, but not lard, contained an essential growth factor for rats, which they termed 'fat-soluble A'.[135] Concomitantly, Osborn and Mendel in New Haven found a similar factor in both cod-liver oil and butter. By the 1920s, the marked effects of a vitamin A deficiency on appetite, growth and tissue differentiation had been widely described. As a result of this research, Jephcott and his team were able to develop a range of products containing vitamin A, including Adexolin liquid and capsules, launched in July 1930. By this time, Glaxo exported vitamin products to India, China, the Dutch East Indies, Greece, Italy, Turkey, Argentina, Brazil and Cuba. However, in those countries where sunshine was plentiful, little demand existed for vitamin D, the anti-rachitic factor being provided naturally, so that Ostelin had few sales in Australia.[136]

Of the various vitamin preparations marketed by Glaxo in the 1930s, 'Glucose D' (later called Glucodin), launched in July 1931, proved to be the most successful commercially. Sold in tins as a health drink, it was the only glucose on the market fortified with vitamin D and calcium glycerophosphate. In 1935, Glaxo's pharmaceutical business grew 'abnormally', this being attributed 'entirely to the heavy increase in Glucose D', which accounted for 50 per cent of turnover.[137]

First pharmaceutical factory: Hayes

The signing of the Steenbock agreement in March 1928 and the prospect of making vitamin D by a novel process,[138] led to the search for a new factory, not least because the irradiation of ergosterol was a potentially hazardous operation. In August 1928 Randall inspected vacant premises at Park Royal belonging to Fuller Horsey & Co., but these were considered unsuitable.[139] In the event, Glaxo took out a five-year lease on the vacant Sanitas factory at Dawley, Hayes, largely because it was situated far from housing and lay close to the Grand Union Canal and the Great Western Railway.[140] Much of the equipment (vessels, condensers, tanks and pumps) was bought second-hand and the plant made Ostelin from a variety of fish oils, including whale, as well as by the Steenbock process. G. P. Dodds, who had originally been appointed by Jephcott in 1920 to work in the Bravington Road analytical laboratory, was the first factory manager. A. R. Lewis, the chief engineer at Hayes, recalled that their remote situation led to the management being given considerable freedom of action and they became like 'the Swiss family Robinson'.[141] As sales of Ostelin grew and Glaxo introduced other vitamin products so modern plant was installed, £3,000 being authorised in October 1931.[142] By the mid 1930s the Dawley factory was also making vitamins E and K and its product range had been widened to include Adexolin (capsules containing vitamins A and D), Minadex (a children's tonic) and wheatgerm extract.[143] In 1936, when the Greenford factory opened, the plant was transferred to what were nicknamed 'the Hayes buildings'.[144] Because it had already become clear that Greenford had insufficient capacity, the Dawley lease was renewed and when the prospect of war became ever more likely it served as a shadow factory, producing vitamins during the hostilities.

Crisis in the milk business: the launch of Ostermilk

While valuable development work was being undertaken into vitamins, the staple product of the Glaxo Department, dried milk, ran into a commercial

23. Joseph Nathan & Co.'s sports day held at Messrs Whiteley's Kildare Athletic Grounds, Wembley Park on 27 August 1921. Harry Jephcott, one of the judges, is standing fourth from the left at the back.

crisis. Sales peaked at over £1.5 million in the post-war boom of 1921 and fell thereafter as the economy stagnated and as other manufacturers entered what was becoming a competitive market. To provide Glaxo with an edge, in 1928 the Department introduced a version fortified with vitamin D.[145] Initially called 'Prescription (Humanised) Glaxo', the brand name was soon changed to 'Sunshine Glaxo'. It proved popular with infant welfare centres which, in turn, upset retail pharmacists who had to sell the dried milk at a higher price. In response to their complaints, Hugo Wolff agreed a plan with Alec Nathan whereby Sunshine Glaxo would be withdrawn from welfare centres. The clinics were then supplied with the same product marketed under the name of Ostermilk,[146] and retailed at about half the price (a 1lb tin costing 2s). Despite the fact that the packaging of Ostermilk was blandly descriptive and no mention was made of Glaxo, the product sold widely and before the end of January 1929 a number of chemists, including Boots, had approached the company to ask for trade terms. At first, the Glaxo Department refused to supply them with Ostermilk but the insistence of their requests led them to change their minds. Nevertheless, the margin was smaller than on Sunshine Glaxo, though a little more generous than applied at the clinics.[147] Accordingly, those pharmacists 'shrewd enough to realise that an infant's food at an economic price was a means of creating trade', stocked Ostermilk, though the limited profit discouraged most retailers. The commercial success of this marketing plan brought its own problems, as Hugo Wolff recalled:

> It was obvious that the general public desired to be able to obtain supplies of Ostermilk from the trade when they were unable or did not wish to do so from the Welfare Centres. It was equally obvious that chemists, when they found they could not supply the food sold at the Welfare Centres, resented their inability to compete with them.[148]

To balance these competing pressures, Glaxo resolved not 'to force the sale of Ostermilk through the chemist, but only to fulfil all demands, but that we should encourage a demand in places where Ostermilk was being used in the welfare centre'.[149]

In 1932 the Glaxo Department was renamed Glaxo Laboratories to reflect the scientific research that supported many of its products. In the same year, it was decided to introduce a full-cream dried milk, marketed as Ostermilk No. 2, fortified with vitamin D. By comparison, the fat and protein contents of Ostermilk No. 1 were modified to equate with the levels in breast milk. At the time, the decision to market a full-cream version was considered 'unsound' physiologically but was driven by the popular belief held by mothers that when a child reached three to four months a richer food was needed. This often resulted in the rejection of the existing Ostermilk in favour of a competitor product. The follow-on milk proved commercially successful and by the late 1930s had overtaken its progenitor in terms of sales.[150] The launch of Ostermilk No. 2 also encouraged the company to advertise the two products in the national press, though the scale of the campaign was muted by fears it might raise in the minds of chemists. Wolff and his team thought that retailers would conclude that such a costly programme had been financed by Ostermilk profits and, therefore, demand that their low margins be increased.[151]

Food diversification: Farex and Minadex

In May 1932, Glaxo Laboratories marketed a new nutritional product sold in 1lb tins called Farex and advertised as 'The *reinforced* cereal food'. It was a pre-cooked mixture of three cereals (oats, wheat and American maize) to provide protein and carbohydrate and was supplemented with vitamins and minerals. In the manufacturing process, water was added to the three flours

24. The hoarding opposite King's Cross station advertising Glaxo in 1921.

to make a slurry, to which salts and vitamins were added; the mixture being roller dried and sieved to produce a medium-fine powder. Farex was reconstituted with milk to make a porridge-like meal. Designed primarily for infant weaning, it was also sold as a convalescence diet. Farex was based on a formula researched at the Hospital for Sick Children in Toronto by Dr F. F. Tisdall.[152] The latter had obtained business sponsorship from Mead Johnson & Co., manufacturers of infant foods. Tisdall undertook considerable research on recipes for them before finding that US patent law prevented the addition of vitamin D. Jephcott came to hear of these developments and in October 1930 requested a sample of the cereal food.[153] In the following year Jephcott travelled to Evansville, Indiana, to visit Mead Johnson's factory and met Tisdall to discuss the possibility of production in the UK. Having obtained his agreement, Jephcott then prevaricated. In his own words, 'pressure of work and the difficulties connected with the project itself, unfortunately, made me hesitate a long time in coming to any conclusion'.[154] In the meantime, paediatricians in the UK heard of these advances and wrote to Tisdall who, in turn, referred them to Glaxo. Under pressure to produce a vitamin-fortified farinaceous food, the company adapted the Mead Johnson recipe. They excluded alfalfa, providing vitamins A and D in a concentrate form, and finely ground the cereals so that they could be used in a feeding bottle. The product was moderately successful in overcoming a popular prejudice against farinaceous foods for infants. Sales, however, remained modest, a mere £84 in the first six months, rising to £254 in 1932–33 and £338 in 1933–34.[155] Demand improved when, in October 1934, Glaxo introduced a new soluble variety (in which the starches had been converted into sugars) called 'New Farex', and in the six months from its launch it generated a turnover of £1,534.[156] Despite this increase, sales remained disappointing and the existence of two products with such similar names had created marketing problems.[157] In the event, the old Farex was renamed 'Farex Cereal Food' and eventually withdrawn from sale. Once they had reverted to a single product, Glaxo simply called the new version 'Farex'.[158]

The company remained equivocal about this excursion into farinaceous foods, though it was acknowledged in 1935 that the product marketing had been insufficiently planned:

> the start of the new product marked the first time that we really did intensive propaganda for the name Farex. This propaganda may have had faults in not making completely clear the fact that there were two products, one 'soluble' and one not, but the prime fact is that it advertised a name and a certain number of people have gone to chemists' and asked for that product by name.[159]

It had, perhaps, been an error to direct the campaign into medical channels, concentrating on paediatricians, chemists, infant welfare centres and children's nurses, rather than consumers and food retailers.

In the meantime, Glaxo's scientists had been devising a formula for a children's tonic that would contain glucose together with essential vitamins and minerals. The composition of the syrup was finalised in November 1933 and launched in the following April as 'Minadex'. Fortified with vitamins A and D, it proved an immediate success, output rising from 8,500 gallons in the year of its introduction to 45,000 gallons in 1941.[160] However, it did not prove a great source of profit as margins remained low in a fiercely competitive market.

By the early 1930s, the Glaxo Department, the truly dynamic and entrepreneurial element in the Nathan empire, had grown to such a size that it required a formal management structure. Accordingly, in 1931, Alec Nathan created a 'local board'.[161] It was not a legally constituted subsidiary but an executive committee granted a defined area of autonomy within Joseph Nathan & Co. Chaired by Nathan, its members (Jephcott, Wolff, Rose, Forster, Richardson, Gwilt and, from 1932, Preston) were called 'local directors'.[162] In the complex family relationships that operated between London and New Zealand, it was a diplomatic preliminary to the grant of full company status to the Glaxo Department.

GLAXO COMES OF AGE

1935–1939

And from Greenford scent of mayfields
Most enticingly was blown
Over market gardens tidy,
Taverns for the *bona fide*

Sir John Betjeman, 'Middlesex'[1]

I N 1932, to reflect the scientific basis of an increasing number of its products, Alec Nathan had changed the trading name of the Glaxo Department to Glaxo Laboratories. In a sense, this was no more than a cosmetic decision designed to give the business a modern and innovative feel. However, the events of 1935 were substantial and far reaching. First, to reflect its growing commercial importance within the organisation, Nathan floated Glaxo Laboratories as a private limited liability company, which functioned as a wholly owned subsidiary of Joseph Nathan & Co.[2] Incorporated on 1 October with a capital of £400,000, Alec Nathan took the chairmanship and Jephcott was appointed managing director, while the other board members included F. C. Randall (finance), Hugo Wolff (sales) and Lieutenant-Colonel E. A. Rose (production); Arthur Dawson, the chief accountant, became the company secretary.[3] The second event, one of even greater significance, was the decision to move from Osnaburgh Street to larger, purpose-built premises at Greenford. This not only facilitated production and provided room for expansion, it also gave Glaxo Laboratories its own sense of identity and a tangible physical presence.

Greenford: a new home

The setting up of Glaxo Laboratories as a private limited liability company had been predicated by the bold decision, taken in September 1933, to unite all sections of its business in new premises outside London in cleaner air and with space for growth. A 15-acre, greenfield site at Greenford was chosen for a factory, warehouse, laboratory and administrative headquarters. The suburb was bounded to the south-west by the Grand Union Canal and to the east by the Greenford Road, which had been laid in 1924 and joined the arterial dual carriageway, the Western Avenue (A40), opened in 1930.[4] The extension of the Piccadilly Line to South Harrow in July 1932 with a station at Sudbury Hill provided a modern rail link from Hammersmith and central London,[5] while the LNER operated commuter services from Marylebone to Sudbury Hill and Harrow, and the Great Western ran from Paddington to Greenford. Later, in June 1947, the Central Line was extended from White City Station to Greenford.[6] A core of the Osnaburgh Street workforce transferred to the new factory, their numbers being rapidly supplemented by staff recruited locally.

Although still rural in the 1920s, the improving communications and its proximity to London made Greenford a focus for light industry. Development had begun in 1900 with the construction of W. A. Bailey's glass-works (later Rockware glass) and the siting of a large munitions factory in the First World War. J. Lyons & Co., for example, opened a tea-blending and confectionery factory in Oldfield Lane in 1921.[7] By the early 1930s, family homes and parades of small shops were being constructed by speculative builders as part of a sustained housing boom. Semi-detached houses with bathrooms and a garage could be bought for as little as £450, while mortgages were available on easy terms with an average interest rate of 4.5 per cent, repayments falling well within the range of most middle-class and better-off working-class families.[8] Greenford lay at the very heart of these developments and this central part of Middlesex with its bright, architect-designed factories, bow-fronted and mock Tudor houses, spacious cinemas and substantial garages was in many respects an expression of modern thirties Britain.[9] J. B. Priestley, travelling along the Great West Road in 1933, described the new factories as 'decorative little buildings', and added that 'if we could all get a living out of them, what a pleasanter country this would be, like a permanent exhibition ground, all glass and chromium plate and nice painted signs and coloured lights'.[10]

By 1933, it had become apparent that the existing factory at Osnaburgh Street, supported by its satellites at Hayes and Bravington Road, were so overcrowded that they inhibited future growth. In May, the Nathan board explored the possibility of separating the food and pharmaceutical busi-

nesses. Because of their in-
terlocking nature (many of
the foods were, for example,
fortified with vitamins), this
was thought impractical. On
22 September, the board decided to buy the land at
Greenford to construct purpose-built premises for
Glaxo Laboratories. A committee consisting of Alec
Nathan, Randall and Jeph-
cott took responsibility for
the implementation of the
project. In March 1934, they
chose Wallis, Gilbert & Partners, the Westminster practice, and in July Frank Cox
agreed to prepare plans,
elevations and estimates.
The partnership, under its
founder Thomas Wallis, had

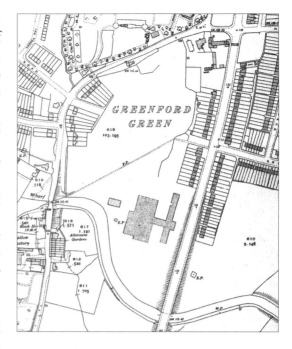

25. An Ordnance Survey map of Greenford showing
the location of Glaxo's new factory constructed
in 1935.

built up a considerable reputation for industrial commissions.[11] Nathan
may have been influenced by the factory they had designed for the Fire-
stone Tyre & Rubber Co on the Great West Road at Brentford, or for
Hoover at Perivale.[12] Indeed, the public profile of the firm had been enhanced by winning the design for the London and Country [Victoria]
Coach Station, completed in 1932.[13]

Although the brief presented to the architects by Glaxo appeared
straightforward (a two-storey office block and laboratory facing the Greenford Road with a manufacturing and warehouse area to the rear), its practical execution presented considerable problems. Separate flow lines were
required for each of the company's many products, while Jephcott's observation that their 'inability to see far into the future as to what requirements
would be' led to a demand for 'maximum elasticity' in the layout.[14] The architects needed great patience in the negotiations with Glaxo, which lasted
for over nine months and during which time they worked without a fee.
Much of the practical decision making fell to Herbert Palmer, Jephcott's
personal assistant. A graduate in commerce from the London School of
Economics, Palmer had joined the Glaxo Department in 1928 as a sales representative. Having attended a high school in Germany, he was a good

26. The construction of the warehouse, canteen and offices for Glaxo in August 1935.

linguist and as a result had been appointed head of the Brussels office.[15] Success there brought Palmer to the attention of Jephcott, who recalled him to the UK where he found himself entrusted with the execution of the Greenford project. Although Palmer later developed into an efficient executive, his correspondence with Frank Cox, the architect, revealed that he lacked the experience to manage such a complex project. Jephcott, too, appears to have floundered and was uncharacteristically indecisive. In August 1934, when Wallis, Gilbert & Partners produced a final set of plans based on Glaxo's detailed proposals, Palmer faltered. He acknowledged that the 'proposed sequence of operations' was as requested but concluded that the arrangement appeared 'somewhat over elaborate'.[16] The operational scheme he had agreed for the milk powder section had 'all the signs of logicality and practicability' but, as Palmer belatedly recognised, if this were executed in a direct line to the packing tables it would impede mobility across the factory floor. These were issues that should have been resolved long before Wallis, Gilbert & Partners were asked to produce detailed plans.

Jephcott, too, was undecided on important questions that wasted the architects' time and delayed the project. As late as September 1934, for example, he had not settled the positioning of the buildings and Wallis, Gilbert were instructed to peg out the two front corners and centre in various positions and erect scaffold poles to give an impression of the structure. Jephcott still vacillated, reporting to the Nathan board that 'we find ourselves not competent critically to examine' the designs of Wallis Gilbert since 'in the absence of plans or proposals from another firm, we have no standard against which to judge the quality of their work'.[17] It was a remarkable admission over a year into the project. In view of Jephcott's concerns and worried about the cost of the factory, Glaxo then decided against formally

The
NEW HOME of
GLAXO LABORATORIES
LTD.
GL
Fully occupied   *December 31st.*
1935

Erected on a 15-acre site at Greenford, Middlesex, the new home of Glaxo Laboratories Ltd., comprises a group of planned and inter-related buildings in which the entire activities of the organisation are now concentrated.

27. An aerial view of Glaxo Laboratories' new factory at Greenford showing that it then had space for expansion.

appointing Wallis, Gilbert. Undaunted, the firm pressed ahead and, on 20 September, Cox offered to revise their sketch plans to effect savings. During the following month, while the architects produced new designs, Jephcott found an effective way of proceeding. Belatedly, he held a series of meetings with departmental heads to draw on their specialist experience and build up an overall plan of their manufacturing requirements. The 'factory committee' met twice a week for a month and produced a businesslike, detailed assessment of the new buildings with dimensions, estimates of space and locations of departments, the very information the architects had needed four months earlier. Once they were given this document and granted direct access to the works managers, the project took off. In December 1934 the new plans and estimates were agreed and at long last Wallis, Gilbert were formally appointed.[18]

The construction of the Greenford factory was put out to tender, and Richard Costain & Co. won the contract with the lowest bid of £138,670. Work began on 18 March 1935, having been preceded by a ceremony in which Alec Nathan cut the first sod. The building advanced at great speed,

28. The main office block and bacteriological and physiological laboratories that faced the Greenford Road designed by the Westminster architects, Wallis, Gilbert & Partners. These brick and black glass buildings were a confident statement of the new company's commercial intentions.

in marked contrast to the protracted design process. In June the structural steelwork was in place, followed by the exterior brickwork in August. By November the offices, laboratories and manufacturing areas were ready for occupation – the entire construction being completed within eight months.[19] The factory employees transferred from Osnaburgh Street that month, followed in December by their office colleagues.[20] Unable to sell the vacated buildings, Glaxo sub-leased them to Conrad Silverman until the Prudential Assurance Co. acquired them for £55,900 at the end of the war.

The Glaxo house magazine for January 1936 described the new factory as fulfilling the 'primary aim of modern industrial architecture', namely 'fitness of purpose within an aesthetically satisfying framework'. In essence, the design comprised two elements: a two-storey office block linked by an overhead walkway to a smaller laboratory building, both of which faced the Greenford Road, and a factory and warehouse area behind. Glaxo had requested that the brick offices present 'a very sober appearance' but were prepared to incur the extra expense of an entrance similar to 'an important banking establishment'.[21] Executed in buff-coloured brick and decorated with black glass panels between the windows, the offices presented a restrained dignity to the passing public. To impress visitors and customers, the entrance was faced in Portland stone, while the moulded architrave over the double oak doors exhibited Egyptian details, popular after the discovery of Tutankhamun's tomb in 1922. The hall itself was designed to impress. Inside it was light, airy and cool, giving a hygienic feel as befitted a

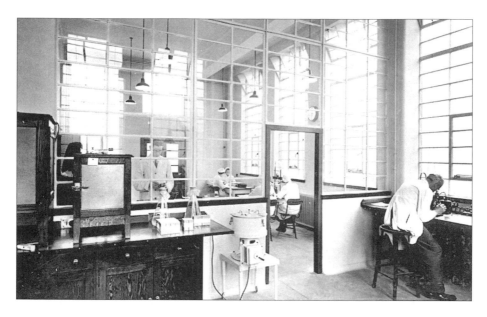

29. *The ground floor of the bacteriological laboratory for the isolation and culture of pathogenic micro-organisms. Through the glass screen was an aseptic room for the packing of vaccines and anti-viruses.*

company that made foods and pharmaceuticals. A stairway led immediately up to the first floor and the offices of Nathan and Jephcott, which overlooked the entrance and faced Horsenden Hill. The Glaxo brief had stated that staff should have an alternative route through the building to use a separate staircase at the rear.

In accord with the benevolent paternalism practised by Alec Nathan, a variety of amenities were provided: a canteen with french windows opening on to gardens and later a tennis court. Subsidised meals and waitress service were available, though the factory staff ate at 12 p.m., followed by office workers at 1 p.m. Sports and social activities were encouraged, though the Nathans were wary of alcohol, which was banned from the canteen. In October 1939, the company purchased a sports field nearby on Oldfield Lane belonging to the Sun Life of Canada for £10,000 when a ground they had rented adjacent to the Northolt aerodrome was commandeered by the RAF.[22]

Although Alec Nathan was prepared to spend on amenities for Glaxo employees, he had also decreed that 'economy' was to be 'practised keenly and vigilantly in all [other] operations'.[23] Much of the plant, equipment and office furniture was moved from Osnaburgh Street. Every attempt was made to reduce costs to the extent that pencils were halved before being

30. The analytical laboratory at Greenford where products were tested for quality and purity.

issued to staff, incoming paperclips collected and out-of-date stationery blocked into pads.[24] Whilst such rigid economy was not applied to the directors, their offices had a restrained decor implying substance without extravagance. Jephcott's room had elm furniture finished in green hide with a matching Axminster carpet and folkweave curtains.[25] Rose, whose daughter Joanna was studying interior design at the Slade, broke with tradition when he asked her to furnish his office. Concealed lighting, fabric-lined walls, inset shelving and a hand-made mahogany pedestal desk with matching blue leather chairs made for a distinctive room, for which Rose himself paid.[26]

The main office block housed the advertising, sales, purchasing and export departments on the ground floor, while accounts, the directors and a conference room were above.[27] A first-floor bridge linked this building to the bacteriological and physiological laboratories, together with the vaccine department and animal rooms.[28] The offices were linked to the factory behind by a two-storey block that contained the postal department and the main analytical laboratory. Food manufacture was separated centrally by cloakrooms, laboratories and small processing rooms from pharmaceuticals. Bulk food supplies (dried milk powder and cereals) were delivered by narrowboat to a dock connected to the warehouse by an overhead conveyor, while a second loading bay on the canal was used for shipments of coal to feed the boiler and generating house.

31. The ground-floor office showing clerks in the sales, filing and invoice departments. All the staff depicted are women and the company's caption to the picture commented that the new building offered 'a spacious open office providing maximum natural light and ideal working conditions'.

Shortly after the opening, it was decided to display Glaxo Laboratories' logo in neon at the top of the central entrance block on Greenford Road. However, as the Great Western Railway's line to Birmingham ran to the south, it was suggested that red or green, being used for signals, could confuse drivers. After a study of the limited alternatives turquoise blue was chosen and became the company's colour. The logo (an inverted triangle with a diamond in its base) had been designed in the early 1930s by Alfred Fisher, Glaxo's first staff artist, and was originally applied to tins of Glucose-D.[29]

The changing shape of the business

In the four years before the outbreak of war, Glaxo Laboratories made steady progress, with both turnover and profits rising in real terms (see Table 4, p. 445). Both almost doubled over this period, vindicating Alec Nathan's decision to relocate the business in modern premises at Greenford. Indeed, in December 1938, the company concluded that

> our margins of net profit are probably higher than safety would dictate. This position has not arisen out of any application of a 'maximum the traffic will bear'

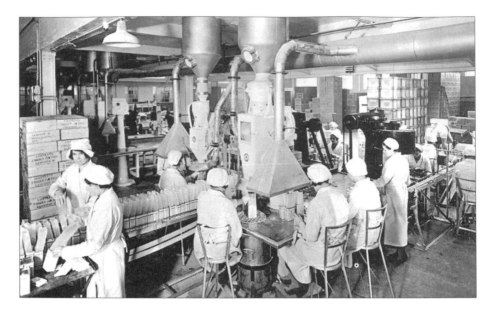

32. The food packing department where measured quantities of powder were poured into tins for sealing. Here women are preparing and filling tins of Glucose-D.

price policy, but has been the gradual result of reduced production costs following upon largely increased turnovers combined with a better spread of both selling and overhead expenses.[30]

The introduction of new products with substantial development costs and limited initial sales may have led to over-conservative prices, though, as Glaxo conceded, subsequent reductions 'with the immediate and calculable loss of net profit calls for courage and conviction as to future turnovers'.[31]

The bulk of Glaxo's medicines were vitamin products, and over 50 per cent of pharmaceutical sales in 1936 resulted from Glucose-D.[32] A vaccine department had been set up in the previous year in the anticipation that it 'would make a profitable addition to our turnover'.[33] Glucose-D continued to dominate, though its low margin encouraged the company to develop other lines.[34] Sales in the UK accounted for almost 60 per cent of turnover during the late 1930s.[35] India was the leading overseas market with 19 per cent, followed by Argentina (4.6 per cent), Italy (3 per cent), while Australia and New Zealand combined generated 4 per cent. Almost half of all pharmaceutical sales were overseas, while the foods business was predominantly in the UK (71 per cent of sales in 1938). Pharmaceuticals generated 58 per cent of Glaxo Laboratories' total turnover in 1938 (see Table 5, p. 446).[36] However, some products defined as pharmaceuticals would not today be

33. The lecture room laid out with a presentation for visiting nurses. The tutor is explaining the roller drying method of making milk powder.

designated as prescription medicines. Glucose-D, in particular, could equally well have been classified as a food and as such would have dramatically altered the balance between the two elements of the business. In 1939, therefore, Glaxo Laboratories remained, in essence, a food company, albeit one with a growing specialisation in vitamin medicines.

The commercial significance of the pharmaceutical element of the business was recognised by October 1935, though the full implications of this diversification had not been understood. Even then, twelve years after the launch of Ostelin, no provision had been made in the company's budgets for research and development. Jephcott was forced to argue that his department

> had been hampered a great deal in the past on account of our inability to incur expenditure … and the lack of physical room in which to carry out research. The moment had arrived when such work must be looked upon as a necessity and provided for as such if the business were to expand and justify the existence of the Greenford factory.[37]

Jephcott spoke of the 'futility of attempting research in a spasmodic manner' and the need for 'continuity' in a planned programme. His case proved

34. *Pharmaceutical packing: there is little evidence of automated machinery to undertake these repetitive tasks. The two tables on the left are capping and labelling vials of Minadex, while the women on the right are working on Ostomalt.*

persuasive and the board agreed that such expenditure should be 'a charge to the business and not dependent upon appropriation of profits'.[38] It is ironic that Jephcott should have been the protagonist of this policy as in the 1950s and 1960s directors of research (Macrae and Jack) found him parsimonious in matters of scientific inquiry and experiment.

In January 1936, Hugo Wolff reviewed Glaxo's marketing strategy, or 'propaganda' as it was then termed.[39] The company made great play of their move to Greenford, doctors and the trade being invited to tour the factory. This exercise had, in turn, led to a debate on future sales policy and it was decided to market pharmaceuticals 'on a strictly ethical basis'.[40] To enforce a uniform price, Glaxo joined the Proprietary Articles Trade Association, and the Chemists Friend Scheme (the National Pharmaceutical Union) so that certain medicines were sold only by pharmacists. Promotional material was directed at the medical profession and representatives called on GPs, hospital physicians, charitable institutions, chemists, nursing homes and maternity and child welfare centres. Employees were instructed to press the claims of products with discretion, as the guidelines issued in 1936 indicated:

Members of our representative staff must always bear in mind when making

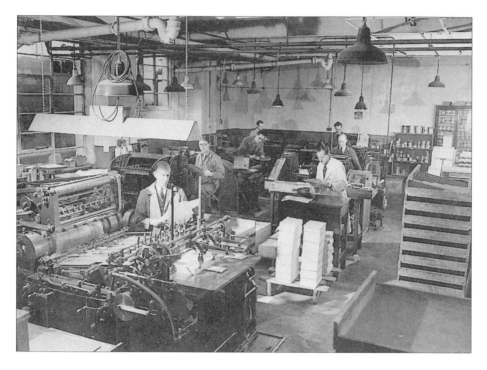

35. The printing department at Greenford in 1946 responsible for labels, medical literature and packing leaflets in a variety of languages.

calls that to the customer they will reflect the policy and character of the House … There is no more important part of a representative's mental make-up than the ability to exercise tact, and a representative should never place himself in such a position that it is difficult, embarrassing or impossible for the House to support his attitude to any particular customer.[41]

Although 'no opportunity must be missed of selling our own organisation and service to customers', it was also decreed that 'in no circumstances' was it 'necessary to disparage a competitive House', many being 'worthy of every admiration, and a representative does not lose anything by acknowledging this on suitable occasions'.[42] In January 1936, Glaxo issued the first *Journal*, a short, illustrated magazine distributed to retail pharmacists, providing them with commercial and technical data on the company's products. The home sales department was restructured into three regions in 1937 because the 'reorientation of the work … simultaneously with the imposition of the increased load which the further expansion of the business imposes, placed a very serious strain upon a large number of individuals'.[43]

The changes introduced to the sales department convinced Nathan and Jephcott that other functions of Glaxo Laboratories required organisa-

36. The crystallisation of vitamin D_2 (calciferol) at Greenford.

tional reform. In 1938, four divisions (production, sales and marketing, technical, and accounting) were created with operational responsibilities.[44] The production division was sub-divided into purchasing, primary (the manufacture of basic ingredients such as vitamin D), secondary (the manufacture of tablets, creams, syrups and so forth) and engineering. The greatest attention was paid to the technical division, which today would be called research and development.[45] It was split into four elements: analytical and control, together with the three research sections (process, chemical and biological). The first was concerned with the continuous monitoring of raw materials and finished products. Process research was in essence chemical engineering and devoted to improving the efficiency of manufacture.[46] The organic chemistry section was 'solely engaged upon research work', while the biological section also engaged in routine testing.[47] As an adjunct, Jephcott set up a medical division to which the bacteriological department (that worked on vaccines and other products of a bacteriological origin) reported. The medical division was established under Dr Hector Walker to provide technical data for the sales organisation and to help with clinical trials.[48] He had qualified in medicine at Glasgow and worked as a general practitioner in Harrow. There Walker treated Jephcott and his family, on one occasion saving the life of his eldest son. Jephcott regularly asked Walker for a professional opinion on medicines and the two became friends. When it became clear that Glaxo's diversification into pharmaceuticals required a full-time physician to advise on technical matters, Walker was an obvious choice.

By September 1938, a total of 741 employees worked at Greenford (of whom 357 were in the factory and 344 were office, scientific and sales).[49] This represented an increase of 19 per cent on numbers in the previous year and suggested rapid growth. Despite the provision made for expansion in the original plans, the Greenford factory soon became overcrowded and as early as June 1936, the board were forced to consider 'the urgent problem of

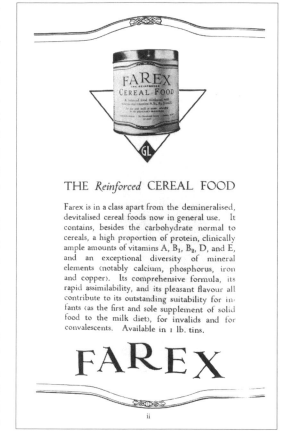

THE *Reinforced* CEREAL FOOD

Farex is in a class apart from the demineralised, devitalised cereal foods now in general use. It contains, besides the carbohydrate normal to cereals, a high proportion of protein, clinically ample amounts of vitamins A, B_1, B_2, D, and E, and an exceptional diversity of mineral elements (notably calcium, phosphorus, iron and copper). Its comprehensive formula, its rapid assimilability, and its pleasant flavour all contribute to its outstanding suitability for infants (as the first and sole supplement of solid food to the milk diet), for invalids and for convalescents. Available in 1 lb. tins.

FAREX

37. *An advertisement for Farex in* Nutrition *for May 1934, a journal published by Glaxo Laboratories.*

accommodation'.[50] They spent £10,000 to enlarge the pharmaceutical packing materials store and the despatch bays in preparation for taking over wholesale distribution. In addition, a two-storey laboratory building was constructed in 1937 alongside what was later called Berkeley Avenue to house bacteriology under R. E. Hunwicke. The manufacture of vaccines, involving the handling of pathogenic organisms, was also moved to this building, which later became known as the headquarters for research.

By March 1939, the introduction of new products such as Farex had increased pressures still further and Glaxo was faced with a major construction programme, which included the excavation of Air Raid Precautions (ARP) shelters as war with Germany appeared increasingly likely.[51] A refrigeration building, extensions to the pharmaceutical factory and a self-contained manufacturing and packing unit for Farex were authorised at a

38. The construction of the milk drying factory for Glaxo at Driffield in 1937 to the designs of Wallis, Gilbert & Partners.

total cost, including ARP trenches and a new garage, of £46,000.[52] In view of the pressing demands made by the government for nutritional products, Glaxo accelerated their expansion plans.[53] Still concerned about possible shortages of capacity, in October 1939 Glaxo extended their lease on the unoccupied Hayes factory, and it was subsequently used under Dr Peter Wilkinson for the irradiation of ergosterol, a potentially hazardous operation in the manufacture of vitamin D.

Safeguarding supplies: Driffield

The success of Ostermilk I and II created shortages in the supply of dried milk powder, then exclusively imported from New Zealand and the Australian factory at Port Fairy. To gain greater control over supplies, the company explored the possibility of building a 'home drying factory' in September 1936.[54] Preliminary discussions were held with Dr Scott-Robertson, Secretary to the Ministry of Agriculture, about a plant in Northern Ireland, but these proved fruitless. It had become an urgent matter as UK demand for 1937 was estimated at 2,000 tons of powder, revealing a deficit of 360 tons.[55] Edward Farmer had investigated the dairy-farm regions of Devon, Wales and Yorkshire and concluded that sufficient quantities of milk were available in either the Kingsbridge area of Devon or in south-east Yorkshire.[56] Negotiations with the Milk Marketing Board narrowed the location

39. Roller drying machines installed at Driffield.

to Driffield, a small town to the north of Hull with good rail links.[57] By January 1937, Jephcott was authorised to take 'drastic action ... to procure powder to meet the deficiencies at any cost and from any source'.[58] Given that Glaxo required about one million gallons of milk a year, it was important to obtain the agreement of the local branch of the National Farmers Union, and as an inducement the company offered to collect the milk themselves at the reduced rates of a farthing per gallon within five miles of the factory and a halfpenny beyond.[59] By April 1937 contracts had been signed to provide the basic minimum supply, while Jephcott and the company's architects, Wallis, Gilbert & Partners, had visited four potential sites.[60] The favoured location in Wansford Road belonged to the LNER, adjoining their line from Hull to Bridlington.[61] The plans for the factory were approved in May and construction, again entrusted to Richard Costain & Co., proceeded apace.[62]

The factory at Driffield was completed on schedule and began drying operations on 1 October.[63] Powder was sent by rail to Greenford, where it was blended with that from Australasia before being packaged. Farmer was appointed the first manager, having been responsible for the co-ordination of the project. Although it made 1,348,000lb of powder in its first year of operation this was far below the volumes at Bunnythorpe and Port

Fairy. The company recognised that Driffield was born of necessity rather than economy:

> the cost of milk for drying at Driffield is out of all proportion to similar costs in the Dominions and it will require all the special advantages of lower packing and transport costs and modern equipment to be able to produce at figures comparable with Dominion imports. On the other hand, the factory has already justified itself by the invaluable services rendered in respect of small quantities of export powder required.[64]

Managers and management

Ultimate authority at Glaxo Laboratories was vested in Alec Nathan as chairman and Harry Jephcott as managing director. Once the move to Greenford was completed, Nathan, by then in his sixties, took an increasingly non-executive role. Although he continued to chair monthly board meetings, the daily running of the business and strategic planning were entrusted to Jephcott. He had become the key figure in the company and, in time, his name became synonymous with Glaxo Laboratories. A skilled planner with an ability to spot talent, Jephcott became increasingly powerful as the years passed; he retained overall control of research and development long after it had advanced beyond the boundaries of pharmacy, sometimes to the detriment of potentially important projects (see p. 112). It was said in the 1950s that when Jephcott sneezed, the board caught a cold. In the 1930s and 1940s, however, his authority was not so well established as many key executives had been recruited by Nathan. The first board appointments in which Jephcott had a hand were in 1936. They followed the sudden death of Frederick Randall on 14 February,[65] which had reduced the board to four: Nathan, Jephcott, Rose and Wolff. In November 1936, Dr Hector Walker (see p. 54) and Edmund Preston both became Glaxo directors, the former taking responsibility for medical matters and the latter for publicity.[66] On graduating in English from Cambridge, Preston had originally worked as Sir Arthur Conan Doyle's travelling secretary, forsaking this to become an advertising copy writer.[67] In 1925, he was loaned to the Glaxo Department by Saward Baker & Co. to write promotional material for Glax-ovo, chocolate-flavoured dried milk, subsequently being recruited by Nathan as the advertising manager. After a dispute with Nathan, Preston returned briefly to agency work, but rejoined the company in 1931, remaining until retirement thirty-three years later. Glaxo-ovo did not capture the public's imagination despite the combined efforts of Nathan and Preston and was withdrawn relatively soon after its 1923 launch.

GLAXO AT WAR

＄

THE SECOND WORLD WAR was a turning point in the fortunes
of Glaxo Laboratories. The totalitarian character of modern warfare
demanded that companies surrender their peacetime commercial
priorities in favour of the pressing needs of the country's conscript armies
and civilian population. Glaxo was forced to divert both its food and pharmaceutical operations to meet government imperatives, and in doing so
transformed the very nature of the business.

The Glaxo board that responded to the declaration of war in 1939 was
small and relatively elderly. Alec Nathan, the chairman, was past retirement
age and had assumed something of a non-executive role, while Rose was in
his early sixties. Wolff had already announced that for health reasons he
wished to leave the company.[1] This left only Jephcott, the managing director,
who was in his prime, together with Walker and Preston, the medical and
publicity directors respectively, who were both middle-aged. The executive
gap created by the departure of Wolff was not filled until November 1940
when Herbert Palmer was appointed to the board.[2] Yet their numbers were
soon to be reduced by the secondment of Walker into the RAF and Jephcott
to the Ministry of Food, where he served as an advisor from 1941 to 1943, while
also chairing the Therapeutic Research Corporation.[3] In essence, a five-man
executive team (Nathan, Jephcott, Rose, Preston and Palmer) steered Glaxo
through the war until November 1944 when the prospect of peace led to a reorganisation of the business on 'progressive lines'.[4] It had become apparent
that Glaxo Laboratories, rather than Joseph Nathan & Co., the parent, was
the driving force within the group and that the existing structure required
urgent reform. To prepare the ground Sandercock, a long-standing board
member of Nathans, and Hutchinson, a pharmacist responsible for the company's North American interests, were 'invited to attend the Glaxo board
meetings'[5] until their formal appointment in January 1945.[6]

In September 1945, with the war in Europe at an end, Alec Nathan, at the age of 73, decided to retire as chairman.[7] He departed on 1 October, the beginning of the financial year. Jephcott as managing director succeeded him, Sandercock taking over as his deputy.[8] This brought to an end the direct involvement of the Nathan family at board level, though Joseph Albert Nathan was appointed joint company secretary with Arthur Dawson.[9] No longer could any serving executive personally recall the early days of the business. Henceforth, Glaxo Laboratories was run by professional managers and the Jewish element in the company's culture rapidly dissipated. The Second World War witnessed the transformation of what had been a family business into a modern industrial corporation, with Jephcott providing the vital executive continuity.

Dried milk powder

With the outbreak of war, the company's main concern was to safeguard supplies of milk powder from New Zealand and Australia. Driffield was unable to make up the shortfall. Given the likely involvement of Italy in the war, there was no guarantee that the Mediterranean would be safe and it seemed possible that shipping passing through the Suez Canal would be attacked. In June 1939, Glaxo opened negotiations with the Milk Marketing Board to increase supplies from UK producers and to establish its quotas from abroad.[10] In an attempt to control the nation's nutritional requirements in times of shortage, the newly created Ministry of Food became the sole importing agency, purchasing milk powder direct from Dominion governments. The Ministry then distributed supplies to Glaxo and other manufacturers at 'a substantially higher cost'.[11] Faced with rising overheads, the company had already increased the retail price of Ostermilk by 3d per lb,[12] and in April 1940 had to consider a further advance of 3d to 6d a tin 'if reasonable profit margins were to be maintained'.[13]

By September 1940, under the impact of rationing and price rises, sales of 'Sunshine Glaxo' fell to such low levels that the company discussed withdrawing the product. This raised concerns about the 'valuable goodwill attaching to the use of the word "Glaxo" [as] it was essential that nothing should be done to prejudice our main trademark'.[14] They sought the opinion of the company's patent agents, Messrs F. B. Dehn & Co., who confirmed that

> the cessation of the use of the name [Glaxo] in connection with foods need not jeopardise the word as a trade mark since the Trade Mark Act provided protection … even for goods for which the mark is not used. Moreover, the continued

use of the word for foods in our export markets affords further protection. We would, however, be well advised to maintain the word 'Glaxo' in conjunction with other trade names as a composite trade mark.[15]

Given this reassurance, the company decided to discontinue the use of the word 'Glaxo' as a trademark for the sale of infant foods in the UK. Henceforth, milk powder would be sold exclusively as Ostermilk so that the name Glaxo could be employed more generally to pharmaceutical products.

As the war deepened and prospects for victory seemed remote, trading became increasingly problematic. Many staff had been lost to the armed forces (see p. 76), shortages of raw materials restricted manufacture, while rationing ultimately determined the limits of consumption. When, in January 1941, Glaxo failed to supply all of its customers, it was decided to call a temporary halt to the advertising of Ostermilk.[16] The moratorium was to be no longer than eight weeks, as the company were concerned that goodwill would suffer. The Ministry of Food did not allow manufacturers to include advertising in their costs and Glaxo chose to continue to promote the Ostermilk name 'even at the sacrifice of net profit'.[17] In May 1941, at the recommendation of Edmund Preston, Glaxo again began to promote Ostermilk, despite the 'considerable difficulty in drawing up press advertisements suitable to the circumstances'.[18]

Despite problems of supply and price rises, consumption of Ostermilk increased during the early war years. However, in 1941 its market was threatened by the introduction of government subsidised 'National Dried Milk Powder'. Glaxo were concerned that this cheaper variant would attract customers. Rather than offer a discount on Ostermilk and attempt to compete, the company decided to raise the retail price of a 1lb tin from 2s 3d to 2s 6d (12.5p).[19] The company concluded that 'we should do nothing that would tend to reduce current rates of gross profit' and that the loss of business to subsidised National Dried Milk, thereby increasing their operating costs, necessitated the higher price.[20] It was a bold decision based on considerable confidence in the brand appeal and quality of Ostermilk;[21] the increase was implemented on 31 March 1941.[22]

In 1942, with the intensification of the war in the Pacific, Glaxo became concerned that supplies of milk powder from Australasia could be curtailed.[23] The company was also worried that in circumstances of reduced supply, the Ministry of Food would intervene to control the distribution of proprietary milk powder. Having seen consumption of Ostermilk grow throughout the war years, Alec Nathan, supported by Rose, concluded that it would be 'ill-advised to expand the business' and that all 'selling propaganda should cease', restricting sales to about 250 tons a month.[24] Preston and Palmer dissented, arguing that the trademark's goodwill could be sustained only by an expenditure of £10,000 on press advertising.[25] The matter was finally resolved in October 1942 when Preston demonstrated the effectiveness of advertising expenditure on sales figures for 1935 and 1939. Nathan agreed that Glaxo

> spend a sum not exceeding that expended in 1939, and that the control of the use of Ostermilk for infant feeding should be the guiding principle in the policy and copy to be employed, coupled with a restricted issue of the *Ostermilk Baby Book.*[26]

By the end of 1942, it was estimated that almost one-third of Glaxo's turnover was on government contracts.[27] Although this work reduced overheads, mounting requests for medicines from the Ministry of Supply endangered the output of proprietary lines.[28] Nathan and Jephcott concluded that the company had a duty to help the 'war effort' and that these orders should be accepted even at the expense of established Glaxo products. However, an inherent and unavoidable conflict of interests arose in August 1944. Paediatricians and Medical Officers of Health had asked the Ministry of Food to add vitamin D to National Dried Milk Powder at the point of manufacture for the benefit of children.[29] Glaxo were concerned that this would transform a subsidised milk powder into an 'infant food' which would trade 'in unfair competition with the like proprietary foods built upon a goodwill of years' standing'. Whilst the company accepted that the 'proposals are in the public interest and we should support them', much effort went into devising an arrangement to fulfil the government's aim without jeopardising the future sales of Ostermilk. Glaxo proposed that Ostermilk be sold at a subsidised rate in infant welfare centres to meet the government's nutritional goals, thereby preventing any necessity to add vitamin D to National Dried Milk Powder.[30] The company was prepared to sacrifice its profit margins 'to maintain its proprietary goodwill'.[31] In the event, the Ministry of Food pressed ahead with its plan to fortify subsidised powder, and Glaxo concluded that an erosion of their dried milk business was 'inevitable' as the public perceived the benefit of the National social schemes.[32]

Despite the company's worries about the future of Ostermilk, the war years, with the emphasis that was placed on a healthy diet and the restrictions imposed by rationing, led to greatly increased sales in the UK (Table 4). Food turnover rose from £496,699 in 1939 to £1,204,879 in 1945, an increment of 89 per cent in real terms (Table 5). Even with the great developments Glaxo made in the field of antibiotics, the food business grew faster than pharmaceuticals, home sales representing 60 per cent of UK turnover in 1945.

The nation's diet: vitamin B_1

By sinking so many merchant ships in spring 1941, German U-boats forced Britain to be increasingly self reliant for its foodstuffs. Disruption to shipments of wheat from the United States and fruit from imperial territories so concerned the Ministry of Food that it explored ways of improving the country's rationed and depleted diet. The Accessory Food Factors Committee of the Lister Institute and the Medical Research Council rec-

40. Alfred Bacharach (1891–1966), a Cambridge graduate, who joined Glaxo in 1920 from Wellcome as a food chemist.

ommended that white flour be fortified with calcium and vitamin B_1.[33] To satisfy a potentially huge demand the Ministry of Food decided to finance the construction of two vitamin factories whose management would be contracted out for a 'marginal remuneration'.[34] Glaxo Laboratories and May & Baker had been approached to run the plant, designed by Hoffman La Roche. Jephcott agreed to undertake this work and the synthesis of vitamin B_1 became a priority.[35] It soon became clear that the plant provided by the Ministry was unsuitable and plans for a new factory at Greenford were put in hand.[36] The contract was awarded to Costain and building began.[37] However, in March 1942, before the factory was finished, the project was halted by the Ministry.[38] Despite the attempts by Glaxo to persuade them to authorise the completion of a small-scale plant within existing premises, the government was adamant and the vitamin B_1 scheme was abandoned.[39] They had belatedly decided to make bread from less refined wheat (extracting 80–85 per cent of the grain rather than 70–75 per cent) which would result in a brown colour. This, in turn, raised the nutritional value of the loaf, increasing its content of vitamin B_1, vitamin B_2 complex, iron and protein. As *The Lancet* observed, it was curious that the government had not adopted this policy from the outset, given the evidence presented by the Medical Research Council; it seemed that they had believed that a popular prejudice for white bread would discourage consumption of the new loaf.[40] Although the Ministry refunded the company's expenses, the considerable research and production expertise diverted to the project could have been more usefully employed in other areas.

Antibiotics: Glaxo makes penicillin

Although Fleming had identified a mould which had antibacterial properties as early as 1928, no one had yet managed to extract the penicillin in a form that could be used therapeutically.[41] In 1938, Professor Howard Florey and Dr Ernst Chain, a biochemist, began to study naturally occurring antibacterial substances at the Sir William Dunn School of Pathology in Oxford and included *Penicillium notatum* in their survey. It soon proved to be the most promising substance but was elusive in preparation. Given the key task of growing the fungus by surface culture, Dr Norman Heatley experimented with different types of vessels in his efforts to generate sufficient quantities for clinical trials.[42] It was discovered that though penicillin itself is extremely labile, its calcium and sodium salts are relatively stable and could provide the basis for a therapeutic medicine.[43] In August 1941, an editorial in the *British Medical Journal* commented that 'we seem to be at the beginning of a new antiseptic era, and not the least promising of the anti-bacterial agents awaiting clinical trial are substances produced by bacteria themselves'.[44] Sampling showed that an incubation period of ten days provided the best yield but the small scale of the operation demanded the use of large numbers of vessels, which had to be attended by hand. With materials in short supply and diverted to military needs, Heatley experienced considerable difficulties in obtaining equipment.

However, news of these discoveries had spread.[45] In August 1940, Bacharach and F. A. Robinson, head of the chemistry department, spotted a paper in *The Lancet* by Chain and Florey entitled 'Penicillin as an antibacterial agent' and showed it to Jephcott.[46] The three agreed that it presented exciting possibilities and Dr B. K. Blount, director of research, was asked to contact Professor Florey at Oxford. A letter sent on 26 September received no reply, and neither did a second. These events contrasted with Florey's later assertion that he had contacted several British pharmaceutical manufacturers without success.[47] The involvement of Blount, an Oxford-trained chemist, was to prove short-lived as he resigned from

Glaxo to serve in the Intelligence Corps and thereafter pursued a career in government service.

Not deterred by Florey's reticence, Bacharach then suggested that Glaxo contact Harold Raistrick, professor of biochemistry at the London School of Hygiene and Tropical Medicine, who in the 1930s had experimented with various methods of extracting penicillin. At the same time, Robinson contacted Dr Wilson Baker of the Dyson Perrins Laboratory in Oxford and was told of the great difficulties Florey's team was experiencing in extracting and isolating penicillin from its broth. Baker believed that they were years from discovering the chemical constitution of penicillin and that the synthesis would prove exceptionally problematic.[48] Robinson recommended active collaboration with other companies exploring the production of penicillin on a commercial scale. Finally, Robinson met Florey and was assured that he wanted

> full collaboration with us, and preferably with everyone else engaged in the field, with regular meetings at which the results obtained by each team of workers will be discussed and plans made for future work. He would be very glad indeed if we would set up a large plant for manufacturing crude penicillin, producing say 1,000 litres of medium a week at first, and possibly more later, because his present output is not adequate even for chemical research and he has at the moment no material available for clinical research.[49]

With these undertakings, Robinson urged Jephcott to begin the experimental production of penicillin at Greenford.

In 1941 Professor Raistrick supplied Glaxo with nine strains of the penicillin mould. An incubator was constructed in the darkroom of the biochemical department and each of the trial strains grown in 1,000ml conical flasks to discover which could produce the greatest yield.[50] Great efforts were made to maintain the temperature at an optimum level and cork matting was placed on the roof during hot weather to supplement the use of electric fans. At first output was low. In October 1942, for example, Greenford produced 380 litres of metabolism solution a month, which with a litre of 12 to 16 units per ml, generated 4.7 to 6.1 mega units. Of this about two-thirds was recoverable for clinical trials.[51] The need to increase supplies had been made greater by the discovery that Florey's original estimate (that a single clinical case required 200,000 units) was too low and that the true therapeutic dose could be six times this amount.[52] Some of the penicillin made at Greenford was sent to the scientists working in Oxford.

While this preliminary work was taking place, Glaxo Laboratories were asked to join a 'research corporation' then being assembled by T. R. G. Bennett, chairman and managing director of the Wellcome Foundation.[53]

The Therapeutic Research Corporation (TRC) was a private limited liability company funded by a select group of pharmaceutical businesses and designed to co-ordinate their research activities. Glaxo was one of the original five members – the others being May & Baker, Boots, the British Drug Houses and the Wellcome Foundation. In the following year, they were joined by representatives of ICI's pharmaceutical division. The TRC had laudable aims (to pool and integrate research, to share manufacturing facilities and to present the views of the pharmaceutical industry to the government) but was limited in achieving these by pre-war, competitive rivalries. Member companies seemed unable to discard their old habits, and often misunderstood each other's businesses.[54] The invitation to Glaxo was, however, a public acknowledgement of the strides the company had made in pharmaceuticals. In October 1941, Dr Lester Smith and Robinson were nominated as Glaxo's representatives on the TRC Research Panel, while Jephcott sat on its main board.[55]

A survey of the TRC's original five members showed that Wellcome had the most impressive record in terms of publications and the most highly qualified scientific staff (Table 6, p. 446). Glaxo took second place in terms of numbers of patents and papers but was fourth in the ranking by doctorates. This was a function, in part, of Jephcott's stated prejudice against scientists who had post-graduate qualifications (see p. 113). The survey revealed that Glaxo Laboratories was not yet in the first rank of UK companies. Membership of the TRC seems to have brought home to Jephcott the importance of drug discovery. In November 1941, he acknowledged the difficulties experienced by the company's chemists in 'having to continuously proceed to London to consult works of reference',[56] and agreed to spend £1,000 on standard works of organic chemistry, including *Beilstein's Handbuch der Organischen Chemie*, then retailing at £550.[57] It was a measure of his reluctance to spend money that these texts were not already in the Greenford library. At the first meeting of the research panel of the TRC, Robinson and Lester Smith discovered that Burroughs Wellcome and Boots had reached a similar stage in their penicillin researches, whilst May & Baker had done very little and abandoned the project.[58] From various reports, they concluded that the scientists at ICI were probably not 'very much further ahead' than the Glaxo team.[59]

No single person, or even a group of individuals, could claim outright responsibility for the progress made by Glaxo in penicillin production. Such were the problems and the complexity of the chemistry that many researchers were involved from a range of disciplines. Although Jephcott was in charge, he was surrounded by a group of independently minded scientists, all with their own specialist departments. The laboratories had grown

in an *ad hoc* fashion in response to product needs and the commercial opportunities presented by scientific advances. The activities of the laboratories were not integrated and no organisational framework existed for the
execution of interdisciplinary projects.

Appreciating the potential importance of the antibiotic, the Ministry of
Supply had formed the General Penicillin Committee by November 1942 to
co-ordinate production, and ICI set up a surface-culture unit at Trafford
Park.[60] Returning to Greenford from Colwyn Bay where he had been acting
as an advisor to the Ministry of Food, Jephcott agreed to give the project a
high priority. In December, production was suspended for a fortnight to
allow construction work to increase the size of the incubator.[61] The design
of the vessels was also improved. Initially, one-litre conical flasks were
employed, but they could not be stacked – a major consideration when
they were needed in their thousands.[62] Heatley at Oxford had tried flat
stoneware bottles but workers found them unduly heavy and they could
not be easily inspected. Milk bottles were widely used, being cheap and
easily cleaned, though they had to be stored at an angle of ten degrees to
prevent the liquid wetting the cotton wool plugs. Glaxo staff designed a
mould culture flask, seven inches in diameter, manufactured by Townson &
Mercer and made of Hysil heat resisting glass to reduce breakages.[63] These
were ideal for stacking and helped to dissipate the heat produced by
fermentation. The flasks were, however, expensive to make and difficult to
wash mechanically because of their awkward shape (earning them the
nickname 'bed pans'). Batches were raised to 200 litres and much of the
experimental work to improve yields fell to Dr Lester Smith assisted by
Austin Bide.[64] The two were also responsible for investigating its
extraction, purification and, in particular, the biosynthesis of penicillin.
Writing in 1946, Lester Smith observed,

> it is probable that more organic chemists, working in collaboration, have at-
> tempted the synthesis of penicillin, than have worked on any other substance ...
> If I may venture a prophecy, it is that no commercial synthesis of penicillin will
> be achieved capable of competing with the submerged culture process.[65]

Because of the limited space at Greenford and the imperative need to
increase output, towards the end of 1942 it was decided to set up a second
incubator. A milk processing factory belonging to the Express Dairy in
Aylesbury was offered by the Ministry of Supply and in January 1943 the
first batch of flasks were installed and inoculated, being harvested in the
following month.[66] In March, however, a crisis arose: the mould turned
white, rather than the usual soft green, and yields fell to alarmingly low

41. Flasks of culture medium being encouraged to grow penicillin mould in 1944. They were needed in large numbers to produce therapeutic doses of the antibiotic. This is probably the Watford factory.

levels. All attempts to restore production failed and an intensive investigation followed. It was concluded that certain trace metals were absent from the water used to prepare the medium. Zinc was added but did not entirely solve the problem, so from July to September water was transferred in tankers from Greenford. Later the phosphate content of the medium was doubled and casein hydrolysate added, though with no great effect.[67] With refinements to the process, increasing yields, and greater numbers of flasks, output at Aylesbury expanded progressively. In January 1944, for example, 23,300 litres of broth were harvested from which 697 mega units of penicillin as a crude sodium salt were extracted, output rising to 3,353 mega units in the corresponding month two years later.[68] The work remained labour intensive, and as L. H. Robinson reported:

> considerable difficulty has been experienced in finding men of the right type as the plant has expanded; at one period we were forced to employ a man of 68 years of age. This difficulty has not been too acute as far as women are concerned

but the Ministry of Labour has been most unhelpful when additional staff were asked for ... Relations between management and staff are excellent. There have been no disputes; in fact, I doubt if it would be possible to find a more industrious set of workers.[69]

By the spring of 1943, supplies of penicillin were sufficiently plentiful to allow the Medical Research Council to allocate the antibiotic to four main centres for clinical trials. These proceeded at pace and it was demonstrated that penicillin had three fundamental properties: 'enormous antiseptic power', 'almost complete indifference to the medium in which it acts' and was found to be 'non-toxic'.[70] As a result, penicillin had a life-saving role in the treatment of certain infective diseases such as staphylococcal septicaemia or meningitis due to *Streptococcus pyogenes* or *pneumococcus*.[71] Yet penicillin could be made only in a relatively impure form and in quantities quite insufficient to treat all potential cases. Consequently, its use was limited to servicemen. Indeed, an editorial in the *British Medical Journal* for 28 August 1943 observed that 'the amount available at present is so small as to make it inadvisable to advertise the names of centres where its use is being studied, lest they should be overwhelmed with requests to treat cases that can only be declined'.[72] Penicillin had to be administered by injection as gastric secretion was sufficiently acid to destroy the medicine. In the autumn of 1943, Florey travelled to forward base hospitals in North Africa to give penicillin to soldiers wounded in the campaign in Sicily and established its use in combating sepsis.[73]

In July 1943, the Medical Research Council approached selected pharmaceutical companies to ask them to increase their production quotas. Glaxo Laboratories was asked to raise its output by five times.[74] Given that there had been no breakthrough in surface culture techniques, this could only be achieved by increasing the number of flasks in direct proportion and the cost Jephcott estimated at a minimum of £50,000. It was apparent that this extra demand could not be met from Greenford or Aylesbury where all available space was occupied. With assistance from the Board of Trade, the company requisitioned the top floor of a rubber factory at north Watford, the most expensive part of the operation being the purchase of thousands of flasks.[75] However, the Ministry of Labour refused to allow Glaxo to employ the numbers of staff needed to meet their production quotas. Because the equipping of the factory was so far advanced, it was decided to proceed rather than seek another location with more plentiful labour.[76] The Watford factory made its first penicillin in February 1944, though yields were variable, in part because of difficulties in maintaining an optimum temperature. At its peak, the plant had 300,000 flasks in a 24-hour continuous process.[77]

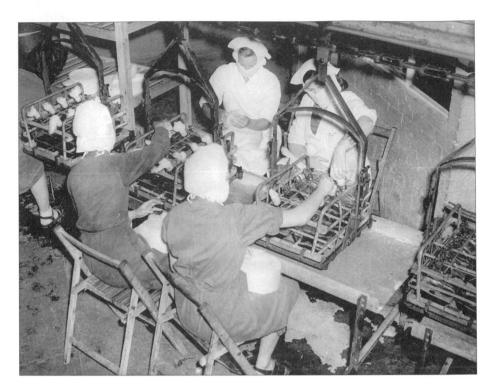

42. Overhead conveyor belts moved the heavy flasks around the factory. Here they are being plugged with cotton wool.

In autumn 1943, the government gave the production of penicillin the highest priority, when it became a 'designated' project alongside aircraft manufacture.[78] Jephcott assumed personal responsibility for the work at Glaxo, appointing Palmer as his deputy. Jephcott had alerted his managers that 'a very high proportion of the total output of this country for many months to come would be dependent upon our efforts', adding 'every additional million units secured by better work, be it better metabolism, or better extraction, may be a life saved'.[79]

Yields at Greenford improved in late 1943 following the discovery in the United States that corn-steep liquor, a by-product of the starch industry, together with lactose, offered an improved culture medium. Corn steep liquor was introduced as a medium at Watford, though Aylesbury continued to employ the synthetic medium and, in fact, achieved higher yields, probably as a result of greater experience and scrupulous care in monitoring the production process. In addition, a new strain of *Penicillium* was introduced from America.[80] Titres rose from 15 Oxford units (a measure of bacteriostatic power) per ml to as much as 75 units per ml. Output at

Greenford totalled around 600 mega units during 1943 and Aylesbury achieved about 2,000 mega units. Although advances in the science of penicillin therapy received considerable coverage in the medical press, the manufacturing operations remained clothed in secrecy. Hence, it was not until February 1946 that the *Buckinghamshire Herald* was able to inform its readers that

Aylesbury was one of the first, if not the first, towns in which a [penicillin] factory was set up. Very few people know that behind the high brick wall of the Nestlé's factory, nine men and 18 women were busily engaged in producing this queer new means of saving life.[81]

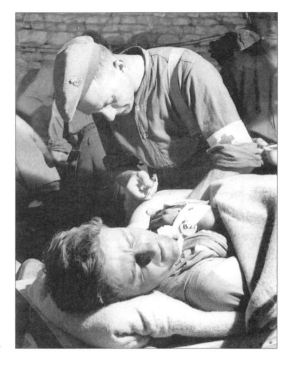

43. *A soldier wounded in the Normandy campaign being given an injection of penicillin by a RAMC orderly in 1944.*

With the prospect of an Allied invasion of Northern France, in February 1944 the Ministry of Supply approached Glaxo to increase their output still further. Capacity at Watford was to be doubled (involving the culture of an additional 80,000 flasks), while a duplicate factory was also to be set up. A site belonging to the British Feeding Meals and Milk Products Co. at Carpenters Road, Stratford, east London, was offered to Glaxo by the Ministry of Supply. A less suitable location could hardly be imagined. In an industrial area targeted by the Luftwaffe, it was adjacent to a feed mill where decaying food and edible waste were allowed to rot in the open air providing a constant source of mould infection.[82] Given the urgent need for extra supplies of penicillin, Glaxo agreed to proceed and construction was completed at the end of October.[83] The factory came on stream at the end of the year despite the roof being destroyed by a flying bomb, though output was seriously affected by contamination from the adjacent dump: not until June 1945 were these production difficulties resolved by the installation of air conditioning and other measures. By January 1946, monthly output had quadrupled that of the previous year, a remarkable achievement given that the factory had been under threat from flying bombs and V2 rockets.[84] It was calculated that about 80 per cent of the penicillin made in the UK and used at the D-Day landings in June 1944 came from factories operated by Glaxo. Yields from each 8-inch flask had risen from 4–12,000 units in 1943 to 50,000 units by September 1945, by which time the company had about 30,000 vessels in use. This was a labour intensive operation, the number of staff involved in penicillin production increasing from 18 in March 1943 to 326 by the autumn of 1945.[85]

By this time, it had become apparent that there were more efficient ways of making penicillin. The major US pharmaceutical companies began to experiment using submerged culture techniques, or 'deep fermentation', as it came to be known. Pfizer, producers of chemicals and ingredients for the food industry, showed late in 1943 that this method could transform the manufacture of penicillin. In March of the following year, Dr W. R. Boon of ICI and Jephcott visited the United States under the auspices of the Ministry of Supply. Impressed by the economies of scale and higher yields permitted by deep fermentation, Jephcott pressed the Ministry to re-design the Stratford factory, then under construction, as a deep culture plant.[86] Because this would have led to delays, the request was turned down, though it was agreed to help finance a modern plant at Driffield, adjacent to Glaxo's milk drying factory, as it was anticipated that lactose would be needed in the production process. Nevertheless, the Ministry of Supply changed its mind because Glaxo had no experience of what was a novel and relatively untried method. Concerned to maximise output in the shortest period of time, the Ministry insisted that the proposed Driffield factory employ both methods: only 40 per cent of output by deep fermentation and the balance (2,500 mega units a week) by bottle production.[87]

Having visited pilot plants in the United States, Jephcott was convinced that the future for penicillin production lay with deep fermentation. Faced with intransigence from the Ministry of Supply, he decided to negotiate a licensing arrangement on the company's behalf. Believing 'that deep culture … is the only method worthy of serious consideration',[88] Jephcott travelled to America in October 1944, where he signed a draft agreement with the Merck, Pfizer, Squibb consortium,[89] although it was estimated that a plant, to be built on the Pfizer model (with a capacity of 10,000 mega units), would cost £400,000, considerably more than the £14,000 originally spent at Aylesbury or £68,900 at Watford.

In the meantime the Ministry of Supply, concerned about contamination from the milk drying plant, decided that Driffield was not a suitable location for a major surface-culture factory. In July 1944 the Board of Trade wrote to Jephcott to suggest two possible sites in the north of England:

> Barnard Castle will be known to you; it is beautifully situated near the River Tees. You may not have heard of Whitburn, which is just north of Sunderland on the coast, but it is a surprisingly unspoilt old English village ... There would be no difficulty in obtaining workers and, as in the case of Barnard Castle, you would receive a welcome from the local people.[90]

In the event, a former sawmill on 20 acres of land adjacent to the LNER's line to Darlington at Barnard Castle was chosen. It was said that Hugh Dalton, President of the Board of Trade and MP for nearby Bishop Auckland, played a key role in the selection as it was an area of potentially high unemployment.[91] The government were to fund the construction, estimated at £420,000, while Glaxo agreed to supervise the installation of plant and its subsequent operation.[92] Although relatively large scale, it too was to be a surface-culture factory in accord with the Ministry's penicillin strategy.

Barnard Castle: deep fermentation

Having signed a provisional agreement with US pharmaceutical companies to use deep fermentation techniques, Glaxo had little interest in the Ministry's scheme at Barnard Castle. The company argued for its abandonment and offered to lease the site to build its own modern factory.[93] Faced with a burgeoning demand for penicillin and being mistrustful of new and relatively untried technology, Sir Cecil Weir, Director General of Equipment and Stores, rejected Jephcott's proposals.[94] A compromise was negotiated whereby the government would wholly finance the surface-culture plant (with a capacity of 2,500 mega units), while Glaxo would pay for a deep fermentation plant (producing 1,500 mega units) on the same site.[95] Construction, to the designs of the company's architects, Wallis Gilbert & Partners, proceeded rapidly and the buildings were completed on schedule in March 1945. However, the execution of the scheme was delayed by differences that arose between the US consortium and the Ministry over the exchange of technical information and the royalties to be paid on penicillin supplied to the government.[96] Jephcott even considered going it alone:

> knowledge of penicillin production was now much greater than at the time when the agreement was first projected, and it might be that we could succeed even in deep fermentation without the American assistance.[97]

Glaxo decided to aim for 'the best product at the lowest price and in the least time' and to achieve this concluded that the 'American information was essential'.

In the meantime, Jephcott had been in touch with the Distillers Company, which had considerable experience of fermentation from their spirit interests. In January 1945 Glaxo pressed ahead with their own scheme and Palmer travelled to America, empowered to close contracts with Merck and Pfizer in New Jersey and E. R. Squibb & Sons in New York;[98] these were duly signed in the following month.[99] However, a new head of the Ministry of Supply convinced of the greater efficiencies of deep fermentation, agreed to finance a submerged culture plant at Barnard Castle (with a weekly capacity of 10,000 mega units) provided that Glaxo renegotiate its licences with Merck, Pfizer and Squibb.[100] The cost was estimated at £350,000 and Glaxo was given the option of acquiring the factory when it was no longer needed by the Ministry. A factory of this size had the valuable side-effect of allowing Glaxo to stop making penicillin at Greenford, where space was at a premium.[101] Under the terms concluded in April 1945, Glaxo paid a royalty of 5 per cent on penicillin produced by the Merck–Squibb process for five years.[102]

In May 1945, a team of four travelled to the United States to study the deep fermentation process in detail. It included Palmer, Dr A. H. Campbell, a senior lecturer at Bristol University, who had been a consultant to Glaxo since 1943, and Frank Anderson, a young production manager involved with the surface culture of penicillin. On their return to the UK, Campbell was appointed general manager of Barnard Castle, and Anderson (who had managed the Watford penicillin factory) subsequently became production manager. Construction proceeded to plan and a technician from Merck arrived from the United States to assist with the installation of plant, though the goal of beginning production in October 1945 proved too ambitious.[103] After considerable teething problems, Barnard Castle came on stream on February 1946 and 24-hour working was introduced later in the year.[104] The first purpose-built pharmaceutical plant commissioned by Glaxo, it was described by Jephcott as 'one of the finest units for production in the world'.[105] In fact, by international standards it was relatively small as Squibb's New Brunswick factory had a monthly output of 460,000 mega units, while the Speke plant belonging to Distillers made 540,000 mega units at a time when Barnard Castle only produced 174,000 mega units.[106]

Deep fermentation techniques were designed to replicate the optimum conditions for the growth of penicillin. Moulds are microscopic plants and require the same living conditions: an abundant supply of nutrients, water and air. If their living conditions are suitable, then they can multiply at an extraordinary rate, doubling their numbers every twenty minutes. First, a liquid supply of corn-steep liquor (the culture medium) was prepared and placed in a 5,000 gallon steel vessel or fermenter.[107] The contents were then

44. The new antibiotic factory at Barnard Castle originally designed for surface culture but constructed largely at Jephcott's insistence for deep fermentation. Shown here in October 1948 before the closure of the railway to Darlington.

sterilised by steam to kill any bacteria present. Penicillin grows only at a certain temperature, which was maintained by special coils. The solution is then inoculated with a selected strain and sterilised air pumped into the fermenter. The contents are stirred to assist the process, which generally takes two to three days. The 'charge' is drawn off from the bottom and the penicillin extracted in a series of operations using selective solvents, the purified chemical then being crystallised and dried.[108]

As construction of the factory at Barnard Castle reached an advanced stage, the Ministry of Supply authorised the closure of Glaxo's surface-culture operations at Aylesbury, Watford and Stratford as soon as their quotas could be absorbed by the new plant.[109] While a rapidly expanding market (through the extension of penicillin for civilian use) provided the demand, economies of scale and progressive technical improvements permitted by deep fermentation reduced the production cost of a single dose from $20 in 1943 to $1 in 1946.[110] Although Jephcott's decision to adopt the latest mass-production techniques was vindicated over the next twenty years, the location of the company's first factory proved ill advised and seemed to have been chiefly influenced by the availability of plentiful labour rather than an understanding of the production process. Indeed, the shortcomings of the site eventually sealed the long-term fate of Barnard Castle as a primary manufacturer of antibiotics. Deep fermentation generated large quantities of non-toxic, odorous effluent which had to be transported by tanker to West Hartlepool where it was poured into the sea. This created considerable costs: by the late 1960s thirty-six tankers were making the journey daily. In fact, the vexed question of sewerage had been raised by the Ministry of Health as early as September 1945 and at a meeting hastily convened with representatives of the Ministry of Supply, the Water Pollution Board and the architects, Wallis, Gilbert & Partners, it was concluded that the existing facilities were patently inadequate to cope with the factory's waste.[111] Glaxo took the view that 'responsibility for providing sewerage or effluent disposal facilities should fall to the Ministry of Supply'.[112] In the event, no satisfactory solution was found, this issue being buried by the imperative need to make penicillin in large quantities.

War service: staff in the front line

In August 1939, Glaxo held its week-long annual sales conference attended by the fifty or so UK representatives. All were present for registration and most, being qualified pharmacists, were exempt from conscription, though many had enlisted in the Territorial Army. By the afternoon, two had been called for training, and on the following day five more had gone. On the final evening at the dinner, three of the diminished sales force attended in uniform.[113] While many volunteered, conscription introduced in September 1939 took away even greater numbers and Glaxo supplemented the pay of those servicemen facing financial hardship, particularly those who had families to support.[114] Although Glaxo already employed large numbers of women in filling and packing operations, the loss of men to the forces encouraged further recruitment. By June 1940, sixty-six staff were on active service and the imminent call-up of a considerable number led the board to introduce longer working hours to maintain output.[115] Saturday morning working was re-introduced and a scale of additional payments calculated if employees were required to exceed the forty-two-hour week.[116] To encourage morale in the foods and pharmaceutical packing departments, it was agreed in September 1941 to relay 'BBC musical programmes' over the Tannoy system, or, as it became known, 'music while you work'.[117]

The decision to conscript female labour under the New National Service No. 2 Act of 1941 led to a further loss of staff even though Glaxo was registered under the Protected and Essential Works Orders because many em-

45. The damage to the food blending floor and analytical laboratory at Greenford caused by a V1 flying bomb on 20 August 1944. Because it was a Sunday casualties were light; had it been a working day, then the consequences would have been grave.

ployees were young and expected to perform more arduous tasks. Faced with the continuing conscription of males, the company decided to apply for deferment only in the case of those with specialist qualifications and, in the case of women, to allow their release without exception.[118] The Ministry of Labour compelled the company to increase the basic working week to forty-four hours and encouraged the use of shifts.[119] To meet orders, Glaxo raised the hours of men in the factory to forty-eight, while female, office and laboratory staff worked forty-four hours.[120]

The bombing of civilians in the Spanish Civil War had encouraged the government to believe that casualties could be high, so a civil defence organisation was established by Sir John Anderson during 1938. As part of its air raid precautions, Glaxo constructed underground shelters in the grounds of the Greenford factory. When, in the autumn of 1940, the Blitz hit London these proved their worth. However, the frequency of raids, together with alarms, led to a considerable loss of production. In September 1940, it was decided to install fifty loudspeakers throughout the factory so that precise instructions could be conveyed to staff from a spotting station

on the roof of the main building.[121] Work continued during raids until
enemy aircraft were sighted. With the need to get workers rapidly into protected areas, more brick shelters were constructed inside the factory. The
scheme reduced lost time, though it was not without risks. In 1944, for example, a V1 flying bomb took the observers on the roof by surprise when it
emerged from low cloud, exploding beyond the Greenford factory before
the alarm could be raised.[122] In January 1941, as raids on London continued, Glaxo set up teams of firewatchers (seventeen every night to report in-
cendiaries and tackle fires).[123] A Home Guard platoon of thirty volunteers
was formed to provide a security cordon around the factory, while the
company also trained and equipped its own firemen.[124]

These precautions could not, of course, prevent attacks by the enemy. At
10.41 on the morning of 20 August 1944 a V1 flying bomb hit the factory, de-
molishing the food blending floor and much of the adjoining analytical
laboratory.[125] Fortunately, it was a Sunday and few workers were present,
only one sustaining serious injury. Had it been a working day, the number
of casualties could have been large. Although the factory was seriously
damaged, temporary repairs and the transfer of all blending and packing
operations to the Farex building reduced the impact of the destruction. In
addition, Allen & Hanburys agreed to pack 100 tons of Glucose-D for
Glaxo over five weeks to ease the congestion. The analytical laboratory was
totally destroyed and staff had to be accommodated in other buildings.
Fortunately, pharmaceutical manufacture was not affected by the flying
bomb.[126] Despite the general disruption caused by war, output was sustained and in many cases increased at Greenford by the recruitment of
women, introduction of longer working hours and sheer determination.

The costs of war

It is difficult to draw up a comprehensive balance sheet to account for the
effect of war on the business fortunes of Glaxo Laboratories. On the face of
it, the company fared rather well. Both sales and net profits grew steadily in
real terms throughout the hostilities, rising by 40 and 73 per cent respectively between 1939 and 1945 (see Table 4). The war had drawn Glaxo into
the very heart of antibiotic pharmaceuticals. It had become one of the UK's
leading producers of penicillin (though much of its plant had been rendered obsolete at the end of the war by technical developments in the
United States). Although most of the scientific research that underpinned
this breakthrough had been at Oxford, Glaxo had played a part in the development work to convert *Penicillium notatum* into a viable, mass-
production medicine. Jephcott showed a commendable determination to

46. Dr Hector Walker surveys the bomb damage through the window of the wrecked analytical laboratory.

acquire the latest technology in the face of intransigence from the Ministry of Supply. Before the Second World War, Glaxo was, in essence, a foods company with scientific interests in nutrition. By 1945, though Ostermilk and Farex remained important products, it had become a significant player in the UK pharmaceutical industry.

Inevitably, the war had distorted the pattern of peacetime demand. In particular, rationing, shortages and a concern with the nation's diet generated an artificially large market for Ostermilk, which accounted for 70 per cent of the company's UK food turnover in 1945, while government contracts for National Dried Milk Powder generated a further 19 per cent. Home food sales rose by 89 per cent in real terms between 1939 and 1945 even with reductions in retail prices. Pharmaceutical turnover, by comparison, increased by only 51 per cent, despite growing orders for penicillin. The inflated figures for Ostermilk (which subsequently declined as peacetime levels of imports were restored) created a false impression in the minds of the Glaxo board, and led them to believe that the foods business lay at the core of the company's prosperity. In 1945, for example, sales of food products were 60 per cent of total turnover (in contrast to 1939, when they were 54 per cent in real terms; see Table 4). In a sense, these figures were a distortion of the true position as they did not include the management fee that Glaxo received from the Ministry of Supply for operating its factories at Aylesbury, Watford and Stratford. Penicillin did not appear as a product in the annual accounts because, strictly speaking, it was not a Glaxo medicine that was sold to customers. The true figure for pharmaceutical revenue was, therefore, higher than these percentages indicated. (In 1945, for example, Glaxo received £256,000 from its contracts to supply penicillin, of which only £41,000 was profit.[127] It was not until 1946 that the company began to earn substantial revenue from penicillin, when turnover rose to £782,000 and gross profits to £243,000.) On balance, Glaxo came through the hostilities strengthened rather than weakened, largely because it manufactured products, both nutritional and medical, that were vital to the war effort.

THE JEPHCOTT ERA,
1946–1961

'One day there'll be someone with real vision. I shall have a
laboratory given to me, a proper laboratory with really modern
equipment and assistants of my own …'

The Man in the White Suit *(1951)*[1]

GLAXO LABORATORIES entered the post-war economy in remarkably good order, with healthy sales figures and substantial
profits. Because expansion had been financed internally, the company was not saddled with vast accumulated borrowings. As Jephcott wrote
in January 1947, 'we ploughed back and ploughed back until it hurt'.[2] Ever
mindful of the disastrous share issues of 1921 and 1922, Jephcott had been
parsimonious with the company's funds almost to the point at which he inhibited growth by refusing to spend on projects that involved an element of
risk. Glaxo grew steadily during the late 1940s and 1950s as new factories
opened at Ulverston (to manufacture streptomycin and penicillin) and at
Montrose in 1952 (to make hydrocortisone and vitamin B_{12}), while a series
of take-overs, including Murphy Chemical, Allen & Hanburys and Evans
Medical, broadened Glaxo's pharmaceutical and chemical portfolio. However, some of this growth had proceeded piecemeal rather than as steps in a
carefully considered plan and by 1960 profits had peaked in real terms.
Jephcott was not a grand strategist. He was a skilled and experienced administrator and tactician who worked according to deeply held principles,
which he followed scrupulously. Rather than pre-judging events or influ-
encing them as they unfolded, Jephcott responded to new situations. Businesses, for example, were acquired in response to offers rather than to
capture a product or market, and factories were built to exploit a medicine
licensed from competitors. He did not encourage the search for novel

drugs. Although important development work was undertaken on griseofulvin (Grisovin), this was not a Glaxo discovery, nor could the company
claim the credit for any new medicine in this period, apart from vitamin
B_{12}. The Glaxo group that emerged in the early 1960s had no clear structure, and this had much to do with Jephcott's management style. He involved himself in every aspect of the business, sat on all the main
committees and regularly visited overseas subsidiaries. Jephcott provided
the essential links between different and distant elements in the group and
believed that his presence was sufficient to maintain continuity. In fact,
Glaxo had already grown too large and complex, entering areas that he no
longer fully understood.

The approach that Jephcott took to other activities followed this pattern.
He had a holiday (and later retirement) home, 'Thalassa', at East Portle-
mouth in Devon, where he bought a number of local farms. They were
piecemeal purchases inspired because he thought that the existing farming
methods were old-fashioned and unscientific. He acquired only the land,
not the farmhouses, and appointed managers.[3] Eventually, Jephcott owned
about fifteen miles of the South Devon coastline and later donated much of
it to the National Trust. However, he ran his farms in much the same way as
he ran Glaxo: by personal involvement, using trusted lieutenants and
retaining ultimate control.

Glaxo Laboratories: 'baby swallows parent'

Having succeeded to the chairmanship of Glaxo Laboratories in October
1945,[4] Jephcott began to restructure the group. Joseph Nathan & Co. was
still the holding company, though it also functioned as a merchant house,
importing butter and dairy products from New Zealand, while exporting
general goods, including machinery, to Australasia, from its headquarters
at 10 King Charles II Street, SW1. By now this business was small in comparison with the turnover of Glaxo Laboratories. Jephcott succeeded to the
chairmanship of Joseph Nathan & Co. when Alec Nathan retired in June
1946, the other board members being Jacobs, Sandercock and Rose.[5] By this
time Rose had retired from active involvement at Glaxo and Jacobs had
always been a non-executive director, having a range of business interests
including the chairmanship of the Palais de Danse, Hammersmith, and a
cinema.[6] Jephcott wound up Joseph Nathan & Co. in 1946, sold the company's warehouse and offices in Wellington and disposed of the agency and
merchanting business there.[7] As a result, the only remaining asset of any
substance left to the company was its £750,000 investment in Glaxo. In January 1947, Jephcott recapitalised Glaxo Laboratories,[8] enabling him to

acquire the assets of Joseph Nathan & Co., which was then placed in voluntary liquidation.[9] In this way Glaxo Laboratories became the parent, truly
reflecting the realities of the business. The influence and, indeed, the name
of the Nathans came to an end.

Post-war expansion

In January 1946, Dr Hector Walker submitted a report recommending that
Glaxo diversify its antibiotic activities by manufacturing streptomycin on a
large scale.[10] In 1944, Dr Selman Waksman and his team at Rutgers University had reported the discovery of a relatively non-toxic metabolite of
Streptomyces griseus, which they named streptomycin, though several years
of research followed before the compound could be made in any quantity.
By 1946, however, it had entered clinical trials and was shown, in combination with para-aminosalicylic acid (PAS) and later Isoniazid, to be an
effective treatment for tuberculosis.[11] Walker had rightly identified streptomycin as an important new medicine. It opened up broad commercial opportunities as armies of patients had suffered for years in large sanatoria
treated with little more than fresh air, graduated exercise and surgery to
collapse inflamed lungs.[12] The effectiveness of antibiotics when used in
combination was startling. Mortality from tuberculosis had declined at
around 3 per cent a year between 1900 and 1945 and thereafter fell at 15 per
cent so that by 1960 the death rate was one-tenth of that of 1940.

In January 1946 the Glaxo board authorised the expenditure of £250,000
on a factory to make streptomycin.[13] The Board of Trade was then contacted
to find a suitable location for what would be the company's second primary
process plant.[14] The briefing, written by Palmer and sent to regional controllers at Glasgow, Cardiff and Manchester, included the following requirements: existing road and rail links, an ample supply of water for steam
raising and cooling in condensers, facilities for disposing of effluent and a
local population that could supply 1,500 employees (of whom two-thirds
would be male).[15] In February 1946, A. Turner, deputy regional controller of
the Board of Trade at Manchester, wrote to Jephcott to recommend

> a site at Ulverston, Lancashire, of 100 acres, with road and rail facilities and elec-
> tric power available … it was occupied by the North Lonsdale Iron Works. The
> site itself is level, is near a canal, and is only a short distance from the sea where
> effluent can be disposed of without passing through filter beds.[16]

Turner also mentioned possible locations at Bromborough on Merseyside
and at Halewood in Liverpool.[17] By April 1946, the Glaxo survey party, con-

sisting of Jephcott, Palmer and Rose, had visited four sites identified by the Board of Trade, of which Ulverston was considered the most promising.[18]

In the meantime, penicillin was made by deep fermentation in ever larger quantities by both Distillers at Speke and Glaxo at Barnard Castle, so that the Ministry of Supply decided to close the less efficient surface culture plants. In April 1946, the Ministry informed Glaxo that it would not require the output from Aylesbury and Stratford from the end of June 1947.[19] Staff at both were immediately given notice of the closures,[20] though it was decided to extend the Stratford factory's lease to make liver extract (for vitamin B_{12}), releasing valuable space at Greenford.[21] The plant at Watford also closed in July 1946.[22] Surface culture had played a vital role in supplying the UK's vital need for penicillin during the war years but it had been rendered hopelessly obsolete by deep fermentation.

Deep fermentation at Ulverston

Having identified Ulverston as having the best facilities, Glaxo approached the Millom & Askam Haematite Iron Co. to buy the derelict 100-acre site. The Board of Trade refused to schedule Ulverston as a 'Development Area',[23] thereby preventing the company from obtaining financial assistance from the government, together with building and labour priorities.[24] Jephcott considered that the project would be greatly delayed without state support and called off negotiations with Millom & Askam. A location in the Seaham area on the Durham coast was investigated further by Jephcott, Palmer and Campbell but proved unsuitable.[25] In the event, the Board of Trade reconsidered and in July Glaxo purchased the land and buildings of the Millom & Askam Co. for £24,000.[26] The triangular site, bounded by the Ulverston Canal, the railway south to Conishead and the road to the sea loch, offered space for future expansion, while water from the canal could be used for cooling processes and effluent pumped into Morecambe Bay. Fermentation requires clean air, which was available in quantity with the closure of the ironworks. Labour was relatively plentiful as the area's industries (coal mining, steel making and shipbuilding) were in decline. Distant from any conurbations, the location was approved by the Ministry of Supply, concerned to ensure the production of vital medicines in wartime. Glaxo authorised the expenditure of £350,000 in November 1946 and construction began in the following year. Provision had been made for twenty-four fermenters, though to save costs only twelve were installed, creating further space for extraction processes.[27]

The four-storey office block, which faced the railway and North Lonsdale Road, bore a resemblance to the company's Greenford headquarters.

47. The newly constructed Ulverston factory designed by Elliott, Cox & Partners and opened in 1948. It was situated beside the Furness Railway's branch line to Conishead.

This was not surprising as both Elliott and Cox, its designers, had been partners of Thomas Wallis, Glaxo's original architect.[28] When Wallis decided to retire, his colleagues set up their own practice and a year later, in 1946, were responsible for the two-storey packing hall ('B' block) at Barnard Castle and subsequently drew the plans for Glaxo's milk drying factory at Kendal (see p. 92). The cost of the Ulverston project rose well beyond the original estimates and finally totalled £485,000.[29] Although the factory had originally been conceived to make streptomycin, the rapidly rising demand for penicillin and the limitations of Barnard Castle (particularly the problems there of effluent disposal) led to a change of priorities, and Jephcott recommended in January 1947 that

> penicillin production shall be transferred from Barnard Castle to Ulverston as soon as the Ulverston production facilities become available. That ... Barnard Castle shall confine itself to streptomycin and other antibiotics ... That, as soon as may be practicable, the whole of the activities in respect to fermentation shall be transferred to Ulverston.[30]

Barnard Castle was then diverted to the secondary manufacture of pharmaceuticals and some food packing transferred from Greenford.

Now that Ulverston was to be the company's principal producer of penicillin, it became apparent in July 1947, before the factory had even opened, that its fermentation capacity was already inadequate:

> the need to produce greater quantities of crystalline penicillin to meet American competition overseas (the yield of crystalline penicillin being approximately one-third that of yellow penicillin) would result in the total output of penicillin being but little greater than that existing.[31]

As a result, Glaxo spent £250,000 on additional fermentation capacity.

Ulverston made its first penicillin G on 19 April 1948[32] and in the following year, when the second fermentation hall was completed, began the large-scale manufacture of streptomycin.[33] Under a fifteen-year royalty agreement signed in November 1948, streptomycin was licensed from Merck.[34] When Ulverston opened the overriding priority was supply; so desperate was the demand for the new medicine that cost was scarcely a consideration. But the construction of additional deep fermentation plants in Europe and the United States soon eliminated the shortfall, and during the 1950s the market became increasingly competitive. As prices tumbled, it became imperative to cut costs. Jephcott wrote in December 1951 to Dr Fred Wilkins, director of Glaxo's northern factories, that

> if the requisite efficiencies are achieved, there is little or no need for additional capital expenditure except as an insurance against failure … and to meet the moral obligation which we have to government to provide some excess capacity against a national emergency.[35]

Marginal pricing was used to assist the bulk sales department in setting competitive rates, which in turn increased volumes to absorb overheads and reduce unit costs.[36] Small teams were sent to the US and Germany to study their production methods. Particular emphasis was laid on improving yields and by the careful selection and modification of *Penicillium* strains, changes to the nutrients and careful control of the temperature and pH of the broth, dramatic improvements were achieved, so that titres rose by a factor of fifty during the period of production.[37] Such was the increase in output that a third fermentation hall, constructed in 1965 as part of a £2 million investment programme, was never used for its original purpose.

The food business: Ostermilk

In one important way, the Second World War misled Jephcott and his senior managers about long-term market trends. The rapid and sustained rise in the demand for dried milk powder had suggested that Glaxo's food business, and Ostermilk in particular, was a major and growing source of sales and profits. In the year to 30 September 1945, for example, UK sales of Ostermilk 1 and 2 had totalled £848,938, while a further £232,695 had been earned from the manufacture of National Dried Milk Powder; together they represented 54 per cent of home turnover, including pharmaceuticals.[38] Because of the commercial importance of infant foods, Jephcott worried about the transition to a peacetime competitive market. During

48. A lunch held in the canteen at Greenford for retired staff and hosted by Sir Harry Jephcott.

the war, the Ministry of Food had controlled the distribution of milk powder, allocating quotas to the various manufacturers. These regulations continued well beyond the armistice as shortages led to ongoing rationing. As
the market leader, Glaxo became increasingly opposed to the operation of
the milk powder pool:

> Our primary objection to the continuation of a pooling scheme was both on
> principle and on commercial grounds ... it facilitated the sale of competing
> foods at high prices. On the other hand, if we declined to participate, the Min-
> istry might be forced to act by the prospective shortage of milk powder and we
> should have little say in what they did.[39]

In these circumstances, Jephcott concluded that Glaxo had little choice
but to co-operate even though this gave the Ministry ultimate control over
production quotas. In May 1948, for example, when sales of Ostermilk out-
ran the company's supplies, the company was forced to ask the Ministry for
an additional allocation of milk powder from Southern Dominion shipments.[40] Having failed to persuade the other commercial manufacturers in
the Infant Food Group to withdraw from the government scheme, Jephcott
decided that Glaxo had little option but to continue making National Dried

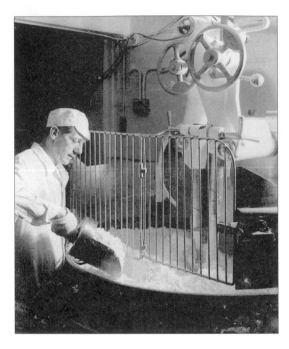

49. *Mixing the ingredients for Complan (the completely planned meal) at Greenford.*

Milk Powder even though it undermined their market for Ostermilk.

The first three years of peace saw a dramatic fall in the turnover of Ostermilk, both in absolute and relative terms. By December 1948, UK sales of foods represented only 15.5 per cent of the company's business, with National Dried Milk Powder accounting for a further 5.3 per cent.[41] Pharmaceuticals had grown considerably, home sales alone generating 53 per cent of total turnover. Edmund Preston, the publicity director, expressed concern about the food business:

while the reputation of Ostermilk would provide sales momentum for a considerable period, the name must nevertheless be regarded as a wasting asset. He calculated that the sales of proprietary infant milk foods might ultimately be reduced to of the order of 4,000 tons per annum and if sales of Ostermilk amounted to about half the total, the tonnage disposed of would still approximate to that sold pre-war.[42]

The progressive encroachment of National Dried Milk on the Ostermilk market was particularly worrying as the former was manufactured at a price agreed with the Ministry of Food. In October 1948, the latter attempted to reduce profits to 2s (10p) per cwt over costs, a figure which Glaxo considered unacceptably low, arguing for a minimum of 4s 8d (23p), or ½d (0.02p) on a 1lb tin.[43] To recover some lost revenue, the company decided to raise the price of Ostermilk in November 1948 to 33s (£1.65) for a dozen 1lb tins, for which the wholesaler would pay 26s 7d (£1.33), thereby increasing the net profit to 2¼d (0.9p),[44] considerably higher than on milk powder sold to the Ministry.

As a result of a concerted promotional campaign for Ostermilk and the introduction of new products, notably Casilan and Complan (see p. 91),

50. A 1930s promotion picture for Glucose-D.

turnover of foods had recovered to 35 per cent of home business by 1956.[45] In the nine months to April 1958, food sales rose by 33 per cent, largely owing to a 50 per cent increase in the turnover of Ostermilk as it recaptured lost ground.[46] The trend continued into 1959 though at a reduced rate: 11 per cent growth for total foods turnover, Ostermilk sales rising by 15 per cent and Complan by 32 per cent.[47] In the early 1960s, however, tougher competition from other dried milk manufacturers, such as SMA, and from evaporated milk eroded the advances achieved by Ostermilk No. 1. To boost the sales of Ostermilk No. 2, attempts were made to improve its homogenisation and the efficiency of the drying process.[48] In 1961, Glaxo decided to switch packaging from tins to cartons, following a trial in Northern Ireland.[49] This change, though not completed until May 1962,[50] ended a long association with their suppliers, Metal Box, in favour of a new arrangement with Bowaters.[51] It was hoped that the new packing machines would generate sufficient savings to obviate the need for a further price rise. However, a detailed investigation of production costs against revenue over the period 1948–61 showed progressively falling returns, and it was decided to increase the retail price of Ostermilk to 4s (20p) for a 1lb carton.[52] The price was determined not by predictions of future sales but by the wish to recover higher costs.

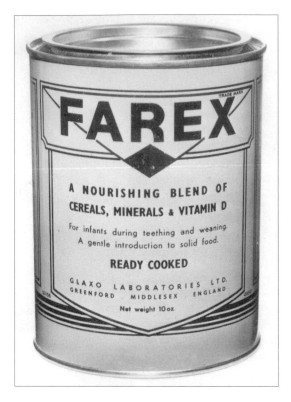

51. The Farex tin in 1953.

Despite the new packaging, the price rise of November 1961 had an adverse effect and sales fell by 6 per cent in the first three months of the following year. Nevertheless, it was decided to hold the retail price of Ostermilk at its higher level,[53] and sales continued to decline until the summer of 1963.[54] Glaxo executives believed that the reputation of Ostermilk would support the greater price and, in view of the need to raise profits, considered that they had little alternative. It seems that they had not fully appreciated the price sensitive nature of the market even for brand leaders. At the same time, efforts were made to improve productivity: in particular the construction of a new spray-drying factory at Kendal (p. 92), and the redesign of the Greenford packing hall together with the installation of extra Job Day machines (see p. 284).[55]

The significant contribution made by infant foods to Glaxo's turnover influenced Jephcott's recruitment of Dr Tom Macrae as head of research. Jephcott had met Macrae, a nutritionist, through their membership of the Accessory Food Factors Committee of the Medical Research Council.[56] Macrae, a Scot, had completed a doctorate at Glasgow on the biochemistry of enzymes before joining the nutrition department of the Lister Institute of Preventative Medicine. During the war he had been commissioned into the RAF as part of a strategy to improve the diet of servicemen.[57] At Glaxo, Macrae appointed George Childs in 1946 to set up a department specifically for nutritional research. Childs had also worked at the Lister Institute before he had been recruited into the air force to assist Macrae, where he tested food samples collected from aerodrome canteens.[58]

Although Ostermilk dominated Glaxo's food business during the war, Farex, a blend of wheat, oatmeal and rye fortified with vitamin D, had established a niche as a weaning product. In 1948–49, when sales totalled 1,780 tons, it was calculated that this specialist line was unlikely to earn orders above 2,500 tons.[59] It was decided that this demand did not justify an advertising campaign for Farex alone, and sales grew slowly to 2,200 tons and a revenue of £420,000 by 1957.[60] In that year, the board spent £47,000 on new equipment and reorganised manufacture and packing in a single building to reduce the risk of contamination and to raise capacity to 3,100 tons a year.[61] Because consumption was confined to infants being weaned from the bottle to solid foods (and, therefore, consumed for a relatively short period), Farex never achieved the revenues of Ostermilk. In a context of increasing competition, Farex suffered a 6 per cent fall in UK sales during 1959 against a background of rising food turnover.[62] To counter this trend, Glaxo introduced a bonus offer in May–June of the following year,[63] though it had only a temporary effect on sales.

Appointed to undertake nutritional research, George Childs was asked by Macrae to devise a high-protein, soluble food that could be given to hospital patients. Having seen how much time was spent on wards preparing special diets for invalids, Childs believed that a market opportunity existed. He showed that it was possible to convert casein, a highly nutritious but unattractive gritty solid, into calcium caseinate formulated as a light powder of which 90 per cent was protein, sodium-free and as palatable as milk. Launched in 1948 as Casinal and later as Casilan, it rapidly gained acceptance in hospitals and became a standard supplement for those suffering from nutritional deficiencies. Childs was then asked to develop a complete food for patients, who were comatose or unable to swallow, that could be fed by a naso-gastric tube. He began work on the project in 1948 and had, in the meantime, produced a feed for piglets (Amvilac) and was developing a veterinary vitamin and mineral supplement, later launched as Vitablend. The knowledge gained in this research contributed to the invention of 'Complan' (the name being chosen by the marketing department as a shortened form of 'completely planned'). It had taken Childs three years to devise the formula, while clinical trials and storage tests took a further two years.[64] Introduced on 1 January 1953, Complan was sold as a dispersible powder reconstituted with water to form a suspension or emulsion, a 1lb packet containing sufficient nutrients for a day. At first, the product was not patented because the marketing department did not believe that it would sell in large quantities. In fact, Complan soon found a wider demand among convalescents, growing children and those wanting a dietary supplement. It proved to be a product with a remarkably long life, continuing to sell long after Glaxo had divested its food interests.

Spray drying: the Kendal factory

By the summer of 1958 the Driffield roller drying factory struggled to supply milk powder in the quantities needed by Greenford. The growth in population in the East Riding, together with a fall in output, resulted in virtually all the milk produced in Yorkshire being required for local consumption.[65] Discussions with the Milk Marketing Board revealed that Glaxo was 'in danger, at Driffield, of being reduced, even in the best of seasons, to a short period of manufacture, probably not exceeding five months'.[66] Glaxo pursued two lines of inquiry: to purchase dried powder from other UK manufacturers (Ambrosia or Fisons Milk Products), or to find a site for a new drying plant.[67] Possible locations in Wales, at Felin Fach and Pont Llanio, were investigated by Palmer but found unsuitable.[68] Glaxo then opened discussions with Ambrosia, whose creamery at Lapford in Devon had supplied much of the company's shortfall in recent years. Ambrosia proposed that the two companies set up a joint organisation to operate the Lapford factory exclusively for Glaxo. The proposal would enable the group to close Driffield and guarantee supplies, though 'at the cost of some reduction in profitability, if only because the price we should pay for Lapford milk powder would have to provide a return to Ambrosia on their half-share in the ownership of the new company'.[69] Negotiations proceeded to an advanced stage but stumbled over the profit target to be set for the factory, Ambrosia aiming for a net figure of £8 per ton on an output of 5,000 tons of powder, which Glaxo believed from their experience at Driffield was over ambitious.

As a result, Glaxo returned to the second option of identifying a site that would enable them to construct a wholly owned factory. The Milk Marketing Board suggested a site at Mint Bridge, a mile north of Kendal in Westmorland, where they were to build their own pasteurising and bottling plant. Glaxo decided to erect their factory alongside the Milk Marketing Board's premises so that it could share boiler facilities and minimise delivery costs. The company also took advantage of the new technique of spray drying, which required higher volumes of milk to be cost effective. Completed in 1962 at a cost of £550,000 and designed by Glaxo's architects, Elliott, Cox & Partners,[70] the Kendal factory's tower-like appearance reflected the modern manufacturing process, in contrast to the single-storey sheds built at Driffield to accommodate roller drying machinery.

The pharmaceutical business: mixed fortunes

In 1945, when penicillin was in effect rationed by the government, sales of pharmaceutical products accounted for only 40 per cent of Glaxo's UK

52. The Kendal spray drying factory: a characteristically tall building in contrast to the single-storey sheds that housed roller dryers.

turnover (see p. 446). By 1958 pharmaceuticals had risen to 59 per cent (of which 19 per cent were antibiotics, chiefly penicillin and streptomycin), while foods accounted for 35 per cent and veterinary medicine and animal feeds earned 6 per cent of UK turnover.[71] Although prescription medicines assumed a growing importance in Glaxo's business, margins were progressively squeezed by pressure from government and later the operation of the Voluntary Price Regulation Scheme (see p. 222) so that they were of modest financial benefit to the business. Indeed, as Table 7 (p. 447) shows, rising sales were not translated into higher surpluses. Profits in real terms were not substantially greater in 1962 than they had been in 1947. Although turnover rose dramatically in real terms from 1956 (in part the result of a series of acquisitions), profits had not moved in step because some of the businesses that Jephcott and Wilson had taken over were ailing. In addition, the group had not been rationalised and subsidiaries allowed to continue as almost autonomous organisations so that the full economies of scale were not realised (see p. 146).

Before the Second World War, Glaxo's pharmaceutical products were almost entirely confined to vitamin preparations. In June 1946, when the

*53. The modern streptomycin filling hall at Greenford during the 1950s from the enclosed
viewing gallery for visitors, which was popularly christened the 'Mappin Terrace' from the
structure at London Zoo.*

Ministry of Supply agreed to allow retail sales, penicillin and streptomycin
became major sources of income, though being manufactured under licence they could never become vast sources of profit. Because antibiotics
were in such demand and were initially costly to produce, they came under
close government scrutiny and the Ministry of Health exerted great pressure on manufacturers to lower their prices. In the *Annual Report* for 1949,
Jephcott documented how penicillin had been subject to five price reductions over three years, reducing the revenue available to Glaxo by two-
thirds.[72] In December 1952, the company agreed to further cuts,[73] and in
the following year were requested by the Auditor-General to demonstrate
that sums being paid for antibiotics sold to the National Health Service
were 'reasonable'.[74] In 1954, the Conservative government set up the Cohen
Committee to investigate the cost of medicines supplied to the NHS and its
report ultimately led to the introduction of the Voluntary Price Regulation
Scheme three years later (see p. 222).[75]

Why, then, did Jephcott become so concerned for Glaxo's future? The
home market for medicines grew progressively as successive post-war gov-

ernments found higher sums for the NHS. The amount spent on drugs, dressings and appliances rose from £43.6 million in 1949–50 to £65.8 million in 1954–55, reaching £100.5 million by 1959–60.[76] Whilst spending grew substantially, the launch of prescription medicines intensified competition. In November 1954, GPs were allowed to prescribe some drugs that until then had been available only to hospitals. These included the tetracycline antibiotics chlortetracycline (Aureomycin) and oxytetracycline (Terramycin) and, from December 1955, the corticosteroids, cortisone and hydrocortisone. Prednisone and prednisolone, for the treatment of inflammatory and allergic disorders, became generally available from February 1957, while the total cost of prescriptions issued for cortisone and hydrocortisone for the first twelve months after their release was estimated at £2.4 million.[77] A combination of market forces and pressure from the Ministry of Health led to a general fall in the price of medicines over the ten years from 1948. Concerned by this trend Jephcott asked the accounts department at Glaxo to prepare indexes to show UK price movements for the company's products.[78] The results confirmed his pessimistic intuition. The index for all Glaxo products fell from 100 in 1948–49 to 57 in 1957–58, while that for foods rose to 134. Most disturbing was the rapid decline in the pharmaceutical index, which collapsed to 49.7 by 1952–53, as a result of successive reductions in the price of antibiotics, and then fell to 27.9 in 1957–58, mainly because of cuts in the price of vitamin B_{12} and the corticosteroids.[79] Food products, by contrast, rose by almost 35 per cent between 1949 and 1953 and remained relatively stable for the rest of the decade. This data fuelled Jephcott's anxiety over the cost of pharmaceutical research, reinforcing his belief that novel medicines might not repay their investment, and encouraged him to think that traditional products, such as Ostermilk and Farex, were a safer commercial option.

How, then, did the group's pharmaceutical products fare during the 1950s and which were the most significant in terms of revenue? From 1946 onwards penicillin was sold in greatest volume, in both an injectable form and as a lozenge for local effect in the mouth. Glaxo had a significant advantage in so far as it was the only UK company that both manufactured and sold penicillin. The largest producer, the Distillers Company based at Speke, was a recent entrant to pharmaceuticals and had no suitable marketing organisation, so it was arranged that six 'independent distributors' (Allen & Hanburys, Boots Pure Drug Co., Burroughs Wellcome, ICI (Pharmaceuticals), Pharmaceutical Specialities (May & Baker) and the British Drug Houses) would undertake secondary manufacture and sales.[80] In January 1947, Glaxo launched crystalline sodium penicillin G (which from September 1952 was marketed as Crystapen).[81] In August 1948, the company launched its first streptomycin preparation, followed in November by procaine penicillin G. Both Crystapen and procaine penicillin G were also sold in ointment form. Glaxo launched phenoxymethylpenicillin (penicillin V) in the late 1950s which, though less active than penicillin G, was gastric-acid stable and could therefore be taken orally. Prescribed to treat respiratory tract infections in children and streptococcal tonsillitis, penicillin V found a ready market in the UK, though it came under increasing competition from the tetracyclines in adult use.[82] In general, the company's penicillin products experienced tough competition during the late 1950s and early 1960s as the number and range of antibiotics increased, leading to successive price reductions.[83] At one stage it was even feared that Glaxo might have excess fermentation capacity by the beginning of 1961.[84] This was, in part, because profitability could be maintained only by a constant drive to improve manufacturing efficiency, with greater yields being achieved from progressively larger vessels. Average quarterly titres at Ulverston for penicillin G, for example, rose from 6,250 in December 1957 to 12,600 in March 1962, while those for streptomycin increased from 4,200 to 6,600 over the same period.[85]

During the 1950s Glaxo continued to make vitamins, and of these the most important medicinally was crystalline vitamin B_{12}, marketed as Cytamen.[86] In September 1954, Glaxo entered a third therapeutic field, corticosteroids, when it launched two ointments for the treatment of inflammatory disorders, cortisone (Cortelan) and hydrocortisone (Efcortelan). By 1957 these had become established products and in that year generated sales in the UK of £800,000, greater than antibiotics (£790,000) or vaccines (£520,000).[87] However, these, too, were soon subject to price reductions, a cut of 15–17 per cent being introduced early in 1959.[88] It proved to be a highly competitive market and though sales rose, profits fell owing to progressively narrower margins.[89]

From the late 1930s Glaxo had also worked on vaccines, and though this remained relatively small-scale, the acquisition of Sefton Park in 1954 (p. 116) led to considerable expansion. In April 1956, with great hopes of its commercial importance, Glaxo launched Polivirin, a vaccine designed to provide immunity against poliomyelitis. Initial sales to the Ministry of Health were high and the company estimated a total annual demand of 4,000 titres generating sales of £800,000 and a gross profit of 67 per cent or £537,000.[90] This proved to be an underestimate and the nine months to March 1958 saw a fourfold increase in UK sales of Polivirin.[91] However, towards the end of the year they fell dramatically[92] and stabilised at a comparatively low level. There had been an initial rush to inoculate the population and once this programme was complete sales were limited to infants and supplementary doses. Glaxo had not foreseen the immediate enthusiasm for the vaccine and had expected the inoculation programme to be more gradual, generating moderate but sustained demand. The actual pattern was, in fact, an initial deluge followed by minimal orders, and in the six months to December 1958, sales of Polivirin fell by £390,000.[93] The effectiveness of the vaccine and the disabling nature of polio, often leading to partial paralysis, accounted for this response. Glaxo and the other pharmaceutical companies responsible for vaccines could rightly claim to have made a significant contribution to the reduction of human misery.

Management and executive change

In the post-war period, ultimate executive authority was exercised by Jephcott and the management of the group was structured to suit his wishes. By 1947, having made Glaxo Laboratories the holding company, Jephcott found the board unwieldy. It was expected to deliberate on both broad group policy and detailed decisions relating to operating subsidiaries. Between March and September 1947, he restructured the organisation almost by trial and error. An executive board was set up to manage the day-to-day operations of Glaxo Laboratories. Under the chairmanship of Jephcott its membership included A. Sandercock (who took the chair in Jephcott's absence), H. W. Palmer (general manager), E. Preston (public relations), Dr H. M. Walker (medical), J. Hutchinson (sales), A. H. Campbell (production), and E. L. C. Gwilt (chairman of the Indian subsidiary).[94]

In September 1947, the board of Glaxo Laboratories was joined by Ida Townsend, then head of the export department.[95] A determined, matronly figure, she remained the only woman ever to become a director of Glaxo Laboratories, an appointment that reflected the company's meritocratic principles. Born and educated in Mexico City of expatriate parents, Ida Townsend moved to London to work for E. F. Harrison, agents dealing with Spanish-speaking countries, based in Gracechurch Street where they shared a building with Glaxo. From 1909, Frederick Harrison served as Glaxo's export agent in South America and ten years later, when this arrangement ended, both Townsend and C. C. Richardson (see p. 139) joined the company. While Richardson travelled to Argentina to set up a local organisation, she worked as his contact in London, making regular visits to Buenos Aires. With her linguistic and organisational skills, Townsend was the natural choice as manager of the export department, which, with one exception, she staffed entirely with women. She retired in December 1955 after twenty-seven years' service with Glaxo.

The minutes of the executive board were reviewed each month by the

*54. The garden party held at Greenford in June 1946
to celebrate the knighthood awarded to Harry
Jephcott. From the clothing of the guests it appears to
have been a cold day.*

group board, also chaired by Jephcott. Its original membership included Sandercock, the deputy chairman and deputy managing director, Palmer and Sir Robert Hutchings together with Sir Nigel Campbell and Sir Cyril Entwistle, both appointed in January 1947.[96] Entwistle, a barrister and company director, had been Conservative MP for Bolton until the Labour landslide of 1945, while Campbell had wide-ranging business experience, having worked in the Ministry of Production during the war and being a board member of the British Overseas Bank, District Bank, Baldwins and Stewarts & Lloyds.[97] At first, selected executive-board directors were invited to attend the group meetings but from December 1948, its membership was closed[98] and henceforth the two committees were united in the person of Jephcott.

The group board initially had only six members, of whom three (Sandercock, Campbell and Entwistle) were part-time and would today be termed non-executive, so that only Jephcott, Palmer and Hutchings were actively involved in the management of the business. Sir Robert Hutchings, once a career civil servant, was given responsibility for personnel training and, for a period, production at Greenford. He had been a senior official in the Indian government's wartime Food Department and afterwards been the Food and Agriculture member on Lord Mountbatten's Executive Council for India.[99] A committed Christian and conscientious administrator, he was described by Viceroy Wavell as 'a good man, sensible and resolute', though some of his proconsular habits seemed incongruous at Greenford. Hutchings relinquished his executive role in 1957, continuing to serve on the main board until December 1967.

In December 1948, Jephcott increased the membership of the group board by three, appointing Sir Jeremy Raisman, Sir Maurice Hutton and Dr Hector Walker.[100] In part, this decision was influenced by the deaths of Sir Nigel Campbell in March 1948[101] and Sandercock in October, but it probably reflected the need to acquire a greater breadth of expertise as Glaxo expanded its activities in peacetime. In November, Herbert Palmer had been appointed deputy managing director (Jephcott combining the posts of chairman and managing director).[102] Palmer, who was Jephcott's right-hand man responsible for the execution of his decisions and for keeping him informed of developments, continued in this role until February 1956 when he became managing director.[103] This appointment was announced in the *Staff Bulletin* under the headline 'Mr H. W. Palmer Takes Over', though in reality Jephcott continued to exercise ultimate control over the group. Raisman and Hutton,

55. *Ida Townsend, head of the export department and the only female director of Glaxo's main board, appointed in 1947.*

by contrast, were both, in effect, non-executive board members. Raisman, a career civil servant, had been the finance member of the Indian government of 1939–45 and chaired the British–Indian delegation to the International Monetary Conference at Bretton Woods.[104] In India, according to Wavell, he had been 'good and sound', being 'patient and tactful in meeting opposition'.[105] Sir Maurice Hutton was given overall responsibility for sales. A stockbroker who had joined the Ministry of Food on the outbreak of war, Hutton headed the British Food Mission in North America and the British Supply Office in the United States in 1947–48.[106] An active and convivial man with considerable business experience, he was said to have lacked authority within the company.[107] In December 1954, Hutton resigned when he emigrated to Australia to become managing director of the Anglo-Australian Corporation (Pty) Ltd of Melbourne.[108]

Thus, in the immediate post-war years, Jephcott appointed five knights (Campbell, Entwistle, Hutchings, Raisman and Hutton) to the Glaxo board, while in April 1952 Sir Henry Tizard was to follow.[109] Jephcott had

56. Joseph Hutchinson. A pharmacist by training he became a salesman and was given responsibility for Canada both before and after the Second World War.

himself received a knighthood in 1946 for wartime service to the Ministry of Food. In a class-conscious society, this may have removed any inhibitions he may have had (coming from a working-class family) about titled executives as close colleagues. Both Hutchings and Raisman had been senior members of the Indian Civil Service and in the preparations for independence found themselves looking for new careers in the UK. Nevertheless, it is curious that Jephcott should have recruited so many knights, none of whom had any knowledge of pharmaceuticals, into a company noted for its unsnobbish and meritocratic culture. In the way that Jephcott had been raised in social status, he may have felt that Glaxo also needed to acquire friends in high places. Jephcott was uncertain of his own social standing and this, perhaps, contributed to his somewhat paternalistic style. Sir David Jack recalled meeting Jephcott in a flustered state having mislaid his invitation to the dinner of the Chemical Industries Association at Grosvenor House at which he was one of the guests of honour with a seat at the high table.[110] Jephcott seemed genuinely perturbed that he would not be admitted without his card and was assuaged only when Jack offered to give him his own invitation if there was trouble. In 1961, Jephcott appointed yet another titled civil servant, Sir Edward Playfair, to the main board. Playfair, who after a lengthy period at the Treasury had served as Permanent Secretary at the Ministry of Defence, had taken a number of business appointments including the chairmanship of International Computers and Tabulators and a non-executive directorship of the Westminster Bank.

Whilst the main board monitored decision making and debated strategy, the executive board, set up in March 1947,[111] was responsible for running Glaxo Laboratories, the largest operating subsidiary in the group. Composed of career managers, each represented a different function in the business. In December 1948,

57. Herbert Palmer, managing director of Glaxo Laboratories from February 1956; he was Harry Jephcott's right-hand man and took charge when Jephcott went on his extended overseas tours. Born in Hammersmith and educated at Ealing Grammar School, Greenford was almost home territory.

for example, Dr Tom Macrae, head of research and development at Greenford, became an executive director,[112] as did Dr F. J. Wilkins in July 1949 when he joined the company to run their northern factories at Ulverston and Barnard Castle.[113] During 1950, both Gwilt and Hutchinson resigned from the executive board as their posts as managing directors of Glaxo Laboratories (India) and Glaxo (Canada) respectively required them to live abroad.[114] Other appointments to the executive board included O. F. Morgan (head of sales) in June 1951,[115] W. J. Hurran (recalled from New Zealand to monitor the group's overseas manufacturing companies) in May 1954[116] and R. A. Langridge in November 1956,[117] who succeeded Ida Townsend as head of the export department.

An important element of Jephcott's management style was frequent visits to the group's overseas subsidiaries in Africa, the Far East and Australasia, often during the British winter. He also regularly crossed the Atlantic to meet his counterparts in the leading US pharmaceutical companies.

58. Dr Fred Wilkins, who joined Glaxo in July 1949 after a chance meeting with Jephcott on a transatlantic liner. Wilkins was appointed to run the group's northern factories at Ulverston and Barnard Castle.

Jephcott was commonly away from Greenford for several months of the year and Sir Jeremy Raisman chaired board meetings in his absence.[118] In December 1950 Raisman was appointed deputy chairman of Glaxo Laboratories.[119] In this way Jephcott was able to preserve his own authority by giving Raisman, a non-executive, the formal supervisory role and leaving Palmer with re- sponsibility for operational matters. Palmer was no longer the inexperienced manager who had prevari- cated over the design of Greenford. Energetic, with a sound grasp of the business, he was a popular figure who took a keen interest in staff matters, becoming, for ex- ample, a member of the Glaxo dramatic society.[120]

Nevertheless, he remained in Jephcott's shadow, sometimes almost literally as their difference in height was marked. Jephcott at 6ft 7in towered over most managers, while the red-haired Palmer was 5ft 3in. Furthermore, he suffered from bronchitis, often at a time when he had been left to manage the UK group while Jephcott was on a winter tour of overseas subsidiaries.

In January 1956, having reached his sixty-fifth birthday, Jephcott re- signed as managing director but continued as chairman of Glaxo.[121] Palmer succeeded him, but Jephcott thought him unsuited for the role of chief executive. In December 1961, Palmer relinquished the managing di- rectorship, though he remained on the board for a further ten years.[122] This was in favour of Wilkins who at the same meeting was appointed chairman and managing director of the executive board of Glaxo Laboratories.[123] In November 1956, Wilkins had been elected deputy managing director of the executive board and, with Jephcott's patronage, appeared to be destined for high office.[124] Jephcott himself was reluctant to retire and in November

1961, when close to his seventieth birthday, persuaded the board to let him continue as chairman.[125]

When, in 1947, Glaxo Laboratories became the parent company, Jephcott decided to hold board meetings not at Greenford, as hitherto, but at 10 Charles II Street, SW1, in the registered offices of Joseph Nathan & Co.[126] This became the secretariat and the formal headquarters building and was used for monthly directors' meetings until February 1952, when a lease was taken on the five upper floors of 1 Carlos Place, at its junction with Mount Street.[127] Formerly occupied as five flats, they were converted into offices, but with the acquisition of a

59. The corporate offices of Glaxo Laboratories at 1 Carlos Place. The company occupied the upper five floors.

variety of operating subsidiaries Glaxo soon outgrew these premises. Glaxo-Allenburys Export, for example, set up in 1960 to co-ordinate the overseas sales of the UK trading companies, was housed in four locations: Avon House, Greenford, Bethnal Green and Carlos Place.[128] It was apparent that more spacious premises were needed for the head office and secretariat. In 1961 a lease was taken out on 47 Park Street, W1, a former residential block converted to commercial use and recently vacated by Richard Thomas & Baldwins, the South Wales steelmakers. The seven-storey building held just over 100 offices and housed the head office, boardroom, secretariat and legal department, together with the staff of Glaxo-Allenburys Export, who occupied the upper floors.

Growth by take-over: Dextran and Murphy Chemical

Concerned by rising costs, uncertainties of research and somewhat intimidated by the size of US competitors, Jephcott sought to build up Glaxo's UK base by a series of take-overs. In 1950, he considered acquiring Herts

Pharmaceuticals, then in the hands of the Custodian of Enemy Property, on the grounds that it 'might provide a useful adjunct to our business'.[129] In the event, Jephcott concluded that its varied interests and book value did not justify the purchase.[130] Not discouraged, he pressed ahead with the strategy of acquiring related companies. In 1947, he had been elected chairman of the Association of British Chemical Manufacturers and held this office for three years, serving as president in 1952–55. In this way, Jephcott built up a circle of friendships with the managers of other UK pharmaceutical companies and in the spring of 1952 became aware of the financial difficulties facing Dextran,[131] manufacturers of substitute plasma. Shortly before the Second World War, research workers at the University of Birmingham had been studying a group of substances, the dextrans, that are produced by fermentation. Later the East Anglian Chemical Co., set up in 1942, separated a dextran that could be given intravenously as a plasma volume expander to treat circulatory failure in shock, arising from excessive blood loss or burns.[132] The practical development of the product was delayed by wartime shortages and it was not until 1947 that it entered commercial production in a factory at Aycliffe, Yorkshire.[133] When the company failed to win approval from the Food and Drug Administration to sell 'Intradex', a new product, in the United States, its problems became apparent. Glaxo paid £56,000 for the issued capital and 'B' debentures of Dextran and made a loan of £16,000 to enable it to redeem the 'A' debentures.[134] A year later, the manufacture of Intradex was transferred to Barnard Castle and the Aycliffe premises closed.[135] Although sales were never large, the substitute plasma was made by fermentation, a process for which Glaxo was well equipped.

The take-over of the Murphy Chemical Co. of Hertfordshire was driven by a need to acquire a sales and marketing organisation for griseofulvin which was initially conceived as a horticultural antifungicide (see p. 118). Founded in 1887 by Albert John Murphy, the company had been set up as a technical consultancy to the fermentation industry and had a laboratory and small factory in Leeds.[136] His investigations into the control of pests and fungal diseases of hops led to the manufacture of insecticides and fungicides at new premises opened in Nottingham after the First World War. The farm and garden department grew so rapidly that laboratories were established at Wheathampstead and, in June 1931, a new organisation, the Murphy Chemical Co., was formed to take over its business. The company built up a strong UK sales force based at forty regional stores. Having no established expertise in horticulture and a novel product in griseofulvin, Glaxo concluded a collaborative sales agreement with Murphy. In view of the growing association between the two companies,[137] Jephcott negoti-

ated a take-over on 22 November 1955.[138]

Further acquisitions: Allen & Hanburys and Evans Medical Supplies

More significant in terms of
size and, indeed, for the future of the group than either
the Dextran or Murphy ac-
quisitions, was the take-over
of Allen & Hanburys on 8
April 1958. Founded in 1715,
when Sylvanus Bevan set up
an apothecary's shop at
Plough Court on Lombard
Street, the company had an
enviable pedigree and reputation. In April 1874, it had
leased an old match factory
in Bethnal Green, which was
progressively rebuilt to become their principal manu-

60. The offices at 47 Park Street, Mayfair, occupied by Glaxo from 1961. Formerly flats, they had been converted to commercial use.

factory until the gradual transfer from 1897 to new premises in unpolluted
air at Ware in Hertfordshire. However, tough competition and an adherence to traditional medicines and galenicals had seen Allen & Hanburys'
profits stagnate during the early 1950s. Aware of the rapid growth and increasing influence of American, Swiss and German companies, The Association of the British Pharmaceutical Industry took steps to protect the
interest of UK producers. Its president, Sir John Hanbury, was asked by the
Council to raise this issue with Jephcott and to invite him to join their assembly. Meeting in his Greenford office, Jephcott agreed to stand for election and added that he felt the time had come for rationalisation. Although
there was no mention of a merger between the two companies, Hanbury
'had the definite impression that something on those lines may well have
been in his mind even at that early date'.[139] By chance, in July 1957, Jephcott
found himself sitting next to Cyril Maplethorpe, the managing director of
Allen & Hanburys, at a luncheon held by the Pharmaceutical Society. 'Con-
versation', Jephcott recalled,

61. A window display of Allen & Hanburys' products including infant foods and proprietory medicines.

turned on the future of the pharmaceutical industry in the UK. I informed him of my enquiries regarding the magnitude of the US companies' interest in the UK market, and their apparent policy to secure a major part of it at any cost. I said that, having regard to the weight of certain US companies in men and money, it was, in my opinion, only a matter of time before British concerns were swamped out of existence, the smaller going to the wall first, A & H consequently before Glaxo. To my surprise, Maplethorpe's reply was one of prompt and emphatic agreement, and an expression of desire to talk the situation over with me.[140]

The directors of Allen & Hanburys, faced with continuing financial difficulties, were almost unanimous in pursuing the question of a merger and discussions continued during 1957, while Palmer and Wilkins visited the Bethnal Green and Ware factories. Wilkins reported to Jephcott that

> he was well impressed by what he had seen, and by those whom he met, particularly some of the younger executives but, in respect of buildings and equipment, there was obvious evidence of a shortage of cash for capital expenditures.[141]

62. *The Allen & Hanburys' pharmacy at 7 Vere Street. It had a staff of fifty during the 1920s and was considered something of a finishing school in the pharmacy profession. Located in the heart of the West End medical community, it attracted custom from many of the leading physicians of the day and did much to enhance the reputation of the company.*

In March 1958 detailed negotiations began.[142] The directors of Allen & Hanburys, especially those drawn from the Hanbury family, insisted that it be called a 'marriage' and not a merger, least of all an acquisition.[143] Given the differences in size between the two companies, this was a difficult fiction to sustain. In 1957 Glaxo was capitalised at £15.8 million in contrast to the £3.8 million of Allen & Hanburys, while their pre-tax profits were £4.2 million and £383,000 respectively. The press rightly interpreted the event as an uncontested acquisition, the *Daily Mail* describing the offer as a 'take-over bid of the best kind'. For an outlay of £633,000, Glaxo took control of assets valued at £1.5 million.[144] There was little attempt to integrate the two companies though it was hoped that communication between them would be aided by two appointments, that of Herbert Palmer to the Allen & Hanburys' board, while Cyril Maplethorpe became a director of the Glaxo main board.[145]

In retrospect, Cyril Maplethorpe believed that it was the decision in 1941 to enter penicillin manufacture that had both transformed Allen & Hanburys into a modern ethical company and paved the way for the merger.[146] The company had taken out licences from both Glaxo and ICI to make penicillin by surface culture and a purpose-built factory was constructed at

63. Building P2 at Ware, designed for the surface culture of penicillin but never used for that purpose. It was subsequently converted for the secondary manufacture of pharmaceuticals.

Ware.[147] Later, Allen & Hanburys also attempted to acquire technical data about deep fermentation from Glaxo but Jephcott refused and, in the event, supplies were purchased from the government factory at Speke, operated by Distillers. In 1950, Allen & Hanburys marketed their first penicillin products (an injectable together with lozenges and creams), while two years later they launched Sulpenin, a tablet containing both penicillin and a sulphonamide for systemic treatment.

In January 1961, Glaxo Laboratories acquired the Liverpool pharmaceutical company Evans Medical.[148] It too was an established family business, having been founded at Worcester in 1809 by John Evans.[149] During the 1830s Evans, in partnership with Joseph Lescher, opened a branch at 15 Fenwick Street, Liverpool, though this soon moved to larger premises at 8 Lord Street.[150] In 1916 the company acquired the Runcorn Gas Works, converting the plant for the manufacture of fine chemicals. However, an enemy raid in May 1941 threatened the future of the business, destroying the company's offices, workshops and warehouse in Hanover Street. Plans were rapidly drawn up to build a factory at Speke and the new plant came on stream in December 1943 (see p. 280). The development of overseas interests after the war brought Evans Medical Supplies commercial success but

64. The Speke offices and factory of Evans Medical constructed in 1943.

its limited size (capitalised at £3 million) made the company vulnerable to take-over. In June 1960 Fisons, who had recently failed to acquire The British Drug Houses, approached the Evans board with proposals for an amalgamation.[151] To defend themselves, Evans in the person of I. V. L. Fergusson, chairman and managing director, contacted Jephcott to discuss whether Glaxo would consider a union along the lines of the Allen & Hanbury's merger. After private consultations, Fergusson recorded that 'Jephcott said that whereas personally he would greatly welcome and be very anxious for an association, cash was the stumbling block. The best he could suggest was one Glaxo 10s share for two Evans Medical 5s stock units.'[152] The offer proved acceptable to the Evans shareholders and, as Fergusson noted, 'the trend towards larger and ever larger units is something which cannot be avoided'.[153] In the event, Evans Medical became a subsidiary of Glaxo on the understanding that it, too, would retain its separate identity and a large degree of commercial autonomy.[154]

The general strategy pursued by Jephcott of growth through take-over was not conducted according to a carefully considered blueprint. He responded to circumstances, taking advantage of other companies' difficulties, to build up a collection of UK pharmaceutical houses each with its own proud tradition, range of products and individual culture. Although Jephcott sought to create a powerful British group that would challenge its US competitors, he failed to take advantage of the potential economies of scale. There was little attempt to rationalise production or eliminate the duplication of specialist functions. By 1962, therefore, when Glaxo Group was set up, Jephcott had assembled a loose federation of semi-autonomous subsidiaries, each with its own name, products and manufacturing capacity. Furthermore, by not imposing a unified structure, he allowed subsidiaries to view the group from their own perspective, nurturing resentments against Glaxo as the ultimate authority and leading to longstanding rivalries and occasional enmities (see p. 146). Structurally, therefore, considerable confusion had been created as company loyalties straddled and conflicted with functional roles. In addition, take-overs and territorial expansion made it increasingly difficult for Jephcott to monitor performance on a personal level.

Although Jephcott dominated the new company and was sometimes authoritarian, he was not without breadth of vision. As he wrote in 1939 to Rupert Pearce, the managing director of the Australian subsidiary:

> although one cannot ignore the financial aspects of living, I do not feel … they are the most important … The greatest thing I know is to go to the office in the morning with a sense of pleasurable anticipation.[155]

In a sense, Jephcott's weakness was a failure to develop such an enthusiasm for life outside Glaxo and he found it almost impossible to leave the company that he had shaped and led. He was intensely paternalistic, dedicated to the welfare of the company and invested with a sense of fair play. Having risen from humble origins himself, Jephcott remained unsnobbish and believed in the selection of talent from whatever background. Under his leadership, Glaxo selected its graduates or school-leavers on a meritocratic basis. Herbert Palmer once commented that 'we are basically a lower middle class company'. This proved to be a significant cultural feature of Glaxo and one that was to endure long after Jephcott's retirement in 1963.

Although Joseph Nathan should be credited with the foundation of the business and Alec Nathan was responsible for the creation of Glaxo Laboratories, Jephcott deserves recognition for directing the company towards pharmaceuticals and grounding its products on a scientific basis. In the early 1950s, Jephcott commissioned a documentary film about the workings of the company and when the cameras paused in his office at Greenford the narrator observed: 'it is indeed a fact that everything revolves around Sir Harry'.[156] A man of integrity and imagination, Jephcott's vision was circumscribed both territorially, largely within former Dominion nations, and in terms of product innovation, believing that the traditional strength of Glaxo in development work and manufacture should not be weakened by risky diversification into research.

RESEARCH IN CRISIS

PHARMACEUTICAL RESEARCH, the search for novel chemical entities, was shaped at Glaxo by Jephcott. As a discipline within the company, it grew from analytical testing designed to monitor the quality of food products and development work to improve their nutritional value. Although he had been responsible for establishing a budget for this work in 1935 (see p. 51), Jephcott never fully appreciated how research had evolved and continued to conceptualise the activity in terms of development. He was at his most happy when taking an academic invention and translating it into a practical product with an efficient manufacturing process. In a paper entitled 'How much research?', written in 1952, Jephcott defined this circumscribed strategy:

A concerted attack by a competent research team coming fresh to a process, unencumbered by a fixity of outlook acquired during years of routine operation, will on many occasions lead to improved techniques. If a minimum improvement of one or two per cent can be attained, this will be well worthwhile … Indeed, it is by increased efficiency gained with little or no capital expenditure that industry can best aid the national economic problems and ward off inflationary pressures.[1]

Uppermost in his mind was the cost and speculative nature of research. Ten years later, in 1962, Jephcott was asked to contribute a chapter in a study of UK research organisations edited by Sir John Cockroft.[2] In this paper, Jephcott outlined his fears:

It is almost inevitable that some project undertaken proves to be much greater in scope and cost than was envisaged. I recall one that had a large sum spent on it over many years and was completely abandoned. Another cost £400,000 without any clear indication of a successful outcome. More recently, a total expenditure approaching £1 million has been incurred on a project and at least half as much again will probably need to be spent on it before the kind of commercial success necessary to make the effort worthwhile is in sight.[3]

In the *Chairman's Review* for 1958 Jephcott described long-term research as 'most hazardous' and added 'yet we have no choice but to pursue it, for out of it we hope will emerge the major advances on which alone we can expect to maintain and expand our business'.[4] He was concerned by both rising salary bills ('though our average cost per graduate is a little more than £6,000 per annum, it ranges in the various laboratories from less than £3,000 to more than £8,000')[5] and the high levels of instrumentation required: 'a chemical laboratory, for instance, that was well equipped twenty-five years ago with a few hundred pounds' worth of glassware and balances, now may need instruments to the value of £300,000 or more, which are expensive to maintain and have a high rate of depreciation'.[6] He calculated that research costs had increased at a rate of 10 to 15 per cent every year during the 1950s and early 1960s.

Jephcott's visits to the larger laboratories of the leading US pharmaceutical companies increased his pessimism. In January 1950, he recorded after a tour of Smith Kline & French's plant at Philadelphia that they spent $1.5 million on research.[7] In his 1952 paper, he quoted the case of an American organisation whose annual expenditure on research was $3–4 million, representing 5.3 per cent of sales. Although he credited them with 'certain outstanding developments', Jephcott thought this level of spending was 'unusually high'. He did not believe that Glaxo could afford such expensive overheads, in part because he adopted an over-simplistic view of the relationship between revenue and research expenditure. Jephcott argued that 'taking one year with another, research must pay for itself by the sale of products amounting from it'.[8] Whilst in the long term he was undoubtedly right, a single project, funded beyond an agreed budget for a short period, could, if successful, transform the commercial fortunes of a company. Flexibility and judgement were required in assessing spending limits rather than rigid adherence to the previous years' profits. Furthermore, Jephcott may have been over influenced by the plentiful budgets and scale of laboratories in the United States into thinking that small or medium-sized enterprises could not discover novel products. The work of Dr David Jack and his team at Ware in the 1960s demonstrated the fallacy of this strategy when they researched and developed salbutamol, launched in 1969 (see p. 331). In September 1962, Jephcott concluded his paper on Glaxo's research organisation in a gloomy frame of mind:

The medium-sized company, such as my own, cannot afford to spend more than a modest proportion of its research budget upon a project that may extend over a long term of years. Moreover, research of this nature calls for men of outstanding research calibre, and such persons are rare; the limitation may be of men rather than money.[9]

Mistrusting academic research, Jephcott regretted the introduction of the doctor of philosophy degree as the key qualification for scientists, arguing that 'it is questionable whether it affords the best training for the chemist who is ultimately to enter industry or a research organisation'. Based upon 'an academic exercise', he thought it too 'highly specialised' and believed that post-graduates would find it hard to

> attack the problems of greater productivity, yet it is to such problems that their activities will need to be increasingly directed, though it will be foreign to their training and perhaps even contrary to the tenets of chemical faith in which they have been trained.[10]

He had forgotten that 'academic research' had been responsible for the initial discoveries that ultimately led to valuable medicines, including vitamin D, penicillin and streptomycin.

At the December 1957 meeting of the research and development committee, Jephcott seemed to have a change of heart. He opened the discussion by

> expressing disappointment at the lack of suggestions as to what work we might undertake. In reply to questions, he emphasised that he was not criticising the technical competence of the work that had been done over the last six months. He felt, however, that the time had come when research should be increasingly directed at projects which, if successful, would lead to new products and that there should be a corresponding reduction in development work.[11]

Dr Tom Macrae, head of research, seemed surprised by this change of direction and added

> nothing would please him better than to devote more time to the search for new products. However, particularly in the field of sterol research, experience had shown that previous attempts to devote more time to the search for new sterols had come to nought because of the need to maintain the company's competitive position in the cortisone field. He cited the work that had been done on prednisone, prednisolone and more recently on the soluble phosphates, contending with Dr Wilkins that the latter could, in any case, be regarded as new products.[12]

65. Dr Tom Macrae in his office at Greenford. A nutritionist and iconoclastic Scot who did much to protect his researchers against Jephcott's more narrow view of appropriate scientific experiment.

Despite his apparent change of heart, Jephcott was not prepared to increase the research budget so that finance for its expansion had to be found by scaling down existing development projects.

In June 1958, Jephcott conceded that 'no important new product for sale was likely to emerge in the foreseeable future from research products now in hand'.[13] The realisation that Glaxo had no novel medicines in the pipeline drove Jephcott to sign a collaborative agreement with Schering, the major US corporation. Glaxo already had licensing agreements with Schering to make diphenatil for the treatment of gastric ulcers, together with the steroids prednisone and prednisolone, which had proved commercially rewarding. Schering were acknowledged leaders in the field of adrenocortical steroids, while Glaxo were 'late comers to this field with much leeway to make up'.[14] Nevertheless, Glaxo had succeeded in designing processes to extract hecogenin, a steroid, from sisal juice to use as a starter material for cortisone and hydrocortisone. 'A marriage of Schering's new product knowledge and [Glaxo's] know-how on high yielding techniques seemed logical and desirable.' Under this arrangement, Schering was to provide scientific data on their latest findings, while Glaxo was to decide within thirty days of disclosure whether it considered these discoveries worthy of further investigation and would 'endeavour to develop commercial synthesis'.[15] Any medicine that resulted would be licensed to Glaxo but with a lower royalty than would have been charged without the collaboration. In a context of fixed budgets, the Schering agreement reduced the finance available for 'true research' carried out at Glaxo. As a result of the joint steroid projects, Macrae observed in October 1958 that 'about 75 per cent of the division's expenditures were now being incurred on development, as distinct from work leading to the discovery of new compounds'.[16]

The full extent of the crisis facing Glaxo had now become apparent. At the January 1959 board meeting, Sir Henry Tizard expressed his concerns and argued that the research teams required an immediate injection of finance for expansion and the recruitment of 'chemists of high quality'.[17] Maplethorpe endorsed this strategy, while Dr Hector Walker 'emphasised the increasing cost of, and need for, external clinical and biochemical work on prospective new products'.[18] It was agreed to vote an extra £50,000 for the chemical research budget and draw up plans for additional laboratory space. In the event, Jephcott agreed to spend a further £100,000 during 1959–60, adding £19,000 to the teams working on griseofulvin and the cephalosporins, and allocated £51,500 for work on a vaccine against poliomyelitis.[19] As a result, total research and development expenditure rose from £818,900 in 1958–59 to £941,400 in 1959–60. In his annual review for 1959, Jephcott outlined the group's race against time:

> A high proportion of our present UK turnover of ethical medical specialities arises from products introduced within the past five years. Five years hence, the proportion will be still higher and many of those products that are now of major importance will be obsolete ... Unless we are adequately equipped, technically and scientifically, to hold our own in this field, we cannot hope to share in the growing economic prosperity of this country or of the world as a whole.[20]

Under pressure from board colleagues and acutely aware of commercial realities, Jephcott agreed to progressively higher spending on research during the early 1960s. The recruitment drive was pushed forwards, though it encountered difficulties in the spring of 1961, because of Glaxo's high standards, competition and the attractive offers being made by US pharmaceutical companies.[21] Research focused on three therapeutic areas: vaccines at Sefton Park, together with cephalosporins and corticosteroids at Greenford. In the event, the corticosteroids produced Glaxo's first novel medicine – betamethasone valerate (Betnovate), launched in November 1963 (see p. 318). As a topical dermatological for the treatment of eczema and psoriasis, it had a relatively limited market and it was not until 1969 that Glaxo was able to introduce two medicines of great commercial significance: cephalexin (Ceporex), an oral antibiotic (p. 315), and salbutamol (Ventolin) for the treatment of asthma, which had been discovered at Ware (see p. 331).

In March 1951, Glaxo sold their laboratory and offices at Bravington Road to Messrs Allnatt for £27,500.[22] Although this event merits little more than a footnote in the history of the company, these were the buildings that

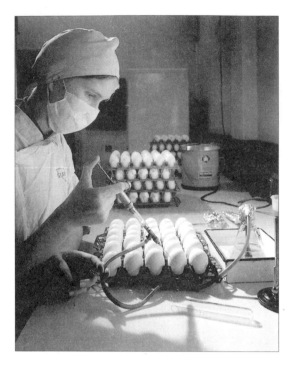

66. *Preparing vaccines: the inoculation of embryonated eggs for Myxilin, a vaccine against bronchitis.*

Jephcott had occupied in 1919 and housed Glaxo's first scientific efforts, albeit quality control. From January 1947, Bravington Road had provided temporary accommodation for the headquarters of the development division. Once the post-war building programme gathered pace and room became available at Greenford, it became redundant and the company disposed of these historic premises.

Vaccines at Sefton Park

By 1949 laboratory accommodation at Greenford had again become overcrowded and Glaxo decided to buy Sefton Park, a medium-sized country house (once the home of the actress Vesta Tilley) near Stoke Poges, in Buckinghamshire.[23] The property itself was acquired for £13,650, and equipped, together with two new laboratories at Greenford, for £175,000.[24] Occupied in 1950, for the first two years the scientists at Sefton Park under Dr Sandy Campbell concentrated almost entirely on fermentation problems designed to improve the efficiency of penicillin and streptomycin manufacture.[25]

Although the bacteriological department at Greenford had worked on vaccines before the war, it was not until October 1944 that Glaxo launched its own product – a vaccine against whooping cough (pertussis).[26] Much of the research had fallen to Dr Joseph Ungar, a refugee from Czechoslovakia who had joined the company in July 1939. Ungar had qualified in medicine before specialising in immunology in Prague and Paris.[27] In November 1946, his department produced the first vaccine to combine protection against both diphtheria and whooping cough. In January 1955, tetanus toxoid was added to provide protection against all three illnesses. In the early 1950s attention turned to the BCG (bacille Calmette–Guérin) vaccine against tuberculosis. Although first prepared at the Pasteur Institute in 1906 by Leon Calmette and Camille Guérin and used in France from the mid 1920s, it encountered resistance from British medical authorities.[28] Only when the Medical Research Council established its efficacy by a controlled trial in 1950 was prejudice overcome and a programme of vaccination in schools followed. Glaxo refined production techniques and became the first pharmaceutical company in Europe to manufacture the BCG vaccine on an industrial scale using freeze-drying techniques. This method enabled the vaccine to be tested for biological efficiency before use and increased the storage time from two weeks to at least a year.[29] In December 1956, a purpose-built biological laboratory, designed by Elliott, Cox & Partners, was opened at Greenford at a cost of £400,000 both for the manufacture of the BCG and tetanus toxoid vaccines and for research into new applications.[30] With the BCG vaccination as an effective preventative measure against new cases of tuberculosis and antibiotics to treat existing patients, the disease was, in effect, eradicated from advanced industrial societies in the twenty years after the Second World War.

In 1952, Ungar and his virology team began work on a vaccine to combat poliomyelitis. Dr Hector Walker had heard about research being conducted by A. J. Rhodes at the Connaught Medical Research Laboratory in Toronto. Jephcott visited him while in North America, reporting in May 1953 that he believed £22,000 would be sufficient to take the laboratory discoveries of Rhodes through to an industrial process.[31] Tizard urged a thorough study of the implications of vaccine research for Glaxo and the undertaking took a more serious turn. In December 1953, the board approved plans to build a laboratory at Sefton Park for work on the poliomyelitis vaccine to be headed by Dr William Wood, recruited from the Connaught Laboratories.[32] The new premises were completed in July 1954 and in just under two years, Glaxo's first supplies of poliomyelitis vaccine, Polivirin, were sold to the Ministry of Health for an immunisation programme aimed at children between the ages of two and nine years.[33] The campaign caught the public's imagination and sales of Polivirin exceeded all expectations in 1957 and 1958, but having surpassed its targets fell to low levels thereafter (see p. 96). The initial boom in vaccine turnover encouraged Glaxo to consider other projects, including that to counter the APC (adreno-pharyngeal-conjunctival) virus,[34] and a range for the protective inoculation of sheep and pigs.[35] Because the virus laboratories at Sefton Park were fully occupied with poliomyelitis work, the board agreed to spend £110,000 on additional facilities.[36]

By 1959, Glaxo had spent £466,000 on facilities at Sefton Park for the manufacture of poliomyelitis vaccine. Although total turnover of Polivirin for the year to March 1959 totalled £1.7 million, estimates suggested a fall to

£500,000 in the following year, while the imminent launch of competitor products threatened Glaxo's investment.[37] Furthermore, a new live vaccine made from attenuated strains (rather than the inactivated type produced by Glaxo) had entered clinical trials, and was soon shown to be more effective. Wilkins recommended that the company build a second laboratory at Sefton Park to work on the attenuated live vaccine to protect Glaxo's existing business.

Griseofulvin

In 1952, Dr Sandy Campbell, director at Sefton Park, submitted proposals for the expansion of their screening processes to include systemic fungicides and insecticides to discover whether they possessed valuable antibiotic properties. Because this was speculative work with no promise of commercial reward, Jephcott refused to grant the additional budget of £20,000 needed to recruit extra staff, though he did agree to the diversion of existing personnel.[38] The idea had originally been put to Campbell in January 1952 by Dr A. Rhodes in a paper entitled 'Griseofulvin: a potential Glaxo product?'.[39] Rhodes, a plant pathologist, had joined Glaxo from ICI where scientists had identified the chemical structure of griseofulvin and demonstrated its potential use as a systemic fungicide against *Alternaria solani* living on tomatoes and *Botrytis cinera* on lettuce. Impressed by this work, Campbell authorised a preliminary study of the action of griseofulvin as a seed dressing. In June 1953, the two presented a paper suggesting a co-operative arrangement with the Murphy Chemical Co. at Wheathampstead, manufacturers of chemical fertilisers and pesticides, for the joint marketing of any agricultural antibiotics developed by Glaxo. In the summer of 1954, following Jephcott's decision to curtail all experiment at Sefton Park into new antibiotics, it was agreed to proceed with the project to find a commercially viable method of making griseofulvin by deep fermentation.[40]

Between 1955 and 1957 researchers at Sefton Park conducted trials on griseofulvin both in the laboratory and at commercial nurseries, while Barnard Castle began trials of its manufacture in their 5,000 gallon fermenters. Trials by Murphy demonstrated griseofulvin's effectiveness against apple scab and protected crops from Botrytis rot.[41] Other studies showed its efficacy against tulip fire, mildew in commercial chrysanthemums and fungal diseases in carnations. In the autumn of 1957, Murphy launched griseofulvin as 'Grisovin 3 per cent Dust', the first commercial antibiotic available to growers in Britain. However, it was expensive in comparison with existing agricultural antifungals and its competitive advantage was confined to valuable, out-of-season crops such as glasshouse lettuce.

The potent antifungal action of griseofulvin combined with its low toxicity encouraged Glaxo scientists to consider whether it could have a role as a medicine.[42] In February 1955, K. A. Lees, who had performed some of the early toxicity tests, approached Dr J. C. Gentles, a medical mycologist at the Department of Bacteriology, Anderson College in Glasgow, to suggest the topical use of griseofulvin in human clinical trials. Gentles, a consultant to the National Coal Board, was exploring the prevalence of athlete's foot among miners and looking for new treatments. However, the surface application of griseofulvin to treat human dermatophytes proved disappointing and Glaxo suspended further clinical investigation. Meanwhile, ICI pursued a parallel path and by 1956 had prepared two patent applications, the first relating to the use of griseofulvin for the treatment of fungal diseases in man and animals, and the second to its oral administration including tablets, pills and syrups. In March 1957, Glaxo researchers learned of the antibiotic's effectiveness against dermatophytic fungi when given orally. This encouraged the Sefton Park researchers to proceed with clinical trials designed to investigate the drug's systemic activity and Dr K. H. Fantes arranged for griseofulvin and griseofulvin oxime to be tested by Gentles on guinea-pigs in Glasgow. The promising results, published in *Nature* in August 1958, [43] led to the first human trials conducted by Professor Gustav Riehl in Austria. Having read of Gentles' successes in *Nature*, Dr Harvey Blank wrote to Glaxo for griseofulvin to treat a patient near death and infected with *Trichophyton rubrum*, the most resistant of dermatomycoses. Supplies were air freighted to the United States and the man recovered.[44] Clinical trials undertaken at King's College Hospital in 1958 by Dr David Williams helped to establish the efficacy of griseofulvin for the treatment of ringworm.[45]

The project almost foundered in 1958 when scientists at ICI reported to Glaxo (under an agreement between the two companies for development work, patent rights and manufacture) that they had discovered abnormal effects on cell division in animals given griseofulvin. If the drug proved to be toxic, the project would have to be abandoned. Yet the findings were not replicated in experiments conducted by Gentles and I. M. Lander, his veterinary colleague in Glasgow. Further investigations were ordered by Glaxo and no toxicity revealed. The issue was finally settled at a meeting held between the two companies in May 1958 when it was concluded that the smaller particle size of the high intravenous doses used by ICI had greatly raised absorption levels and led to a poisonous effect.

No sooner had this matter been resolved than a fresh and more acrimonious dispute broke out between the two companies. An ICI researcher named A. R. Martin contested the originality of Gentles' observations and Glaxo's associated claims. He argued that these results simply confirmed earlier evidence gathered by ICI that had led to the filing of the provisional patents in 1956. An internal inquiry conducted by Herbert Palmer concluded that Glaxo had no knowledge of Martin's experiments on fungal infections in guinea-pigs and confirmed that Gentles had been looking for an antibiotic to treat resistant dermatological conditions before any contact had been made with the company.[46] The report re-established the integrity of Gentles and of Glaxo, and co-operation with ICI was restored. On 6 April 1959 griseofulvin was simultaneously launched in the UK by Glaxo as Grisovin and by ICI as Fulcin.[47] In the United States, Glaxo licensed Grisovin to Johnson & Johnson and Schering, while ICI licensed it to Wyeth. Griseofulvin proved to be a breakthrough treatment for ringworm in the way that streptomycin and other antibiotics revolutionised the management of tuberculosis. Until its introduction, there was little that pharmacology could offer, resistant cases having to suffer lengthy and potentially hazardous radiation. Although the compound had not been discovered by Glaxo, it was one of the first novel medicines that the company succeeded in taking from the laboratory bench through to clinical use.

Vitamin B$_{12}$

In 1946, Dr E. Lester Smith, head of the biochemical unit, returned to his pre-war studies of vitamins and began to look in particular for a treatment for pernicious (Addisonian) anaemia.[48] It had been shown that folic acid could restore the shortage of haemoglobin in the blood but could not arrest the associated neurological degeneration, sometimes leading to partial paralysis. In 1926, G. R. Minot and W. P. Murphy of Boston, Massachusetts, had discovered that lightly cooked liver in large quantities benefited patients with the disease. This, in turn, led to the manufacture of purified liver extract. Lester Smith, who joined Glaxo in 1926 having studied chemistry part-time at Chelsea Polytechnic, carried out work on the production of calciferol and vitamin concentrates. In 1936, Glaxo had acquired a licence from the Norwegian pharmaceutical company Nyegaard & Co. to make the extract and Lester Smith travelled to Oslo to learn about the process. Plant was installed at Greenford and Glaxo marketed the product as Examen. Research under Dr B. K. Blount began to identify the chemical nature of the anti-anaemia factor but made little progress, partly because no reliable test existed but also because of a relative scarcity of patients.[49] Although Glaxo scientists improved the potency of the extract and modified the manufacturing process during the war years, they came no closer to discovering the cause of its therapeutic effect.[50]

The breakthrough came when Lester Smith, assisted by L. F. J. Parker and K. H. Fantes, adopted the relatively novel technique of partition chromatography devised by A. J. P. Martin and R. L. M. Synge. This enabled them to separate purified liver extracts into different coloured zones.[51] In August 1946, in an internal report to Jephcott, Lester Smith stated that clinical activity seemed to be associated with the pink zone.[52] Further work confirmed this observation and, after a series of delays, repeated chromatography of the pink material led to an intense red preparation which in May 1948 was crystallised from acetone in the form of needles.[53] The vitamin was found to be potent and effectively treated both the blood and neurological deficiencies of pernicious anaemia patients in relapse. For his pioneering work Lester Smith was elected a Fellow of the Royal Society, the first Glaxo scientist to be honoured in this way. However, Lester Smith had been forestalled by Karl Folkers and the team at Merck in Rahway, who had obtained red crystals (which they christened vitamin B_{12}) five months earlier but had delayed publication.[54] The American crystals, which were soon shown to be identical to those made at Greenford, had been made from a mould found in the fermenters that produced streptomycin.[55] Since Glaxo had a licence to use this method, they were able to adapt the antibiotic manufacturing process to produce supplies of vitamin B_{12} as well.

Crystalline vitamin B_{12} was marketed by Glaxo under the name Cytamen and launched on 14 November 1949 at the London Medical Exhibition.[56] It retailed at 21s (£1.05) for six 1cc ampoules, though a succession of price reductions followed at the behest of the Ministry of Health,[57] and as a result of competition with Merck.[58] Although a significant medical advance, Cytamen did not prove of great commercial advantage to Glaxo. Patients were comparatively few in number and the maintenance dose was calculated at one-twentieth of the treatment regimen.

Cortisone: Montrose

In April 1949 a report appeared in the *New York Times* suggesting that a treatment had been found for rheumatoid arthritis. Patients given cortisone, an anti-inflammatory corticosteroid, by Hench and Kendall went into remission, spurring a hunt to find a viable commercial synthesis. In March 1951, the Medical Research Council asked Glaxo whether the company would take part in collaborative research to discover ways of making cortisone from raw materials other than ox gall.[59] Jephcott was enthusiastic and met Sir Charles Harington at the National Institute for Medical Research, Mill Hill, where he was told of work to extract hecogenin, a natural though inactive steroid, from sisal waste. About a kilogram of hecogenin had been prepared and the scientists had developed six of the stages in a complex process designed to synthesise cortisone. Their findings were made known to Glaxo and other pharmaceutical companies to accelerate the work. Jephcott arranged for a quantity of sisal waste to be delivered to Greenford from East Africa so that work could begin immediately.[60] In the meantime, the chemists at Glaxo also experimented on producing cortisone from ergosterol, which the company had made at its Hayes factory as a source of vitamin D. Although ergosterol was expensive, theoretically it could be produced in large quantities by fermentation at potentially lower costs. However, privately Jephcott was not optimistic about Glaxo's chances of success and wrote in November 1951 to Herbert Palmer to question the company's

> real prospects with cortisone and what are the dangers that at some future date … we may find that we have spent half a million… and have nothing by way of an asset … It's difficult to avoid the conclusion that, both in the academic and in the more technical field appropriate to ourselves, we are well behind the US – by 'well' I mean years … We [are] mere pigmies compared with Merck.[61]

Even when the synthesis was achieved in July 1952, Jephcott remained pessimistic: 'there is much yet to be done before we are in a position to produce even small quantities for human use'.[62]

The scientists and laboratory staff involved in the synthesis from ergosterol held a cortisone party in The Oldfield, a public house near the Greenford factory, though the high absentee rate the following day discouraged future events. Despite the celebrations, it rapidly became clear that the ergosterol route to cortisone could never be commercially viable. As a result, great efforts were put into the synthesis from hecogenin. By May 1953, the development programme had reached the stage where the economic success of the project was 'in large measure dependent on the cost of hecogenin'.[63] Estimates based on sisal grown in Kenya by the National Research and Development Corporation suggested that cortisone derived by this route could be competitive.[64]

In June 1951, despite the plan to make ergosterol by fermentation, Jephcott decided against housing cortisone plant at Ulverston, and to find an entirely new location. Some believed that Jephcott was sceptical about the future of cortisone and decided that any success or failure should be clearly apparent. Various sites were explored, including Wern Tarw, northeast of Bridgend in Glamorgan,[65] Leven in Fifeshire and Barnsley. Finally, the board bought six acres of land in Cobden Street, Montrose, Angus, for

£40,000 in May 1952.[66] In addition, Bide, as the first factory manager, acquired the option to buy thirty-three acres of the South Links, a nine-hole pitch and putt, adjacent to the proposed plant and this later provided valuable space for expansion.[67] The site, which belonged to Purvis Industries, manufacturers of pre-cast concrete blocks then in liquidation, included two single-storey buildings that could be converted for pharmaceutical production. Its location on the estuary of the River

67. The Montrose factory situated beside the River South Esk.

South Esk provided a ready outlet for the disposal of effluent. The town council, wishing to attract new businesses, were receptive, while the Board of Trade had stipulated that companies could obtain a development licence only if they used existing structures. One of the buildings, a wartime hangar, was used to make purified liver extract, and another (building 15) was employed for the production of cortisone. Initially, the plant was set up to work from ergosterol but, by November when it had been shown this was uneconomic, Glaxo decided to buy an intermediate compound ('EAX') from Merck which in relatively few stages could be converted into cortisone and hydrocortisone. Development work on the hecogenin route was by no means complete and the company had little option but to purchase the Merck compound if Montrose were to enter the corticosteroid market. Montrose made its first batch of cortisone in January 1954 and Albert Hall, the factory analyst, recalled going to the laboratory on a Saturday morning to test its purity. When it was shown to have reached the required standards, a party was held in the Park Hotel, while Norman Jeffrey, who had just been appointed factory manager, travelled to Greenford on the sleeper with the compound in a polythene bag inside a biscuit tin.[68]

When the factory was occupied in May 1952, it had very few staff, but numbers increased to nineteen by June and fifty-two a year later. By 1960 they had only reached 195. Although Austin Bide remained the manager until December 1953, he was based at Greenford and commuted to Montrose on a monthly basis. In his absence, executive control was exercised by

Jimmy Green, who had the entire plant painted in eau-de-Nil. Great effort was made to commission the nineteen-stage process from hecogenin on schedule in March 1955, and the same year Glaxo's first steroid products (Cortelan and Efcortelan) were launched in the UK. The former had initially been registered under the trade mark 'Cortesan', when presumably the full implications of the name had not been considered.[69] Yet these remained difficult years for the Montrose factory. Its reliance upon three products, not exclusive to Glaxo and so subject to fierce competitive pressures, kept its future in doubt.

Neither Cortelan nor Efcortelan earned high profits. Initial returns were limited by use of the Merck intermediate, and after production had switched to the company's own supplies of hecogenin, competitive pressures forced a series of price cuts. Nevertheless, the corticosteroids generated considerable turnover and in 1958, for example, UK sales earned £860,000 or 21 per cent of the group's pharmaceutical business.[70] This success proved shortlived and in the following year sales fell by £158,000, almost all of this being the result of rebates.[71] Despite keen competition, UK sales of corticosteroids continued to rise in the early 1960s, though ongoing price reductions led to ever tighter margins.[72] The real commercial and therapeutic breakthrough in anti-inflammatory medicine for Glaxo was to come from another corticosteroid, betamethasone 17-valerate in November 1963, the first of a new portfolio of dermatologicals (see p. 318).[73]

IMPERIAL GLAXO

§

AS MERCHANTS, Joseph Nathan & Co. traded agricultural goods
from New Zealand for industrial products made in the UK. Until the
company became involved in manufacture there was little need to
broaden its territorial horizons. Once it had begun to export dried milk
powder then the Glaxo Department sought wider sources of supply and
new markets. In 1909 an agency was opened in Buenos Aires to serve South
America and just before the outbreak of the First World War agents were
appointed for India and the Far East. The company remained within Imperial and later Commonwealth boundaries of business until the mid 1960s
when, under the chairmanship of Sir Alan Wilson, greater attention began
to be paid to Europe.

New Zealand and Australia

Greatly increased demand for milk powder during the First World War
made it necessary to find additional manufacturing capacity in New
Zealand. Rather than incur the capital costs of building a new plant, in June
1916 the Nathans acquired an interest (and the agreement to purchase) in
the Waihou Valley Dairy Co. and installed nine roller drying machines in
their dairy at Te Aroha.[1] In the following month, a creamery at Matamata
was rented from the New Zealand Co-operative Dairy Association on the
understanding that it, too, would be converted into a milk drying factory.[2]
However, this additional plant did not prove sufficient and, in November
1917, Nathans rented a third factory built by the Association on land formerly owned by the Matangi Cheese Co. This was the largest of the three
with eighteen roller dryers, and constructed at a cost of £122,000. When he
visited New Zealand in 1920, J. A. Nathan recorded that Matangi had a potential annual output of 2,000 tons of powder, while Bunnythorpe and

Matamata each produced 1,500 tons and Te Aroha a further 900 tons.[3]

In December 1919, Fred Nathan, chairman of the New Zealand board, signed a seventeen-year agreement with what was now the New Zealand Co-operative Dairy Co. for the supply of milk powder based on inflated wartime demand and prices.[4] In the following year a new subsidiary, Glaxo Manufacturing Co. (N.Z.), was set up to run the four milk drying factories that supplied Greenford. The hard-fought negotiations between the Nathans and the Dairy Association had one important side effect: it brought Herbert Edward Pacey to the attention of the company. The son of emigrants, Pacey had joined the Association as an office boy in 1888. An obvious administrative talent led to rapid promotion and Pacey became its chairman and managing director. In 1919, when his future seemed less certain, he was persuaded to join Nathans as the director in charge of milk powder production and in July of the following year at the age of 46 was appointed managing director of the manufacturing subsidiary.

Glaxo's good fortune proved shortlived, and in the disastrous post-war slump of 1921 orders collapsed. In the following year, London informed the Wellington office that future annual requirements of milk powder would be 2,000 tons rather than the 5,000 tons the four factories currently produced.[5] The New Zealand company found itself in an impossible position as the Association insisted that the terms of the 1919 contract be honoured. In the event, it was decided to concentrate drying at Matangi, while at Bunnythorpe and Te Aroha plant was installed to turn the milk into cheese and casein. Heavy losses were incurred on these operations as milk was purchased at prices based on the value of powder. At Matamata the milk was simply separated and the cream sold to the Association as Glaxo was prevented, under the contract, from manufacturing butter. In 1925, the Association agreed to close the Matamata factory with the proviso that Glaxo remove the drying plant and, reimburse them £37,000.[6] Matters deteriorated still further in 1931 when the world-wide depression precipitated the Nathans into a financial crisis. The minimum price for milk powder, 1s 3½d (6.5p) per lb, which had seemed impossibly low when the agreement had been signed, now became so burdensome that it threatened the profitability of the business. Pacey was ordered to negotiate a discount and a reduction in the minimum order from Matangi of 15,000 gallons. This and subsequent annual concessions saved Nathans from possible bankruptcy.[7] After a visit to the UK in March 1929, Pacey reached an understanding with Alec Nathan to combat the eccentric and autocratic leadership of Fred Nathan, chief executive of the New Zealand organisation. Pacey assumed financial control of the company and introduced proper administrative systems, though he remained constrained by Nathan family pressures until the death of Fred in 1938.

The rationalisation of the New Zealand factories may have solved their financial problems but it simply served to exacerbate the problems of supply experienced by Greenford. The UK packing factory required powder of uniform quality delivered regularly every month and because it now relied on consignments from the single drying plant at Matangi, these could not be guaranteed. Output in New Zealand peaked between October and January, dwindling to almost nothing from April to August so that Greenford had to stockpile during the winter months to maintain production in the summer, thereby increasing their costs. In 1933, when the market began to recover, Alec Nathan sought to raise output from Australia to make good the deficiencies (see p. 128). The situation improved in 1936 when the agreement with the Dairy Association expired, and Glaxo could again operate its milk drying plant at Bunnythorpe. In addition to these supply problems, the Nathans' merchanting business, which handled the sale of Glaxo products in New Zealand, had been hit particularly hard by the interwar slump. In September 1927, they had engaged a representative, S. H. Martin, to sell milk powder and vitamin preparations to pharmacists.[8] Nevertheless, in February 1932 the New Zealand company recorded a net loss of £3,158 of which £2,044 had been incurred by the Glaxo Department.[9] In an attempt to stimulate trade, Glaxo milk powder was substantially discounted, with the result that in 1935 the business recorded a modest profit of £6,770.[10] With the formation of Glaxo Laboratories as a distinct organisation in 1935, it was decided to separate the dried milk and pharmaceutical business from the hardware, merchandise, tobacco and butter trade of Joseph Nathan & Co. and in the following year a new private limited liability company, Glaxo Laboratories (N.Z.) was floated to manage the factories and local trade in pharmaceuticals imported from the UK.

In 1919, when the Glaxo Department was desperate to increase the supply of milk powder, David Nathan had investigated the dairy farm areas of Victoria with a view to setting up a rollerdrying factory in Australia.[11] A protectionist Labour government in Canberra had imposed tariffs on bulk imports of Glaxo in 1915 and the emergence of a competitor product persuaded the Nathans to attempt local production, an earlier project having been abandoned.[12] At the end of the First World War, the citizens of Port Fairy, a coastal town 180 miles west of Melbourne, sought new businesses to supplement its traditional agricultural interests, and T. G. Guyett, a local businessman, approached the Nathans.[13] The formation of the South Western Co-operative Milk and Trading Co. under the chairmanship of James Steele, to guarantee a local supply of milk impressed David Nathan and an agreement was signed in August 1919. Twenty-seven acres of land were purchased at Port Fairy North near the railway crossing and construction began in the autumn, the contract for the brick buildings being won by Thomas Guyett & Sons. At a cost of £30,659, the factory was completed in October 1920. J. E. Nathan, a son of David, was given overall responsibility for the manufacture of Glaxo dried milk, while Victor Hyams, who had married a granddaughter of Joseph Nathan, was appointed general manager, based in Sydney.[14]

No sooner had it come on stream than the Wellington headquarters of Joseph Nathan & Co. asked the management at Port Fairy to implement a partial closure.[15] Demand for milk powder collapsed in 1921 and its output was no longer needed. To recoup part of their investment in the factory, the Nathans transferred its ownership to a new company, Glaxo Manufacturing Company (Australia) Ltd., so that Joseph Nathan & Co. (Australia) was solely responsible for the distribution and sale of dried milk.[16] Because the Nathans had committed the factory to buying large quantities of milk under the contract with the Co-operative, Alec Nathan was instructed to find ways of saving the business from bankruptcy. A dairy and casein plant were added and Port Fairy diversified into cheese and butter, marketed under the 'Bonnieport' brand (derived from the slogan 'Glaxo builds bonnie babies'). So popular was its cheese that the company began to supply the Kraft-Walker Co. in 1926. The virtual cessation of milk powder orders between 1927 and 1933 led to the proposal that Port Fairy be sold to Kraft, though this was not carried through, perhaps because of the variability of supplies from New Zealand.

During the early 1930s, Port Fairy had the capacity to meet Greenford's additional needs but the factory manager, Paddy Walsh, an Irishman recruited from the New Zealand company in 1919, was reluctant to raise output as this would interfere with the plant's successful export trade in cheese. During the 1920s Walsh, a tough and autocratic leader, had been told by the Nathans that the factory would be closed unless it remained in profit. Walsh was reputed to have stood over workers loading railway wagons brandishing a shillelagh and would pay his men for only five hours even though they had done an eight-hour day.[17] His dislike of authority was revealed by his habit of racing his chain-driven Mercedes saloon past the Borough Council Chamber when it was in session. By the late 1930s the Nathans had decided to limit Walsh's power and younger managers were sent from the UK to Port Fairy, though the strife that ensued was not resolved until his departure at the end of 1950. Following the formation of Glaxo Laboratories (Australia) Proprietary in 1938, milk drying for the UK because a priority. Four years earlier, Alec Nathan had travelled to Melbourne to reorganise the Glaxo side of the business, appointing a new sales force and arranging for the direct import of medicines. Nevertheless, the decade closed disappointingly for the Australian subsidiary with a modest profit of £13,646 and pharmaceutical sales falling below their targets.[18]

The Second World War disrupted the export of milk powder from both Australia and New Zealand and the return traffic in pharmaceuticals. In April 1945, cheese production at Port Fairy finally ended, having been greatly reduced under pressure from the UK Ministry of Food to increase the output of milk powder. The building was converted for the manufacture and packing of Farex, which had sold in ever increasing quantities during the hostilities. However, the immediate post-war years presented a range of problems which threatened the future of these overseas subsidiaries. Both governments had subsidised milk production so that in 1946, for example, a ton of powder delivered to Greenford from Australia cost £88, and from New Zealand £97, in sharp contrast to the £157 from Driffield.[19] If the Dominion administrations abolished the subsidy then the price of Ostermilk would of necessity have to be increased and sales were likely to fall dramatically. Even though R. C. Pearce, managing director of Glaxo Laboratories (Australia) Pty was able to contain the problem, price controls on dried milk, together with rising production and transport costs, steadily eroded domestic profit margins, which fell to under 3 per cent. As the Australian company had a profitable export business, consideration was given to withdrawing Glaxo from sale at home to divert the powder abroad but, in view of the established and widespread goodwill associated with the product, this plan was abandoned.[20] Farex, which had been launched in 1936–37, fared better, sales rising from 970,000lb in 1949 (representing 5.35lb per Australian birth) to 1,015,000 lb in 1950 (5.32 lb) and 1,094,000 lb (5.41 lb) in 1953, when the demand appears to have reached a plateau.[21]

Pharmaceuticals at Port Fairy

For its pharmaceutical business the Australian subsidiary was almost wholly reliant on imports from the UK in the post-war years. Sales of penicillin grew rapidly in 1950–1951 and Glaxo was asked whether it could meet the entire Australian demand for streptomycin.[22] The company agreed but rapidly growing orders caught Glaxo by surprise and complaints of irregular supplies were made to the Ministry of Health together with requests for a resumption of imports from the United States. In response, Glaxo raised the quota of 4kg per million per month by 50 per cent, though this entailed cutting orders to other parts of the world. To provide a long-term solution Jephcott travelled to Australia to discuss setting up an antibiotics factory at

Port Fairy, but was discouraged by both the Ministry of Health and successive Ministers for National Development, because they believed such a plant would prejudice the Commonwealth Serum Laboratories (CSL), a government-owned organisation which manufactured penicillin. Jephcott concluded after several interviews that

> their attitude is clear. They would give no encouragement, indeed, would react most unfavourably, to any proposal for erecting another penicillin plant. On the other hand, they would favour the production of antibiotics (streptomycin a little regretfully, since CSL had contemplated its manufacture) and especially of other essential medicinal substances not at present manufactured in Australia.[23]

Facing official resistance, Jephcott postponed plans to invest in a capital-intensive primary plant. He was aware, too, that the Australian subsidiary needed strengthening, particularly in the areas of technical support and secondary production. His visit in 1951 led him to several unpalatable conclusions:

> the present disjointed nature of the Melbourne organisation is a serious weakness, resulting in delays, waste of time and a degree of general inefficiency … Pearce is pre-occupied with day-to-day affairs and, indeed, is himself often uncertain what should be done. The absence of a senior officer technically competent and with initiative is all too obvious.[24]

Pearce, a South African accountant, found the management of the Australian company in the post-war period increasingly stressful as technology raced ahead of his own understanding. Always parsimonious, he was unwilling to spend on equipment, creating extra problems for the fermentation teams. Matters became more serious in 1952 when the Australian government abruptly introduced severe tariff restrictions on the import of all goods from the sterling area, which included both penicillin and streptomycin made in the UK. Although Pearce believed that these controls could not last, Jephcott concluded that it was imperative to begin primary production in Australia and to widen secondary manufacture as a way of reducing costs and avoiding import duties. It was agreed to set up a fermentation plant at Port Fairy to make streptomycin and vitamin B_{12}, at an estimated cost of £250,000.[25] Modifications and difficulties in importing plant and machinery delayed the completion of the fermenters until February 1955 and raised the final cost to £360,000.[26] This was a source of concern as profits in 1954 amounted to only £35,621 (and had been £25,059 in 1953). Although specialist staff were sent from Ulverston to improve its

efficiency, low yields characterised the factory's early
operation.

The relatively limited scale
of the factory made it difficult for Port Fairy to
compete.[27] As Pearce had
reported in July 1955, their
overheads were high and he
could envisage little reduction

> because we are enjoying most
> of the refinements – if I can
> use such a word for extensive
> analytical control, air-condi-
> tioning, cleaning, security,
> depreciation and a fairly ex-
> tensive technical staff …
> There is only one thing that
> can help us to bear this bur-
> den, and that is a very consid-
> erably increased trade.[28]

68. *Griff Hunt, managing director of Glaxo's
Australian subsidiary.*

A solution, as Pearce recognised, was to diversify into penicillin manufacture and in July 1955 he calculated that Port Fairy had the capacity to make
4 million mega units.[29] Limited production began in November 1955. As
part of the attempt to reduce production costs, Brian Jones, a manager at
Ulverston, was seconded to Port Fairy for twelve months in 1957, where he
discovered that his presence was not entirely welcomed by the local staff.
All the manufacturing guides were kept locked in the factory manager's
office while his relationships with the Australian section heads deteriorated
after a rumour was spread that he had been sent to spy on their performance and was sending back reports to the UK.[30]

In 1957, when Griff Hunt, Pearce's heir-apparent, visited Greenford, it
was decided to expand the range of antibiotics made at Port Fairy even
though it would lead to problems with CSL and require a new licensing
agreement with Distillers, as the existing arrangement precluded the manufacture of penicillin V by subsidiaries.[31] After protracted negotiations, an
arrangement was concluded with CSL, the sole domestic producer,
whereby Port Fairy made penicillin G and streptomycin while the former
manufactured penicillin V. Together with the redesign of the plant, this

division of trade allowed the company to return to profit in 1963, having in-curred a loss of £A88,078 in the previous year.[32] The 1950s had proved tur-bulent times for the Australian subsidiary, operating in an unpredictable and inconsistent political and commercial climate. The company had been kept alive by food manufacture and imports of pharmaceuticals from the UK. In 1954, for example, the former (in particular Farex) generated sales of £133,007 and gross profits of £30,225, while pharmaceuticals had a turnover of £163,963 of which £60,167 was profit.[33]

India and Pakistan

In October 1914, Joseph Nathan & Co. gave Herbert James Foster, a general agent, the exclusive right to sell Glaxo milk powder in India, Ceylon, Burma and the Malay States, the tradename having been registered a year earlier.[34] Under the Nathans, India had fallen within the remit of the Wellington of-fice and been supplied from New Zealand. Although problems of quality and continuity existed during the First World War, it was not until 1919 that London took responsibility for the manufacture and despatch of milk pow-der.[35] Foster continued to serve as the company's agent, though work for Glaxo occupied an increasing proportion of his time. In June 1919, faced with large stocks of milk powder sold back to the company by the UK gov-ernment, the directors of Joseph Nathan urgently considered expanding their export trade, and in particular that to India.[36] Furthermore, in order to keep the four drying factories in New Zealand working at full capacity, it was decided to seek short-term agency arrangements in territories not cov-ered by existing contracts.[37] H. J. Foster was encouraged to extend Glaxo business in the Far East, though in 1921 a plan to develop a market in China was abandoned.[38] Three years later, finding that he could no longer finance the growth of his agency, Foster set up a private limited liability company, in which the Nathans acquired an interest.[39] When Foster died in Decem-ber 1925, the Nathans purchased the remainder of the shareholding from his estate.[40]

The management of Glaxo affairs in India was then entrusted to Edward W. Foster (no relation of H. J.), who in 1914 had worked in Nathans' Lon-don office on trade connections with China.[41] Exhibiting an uncharacter-istic error of judgement, Alec Nathan placed great faith in Foster and gave him considerable authority to develop Glaxo's business in India and the Far East. Convinced that Foster had been a success, in 1930 Nathan decided to put him in charge of the export department in London with a seat on the board. Other directors, who thought that Hugo Wolff 'by reason of his work and the length of his service' should have prior consideration,

objected.[42] In the event, neither manager was promoted and Foster remained in India until his sudden death in 1933. In the following year, Jephcott made a long-planned visit and was horrified by the disorganised and
parlous state into which the business had been allowed to fall by Foster. An
autocrat, he had taken none of his subordinates into his confidence and
had neglected personal contacts with his sub-offices, paying little attention
to reports from Calcutta or Madras. As Jephcott recorded in March 1934,
many of his decisions had lost the company vital customers:

> Whatever the reason for getting rid of our old agent Katarah in Karachi, it has
> been a great mistake. We picked up a dud with no organisation. K[atarah] is a
> power in the area. He took up C[ow] & G[ate] and has just wiped us out of the
> North West District. In Colombo for many months C[ow] & G[ate] have been
> underselling us. We have now only the shreds of the trade.[43]

Because Foster mistrusted his subordinates and rarely took people into
his confidence, Jephcott was forced to guess his commercial strategy. He
concluded that 'Foster's conception … was that of an agency business and
of ourselves merely as principals', rather than as Glaxo's sales and
marketing arm in India.[44] After the events of 1930 and the withdrawal of
the offer to run the export department, he sought non-Glaxo business to
increase the company's turnover, taking on the marketing of soap for the
Tata Oil Mills and selling products such as Maclean's toothpaste and
Aspro's aspirin.

Jephcott and E. L. C. Gwilt, appointed as Foster's successor, then interviewed every European member of staff in the Bombay, Calcutta and
Madras offices, together with every Indian medical representative and Indian broker, to identify the causes of the progressive decline in Glaxo milk
business, which had dwindled to the point where 75–80 per cent of sales
were to the poorer native population.[45] Few Europeans or Europeanised
Indians bought Glaxo powder and their custom had fallen into the hands
of competitors such as Cow & Gate. A key consideration was the fact that
tins of Glaxo were undated and, therefore, mistrusted. Indeed, falling sales
had led to overstocking such that many tins had, indeed, outlived their shelf
life. Belatedly, in 1933, a system of stock examination and replacement had
been adopted but was both inadequate and haphazardly implemented. Following Jephcott's whirlwind tour improvements to the packing and dating
of tins were implemented.[46]

Under Gwilt, H. J. Foster was run as a direct Glaxo subsidiary and the
unrelated agency business was gradually relinquished. Edward Foster had
refused to appoint a local firm of advertising agents to avoid paying their

69. An aerial view of Glaxo's Worli factory in the suburbs of Bombay. It was their largest plant in India and represented a significant capital investment.

commission. Jephcott arranged that the Bombay practice, Stronachs, were given responsibility for the company's promotional campaigns in future. The recruitment of a qualified pharmacist, Reg Harryot from Greenford, in 1932 had marked a change of emphasis, with Glaxo pharmaceuticals taking an increasing share of the business. In 1937, for example, turnover had risen to £200,000 and profits amounted to £38,000, of which 54 per cent derived from medicines.[47] Prompted by the boycott of British goods organised by Gandhi, manufacture, or rather packing, had begun on a small scale in 1933 at leased premises in Sewri, Bombay, where tins were filled with powder imported from Australasia.[48] In 1938 work began to construct a new factory and offices at Worli, being completed at a cost of £36,600.[49] As a result of this investment the capital of H. J. Foster was increased from Rs1,50,000 (£11,250) to Rs95,00,000 (£71,250).

E. L. C. Gwilt, the managing director of H. J. Foster & Co. for twenty years from 1934, became a figure of political and social importance in Bombay. He served as a member of the Central Legislative Assembly from 1939 until independence in 1947. It was through his intervention that Jephcott was invited to India on official wartime missions to advise on milk powder production.[50] In the run-up to independence, Gwilt believed it was important for H. J. Foster to set up a milk drying plant and begin the secondary manufacture of pharmaceuticals. Jephcott readily agreed and in 1946 construction of a pharmaceutical plant at Worli began, though difficulties in obtaining equipment delayed its completion until 1950. That year the subsidiary's turnover exceeded £2 million and the name of the company was changed to Glaxo Laboratories (India). However, the Bombay factory did not undertake primary production and political pressure was exerted on the subsidiary to undertake the manufacture of crystalline penicillin. In 1949, Jephcott, who took a close interest in the Indian company, recorded that Indian officials discounted 'the kind of activities which we indulge in by way of secondary manufacture [processing, filling and packing], not regarding them as importing essential technique and know-how into India'. He also urged that the number of Indian staff be increased even though Gwilt found this an 'unpalatable' idea, being 'reasonably satisfied if the fellow has a white face and [wears] the old school tie'.[51] Despite the conservative outlook of Gwilt and some official suspicion, Glaxo Laboratories (India) grew rapidly in the early 1950s, its pharmaceutical business being driven forward by rising demand for penicillin. By 1952 the Worli factory was filling a million vials a month and an application to increase its capacity by 60 per cent had been agreed. In terms of turnover, the Bombay office was the most important with sales of £81,200 in 1954, followed by Calcutta (£74,900), Madras (£68,100), and Delhi (£24,400). Strong sales of vitamin B_{12}, accounting for over 50 per cent of the market in 1956, helped to establish Glaxo as a supplier of pharmaceuticals. As regards milk powder, the ground lost in the 1930s had been recaptured and the company had a 65 per cent share.

In the late 1950s, Glaxo built a roller drying factory at Aligarh, eighty miles south-east of Delhi. This capital investment had been prompted, in part, by the Indian government's withdrawal of licences for the import of milk powder from Port Fairy. In its first year the Aligarh factory manufactured 1,500 tons of powder, though problems had been experienced over the supply of buffalo milk because of poor roads. In addition, a secondary plant for the production of vitamin A from an intermediate was installed at Worli. More importantly, and to establish Glaxo's credentials as a company committed to the Indian economy, it was decided to build a primary process factory to make corticosteroids from intermediates. A site at Thana, twenty miles from Bombay, was acquired and came on stream in 1962. The factory also made a laxative from senna pods, and vitamin A from the synthesis of lemon grass oil into beta-ionone. The opening of this

70. Plant for making vitamin A from lemon grass at the Thana factory.

primary process plant assured Glaxo Laboratories (India) of its place as the largest subsidiary in the group, marginally ahead of Allen & Hanburys in terms of capital employed and profitability, a significant achievement given the economic and political complexities of the market.

Following the partition of the Indian sub-continent and the creation of the separate state of Pakistan in 1947, Jephcott and Gwilt decided that if Glaxo were to retain its business there they would need to set up a new subsidiary, rather than attempt to manage the existing trade from Bombay. Indeed, partition nearly destroyed the business as almost all of the Glaxo staff in what became Pakistan were Hindu or Sikh and had fled to India. In 1937, R. A. M. Henson, one of the directors of the Indian subsidiary, had been sent to Lahore to open a branch to serve the Punjab and North West Frontier province. In March 1948, Henson became managing director of Glaxo Laboratories (Pakistan) with a head office in Karachi, rather than Lahore, where H. J. Foster had been based.[52] However, in view of both political and economic uncertainties, the company received only the barest capital investment – £7,500. This was soon shown to be inadequate and net profits after fifteen months of trading proved insufficient to cover royalty payments and overheads. If it were to be viable, the subsidiary needed to expand and also begin secondary production. Late in 1950, protracted negotiations with the Pakistan government approved the company's plan to increase its issued capital from £7,500 to £375,000 on condition that

1. A tin of Glaxo dried milk blended and packed at Joseph Nathan & Co's factory in King's Road, St Pancras, dating from the Edwardian period.

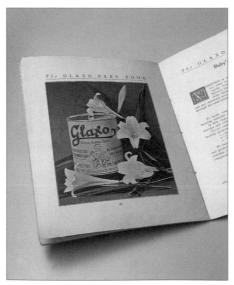

2. The first Glaxo Baby Book *published in 1908 and subsequently edited by a qualified nurse, Margaret Kennedy. Over a million copies were distributed over the next fourteen years.*

3. An Edwardian enamelled sign for Glaxo with the famous slogan 'builds bonnie babies'.

4. A portrait of Alec Nathan (1872–1954) by Sir James Gunn (1893–1964). Nathan was appointed a director of Joseph Nathan & Co. in 1915 and served as chairman from 1927 until 1946. Nathan was also chairman of Glaxo Laboratories from its foundation in 1935 until 1945.

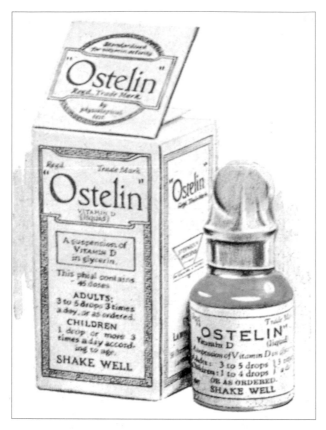

5. *An early advertisement for Ostelin, vitamin D drops. This was the Glaxo Department's first pharmaceutical product and was launched in October 1924. For his efforts in developing the vitamin supplement, Harry Jephcott received a royalty on sales.*

6. *The tradition of supplying young mothers with medical and nutritional facts continued and these* Ostermilk Baby Books *date from the 1930s and 1940s.*

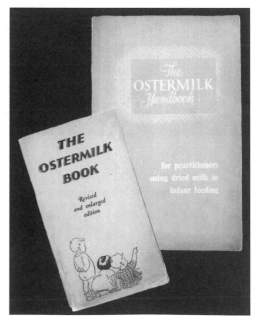

7. A portrait of Sir Harry Jephcott (1891–1978) by Sir Gerald Kelly (1879–1972). Jephcott was chairman of Glaxo Laboratories from 1945 and of Joseph Nathan & Co. from 1946.

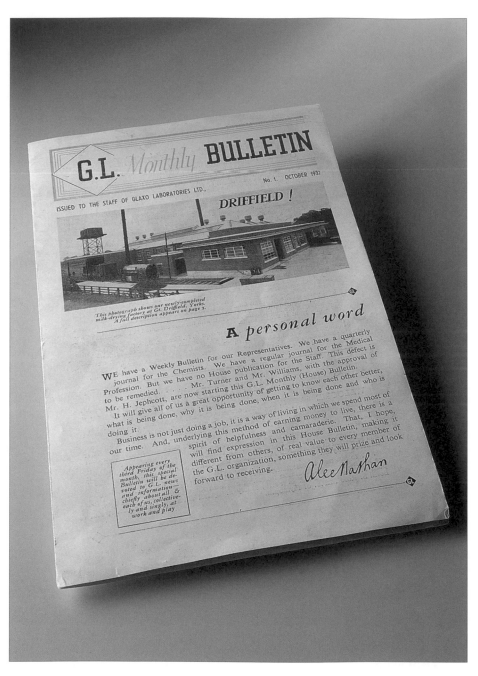

8. *The first G.L. Bulletin,* published in October 1937, *reported the opening of Glaxo Laboratories' first UK milk drying factory at Driffield. Typically, it began with a personal word from Alec Nathan.*

9. A tin of Glucose-D, marketed as a health drink by Glaxo Laboratories in July 1931. Re-launched as Glucodin after the Second World War to provide a protected name, it continued to be a significant food product well into the 1970s.

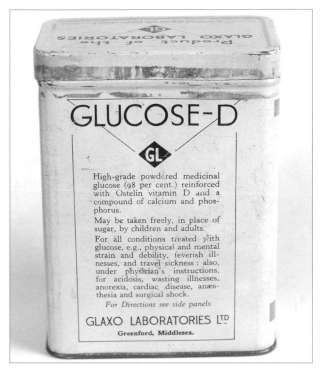

10. The isolation of vitamin B$_{12}$, the anti-pernicious anaemia factor, by Dr Lester Smith (left), Dr L. Parker and Dr Karl Fantes (right), depicted by Liam Breslin.

11. The construction of the Ulverston antibiotic factory in October 1947 on the site of the North Lonsdale Iron & Steel Co.'s ironworks. A pencil sketch by J.C. Moody (1884–1962), formerly principal of Hornsey College of Arts and Crafts.

12. The fermenter hall at Ulverston built for the manufacture of penicillin. A watercolour by J.C. Moody.

71. The Madras office and factory illuminated by night in 1957.

there was 30 per cent local participation and that vital import licences were granted. In 1953, it became the first Glaxo subsidiary to become a public limited liability company. Penicillin was the most important product, generating 34 per cent of sales in 1951.

Henson was particularly keen to begin local manufacture, and planning began at the end of 1950 for a factory in Karachi to fill vials with antibiotics and to pack infant foods. Its completion was delayed by a forced change of location and it came on stream in July 1955. Perhaps the most radical concept, considering the structure of Pakistan society, was the decision to recruit almost half of the 360 staff from the female population. In the early 1950s this was unusual and the literacy requirement resulted in a workforce drawn from middle- or upper-class families, though this grouping was later broadened as educational opportunities widened. Henson had also filed applications for the manufacture of injectables, tablets and ointments and even proposed the construction of a light chemical plant. Both Jephcott and Palmer were unimpressed, partly because of the general shortage of funds within the group, but also because of the dependence of such a scheme on imported raw materials.[53] In the event, it was agreed to build a factory at Lahore, completed in 1964, to make liquid glucose, dextrose monohydrate and vitamin A. Given the almost mystical awe in which the medicine was held and the great disparity between supply and demand, the company could have earned large profits by ruthless pricing and an inequitable distribution policy. Henson resisted any temptation to adopt these methods and greatly enhanced the company's reputation with the government and medical profession.

At first, executive posts were confined to expatriates and it was not until November 1951 that the first national, Izzat Hyat Khan, became a management trainee and in the following year was sent to Greenford for sixteen months' study. His success led to others being sent to the UK to gain professional qualifications and several were later promoted to the board, including Dr Rashid Ahmad (technical director and later chairman), K. M. M. Shah (finance director), R. H. Usmani (production director) and S. M. Mohsin (company secretary). Ahmad ultimately became chairman of Glaxo Laboratories (Pakistan).

Henson also had ambitions to begin production in East Pakistan (now Bangladesh), where by the mid 1950s the annual demand for milk powder and glucose totalled 100–125 tons and 300 tons respectively, just over half the entire total for the company. His scheme involved replacing the rented premises in Chittagong with a small purpose-built factory. In 1959 Renala Khurd in the Punjab was chosen as the most suitable site for a milk collecting and drying operation, where a 600-ton plant was costed at £150,000 and completed four years later. To make glucose, a joint arrangement was concluded with Rafhan Starch and a factory constructed beside their premises at Sargodha, 100 miles north-west of Renala. Costing £225,000, the scheme had the advantage of generating two by-products: hydrol sold to tanneries and corn steep liquor sold to the government penicillin factory at Daudkhel.[54] These developments, together with a rapid and sustained increase in sales, gave the subsidiary second place by turnover in the group's overseas league after only fourteen years of trading (see Table 8, p. 447).

South America

In June 1921, anxious to increase demand for milk powder, the Nathan board agreed to spend £10,000 on 'the exploitation of the South American market'.[55] Until then sales had been entrusted to Frederick Harrison, their agent from 1909, though this had remained the least profitable of the Glaxo Department's overseas territories characterised by the threat of litigation and bad debts.[56] Alec Nathan had little faith in Harrison and clashed with him in February 1917 over the proposed formation of a South American subsidiary. When Harrison demanded a decisive voice in its policy, Nathan

*72. Filling tins of Ostermilk in the Colombo factory. Here, too, this was exclusively a job
for women.*

abandoned the scheme, prompting David Nathan to supply South America
direct from New Zealand. Harrison resigned and sued the Nathans for
breach of contract but died before the case came to court. In November
1921, Charles Cerda Richardson, who had worked for the Nathans in Belgium as a sales representative, was sent to Buenos Aires.[57] Although he
spoke Spanish fluently, Richardson arrived almost at the trough of a severe
economic depression which arose in the context of declining British influence. Nevertheless, Richardson showed enthusiasm, opening an office at
Calle Florida 251, Buenos Aires in February 1922, clearing the Argentinian
market of outdated stocks and replacing them with fresh supplies imported
from the UK. [58] Soon afterwards larger premises with a laboratory were
opened at Calle Tucuman for the filling of vials with Ostelin. Sales grew impressively in the mid 1920s with staff recruited from Britain. In 1930,
Richardson added Colloidal Calcium with Ostelin, imported from Osnaburgh Street, to the agency's portfolio, followed by Ostomalt and Adox-
olin capsules and drops. During Alec Nathan's visit to Argentina in 1931, it
was decided to manufacture infant foods locally and an experimental dairy
farm was leased from the Buenos Aires Great Southern Railway in Quequén, 350 miles south of Buenos Aires. Second-hand roller dryers were

73. Glaxo deliveries by camel drawn wagon in Karachi.

installed from New Zealand, and locally made milk powder was launched in November 1932.[59]

In 1933 the Nathans ended the agency arrangement and set up a subsidiary called Ch. C. Richardson S.A., C.e.I. A number of new pharmaceutical products were added to the company's range during 1934 with local manufacture under the supervision of a qualified chemist from London. Although Richardson successfully introduced Glaxo foods and pharmaceuticals into Uruguay, Chile and Paraguay, sales remained far lower than in Argentina, in part because of smaller teams of representatives but also because he was unable to establish direct local packing or manufacture there, though a company, C. C. Richardson S.A. was established in Brazil during 1936.[60] In Chile, for example, Richardson appointed a sales agent and representative in the late 1920s to handle the introduction of Ostelin and other vitamin preparations. When the government imposed import restrictions in 1933, local manufacture was contracted to the West Coast Service Laboratory, owned by Gustavo Bowski, though it remained a small-scale operation.[61]

The Second World War and the rise of pro-German interests caused considerable disruption to Glaxo's trade with South America. The immediate post-war years also saw the progressive rise of American interests as US

74. The factory and laboratories constructed for Glaxo Laboratories (Pakistan) in West Wharf Road, Karachi, and photographed in 1957.

pharmaceutical corporations increasingly dominated the region. Glaxo Laboratories had little capital to invest in South America and the company's representation remained weak. In line with Jephcott's federal policy, the established subsidiaries in Argentina and Brazil were renamed Laboratorios Glaxo (Argentina) S.A., C.e.I. and Laboratorios Glaxo (Brazil) S.A., while new subsidiaries were formed in Uruguay (1947), Chile (1951), Cuba (1953), Colombia (1957) and Venezuela (1959).[62]

Towards the end of 1948 the lease at Quequén expired and a dairy was purchased from the River Plate Dairy Co. on the outskirts of Chivilcoy.[63] In 1951 modern plant was installed for the manufacture and packing of infant foods, allowing the factory at Buenos Aires to concentrate on pharmaceuticals. With the introduction of Farex in 1952, the turnover of food products expanded and two years later accounted for almost a third of sales, though margins were increasingly squeezed following the introduction of price controls. The highest profits were in pharmaceuticals, and penicillin, introduced in 1946, became the company's leading product. Four years later Glaxo was dislodged from this market when its import licences were suspended to support the local production monopoly granted to E.R. Squibb. Henceforth, Glaxo could sell penicillin only when Squibb failed to meet the domestic demand. When, in 1952, the Argentinian Ministry of Health announced that only bulk streptomycin could be imported Glaxo quickly planned the installation of a vial filling and packing plant at Buenos Aires.

75. The roller drying factory at Chivilcoy in Argentina.

However, the continued growth of the business and the need to introduce new products necessitated a move to larger modern premises. In 1956 land was acquired in the industrial suburb of Munro and a new factory, laboratory and offices were built. Opened in September 1960, it represented a tangible commitment to Argentina and its construction coincided with the launch of several new medicines including vitamin B_{12}, L-Thyroxine and Ef-Cortelan nasal spray.[64] Turnover grew more rapidly in the late 1950s and by 1962 was four times that of 1957, largely because of increased sales of pharmaceuticals (see Table 8).[65] Staff numbers also grew fast, rising from 45 in 1930 to 219 in 1945 and 412 in 1960.[66]

Overseas strategy

As part of the post-1945 review of Glaxo's operations, Jephcott travelled to virtually all the group's overseas subsidiaries. He continued to make regular tours throughout the winter months during his chairmanship, favouring Commonwealth countries. With the exception of Italy (see Chapter 14), the Continent was largely ignored, partly because he believed that it was too devastated by the effects of war to offer profitable opportunities. To give the group a sense of cohesion, it was decided to foster the name of Glaxo Laboratories ubiquitously in these territories. Although Glaxo Laboratories had consciously developed a local nationalisation policy before 1939, this strategy matured after the Second World War. In essence, Jephcott devolved executive authority to an expatriate managing director with considerable freedom of action but who was encouraged to recruit the majority of his staff from the indigenous population. During the 1950s, a number of these chief executives were trained pharmacists who had worked for Glaxo as medical representatives before the war. In the absence of rapid and reliable communications, Jephcott kept in touch by regular winter visits. He was often accompanied by his wife ('the best honorary member the firm ever had' as she was described by H. E. Pacey, when on a trip to New Zealand in 1921[67]), who was suspected of keeping notebooks on the family circumstances of staff. With her information, Jephcott could ask apparently impromptu but informed questions of employees that he had not seen for many years and so build up a sense of personal loyalty and belonging. In 1961, a report prepared by Sir Robert Hutchings, the group personnel director, summarised the strategy for the overseas subsidiaries:

> Ex-patriate staff desirably must be reduced to the essential minimum and local staff recruited and trained to accept top management responsibilities. There must not be so wide a disparity between the total emoluments of ex-patriates and ... locally recruited staff as to cause ill feeling ... In making appointments to the boards, management will have unfettered discretion to choose the best men, but ... we could always endeavour to have at least two directors.[68]

By the late 1950s, as these overseas subsidiaries grew in size and complexity, weaknesses inherent in the loose federation established by Jephcott began to appear. Great responsibility fell upon the expatriate managing directors, who, though competent to run sales and marketing organisations, sometimes lacked the management skills or technical knowledge to lead diversified companies engaged in manufacture. In the early 1950s a Subsidiary Companies Unit had been set up in the London head office to serve as an intermediary, while the Central Technical Services Unit, established at Greenford in 1958, was designed to assist with production problems and the training of technical staff and to provide an exchange of scientific information.

India and Pakistan dominated Glaxo's overseas trade (in 1961, for example, they accounted for 76 per cent of profits earned abroad). Although important historically for the development of the group, both New Zealand and Australia were considerably smaller in terms of turnover, and in Europe, only Italy was of any consequence.

Jephcott never tried to break into the American market, feeling overwhelmed by the size of the major US pharmaceutical corporations. He was perturbed to discover in May 1958, when Glaxo was capitalised at £15.8 million, that Eli Lilly had assets of £61.1 million, Merck £52.9 million, Pfizer

£45.4 million and Parke Davis £41.8 million,[69] and that 'only one (Searle) of the eight US companies employed smaller resources and had a lower total turnover than our own'.[70] Recognising that these corporations commonly earned at least two-thirds of their business at home, Jephcott fought shy of attempting to trade directly in the US. Accordingly, he concentrated on Commonwealth nations, where the Nathans had traditionally traded, and where he believed cultural, political and linguistic factors worked in the group's favour. This low-risk strategy was founded in pessimism and doomed to long-term failure. If Glaxo had discovered a breakthrough medicine in the early 1960s, its market focus, directed towards comparatively low-income or slow-growth areas, would have significantly limited any financial returns. If Glaxo had any ambitions to improve its position in the international league table of pharmaceutical companies it needed to trade competitively in the world's leading markets.

GLAXO GROUP:
STRUCTURE AND MANAGEMENT
1962–1971

Under today's conditions I have no doubt but that a group
organisation has become an imperative need.

Sir Harry Jephcott, 'Company organisation' (1961).[1]

BECAUSE OF the growing complexity and size of Glaxo Laboratories, Sir Harry Jephcott decided to set up a non-trading holding
company to oversee the operations of its increasing number of subsidiaries and to provide a framework for its relatively limited head office
functions. Until then, Glaxo Laboratories had served as the principal manufacturing and sales company in the UK and as the supervising executive
body. Glaxo Group was formed in January 1962 and continued in its executive role for a further ten years when the attempted takeover by Beecham
led to the creation of Glaxo Holdings. Yet as Jephcott and his successor Alan
Wilson continued to acquire businesses the organisation became increasingly unwieldy. Formal lines of communication between subsidiaries were
poor, while a number of head office and specialist roles were unnecessarily
duplicated. Each trading company, for example, had its own commercial
director, sales force, distribution methods and promotion strategies with
little, if any, attempt to co-ordinate these across the group. Indeed, it was
said that the rivalry between Glaxo Laboratories and Allen & Hanburys was
as great as between two competitor businesses. Neither Jephcott nor Wilson attempted to introduce divisionalisation as company loyalties remained strong and it was thought counter-productive to interfere with
them. As a result, little attempt was made to gather the economies of scale
that could have accrued from the enlarged business. Despite some structural changes, Glaxo Group in 1972 was more confused and ill-defined than
when it had been founded a decade earlier.

The structure of the group

By 1961, Jephcott had become increasingly aware of the holding-subsidiary company's deficiencies. In the past, its informality, he believed, had served the business well:

> Traditionally, there has been little by way of formal organisation within Glaxo in the sense of the ambit of individual responsibilities being precisely defined and, indeed, during the immediate post-war years when the business ... was rapidly expanding, this fluidity had positive advantages.[2]

However, the expansion of Glaxo's overseas subsidiaries, particularly those in India and Pakistan, together with takeover of Murphy Chemical, Allen & Hanburys and Evans Medical, convinced Jephcott that 'a group organisation has become an imperative need'.[3] By 1961, for example, Glaxo comprised over sixty subsidiary enterprises.[4] In April, Jephcott proposed setting up a non-trading holding company to which

> all subsidiaries, whether at home or overseas ... would be responsible ... for policy, finance, for the results of their trading, and for all other matters adjudged desirable.[5]

Under this scheme, Glaxo Laboratories was to become 'a self-contained unit' engaged in manufacture and trading.

In 1961 detailed proposals were drawn up after advice from the company's solicitors, Linklaters & Paines, and discussions with other industrial groups, notably Albright & Wilson. It was also concluded that the name Glaxo Laboratories was 'unduly restrictive ... for group activities'[6] but should be preserved 'without alteration for the UK trading company'.[7] Glaxo Group, the holding company, was given financial control over the subsidiaries, including the power to retain the cash surpluses of the operating businesses for investment purposes. It approved all senior executive appointments and provided a range of head office functions organised centrally, such as corporate accounting, patent and legal matters, relations with government and public representation.[8] It was envisaged that Glaxo Group would be small in scale with 'possibly no more than half a dozen persons, apart from the staff of the [Company] Secretary's office, but ... it will need to expand as soon as appropriate accommodation can be secured'.

In a sense, these organisational changes were little more than cosmetic. The two-tier system that Jephcott emphasised in 1962 had, in fact, been created in March 1931, when Alec Nathan, as chairman of Joseph Nathan & Co., set up a local board for Glaxo Department (see p. 40).[9] This structure

Figure 1 Glaxo Group: organisational structure 1962–1972

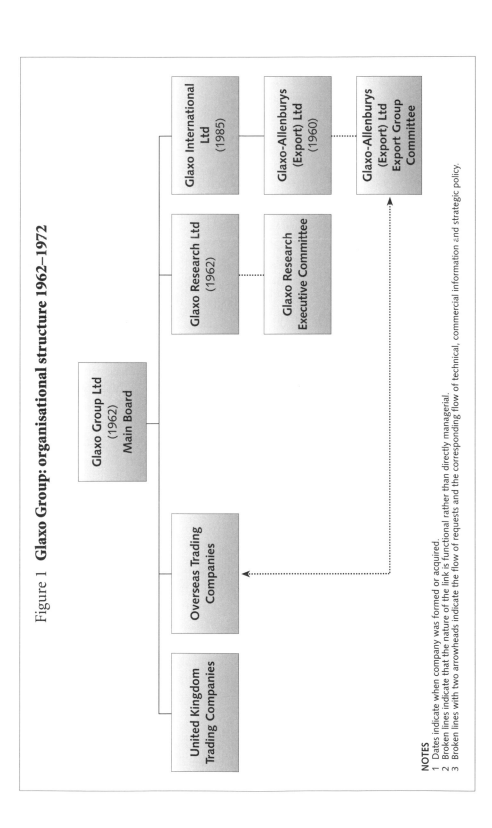

NOTES
1 Dates indicate when company was formed or acquired.
2 Broken lines indicate that the nature of the link is functional rather than directly managerial.
3 Broken lines with two arrowheads indicate the flow of requests and the corresponding flow of technical, commercial information and strategic policy.

was replicated in 1947 when Glaxo Laboratories became the new holding company. Jephcott drew a distinction between main-board directors, who considered strategy and ultimately took decisions, and executive directors, each with a defined functional role, entrusted with the management of manufacturing, research and sales activities. The establishment of Glaxo Group failed to tackle the inherent weaknesses in the company, in particular the inefficiencies associated with an unintegrated federation of subsidiaries.

Under the new structure, Glaxo Laboratories continued as a manufacturing and sales organisation, responsible for the plants at Greenford, Ulverston, Barnard Castle, Montrose and Kendal. Dr F. J. Wilkins was appointed chairman and managing director, assisted by two deputy managing directors, O. F. Morgan (commercial) and W. J. Hurran (technical). Until then the company had also overseen the laboratories at Greenford but, given their growing size and the specialist nature of their tasks, it was decided to set up a separate subsidiary, Glaxo Research.[10] Jephcott was anxious to retain control over this activity and assumed the post of chairman on the pretext that they had not been able to find 'an appropriate managing director for the research company'.[11] In the event, Jephcott relented and allowed Dr Tom Macrae, the head of research at Greenford, to take the post. Jephcott also suggested that a scientist from both Allen & Hanburys and Evans Medical be nominated to join the board to provide an element of co-ordination. Dr David Jack, who in 1961 had been appointed head of research and development at Allen & Hanburys, refused to become a director of Glaxo Research realising that Jephcott would simply use the company as a vehicle for imposing financial limits and blocking projects that he considered too risky. As a result, the Ware laboratories became a division, which officially reported to Glaxo Research, and Jack retained an important element of autonomy.

Although Jephcott's successor, Sir Alan Wilson, was not primarily interested in organisational matters, on becoming chairman he recognised that there were inherent weaknesses in the existing structure. He concluded that co-ordination between the four principal subsidiaries (Glaxo Laboratories, Allen & Hanburys, Evans Medical and Edinburgh Pharmaceutical Industries) had been 'patchy, time-consuming and largely ineffective'.[12] To integrate the group's operations and eliminate unnecessary duplication, he proposed in 1963 that the company be organised 'on a functional and not an historic basis'. This, Wilson suggested,

> means putting like with like, so that all production is the responsibility of one director, all sales are the responsibility of another director, and so on. On the other hand, if we are not to lose a considerable turnover, it will be necessary to

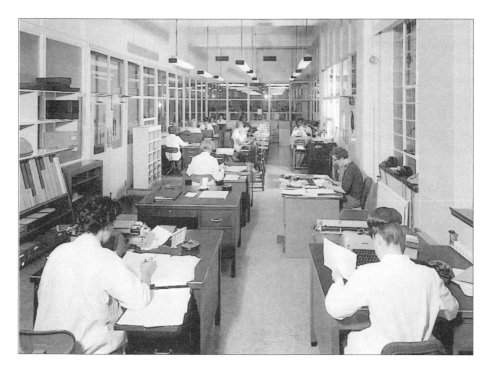

76. The Greenford offices in the 1960s (compare with their 1930s counterparts, page 49).

retain three, or possibly even four, sales forces, and this makes it desirable to keep the present constituent companies in being, with separate public images but with their activities confined to selling only.[13]

Wilson then outlined a radical plan, which in view of the changes required, was never fully implemented. He proposed that

> there should be two major UK companies, namely (1) Glaxo Group Ltd., a holding company with its headquarters at Park Street, and (2) a new operating company which ... I denote by Glaxo UK, with its headquarters at Greenford.[14]

The latter was to take responsibility for research and development, manufacture and commercial policy, together with a number of more general functions. Wilson proposed that central secretarial and legal matters, agreements, patents and trademarks, finance, taxation, group accounts, pensions and economics would fall to Glaxo Group, and concluded that 'central purchasing and research would logically form part of Glaxo UK', while 'Personnel, labour relations, public relations, publicity and advertising might be split between the two companies.'[15] Glaxo Laboratories, Allen

& Hanburys and Evans Medical would each surrender their research and production roles to Glaxo UK, becoming sales companies (see below). Under this scheme, the overseas operating companies would become the responsibility of a main board director based at Park Street.

To assuage any ill-feeling that might be engendered by disturbing established company loyalties, it was decided to proceed gradually. During the protracted transitional period, two executive bodies were to co-exist with overlapping responsibilities. It was planned to set up a management committee, composed initially of the executive directors of Glaxo Group, which would ultimately become the board of Glaxo UK. This was then to be entrusted with the integration of the various production units, the redesign of the information systems and the establishment of a new managerial hierarchy before itself assuming sole executive authority.

In the event, the restructuring proposed by Wilson never came into being. The acquisition of Edinburgh Pharmaceutical Industries served to complicate matters, while the strength of existing company loyalties proved a powerful barrier to organisational change. Wilson did succeed in setting up a separate wholesaling business, Vestric (see p. 155), in 1966, and attempted to rationalise the activities of the group's UK trading companies by the creation of Duncan Flockhart & Evans in 1965, a sales organisation to market the prescription medicines formerly traded by Duncan Flockhart, Allied Laboratories and Evans Medical, to which the products of BDH were added in 1968. However, the acquisition of Matburn, manufacturers of brass tubing and medical equipment, in 1967, followed by BDH and Farley's Infant Food, both in 1968, increased the number of subsidiaries and complicated organisational and production issues still further. In 1972, when Glaxo Holdings was formed, the group had nine major businesses operating in the UK (Glaxo Laboratories, Allen & Hanburys, Evans Medical, Murphy Chemical, BDH, Vestric, Macfarlan Smith, Farley's Infant Food and Matburn Holdings) such that any attempt to rationalise production and sales functions was fraught with difficulties. It had become an unwieldy and labyrinthine group without a clear operational framework.

Wilson was aware of these complexities and of their potential for creating costly managerial inefficiencies. He sought to integrate the group by a hierarchy of executive appointments. Group directors were appointed to the boards of the operating companies as part-time members, usually serving as the chairman in the case of those based in the UK.[16] Since many subsidiaries also themselves had subsidiaries it was necessary to extend this principle of representation: each of these companies had a part-time director drawn from their parent subsidiary. Although the overall structure of

Figure 2 Glaxo Group in 1967: principal UK trading companies

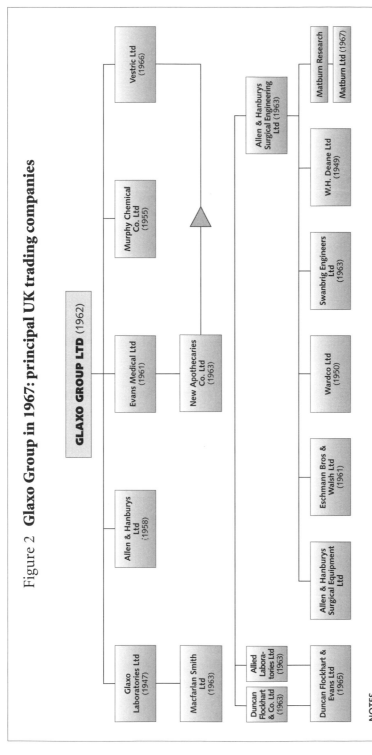

NOTES

1 Edinburgh Pharmaceutical Industries Ltd (EPI) acquired in 1963 was initially a front line subsidiary. In 1964 EPI ceased to exist and its subsidiaries Macfarlan Smith Ltd, Duncan Flockhart & Co. Ltd and Allied Laboratories Ltd were transferred to other Group subsidiaries as shown.

2 In 1965 Duncan Flockhart & Co. Ltd, Allied Laboratories Ltd and the specialist pharmaceutical activities of Evans Medical Ltd were amalgamated to form a new trading company, Duncan, Flockhart and Evans Ltd.

3 Vestric Ltd was a joint venture launched in conjunction with BDH Group Ltd. The activities of the New Apothecaries Co. Ltd were absorbed by Vestric when the new company began operating in 1966.

4 Dates indicate when a company was either acquired or formed.

77. Looking north up Clarges Street, off Piccadilly, in 1966 with Clarges House, Glaxo's new corporate headquarters on the right.

Glaxo Group appeared straightforward, the network of UK operating subsidiaries was, in fact, inordinately complex, resulting in much duplication and confusion over functional roles. It was not until the 1970s, when divisionalisation involved a further layer of management, that this structure was simplified (see p. 197).

In 1965, Westminster Council decided to zone the Park Street area for residential purposes and Glaxo were forced to seek new accommodation for their head office. These premises had been converted from self-contained flats and lacked sufficient conduiting for electrical typewriters and computers so the opportunity was taken to find a modern, purpose-built structure. In August 1965, Glaxo leased Clarges House, 6–12 Clarges Street, 40,590sq.ft. of offices, for forty-one years from The Land Securities Investment Trust at an annual rent of £130,000.[17] The group's architects, Elliott, Cox and Partners, estimated that an expenditure of £97,000 was required to fit out the interior 'including floor coverings, new partitioning, new decorations, alteration of flat, furnishing of board room and directors' rooms, service installations'.[18] This work proceeded within budget and was completed by June 1966, when the transfer from Park Street followed. Although Clarges House was modern and had been acquired to provide space for expansion it soon became overcrowded, forcing Glaxo to lease three offices and renovate the recently vacated premises of The British Drug Houses in Graham Street, Islington.[19]

Edinburgh Pharmaceutical Industries

Jephcott's policy of growth by acquisition to match Glaxo's major competi-

78. A late-nineteenth-century view of Duncan Flockhart's Edinburgh pharmacy.

tors continued after the formation of Glaxo Group. The first approach may
have come from Edinburgh Pharmaceutical Industries (EPI) aware that
they were vulnerable to takeover and concerned to preserve their identity.
EPI was an amalgamation of three historic businesses: Duncan Flockhart &
Co., Macfarlan Smith, and Allied Laboratories. Edinburgh had become a
centre for medical excellence during the eighteenth century following the
establishment of the Royal Infirmary in 1729, together with the Royal Maternity Hospital and the Royal Dispensary.[20] In the Victorian period, the
city became a centre for the manufacture of anacsthetics and medicinal
chemicals, principally opium alkaloids, both encouraging and responding
to advances in surgery. The three Edinburgh firms most closely associated
with these developments were Duncan Flockhart & Co. (founded by John
Duncan who in 1833 was joined in partnership by Andrew Flockhart, a surgeon),[21] J. F. Macfarlan & Co. and T. & H. Smith. It was, for example, Duncan Flockhart & Co. that had produced the batch of chloroform which Sir
James Young Simpson used as an experimental anaesthetic on 4 November
1847. The success of the substance encouraged the company to focus on its
manufacture, especially when demand was boosted by the Crimean War,
and in 1876 they moved to a larger factory in Holyrood Road. Anaesthesia
continued to be Duncan Flockhart's principal specialism in the twentieth

century, its leading products including chloroform, ether and procaine hydrochloride. John Fletcher Macfarlan was a surgeon apothecary who in about 1800 acquired a pharmacy at 17 North Bridge.[22] In 1830 he took into partnership David Rennie Brown, formerly his apprentice, and they succeeded in building up a trade in laudanum, and subsequently morphine, which was manufactured in their factory at Abbeyhill. The company also made carbolic gauzes and wound dressings for Lister under his personal guidance, and during the First World War made over seven million bandages. Drs Thomas and Henry Smith, the sons of a prosperous master weaver in Paisley, both graduated in medicine at Edinburgh, before opening a chemist and druggist shop at 21 Duke Street.[23] They, too, began to make morphine and purchased vacant land in the Canonmills area, where their Blandfield Chemical Works was built. Although Thomas left no descendants, Henry was followed by his sons, Peter and James, who had both studied chemistry in Germany. The firm became a limited liability company in 1904 and thereafter was led by professional managers, notably Dr James Watt, a partner in the lawyers, Davidson and Syme, who as chairman from 1920 organised a substantial reinvestment in plant at the Blandfield Works, Wheatfield Road. Growing rapidly with a specialism in alkaloids and opium derivatives, T. & H. Smith became one of the leading Scottish fine chemical and pharmaceutical businesses. Set on an expansionist strategy, in 1957 the company began to acquire the share capital of J. F. Macfarlan & Co., a formal merger being completed three years later.[24] In 1961 the new company, Macfarlan Smith, joined forces with Duncan Flockhart, the group subsequently being called Edinburgh Pharmaceutical Industries.

In January 1963, EPI accepted Glaxo's offer to acquire their entire ordinary stock for £1.25 million.[25] Glaxo then decided to divide up EPI's constituent parts and to attach them to relevant subsidaries in the group. Macfarlan Smith, which manufactured opiates and other fine chemicals, became the responsibility of Glaxo Laboratories, while the speciality pharmaceutical businesses, Duncan Flockhart and Allied Laboratories, fell to Allen & Hanburys. EPI was also involved in the wholesale distribution of drugs, an activity hitherto eschewed by Glaxo but which formed an important part of Evans Medical. These wholesaling elements were brought together in an informal organisation, and joined by the New Apothecaries Co. of Glasgow, which had been acquired by Glaxo in 1963.[26] Turnover from this activity rose from £13 million in 1963–64 to £16 million in 1964–65, while profits were £0.5 million and £0.7 million respectively.[27] The commercial success of these wholesaling operations led Glaxo to consider its expansion and ultimately to set up Vestric.

79. A promotional display of Duncan Flockhart products at the Edinburgh Medical Exhibition in May 1955.

Wholesaling: Vestric

Although Glaxo Laboratories had a well-established national network of sales representatives who visited GPs, pharmacists and hospitals, the distribution of its products was entrusted to independent wholesalers. However, the take-overs of both Evans Medical and Edinburgh Pharmaceutical Industries brought the company into this activity. In the 1930s, Evans had set up a small network of depots[28] and by 1945 had distribution warehouses in Newcastle, Manchester, Sheffield, Birmingham, Bristol, Swansea and Belfast. As the number and range of medicines increased, retail chemists found it difficult to predict demand and began telephoning on a daily basis. Evans' delivery vans could not always respond in time and arranged for the New Apothecaries Co. in Glasgow to carry a full range of their products. In 1952 a warehouse was built in Ruislip and another in Swansea. Gilbert Jackson of Sheffield was acquired in 1960, together with Lofthouse & Saltmer, the only pharmaceutical wholesaler in Hull, during the following year. Hence, when Glaxo Laboratories acquired Evans in 1961 it gained an established, medium-sized wholesale network. The take-over of Edinburgh Pharmaceutical Industries two years later (p. 152), added the wholesale

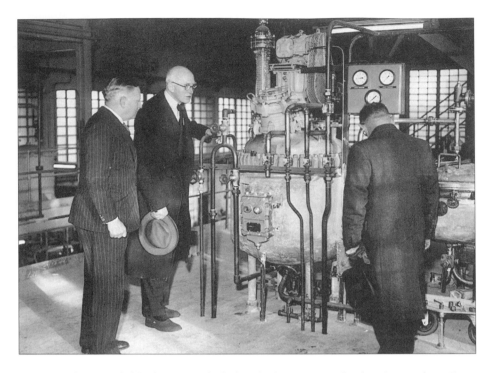

80. Lord Ferrier (left), chairman of Edinburgh Pharmaceutical Industries, conducts Sir Harry Jephcott and Herbert Palmer (back to camera) on a tour of the Blandfield Chemical Works in Edinburgh shortly after the acquisition by Glaxo Group.

business of T. & H. Smith with premises in Edinburgh and Glasgow.

In London, The British Drug Houses (BDH), manufacturers of prescription pharmaceuticals and laboratory chemicals, expanded its distribution organisation by acquiring a number of regional wholesalers during the early 1960s. These included Ferris of Bristol, J. R. Gibbs of Paignton and Bristol, Bradley & Bliss of Reading and Sandwich, Woolley & Arnfield of Manchester and Stockport, Knights of Nottingham and Birmingham, and Rowland James of Swansea and Cardiff. In this way, they rapidly assembled a national network of depots stocking a full range of prescription medicines. By 1964, Glaxo and BDH had wholesaling interests of a similar size, with the former particularly well represented in Scotland and the north and the latter stronger in the south. In spring 1965, when vertical integration served as a defence against government pressure on margins, Palmer and Bide approached BDH with proposals for a jointly owned company. The management consultancy arm of Cooper Brothers was asked to assess the feasibility of a 50/50 organisation and recommended a merger. The number of retail pharmacies was decreasing as multiples, such as Boots and

Timothy Whites, took over competitors and closed their smaller shops. Facing the power of larger buying groups,[29] Glaxo and BDH together were in a stronger position to negotiate terms with both customers and manufacturers and provide specialist coverage.

In June 1965 the merger proceeded and a jointly owned company was formed.[30] Its board was composed of executives from both parents: F. W. Griffin, the managing director of BDH who had extensive experience in wholesaling was the first chairman and Bide the deputy chairman, while W. A. Kinnear and K. M. N. Fergusson, both of Evans Medical, became the managing director and finance director respectively.[31] The name of the new organisation had to be easy to give over the telephone. It was discovered that Glaxo had registered Vestric as a tradename for a veterinary product and the registrar of companies accepted this two-syllable word. Much debate surrounded the location of the head office with Evans favouring Liverpool and BDH preferring Reading. In the event, Runcorn was chosen and within eight weeks of the decision a prefabricated headquarters was constructed and occupied.[32] In 1966 Vestric earned sales of £35.4 million and a net profit of £1 million, lower than forecast because of a wage increase, the introduction of Selective Employment Tax, and the opening of a branch in Sunbury.[33] Costs continued to rise during the late sixties, reducing the company's profitability. This, in turn, encouraged Glaxo to take over BDH, in part so that it could gain control over Vestric.[34]

The British Drug Houses

The British Drug Houses had been formed in 1909 by the amalgamation of three wholesale London druggists: Barron, Harveys & Co. of Giltspur Street, Davy, Hill & Hodkinsons of Park Street and Heron, Squire & Francis of Southwark Street.[35] The merger also involved the formation of a private limited liability company and the transfer to a new warehouse and factory at Graham Street, Islington. In 1923, BDH took a significant step beyond the manufacture of traditional galenicals when it entered a consortium with Allen & Hanburys to supply the entire UK demand for insulin.[36] The extraction took place at Graham Street while crystallisation and vial filling were undertaken at Allen & Hanburys' Bethnal Green factory, the final product being marketed jointly under the trade name Insulin 'A.B.'[37] During the First World War, at the request of the government, BDH had begun to manufacture laboratory reagents as many had hitherto been imported from German chemical companies. This business continued to grow and a new factory was opened at Poole in 1946 for the production of laboratory chemicals. In 1961, BDH entered into an arrangement with

Mead Johnson & Co. of Evansville, Indiana, to collaborate in research and marketing, this prompting the latter to acquire a 35 per cent holding in the ordinary shares of the former. The pharmaceutical division of BDH manufactured a considerable range of products including vitamins, Radio-Malt, and two steroid contraceptives (Volidan and Serial 28). By 1966, the turnover of BDH Group had reached £27.2 million and its pre-tax profits were reported at £1.8 million.[38]

In August 1967 Glaxo approached David Robertson, chairman of BDH, to discuss the possibility of a merger, and agreement was soon reached in principle with the UK board and Mead Johnson.[39] Discussions with BDH then reached an impasse. Although the margin of dispute had been reduced to 1s 6d (7.5p) per BDH share, Sir Alan Wilson believed that it had become an emotive issue and a break in talks would prove beneficial. The gains to Glaxo from a take-over were based on a programme of rationalisation, but the share price had risen to a point where to obtain any benefits the company would be forced to make drastic economies. At the same time, the BDH directors were asking for increasingly specific guarantees about staff levels. After a short period of reflection and on the advice of Lazards, Glaxo resolved to proceed with the merger strategy and on 13 November turned their informal offer into a formal bid to acquire the remaining ordinary capital and preference stock of BDH.[40] At the close of business on 5 January 1968, Glaxo's offer had been overwhelmingly accepted by 81.4 per cent of ordinary stockholders and 82.5 per cent of preference stockholders.[41] Having purchased more than 90 per cent of the equity in BDH Group, Glaxo moved to acquire the outstanding shares compulsorily. This, in turn, gave them complete ownership of Vestric.[42]

Surgical engineering: restructuring

During the 1880s, having moved into larger modern premises at Bethnal Green, Allen & Hanburys began the manufacture of surgical instruments, recruiting skilled workers from Sheffield.[43] Although the company's instruments won the approbation of the Royal College of Surgeons for their quality and ingenuity, it remained an unprofitable business until after the First World War. By this time, Allen & Hanburys had diversified into the production of aseptic hospital furniture, including operating tables and high-pressure steam sterilisers.[44] Whilst the business flourished during the 1950s with the introduction of the 'MC' operating table, the profitability of surgical instrument manufacture was undermined in the following decade by both domestic competition and the import of cheaper products.[45] To try to save the business, Maplethorpe proposed organisational change and prod-

81. Surgical engineering products made by Allen & Hanburys displayed at the Manchester surgical exhibition of 1927. The centrepiece is the St Bartholomew's Hospital pattern operating table.

uct innovation.[46] Allen & Hanburys had taken over three related businesses: W. H. Deane (High Wycombe) in 1949, Wardco in 1950 and Eschmann Bros & Walsh in 1961. W. H. Deane made wooden hospital furniture, including lockers and examination couches, and held about 90 per cent of this specialist market in the UK. Eschmann Bros & Walsh had been founded in Bartholomew Square, Clerkenwell, during the 1830s for the manufacture of surgical instruments and braided gas tubing. In 1955 they had merged with George Carsberg (established in 1793) and four years later acquired Portslade By-Product in Sussex, makers of latex rubber equipment. In April 1963 Maplethorpe rationalised these subsidiaries under a new organisation, Allen & Hanburys (Surgical Engineering). He believed that the continuing advance of medical science would lead the NHS to implement a massive hospital building programme and would, in turn, generate a growing demand for a wide range of equipment. In the event, construction was subject to severe capital constraints and proceeded on a 'stop–go' basis, which in turn led Glaxo to rationalise its surgical engineering subsidiaries.

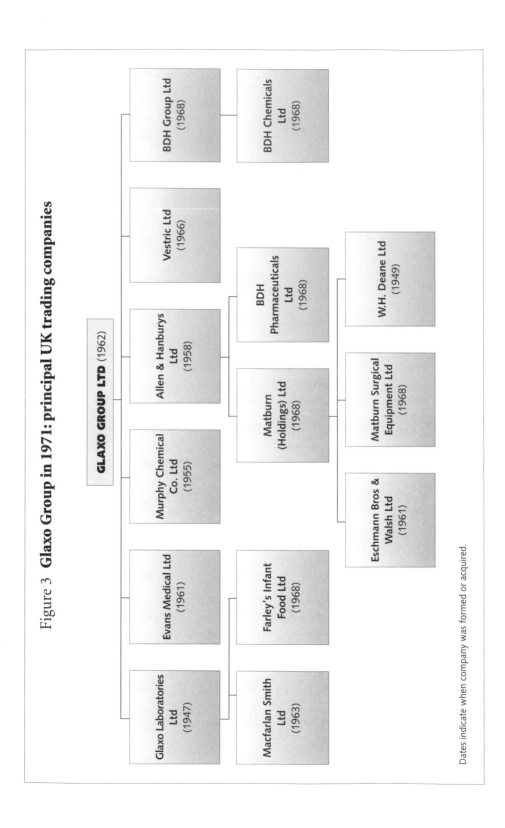

Figure 3   Glaxo Group in 1971: principal UK trading companies

Dates indicate when company was formed or acquired.

Maplethorpe also predicted that electronic equipment would play an increasing part in medicine and surgery and had opened discussions with Elliot Automation for a collaborative venture.[47] In the event, no agreement could be reached and a commercial opportunity was lost. However, Maplethorpe did succeed in streamlining production following the creation of Allen & Hanburys (Surgical Engineering). The production of operating tables and sterilisers was transferred from Bethnal Green to a new factory at Farlington, Portsmouth, under the name of Swanbrig Engineers.[48] In addition, plastic products, including catheters, and a range of surgical instruments were made by Eschmann Bros. & Walsh at Lancing, Sussex, and in London, while Wardco at Sheffield forged surgical instruments and scissors, for both medical and domestic use.

Despite these organisational economies, the surgical business, with the exception of Eschmann Bros & Walsh (which earned over 70 per cent of its turnover from export sales through dealers established in over 120 countries), did not flourish and was re-appraised by Bide in spring 1968.[49] The situation had been complicated by the take-over of Matburn Research and its subsidiary, Matburn, two small companies that specialised in the manufacture of surgical suction pumps, diathermy apparatus (the use of a high-frequency electric current to cut tissue and then to char it to stop bleeding) and laboratory equipment.[50] Bide reported that, with the sole exception of Eschmann,

> no section of our surgical business, at present levels of turnover, can show more than a trivial return on the capital it employs and most parts show a substantial loss. The greatest contributor to losses is the instrument and miscellaneous small equipment side of the business where a 'full line' policy with commensurate heavy stocks and disproportionately large overheads gives rise to a ruinous situation.[51]

A working party, headed by B. R. Jones, managing director of Allen & Hanburys (Surgical Engineering), recommended that the business be retained in its current form but concentrated in the Swanbrig factory at Portsmouth. However, this plan was considered 'too optimistic' by the Glaxo board, which favoured Bide's recommendation to 'reduce or eliminate those activities which are unprofitable and concentrate on those which have a reasonable future'.[52] In essence, this involved selling or winding up the surgical instrument businesses at Swanbrig and the factory at Rigg Approach, Walthamstow, and focusing upon Eschmann as the core activity.

David Smart, then commercial director of Allen & Hanburys, was entrusted with the task of preparing a scheme for the reorganisation of the group's surgical activities.[53] He proposed the creation of a holding company, which would not itself trade but would co-ordinate the activities of the three manufacturing subsidiaries divided according to their specialist activities. Matburn (Holdings), under the chairmanship of Bide and with R. D. Henshaw as managing director, was to be the policy-making body, while the three trading companies were to comprise Eschmann Bros & Walsh, which would continue to make disposable items in rubber and plastic (such as catheters, including the Foley balloon catheter, and tubes), Matburn (Surgical Equipment), whose Farlington factory would concentrate on the production of operating tables, surgical suction pumps, autoclaves and diathermies, and W. H. Deane (High Wycombe), which would continue to manufacture wooden hospital furniture. Wardco of Sheffield would be wound up as a company, though its factory was to remain in operation as a division of Eschmann Bros & Walsh. Allen & Hanburys (Surgical Engineering) and its subsidiary, Allen & Hanburys (Surgical Instruments), were both placed in voluntary liquidation, the Rigg Approach factory having first been vacated.[54] One reason why Smart arranged the four companies into a self-contained group with its own holding organisation was because Wilson believed that the long-term prospects of the business were limited. He intended to sell Matburn as soon as it became profitable.

Farley's Infant Food

In March 1968 Glaxo Group took over Farley's Infant Food for £3,035,000.[55] Although primarily a pharmaceutical company, Glaxo still had a healthy food business, which in 1967 generated a UK turnover of £4.7 million in comparison with £8 million for medicines. Yet, despite rising sales, profit margins on foods remained modest and in 1965 Glaxo signed a collaborative research agreement with Bovril.[56] To secure greater economies of scale, Glaxo approached Farley's, their principal rival in the UK, with proposals for a merger. Wilson predicted that they might have to pay upwards of 45s per share and commented that

> such a price could not be justified if the transaction were considered in isolation, and the whole argument for the acquisition hinges on the past history and future prospects of our own cereal foods. The profitability of these has sharply decreased in recent years, largely due to competition from Farley's, and in 1966/67 the UK turnover of Farex, Farex Fingers etc. fell to about £300,000, with a gross profit of about £40,000.[57]

The take-over, therefore, was 'partly a defensive measure and partly as a means of acquiring a commercially-minded organisation which, together with our technically-orientated staff, will be much more effective in the nutritional field than the present Glaxo foods organisation seems likely to be'.[58] Negotiations proceeded during 1968 and the Trahair family, who owned 75 per cent of the ordinary shares, accepted an offer of 45s per share.[59]

Farley's Infant Food had its origins in a family bakery established in the Barbican district of Plymouth during the early Victorian period. In the latter part of the nineteenth century the Farley family were approached by Dr William Penn Eales, who had become concerned about the quality of infant foods, to make a biscuit-type cereal to a formula he had devised.[60] It was not an ordinary teething rusk but a nutritional pre-cooked food. As a result of their collaboration Farley's introduced a golden-brown 'Feeding Biscuit' later called a Farley's Rusk. In the early twentieth century, when Edwin Farley emigrated to Canada to join his eldest son, he sold the bakers and the secret formula to William Bolitho Trahair, the owner of the Globe Stores and the agent for a number of proprietary lines, including John Master's Matches and Globe Metal Polish. He gradually built up the rusk business from a small bakery at 14 Notte Street where two men and two boys originally turned out 36,000 biscuits a day. The rusks were known as the 'four Bs' as 'Bright Bonny Baby Biscuits' was imprinted on each one with a hand roller. In 1919 the Trahair family formed a limited liability company, Farley's Infant Food and shortly afterwards the Notte Street bakery was closed when modern, semi-automated ovens were installed at the Woolster Street warehouse. This, in turn, was superseded by a purpose-built factory constructed in the outskirts of Plymouth at Torr Lane and opened in 1931.

Commercial performance

In 1962 when Glaxo Group was incorporated, the organisation was at best medium-sized in the world order of pharmaceutical companies. Although it was the largest British manufacturer of prescription medicines (with a greater turnover than Beecham, ICI or Wellcome), both Pfizer and Lederle had higher sales in the UK.[61] As a business, Glaxo ranked, in the 1965 edition of *The Times 300* largest industrial companies, 98th by capital employed and 52nd by profits.[62] Twenty years later there had been little change in the relative position of Glaxo Holdings. In 1982, for example, it was 20th in the world league table of pharmaceutical companies and its global turnover was less than half that of the three leaders, Hoescht, Bayer and Merck,[63] though Glaxo had achieved first place in terms of UK sales.[64]

82. A delivery van for Farley's Infant Food at work in the 1930s.

Nevertheless, within Britain Glaxo could not be considered a corporate giant, being ranked 103rd by turnover and 55th by profits.[65]

Throughout the 1960s Glaxo earned respectable levels of profit, rising from £6.8 million in 1962 to £24 million in 1970, an increase of 253 per cent (Table 9, p. 448). Yet this growth was a reflection of inflationary pressures in the UK economy and was appreciably lower in real terms (155 per cent). Improvements did not outweigh the effects of greater competition and tighter margins on products; thus in 1962 trading profit represented 15.9 per cent of turnover, falling to 15.3 per cent in 1969 and 14.9 per cent in 1970. The increase in turnover of 88 per cent in 1968 was not a result of greatly increased sales but followed the acquisition of BDH and of Farley's Infant Food, aided by the devaluation of the pound, which reduced the price of Glaxo's exports from the UK and raised the sterling value of sales by overseas subsidiaries.[66]

The pessimistic outlook expressed by Jephcott towards the end of his office as chairman tended to cloud the thinking of the group for much of the 1960s. A lengthy paper entitled 'Future policy', prepared by Palmer in June 1962, provided an analytical basis for these concerns.[67] First, Palmer argued, Glaxo's opportunities for concluding licensing arrangements to acquire the right to manufacture and sell novel medicines from America were 'rapidly diminishing in number and importance' because US firms were ambitious to develop their own overseas subsidiaries rather than entrust products to rivals.[68] Palmer also identified higher levels of competition in both the UK and Europe:

Before and immediately after the war the representation in the UK market of foreign pharmaceutical houses was limited to Parke Davis & Co. (of Detroit, USA), May & Baker (Rhône-Poulenc of France), Bayer (Bayer, Meister & Lucius of Germany) and Sharp & Dohme (Philadelphia, USA). Today the only companies in the top *twenty* USA houses who are *not* directly and importantly active in this market are Schering, Robins and Wallace and even the last two have UK subsidiaries.[69]

On the Continent, he noted the existence of a growing number of major producers: Roussel in France, Carlo Erba and Lepetit in Italy, Hoechst and Boehringer in West Germany and Leo in Denmark. Palmer believed that nations in the Common Market would defend their borders against US competition more effectively than Britain had done, and this would, in turn, make it more difficult for Glaxo to sell its products in Europe.

A third concern of the Glaxo management of the early 1960s was the growing public and official criticism of pricing policies and threats to 'encourage or expand generic pricing'.[70] What particularly worried the board was that the greater part of the group's profits were earned in Britain. If Glaxo was unable to sustain its position in the home market in the face of mounting US competition then its future was indeed bleak.

Faced with this 'gloomy' outlook, Palmer asked 'whether we should not rather seek alternative avenues for the employment of our capital resources than continue in courses which look like becoming more and more doubtfully productive of a profitable outcome'.[71] Before Glaxo considered abandoning pharmaceuticals, he proposed a number of remedial measures: first, 'long-term co-operative agreements or even merger ... with foreign firms of standing that are not established or not well established in the UK and the major Dominion markets'; these included manufacturers based in the US, France, Germany or Japan, territories in which Glaxo was poorly represented or had 'no marketing operations of our own'.[72] Secondly, Palmer suggested that Jephcott's policy of horizontal integration be pursued further and that smaller UK companies in related fields be acquired:

> Any worthwhile investment which served to broaden the base and increase the profitability of our interest in foods, veterinary products, surgical equipment, proprietory medicines, and agricultural chemicals ... would stabilise the Group's profitability and improve its staying power particularly during periods of poor return from our continuing major research expenditure.[73]

The third strategy involved a measure of vertical integration, and was designed to strengthen the wholesaling organisation that Glaxo had inherited in 1961 by its takeover of Evans Medical. This, Palmer believed, could be expanded

> not necessarily because pharmaceutical wholesaling is demonstrably a profitable field for investment, but also to develop an effective national distributive network capable of handling other products that may be associated with those at present sold – agricultural chemicals, foods, laboratory or surgical apparatus etc.[74]

All of these options were explored over the remainder of the decade, though only the last two were acted upon immediately.

A fourth strategy, one not considered seriously by Jephcott, was adopted by Sir Alan Wilson in the mid and late 1960s. As a scientist he had become acutely aware of the group's need for new products and recognised that research at Greenford had been underfunded, while that at Ware had operated with limited resources. His chairmanship was characterised by increased spending on research and development, which rose to 3.8 per cent of turnover in 1972 (see Table 21, p. 455). Wilson also adopted a more positive attitude to Europe and sanctioned investment in existing but embryonic companies in Belgium and France, together with the setting up of subsidiaries in Switzerland (1963), Germany (1964), Sweden (1967) and Denmark (1968) – see Chapter 16. Towards the end of the decade, Wilson authorised a programme of heavy capital investment. Between 1965 and 1969 spending on fixed assets averaged about £5 million per annum.[75] In 1969, it was raised to £9 million, grew to £20 million in 1970 and continued at £18 million in the following year (see Table 10, p. 449); the bulk of this was spent on improving and expanding the group's primary and secondary production facilities. Extensions to the factories at Ulverston and Montrose cost £10 million, while a new penicillin facility at Cambois, Northumberland, required an investment of £6 million. The construction of new plant for the manufacture and packaging of medicines at Barnard Castle, together with the rationalisation of production between Greenford, Stoke Poges and Speke cost a further £6 million. Considerable expenditure was required to enhance the research capacities of the group, including £5 million to extend the laboratories at Greenford and Ware.[76]

Management: appointments and culture

On its establishment in 1962 the board of Glaxo Group, chaired by Jephcott, consisted of six executive directors, drawn mainly from the principal operating companies. They were Palmer, the general manager, Dr F. S. Gorrill, a doctor by training and latterly chairman of Evans Medical, Maplethorpe, managing director of Allen & Hanburys, and Wilkins, chairman of Glaxo Laboratories. In addition, there were two specialists: Hutchings, who ran the personnel and training functions, and Dr Hector Walker, the medical director. There were three non-executive directors: Sir A. Jeremy Raisman, the group deputy chairman, Sir Cyril Entwistle, a barrister and Conservative MP for Bolton until 1945, and Sir Edward Playfair, a former civil servant. As set up by Jephcott, Glaxo Group had no managing director. Initially, Palmer had been appointed but he resigned on 1 January 1962, and the post remained unfilled.[77] Something of an executive vacuum existed, given that Jephcott was elderly and Raisman, his deputy, was non-executive. In fact, the post of managing director remained in abeyance until November 1980 when Paul Girolami became 'chief executive'. This was an unusual policy, though Palmer did continue as 'general manager' until 1968 when he was appointed deputy chairman, in succession to Raisman, holding this post until his retirement, after forty-three years with Glaxo, in 1971.

In the autumn of 1962, Jephcott approached his seventy-second birthday but showed no real enthusiasm to retire from the management of Glaxo Group. In November, Raisman recommended that a search begin for a successor to ensure the smooth transition of authority.[78] The non-executive directors concluded that there was no obvious candidate within the company. Wilkins and Maplethorpe (who was also close to retirement) were too closely identified with their respective subsidiaries to convey a spirit of impartiality when dealing with group affairs, while Palmer, who had worked as Jephcott's second-in-command for many years, suffered from bronchitis and was considered to lack the forcefulness required of a leader. As a result, they looked outside Glaxo for a new chairman. Sir Alan Wilson emerged as the front runner. He had resigned as deputy chairman and chairman-designate of Courtaulds in March 1962, following ICI's unsuccessful bid to take over the company.[79] With an established reputation as a scientist, Wilson had acquired considerable industrial experience. In January 1963, he was elected to the board, and Austin Bide, then company secretary, was appointed to a directorship at the same meeting.[80] Three months later, Jephcott announced his intention to retire from 30 June 1963 and that Wilson would succeed him.[81]

Jephcott was made honorary president of Glaxo and continued to work in an office at Greenford for many years. Free from executive responsibilities and yet still deeply attached to Glaxo, he began to research and write *The First Fifty Years: An Account of the Early Life of Joseph Edward Nathan,*

83. A dinner for Sir Alan Wilson (centre) *attended by his predecessor Sir Harry Jephcott* (right) *and successor Austin Bide* (left). *Between them they spanned 66 years of Glaxo history, Jephcott having joined the company in 1919 and Bide retiring in 1985. One reason for the strong corporate spirit at Glaxo was the long tenure of its chairmen.*

publishing this privately at his own expense in 1969. Although paternalistic and, like many business leaders, reluctant to surrender authority, Jephcott had many outstanding qualities. Forthright and dedicated, he possessed a genuine self-deprecating side. In 1959 the *New Scientist* carried a profile of Sir Harry Jephcott and although he 'was none too pleased with it',[82] the description had elements of truth:

> There was no question that this expansion [of Glaxo Laboratories] had been due above all to his vigorous and imaginative leadership, with which he coupled the ability to select able colleagues. He was undoubtedly a driver of men, but he would never drive them harder than he drove himself; and if his unwavering, penetrating blue eyes suggested a rooted unwillingness to suffer fools gladly he also has much charm of manner and a pleasant humour.[83]

In his own behaviour and in the selection of key executives, Jephcott did much to mould the managerial culture of Glaxo in a fashion that survives to the present. He helped to create an unsnobbish meritocracy in which individuals were valued for their capacity to perform tasks and not for their background or social class. Perhaps because he had risen from humble origins himself, he selected young men of talent who had shown a similar aptitude. Managers were rarely recruited from the public schools or from Oxbridge. Wilkins, for example, later to be chairman of Glaxo Laboratories, had been principal director of Scientific Research (Defence) when he met Sir Harry crossing the Atlantic on the *Queen Mary*.[84] Jephcott was impressed by his energy and enthusiasm and offered him a post in charge of the company's antibiotic fermentation factory at Ulverston. Born in Cardiff, the son of a salesman, Wilkins went to school in the city before obtaining an external London University B.Sc. and a Diploma in Industrial Chemistry from University College of South Wales.[85] Although he subsequently completed a doctorate at Christ's College, Cambridge, Wilkins was not from a privileged background and earned his appointment to the Glaxo main board in 1956 by determined application. During the war he was seconded to the Ministry of Supply to improve productivity and safety at the Royal Ordnance filling factories at Bridgend, Glascoed and Hereford.[86] An avid collector of antiques, particularly Chinese porcelain, he would tour dealers' shops after an air raid in the hope of being able to purchase damaged pieces at a reduced price.

Wilkins inspired loyalty and affection in those staff for whom he was responsible, and when he died some wept openly,[87] while the flag at Greenford was flown at half mast.[88] He had been to Edinburgh for a Scottish Area Sales Conference and board meeting of Edinburgh Pharmaceutical Industries. He, together with five others from Greenford, was to return on the 5.30 p.m. flight but because of earlier fog at Heathrow no aeroplane was available, and the next, at 8 p.m., was cancelled. Four of the group decided to stay overnight, while Wilkins and Laurie Gullick, the sales director of Glaxo Laboratories, chose to travel by the night train but then accepted seats on the 11.17 p.m. flight in order to save time.[89] The BEA Vanguard crashed on landing in the early hours of Wednesday 27 October 1965 and all on board were killed. Writing an obituary, Sir Alan Wilson observed,

> His outlook was partly that of a scientist with a highly analytical mind, and partly that of an artist, for he took a great delight in music, in ballet and the art of the High Renaissance. He was never at a loss for a new idea and he was always anxious to give the younger members of the staff the best possible chance of proving themselves. He was warm-hearted and volatile, and, as he liked saying, a true Welshman.[90]

Energetic and forceful, Wilkins was also ambitious and some of his colleagues thought that he sought to succeed Wilson as chairman. Wilkins appeared to have advanced his cause early in 1963 when he became deputy managing director of Glaxo Group, though this appointment proved short lived.[91] In May for reasons that were not disclosed, he resigned from the post and two years later Wilkins' career was cut short by his untimely death.

Austin Bide, who succeeded Palmer as deputy chairman in May 1971, had also been selected by Jephcott and prepared for high office. He had, by his own admission, 'come up the hard way', having decided at an early age that he wished to be a chemist.[92] Born in 1915 and educated at the County School, Acton, he entered the Department of the Government Chemist at the age of seventeen. He studied in the evenings and weekends at Birkbeck College and Chelsea Polytechnic where in 1939 he achieved the rare distinction for a part-time student of first-class honours.[93] When war broke out, Bide attempted to join the RAF but was informed that he fell within a reserved occupation and had been seconded to work for Glaxo Laboratories. Needing scientists to work on war-related projects, Jephcott had contacted the Department of the Government Chemist, in which he had himself worked during the First World War. Bide was one of five chemists recruited and was allocated to research, the other four (Jim Caygill, Albert Hickman, Bob Peevers and Eric Winter) went into production. Although initially engaged on the synthesis of Vitamin B_1, Bide was then assigned to Dr E. Lester Smith to work on the development of penicillin. In 1944, Bide was appointed head of the Chemical Investigation and Development Department, and with his deputy Dr Peter Wilkinson planned and set up a pilot plant for the experimental manufacture of novel compounds.

In October 1946 Bide became personal assistant to Palmer, then deputy managing director of Glaxo Laboratories, whilst retaining responsibility for patent and trademark matters. To broaden his business knowledge he was sent to lectures at the LSE organised by Professor Ronald Edwards on economics and law, and continued to attend his seminars for several years after the course had ended. The two were to encounter each other in very different circumstances in 1971–72 when Edwards had become chairman of Beecham and Bide was deputy chairman of Glaxo. In 1951, at the age of 36, Bide was asked by Jephcott to set up a factory in Montrose for the production of cortisone. He became its first manager when the plant opened in the following year, commuting from Greenford. In 1954 he returned full-time to Greenford to join the secretariat and became joint company secretary two years later.

Others whom Jephcott recruited were Dr Hector Walker, Dr Tom Macrae and W. J. Hurran. Walker, a young GP practising in Harrow, treated

Jephcott and his family, on one occasion saving the life of his elder son. Jephcott regularly asked Walker for professional opinions on medicines and the two became close friends. In 1934 Walker joined the company and two years later was appointed medical director of Glaxo Laboratories. Although many found him courteous and sympathetic,[94] he could be outspoken and an early dispute soured his relations with Macrae. This had damaging results as both were involved in research. For example, Walker, in opposition to Macrae, argued that work on penicillin should concentrate on injectable versions, ignoring the vast commercial value of oral formulations.[95] He also maintained that pharmacological research should always be undertaken by medically qualified scientists to ensure a proper appreciation of the toxic effects, while Macrae believed that the discoveries achieved by the pharmacologists at Ware were largely as a result of their specialist training.

Although Sir Alan Wilson was chairman of Glaxo for nine years, he had less influence than Jephcott on the composition of the board. Nevertheless, two important appointments were made during his period of office, those of Paul Girolami and David Smart, both in 1968. When Maplethorpe retired from Glaxo Group it was natural that Smart, his successor at Allen & Hanburys, would take his place representing this major subsidiary. The latter had been educated at Rugby School and Cambridge University, where he read natural sciences as a preliminary to medical training at St Mary's Hospital in London. However, following a serious rugby injury, Smart did not complete his studies and joined Allen & Hanburys in 1952 as head of their medical information department, later becoming marketing director. His commercial expertise led to him being given overall responsibility for group marketing when appointed to the board, a function that he retained until April 1979. During the 1950s he formed a close friendship with Austin Bide, which subsequently served to soften the rivalry and competitiveness that existed between Glaxo Laboratories and Allen & Hanburys.

Paul Girolami had been recruited by Wilson in 1965 as the group's financial controller with a view to appointing him as its first financial director. Born in 1926 in the northern Italian village of Fanna, he was the eldest son of a mosaicist, who then emigrated to England. The family settled in Highgate and Girolami went to William Ellis Grammar School and then to the LSE, where he studied for a Bachelor of Commerce degree.[96] After graduating in 1950 with a lower second, Girolami was articled to Chantrey & Button and in 1953 won the fourth certificate of merit in his chartered accountancy finals.[97] This gave him an entrée to the major firms and he joined Cooper Brothers in the following year, working for their embryonic international consultancy. Made a director in 1963 and still ambitious,

Girolami decided to seek a new challenge elsewhere. Another chartered accountancy firm, Arthur Youngs, offered him a post in Paris, and Wilson approached Coopers looking for a financial director. Although Glaxo paid less and he was not guaranteed a seat on the board, Girolami opted for the pharmaceutical group.

Having joined Glaxo on 1 January 1966, he soon became a confidant of Wilson. Monica Hayes, then his secretary, believed that they had a similar style of thinking, both enjoying solving complex theoretical problems such as mathematical formulae.[98] Appointed finance director in May 1968, Girolami was given ever wider responsibilities by Wilson.[99] For example, he introduced budgeting systems and forward planning and sought to automate internal accounting with the use of computing systems. Girolami kept two hats in his office, a brown trilby for visits to Greenford and a black bowler for meetings in the City. He was part of a small executive team based at Clarges House that reported directly to Wilson, and included Bide, the deputy chairman, and M. R. Camp, who in November 1965 had been appointed company secretary.[100]

In May 1970 Sir Edward Playfair, a non-executive director, was asked to take soundings about the chairmanship, given that Wilson would be 65 in August 1971 and therefore due to retire. It was decided that he should be asked to continue 'up to mid 1974' in view of his 'greatly valued leadership'.[101] Although Wilson accepted the invitation,[102] he exhibited some reluctance about continuing: 'as I mentioned to the board, circumstances may change and may make it desirable for a new chairman to take over at an earlier date than that now anticipated'.[103] His premonition proved well founded and the take-over bid mounted by Beecham in the following year exhausted Wilson's enthusiasm for the role. In March 1972, while the battle for Glaxo's independence still raged, it was agreed that Austin Bide, the deputy chairman, would succeed him.[104] However, a formal announcement was delayed for a year until the Monopolies Commission had issued its report and the future of the group was assured. In the event, Sir Alan Wilson retired on 31 March 1973.[105]

THE BEECHAM BID

O N T H E morning of 2 December 1971 Sir Ronald Edwards, chairman of Beecham Group, together with his fellow directors, Sir Kenneth Keith and G. J. Wilkins called on Sir Alan Wilson at his office in Clarges House to bid for Glaxo. They offered eleven of their 25p shares, together with £3.60 of 5 per cent convertible loan stock unsecured, for every nine Glaxo shares.[1] Although rumours had circulated amongst analysts (driving Glaxo's share price to a new peak of 440p early in September from 284p earlier in the year), there had been no formal discussions. By making the offer so close to Christmas, Edwards tried to catch Glaxo off guard and hamper their defensive measures. However, a response was swift. At a rapidly convened board meeting held at 4.10 p.m. in Clarges House, it was unanimously agreed to oppose the take-over and Wilson issued the following public statement:

> The board of Glaxo Group Ltd. is considering proposals submitted to-day by Beecham Group Ltd. Prima facie these proposals do not seem ... to be in the interests either of the shareholders of Glaxo Group Ltd. or of the British pharmaceutical industry. It is presumed that the Department of Trade and Industry will consider whether this matter should be referred to the Monopolies Commission.[2]

An intense battle followed for the survival of Glaxo. This was to take a number of turns, including the financial restructuring of the group, and a defensive merger with Boots, which led to a referral to the Monopolies Commission. Had the Beecham bid succeeded, Glaxo would have become a subsidiary and its very name might have disappeared. What follows is an account of the complex interplay between the rival factions, an assessment of the tactics they employed and how Glaxo succeeded in preserving its independence against a determined attack.

Background to the take-over bid

The Beecham bid took place at a time when the world pharmaceutical industry was dominated by the United States, together with Switzerland and West Germany in slightly lesser positions.[3] The largest ten companies all came from these three nations. Although Britain had a number of pharmaceutical businesses (notably Glaxo, Beecham, Wellcome and ICI), none ranked among the leaders, and there was concern that they could ever compete on an increasingly international stage. In 1971 this belief was reinforced by a report prepared by the Centre for the Study of Industrial Innovation (CSII) and commissioned by the Pharmaceuticals Working Party of the National Economic Development Office (NEDO).[4] A key conclusion of the survey was that 'the main characteristic of the pharmaceutical trade is the marked and sustained dominance of a small number of exporting countries'.[5] At the end of the 1960s, for example, two-thirds of all export sales came from five nations (West Germany, United States, Switzerland, UK and France). Of these, the outstanding performance was by West Germany, which had quadrupled the dollar value of its sales over the period 1959 to 1969. With a vast home market, the United States was least reliant on overseas trade, increasing its exports by only 32 per cent over the decade. The CSII report concluded that the need to maximise the gains from costly research and development programmes could be satisfied only by spreading further into overseas markets.[6] This, in turn, required them to extend the range of their marketing and production facilities across the world.

The CSII investigators were concerned that the changing pattern of global trade was undermining the commercial attractiveness of the UK as a base for pharmaceutical companies. In the past, its historical links with the Commonwealth had provided fruitful market opportunities, but the rise of the Common Market had resulted in the UK becoming 'one among several possible locations of investment to supply European markets'.[7] The tariff structure in the Common Market (which Britain had yet to join) and the promise of standardised product registration procedures had moved the investment advantage towards the six member states. Although the growth in demand for pharmaceuticals had been steady and the existence of the NHS guaranteed stability, the fact that about 75 per cent of medicines pre-scribed in the UK were made by foreign competitors was a cause for con-cern. The 'pessimistic' forecast of the report was that

> such factors presage the beginning of a decline in the UK's status as a location of pharmaceutical activity. If such a decline does materialise, it could occur rela-tively rapidly. Because of production flexibility it is possible that the overseas-

owned firms can change the location of production more swiftly than those in the 'heavier' industries.[8]

These findings, the researchers concluded, applied equally to British-owned pharmaceutical companies, of which the larger were well-established in some world markets. In 1970, for example, Beecham earned 71 per cent of its profits from abroad, where profit margins were commonly double those at home.[9] The CSII had interviewed a number of executives from the pharmaceutical industry, including J. D. Pollard, vice chairman of Beecham Pharmaceutical Division, and R. H. Clarke, director of its overseas operations, and they also quoted Sir Ronald Edwards, chairman of Beecham, in his annual report for 1970 as saying:

> The importance in operating across the world is almost self-evident: it gives us the flexibility and resilience to be able to absorb setbacks or difficulties in particular markets and to make them up elsewhere. In other words, it reduces our vulnerability to local political, economic or other problems.[10]

Thus, a key conclusion from the CSII report was that the industry, by its very nature, was set irreversibly on a multinational course and that UK companies needed to develop their overseas activities if they were to survive.

Given that the largest British pharmaceutical companies were medium-sized in world terms, officials at NEDO, who had commissioned the study, understandably came to the conclusion that the best way to safeguard the UK's position was to encourage mergers. NEDO was chaired by a former colleague of Wilson's at Courtaulds, and he called a meeting at which it was suggested that Glaxo, Beecham and ICI should pool their pharmaceutical interests into a single commercial organisation.[11] In 1970 the combined pharmaceutical turnover of the three companies (Glaxo $261 million, Beecham $132 million and ICI $67 million) would have totalled $460 million, well below the figure for Roche ($840 million) and Merck ($670 million) but equivalent to Germany's Hoechst ($497 million).[12] The talks were held on an informal basis but were never referred to the Glaxo board.

Wilson was in essence a distinguished scientist who found himself as a captain of industry. Born in Wallasey in 1906, his precocious intellect won him a scholarship to Emmanuel College, Cambridge, at the age of 16 where he read chemistry and mathematics before settling on physics as his favoured discipline. Elected to a fellowship at the age of 23, four years later be became a university lecturer in mathematics with a fellowship at Trinity

College. It was during this period that Wilson produced his two outstanding works, *The Theory of Metals* (1936) and *Semi-Conductors and Metals* (1939), which established his academic reputation and led to his election to the Royal Society in 1942. During the war, he was pressed into military projects and worked on radio communications and atomic energy. In December 1944, then 39 years old, Wilson was approached by Courtaulds, who were looking for a scientist to head the company's research and development department. Wilson accepted and joined the board in September 1945.[13] He was later to comment on his dual experience:

> I have never found it [industry] very different from the academic world. The technical problems are of the same order of difficulty, and human relations are very much the same in a laboratory as in a factory, and at a high table as at a board table, and I am at a loss to understand why so many people find the transition from one to the other so much of a stumbling block.[14]

In writing this, Wilson was, no doubt, attempting to encourage scientists to enter business, but the passage also revealed his weakness as a leader. Although he had a lucid and penetrating mind, Wilson was unable to convey enthusiasm to others; he lacked the capacity to inspire. Junior executives dreaded having to sit next to him at formal dinners, knowing that much of the meal would pass in silence. David Jack, head of research at Ware, observed that this was reserve, since on those occasions when his interest was engaged (discussing computers or scientific conundrums), he would become animated and engaging.[15] Despite his cool exterior, those who worked closely with Wilson found him a likeable and sympathetic personality. Some believed that Wilson would have achieved more had he remained at Cambridge, though that underrates the value of his business decisions. As Girolami wrote for Wilson's obituary:

> He initiated a truly international approach by breaking the 'Commonwealth' mould in which Glaxo had been fixed and entering the European markets head on. A decisive step was the establishment of effective basic research in the group. The small unit he created and quietly nurtured and sustained was to become one of the most fruitful centres in the world and the source, with some exceptions, of all the Glaxo products sold today.[16]

Whilst ideas of merger between leading pharmaceutical companies were floated in a speculative manner during the late 1960s, neither Wilson nor the Glaxo board had any plans for a major take-over. Hence Wilson was somewhat bemused when the notion was taken up in an informal manner by Sir James Taylor, a distinguished scientist and a former research director of ICI, who had been a non-executive director of BDH before its acquisition by Glaxo. In January 1971, he wrote personally to Wilson:

> I have been studying the position of the pharmaceutical industry in this country and have come to the conclusion that the time is opportune for an attempt to be made to establish a much larger and more powerful British concern than exists at the present time ... It further seems to me that Glaxo and ICI Pharmaceuticals have complementary strengths and capabilities that would make them possible partners for uniting to form a nucleus, as a first step, for a really powerful British pharmaceutical company, capable of holding its own in international markets and world competition.[17]

Wilson discussed the matter with his fellow directors who agreed that the proposal should be firmly rejected. He replied to Taylor on 12 January:

> I must say that I am singularly unimpressed by this argument. Glaxo is, at this moment, a highly successful organisation which has over a long period been able to keep in the forefront of progress ... we feel that we are much more likely to be successful by being subject to competitive pressures than by being partially insulated from them. If we fail to innovate, we should not feel that it was right that we should be supported by others.[18]

Wilson argued in more detail, along the lines he later developed when giving evidence to the Monopolies Commission, that the pharmaceutical industry presented a special case because its members 'must stand or fall by the success of [their] research departments in discovering new products'.[19] He believed that inventiveness beyond certain minimum staff and laboratory requirements was not a direct function of size. Since neither company appeared to be short of funds for such activities, Wilson concluded that a merger would be counter-productive. He illustrated his case by reference to Glaxo's own experience:

> as a result of our acquisitions, we were forced to decide whether to have one research department or several. We came down against one integrated research department and decided to have two, which are separately managed but loosely co-ordinated in what one might call a federal structure ... I am convinced that, if we had one research department, centrally directed, we might increase our efficiency in the short run, as measured by the successful conclusion of the work at present in hand, but in five years or so, the number of our streams of inventiveness would have diminished.[20]

Despite this rejection, Sir James Taylor was not deterred and replied by return that 'I do believe that there is a strong case for an opposite view and I would like to develop the case at some length for your consideration'.[21] Wilson replied, reiterating his opposition to such a scheme.[22] Taylor agreed to respect his position and abandon the proposal and, in doing so, suggested that there were lessons to be learned from the evolution of the dyestuffs industry:

> Dyestuffs were originally natural products which were replaced by man-made chemicals and the industry gradually became a scientifically based one. Again, like the pharmaceutical industry, it was originally non-capital intensive, manufacture comprising vats, and so on. It was also much fragmented in small units. Germany took the lead in forming a national large industry and captured most of the world trade. Britain was finally forced to set up a national industry itself as a means of halting German competition and ensuring that Britain had a healthy home potential in this strategically important field. Creating a powerful industry in Germany improved its R & D and manufacturing strength and its innovative success instead of detracting from it.[23]

Wilson stood by his decision not to explore a merger.[24] Yet rumours of a take-over continued to circulate throughout the rest of 1971.[25] The first indication that Beecham might be preparing a bid followed a report in the *Daily Mail* for 8 September under the headline 'Glaxo's an unwilling bride', followed more specifically in November by a report in the *Daily Telegraph* entitled 'The LSD of merging Beecham and Glaxo'.[26] Throughout the 1960s Glaxo had, in fact, been the target of press speculation that it was about to be subject to a bid. In the autumn of 1965, for example, when Paul Girolami joined the group as financial controller, reports circulated that this had been prompted by a need to strengthen its defences. Because Glaxo had grown under Jephcott as a loose confederation of a diverse range of businesses, it was ripe for rationalisation and in the view of outsiders could be transformed into an efficient and profitable organisation if the group concentrated on a limited range of core activities.[27]

Beecham Group

Beecham was marginally the larger of the two groups. In 1971 it was capitalised at £133 million, compared with Glaxo's £109 million, and made a profit of £35 million (on a turnover of £182 million) compared with £25 million (on £173 million) for Glaxo.[28] However, almost two-thirds of Beecham's sales were composed of consumer products (£117 million), while pharmaceutical and veterinary medicines accounted for only £55 million.[29] Glaxo, by comparison, had a far larger ethical business, its pharmaceutical and food products generating sales of £119 million.[30] Glaxo, too, had more employees, 31,000 (of whom 17,500 were in the UK) compared with 23,000 (14,000 in the UK) at Beecham.[31] Thus, in scale the two businesses were not dramatically different, although Beecham through the sale of its patent medicines, drinks and toothpaste, had the higher public profile, and this, together with its capitalisation, led commentators to believe that it was the dominant company.

Beecham, like Glaxo, could trace its origins to nineteenth-century entrepreneurship: Thomas Beecham had traded in Wigan during the 1850s as a 'chemist, druggist and tea dealer' with a licence to sell medicines. His most notable product was a laxative pill. Nevertheless, the business developed not into prescription drugs but patent medicines, and it was not until 1926 that Beecham launched its first pharmaceutical product – an aspirin-based powder to treat influenza and colds.[32] The acquisition of Veno Drug Co in Manchester during 1928 brought a cough medicine (containing glycerine, chloroform and resin) and Germolene ointment. Also in that year Beechams Pills was set up to manufacture and sell a variety of proprietary medicines. Under the guidance of Philip Hill, the property developer and financier, a more adventurous and expansive course was taken and in 1937 the Beecham laboratory was endowed at the Royal Northern Hospital in London.[33] During the war, Hill kept in close contact with the scientific consultant Sir Charles Dodds, and in 1942 secured the Beecham board's approval for the creation of a central laboratory for biological and bacteriological research. In 1945 Beecham Research Laboratories Ltd was set up in temporary accommodation at Brentford, while a year later work began upon a 'research station' at Brockham Park, Surrey.[34] However, the death of Hill in 1944 and the appointment of a new chairman, Sir Stanley Holmes, who lacked a whole-hearted commitment to research and development, led to a temporary loss of direction. Institutional concern resulted in the appointment of Leslie Lazell as group managing director in 1951. Beecham was restructured along functional or geographical lines and investment in the discovery of ethical medicines rapidly increased.[35] In 1954 Sir Ernst Chain, a Nobel laureate and one of the original researchers into penicillin, became a consultant, and the group's laboratories began to work on the modification of known strains of penicillin.[36] Early in 1959, the Beecham team successfully isolated the nucleus (6-APA or aminopenicillanic acid) which opened the way to adding molecular side-chains and the production of semi-synthetic penicillins.

Having concluded a licence with Bristol-Myers to sell their products in America, Beecham launched their first semi-synthetic penicillin, phenethicillin (Broxil), in 1959.[37] Between then and 1967 the group more than doubled the number of scientists, and tested over 2,000 compounds, from which a further four semi-synthetic penicillins were chosen for marketing. Notable among these were ampicillin (Penbritin), introduced in 1961, and amoxycillin (Amoxil) in 1972. They had distinct advantages over the earlier antibiotics, having a wider spectrum of activity, and were efficient against resistant bacteria in hospitals. The production of these new medicines transformed Beecham's pharmaceutical business and sales rose from £2.8 million in 1960–61 to £44 million in 1969–70, at a time when the group spent £4.9 million on research and development (over a fifth of the estimated £22 million expenditure for the entire UK pharmaceutical industry).[38] In addition, Beechams had developed a business in veterinary medicines, which was reinforced in 1967 by the acquisition of Vitamins Ltd, which produced vitamins for both human and animal use, together with feed supplements. In 1969 Beecham had strengthened its position in the drinks market (the company already owned Lucozade, and H. W. Carter & Co. makers of Ribena) by taking over Horlicks. Thus, in many respects the group had a similar shape to Glaxo.

Origins of the take-over bid

At the time of the bid, Sir Ronald Edwards had succeeded Lazell as chairman of Beecham. Lazell had decided that there were no executives within the group of sufficient experience and brought in an outsider to negotiate with government and carry the responsibilities of a diversified pharmaceutical company. Disquiet had been expressed in the House of Commons at the cost of medicines, including Beecham's semi-synthetic penicillins, and the thalidomide disaster had raised concerns over the testing of new products (see p. 223). Lazell chose Edwards, formerly chairman of the Electricity Council and a professor of economics at the London School of Economics where he had specialised in industrial organisation.[39] With his knowledge of finance, long association with politicians and civil servants, Edwards at 58 was exactly what Lazell wanted. Once in office, he pursued an expansionist policy acquiring the Fisher Group of Buhl-Baden in 1970 and a US subsidiary, S. E. Massengill, the following year.

The bid for Glaxo was not a strategic change of direction for Beecham as Lazell had pursued a policy of growth through acquisition, arguing that a company should be targeted if either (a) its products would fit into and strengthen the group's existing structure, or (b) it would provide a base for a major new field of activity.[40]

Glaxo fulfilled the first of these criteria. Edwards believed that if Beecham were to compete successfully with the industry leaders, the group needed to double in size and this was unlikely to happen solely from internally generated growth in a UK environment where there were political rumblings over excessive profits (see p. 229). Furthermore, Glaxo was financially healthy; it had no borrowings and ample reserves that could be re-invested.[41] Edwards recognised Glaxo's reputation for research and development and was aware of the complementary nature of their respective product ranges. This thinking was summarised in Beecham's subsequent submissions to the Monopolies Commission:

> Substantial research and development advantages would arise from a merger in two ways. First, the greater volume of business which the greater marketing capability of the combined groups would generate would help to sustain economically a larger research effort than they could sustain separately, and thus the new company would be in a better position to compete with the much larger overseas based international companies. Secondly, the combining of the two research efforts, and the redeployment of those resources … would facilitate the investigation of more therapeutic areas in greater depth, so improving the chances of discovering major new products.[42]

The defence of Glaxo

Although the first public pronouncement from Wilson on 2 December 1971 did not reject the Beecham bid outright, it soon became clear that there was implacable opposition to the merger. There had been two important absentees at the hastily convened board meeting, Paul Girolami, the finance director, and Ray Camp, the company secretary, who were in Madrid helping to set up a Spanish subsidiary.[43] Both considered the union unwarranted and were to play key roles in the defence of Glaxo. Within the group as a whole, the bid was greeted with incredulity and annoyance. Managers and scientists, who believed that Glaxo was the leading pharmaceutical company in Britain, considered Beecham's actions an affront. They thought it inappropriate for a business that manufactured soft drinks and OTC products to take over a company engaged in the discovery of ethical medicines. This sense of outrage revealed a measure of complacency in Glaxo and perhaps something of the business naivety which led to the epithet 'the university of Greenford'.

In the eleven days before Glaxo's AGM on 13 December, a series of discussions and two board meetings were held. Bide, who had been appointed deputy chairman in October 1971, Girolami, Smart, the commercial director, and Camp, were all agreed that the bid should be firmly opposed.[44] Although Wilson as chairman always resisted the take-over in public, he

appears to have been ambivalent in private. His experience of the attempted take-over of Courtaulds by ICI in the winter of 1961–62 had been
a salutary one, and he may have been impressed by the force of Edwards'
strategy. Sir Arthur Knight, finance director of Courtaulds from 1961 and a
close colleague of Wilson, recalled that the latter had initially expressed an
interest in merger when approached by ICI. In the subsequent defence of
the textile group, Wilson had been eclipsed by the forthright C. F. Kearton.
In March 1962, Wilson had been asked by H. R. Mathys, a fellow board
member, to honour his promise to relinquish the post of chairman-designate.[45] Exhausted and depressed by internal politics and the perilous situation in which Courtaulds found itself, Wilson agreed and announced his
resignation on 25 June.[46] Moreover, when Knight had been a student at the
London School of Economics, he had been taught by Edwards and, having
kept in contact, was surprised by a telephone call from him during the early
stages of Beecham's bid for Glaxo. Edwards expressed frustration with Wilson, saying that he believed that the two had reached an agreement over the
proposed amalgamation.[47] Wilson was a man of considerable integrity, an
observer of proprieties, and would not have given his word lightly. It is possible that, as in the case of Courtaulds, Wilson was simply exploring the options in a theoretical way, rather than committing himself to a definite
course of action. Girolami recalled that in discussions at Glaxo Wilson had
always firmly opposed the bid and, indeed, had reservations about the
merger with Boots, though in the practical handling of the defence, he delegated matters to his board colleagues.[48]

   At a meeting on 6 December Glaxo informed Beecham, via Lazard
Brothers, the company's merchant bankers, 'the principles (political and
otherwise) on which Glaxo based its unreserved opposition to the take-
over bid with a view to affording an immediate opportunity to Beecham to
consider the wisdom of continuing with its proposals'.[49] Three days later a
third board meeting was convened at which it was decided, largely at Bide's
suggestion, that the Monopolies Commission should be encouraged to
investigate the matter.[50]

   Wilson and Smart called on Sir Keith Joseph, Secretary of State for Social
Services (the sponsoring Ministry for the pharmaceutical industry), to
make representations about the 'public interest' consequences of the bid.
They gained his support and it was agreed to deliver the case outlining its
monopoly implications to the Minister of Trade and Industry, John Davies,
by Friday, 10 December.[51] To allow a rapid response, the Glaxo board
resolved that a quorum of four directors (including the chairman and or
the deputy chairman) should negotiate with Group's 'financial advisors,
auditors and solicitors' and take 'all steps' that might be required in con-

ducting opposition to the Beecham bid.[52] In practice, the defence was conducted by Wilson, Bide, Girolami, Smart and Camp.

At the AGM on 13 December 1971, Wilson delivered a statement to shareholders outlining Glaxo's reasons for opposing the take-over:

> In the first place, the bid, if successful, would result in a reduction of the competitive pressure on the two enterprises. In the pharmaceutical industry, this pressure largely takes the form of competition in ideas and research, and there is a constant need to invent and market major new medicines. Secondly and specifically as regards a 'monopoly' in the narrow sense the bid, if successful, would result in the whole of the production of penicillin G in Great Britain coming under the control of one company. Penicillin G is an important medicament in itself, and in addition is largely used as a starting material for other antibiotics, namely, semi-synthetic penicillins, produced by Beecham and a cephalosporin, produced by Glaxo.[53]

Sir Alan was, in fact, slightly overstating his case as Beecham did not manufacture their own penicillin G, purchasing the bulk of their supplies from Glaxo. The desire to control one of their major sources of basic materials may have been a further motivation behind the bid.

Sir Ronald Edwards argued that merger was the only way to create a UK company with the 'size, speed of impact and marketing muscle' that could compete successfully on a world stage with the largest American, German and Swiss rivals.[54] The combined turnover of the two companies amounted to £350 million (of which £150 million derived from pharmaceutical and veterinary products) and the merged business ranked ninth in the global league table.[55] Nevertheless, their amalgamated research budgets totalling £10 million per annum were considerably less than the £29 million spent by Merck or the £25 million at Eli Lilly. Edwards concluded,

> medium scale has its virtues and hitherto has served the UK industry well, but times are changing. In view of the market strength now needed by British companies to match our competitors internationally and the resources required to sustain and develop high and widespread investment, an increase in size becomes imperative.[56]

Beecham had originally attempted to present the take-over as a 'friendly merger',[57] though the press viewed it as a battle between two captains of industry. As *The Times* put it:

> Sir Ronald Edwards and Sir Alan Wilson ... have known each other for a considerable length of time. For years they worked together on the Electricity

Council, Sir Ronald as chairman, Sir Alan as deputy chairman. Both men were eminent academics before they immersed themselves in the practical life of industry.[58]

They were presented as the proponents of two different strategies: Edwards as the advocate of the large-scale organisation and Wilson of the medium-sized firm. Two years earlier, Sir Alan had argued that these businesses were the only ones 'which have been successful innovators over long periods' and that 'giant corporations do not seem to provide an atmosphere in which the creativity demanded in the pharmaceutical industry can flourish'.[59] He supported this case by pointing to Glaxo's recent launches of Betnovate, Ceporin and Ventolin. Alan Wilson pointed out in a letter to its shareholders that in three years' time Beecham's patents on ampicillin (Penbritin), which accounted for over 70 per cent of the company's pharmaceutical sales to chemists in 1971, and their other semi-synthetic penicillins, would begin to expire. He suggested that the take-over was motivated, in part, by the need to obtain a fresh portfolio of products at a time when their own laboratories had failed to discover commercial successors,[60] a view supported by some press commentators.[61]

The defence of Glaxo proceeded on two fronts. While Bide organised submissions to government for an inquiry by the Monopolies Commission, Girolami raised the matter of a white knight with Camp. They settled on Boots, a company with which Bide had connections through his friendship with Dr Gordon Hobday, the managing director. Negotiations between the senior managements then proceeded at great speed, Glaxo being represented by Lazards and Boots by Schroder Wagg. Bide, Girolami and Camp agreed a broad strategy and the outlines of a merger between the two companies were drawn up.

On 6 January 1972 to the 'surprise and regret' of the Glaxo board, John Davies, Minister for Trade and Industry, refused to refer the Beecham bid to the Monopolies Commission, drawing protests from some MPs and sections of the trade and City press. He had, perhaps, concluded, quite rightly, that should the merger take place, there were sufficient producers in the UK to preclude the creation of a monopoly.

On 10 January, Beecham sent details of their offer to Glaxo shareholders. In the lengthy document, Edwards summarised the rationale for the bid:

> The pharmaceutical industry is an international one. Firms of consequence are characterised by large research and development investments, significant exports, factories in different countries and powerful marketing forces across the world. Our principal international competitors are already substantially

larger than either Beecham or Glaxo, but Beecham and Glaxo together would achieve about tenth place by sales value and thus would be enabled to compete more effectively. Since the United Kingdom market represents less than 4 per cent of the world total, British companies must concentrate more and more on overseas markets and it is from combined efforts overseas that some of the major advantages of the merger would accrue.[62]

Glaxo responded swiftly with advertisements published in the major national newspapers stating their clear opposition:

> This is a take-over attempt. It must not be allowed to succeed. It would harm the Glaxo shareholders. It could harm Glaxo employees. You will shortly receive a letter refuting the Beecham arguments. In the meantime, do not complete the Beecham acceptance form.[63]

On 12 January Glaxo announced their own merger with Boots to create 'the largest pharmaceutical enterprise in the United Kingdom'.[64] The preliminary terms were nine Boots shares and £4 of 5 per cent convertible stock for every five Glaxo shares, valuing Glaxo at £350 million and the amalgamated companies at £750 million. Thus, Boots effectively valued Glaxo at 503p per share in contrast to their market price of 366p before the Beecham bid, and the latter's offer of 430p.[65] The public statement argued that

> the two companies fit together in harmonious and complementary fashion and their outlook and philosophy is also similar ...
>   The procedure proposed may have the appearance of a take-over and your directors accordingly wish to stress that it is in fact no more than an adoption of the most convenient technique to achieve the desired end. IT IS NOT A TAKE-OVER. IT IS A TRUE MERGER.[66]

The *Sunday Times* commented that

> a Boots–Glaxo combine would have the financial strength to match the drug giants but nowhere near such a powerful marketing strength as Beecham–Glaxo. It would also be inherently more insular. Such a trend may not be healthy for the relatively small UK drug industry but in the absence of a Government monopolies probe such questions will be submerged in short-term financial interest.[67]

The proposed amalgamation with Boots was presented as the union of equals, and an article in *Glaxo Group News*, the staff newspaper, stressed that it 'is a merger in fact and in spirit'.[68] The complementary nature of the two businesses was stressed, together with their similar philosophies and outlook. Although both sides had entered the arrangement voluntarily, the balance of power, almost of necessity, was to favour Boots as the rescuer. Initially Glaxo had proposed an amalgamation with Boots, but the latter's advisors argued that this would not provide shareholders with an attractive alternative to the Beechams offer. As a result, Glaxo agreed that Boots would bid competitively for the group. The *Pharmaceutical Journal* commented that a Boots–Glaxo merger

> would create a group different in many ways from that resulting from a Beecham–Glaxo link up. Boots–Glaxo would be a vertical grouping (manufacturing–wholesaler–retailer) quite different from the horizontal alignment of two manufacturers which would result from a coming together of Beecham and Glaxo.[69]

Boots owned 1,398 chemists shops and in 1968 had taken over the business of Timothy Whites with a further 618 houseware and chemist outlets.[70] It was the largest pharmaceutical retailer in the UK, while Glaxo, through its subsidiary Vestric, was the biggest wholesaler. These points increased pressure on the government to refer the whole matter to the Monopolies Commission. It was argued that since many GPs, when writing prescriptions, simply use the generic rather than the branded name, Boots pharmacists (who handled about one-sixth of NHS scripts) would in future favour Glaxo products.[71] Others, including independent chemists, were concerned by 'the concentration of manufacturing and buying power which would arise from such a merger'.[72]

Under the proposed amalgamation, Wilson agreed to step down as chairman in favour of the Boots managing director, Hobday, while Bide was to become deputy chairman, and Girolami chief executive of the pharmacy division. The initiative passed to the Boots management partly because Glaxo was the passive partner in the scheme of arrangement. This was understandable. Boots was the larger company with net assets of £125 million and world sales of £304 million (of which £288 million were in the UK) earning profits of £34 million for the year ended 31 March 1972.[73] Although they manufactured medicines and conducted their own research, the ethical side of their business represented a small proportion of the whole. Whilst Glaxo needed Boots as an essential part of their defensive strategy, the latter could have survived perfectly well without resort to merger. Boots had an advantage over Beecham in being more highly rated on the stock market and could, therefore, pay a higher price for Glaxo shares.[74] To convey the notion that the Boots–Glaxo merger was a mutually agreed strategy, it was arranged that a 75 per cent majority was required, whereas the Beecham offer required only 50 per cent.

On 24 January the impending Boots offer prompted Beecham to increase their bid, which, with the rise in Glaxo–Beecham stock, was equivalent to approximately 535p per share.[75] This, in turn, had forced Boots to revise their draft proposals and raise the offer to two ordinary shares of 25p each and £1 nominal of 5 per cent convertible unsecured loan stock for every Glaxo ordinary stock unit of 50p.[76] The merger document was finally approved by the Glaxo board on 28 January and despatched to shareholders three days later.[77] At this point Glaxo shares stood at 532p, while the Beecham bid valued them at 535p and the Boots' offer at 573p. W. R. Norman, chairman of Boots, summarised the advantages of the union in the offer document as follows:

> To the Boots' shareholders the merger with Glaxo provides a unique opportunity to expand the interests of their company into the world at large. Glaxo will gain access to Boots products, both ethical medicines and consumer products, for marketing through their extensive international companies. In addition Glaxo will have the great advantage of the support of one of the best known and most successful retail operations in this country to provide a powerful buffer against the vicissitudes of international trading.[78]

Voting on the Boots–Glaxo merger was timetabled for 22 February, but events intervened to prevent the ballot from taking place.[79]

John Davies had come under increasing pressure from the Commons to refer the two schemes to the Monopolies Commission. On 17 January, shortly after the Boots–Glaxo merger had been publicised, questions were raised by Edward Milne, MP for Blyth, whose constituency included Glaxo's Cambois factory, but Davies stood by his earlier judgement.[80] However, increasing press comment and parliamentary pressure persuaded Davies to reverse his decision on 3 February. *Glaxo Group News* covered their front page with the banner headline: 'Beecham and Boots Bids referred to Monopolies Commission'.[81] Hearings were arranged for March and it was anticipated that a report would be issued in July.[82] Glaxo had earned a respite of about five months in which to conduct its defence.

Financial restructuring: Glaxo Holdings

While information was being gathered for the Monopolies Commission, Girolami worked on a financial reorganisation designed to cut the ground

from under the Beecham offer. The scheme was authorised by the board on
15 March 1972 and announced with the half-yearly results.[83] A new company, Glaxo Holdings, was formed to compete with the bids from both
Beecham and Boots. It enabled the existing shareholders to give themselves
the same financial benefits that the two rival groups were offering. The
scheme removed at a stroke the financial advantages inherent in Glaxo
Group's balance sheet and created a poison pill for a bidder that could not
afford to pay in cash.[84] In practice, Glaxo Holdings exchanged one of its
shares, together with 60p of 7½ per cent convertible loan stock, for each existing share in Glaxo Group.[85] Between 1975 and 1984 shareholders then
had the option of exchanging the 500p of convertible stock for another
share in the holding company. The effect was to increase the income of the
stockholders at no extra cost to the company as the interest on the loan
stock was to be paid out of pre-tax income, whereas if Glaxo had decided to
offer a higher dividend on its ordinary shares, this would have come from
net profits. A total of £41.3 million of the company's reserves had also been
capitalised and distributed to shareholders as convertible loan stock. In a
unique and ingenious move, each loan stockholder was given the option,
up to the first conversion date, of selling his stock for cash in the event of
Glaxo being taken over. The effect of this asset transfer was to yield a gain
of 18 per cent for Glaxo shareholders, closely matching the Beecham offer,
and yet leaving the group in the hands of the existing management. Glaxo
Holdings was incorporated on 23 March 1972 and the scheme of arrangement was sanctioned in the High Court of Justice and filed with the Registrar of Companies on 19 May.[86]

In introducing the scheme to Sir Harry Jephcott by letter, Wilson argued

> We cannot be certain that the Monopolies Commission will come down on the
> side of the angels, and the capital reconstruction will be a formidable defence
> against the possibility of Beecham returning to the attack. You will readily ap-
> preciate that the extra income that a shareholder will receive will come from the
> Exchequer. (This is one of the effects of corporation tax ...). The same was true
> of the income from the loan stock offered by Beecham, but none of the financial
> pundits seemed to spot it! The capital reconstruction therefore removes a very
> large advantage from Beecham.[87]

It had only been possible because of Glaxo Group's freedom from debt.
The tight housekeeping vigorously adopted by Jephcott and maintained by
Wilson resulted in the business having valuable assets. As Glaxo explained
in a public statement, this financial probity had been a source of concern as
the management had been aware that 'in certain circumstances our
ungeared structure might attract bids offering apparent increases in in-

come and capital value'.[88] The group justified the timing by saying that a major investment programme had recently been completed, and that improved profit prospects and a healthy cash flow had combined to create an opportunity 'to increase shareholders' income, and to do so as economically as possible'.[89] The press appeared impressed by the ingenuity of the scheme, the *Guardian* commenting that 'like many of the nuances of takeover strategy, this proposal is touched with a degree of sophistication, which threatens to leave Glaxo's band of small shareholders gasping'.[90] The immediate reaction to the announcement was an increase in Glaxo's share price from 503p to 512p, and this was interpreted by the press as a sign that the stock market considered the higher income available to shareholders outweighed the slight reduction of earnings per share implied by the new capital structure.

Girolami, the author of this strategy, had driven it forward despite opposition from the group's merchant bankers, Lazards, and other City institutions. In addition, several members of the Glaxo board became apprehensive, though their worries were overcome by Bide, who showed considerable determination in getting it approved. The scheme required a 75 per cent majority for ratification and this was comfortably achieved at a poll on 24 April, held at Grosvenor House, Park Lane.[91] In fact, the holders of the ordinary stock of Glaxo Group voted 83.5 per cent in favour of the arrangement. The restructured finances of Glaxo Holdings and the rise of its share price to 512p almost made the group too expensive to acquire. Beecham had offered 536p and the Boots bid was worth 617p, though as the *Daily Telegraph* pointed out the reconstruction had reduced the market capitalisation of Glaxo by £41 million, by substituting loan stock, so that any bidder could afford to increase his offer by this amount less only loan stock interest.[92] In the event, Beecham did not raise their bid and waited for the outcome of the Monopoly Commission's deliberations. The Inland Revenue subsequently ruled that the issue of bonus loan stock could no longer be allowed for tax purposes, and effectively prevented the manoeuvre from being repeated.

Monopolies Commission hearing

The bids for Glaxo by both Beecham and Boots were the fortieth reference to the Commission since the passing of the Monopolies and Mergers Act of 1965.[93] The nine-member team was chaired by Sir Ashton Roskill QC.[94] Glaxo's *Submission* had been assembled in little over two weeks, under the supervision of Bide and Camp, though preparations had been underway since December. [95] The company argued that Beecham was on a risk-spreading venture 'to escape from the otherwise insoluble problem which would be provided by a large, costly but unremunerative, research organisation, against the background of prospectively falling profits'[96] and to acquire new chemical entities 'nearing the end of successful clinical trial'.[97] Stressing that Glaxo was opposed to the union, they argued that Beecham's assessment of the advantages that would accrue needed to be 'heavily discounted'.[98] Glaxo suggested that the philosophies of the two groups were 'alien to one another' because Beecham was 'an industrial organisation existing merely to exploit a commercial demand for medicines'. Beecham, the *Submission* argued, had only entered the ethical pharmaceutical field during the last twenty years and around 65 per cent of its turnover came from consumer products such as shampoos, soft drinks, toothpaste and hair cream. Glaxo, by contrast, was 'predominantly an ethical pharmaceutical company'.[99] In fact, Beecham had been engaged in pharmaceuticals for much longer than twenty years, and Glaxo itself was far from exclusively engaged in the discovery of novel medicines, manufacturing a number of OTC products (such as Malt Extract, Sea Legs, antacids, tonics and anti-diarrhoels) and a range of agricultural and horticultural pesticides, deriving about 40 per cent of its turnover from its non-pharmaceutical businesses.

On the other hand, when assessing the consequences of a merger between Boots and Glaxo the *Submission* sought to highlight the complementarity of the two groups.[100] For example, it was suggested that,

> Glaxo has already a world-wide marketing organisation … Boots has a number of excellent 'young' products with real potential but is handicapped in realising their potential by the relatively slight territorial coverage and sources of its overseas marketing. Since the products in question do not compete with Glaxo's existing lines, and since the research of the two companies is directed to innovation in different therapeutic categories, the whole weight of Glaxo's marketing organisation can be put unreservedly behind these existing products …[101]

The first hearings were held at New Court, 48 Carey Street, on Friday, 3 March 1972, and the Glaxo delegation, led by Wilson, included Bide, Back, Girolami, Smart, Hurran and Camp, supported by Ian Threlfall QC.[102] Initially, the questions focused on the proposed Boots–Glaxo merger and Bide, who had been responsible for the initial contacts and overseen the negotiations, gave most of the replies.[103] Evidence was provided by Smart on marketing and commercial matters[104] and Girolami provided data on financial questions.[105]

A major point of Glaxo's defence was the strength of its research and development function and the threat to it should Beecham secure control of the company. Sir Alan Wilson found himself on home territory. He drew a distinction between pragmatic and 'ivory tower research' in the pharmaceutical industry, the latter failing to generate any new medicines.[106] He suggested that there is little correlation between 'chemical structures and pharmacological effect', which, in turn, presented special problems:

> In an acute form scientific research is not possible. You do not do things in [a] logical order. There is a very large element of intuition and a feeling for the market … What we have to do is take somebody who has a feeling in his bones, not for any reasons which would convince a board of directors, or certainly not for financial reasons, he knows he has got something and it is up to him.[107]

He argued that the real factor limiting pharmaceutical research was not money but ideas.[108] Wilson believed that merging departments through take-over would not increase the stock of inventiveness, but could produce an unhappy and poorly motivated organisation:

> Our staff could not make Beecham have new ideas. The ideas are in the individual, and if you are putting somebody who has no ideas together with somebody who has you do not produce any more ideas … If you have a lot of people, you can put 10 people together and they will have one idea, or you can put 500 people together and they will have two ideas. You tend to think on establishment lines [in business], but you cannot.[109]

Wilson believed that intangible factors were involved in nurturing a productive research and development department which went beyond funding and administrative efficiency. Drawing on his own experience at Courtaulds, where he had been forced to rebuild the research function, Wilson concluded

> if you have an unsuccessful research set-up, it is a most difficult thing to deal with, and the only way I know of reviving an introverted research department is to demolish it and take the best people out, put them elsewhere in a different environment, and you ventilate it, break up the deadlock.[110]

Such opinions, expressed by a scientist with a high reputation in both academic and industrial research, carried considerable weight with the Commission and his evidence on the question of industrial research was Wilson's last significant contribution to the future of Glaxo.

The Monopolies Commission continued to gather evidence throughout April and June, presenting Glaxo with a series of detailed written questions concerning a possible duplication in sales forces and production facilities between Glaxo Laboratories, Allen & Hanburys and BDH, and the organisation of the group's food and bulk chemicals businesses.[111] The company also continued to lobby and to argue its case through the media.

Report of the Monopolies Commission

It was with great relief and celebration that the report of the Monopolies Commission was received by Glaxo on 13 July 1972.[112] John Davies accepted the recommendation that neither acquisition should be allowed to proceed, thereby bringing to a close the 'fateful nine [months]' that had elapsed from Beecham's initial offer.[113] The Commission concluded that

> the mergers could be expected to operate against the public interest ... They accepted that in the long term there could be some marketing advantage from increased size, particularly overseas. But they considered that the success of the British pharmaceutical industry depended on its ability to innovate and the main issue was the effect of the proposed mergers on the companies' research and development. They took the view that each of the companies was large enough on its own to support worthwhile research and development and that the effect ... in particular that which might result from the loss of an independent centre for the taking of decisions about the direction of future R. & D., outweighed the other benefits which might accrue from the merger.[114]

The Commission accepted Wilson's argument that all three companies were sufficiently large to fund costly and risky research and that effectiveness in research was not necessarily a function of size. The prospects for 'promising ideas' would not, in the Commission's view, be improved by merger and, indeed, the elimination of competition between Beecham and Glaxo in similar therapeutic areas, could lead to less innovative enterprise. The *Financial Times* added that a union between Boots and Glaxo would have deterred the new organisation from broadening the scope of its research, while in the case of victory by Beecham, there would have been the added question of damage to the morale of Glaxo staff as they were compelled to amalgamate.[115]

Consequences of the take-over bids

The first and most important consequence of the Monopolies Commission report was that Glaxo had been granted a period of grace from the threat of future take-overs.[116] The confidence of the senior management had been shaken by the contest and any doubts that the business appealed to acquisitive corporations had been emphatically dispelled. The group was to embark on a period of self-examination to explore weaknesses in strategy, structure and manufacturing to lift it from what had become a plateau in profitability.

The Glaxo case offered parallels with Courtaulds' successful defence against ICI. During that campaign, Wilson had also resigned from the board. When planning the merger between Glaxo and Boots, Wilson offered to retire in favour of Hobday, the managing director of Boots.[117] Having indicated his willingness to step down, it was then difficult for Wilson to continue in office once the union had been blocked by the Monopolies Commission. Due to retire, aged 65, in August 1971, a year earlier Wilson had been asked by the board to continue as chairman 'for a period, say up to mid 1974'.[118] He had accepted with one qualification:

> In view of the great demands on the top management of the company, I gladly accept this invitation. But as I mentioned to the board, circumstances may change and may make it desirable for a new chairman to take over at an earlier date than that now anticipated. In such circumstances you will have my fullest co-operation.[119]

The stress of the defence, and doubtless the painful memories that it evoked, encouraged Wilson to accelerate his retirement plans and in March 1972, while the Commission was still collecting evidence, he decided to go and Austin Bide, the deputy chairman, succeeded him.[120] In view of the uncertain outcome of events, a public announcement was delayed until September, though it was not until a year later on 31 March 1973 that Sir Alan formally left the board.[121] The forthright and determined campaign fought by Bide won him the respect of both the senior management of Glaxo and its shareholders. He became, in effect, the only candidate to succeed Wilson.

Wilson was not the only executive casualty of the failed bids. The outcome was a major disappointment to Edwards. In 1972, having developed a minor heart condition, which might have exacerbated his glaucoma, he resigned as chairman of Beecham, though he remained as president until his retirement three years later.[122]

The question remains whether Beecham were right to bid for Glaxo, knowing that it would be contested. In the light of the merger movement that swept subsequently through the pharmaceutical industry, which included Glaxo's take-over of Wellcome and merger with SmithKline Beecham, it seems that Edwards was justified. Had he been successful, Beecham would have acquired a first-rate research and development facility that was beginning to generate outstanding products. He would have broadened the group's therapeutic base, doubled its sales force and extended its overseas representation, particularly in Commonwealth countries. Beecham would have emerged a richer and more powerful force. Edwards' mistake was not that he undertook the take-over bid but that he failed to bring it to a satisfactory conclusion.

Was the Centre for the Study of Industrial Innovation correct in its conclusion that UK-based pharmaceutical companies were likely to decline unless they increased their size and widened their territorial coverage? In July 1989 Beecham concluded an amalgamation with SmithKline Beckman.[123] The group had not grown as rapidly as Glaxo and that year was ranked third in the UK and twenty-second in the world with annual pharmaceutical sales of $2,006 million.[124] Glaxo was then second in the world with a turnover of $4,578 million.[125] Although proponents of the Anglo-American merger estimated that the combined business would generate sales of $4 billion and lift SmithKline Beecham to second place in the world ranking,[126] these proved to be inflated and in 1990 the united group recorded sales of $3,669 million and held eighth place.[127] Glaxo retained second place behind Merck, then the market leader. In 1989, at the time of the Beecham merger, Boots were ranked sixth in the UK and sixty-first in the world. However, the production of pharmaceutical products, totalling a mere $485 million, represented only 10 per cent of the group's turnover ($4,817 million), the bulk of which was generated by their highly successful retailing chain. Boots remained committed to the discovery of new medicines and in 1991 earned $1,122 million or 17 per cent of their turnover from the sale of their own ethical pharmaceutical products.[128] Yet the withdrawal of their new cardiac vasodilator, flosequinan (Manoplax), in 1993, after a twelve-year development programme costing £100 million,[129] caused commentators to question the commercial sense of Boots continuing in the field of pure research. In March 1995, despite sales of £442 million and a profit of £86 million, Boots Pharmaceuticals was sold to the German company BASF.[130] Thus, it is a curious irony that Glaxo, which according to both merger schemes was the business to have been taken over, proved to be the company that flourished and eclipsed both its prospective acquirer and its white knight.

RESTRUCTURING AND
MANAGERIAL CHANGE
· 1972–1985

§

THE SHAPE of Glaxo Group owed as much to chance as design: a loose federation of related and unintegrated businesses. For Sir Alan Wilson structural issues were not a priority and the group became even more complex under his chairmanship, following the setting up of Vestric and the takeover of BDH and Farley's Infant Food. Acutely aware of the need for change, Bide used the failed Beecham bid as a catalyst for a programme of administrative reforms. Bide believed in the centralisation of authority and the reorganisation of Glaxo's activities along functional lines. As a result, new supervisory bodies were created, including the Group Management Committee, while production and marketing were rationalised in the UK with the establishment of Glaxo Operations in 1978. Directors were given specific responsibilities by both activity and regions of the world. To break down the barriers that arose from traditional company loyalties, a programme of integration was put in place, designed not to eliminate them but to permit the growth of a compatible group culture. Wide-ranging structural and administrative reforms, essential to the group's performance, followed the setting up of Glaxo Holdings.

Structural reorganisation

1972 was in many respects a pivotal year for Glaxo. First and foremost, the group succeeded in defending itself from the predatory advances of Beecham, and the Monopolies Commission ruling granted a breathing space to reinforce its independence. Secondly, the new pharmacology building at the Ware laboratories was opened and work began there on the projects that were ultimately to lead to the discovery of Zantac, Zofran and Imigran (see p. 335). Thirdly, the group was restructured financially to create Glaxo Holdings (see p. 188) and the long-considered managerial

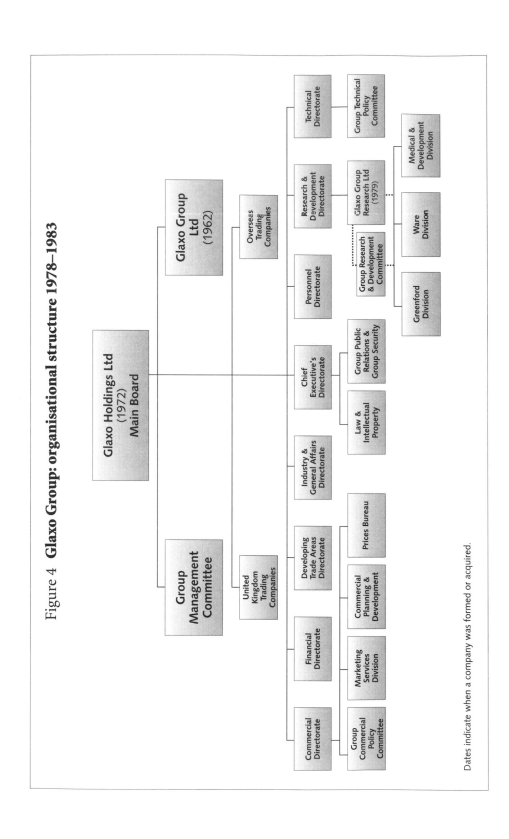

Figure 4 **Glaxo Group: organisational structure 1978–1983**

Dates indicate when a company was formed or acquired.

reorganisation was finally implemented, following approval at the July board meeting.[1] The need for reform had become pressing and ideas for streamlining management were often discussed informally.[2] The design of a new structure for the group was made easier by the experience of implementing more limited reorganisation. In 1970 David Smart, as managing director of Allen & Hanburys, had introduced the principles of functional responsibility and greater centralised control within that company. Earlier, Austin Bide had played a key role in setting up Vestric, which focused the group's wholesaling operations within a single business, achieved through a 'policy audit', by which all its major activities were reviewed to ensure consistency and coherence within Glaxo as a whole. In addition, both Smart and Bide had been involved in the restructuring of the surgical engineering subsidiaries and the creation of a sub-group under Matburn Holdings (see p. 162).

The shock of a threatened take-over created the impetus for change. Once it had become clear that Glaxo would survive as an independent entity, Bide's blueprint to restructure Glaxo Holdings was published in the autumn of 1972; it was subsequently known as the 'orange book', the colour of its cover.[3] It drew a fundamental distinction between the 'central function' of the Holdings (Parent) Company, which was responsible for 'the formulation and direction of strategic policy', and 'local managements', which were empowered to develop 'tactics within the framework of such policy'.[4] Bide believed in the virtues of sound administration[5] and, as a scientist, disliked the general corporate disorder in which the UK subsidiaries operated. He had become acutely aware of the need to bring the various 'barons' (heads of factories or managing directors of overseas companies) within the executive hierarchy. Bide had been responsible for the group's intellectual property rights, and patent protection remains a feature of the pharmaceutical industry that has to be organised centrally to ensure uniform and coherent implementation (see p. 260). Serving as company secretary from 1956 to 1965 and studying the workings of the group from a head office perspective, it was not surprising that his guiding principle was 'to bring about a somewhat greater degree of centralisation'.[6]

In November 1972 this strategic change took three forms. First, a Group Management Committee was set up and located between the Holdings board and the individual operating subsidiaries. Its membership was limited to the executive directors of Glaxo Holdings, chaired by the chief executive. Designed to remain in close contact with the tactical questions being addressed by the major subsidiaries, the Group Management Committee served as the principal forum for strategic decision making. The company secretary, initially Ray Camp and from 1978 Michael Allan, acted as the conduit for agenda items. If, for example, the chairman of Glaxo Laboratories (India) wished to build a new milk drying plant, informal soundings would be made and, if they received a favourable response, he would submit a costed proposal to the Group Management Committee. Should the project fall within the overall group strategy, the Group Management Committee would refer the matter to the Holdings board for ratification. In this way the group was able to take closer control of the activities of its subsidiaries to ensure that they accorded with its overall strategic policies. In the past, overseas operating companies had been granted a great degree of autonomy and could, for example, have made significant marketing decisions without direct reference to Glaxo Group. The system had worked efficiently as long as the business was of limited size and could be supervised on a personal basis by a touring chief executive.

The second major change was the focusing of head office functions, gathered under a series of 'directorates'. In essence, this involved each main board director being assigned to a specific role with nominated operating companies and geographical areas. Five functional directorates were created: finance (Girolami), developing trade areas (Back), commercial (Smart), technical (Hurran) and personnel (Drewitt), together with a sixth, deputy chairman (Bide) with a general executive role.[7] In the past, the directors of Glaxo Group had been drawn from the principal trading subsidiaries and might therefore duplicate expertise and experience within the main board. Directorates were not companies in their own right but, in effect, head office departments with supervisory powers over individual businesses (see Figure 4). In June 1973, Bide added the research and development directorate, which he, as a chemist, chaired and to which Hems, managing director of Glaxo Research, and Jack, managing director of Allen & Hanburys Research, were key appointments.[8] Later an industry and general affairs directorate was created under Smart.

The third important change was the rationalisation of executive authority between the board and its overseas subsidiaries. In the past, responsibility for the provision of management services to these was divided between several head office departments and Glaxo International, together with its subsidiary Glaxo-Allenburys (Export). To provide clearer lines of authority, these two companies were absorbed within the various directorates. The countries in which Glaxo operated were divided into 'mature trading areas' and 'developing trading areas', though some could be granted 'special trading area' status.[9] Mature trading areas were nations where Glaxo had a well established sales and marketing base, and sometimes had secondary manufacturing facilities. They were: Argentina, Australia, Canada, France, India, Iran, Italy, New Zealand, Pakistan and

South Africa. Each main board director, in addition to his functional role, was appointed as a 'parent board counsellor', a position initially suggested to the Glaxo board by Sir Edward Playfair, whose classical education had introduced him to the concept. In ancient Rome, counsellors were appointed by the Senate to explain its policy decisions to local rulers in far-flung Imperial dominions and to assuage their fears or objections. Bide modified this system, allocating each executive director a territory which they were expected to visit and maintain a supporting brief. In November 1972, when the new structure came into being, David Smart, who headed the commercial directorate, was parent board counsellor for Italy and France, while Napier Drewitt, in charge of the personnel directorate, looked after Australia, Canada, India, New Zealand, Pakistan and South Africa. Parent board counsellors were not responsible for business decisions and operations within their territories but were to serve as a source of information and advice.[10] They were encouraged to visit their regions regularly to build up informal lines of communication, replicating the personal contacts formerly established by Jephcott on his winter travels. The parent board counsellor network was designed to give subsidiaries a sense of belonging and representation, whilst expanding the knowledge of those operating within an increasingly centralised head office.

'Special trading areas' were defined as territories with acute problems whether caused by politics, trading difficulties or legal issues. In 1972 six were created: Bangladesh, Brazil, Japan, Nigeria, Pakistan and Spain.[11] 'Developing trade areas' were of two varieties, either countries in which Glaxo operated through appointed distributors or agents, or countries in which the group's subsidiaries or associated companies were heavily reliant upon the UK for services and advice. They were largely territories which had been supported by Glaxo-Allenburys (Export) and Glaxo International and now became the responsibility of the developing trade areas directorate, headed by Douglas Back.

In its fundamentals, this centralised structure remained in place until the early 1980s when Paul Girolami, chief executive from November 1980, began a process of introducing 'delegated management', which returned greater autonomy to executives within defined territorial and functional boundaries (see p. 217).[12] Although the creation of 'parent board counsellors', a term coined by Bide, and the division of Glaxo's overseas subsidiaries into three market categories were unique to the group, the emphasis on centralised control and splitting of executive authority on functional lines were features of the 1970s and took place in other multinational companies.

Integrating the business

On becoming chairman in April 1973, Austin Bide made the integration of the group's activities in the UK one of his priorities. At the same time, he was concerned to protect the goodwill associated with the names of Allen & Hanburys, Evans Medical and other well-known businesses such as Duncan Flockhart. To create a more coherent organisation without alienating managers and staff, he decided that drawing them together had to be a gradual process. Bide was helped considerably by David Smart, whom he had come to know and trust from the mid 1950s when the two had met whilst representing their respective companies in the United States. Smart, as managing director of Allen & Hanburys, and Bide, as a former Glaxo Laboratories executive, representing the two major constituent companies in the group, were able to present a united front and persuade employees that this was an impartial process. Their aim was to instil a further level of loyalty, not just to an individual company but also to the group in the way that a citizen might feel regard for a town or county and also to a nation.

In practice, the integration was achieved by first exchanging key managers. David Smart, for example, as the managing director of Allen & Hanburys was appointed to the board of Glaxo Laboratories, while John Hurran, the managing director of the latter became a director of the former. Austin Bide himself also sat on the Allen & Hanburys board to break down established cultural barriers. Managers were deliberately drawn from different companies to work on specific projects to foster a spirit of co-operation and establish personal links.[13] In addition, new levels of management were created to oversee common or related operations that had formerly fallen under the remit of autonomous subsidiaries. In 1974, for example, the Primary Product Division was set up to provide a forum for the managers of the group's factories at Ulverston, Montrose, Cambois and Edinburgh to rationalise manufacture between them and exchange ideas readily. It was not constituted as a company but operated as a functional gathering with defined meetings to co-ordinate activity and foster an exchange of technical information.[14]

Having gathered together the primary manufacturing plants and exchanged executives throughout the group, in January 1978 Bide judged that the moment was right to introduce a formal reorganisation. Having gained the consent of all but one of the executive directors, he proposed the creation of a 'first-line' subsidiary to be entrusted with operational responsibility for all primary and secondary manufacture in the UK, together with sales of ethical pharmaceuticals.[15] Entitled Glaxo Operations UK, it served as the key executive body in Britain, responsible for all activities apart from research and development. Medicines continued to be sold under their

*84. Austin Bide as chairman addresses a meeting of shareholders supported by his senior executives (*left to right*): Ray Camp, Douglas Back, David Smart, Paul Girolami (*partly obscured*), Napier Drewitt and John Hurran.*

established trademarks, with the Glaxo Laboratories, Allen & Hanburys and Evans Medical packaging, but the companies from which they originated henceforth functioned as 'shell subsidiaries'. Napier Drewitt was appointed chairman and parent board counsellor of the new company, and E. R. C. Farmer its managing director.

Drewitt was chosen in part because he had come to Glaxo relatively recently from a career in Courtaulds and could be viewed by staff as impartial. The same was true of Farmer, who had joined the group in 1974 after broad experience in management, including seventeen years with Sterling-Winthrop, latterly as director of Sterling Drug International.[16] He originally worked in the food products division at a time when the group was attempting to rationalise manufacture between the Glaxo factories at Greenford and Kendal and the former Farley's plants at Plymouth and in Ireland. Given that costs exceeded turnover, Farmer took a dispassionate view of the business and with the aid of an accountant dissected its operations. He prepared a plan designed to eliminate duplication and to concentrate production at the most efficient centres whilst introducing higher standards of quality control. In February 1975 this scheme was approved by the Glaxo Holdings board and it was agreed to transfer production from Greenford to Plymouth and Kendal,[17] while the Irish factory was to be closed, at an estimated annual saving of £206,000.[18] Two new subsidiary companies (Glaxo-Farley Foods and Glaxo Health Foods) were created in order that the business could be run along product lines rather than its historical antecedents. Although the foods business recorded a loss in 1974, relocation and staff cuts led to a return to profitability two years later. The success of these organisational reforms brought Farmer to prominence and he became a candidate to take over the more demanding task of welding together Glaxo's pharmaceutical manufacturing and sales operations in the UK.

The setting up of Glaxo Operations UK was the culmination of an ambitious plan to unite the company in Britain into a coherent whole. Farmer gathered together a team of executives deliberately drawn from diverse parts of the group. They included Dr J. C. Hamlet (secondary manufacture), Dr E. N. Taylor (primary production), A. J. Greenacre, an accountant recruited by Paul Girolami (finance and computerisation), and Berkeley E. Baker, formerly of Allen & Hanburys (marketing). The results were dramatic as economies of scale and efficiencies were realised. In 1978, Glaxo Operations earned a revenue of £55 million and a trading profit of £20 million, figures which rose in inflationary times to £104 million and £49 million respectively by 1982, partly as a result of a reduction in staff numbers from 8,550 to 7,250.[19]

Following the success of Glaxo Operations, in 1981 it was decided to review the group's UK activities. In part, this followed the appointment of Paul Girolami as chief executive in November 1980,[20] and was the result of extensive discussions between him and Farmer throughout the following year. Although it had only been in existence for three years, Girolami believed that Glaxo Operations was too unwieldy and sought to divide up its responsibilities on functional lines. Consequently, two new subsidiaries were created, Glaxo Pharmaceuticals UK and Glaxochem, the latter comprising the primary process factories in Britain and the former secondary manufacture together with sales and marketing. Farmer became chairman of Glaxo Pharmaceuticals with Hamlet as the managing director. Girolami believed in devolving authority on functional lines, a managerial feature characteristic of the 1980s. Primary production was a very different activity from secondary manufacture and Glaxo was still actively involved in the sale of bulk chemicals to other pharmaceutical companies. Glaxochem was the natural successor of the Primary Product Division and supervised manufacture at Ulverston, Cambois and Montrose, together with the new factory opened in 1980 at Annan for the production of labetalol hydrochloride.

The group's veterinary business was separated under a new holding company, Glaxo Animal Health. The number of products had increased (principally antibiotics, vaccines and anti-inflammatory corticosteroids) and had generated its own research and development functions at Greenford. Based at Harefield, near Uxbridge, it had trading subsidiaries in the UK (called Glaxovet and originally formed as a first-line subsidiary in 1978), Ireland, Italy, New Zealand, South Africa and Zimbabwe, which were integrated on an international basis in July 1985 with the creation of the Harefield Animal Health Group.[21]

Under Bide, the research and development functions had been gathered together in a unified structure by the setting up of Glaxo Group Research in 1979. Although the Ware laboratories of Allen & Hanburys originally had the status of a division and reported to Glaxo Research, they operated, in practice, as an autonomous organisation responsible to the main board for major items of expenditure. Their growth throughout the late 1960s and early 1970s, combined with the discovery of a number of novel and commercially significant products, led to the creation of Allen & Hanburys Research in 1973 with Dr David Jack as the managing director. In October of that year, Glaxo Research had 612 scientific and technical staff, while the Ware laboratories totalled 301.[22] The sustained expansion at the latter, driven by its success in pharmacologically based research, saw the gap in their relative size reduced, though Greenford remained the larger organisation. The formation of Glaxo Group Research was designed to initiate a process of integration since the two laboratories had worked largely independently of each other, pursuing different approaches and developing distinct therapeutic specialities. The process of uniting their activities and cultures proved to be a protracted one and could be said to be formally complete only when the research function was focused in a single site at Stevenage in 1995.

The commercial record

Throughout the seventies turnover rose every year except 1979, when it was calculated that the increase in the foreign exchange value of sterling reduced overseas sales by as much as £40 million.[23] However, this picture of progressive growth is not so apparent when the results are adjusted for the effects of inflation, which in 1974 ran at 16 per cent and in the following year topped 24 per cent, remaining in double figures until 1982 with the sole exception of 1978 (8.3 per cent). In real terms, the sales recorded by Glaxo did not fluctuate greatly between 1973 and 1982 (Table 5). The picture was more complicated regarding profits. The published figures showed increments

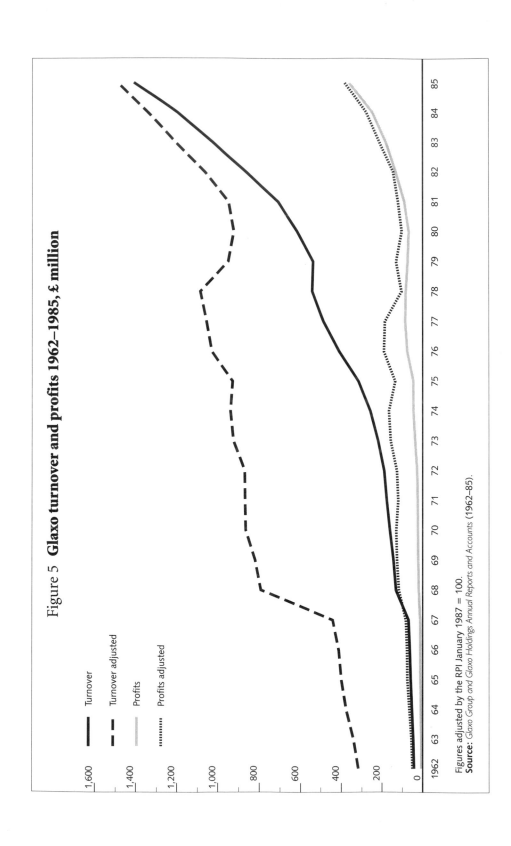

Figure 5 Glaxo turnover and profits 1962–1985, £ million

Turnover
Turnover adjusted
Profits
Profits adjusted

Figures adjusted by the RPI January 1987 = 100.
Source: *Glaxo Group and Glaxo Holdings Annual Reports and Accounts* (1962–85).

every year from 1972 to 1985 with only three exceptions, in 1978, 1979 and 1980. In real terms, however, the profits for 1973 and 1974 were both higher than those for 1982. A progressive rise to a peak in 1976 was followed by a sustained fall to a low in 1980. Then a gradual recovery led to rapid growth from 1983 (see p. 448). From 1973 onwards, an increasing budget was allocated for capital projects and research and development, rising from £11 million in 1973 to £47 million in 1980 and £126 million by 1985 (Table 10, p. 449). This represented an apparent growth of 1,045 per cent, a figure much less dramatic but still impressive when expressed in real terms (189 per cent). The seventies and early eighties were, therefore, years of sustained spending on research and capital projects which, in the nature of the pharmaceutical industry, did not produce an immediate or dramatic improvement in the group's published results. Indeed, in the late 1970s and early 1980s the return on capital employed fell from the 40 per cent of the mid 1970s to around 20 per cent and even below (Table 10), not regaining the higher levels until 1985.

Despite the relative stability of Glaxo's profits in real terms, earnings per share grew considerably over the period, rising from 0.2p in 1963 to 1.5p in 1980 and 8.9p in 1985 – an increase no less dramatic in real terms, 1.5p, 2.2p and 9.4p respectively (Table 11, p. 450). This improved performance was achieved because Glaxo was able to finance its capital investment programmes from internally generated funds, largely without resort to the stock market. Although there had been share issues in November 1967 and January 1970 (involving the issue of one new share for every four held) and a further split in August 1975 (one for five, together with one ordinary share of 50p for each £25 of convertible unsecured loan stock at 200p), these remained modest in their scale. Further capitalisation issues (one for one) followed in January 1980, 1983 and 1989. Because their value had risen so dramatically, and to make them more readily priced, in October 1991 each ordinary share of 50p was subdivided into two ordinary shares of 25p each.[24]

As regards the geographical distribution of sales, there was a significant shift during the late seventies and early eighties (Table 12, p. 451). In the previous decade, the UK accounted for the largest share of turnover with India coming a close second (Table 13, p. 451). By 1972, when Glaxo Holdings was created, this pattern had not altered greatly except that rising sales throughout Europe had begun to erode the dominance formerly exerted by the UK. North America remained of minor importance despite the fact that the United States was the world's largest national market for pharmaceuticals. At first, the acquisition of Meyer Laboratories in 1978, together with a determined attempt to sell directly in America, rather than license products to indigenous companies, generated a modest increase in sales, and it was not until the early 1980s that they began to climb at a steep rate. In percentage terms, the contribution of North America rose from 4.8 in 1972 to 5.1 in 1980 and then rose rapidly to 28.1 in 1985 and 41.4 in 1990. Sales in the rest of the world (excluding Europe) failed to keep pace with the rapid growth of the company and the US market as a whole, their percentage contribution falling from 40.4 in 1972 to 36.9 in 1980, 20.4 in 1985 and 16.5 in 1990 (see Table 12). Europe generated a rising percentage of sales throughout the 1970s as new subsidiaries were established and existing companies, such as Laboratori Glaxo S.p.A. in Italy, grew and were the recipients of capital investment. In 1972 Europe generated 54.8 per cent of turnover rising to 58.1 per cent in 1980. However, as Glaxo Inc. grew at such rapid pace in the eighties, the percentage contribution of the European subsidiaries fell to 51.5 in 1985 and 42.1 in 1990.

The changing balance in the make-up of the group's sales was reflected in the location of staff. In 1963, for example, 60 per cent of employees were based in the UK (Table 14, p. 452). At this time, the entire primary production of Glaxo and a high proportion of its secondary manufacture was in Britain, together with the research and development laboratories and its head office. As elements of production and laboratory work were established abroad, so the dominance of the UK was weakened. In 1970, 58 per cent of staff were at home, though by 1975 the proportion had fallen to 54 per cent and in 1980 was 51 per cent. A small rise to 53 per cent by 1985 followed, though the trend henceforth was significantly and rapidly away from Britain as Glaxo assumed an increasingly international character so that by 1994 only 25 per cent of its 47,189 workforce were based in the UK.

By today's standards, the product portfolio held by Glaxo during the early eighties was broadly based. Because the group had experienced such difficulties in raising both turnover and profits in real terms, the managing directors of its overseas subsidiaries were encouraged to diversify further. In 1980, for example, Sir Austin Bide announced that the Australian company had acquired an enterprise bottling and selling spring water, Deep Spring, from Conga Amalgamated Pty as part of 'the long term aim to broaden our business base'.[25] This enterprise was not particularly successful, largely because Glaxo did not have the expertise to compete with the major drinks companies. At the time, the group was involved in foods, generic and OTC medicines, the bulk sale of medicinal chemicals, the manufacture of surgical equipment and in pharmaceutical wholesaling. This policy of spreading risks continued well into the decade, Glaxo announcing in 1985 that their New Zealand subsidiary had launched, under licence, a brand of yoghurt called 'Yoplait'.[26] Within the UK, Glaxo Holdings were not unusual in this respect as two of its major competitors, Beecham and ICI, were equally diversified, the former manufacturing a range of OTC preparations and other products such as toothpaste, hair cream and carbonated drinks, while for the latter pharmaceuticals were only one aspect of their output which included paints, pesticides, fertilisers, industrial chemicals and even petrol.

The first signs of a significant and sustained improvement in the group's fortunes showed in 1983 when, in real terms, turnover rose by 13.5 per cent and profits by 47.3 per cent (Table 9), and began to lift Glaxo above the levels it had achieved in the mid and late 1970s. 'These welcome advances', commented Bide,

> have been brought about by the expansion of our ethical pharmaceutical business, which was and remains, by far, our most important activity … the main contributor to our growth was our anti-ulcer drug ranitidine (Zantac). By the end of June 30 [1983] … it was being sold in all major markets except the United States, France and Japan.[27]

Ranitidine was launched in the United States in June 1983 with spectacular results (see p. 401), raising the turnover of Glaxo Inc. to £147 million in 1984, an increase in just twelve months of 345 per cent.[28] The high levels of growth in real terms continued as group turnover and profits rose by 10.9 and 37.7 per cent respectively in 1985. Bide announced his retirement as chairman that year, adding that 'the group's balance sheet is now outstandingly strong'.[29] Indeed, because the capital assets of Glaxo had accumulated significantly, it was decided to issue ordinary shareholders with one 50p share for every share they already held to improve their marketability.

International reporting: computer systems

In 1959, Glaxo Laboratories acquired its first computer, the Emidec 1100, an experimental machine supplied by EMI at a cost of £136,000.[30] It was used to produce home sales invoices and to prepare payrolls. Prone to breakdown, its unreliability prompted Jephcott to respond to a visitor's request to see the company's 'fascinating new computer' with the reply 'for a fiver you can take it away'.[31] Despite these setbacks, the group saw the virtues of electronic data handling and in 1964 Cooper Brothers were instructed to prepare a report on its future needs. As a result, an ICT 1903 (16k) was purchased for £123,000 to take over from the Emidec and, in addition, undertook stock control, sales analysis for the Murphy Chemical Co. and

85. The computer room at Greenford in the early 1970s.

publicity mailing.[32] One of the first presentations made to the board by
Girolami was on the group's computer needs. By 1968, the electronic data
processing department at Glaxo already numbered 110 staff (30 on systems
and programming and 80 preparing data and operating machines). Allen &
Hanburys had installed an ICT 1004 in 1965 at Bethnal Green, while the Ulverston factory had bought an IBM 1130 for development projects. BDH
and Vestric also had their own computers, while Evans Medical used an external bureau to process punched cards prepared at their offices.[33] Girolami recognised not only that Greenford needed a more powerful
computer (and an ICT 1904 was ordered) but that it was also necessary to
co-ordinate and standardise the various systems operating in the group's
UK subsidiaries. He proposed the introduction of uniform and inter-
changeable programs and the centralisation of electronic processing at
Greenford.[34] As the range of computer applications increased, considerable
effort was devoted in the 1970s to developing an international network of
reporting. The design of management information systems based on computers helped to establish the authority of the UK board over what had
been semi-independent subsidiaries.

Until the mid 1980s, with the exception of Glaxo Inc., the US company, virtually all the computers in operating subsidiaries were mainframe. Subsequently, large numbers of mini-computers were bought from Hewlett Packard and distributed from the centre.[35] These, too, were used for sales, payroll, purchasing, personnel, stores management and later for word processing. More flexible and not requiring dedicated rooms, they provided rapid access to information and offered further means of direct communication.

Sale of Murphy Chemical Co.

In spring 1973, Bide decided to sell Murphy Chemical.[36] The subsidiary had been acquired as a vehicle to market griseofulvin as a plant antibiotic (see p. 104), but it had become clear that the product's commercial value for Glaxo lay as a systemic anti-fungicide for humans and that agricultural and horticultural chemistry would remain peripheral in the group's research and development programmes. May & Baker, the UK pharmaceutical firm, were involved in this area and Bide, who knew their company secretary well, dropped him a hint that Glaxo might no longer wish to retain Murphy Chemical.[37] Shortly afterwards Rhône-Poulenc, who owned May & Baker, approached the group to express an interest in its acquisition. Glaxo, concerned to protect the interests of the Murphy staff, agreed that Pepro S.A., another Rhône-Poulenc subsidiary, would undertake the purchase.[38] As discussions drew to a conclusion, Glaxo discovered that May & Baker were, in fact, to acquire the company with job losses for the Murphy management and employees. Facing the threat of rationalisation, morale collapsed and a senior Murphy director resigned.[39] To re-establish its credibility and allow equilibrium to return, Glaxo abandoned the projected disposal. However, the reasons for the sale remained valid and when, in September 1977, the Dalgety Group, through its subsidiary, ABM Chemicals, expressed an interest in taking over Murphy as a going concern at net asset value, Glaxo opened fresh negotiations.[40] Terms were agreed in November and the disposal proceeded.[41] Although this event was not part of a general strategy of narrowing the group's activities, it was, in fact, to be the first in a series of divestments that were to gather pace in the mid 1980s (see p. 213).

Managerial change

Under Wilson, the board had been an amalgam of powerful factory or subsidiary executives and a few specialists. Among the latter were Paul Girolami, elected in 1968 as the group's first finance director, and W. D. Scott, recruited three years earlier from ICI where he had served as the commercial director. In May 1965, having suffered a heart attack, Scott took early retirement and was succeeded as commercial director by David Smart, then managing director of Allen & Hanburys. W. J. Hurran, a chemist by training and having been managing director (technical) of Glaxo Laboratories from 1961 and later its chief executive, was given responsibility for technical matters. When Hurran retired in December 1976 after forty years of service with Glaxo, he was succeeded by Dr Alan Raper who was then working as his technical manager.[42] The latter had joined Glaxo at Barnard Castle as a chemist in 1954, having completed a doctorate at Leeds University. Raper investigated various extraction and purification processes to improve the yield of antibiotic manufacture.[43] After a period working for Wilkins at Greenford, Raper returned to Barnard Castle, where in 1967 he became factory manager. When Napier Drewitt surrendered his personnel responsibilities in March 1978, Raper added them to his technical role and played a key part in extending company medical insurance beyond board directors.

Among the key appointments made by Wilson was that of Napier Drewitt, who in 1972 became personnel director.[44] Two years earlier Wilson had introduced him as a consultant, having worked with Drewitt when they both sat on the Courtauld board. Educated at Kendal School and Keble College, Oxford, where he read chemistry, Napier Drewitt joined British Celanese in 1936, becoming head of the chemical research laboratory and later their personnel manager.[45] Following the takeover of British Celanese by Courtaulds in 1957, Drewitt was appointed to the parent board five years later.[46] In Glaxo, personnel questions had fallen to Sir Robert Hutchings and his retirement in December 1967 had created a functional gap. Drewitt continued to take responsibility for such matters until 1978, when he became chairman of Glaxo Operations. Although a man of charm and integrity, Drewitt, rather in the mould of Jephcott, believed that it was essential to keep costs at a minimum in order to generate profits for investment. As a result, he pursued a parsimonious salary policy, driving a Morris Minor car himself as an example to his fellow executives. This lack of generosity discouraged some managers who moved to better paid posts with other companies.

The functional nature of the board was emphasised in March 1978 with the appointment of two additional directors.[47] Dr David Jack was elected as the first research and development director. Until then, successive chairmen Jephcott, Wilson and Bide, each having trained as scientists, had themselves retained responsibility for this role. However, the advances in pharmacology were so rapid that a specialist representative was now needed at the Holdings level. John Farrant became technical director when Raper took the personnel role in succession to Drewitt. Farrant had studied chemical engineering at University College London before working for ICI at Billingham.[48] Having met Dr Fred Wilkins and looking for new opportunities, he joined Glaxo in 1960. After terms at Barnard Castle and Greenford, in 1963 he was appointed factory manager at Ulverston before moving to Glaxo Laboratories (India) as commercial director and from 1970 as its managing director. Returning to the UK three years later, Farrant served as technical director of Glaxo Laboratories and then as group technical manager before assuming board responsibilities.

In April 1979, when David Smart was elected to a two-year term as president of the Association of the British Pharmaceutical Industry, he was appointed industry and general affairs director of Glaxo Holdings so that he could devote all his time to public matters. His role as commercial director was taken by Douglas Back. Educated at Queen's College, Oxford, he joined the sales department of Glaxo Laboratories in 1948, becoming one of Jephcott's personal assistants. In 1950 Back was appointed head of the Central Secretariat and after several managerial posts ran the bulk sales department at Greenford. The commercial director and, from July 1968, managing director of Glaxo Laboratories, his experience had largely been in the field of sales and marketing.

The major executive change for the future was the appointment of Paul Girolami as chief executive from 1 November 1980.[49] Sir Austin Bide had reached his sixty-fifth birthday in September and decided to reduce his responsibilities to prepare the ground for a successor, though he continued to serve as chairman of the group until his retirement in December 1985.[50] This represented a change of emphasis because until then the chief executives of Glaxo had all had scientific or production backgrounds. Girolami, a chartered accountant and the finance director, was from a different culture. He had been given considerable responsibilities by Wilson, with whom he had a natural intellectual affinity and he had consolidated his position with Bide. Along with Ray Camp, the company secretary and later the group's solicitor, he would often gather in Bide's office in the early evening to discuss the day's events in an informal way.[51] The involvement of Girolami in the defence of Glaxo against the Beecham bid had established his credentials as a heavyweight executive.

When Girolami became chief executive, he was succeeded as finance director by G. D. Neely, a chartered accountant, formerly chief accountant with Cadogan Investments, a management consultant with Unilever and finance director of the National Bus Company.[52] Latterly he had served on the board of Linfood Holdings. The appointment was not, however, to prove a lengthy one. On 13 June 1983, he offered his resignation in order to pursue a career in the City.[53]

Neely was succeeded as finance director by Charles Newcomb, who had an extensive knowledge of the group's financial arrangements, having been its auditor when a partner of Jackson, Pixley & Co.[54] In 1976, however, Coopers & Lybrand were elected as joint auditors of Glaxo Holdings, whilst also being appointed as sole auditor to every overseas subsidiary.[55] Although Clark Pixley were a medium-sized practice with a London headquarters, they could not provide the international coverage and broad range of financial advice that multinational corporations now required. Coopers & Lybrand as one of the 'big eight' firms had this expertise across the globe and had well established professional links with Girolami. In 1978, having become senior partner of Clark Pixley, Newcomb was approached by Girolami to offer him the post of group financial controller. Arthur Axe, formerly financial director of Allen & Hanburys, had retired and Girolami sought an experienced accountant who knew Glaxo well to improve the quality of reporting by subsidiaries. Regular, standardised returns were prepared assisted by the progressive introduction of computerised techniques. As a result, the centre became better informed and was able to produce fuller and more precise annual returns. In 1981 Newcomb resigned as financial controller to become an independent consultant, but two years later when Neely departed he was persuaded to return as finance director serving for a five-year period.

In November 1984 Bernard Taylor was appointed to the Holdings board as commercial director to take over these responsibilities from Douglas Back, who had retired in February. Having been a representative for Smith Kline & French, Taylor had joined Glaxo in 1963 as a sales manager based in New Zealand.[56] He remained there for four years before returning to the UK as new products manager of Glaxo Laboratories based at Greenford. Awarded a Sloan Fellowship at the London Business School in 1970 and identified as a potential senior executive, Taylor joined Glaxo Australia on the understanding that he would become its managing director in January 1972 when Griff Hunt retired. Over a period of ten years, Taylor established the company as one of the group's most important overseas subsidiaries, increasing its share of the market for prescription medicines from 1 to 4 per cent. In 1983, Sir Austin Bide invited him to return to Greenford to serve as chairman and managing director of Glaxo Pharmaceuticals UK – the principal manufacturing and sales subsidiary. This key appointment, set at the heart of the group's operations, was doubtless designed to broaden Taylor's management experience with a view to giving him greater responsibilities. These followed in April 1985 when he was appointed deputy chief executive at the same meeting that Paul Girolami became deputy chairman,[57] the two changes effectively settling the transfer of managerial authority. When Sir Austin Bide retired as chairman at the Annual General Meeting in October,[58] he was succeeded by Girolami. Taylor, in turn, became the chief executive.

The facilitating role of the company secretary had become an important one in Glaxo, not least because Bide had held this position for a number of years, latterly combining it with his main-board responsibilities. This office had the task of liaising with the management of subsidiaries, both at home and abroad, to advise them on policy issues and act as a sounding board for agenda items. In 1965 M. R. Camp became company secretary of Glaxo. A pharmacist who later qualified as a barrister, Camp had joined the sales department of Glaxo Laboratories in 1952, transferring a year later to the patents and trademarks department, and subsequently becoming company secretary of Glaxo Laboratories. As the group and its head office functions expanded, so it became necessary to employ an increasing number of specialists, particularly in the legal field to deal with patent and trade agreements. In December 1976, Camp relinquished the secretaryship in order to serve as Glaxo's solicitor, while Michael Allan, the assistant group secretary, was appointed in his place.[59]

Focusing the business: divestments

Initially most of Girolami's energies as chief executive were directed towards the launch and marketing of Zantac (see p. 251) and, following its success, the implementation of the decision to enter the United States as an effective trading organisation. However, it had become increasingly apparent that the group's resources were spread across too many disparate enterprises. Aware of the rising costs of pharmaceutical research and the need to concentrate on core activities, Girolami began a programme of divestment in 1984. E. R. C. Farmer, until then chief executive of Glaxo Pharmaceuticals UK, was given the task of putting this strategy into practice. The first subsidiary selected for sale was Vestric, the group's wholesaling company. During the latter part of the year, Farmer investigated the possibility of setting up Vestric as a wholly independent business.[60] This proved impractical and as an alternative he sought to establish a network of partnerships with as many as thirty other UK pharmaceutical companies, which Farmer believed, would 'have an interest in preserving an independent efficient wholesaler such as Vestric'.[61] No manufacturers expressed an interest, largely because of its poor financial performance and the collapse of resale price maintenance in 1979, followed by an increase in parallel imports (medicines manufactured overseas and shipped to the UK to be sold cheaply). Vestric had countered these adverse developments by reducing

Figure 6 **Glaxo Holdings in 1985: principal UK trading companies**

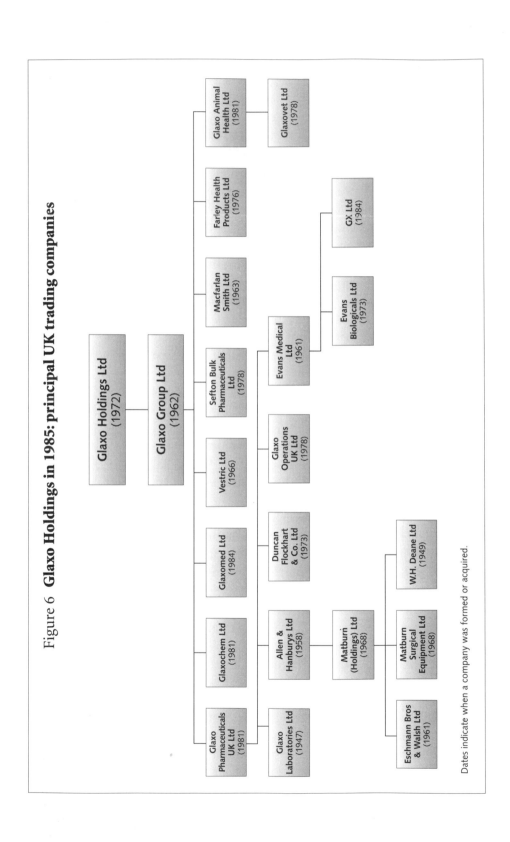

Dates indicate when a company was formed or acquired.

staff and operating costs, closing twenty-four of the original forty-six depots. Despite these enforced economies, profits continued to fall and in 1984 the company recorded a loss. With at best only a modest improvement forecast, Glaxo decided to sell the subsidiary to A. A. Holdings, a distribution group traditionally specialising in fuels but with a growing interest in pharmaceuticals. In the event, the sale proceeded for £10 million, which recouped about half the accumulated investment in Vestric.[62]

Glaxo also disposed of Matburn (Holdings) in 1985. The group had been created in 1968 to gather together the three surgical engineering companies owned by Glaxo: Eschmann Bros & Walsh, Matburn (Surgical Equipment) and W. H. Deane (High Wycombe). With cuts to capital spending by the NHS, they had falling orders and in 1984–85 Matburn had recorded a loss. In June 1985 W. H. Deane was subject to a management buy-out,[63] while the other companies in the surgical engineering group were sold to Smiths Industries in October.[64]

Although the disposal of Matburn had long been contemplated and represented only a very small element in the Glaxo Group, the same was not true of the decision to sell Farley Health Products in November 1985.[65] The company had been formed in 1975 by merging Farley's Infant Food with the food business formerly operated by Glaxo Laboratories and which included products such as Ostermilk, Glucodin, Complan and Farex, all of great historical significance to the company. Although the turnover of Farley Health Products had risen from £31.5 million in 1980–81 to £40.4 million in 1984–85, fierce competition and narrow margins had seen trading profits fall from a peak of £4.2 million in 1981–82 to £2.6 million in 1984–85.[66] By then, food sales accounted for only 5 per cent of the group's total turnover (excluding Vestric) and generated only 3 per cent of gross profits.[67] Substantial capital expenditure, particularly on spray drying plant at Kendal, was not expected to improve dramatically the company's financial performance. Given that Glaxo had taken the strategic decision to concentrate on its core pharmaceutical business, there seemed little alternative but to seek a buyer for Farley Health Products. Both Boots and Beecham expressed an interest and, in the event, Glaxo agreed to sell to the former in November 1985.[68] However, the disposal was not straightforward as the company's factory at Kendal was hit by an outbreak of salmonella shortly after a sale for £42 million had been agreed. The plant was shut down to eradicate the infection and the business put into voluntary liquidation.[69] In the event, Boots acquired Farley Health Products from the receiver for £18 million.[70] It was a particularly sad and undistinguished way for the group to have left foods after what had been a long and successful involvement.

Not only did Girolami decide to focus on pharmaceuticals, he also

decided to limit Glaxo's activities to novel, prescription medicines. As a result of acquiring smaller UK manufacturers, Glaxo made a host of drugs,
many of which had long since lost any patent protection and some were
common OTC preparations. Subject to widespread competition and tight
margins, they were not a source of great profit but absorbed considerable
resources in their production and marketing. In 1982, Evans Medical had
been given responsibility for the group's generic business in the UK. The
subsidiary was encouraged to expand and given the authority to invest at
its Speke factory within designated budgets. Over the three years from 1982,
turnover rose from £11 million to £29 million and its trading profit increased from £1.3 million to £3.1 million.[71] The improvement resulted from
sales of new generics and diamorphine, whilst their established products,
including vaccines, had tended to stagnate. Bernard Taylor, appointed to
the Holdings board in November 1984 as commercial director and later
chief executive in succession to Girolami, concluded that

> commercial success in generics arises either from the exploitation of the brief
> period of price firmness and limited generics competition, which immediately
> follows patent expiry of a branded pharmaceutical, or through some product
> advantage, which provides patent-like protection. Examples of the latter are di-
> amorphine which, in effect, is a monopoly for Evans and which through price
> increases now enjoys a 70 per cent gross margin and contributes 25 per cent of
> Evans' gross profit in the UK.[72]

Falling margins appeared to be an inevitable trend for new generics as
smaller competitors, with lower overheads, began to manufacture cheaper
variants. To combat this, Evans introduced the GX brand to identify the
medicine as having a guarantee of Glaxo quality and to justify a slightly
higher charge. Physicians were asked to prescribe GX products and
pharmacists to dispense them, while the DHSS had to pay a premium over
the tariff price. The campaign failed to convince health professionals that
the increment was merited and in 1985–86 sales totalled only £250,000
against a target budget of £3 million, generating losses of £1 million. Taylor
argued that 'the major part of the generics business will always be short-
term, low margin and of little interest to the group'.[73] He also identified an
inherent conflict with the patented element of Glaxo's pharmaceutical
business, where one of the aims was to build a brand loyalty that would
endure after legal protection had expired. The competition between GX
salbutamol, promoted by Evans, and Allen & Hanburys' Ventolin
illustrated the case, the price differential being more obvious than if it were
between Glaxo and a third party. As a result, Taylor recommended that 'the
group's interests would be best served by disengaging from the generics

business, thus removing the dichotomy of purpose which arises from our current policy'.[74] In the event, Evans Medical was subject to a management buy-out in July 1986 for £27 million.[75] Ironically, Taylor himself was to resign from Glaxo three years later and subsequently became chairman of Medeva, the group which, in turn, acquired Evans. Thus, the executive who argued for the company's disposal ultimately took responsibility for its continued existence.

The devolution of management

Although Girolami recognised the need to centralise authority during the 1970s to establish control over the group, he also believed that these achievements had come at a price. The emphasis on structural matters had, of necessity, led to the neglect of other strategic issues, particularly policy relating to sales and marketing. The gathering of power to the centre and largely into the hands of pharmaceutical specialists, who had no great knowledge of the group's other activities (foods, surgical equipment and wholesaling), contributed to their relative decline and encouraged the decision to dispose of these subsidiaries. Girolami also considered that many of Glaxo's overseas companies, particularly those in the developing trading areas, had been inhibited by centralised controls and he began a gradual process by which sales and marketing initiative was handed back to national subsidiaries. This policy took a number of years to work through and it was not formally announced until the winter of 1986, when it had been in operation in various territories. Outlined in the first issue of an international staff magazine, *Glaxo World*, Girolami observed that the group was like 'a far-flung empire made up – in many cases – of powerful independent companies'.[76] It was this very independence which he sought to encourage within defined parameters. His strategy, or 'philosophy' as he termed it, was based on the belief that the group had become centralised to the point that the natural enthusiasm and innovative spirit of managers had been dampened by the powerful core executive. The solution proposed by Girolami was not to delegate 'control' or 'direction' but as in the days of Jephcott and Wilson to devolve decision making about trading to those in the marketplace. Because the executives of national sales companies were closer to events, he argued, their responses would be more specific and more closely attuned to the culture in which they operated. 'When the group was less delegated', Girolami observed,

> when the centre sought to control almost everything, a result was to reinforce the concept of a geographical centre. However, as more and more regional re-

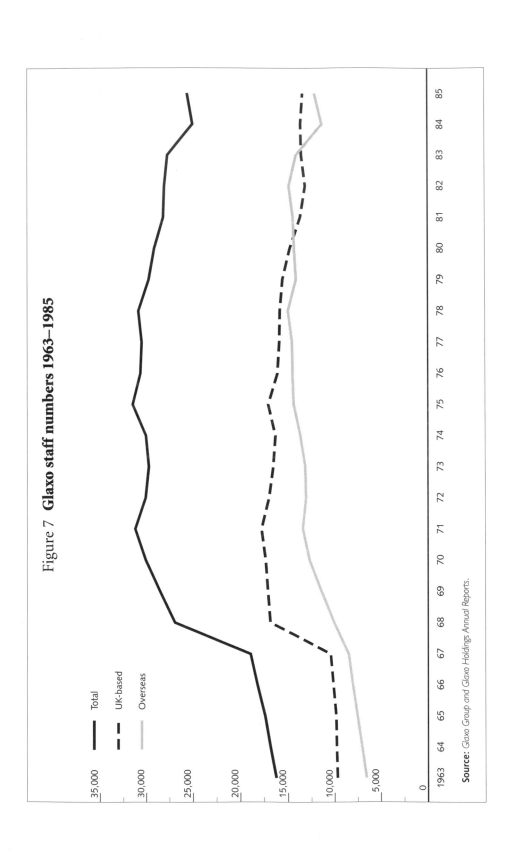

Figure 7 **Glaxo staff numbers 1963–1985**

Total

UK-based

Overseas

Source: *Glaxo Group and Glaxo Holdings Annual Reports.*

sponsibilities are passed to people offshore, then the centre becomes less a geographical than an organisational idea ... This question of 'centre', the meaning of
it is going to change. I think that the centre is not just Clarges Street [the executive location of Glaxo Holdings] – it is the international layer of management.[77]

Because operational responsibility was being devolved to those in the
front line of business, Girolami argued that the centre had to be restructured to provide the appropriate leadership and supervision. He suggested
that 'this role of direction' had three elements. First, the centre was the
repository of executive authority and ultimately responsible for drawing
up rules of conduct. Secondly, Girolami argued that it should have an international role, involving 'the worldwide co-ordination of the functions,
operations and activities of an integrated group business'. Thirdly, the centre was 'concerned with the setting of standards of quality in all its
processes, from research and development through to production and
marketing'.[78] Girolami's dynamic personal style, his seats on the boards of
major subsidiaries and his policy of travelling regularly to these overseas
companies enabled him to provide a strong strategic direction to foreign
marketing even while allowing substantial operating independence. In the
case of Zantac, which Girolami viewed as Glaxo's key product, the pricing,
marketing platform and other major decisions constituted strategic matters for the group and were generally determined centrally with input from
the operating companies.

Non-executive directors

In 1962, when Glaxo Group was formed, there were three non-executive directors: Sir Cyril Entwistle, appointed in 1947 (see p. 98), Sir Jeremy Raisman
who was also deputy chairman, appointed in 1948 (see p. 99), and Sir Edward
Playfair who had joined the board in 1961 (see p. 101). As in other major companies, Glaxo's non-executive directors were appointed either because they
were individuals with a proven record of decision making who could be
called upon to give impartial advice about a new strategy or key decision, or
because their background or experience made them particularly useful to
the group. They served as a collective sounding board and, because they were
not reliant upon Glaxo for their status or income, could speak without the
constraints that might apply to a salaried, career executive.

When Entwistle retired in 1964, Sir Alan Wilson appointed J. G. Beevor,
chairman of the Lafarge Organisation, Doulton & Co. and the Tilbury
Contracting Group, in his place. Beevor, a solicitor by training, was selected
for his general experience of business and he continued to serve on the

main board until December 1975. Sir Jeremy Raisman retired as deputy chairman in December 1968 and was succeeded in that role by Herbert Palmer (see p. 167). Palmer was, however, an executive director and to maintain the representation of non-executives, Wilson recruited Sir Henry Lintott, who had recently retired as British High Commissioner in Canada. When Sir David Barran retired as one of the managing directors of Royal Dutch Shell in 1972, the opportunity was taken to appoint him to the Holdings board.

After the retirement of Beevor in 1975, Bide recruited Lord Fraser of Kilmorack. He had recently served as deputy chairman of the Conservative Party Organisation after a lengthy period as the director of its research department. Bide had become acutely aware during the defence of Glaxo against the Beecham bid that the group had few established links either with the pharmaceutical industry or with public bodies and government. Once chairman, he consciously sought to build external connections, encouraging others to follow his lead. The introduction of Lord Fraser was, in part, a feature of this policy. With the retirement of Lintott, Sir Philip Rogers joined the board as a non-executive director in 1978. A career civil servant, he had served in the Colonial Office and elsewhere before becoming permanent secretary at the Department of Health and Social Security in 1970. Rogers was, therefore, well placed to advise the company on government policy relating to the NHS and in particular the supply of prescription medicines. With the retirement of Playfair in 1979 and that of Barran in May 1982, two vacancies were created. The first was filled in October 1982 by J. M. Raisman (the elder son of Sir Jeremy Raisman), then chairman and chief executive of Shell UK. Sir Ronald Arculus, a career civil servant, was appointed to the second post in May 1983. He had recently retired as British Ambassador in Italy after a lengthy career in the diplomatic service, during which he had held both commercial and technical posts. With the departure of Sir Philip Rogers in May 1984, Professor Ralf Dahrendorf joined in a non-executive capacity, having just retired as director of the London School of Economics. The departure of Lord Fraser in October 1985 was followed by the appointment of Sir Alistair Frame, a chemical engineer and businessman of wide experience, then chairman of the Rio-Tinto-Zinc Corporation.

GOVERNMENT REGULATION
AND THE MARKET

꭛

> The national health service, which pays almost the entire bill for
> prescription medicines, is not an ordinary buyer. The medicines
> are developed, manufactured and supplied by the pharmaceutical
> industry; they are prescribed by doctors; they are consumed by
> patients; and, through the National Health Service, the taxpayer
> eventually pays for them. But neither the doctor who prescribes
> nor the patient who consumes is immediately concerned with
> prices. It is the indirectness of their relationship with the industry
> which imposes on the Health Departments both a difficulty in
> controlling costs and a special duty to exercise a surveillance over
> prices to ensure … that they are both fair to the industry and the
> taxpayer.
>
> Report of the Committee of Enquiry into the Relationship of the Pharmaceutical
> Industry with the National Health Service 1965–1967.[1]

UNTIL THE passing of the 1968 Medicines Act, there were few
statutory limitations on the freedom of pharmaceutical companies
to market drugs in the UK. Indeed, the need for legislation was
being considered when, in November 1961, the toxic side-effects of thalidomide were revealed.[2] Although physicians had long been aware of adverse
reactions, it was not until the latter part of the nineteenth century that tests
were devised to measure their effects. In 1877, for example, the British Medical Association had set up a committee to investigate sudden and unex-
pected deaths linked with the use of chloroform anaesthetic.[3] At the end of
the First World War, a major outbreak of jaundice and fatal liver disease
among soldiers, prompted the Medical Research Committee to fund a
study into the use of arsenicals to treat syphilis. As regards the efficacy of

new drugs, however, it was not until the 1960s that serious thought was given directly to the design of clinical trials. Until then, the use of controls, to monitor a placebo response was rare and the statistical interpretation of results remained rudimentary. Some protection to the public was provided by various Food and Drug and Therapeutic Substances Acts. The Pharmacy and Medicines Act of 1941, which required that promotional material be consistent with the terms of the product licence, prohibited the advertisement of OTC preparations for the treatment of serious disorders. In addition, the Poisons Regulations and Dangerous Drugs Acts initiated a system for classifying the potency of medicines, designating those that required a doctor's prescription.[4] Statutory control of the use of medicines had been achieved in an *ad hoc* fashion by an accretion of specific but relatively limited laws that created innumerable loopholes. During the early sixties, for instance, anyone could launch a product in the UK no matter how inadequately tested or dangerous without a requirement to seek an independent opinion about its toxicity and the adequacy of conditions under which it was manufactured.

In the UK the Voluntary Price Regulation Scheme (VPRS), agreed between the Ministry of Health and the Association of British Pharmaceutical Industry, governed medicines supplied to the NHS. Introduced in June 1957 for a trial period of three years,[5] it offered three methods of price evaluation: the 'export criterion', the 'standard equivalent' and the 'trade price formula'. For the first, which was to prove the most important, the home price of medicines which had substantial exports (defined as 20 per cent or more of output), was not to be greater than the average overseas price.[6] Secondly, a drug that had limited exports was not to be priced higher than an equivalent medication. Thirdly, if neither of these two formulae were applicable, the price was to be computed on the basis of ingredient costs plus overheads, processing and a provision for wholesalers' discounts. However, manufacturers were at liberty to ignore all three arrangements and negotiate a price separately with the Ministry of Health. Finally, the most important concession granted to the pharmaceutical industry related to the first three years of a new drug's life, when companies were permitted to set charges without limitation, the so-called 'freedom period' to recoup research and development costs. Three years was considered adequate to allow a new medicine to establish itself at home and in overseas markets. This, in turn, provided evidence for the export price criterion.[7] By 1959, the prices of some 3,200 proprietary medicines had been negotiated under the VPRS, representing 88 per cent by value of those drugs that fell within its remit.[8]

Just as the scheme came into being, the cost of medicines consumed by the NHS rose dramatically by £9.6 million in 1956–57 to £67 million, after a period of relatively minor price rises. An official inquiry into prescription costs under Sir Henry Hinchliffe, the Manchester industrialist and governing director of Glazebrook Steel & Co, was ordered by the government. His report, published in 1959, revealed that these escalating figures did not result from a greater number of prescriptions but were the consequence of more expensive drugs: 'while there is no evidence of widespread and irresponsible extravagance in general practitioners' prescribing, there is scope for economy'.[9]

The report demonstrated that the gross cost of medicines had risen from £31.7 million in 1949–50 to £62.8 million in 1957–58 (Table 15, p. 452) at a time when the total number of prescriptions had only grown from 206.4 million to 209.1 million, the average cost of each one having doubled.[10] Although general practitioners and hospital consultants were urged to be more economical, and the public was chastised for its growing reliance upon 'the medicine habit',[11] no legislation followed and the VPRS remained intact.

Nevertheless, pressure for reform was heightened by evidence from the US Subcommittee on Anti-Trust and Monopoly, chaired by Senator Estes Kefauver. Inquiring into the costs and prices of four groups of medicines (corticosteroid hormones, tranquillisers, oral anti-diabetic drugs and antibiotics), it alleged that advertising abuses, and the practice of prescribing by brand rather than generic names, had undermined effective competition. Kefauver concluded that many of these products earned 'unreasonably high' profits,[12] while price fixing by some US companies later led to court convictions.[13] When the UK government reviewed the VPRS in January 1961, the Ministry of Health strengthened its control, especially over medicines that earned sales to the NHS in excess of £500,000. The Ministry established its right to negotiate direct with manufacturers to agree prices based on costs of production.

Safety of medicines

A powerful impetus to test for dangerous side effects was provided by the thalidomide disaster. The drug had been discovered by the German company Chemie Grunenthal in 1954, which claimed that it was an effective tranquilliser with no adverse side-effects. In 1956 the Distillers Company acquired its UK rights and tested its potential toxicity in animals with negative findings. Clinical trials in humans appeared to show that the drug was safe and in 1958 it was launched as Distaval. Thalidomide was withdrawn from the market in November 1961 following preliminary reports in the

BMJ of peripheral neuritis, and evidence from Australia that it was impli-
cated in foetal deformities. As a result, the medical profession campaigned
for standardised testing procedures and the setting up of an independent
organisation to supervise the introduction of new drugs. In July 1962,
Enoch Powell, the Health Minister, accepted the principle that an advisory
body should be established to review evidence on the toxicity of drugs before they entered clinical trials in humans.[14] To advise the government, a
sub-committee of the Standing Medical Advisory Committee was set up
under the chairmanship of Lord Cohen, then professor of medicine at the
University of Liverpool and president of the General Medical Council.

Wishing to demonstrate its probity, Glaxo considered establishing its
own 'Advisory Panel', involving independent experts, to make recommendations on the approval of new drugs.[15] Sir Charles Dodds, Courtauld professor of biochemistry at the University of London, was asked if he would
chair the panel and, in declining, suggested that Glaxo delay taking any
such action until the government had issued its own guidelines.[16] In April
1963, the Cohen Committee recommended that a central regulatory agency,
subsequently known as the Committee on Safety of Drugs, should be established on a voluntary basis. It would be official only in the sense that its
members were appointed by the Minister of Health, who would also provide its finance, accommodation and secretariat. Despite the fact that it had
no legal sanctions, both the Association of the British Pharmaceutical Industry and the Proprietary Association of Great Britain agreed that their
members would not submit for clinical trial or market a drug against its advice before the Committee on Safety of Drugs began to function on 1 January 1964. The new body was established with three sub-committees: that on
toxicity to evaluate data derived from studies on animals and healthy
human volunteers to determine whether the compound should be tested
on patients; that on clinical trials to assess the findings from such studies to
decide whether the drug could be approved for marketing; and that on adverse reactions to monitor undesirable side-effects of the drug once it had
been launched.[17] However, the voluntary approach advocated by Lord
Cohen's committee was not without its critics. Two pharmacist members
wrote a dissenting minority report urging immediate compulsory legislation. The majority, who did not rule out statutory controls, thought that
this would entail a lengthy parliamentary procedure and that a rapid
response was required to assuage public concerns.

Sir Derrick Dunlop, formerly professor of medicine at Edinburgh, was
appointed first chairman of the Committee on Safety of Drugs in June
1963. He and its first medical assessor, Dr Dennis Cahal (until then medical
advisor to Allen & Hanburys), placed great emphasis on the efficient han-

dling of submissions, which helped to win the confidence of the pharmaceutical industry. Whilst the Dunlop Committee set about establishing formal procedures for the regulation of new chemical entities, considerable debate took place about the methodology to be employed in clinical trials. In May 1964, for example, Dr T. B. Binns of Glaxo Laboratories and Dr W. J. H. Butterfield, professor of medicine at Guy's Hospital, argued in *The Lancet* for active co-operation between the pharmaceutical industry and academics in medical schools. 'Since the war', they argued

> clinical trials have revolutionised therapeutics. They have become the criterion by which the previous research is judged … It is abundantly obvious that clinical trials are a bottleneck in the development of drugs, but so far next to no attempt has been made to study, let alone to cater for, this new situation.[18]

In 1959, the Hinchliffe Committee had concluded that 'the present arrangements for the organisation and interpretation of clinical trials and for publication of results are inadequate … New drugs should be subjected to independent clinical trials as early as possible'.[19] Binns and Butterfield argued for the use of rigorous statistical tests, the expansion of departments of clinical pharmacology and greater levels of interest by hospital physicians in these inquiries. The theme was taken up in an editorial published in *The Lancet*, which described a ten-stage process of two and a half years' duration between the beginning of clinical trials and the drafting of a paper describing their results.[20]

In addition, concerns were expressed that the increasingly competitive environment might encourage pharmaceutical companies to exaggerate the therapeutic qualities of their products. The early 1960s had seen a form of medicinal mania sweep the UK as the public uncritically accepted advances in pharmacology and provided manufacturers with welcome opportunities to promote their drugs. In October 1963, for example, the *Evening Standard* had carried a story under the headline 'Super drug is a knockout discovery', concluding that the 'orange-white capsule will beat 'flu, pneumonia, bronchitis'.[21] A month later the *Sunday Times* printed an article under the heading 'New British drug is more effective than penicillin', in which it was claimed 'the first large scale trials suggest it is the perfect antibiotic, without the drawbacks of the existing ones'.[22] When Ceporin, Glaxo's injectable cephalosporin, was launched in 1964, the *Daily Mail* devoted a front-page spread to the antibiotic under the headline 'Wonderful new drug'. An interview with Sir Alan Wilson reported, whether accurately or not, the chairman as having said that Ceporin killed bacteria with 'almost miraculous speed' and produced 'no side effects or allergies'.[23] The hype that surrounded the launch attracted adverse comment in the medical press, the *BMJ* arguing that

> It is unfortunate that the discovery has been heralded with so much publicity in the mass media – press and television. Publicity of this kind makes it difficult for the practising doctor to make a sober assessment of the qualities of a new drug, especially in the face of importunity from patients whose ideas about the new 'wonder drug' are bound to be confused by propaganda.[24]

In 1965, the *Drug and Therapeutics Bulletin* suggested that some of the statements issued by Glaxo about Ceporin were 'misleading or need qualification'. The company had, for example, advised that 'Ceporin is indicated for use whenever mixed infections are present or suspected.' The *Bulletin* argued that

> the widespread use of cephaloridine (Ceporin) as a cover for mixed infections is to be deprecated for two reasons. First, since there is a cross-resistance between cephaloridine and the penicillinase-resistant penicillins, any drug in this group should be used with discretion to prevent the emergence of staphylococci resistant to the whole group. Secondly, a few of the small number of patients already treated with cephaloridine have developed rashes or drug fever, suggesting that sensitisation may occur fairly readily.[25]

Glaxo had also suggested in its promotional material that Ceporin's 'intense bactericidal activity means that resistance is unlikely to develop', to which the *Bulletin* countered

> Bactericidal action of an antibiotic does not mean that resistance is unlikely to develop. Streptomycin, for example, is intensely bactericidal, but resistance to it develops with unparalleled rapidity.[26]

According to the *Bulletin*, Glaxo had agreed to revise the content of their literature, though this remained a voluntary process.[27]

In the meantime, pressure on the government by the medical and pharmacy professions to broaden the scope of statutory controls continued. In September 1967, a White Paper, 'Forthcoming Legislation on the Safety, Quality and Description of Drugs and Medicines', was published and provided the basis for the Medicines Act, passed in the following year.[28] The patient was to be protected in two ways:

> first, existing law will be fortified to ensure that the product supplied to the customer is what he asks for, and that he is not misled by description and labelling

or by unsupported therapeutic claims; and secondly, the law will provide, so far as possible, that doctors, dentists, veterinarians, and pharmacists can rely on the purity and efficacy of the substances they prescribe, supply and use, and be fully informed about their properties – desirable and undesirable.[29]

Under its terms, the Secretary of State for Social Services and the Minister of Agriculture were to act as the licensing authority governing the marketing, importation and manufacture of drugs for human and veterinary use.[30] The Act also established a Medicines Commission that was responsible for advising the two ministers on broad aspects of policy regarding drugs and to direct the preparation of the Pharmacopoeia. The Committee on Safety of Medicines, as it was renamed, together with the Veterinary Products Committee, both fell under its jurisdiction, and the former was responsible for making recommendations about whether new compounds should be granted a licence on the basis of their safety, efficacy and quality.[31] In this way a comprehensive system of controls, procedures and penalties was implemented with the co-operation of the pharmaceutical industry and the medical profession.

In the United States the process for approving new medicines fell to the Food and Drug Administration (FDA), which, from the passing of the 1962 Drug Amendments legislation, was required to collect evidence of adverse reactions to new products. The American approval process was regarded as more demanding and generally took longer than that in the UK during the twenty years from 1964. As a result, fewer drugs were licensed in the US than in Britain over this period. However, a study of those medicines authorised for use in the two countries but subsequently withdrawn when side effects became a cause for concern showed a similar rate, suggesting similar safety procedures. Among those drugs introduced between 1964 and 1983, five had been withdrawn in America and eight in the UK, while of those launched after 1974, four had been discontinued in the former and three in the latter.[32] The total number of withdrawals represented only 2 per cent of all new drugs in the two markets and suggested, therefore, that each regulatory system was effective in identifying compounds associated with toxic side effects.

The regulation of price

Concerns about the rising costs of medicines supplied to the NHS were raised as early as 1957 and led to the appointment of the Hinchliffe Committee (see p. 223). As the drugs bill continued to rise, Enoch Powell, the Minister of Health, announced to the House of Commons in a short written answer in May 1961 that he proposed 'to use section 46 of the Patents Act 1949, which enabled a government department to use patented goods for services of the Crown, in obtaining certain drugs for the hospital services either from manufacturers in this country or from abroad'.[33] Less expensive equivalents of widely used medicines, notably the tetracyclines, chloramphenicol and chlorothiazide, were produced in other countries where patent laws were less stringent. Some hospitals had begun importing small quantities, for as little as half the UK price, but were wary of ordering more for fear of prosecution under the existing patent legislation. By invoking section 46, Powell was able to obtain supplies legally and, through central bulk buying, to effect substantial economies. He was aware that manufacturers needed adequate profits to finance future research but wished to demonstrate such power as the government possessed. By putting the supply of British hospitals out to tender, Powell concluded contracts with one Danish and four Italian companies for the supply of tetracyclines and saved an estimated £984,000 during 1961.[34] Pfizer decided to challenge the Minister's action in the courts but, after an appeal to the House of Lords, lost the case by the narrowest of margins.

In June 1965, the Ministry of Health, content with having established the principle, announced that it would stop importing cut-price medicines when the current contracts expired in the following October. They had been influenced by finding that some cheaper drugs bought overseas did not meet UK quality standards. In addition, the government was also concerned that if excessive price reductions were implemented domestic manufacturers, who exported about one-third of their output, would be driven into financial difficulties with consequences for the balance of payments. Indeed, Glaxo derived almost two-thirds of its turnover from overseas business in the late 1950s and early 1960s.[35] Furthermore, three-quarters of the pharmaceutical industry in Britain was owned by foreign multinationals and it was felt that draconian measures would simply encourage them to withdraw their investments.[36] Nevertheless, armed with the power of section 46, officials were able to negotiate lower prices. The end of government purchasing from abroad rapidly followed the setting up of the Sainsbury Committee in May 1965 to examine the relationship of the UK pharmaceutical industry and the NHS. Lord Sainsbury, the chief executive of the retail grocery chain, was appointed as the chairman, its other members being drawn largely from the medical profession. At Glaxo, Palmer and Bide prepared representations[37] and their 'Memorandum of evidence', submitted in July 1966,[38] argued that the transactions between the Ministry of Health and the pharmaceutical industry are in essence those existing between a monopoly purchaser and a number of suppliers ... Such a monopoly purchaser required fewer safeguards than a large number of unorganised purchasers, but in settlement of a large number of individual transactions and in avoidance of elaborate and expensive administrative machinery, there is need for, if possible, simple procedures for the determination of fair and reasonable prices.[39]

As a result, Glaxo favoured the retention of the VPRS in a modified form, given that the British pharmaceutical industry 'can only export successfully in competition with other companies of other origin if its customers believe that the drugs that it produces are of the highest quality, of reasonable price and acceptable to the National Health Service'.[40] They concluded that 'there is no evidence to suggest that pharmaceutical invention would be improved in quality or quantity by government direction or control'.[41]

The Sainsbury Report, published in October 1967, concluded that 'the cost to the National Health Service has been inflated by excessive prices to the extent of several million pounds' over the three years from 1963 to 1965.[42] Although its authors acknowledged that the industry had provided 'the people of this country with medicines of great value', they argued that the 'profit on capital employed on pharmaceuticals has in some cases been less than might be expected and in some others much higher than is reasonable, even taking into consideration the risks involved'.[43] Although the Sainsbury investigation showed that reductions in the costs of medicines no longer covered by the three-year 'freedom period' were sometimes delayed, this was not Glaxo's practice. In fact, the company could have been accused of undercharging for certain innovative medicines such as Ventolin, a point repeatedly made by its US collaborator, Schering (see p. 374). Glaxo cut the price of Betnovate by 13 per cent when the drug emerged from the freedom period in 1966.[44] In the case of phenoxymethylpenicillin (Crystapen V), introduced in 1957, the company reduced its price by 10 per cent when it emerged from the protected three years, while the competitive nature of the antibiotic market and the sensitivities exposed by the Pfizer case led to a series of reductions which produced a cumulative drop of 66 per cent by 1966.

Given the shortcomings of the VPRS, the Sainsbury Committee proposed a revised system:

For any existing medical speciality product ... and for any new medical speciality product on its introduction, the Ministry should be entitled to obtain from the manufacturer a Standard Cost Return, showing direct costs of labour and materials and indirect costs comprising works overheads, administration and general overheads, and the allowances for sales promotion and for research and development that are apportioned to the product. Standard Cost Returns should be required for all new medicines on being licensed ... for all existing medicines with National Health Service sales exceeding £250,000 per annum ...[45]

The Committee recognised that this, in itself, would not solve the problem of overcharging as the definition of 'reasonable profits' was open to interpretation, given the need to finance future research.[46] However, without the proposed Standard Cost Return

the Ministry would have no way at all of judging the reasonableness of the firm's proposed prices. The Ministry must satisfy themselves that high rates of expected return are indeed justified by unusual enterprise or willingness to accept risk, or are due to particularly favourable export prospects.[47]

Following these recommendations, the accounting controls on UK pharmaceutical companies were tightened. All businesses with sales of medicines over £750,000 were to supply the Department of Health with a standardised Annual Financial Return, giving details of costs and capital employed in the previous year; information that would play an important part in the negotiation of prices.

However, these changes to the VPRS did not meet with universal approval and Roche refused to accept the new system. Reaping the benefits of their benzodiazepine anxiolytics, chlordiazepoxide (Librium) and diazepam (Valium), Roche feared their profits would be greatly curtailed.[48] Resorting to legislation passed in the First World War but never implemented, the Conservative government issued the first compulsory patent licences, allowing generic manufacturers to make diazepam. The upshot was a price war that forced Roche to cut the cost of Valium. When Roche subsequently refused to grant the NHS the usual rebate for large-volume purchases of the drug, the government threatened to investigate its pricing policies. Roche offered to provide the necessary calculations and details of turnover on condition that they were treated confidentially. The authorities refused and referred the matter to the Monopolies Commission. Reporting in April 1973, it recommended a reduction of 40 per cent for Librium and 75 per cent for Valium, which the Ministry of Health sought to enforce by government orders. Roche fought the cuts, taking the matter to the House of Lords, where they lost their appeal. Adolf Jann, chairman of Roche, then sought a compromise.[49] In November 1975, Roche agreed to the revised terms of the VPRS and settled the back payments in return for increases in the prices of its tranquillisers.

The Office of Health Economics estimated that the cumulative effect of reductions secured under the VPRS over the previous five years resulted in a saving of £18 million in 1970 on sales totalling £170 million.[50] Given that it has proved impossible to define 'reasonable' profits or costs, the scheme continued to rely on negotiation and goodwill. Its survival throughout the 1970s and 1980s has been cited as a reason for the continuing strength of the UK pharmaceutical industry, providing manufacturers with a secure home market in which to launch products before attempting to compete overseas (see p. 235). In 1977 the VPRS was renamed the Pharmaceutical Price Regulation Scheme (PPRS) to reflect the 'sanctions' and procedures of last 'recourse', which ministers had available under Section 46 of the 1949 Patents Act, though it remains a voluntary agreement without statutory powers.[51]

In practice, the PPRS controlled profits rather than charges. The Department of Health decided that 'it is unrealistic to allocate all of a company's costs ... between the different medicines that it supplies', preferring to assess the overall return on capital on the assumption that if this appears to be reasonable then the same should be true of what the NHS paid for all of its medicines.[52] The proportions of a company's cost and capital bases attributable to NHS sales formed the basis of a profit and loss account, the surplus being expressed as a percentage of capital. Companies were given a target return of between 17 and 21 per cent, depending, in part, upon research and development commitments. Although the drugs bill paid by the government has continued to rise in real terms, it has not increased disproportionately, remaining below 10 per cent of total NHS costs (see Table 16, p. 453). When judging a reasonable level of profit, the PPRS deliberately discriminated in favour of those companies with major operations in the UK. The Department of Health was mandated to take account of 'the contribution which the company makes or is likely to make to the economy, including foreign earnings, investment, employment or research'.[53] Those groups with laboratory and production facilities in the UK were allowed higher margins than a foreign business with little more than a sales organisation.

Even supporters of the pharmaceutical industry conceded that competition over price was not the major expression of inter-company rivalry. The peculiar nature of the market, in which the effective decision maker (the physician) is separated from the buyer (a government or health care scheme), the inelasticity of demand and the need for effective, reliable products, was believed to render active price competition a secondary factor for most major drug companies. Their strategies aimed not at cutting costs to make their medicines cheaper than other producers, but at discovering more potent or innovative therapies or at worst finding new uses for existing remedies, which, in turn, would enable them to set an equivalent or possibly slightly higher charge to capture business from their rivals. However, the notion that price competition did, in fact, play an important role even in regulated economies was revitalized in 1975 by George Teeling-Smith, director of the Office of Health Economics, in collaboration with Duncan Reekie. Together they published a booklet entitled 'The Canberra hypothesis', which argued that companies took account of the cost of existing therapies when assessing the price of a new drug.[54] Teeling-Smith and Reekie included data to show that the highest priced of the first four non-steroidal anti-inflammatories introduced in Britain had the lowest market share. Furthermore, an analysis of two UK topical steroids revealed that the second, launched at a discount, captured the greater market share. Although not identified, this case probably referred to the lower price that Glaxo charged when launching Betnovate as a challenge to ICI's existing product, Synalar (see p. 246). Teeling-Smith and Reekie concluded that this evidence demonstrated the influence of actual and expected price competition.[55] Their general contention was that in a research-based industry such as pharmaceuticals, innovation played a greater part in determining price levels than classical competition between rival businesses and that companies would charge a premium rate only if the product was of particular novelty.[56]

In fact, pharmaceutical markets, whether highly regulated or left by the state to find their own price levels, are not homogeneous but divided into distinct sectors determined by the nature of the disease, the number and type of patients that suffer its effects, the availability of rival therapies and perceived values of medicines. A life-threatening and widespread disorder, such as hypertension, which is treated effectively by medication, has attracted fierce competition for potentially vast commercial rewards. Some severe or distressing disorders, such as cystic fibrosis or Huntington's chorea, may only affect a very small proportion of the population, while others, such as autism, may not readily lend themselves to traditional pharmacological interventions. In these cases pharmaceutical companies have found it difficult to justify the high cost of research and development programmes, leading to relatively few modern competing therapies.

The effectiveness of the PPRS in preventing manufacturers from charging excessive prices was examined by a comparative study of identical drugs marketed in Japan, the US and Europe.[57] A sample of eight companies was selected and their selling prices, net of taxes and retail margins, were contrasted for 1980–81 by both standardised packs and dosage unit. The general finding was that charges in Japan tended to be approximately twice those of America, but that European prices were only marginally higher

than those in the US.[58] The cost of medicines in the UK was consistently
below those recorded in Europe (France, Switzerland and Germany).[59] It
was concluded that controls in Japan were less rigid than in the other nations, allowing prices to rise to higher levels and generating greater profits,
which, in turn, could encourage multinational pharmaceutical groups to
invest more widely there.[60]

Under the auspices of the VPRS and its successor body, Glaxo took a responsible position in the pricing of medicines. The paternalistic philosophy established by Jephcott was designed to generate high quality
medicines at a fair price. Indeed, in the group's annual report Jephcott regularly complained of the pressure on margins and calculated that over the
twelve years to June 1960 the price of medicines sold to the NHS had fallen
on average by 6.5 per cent each year, whilst basic wage rates had risen by a
cumulative 70 per cent and raw material costs by 20 per cent.[61] Although it
appeared that the company had been swept along in the general euphoria
of the mid 1960s for antibiotics and corticosteroids and that this influenced
the tone of its promotional material, there was no suggestion that Glaxo
had overcharged for these medicines. Indeed, David Smart, the group commercial director for much of the 1970s, believed that with public concern
over the rising cost of drugs sold to the NHS, companies were obliged to
moderate their prices and that excessive increases in a context of finite budgets would simply result in fewer prescriptions, ultimately to the detriment
of patients. This, he argued, would eventually undermine the established
reputation of the company.[62]

Nevertheless, Glaxo also tried to avoid underpricing its medicines in the
UK. In October 1974, for example, when high levels of inflation had eroded
the company's returns, representation was made to the Department of
Health to grant increases to the price of Glaxo's prescription medicines,
and an overall increment of £2 million was authorised.[63] A complicated
two-way relationship existed between the price of medicines at home and
abroad. In the 1950s and 1960s, Glaxo usually set the price of a new product
by what it felt the UK market would bear and often sought to undercut
competitor medicines. Prices overseas were then related to this figure and
often considered modest by their US counterparts. Aware of this crucial relationship, successive governments resisted the temptation to cut NHS expenditure by forcing down the cost of medicines. Furthermore, under the
VPRS, the UK price for drugs with substantial exports (defined as over 20
per cent of output) was not to be higher than the average overseas price.
Hence, it was important not to undersell products abroad as this could
have the effect of depressing UK returns.

A sea change for Glaxo occurred in 1981 when Girolami argued that

Zantac should be priced considerably above that of its main competitor, Tagamet. Received wisdom dictated that the second drug in a new thera-peutic area should be launched at a small discount. Girolami believed that its superior qualities (some of which were only beginning to emerge) justi-fied a higher price (see p. 250). It was a view which did not meet with com-plete agreement. David Jack, the research and development director, who was responsible for the discovery of ranitidine, thought that in the long run society would suffer as finite resources were consumed more rapidly by ex-pensive new medicines:

> My fear was that if the price was too high, the drug would not be used ... The biggest problem is the trouble the government and society will have in provid-ing good healthcare for an ageing population with greater and greater need. The economics of the provision of healthcare is the big problem ...[64]

The higher price asked for Zantac over Tagamet was justified by clinical superiority and helped to defray the group's rising expenditure on research and development. Pharmaceutical companies argued that it was unreason-able to price new medicines on a cost-plus basis;[65] that is to calculate what it had cost to discover Zantac and take it through the development pro-gramme and then to attempt to recoup that sum, together with a profit el-ement. Glaxo, in common with other leading manufacturers, maintained that, because they relied for their future existence on the discovery of novel drugs, the costs of current and future research should determine the price of existing medicines. Zantac was needed, therefore, not to pay for past en-deavours but to generate funds for products about to enter the pipeline. Whilst the force of this case was undeniable, it could, perhaps, be claimed that over a period of ten years Zantac earned more than enough income for prospective research and development projects. The commercial success of the drug was phenomenal and, when setting the price in 1981, Glaxo could not have reasonably predicted that it would become the highest-selling pre-scription medicine of all time.

In the 1980s, pharmaceutical companies increasingly sought to estab-lish prices in terms of overall reductions in health care costs. If, for ex-ample, a novel and potent medicine could be shown to shorten treatment times, so that patients were discharged from hospital more rapidly, then the savings could be far greater than the additional cost of the drug. A medicine with a higher price could be justified if a cost-benefit calcula-tion demonstrated an overall gain to the health service and society as a whole. As a result, pharmaceutical companies found themselves increas-ingly involved in the discipline of pharmaco-economics.[66] In 1990, for example, Glaxo launched ondansetron (Zofran) for the prevention of nausea in patients receiving chemotherapy to treat cancer. Two years later a cost-benefit analysis compared the efficacy of ondansetron with an existing generic medicine, metoclopramide. The number of emetic episodes from a clinical trial were compared and the treatment costs (including nursing care and junior doctor time) were calculated. The study showed that 'if therapeutic success is defined as the avoidance of emesis and antiemetic side-effects, then the two therapies would be equally cost-effective at a drug price ratio of 5 to 1'.[67] In practice, however, Glaxo priced ondansetron at £81 for a pack of ten 8mg tablets, while twenty 10mg tablets of generic metoclopramide sold for only 46p.[68] The company justified the differential on the grounds of ondansetron's superior therapeutic qualities and the length of the research programme.

After the launch in 1991 of Glaxo's anti-migraine drug, sumatriptan (Imigran), *The Lancet* explored the wider value to society of such a novel medicine.[69] Although the direct cost to the NHS of treating migraine sufferers was estimated at only £23 million, the potential benefits appeared far larger. On the basis that 10 per cent of the UK population experienced one attack a month, it was estimated that the 67 million migraine episodes a year could cost the national economy between £150 and £300 million. Calculations of this kind were used by Glaxo to justify charging for a relatively expensive medicine, together with the fact that its novelty had demanded a nineteen-year research and development programme.

National regulations: their commercial impact

Some economists have argued that one reason for the comparative success of the UK's pharmaceutical industry has been the liberal attitude taken by governments, particularly after 1979, and the commercial opportunities provided by the PPRS. In practice, the NHS purchases over 98 per cent of prescription medicines sold in the UK, the sixth-largest pharmaceutical market in the world.[70] The NHS does not operate a national reimbursement list (a categorisation of medicines with varying levels of state funding) and there are no price-setting criteria. The UK also has one of the most liberal regulatory systems in Europe.[71] The fact that many of the leading US, Swiss, German and Swedish pharmaceutical companies have established substantial research and manufacturing bases in Britain is perhaps evidence of the industry-friendly nature of this policy. Furthermore, it has been suggested that the relative strength of the UK (with four major companies and a host of smaller producers until 1995) was, in part, a function of an established domestic market into which new medicines could be

launched at favourable rates of return. In France, by comparison, a more
fragmented and less consistent system of regulation may have made it more
difficult for major companies to emerge, despite the relative size of the
market (almost three times that of the UK in terms of sales).[72] In 1993, for
example, not a single French company was in the top fifteen ranked by
pharmaceutical sales, a listing which included two UK, two German and
three Swiss groups.[73]

The British system, where the government purchases medicines on behalf of its patients at the recommendation of doctors, is, of course, very different from that in the US. There, the individual is largely responsible for
making financial provision for the cost of health care. As servicemen returned to civilian life after the Second World War, many enrolled in private
insurance schemes, such as Blue Cross, recognising how expensive hospital
treatment had become. By 1980, over 80 per cent of the population had
some form of health care coverage.[74] Blue Cross was originally established
as a 'fee-for-service' plan, by which the provider was paid direct for treatment administered according to the terms of a contract that defined the
limits of care. In addition, health maintenance organisations, including
Kaiser Foundation Hospitals, were founded, where those insured (or their
employers) paid a monthly fee to cover physicians' visits, medication and
other non-hospital treatments. These pre-paid plans have an inbuilt incentive to keep patients out of hospital as a way of keeping costs to a minimum. Preferred provider organisations were also established which
negotiated contracts with doctors and hospitals to offer a range of medical
services to their subscribers. Medicare and Medicaid, set up in the 1960s,
were schemes sponsored by the federal government to ensure that the
elderly and poor could obtain treatment, while other state programmes
included the Veterans Administration.

In the 1970s, when health care costs in the US reached 7.5 per cent of
GNP, President Nixon declared a national crisis about the rising trend of
expenditure. By 1989 costs had increased to 11 per cent of GNP and in 1992
reached 14 per cent.[75] In 1993, the US Office of Technology Assessment,
having been commissioned by Congress to investigate claims that prescription drug prices were too high, issued its report, which showed that pharmaceutical companies did, indeed, record returns 2 or 3 per cent higher
than those in comparable industries.[76] Profits on new drugs introduced in
the early 1980s were calculated as being 4.3 per cent of their estimated life-
time sales, though there was considerable volatility. Defenders of the US
system pointed to the success of its domestic industry, which has more
companies in the league table of the largest twenty than any other nation.
The margins have been justified in relation to escalating research costs,

which grew in real terms by 10.6 per cent per annum during the 1980s, or by 6.9 per cent over the thirty years from 1961.[77] In contrast to the UK, successive administrations in the US have declined to introduce wide-ranging regulations to manage the provision of health care, leaving the matter to market forces. While all sides appear to agree that the continuing escalation in spending cannot be supported in the context of an ageing population, the various interests have failed to find a solution acceptable to the medical profession, the pharmaceutical industry and legislators.

The relationship between regulatory systems and the health of a nation's pharmaceutical companies is complex. In the UK and US, a liberal attitude towards pricing appears to have enabled well-established domestic industries to flourish. However, minimal controls may not of themselves provide an encouraging environment. In Italy, for example, the absence of patent protection until 1979 discouraged innovation as companies were aware that they could not defend a novel and costly product when it was copied by their competitors. Furthermore, no clear correlation existed between price regulation and consumption expenditure on medicines. Denmark, Germany and the UK, nations in which certain pricing freedoms are allowed, have some of the lowest growth rates in public drug spending, while in Portugal a sharp increase during the 1980s, higher than the country's rate of inflation, suggested that their efforts at price control had not proved effective.[78]

Brand v. generic pharmaceuticals

One American study published in 1962, which drew heavily upon the findings of the Kefauver Report, concluded

> on the basis of experience in the corticosteroids, tranquilizers and antibiotic markets, that genuine price competition among ethical drugs is effectively prevented, for the most part, by the existence of product patent privileges. Patent or patent application holders may exercise restrictions on output, and the resulting high levels of prices used to finance selling campaigns which contribute to the otherwise serious imperfections of market information and make it impossible for small sellers of generic name products to obtain any significant share of the retail prescription market …[79]

In the UK novel chemical entities were protected by patent, which during the 1960s and 70s had a life of sixteen years (see p. 260). During this period, the medicine could be manufactured and sold only by the patentee, who marketed the product under its brand name. Drugs were also given a generic name that related to their scientific characteristics. The brand name, by comparison, bore no relationship to the medicine's chemical composition and was designed to appeal to physicians in the form of a memorable epithet, often with healing connotations. For example, Glaxo's bronchodilator received the generic name salbutamol but was called Ventolin for marketing purposes, while its longer-acting variant, salmeterol was named Serevent. Objections to this system had been raised by the medical profession during the 1960s on the grounds that brand names gave no clue to a drug's active ingredients and could lead to prescribers being unduly influenced by promotional material. The government favoured reform to reduce the cost of medicines supplied to the NHS as pharmacists were compelled to supply a branded product when prescribed even if a generic version were available at considerably reduced price.

One of the boldest recommendations of the Sainsbury Report was that brand names be abolished. It argued that medicines, whether subject to patent or not, should be marketed under an official name approved by the Medicines Commission, with or without a 'house mark'.[80] The Sainsbury Committee believed that this would lead to

> a more scientific approach to prescribing. We think it impracticable to ask doctors to prescribe by approved [generic] names while brand names are still heavily advertised. We do not think that the choice of medicines to fill doctors' prescriptions should automatically lie with the pharmacists outside the doctors' control.[81]

Following representations by the pharmaceutical industry, the government decided against this reform and no such changes were included in the Medicines Bill of 1968. The Ministry of Health had been persuaded that the effectiveness of a particular drug was not solely related to its active ingredients and that an individual's physiological response could also be a function of its pharmacological formulation. The import of poor quality generic medicines had convinced the government of the need for quality controls and it was thought, in the absence of elaborate testing procedures, that the best safeguard was the reputation of an established manufacturer, selling medicines by brand name. As a result, the dual system of nomenclature has remained in place in the UK, as in other Western countries, while a continuing debate has flourished over the nature of patent protection (see p. 260). Even the *BMJ*, which had been campaigning for reforms, concluded in March 1968 that the abolition of brand names was probably not 'practicable or even desirable'.[82]

During the 1970s and 1980s, the Ministry of Health encouraged physicians to substitute generic for branded medicines in the hope that this would lead to important savings. Even in the US, where the regulatory authorities were relatively liberal over the issue of price, 'drug product selection' legislation was passed in fifty states and the District of Columbia permitting pharmacists to dispense generic equivalents.[83] However, two studies conducted in 1974 revealed that the assumption that such substitutions would substantially reduce expenditure was over optimistic. The first investigation, which compared seven leading medicines (including tetracycline, penicillin G and prednisone), established that the price to the consumer of the generic was lower than the branded product for five of the drugs at all but one of forty-six pharmacies in a single Midwestern city.[84] The second inquiry, which compared the retail prices of three groups of penicillins (Gram-positive, broad-spectrum and anti-staphylococcal), revealed wide variations. Although branded products were in general more expensive, the great range in generic prices could result in some costing more than the cheapest trademarked product.[85] Generic prescribing did not guarantee that the patient received the lowest-cost, equivalent therapy. However, a further study, conducted ten years later (between April and June 1984), demonstrated that the price paid by 1,363 pharmacies in thirty-nine states to manufacturers for twenty-one leading medicines was always lower in the case of generics.[86] The survey also showed that the consumer usually paid more for branded products, though a far wider variation in prices suggested that the selection of a generic was not in itself a guarantee of lowest-cost therapy.[87] The fact that pharmacies were consistently charged less for generics by 1984 implied that physicians and hospitals had become increasingly cost conscious over the previous decade and chose medicines more selectively than before.

Nationalisation of the pharmaceutical industry

Following the findings of the Sainsbury Committee that the NHS had been overcharged for medicines by some companies, the Labour Party turned its attention to the pharmaceutical industry. The party's 'Programme for Britain', presented at the 1972 Party Conference, outlined a number of proposals to extend public ownership and study groups were set up to work on specific economic sectors, including pharmaceuticals.[88] The plan was given an impetus in the following year on the grounds that 'the NHS was the major customer of the drug industry', while the Manifesto for the February 1974 election outlined Labour's intentions:

> We shall also take over profitable sections or individual firms in those industries
> where a public holding is essential to enable the Government to control prices,

stimulate investment, encourage exports, create employment, protect workers and consumers from the activities of irresponsible multi-national companies ... We shall therefore include in this operation, sections of pharmaceuticals, road haulage, construction ...[89]

Harold Wilson won the election by the slimmest of margins. When, in the summer of 1974, Tony Benn, the Minister for Industry, supported by Wilson and Edward Short, the Leader of the House, reiterated his intention to take UK pharmaceutical companies into state ownership, Glaxo began a concerted defence.[90] Bide, as chairman, prepared a board paper which recommended that the group raise the level of support it gave to the Association of the British Pharmaceutical Industry and considered the question of political donations. Recognising that this represented 'a departure from its traditional attitude of neutrality and non-involvement', it was concluded that the very survival of Glaxo merited such a change of policy. As a result, the directors voted to give £20,000 to the Conservative Party together with a donation of £1,000 a year for three years to the Centre for Policy Studies.[91]

Although the Labour Party won the October 1974 election with an increased majority, it had made no mention of the proposed nationalisation in its Manifesto, aware that it would have aroused considerable opposition from potentially powerful lobby groups.[92] The proposal was never formally abandoned and in June 1978, with the prospect of a further election at hand, Glaxo voted to donate £25,000 to the Conservative Party because of the continuing 'threat of nationalisation'.[93] Under the leadership of Margaret Thatcher, the Conservative Party had pledged to reduce the power of the state and thus end any prospect of nationalisation. Nevertheless, Glaxo continued to make annual gifts to the Conservative Party throughout the eighties, increasing the sum from £25,000 in 1984 to £35,000 in 1986, and raising its donation to the Centre for Policy Studies to £5,000 per annum.[94] In May 1987, with an election imminent, Norman Tebbit, chairman of the Conservative Party, requested that the payment be brought forward by one month,[95] and, as the *Annual Report* stated, the group's contribution was raised to £50,000 for Conservative Central Office and £10,000 to the Centre for Policy Studies.[96] The donation continued during the early nineties and was subject to a series of small increments, so that in 1994 the two contributions stood at £60,000 and £12,000 respectively.[97]

The continuing threat of nationalisation during the seventies had also influenced the appointment of Lord Fraser as a non-executive director in November 1975. After a long career at Conservative Central Office, Fraser had recently retired as deputy chairman of the party and was permitted to hold two external consultancies.[98] In the summer of that year he was approached by Bide and offered a seat on the Glaxo board, which he continued to hold until 1985. Although he was not immediately replaced, Lord Howe, formerly Chancellor of the Exchequer and Foreign Secretary, was elected to the Glaxo board in the summer of 1991, an appointment in tune with a general corporate climate in which major international companies found it valuable to have retired cabinet ministers as advisers. In 1995, after Sir Colin Corness had become the non-executive chairman of Glaxo, the group announced that it would cease to make political donations and return to its earlier policy of neutrality. It had become increasingly difficult to justify payments to the Conservative Party on grounds of self-defence and when shareholders on occasion questioned the validity of such donations at the annual general meeting.

Regulation and innovation

A study of seven UK pharmaceutical companies revealed that they had researched 197 new chemical entities (defined as novel chemical or biological compounds, excluding esters or salts unless they conferred a major therapeutic advantage) in human clinical trials over the period 1964 to 1981 – an average of twelve a year.[99] By the beginning of 1984, thirty-five had completed their development programmes and been launched on the market, 137 had been abandoned and twenty-five were still being evaluated. Analysed by therapeutic class, most new chemical entities were anti-infectives (42 per cent), while the other significant categories included medicines for cardiovascular disorders (10 per cent), the central nervous system (16 per cent) and the treatment of allergic conditions (11 per cent). The average development time (synthesis to marketing) for those drugs that were launched was four and a half years in the 1960s, rising to nine years in the following decade,[100] a key factor being the need for ever more rigorous toxicity studies.

A survey of prescription medicines licensed in the UK during the decade from 1971 showed that the number of new chemical entities brought to the market remained constant at around twenty a year,[101] despite a growing volume of product launches. This suggested that most new medicines were not of a particularly innovative nature, and that these applications related to line extensions or to other uses for drugs already in the pharmacopoeia. The study also revealed that these new chemical entities fell within a limited range of therapeutic groups, including non-steroidal anti-inflammatory agents, corticosteroids, B-adrenergic receptor blocking agents, antidepressants, benzodiazepines, penicillins, cephalosporins, oral hypoglycaemic agents and anti-hypertensives. In general, these medicines treated common, chronic conditions. The direction and focus of innovation had been influenced by the market, in the way that war had diverted research towards the treatment of wound infections and the discovery of antidotes to poisons. The key question for government during the 1970s was whether greater regulation of the industry (either providing financial incentives to undertake particular forms of research or limiting profits to fund work in other scientific institutions) would encourage the search for novel chemical compounds, or whether such controls would simply stifle enterprise. There may, however, be a strong case for regulation to ensure that rare diseases or those where the costs of failure (as in obstetrics, where fears of a disaster on the scale of thalidomide have deterred the search for new drugs) are potentially ruinous to companies do not continue to be neglected.

The study also found that the number of new chemical entities reaching the UK market during the 1970s was considerably fewer than the figure for the previous decade, twenty a year in contrast to the earlier fifty.[102] A worldwide investigation showed that there had been a fall in the total number of novel compounds being introduced from 90–100 per annum in the early 1960s to 40–50 in the late 1970s.[103] The decline in the number of truly novel medicines launched in the UK was not a regulatory effect but part of an international trend arising from the difficulties of making scientific advances in thoroughly researched therapeutic areas. Doubtless, certain rare disorders would have offered scientists further opportunities but in view of the limited returns that any drug would generate, companies were understandably reluctant to commit substantial resources to their discovery. In October 1967, *The Lancet* commented on these problems in the aftermath of the Sainsbury Report:

> Pharmaceutical firms are of many sorts, ranging from those interested only in innovating to those content to imitate. Between these extremes, the bulk of the firms innovate as best they can … It may seem incongruous that further progress in pharmacology now depends heavily on commercial undertakings whose directors owe their first duty, not to doctors or patients, but to shareholders.[104]

An analysis of 118 UK product licence applications submitted to the Committee on Safety of Medicines between 1987 to 1989 contrasted the success ratios and therapeutic classes of 'fully innovative' and 'semi-innovative' drugs.[105] There were thirty-two 'fully innovative' drugs and of these eighteen (56 per cent) were approved, while only twenty-nine of the 'semi-innovative' (34 per cent) were granted a licence. The range of therapeutic categories offered by the semi-innovative applications was narrow: fifty-two (60 per cent) fell into three areas, cardiovascular, central nervous system and anti-infectives. Only thirteen (41 per cent) of the fully innovative applications were in these groups. The higher approval rate for truly novel compounds had two causes. First, pre-market development programmes often undertaken by experienced pharmaceutical companies had been performed with skill and thoroughness. Secondly, the Committee on Safety of Medicines adopted a more liberal risk–benefit assessment for innovative compounds particularly if the clinical condition was poorly served by existing medicines. The companies themselves had broadened the scope of their research to include comparatively neglected diseases or disorders. The study showed that the numbers of patients used in clinical trials varied widely. In part this too was a feature of the risk–benefit assessment. For agents designed to treat otherwise lethal conditions, the Committee has required relatively few subjects to demonstrate safety and efficacy, while greater numbers were requested for products intended for common conditions (those with a more benign natural history or those for which effective alternative treatments existed).[106]

A survey of medicines approved in the US by the Food and Drug Administration over the same period, 1987 to 1989, revealed a similar overall pattern. Of the fifty-five new medicines that were approved nine (16 per cent) were classified by the FDA as representing an 'important therapeutic gain', fifteen (27 per cent) as 'modest gain' and twenty-nine (53 per cent) as 'little or no gain'.[107] The assessment time for the most novel medicines was reduced to an average of 2.4 years, while that for those of little or no gain was 3.1 years.[108] However, a comparison with earlier three-year periods showed a modest deceleration in the total number of drug approvals. Between 1987 and 1989 the annual average was 18.3, which represented a 16 per cent fall from the 21.7 of 1984–86, and was 4 per cent below the 19.0 for 1981–83.[109] Some have argued that the decline is the result of the introduction of increasingly stringent FDA regulations from 1962.[110] The reduction in the number of novel chemical entities reaching the market may also relate to the nature of pharmaceutical research. The accumulated volume of investigatory work by established methodologies had, perhaps, made it increasingly difficult to discover novel but effective compounds, while the rising cost of development programmes deterred companies from speculative projects – an hypothesis supported by a general fall in science-based innovation in the US from the late 1960s.[111]

SALES AND MARKETING

THE EARLY success of Glaxo had been largely dependent on the skilful marketing strategies of Alec Nathan. Although the Nathans employed a small number of regional representatives, the main thrust of Alec's promotional campaigns was delivered through advertising in newspapers and specialist journals together with postal communications. As the volume of trade grew, Nathan delegated to Hugo Wolff, head of sales, and Alexander Cox, director of propaganda. When Glaxo launched its first pharmaceutical product, Ostelin, it became clear that the sales force, recruited to sell foods, needed additional technical expertise. Accordingly, Charles Jephcott, elder brother of Harry and recruited as assistant to Wolff during the post-war boom, began to hire qualified pharmacists as representatives and to train them.

A pharmaceutical sales force

From the 1930s onwards, only qualified pharmacists were recruited as representatives even though they had to promote the entire range of Glaxo products. Detailed guidelines were prepared by Alec Nathan governing their duties and demeanour. The watchword was 'service' and representatives were instructed never to 'hesitate in an instance of emergency to incur expense by sending telegrams, or by asking for goods to be despatched in some special way, as for example, by first passenger train'.[1] Representatives were expected to adopt a courteous and professional manner, while aggressive selling was prohibited as detrimental to the company's image:

> There is no more important part of a representative's mental make up than the ability to exercise tact, and a representative should never place himself in such a

position that it is difficult, embarrassing or impossible for the House to support his attitude to any particular customer.[2]

Rival manufacturers were to be respected and never disparaged.[3] Although not a dynamic or inspirational leader, Charles Jephcott was a stickler for detail and imbued the sales force with a sense of propriety which did much to establish Glaxo's reputation as responsible and trustworthy. By 1939, there were just over forty on the 'home representative staff'. All were men, though a photograph taken at the annual conference in August 1938 shows a woman present.[4] There was no specialisation within the sales force, each representative being expected to promote the full range of Glaxo foods and pharmaceuticals and to call on retail pharmacists, GPs, hospital doctors, pharmacists, welfare clinics and nursing homes.[5] At first, representatives had to cover their territory using public transport but in the 1930s they were given the option of a company car. In May 1939 a garage with its own petrol pump was constructed at Greenford, at a cost of £4,500, to accommodate a fleet of cars and three vans.[6] By the early 1940s, Glaxo had forty Hillman Minx four-cylinder saloons for its sales force,[7] though many were laid up or sold during the war years.[8]

The sales force was greatly disrupted by the Second World War as its members volunteered for military service and pharmacists were recruited into government departments, but many returned to Glaxo after demobilisation. The *Working Instructions* issued in the 1950s were identical to those devised in the 1930s, though now staff had to promote a growing range of pharmaceuticals, notably antibiotics and corticosteroids.[9]

Hugo Wolff's early retirement for health reasons in January 1939 left the sales directorship of Glaxo vacant during the war years.[10] With rationing and control of raw materials, the post was almost made redundant, responsibility for sales being taken by Palmer and Preston. In 1947, however, Jephcott appointed Joe Hutchinson as sales director. A pharmacist, Hutchinson had joined Glaxo as a UK representative in 1920, subsequently working in Canada and Philadelphia.[11] But he fell out with Jephcott, who had him posted back to Canada in 1950 as the managing director of a new subsidiary.[12] In June 1951, O. F. Morgan, another former Glaxo representative, became sales director in place of Hutchinson.[13]

By the late 1960s, Glaxo's UK representatives sold a bewildering variety of products: dried milk powder, Farex, vitamins, vaccines, antibiotics, corticosteroids and even veterinary medicines. Although all had qualified in pharmacy and received regular in-house training, it was difficult for them to promote such a broad portfolio. Typically, they would spend the early part of the morning calling at GPs' surgeries, usually without an appointment, and, in an era before large group practices, were often able to build up trusted personal contacts. Later in the day, they visited retail chemists, hospital staff including pharmacists, and called at maternity and child welfare clinics to promote Glaxo foods, vitamins and vaccines. When pharmaceutical products were to be launched, the representatives paid particular attention to hospital consultants and it was thought that the success enjoyed by Betnovate was, in part, because dermatologists had been targeted before the campaign was broadened to GPs.[14]

Representatives were given considerable freedom of action, while their area managers, particularly those distant from Greenford, had a great measure of independence in deciding how individual medicines were sold. Company policy was disseminated by means of an annual conference, 'Representatives' bulletins' and an interview order that identified product priorities. Reporting to O. F. Morgan, the sales director, were Leonard Kitch, general manager home sales, who sent technical information to physicians and replied to their queries, and Bill Deacon, who organised the sales force. The latter was succeeded in 1972 by John Hunt, then sales manager responsible for north London. Unlike today, when the post of representative is considered a first step in a managerial career in marketing, many employees viewed the job as a life-long commitment. By the standards of the time, they were well qualified, given ample opportunities for individual initiative, and took a pride in building up a strong professional relationship with GPs and pharmacists. A cultural change occurred in 1968 when, after considerable debate, it was decided to open these posts to science graduates. Hitherto pharmacists had been preferred because it was thought that their professional qualification and practical expertise enabled them to establish a rapport with both retail chemists and hospital pharmacists. All the representatives appointed in the post-war period were male, the first woman, Beryl Gibbs, being appointed by John Hunt in 1973.

Marketing Betnovate

During the 1960s and 1970s investment analysts commonly compared Glaxo and Beecham, suggesting that the former as the 'University of Greenford' had the superior science but was weaker at marketing and sales. This distinction, though not without a measure of truth, was an over-simplification. The decision to recruit only professionally qualified representatives resulted in Glaxo having a high quality team which amply showed its effectiveness in November 1963 when the company launched Betnovate.[15] The market for a topical corticosteroid was securely occupied by ICI's product, Synalar. Yet, within a few years, Betnovate overtook its competitor and

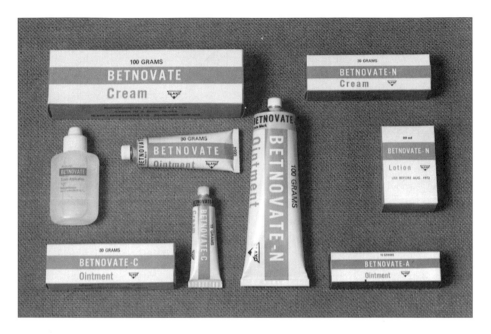

86. Betnovate creams, ointments and lotions for the treatment of skin disorders such as eczema.

dominated this dermatological field. Since the medicines were of similar potency, its success was due in no small part to the company's carefully planned promotional campaign. However, this episode also illustrated the weaknesses in Glaxo's sales and marketing strategies. In retrospect, Betnovate may have been underpriced when it was introduced at a discount to Synalar, whilst a higher charge would have conveyed greater confidence in the medicine and widened the opportunities for promotion. Pressured by the Department of Health, Glaxo cut the original price of Betnovate in July 1966 and following the introduction of the VPRS in November agreed to a second reduction of 10 per cent by the end of 1967. Betnovate continued to be marketed at a discount; a 15g tube sold to retailers at 6s 6d (32.5p), 17 per cent less than Synalar which cost 7s 10d (39p).[16]

Despite the low price, sales of Betnovate in 1966–67 accounted for 36 per cent of the group's UK pharmaceutical turnover and 20 per cent of exports.[17] Home sales rose rapidly from £408,986 in the first eight months of trading to over £2 million by 1966–67 (see Table 17, p. 453). Income from Betnovate surpassed that from all Glaxo's antibiotics by 1969 and was greater than that for sales of bulk chemicals. This commercial success owed much to a skilful and determined marketing campaign by Glaxo Laboratories. A key decision had been to target hospital consultants, rather than GPs, in the sales drive surrounding the launch. Dermatologists, though far fewer in number, had been identified as the crucial decision makers and if they could be persuaded to change their prescribing patterns it was believed that family doctors would follow their lead. To establish Betnovate as the drug of first choice and maintain interest in the product, Glaxo sponsored a large number of clinical studies at London medical schools, notably St Mary's and King's. Because corticosteroids had been shown to suppress the natural function of the adrenal cortex, many doctors were concerned that the side-effects would be more damaging than the therapeutic benefits. However, Dr Dowling Munro demonstrated that in adults treated topically with Betnovate for short periods the inhibition of pituitary-adrenal function was only slight, justifying the clinical gains.[18] Other papers confirmed these findings[19] and had the effect not only of reassuring GPs but also of keeping the name of Glaxo's product to the fore in dermatology.

Although the Glaxo sales force was professionally managed, weaknesses were apparent in the group's marketing functions. There was little co-ordination, for example, between the publicity department run by Preston and Morgan as head of sales. Advertising campaigns were implemented without being co-ordinated with the promotional priorities of the representatives and there was little discussion to ensure that they were attempting to convey a common message. It was the same at Allen & Hanburys, where a professional team of representatives attempted to sell a wide variety of products. Their leading prescription medicines in 1967 were: chlorpheniramine maleate (Piriton), an antihistamine (with sales of £391,000); choline theophyllinate (Choledyl), a bronchodilator (£361,000); Triptafen, an antidepressant containing amtitriptyline (£225,000); and perphenazine (Fentazin), a neuroleptic (£207,000).[20] In addition, Allen & Hanburys had launched an important veterinary speciality in 1959, Dictol, an oral vaccine for lungworm in cattle, which earned sales of £444,000 in 1967, while their leading OTC preparations included Haliborange tablets (£613,000) and Dequadin lozenges, an anti-bacterial treatment for throat infections (£239,000). With such a diverse product range it was difficult to give their marketing strategy a consistent focus, and earnings from any single medicine were destined to remain limited.

Reform and restructuring in the 1970s

The 1970s witnessed a transformation in the sales and marketing functions of Glaxo, albeit a gradual one. The decade saw a change away from repeated calls by representatives towards promotional meetings of invited audiences. Special conferences were organised targeting particular disorders and their specialist physicians, so that a carefully prepared message could be delivered to key decision makers. In January 1972, for example, Glaxo funded a conference held at the Royal College of Physicians on steroid anaesthesia to promote its product Althesin (see p. 319). The presentations by both anaesthetists and Glaxo scientists were later published in a supplement to the *Postgraduate Medical Journal*.[21] The success of this approach led to the organisation of a Zantac symposium held at the Barbican Conference Centre in October 1981 and later at the Seventh Congress of Gastroenterology in Stockholm.[22]

By the early 1970s it had become apparent that Glaxo representatives were attempting to promote too many products. A veterinary sales force had already been formed, and the separation of the food and pharmaceutical lines was overdue. In 1973 Peter Scruton, then marketing director, proposed the divisionalisation of the UK sales force and four groups were created: Pharmaceuticals under John Hunt, Animal Health (Bob Maskell), Glaxo-Farley Foods (Harry Purdom) and Marketing Services (Paul Baker), the last to provide publicity for products. Glaxo-Farley Foods Division was centralised at Plymouth, leaving Greenford to focus on the group's prescription medicines. Despite these reforms, the sales and marketing organisations of Glaxo Laboratories and Allen & Hanburys, based at Greenford and Bethnal Green respectively, continued to function as separate entities. It was not until January 1978 and the creation of Glaxo Operations UK (see p. 202), that the two departments were brought together in a single organisation located at Greenford, though the sales forces retained their historical names and the traditions of their parent companies.

In 1977, having implemented these strategic reforms, Glaxo had high hopes that their new anti-hypertensive, labetalol (Trandate) would prove commercially successful. Because labetalol had been shown to block both alpha- and beta-receptors, the scientists believed that this effect could be translated into a significant market advantage. In April 1976, a year before the launch, a symposium was held at Torquay for cardiologists to explain the novel action of labetalol. Introduced in March 1977, initial sales were not promising (those to UK chemists totalling an estimated £590,000), though the group maintained its faith in the medicine. In the *Annual Report* for 1978, Bide stated that 'clinical experience reinforces our confidence that Trandate will become one of our most important and profitable products'.[23] In March 1979, a second labetalol symposium was held at the Royal College of Physicians, papers being published in the *British Journal of Clinical Pharmacology*.[24] This meeting was followed three months later by a conference at the Scanticon Centre, Aarhus, Denmark.[25] The intensified campaign of 1979 lifted UK sales to chemists to £1.8 million, though they did not achieve a dramatic take-off and returns grew to a modest peak in 1982.

In 1979 the market research department of Glaxo Operations UK prepared a report on the prescription pharmaceutical market in Britain, inspired by the recognition that sales of new products had failed to generate a real rise in turnover and profits during the mid and latter parts of the decade.[26] It had become crucially important that Glaxo target those clinical areas likely to yield the most favourable returns. Analysing the five years to 1979, Glaxo identified three major therapeutic classes with an annual income from chemists' purchases of over £100 million: the cardiovascular system, the central nervous system (CNS) together with the alimentary tract and metabolism. Over this period the first and last had grown by 52 per cent and 38 per cent respectively, while CNS medicines had risen by 19 per cent.[27] The respiratory system provided the fourth largest total of chemists' purchases, with sales in 1979 of £86.1 million, and a growth rate of 29 per cent over the previous five years. This market intelligence helped Glaxo to define its research priorities. Furthermore, it served to justify the significance attached to the launch and promotion of ranitidine (Zantac) in October 1981, falling within one of the biggest and most rapidly expanding therapeutic areas. It also explained why Betnovate failed to transform Glaxo's fortunes as the dermatological sub-market ranked seventh with a value of £43.6 million in 1979 and a growth rate of only 9 per cent in real terms in 1975–79.[28]

Marketing Zantac

By 1981, when Glaxo launched Zantac in Italy and the UK, the home market had settled into a period of stability and calm. The PPRS had reassured critics that the returns on new products were subject to scrutiny. Furthermore, the climate of popular opinion had switched away from criticising businesses thought to be making excessive profits towards the encouragement of enterprise as a means of generating economic growth. With income from its asthma, corticosteroid and antibiotic products, the group had grown to the point where it could mount an assault on the market for anti-ulcer medication – a field of potentially vast dimensions occupied by only one modern medicine. The experience of promoting and selling Zantac was to prove to be a turning point in the commercial strategy of the group.

Early in 1981, the marketing team of Glaxo Pharmaceuticals (UK), under John Reece, drew up a corporate plan for the launch and sale of Zantac.[29] They concluded that the drug should be marketed 'as a direct competitor to the breakthrough H_2 antagonist cimetidine (Tagamet)'.[30] This approach was recommended for three reasons, first,

Zantac has the same mode of action as Tagamet which is the global competitor in the anti-ulcerant market ... [Secondly] market research indicates that when doctors are told of Zantac, they immediately classify it as 'another Tagamet'. By adopting this strategy, Glaxo can capitalise successfully on the considerable educational work relating to the mode of action of H_2 blockers already undertaken by SKF and the Glaxo sales force can then concentrate on 'selling the benefits of Zantac' viz a viz Tagamet. [Thirdly] medical and lay press articles already relate to the two products as 'the same' in their mode of action.[31]

This strategy was supported by their assessment of the other therapeutic agents available to treat peptic ulcers.[32] Most seemed inferior: carbenoxolone and bismuth type products sold in limited quantities, while antacids, a traditional way of relieving symptoms, required large daily doses and did not treat the underlying condition. It was decided to adopt

the platform of presenting the unique selling benefits of Zantac with only indirect comparison to cimetidine because this would allow the doctor to be presented with a therapeutic alternative which is equivalent to, or better than, cimetidine, the market leader. The unique selling benefits of better patient compliance with twice a day dosage, without the risk of sex related side effects [gynaecomastia] and drug interaction could then be stressed.[33]

On pricing, the marketing team drew no firm conclusions, but worked on the assumption that Zantac would be priced at, or just below, parity with Tagamet for daily maintenance treatment; that is one ranitidine tablet being equivalent to two of cimetidine, giving a therapeutic treatment cost per day 20 per cent below the price of Tagamet.[34] The UK was thought to be particularly price sensitive (hence the need to sell at a small discount), while other nations, such as Italy, had less stringent regulations, or, like the United States, were less influenced by differentials in charges.[35]

In April 1981 the issue of price still remained 'under active assessment'.[36] At this stage, three rates were considered, each with a considered outcome: 'High volume – low price. High price – low volume. Medium price and volume'.[37] Conventional marketing wisdom taught that the second product in a novel therapeutic field could never gain more than 50 per cent of sales.[38] Accordingly, Reece's team prepared three sets of forecasts based upon Zantac being priced at a discount, at parity and at a premium of about 10 per cent. A meeting was convened on 21 July 1981 under the chairmanship of Paul Girolami, then chief executive of Glaxo Holdings, to decide on the pricing strategy. It was attended by Douglas Back, the commercial director, E. R. C. Farmer, chairman of Glaxo Pharmaceuticals, Berkeley Baker, its commercial director, John Reece, and Michael Allan, the company secretary of Glaxo Holdings.

Girolami immediately countered the pricing assumptions which had determined the three projections, arguing that these 'figures indicated the product would be a commercial failure in the UK', with total sales of £6 million by 1986 and a gross profit of 43.7 per cent.[39] Farmer and Baker believed that Zantac should be launched at a small premium over Tagamet, which sold for £13.50, and suggested a figure of £15 for a 60-tablet pack.[40] They considered that any higher charge would lead to Zantac being 'relegated to a "special treatment" product, particularly as there was firm evidence that SKF were moving to a twice daily dose', thereby removing one of the advantages of ranitidine.[41] Farmer and Baker feared that a high price would lead to doctors prescribing the drug only when side effects from Tagamet indicated a substitution. Furthermore, market intelligence showed that the medical profession regarded Zantac simply as a monopoly breaker without any particular medicinal gains:

> British GPs did not consider Tagamet as having a major defect other than its high price. They were ... still very worried about the possibility of unknown side-effects with a new drug.[42]

In the lively debate that followed, Girolami took a radically different line and argued that

> it was important for Zantac to be seen to succeed in the UK because of the undoubted lead and impression the UK market for new products gave the other group companies ... Zantac was a product crucial to the group's future. Rather than see it fail in the UK, he [Girolami] would therefore be prepared to see the product licensed for co-marketing in the UK.[43]

In other words, Girolami was so convinced of Zantac's commercial importance that he threatened to offer co-marketing rights to a rival pharmaceutical company if they rejected his radical strategy. He believed that the Glaxo projections (which assumed a remarkable price sensitivity, changing by a factor of nine between £13.60 and £20) were based on the false assumption that Zantac would be viewed solely as 'a slightly improved mark 2 version of Tagamet'.[44] Girolami suggested that the UK could be seen as a special case, while some of the group's overseas companies had produced more optimistic estimates for potential sales and profits. He proposed that Zantac be sold at £24 per pack, yielding a gross profit of 67 per cent and at the very minimum at £20 (60 per cent).[45]

John Reece presented a summary of their findings to the September meeting of the Group Management Committee at which it was agreed that Zantac would be marketed not as a Tagamet monopoly breaker but as 'a major evolutionary advance in the treatment of peptic ulcer and other acid-aggravated disorders'.[46] The claim was supported by the fact that ranitidine was more potent than cimetidine and could, therefore, be administered in fewer doses (twice daily for major indications rather than four times for Tagamet) and had a better safety profile. It did not represent, as Tagamet had done, a radically new way of treating ulcers, but was a step improvement to an existing therapy. The gamble taken by Girolami was in suggesting that these gains merited a premium of around 80 per cent, the price to the wholesaler for a 60-tablet pack being set within the range of £23 to £28.[47] Glaxo obtained approval from the Department of Health to price the daily treatment of Zantac (91p) 75 per cent higher than that of Tagamet (52p).[48] This was justified partly on grounds of a shorter course of medication (four weeks rather than six), reducing the premium to 17 per cent, though in practice physicians tended to give Zantac for the habitual six weeks. The launch of Zantac was arranged for 8–10 September in Italy, and for 1 October in the UK, where a symposium for 800 invited physicians was held at the Barbican. After one year on the market, sales had totalled £42.5 million in Italy and £6.5 million in the UK. Limited business was also achieved in Australia, Hong Kong, Malaysia, Nigeria, Portugal, Singapore and Switzerland, where Zantac was introduced during the twelve months from October 1981. In the first year world-wide sales revenue totalled £49.8 million.[49]

The commercial success of this strategy was remarkable (see Tables 9 and 18, pp. 448 and 453), and probably surprised Girolami himself. By 1985, for example, Zantac had captured over half the UK market for anti-ulcer medication with annual sales of £46 million, a growth of 344 per cent in four years. World-wide the medicine recorded sales of £432 million, upsetting received wisdom about second products. Why, then, did this pricing policy prove so rewarding? Few comparable examples exist in the pharmaceutical industry and, indeed, in business generally where a product which was not a radical innovation has achieved such commercial supremacy.

The key to Zantac's commercial success was the effective marketing of the product's favourable attributes compared with Tagamet. Rather than presenting ranitidine as yet one more medicine designed to treat peptic ulcers, it was targeted against the market leader and what had become the world's largest selling prescription drug. If Zantac could supplant Tagamet, it was guaranteed to generate significant earnings. The incremental gains of ranitidine were stressed and much made of the simpler dose regimen and limited side-effects (though some of these advantages could, by their very nature, only become clear over time). By pricing Zantac at a premium well in excess of Tagamet, Glaxo conveyed the message that this was an important drug worthy of a higher charge and, as Girolami had predicted, demand for this potentially life-saving medicine proved remarkably price inelastic. Zantac's ultimate success demonstrated the medical profession's acceptance of these product characteristics. There had been an element of risk in the strategy as the higher price could have depressed sales considerably if prescribers had been unimpressed by the therapeutic advantages of the medicine, a case urged by those who advocated the launch of Zantac at a discount. But as Girolami observed in the July price meeting 'the group's need for success with Zantac was greater even than Glaxo Operations'.[50] By this he meant that the company as a whole required a new medicine to take on its major competitors. Glaxo had recently set up a subsidiary in the United States and, though it had made steady progress marketing a selection of the group's established products, a novel product and major sales initiative were needed to cement the commercial fortunes of Glaxo Inc. In the event, Zantac proved to be the key to the company's success in the United States and was based on yet another novel strategy; a co-promotional and sales programme with Roche (see p. 392).

The marketing success of Zantac owed much to the lessons learned from Glaxo's previous major launch, that of labetalol (Trandate), which had not lived up to expectations. Because the vast majority of prescriptions for preventative cardiac medicines are written by GPs, Glaxo had taken the decision to focus its promotional strategy on them rather than hospital consultants. However, the Trandate campaign had not taken sufficient account of the fact that in many cases the initial prescription would have been written by a cardiologist for hospital out-patients. Although these specialists were directly responsible for only a small volume of sales, they were the key decision makers and GPs tended to follow their lead when it came to repeat prescriptions.

In addition, Trandate entered a far more competitive market than Zantac. It was not the second drug in the field but faced at least half a dozen well-established rivals. Although it could claim therapeutic novelty in being both an alpha- and beta-blocker, this required an elaborate scientific explanation which some of the sales force believed was too complex to convey in a short meeting with a busy GP. Indeed, this message did not impress the compilers of the *British National Formulary*, which in 1985 declared that 'there is no evidence that labetalol is more effective than pure beta-blockers'.[51] Like Tagamet, Trandate did not have a straightforward dose regimen. To minimize side effects, labetalol had to be titrated and the patient's physiological response monitored, which discouraged its initial use outside hospitals. Launched in 1977, Glaxo had fewer resources to market the drug and at that time had no US subsidiary for a major sales campaign. In addition, the group had no established reputation in cardiac medicine, having built up a portfolio of drugs in the respiratory, dermatological and antibiotic fields. Trandate was unfortunate in being launched at a time when the Department of Health, worried about the potential toxicity of novel medicines, introduced a monitoring system by which GPs were asked to complete reports of adverse reactions to all new drugs – a system that developed into the yellow cards submitted to the Committee on Safety of Medicines. This inadvertently created the impression in the minds of prescribers that there was an inherent problem with Trandate and impeded its uptake.[52] In retrospect it was not surprising that sales of Trandate never took off (and had the medicine been priced at a premium above its competitors, then it would probably have performed even more poorly).

Respiratory medicines: Ventolin and Becotide

Although Ventolin had been launched in January 1969, it proved to have a remarkably long product life, with growing world-wide sales up to 1995.[53] Although the Allen & Hanburys' board recognised the commercial importance of this novel medicine from the outset they appear to have been rather conservative in their expectations. It rapidly became the company's most important drug, accounting for about half the £606,400 increase in home sales during 1970.[54] By the following year the Ventolin inhaler had gained 33 per cent of the UK market, while in its tablet and syrup form salbutamol captured 9 per cent,[55] figures that in 1973 were to rise to 52 per cent and 30 per cent respectively.[56] In that year Allen & Hanburys recorded an increase of UK sales of 20 per cent, adding that Ventolin had probably reached 'market saturation'.[57] This pessimism proved unfounded as Ventolin's share of the market for bronchodilators continued to rise, reaching 65 per cent in 1977.[58] Judged against its returns for the following decade, however, these figures appear less impressive, for in 1980 UK sales almost doubled and climbed steadily thereafter. It was not until 1981, for example, that Ventolin became the leading ethical medicine in the UK as measured by the number of prescriptions.[59] Promoted by Glaxo Inc. in the United States, Ventolin rapidly captured a dominant market share and became the subsidiary's second most important product after Zantac. In 1985, with a global turnover of £174 million, Ventolin was ranked twenty-third in a league table of prescription medicines.[60] As the market for anti-asthma products continued to expand at around 18 per cent annually, Ventolin

climbed to fourteenth place by 1987 with sales of £200 million[61] and captured over 25 per cent of the global market for inhaled medication.[62]

Why has Ventolin had such a long product life, and why did it achieve its
greatest commercial success eleven years after the UK launch? Three factors
were important. First, the incidence of asthma in industrialised economies
increased, creating a growing demand for bronchodilators. Because they
treat symptoms, rather than addressing underlying causes, such medicines
are commonly employed on a regular basis over long periods of time.
Secondly, the marketing reorganisation of the 1970s and the emphasis on
promotional campaigns by the various Allen & Hanburys sales forces
began to pay dividends. Furthermore, the commercial success of Zantac
generated such income that the marketing budget for Ventolin could be
progressively increased throughout the 1980s. In the US salbutamol had
originally been licensed to Schering, but the formation of Glaxo Inc.
allowed the group to market the medicine itself with conspicuous success.
Salbutamol became the drug of first choice in the treatment of asthma and
because of its established efficacy many physicians chose to prescribe
Ventolin rather than substitute a generic preparation when it lost UK
patent protection in September 1987. Thirdly, Glaxo put considerable effort
into designing product extensions to preserve an element of novelty. In
1988, for example, Allen & Hanburys launched two new ways of delivering
salbutamol, either in the form of a dry powder (the Ventolin Diskhaler) or
as a slow-release tablet (Volmax).

Launched in 1972, beclomethasone dipropionate (Becotide) also had a
lengthy gestation period before sales took off, though for different reasons.
An inhaled corticosteroid, Becotide was designed to reduce inflammation
of the bronchial mucosa and keep the airway clear by reducing odema and
the secretion of mucus. At first, physicians were wary of potential side-
effects and sales in the mid 1970s were described as 'sluggish'. As Becotide
required considerable explanation, it was not thought to be a product for
the 'lazy doctor', and by 1977 its UK market share was only 24 per cent.[63]
However, respiratory physicians were beginning to change their ideas
about how to treat asthma. Specialists thought it important not simply to
dilate the airway during acute episodes but to attempt to address the
underlying inflammation. As a result, the use of inhaled corticosteroids
was increasingly recommended as an adjunct to a bronchodilator in
children over the age of five and adults with chronic asthma.[64] Glaxo
stepped up its promotion of Becotide (or Beclovent as it was called in
North America) to take account of this therapeutic strategy and sales grew
strongly from the mid 1980s. World-wide revenue from Becotide increased
by 29 per cent in 1987, and it moved from 51st to 39th place in the league

table of prescription drugs and became the second largest selling inhaled anti-asthma medicine, after Ventolin.[65] Global sales rose by a further 36 per cent in 1988 reflecting the importance of the US market, where it became the leading inhaled corticosteroid.

The nature of pharmaceutical selling

The use of representatives remains a key element in the sales strategies of the major pharmaceutical companies, accounting in many cases for over half of the marketing budget.[66] The Sainsbury Committee calculated that UK expenditure on product promotion totalled £15.4 million in 1965 and was equivalent of 13.9 per cent of the cost of sales to the NHS.[67] The report was critical of these high levels of expenditure:

> It is even more questionable whether the nation … obtained value for money for the £7 million spent on representatives in 1965 … Nor were all the doctors appreciative of the visits of representatives. A substantial proportion said that they would not lose an important source of information if they saw no representatives … Over half said there had been occasions during the last year when they felt a representative had insufficient knowledge to tell them what they wanted to know about a product.[68]

Although the committee were convinced that some companies demonstrated care 'not only about the recruitment and training of their representatives but also about briefing them', this was not universal.[69] They calculated that the time clinicians spent in sales meetings cost the nation £250 per doctor annually and argued that this was a 'wasteful' method of promoting products. Acknowledging that the industry had a legitimate role of 'informing doctors about medicines', the committee concluded that 'some of the sales promotion effort of pharmaceutical manufacturers fails to measure up to this responsibility'.[70]

Several studies have shown that physicians rely on representatives for information about new drugs. In the 1970s a sample of 453 GPs in the UK showed that 51 per cent believed that representatives provided valuable data,[71] as did 56 per cent of Canadian family doctors,[72] and 70 per cent of 284 New Zealand practitioners.[73] Nevertheless, it has also been shown that most clinicians do not regard them as a completely trustworthy source of information because of the inherent commercial bias in their role. In 1986 only 36 per cent of a sample of doctors in North Carolina saw them as accurate.[74] There is considerable evidence that representatives influence prescribing patterns (indeed, why else would major companies employ them?) and, given business pressures, that they can, on occasion, be overzealous in their promotion. One study argued that physicians should rely exclusively on scientific papers for data about novel medicines and, while pharmaceutical companies should be permitted to advertise in such journals, the effect of 'detailing is to increase the consumption of drugs, and in doing so detailing adds unnecessarily to the economic cost of prescribing and results in significant adverse health costs'.[75] Whilst some authors in America have called for a ban on such sales techniques, there have also been criticisms of the system in the UK and calls from the medical profession for 'an expert capable of independently assessing the claims of a company' to be present at promotional meetings:

> A further possibility would have been to suggest a clear system – like that operating in many Swedish hospitals – of determining in advance the scientific and educational value of what is presented ... Many drug companies would welcome such a scheme: they do not like dealing in an unseemly trade of ballpoint pens and Italian red wine – they want to make their case and be off.[76]

Potential conflict extends beyond individual prescribers to medical institutions. A review conducted in the United States during 1984 reported that the pharmaceutical industry's 'goal of increasing sales of its products may be in direct conflict with the responsibility of the pharmacist to reduce or contain the hospital drug budget'.[77] Whilst the major contribution made by pharmaceutical companies to the discovery of innovative medicines was acknowledged, it concluded that opportunities existed for clinical pharmacists to apply their technical skills to 'the evaluation of the manufacturers' promotional and package insert material',[78] and that the marketing of new medicines should be balanced:

> Manufacturers should not expect to promote their products in institutions without evaluation or limitation. Pharmacists must allow for a full and fair presentation of drug products in their institutions ... In the future, the evaluation of drugs will include an assessment of the economic impact with the evaluation of the clinical efficacy, and industry should draw its attention to the cost–benefit ratio of the drugs it promotes.[79]

In response to criticisms from the medical and pharmacy professions, there has been a general improvement in the training and regulation of representatives. Set up in 1968, the International Federation of Pharmaceutical Manufacturers Associations (IFPMA) was pledged to promote 'ethical principles and practices' throughout the pharmaceutical industry.[80] In March 1981 it promulgated a Code of Pharmaceutical Marketing

Practices which its fifty-one national member associations agreed to observe. The following year a complaints procedure was established and from 1983 its findings were regularly published. The code of practice was revised in 1988 to bring it in line with the World Health Organisation's *Ethical Criteria for Medicinal Drug Promotion* and its acceptance was made a condition of membership to IFPMA.[81] Although not a detailed document with specific regulations, it set out general standards and required, for example, that 'information in promotional material should be based on an up-to-date evaluation of evidence that is scientifically valid'.[82] Medical representatives were to be 'adequately trained and possess sufficient medical and technical knowledge to present information on their company's products in an accurate, responsible and ethical manner',[83] while full advertisements were to include 'a succinct statement of the contra-indications, precautions and side-effects'.[84]

In the UK representatives employed by companies registered with the APBI are required to pass professional examinations within two years of being recruited. Traditionally, the most experienced staff have been assigned to hospitals, especially those with medical schools, because their consultants have the greatest influence over the existing and future doctor population. If a cardiologist with an international reputation, for example, recommends the use of a new beta-blocker, it is likely to be adopted by juniors and medical students. Hospital representatives, covering one or two therapeutic areas, tend to have greater specialist knowledge than those visiting family doctors with a range of medicines. Indeed, part of their role has been that of educator, providing copies of scientific papers and financial assistance to attend conferences. Obviously a key goal of any hospital representative is to get his or her company's latest medicine into the institution's formulary – a compendium of those drugs that the health authority will routinely dispense. New products are usually considered by a panel of physicians and pharmacists who consider the merits of new medication and, on the basis of novelty or price, determine whether it should enter a trial period. Hospital formularies usually include clear recommendations on prescribing policy and can, therefore, exercise a significant influence on practice.

Patent protection

The principle of patent protection lies at the heart of the prescription pharmaceutical industry. The law of intellectual property is employed by companies to safeguard both molecules and manufacturing processes so that they alone can produce or sell a medicine for a defined period of time.[85] By surrendering the secrecy surrounding a discovery, the inventor is granted a monopoly, which in the case of pharmaceuticals increases the chances of recouping the large sums invested in research and development and provides an income for future endeavour.[86] Without this commercial protection, the industry could not survive, for as soon as a novel chemical entity was launched, it would be copied and sold at a discount by businesses which had not incurred the costs of discovery and clinical evaluation. Almost all countries have specified that an invention, to qualify for patent status, must exhibit three qualities: it has to be novel, it should involve a degree of inventiveness and it should be of practical utility, so that new chemical entities for which there is no obvious use cannot be patented. (Nor, indeed, can scientific theories.)[87]

In the pharmaceutical industry, patent protection is commonly sought from the point at which the molecule is found or created in the laboratory rather than when the approved medicine is launched in the market. In the UK, the Statute of Monopolies (1623)[88] provided for a period of fourteen years, which was increased by the Patents Act of 1919 to sixteen years.[89] Recent legislation extended protection to twenty years, which has become an international standard enshrined in the European Patent Convention and the Trade Related Intellectual Property Rights (TRIPs) agreements organised by GATT. The introduction of ever more rigorous safety and efficacy standards has greatly increased the work required to meet national regulatory requirements. Given that a full research and development programme can take as long as twelve years, the effective period of protection for a marketable drug can be reduced to as little as eight years.[90] As a result, the pharmaceutical industry has campaigned for increased periods of patent protection. In 1992, the European Economic Community introduced a Supplementary Protection Certificate which granted a product a further five years of patent life, though the effective term was limited to a maximum fifteen years. If a medicine had eight years of its patent remaining when it was launched then a Supplementary Protection Certificate would extend its effective life in the market to only thirteen years. 'Line extensions', that is, improvements to an existing product, such as a reduced dose regimen or more efficient means of administration, can lead to new patents being granted towards the end of a medicine's protected life. When the original patent expires, other companies can gain approval to copy the drug but cannot get access to the updated formulation or the originator's tradename. The rival product is usually sold under its generic name and because the manufacturer has no research and development programme to support can be sold at a considerably reduced price.

Although there are important differences among nations in the law of intellectual property, there has been a considerable degree of standardisation, particularly within Europe, based upon the Strasbourg Convention of 1963.[91] This formed the basis for the European Patent Convention of 1973 which led to the establishment of the European Patent Office (EPO) five years later. As a result, companies have been able to file a single application at the EPO in Munich designating as many as twelve countries within Europe and be granted patents valid there under a single examination procedure. However, some nations have refused to allow chemical compounds protection. Austria only granted this right in 1987, while Spain and Greece followed suit in 1992.[92] Other countries have continued to exclude pharmaceutical compounds, issuing patents for manufacturing processes alone. In those nations where the law of intellectual property is weak or poorly administered, Glaxo and other major companies have been reluctant to develop sales organisations, fearing that their products will be copied without any form of redress.

From almost its foundation, Glaxo took out patents in the UK and abroad to protect its products. From the late 1930s, this activity became increasingly important as the company added vitamins to their foods business. At a time when head office expenditure was pared to an absolute minimum, legal advice was sought from specialists and Jephcott contracted this work to Frank B. Dehn & Co., patent and trademark agents. As the number of medicines manufactured by Glaxo increased, Jephcott recognised the need for in-house expertise and arranged for Austin Bide to work with Dr Frank Dehn, the senior partner. It was planned that Bide would set up a department to look after the group's patents and trademarks. In October 1946, when personal assistant to Palmer, Bide retained responsibility for the administration of intellectual property matters, introducing a manual reference system which recorded details of all patents and trademarks held by the company and its subsidiaries. When Bide took on general management duties, responsibility for intellectual property fell to Ray Camp, the company secretary who had qualified both as a pharmacist and a barrister, and to Harold Martin.

As patent issues became increasingly contested by rival companies across the world, requiring a highly specialised knowledge of national variations in intellectual property law, so Glaxo began to hire and train a growing body of lawyers. In January 1986, Jeremy Strachan was recruited from Standard Telephone & Cables to be director of group legal services and took responsibility for Glaxo's increasingly complex body of patents. A barrister with a career in industry, Strachan introduced formal in-house training whereby staff could become chartered patent agents. Career development programmes were gradually introduced, partly as a result of pressure from staff concerned to enhance their professional skills and partly in response to the growing need for comprehensive product protection.

The patent department is one of the few within Glaxo's devolved culture that is unashamedly centralised. Although nations have different procedures and levels of protection, it is essential that products are safeguarded on a global basis. A loophole in a single market can have wider implications if that country seeks to exploit its position by exporting cheap copies. To safeguard their most important assets in a consistent and effective manner throughout the world, medicines have to be protected by a single organisation, even though they may be advised by the legal departments of national subsidiaries. A weak or failed defence could threaten the very livelihood of these international businesses.

Parallel trading

By the late 1980s Glaxo estimated that about 7 per cent of the UK market for Ventolin and 10 per cent of that for Zantac was supplied by parallel imports from within the EEC.[93] Wholesalers in EEC territories were permitted to purchase supplies of a patented drug at a price set for their local market and then sell it preferentially in other nations where the official charge was higher, thereby depriving the manufacturer of business. The basic provisions of the Treaty of Rome, which favoured the free circulation of goods and prohibited anti-competitive practices, legitimised parallel trading.[94] Wholesalers in the UK, France, Netherlands and Italy with modern information technology systems set out to exploit the differences that existed in the price of branded medicines in EEC markets, which resulted from both currency fluctuations and controls exercised by national governments. In 1988, the net annual reduction to group profits from this form of commerce was calculated at £6 million for Zantac alone and it was anticipated that the total could rise to £10 million. Parallel trading, therefore, was mainly confined to relatively expensive products such as Zantac and the group's respiratory medicines, which together accounted for 71 per cent of Glaxo's turnover in the EEC by 1988.[95] It has not affected the group's systemic antibiotics, mainly because sales were made direct to hospitals and so resulted in more specific price arrangements.[96]

Whilst parallel trading was largely confined to the EEC as a legitimate activity, it continued to exercise a perceptible, though not a dramatic, overall effect upon Glaxo's revenues and profits. As a result, it considered two key options to reduce its impact: first, to try to ensure that secondary production factories had the capacity only to supply the needs of their local and designated markets, and to launch products only in those territories where satisfactory prices could be obtained, attempting to limit any introductory discount to 15 per cent of the target price set by the group. In the longer term, Glaxo believed that the search for economies in health care expenditure, the anti-trust rules of the European Union and active competition would lead to a convergence of prices at lower average levels. Parallel trading would be one of the instruments leading to this general reduction.[97] The most effective defence has been to limit output in low-price countries because to stop production there would simply encourage the manufacture of copies that would also find a ready export demand.

MANUFACTURE:
FOODS TO PHARMACEUTICALS

§

O N T H E outbreak of the Second World War, Glaxo Laboratories had only two factories both of which were primarily designed for the manufacture of food products. Greenford, opened in 1935, prepared and packaged Ostermilk and Farex together with a variety of vitamin supplements, while Driffield, in the East Riding of Yorkshire, came on stream in 1937 using roller drying to make milk powder. The nation's desperate need for penicillin led to rapid expansion in the company's plant. The labour-intensive operations of surface culture led to the opening of factories at Aylesbury, Watford and Stratford.[1] Having supplied penicillin for military purposes, Glaxo Laboratories was called upon by the Ministry of Supply to increase its production for civilian needs in peacetime. A purpose-built factory, employing deep fermentation techniques constructed at Barnard Castle, came on stream in January 1946, followed by a second larger plant at Ulverston two years later. In March 1952, Glaxo Laboratories bought six acres of land for £40,000 on the north bank of the South Esk estuary at Montrose to experiment on the production of corticosteroids. Hence by 1960 Glaxo Laboratories had three primary-process factories in the UK: Ulverston and Barnard Castle (both of which made antibiotics) and Montrose, which had yet to find a product of guaranteed commercial significance.

As regards secondary production, that is taking active chemical ingredients and turning them into consumable medicines in the form of tablets, vials, creams, syrups and so forth, Glaxo Laboratories initially undertook all of these operations at Greenford. During the late 1950s and early 1960s there were four key manufacturing departments in the factory: tablets, ampoules (for antibiotics and vaccines), ointments and creams (penicillin and corticosteroids) and food blending (Farex, Glaxo, Ostermilk and Complan). Packaging and labelling was automated when possible though some overseas orders were too small to justify setting up machinery and were finished by hand. At this time, Greenford embraced a bewildering number of secondary processes, ranging from the individual packing of tins with bags of milk powder to the semi-automatic and aseptic filling of streptomycin vials in a specially designed hall.

With the take-over of Allen & Hanburys in 1958 and of Evans Medical in 1961, Glaxo acquired two secondary-process plants at Ware and Speke. Ware, like Greenford, produced a myriad of products ranging from Dictol, a lungworm vaccine for cattle, Steriflex, an intravenous infusion, Dequadin (antibacterial throat lozenges) to Haliborange vitamin tablets, together with a growing range of prescription medicines. The Speke factory of Evans Medical, a wartime construction completed in 1943, suffered from an inflexible layout. It made a great number of products, generic medicines accounting for 80 per cent of the output, but also made OTC preparations, including Mycil foot powder. In total, Speke manufactured 400 different types of tablet and had a range that demanded 1,000 different packs for the home market alone.[2] The Allen & Hanburys acquisition also brought them the Bethnal Green factory, which manufactured surgical instruments and served as a warehouse. Thus, when Glaxo Group was formed in 1962, the company had eight major factories in the UK (Greenford, Barnard Castle, Ulverston, Montrose, Ware, Speke, Bethnal Green and Kendal), together with a number of smaller operations, which performed a wide variety of manufacturing tasks often without reference to each other. An urgent need existed to integrate and rationalise this activity, particularly as increasingly stringent government safety regulations drove up the costs of production and required ever more effective precautions against contamination.

Primary production

Primary production involves the manufacture of active chemical or biological ingredients in bulk from basic raw materials. Primary plant is usually capital-intensive and purpose-built for each new medicine that is discovered. To ensure a reasonable return, it has to be operated continuously. Although these factories had always been run intensively, in the 1980s Glaxo made a concerted attempt to reduce the number of compounds produced, not only to cut unit costs but also to focus on areas of added value and to ensure that plant was more effectively responsive to market forces. Ulverston, for example, became the group's sole producer of cephalosporins, abandoning the manufacture of vitamin B_{12} in 1991 and penicillin in 1993, having ceased to make streptomycin in 1981. In addition, technological innovation has progressively improved control and monitoring at every stage. In 1965, ultrasonic probes were introduced at Ulverston to detect when liquid levels fall in fermentation tanks, while a digital system was installed to record temperature changes in the vessels.[3] More recently, the application of computer-guided controls have enabled staff not only to measure accurately each production process but also to calculate unit costs. Given that plant often operated with explosive liquids and gases under great pressure, safety has always been of paramount concern. With little margin for error and potentially catastrophic consequences to themselves and the local population, the scientists had as a priority the elimination of dangerous side-effects.

From the 1940s onwards, much of Glaxo's manufacturing expertise lay in antibiotics using deep fermentation. The launch in 1964 and subsequent commercial success of cephaloridine (Ceporin), the first injectable cephalosporin manufactured by Glaxo, created a rising demand that led to sustained capital investment at Ulverston and Barnard Castle. Manufactured from cephalosporin C, this was a relatively expensive medicine compared with existing antibiotics. Glaxo had attempted to use penicillin G or penicillin V as the starter material but these had proved uneconomic. In March 1965, it was predicted that the strength of overseas orders would raise demand to 5,000kg per annum within two years.[4] As this was five times the existing capacity, it was agreed to spend £200,000 increasing output to 2,500kg, a quantity estimated to yield a profit of £2.5 million a year.[5] However, it rapidly became clear that this expenditure would not be sufficient for the continuing growth in sales and in July the board agreed to invest £2.14 million, together with working capital of £830,000 in additional plant for the manufacture of antibiotics at Ulverston on the grounds that 'although the cost of the new assets for the expansion was considerable, the estimated return was extremely favourable and the pay back period very short'.[6] The demand for cephaloridine grew steadily during the sixties, production at Ulverston rising from 833kg in 1965 to 13,989kg in 1970. The initial fermentation and extraction processes employing 400 men were undertaken at Barnard Castle.[7]

Yet the labour disputes which troubled Ulverston in the late 1960s (see p. 290) encouraged Glaxo to establish an additional source of supply. Furthermore, the fermentation plant at Barnard Castle was drawing to the end of its useful life.[8] Lacking the ready means to dispose of noxious effluent, it was considered counter-productive to invest further in the primary manufacture of antibiotics.[9] Additional demand was satisfied in the short term by spending £250,000 on enlarging the cephalosporin C extraction plant at Barnard Castle, £100,000 on chemical conversion and sterile stages plant at Ulverston and £50,000 at Montrose to enhance its thienylacetyl chloride

87. Glaxo's new factory at Cambois, Northumberland, for the manufacture of penicillin. Viewed from the north-east, it shows the solvent recovery plant and the fermentation hall in the background.

manufacturing capacity.[10] However, these were seen as interim measures, and approval in principle was given to the expenditure of £1.1 million to establish a cephalosporin C facility at Ulverston, enabling similar operations at Barnard Castle to close. The board were also aware that Eli Lilly were on the point of launching an oral cephalosporin called cephalexin for which it was anticipated there would be 'a very significant' market.[11] So that they could produce their own supplies, Bide proposed that the plant be cannibalised and improvised facilities prepared at Ulverston and Montrose. Lilly were using penicillin G as their starting material, rather than cephalosporin C, and Glaxo chose to follow a similar route using penicillin V acid, not least because it would not disrupt the output of cephaloridine.

Penicillin at Cambois

In the event, Glaxo decided to build their new antibiotic factory not at Montrose but on a greenfield site owned by the National Coal Board at

Cambois, fifteen miles north of Newcastle.[12] Two other locations, Girvan and Leven, had been considered, but offered fewer advantages. Cambois, situated half a mile from the coast, had facilities for the disposal of effluent into the sea, road and rail connections to Barnard Castle and Montrose, could take water from the North Sea for cooling purposes and had a varied workforce. The Cambois factory was constructed in two phases: initially eight 25,000 gallon vessels were installed for the fermentation of penicillin at a final cost of £7.6 million (of which £2.5 million came from the Board of Trade);[13] then in 1971 Glaxo spent a further £2.65 million at the site on a further six 25,000 gallon vessel fermenters in order to raise its capacity by 330 million mega units of penicillin.[14] This had been necessitated by the diversion of fermentation capacity at Ulverston to vitamin B_{12} and griseofulvin at a time when overseas demand for the antibiotic was rising. In the meantime, the need to set up manufacturing facilities for cephalexin had resulted in the board authorising the expenditure of £1.4 million at Montrose and Ulverston,[15] to which a further £500,000 was added in March 1970 in order to raise its annual output to 40,000kg.[16]

Diversification at Montrose

During the 1950s, the manufacture of penicillin and other antibiotics stood at the core of Glaxo Laboratories' pharmaceutical business. Although profits remained modest and actually fell in real terms for part of the decade (Table 7), finance for capital projects was always found if penicillin production were threatened. Both Ulverston and Barnard Castle benefited from the priority status awarded to penicillin and felt secure as world demand for the medicine rose. However, the same was not true of the group's third primary-process factory at Montrose, which by the mid 1960s was fighting to survive. It was reliant on a limited product range, virtually all drawn from the corticosteroids. As part of a general strategy of lowering unit costs at Montrose, in 1965 Wilkins transferred Dr Chris Hamlet from Ulverston as production manager with the intention that he would eventually take charge at the works. As Hamlet recalled, small volumes made it impossible to achieve the economies of their larger competitors in the United States.[17] At the time of his transfer, the factory employed a total of 170 staff of whom eighty were in production, though Hamlet estimated that output could be maintained with just thirty-five.[18] Montrose had recently begun the manufacture of betamethasone 17-valerate (Betnovate) and its commercial success proved a life saver as the plant rapidly reached capacity, while other parts of the factory remained underused. Financial constraints delayed the investment requested by Hamlet until the 1970s.

Output of betamethasone grew gradually from 0.3 tons per annum in 1965 to 1.3 tons in 1975, when £900,000 was spent to raise the capacity of the plant by 500kg to 2,500kg.[19] In the event, output ultimately climbed to over 2 tons in 1980 and over 3 tons by 1991.

The nature of the manufacturing process itself contributed to the problems experienced at Montrose. Corticosteroids could only be made economically in a large number of stages so that it became both a labour-intensive and time-consuming operation.[20] As a result, the plant at Montrose was characterised by numerous small or medium-sized vessels each with its own temperature and pressure

88. Montrose factory with a vessel for the production of a special reagent that played an important part in the chemical conversion of cephalosporin C to Ceporin.

controls. Unlike Ulverston, glass was used extensively, being resistant to corrosion, cheaper than stainless steel and favoured by the many chemists at Montrose who liked to observe reactions as if in a laboratory.[21] The multitude of vessels added to the plant's flexibility, though they created fewer opportunities to reduce costs by solvent recovery.

In 1969 Montrose embarked on a process of diversification to reduce its reliance upon corticosteroids. A new building was constructed to undertake the final stages in the manufacture of cephalexin, the intermediate being supplied by Ulverston. In 1974 Montrose began to manufacture salbutamol, which until then had been made exclusively at Ware. Earlier, Dr Arthur Hems had persuaded Cyril Maplethorpe, chairman of Allen & Hanburys, the subsidiary which had discovered and marketed the medicine, that Montrose should undertake some of the production because of the rapidly growing demand. Plans were drawn up for the installation of dedicated plant with a capacity of 5 tons per annum. Objections were then raised within Allen & Hanburys at a time when enmities between the two subsidiaries were still alive. Following an intervention by Dr Alan Raper the plant was commissioned, though it soon became clear that it was inadequate and additional capacity had to be installed. Salbutamol was made by a relatively straightforward five-stage process and ultimately its production was concentrated at Montrose. The steroid induction anaesthetic, alphadione (Althesin), was also manufactured there until its withdrawal in 1984 (see p. 320), as was clobetasol propionate (Dermovate), staff numbers rising to 523 by June 1975.

Rationalising primary manufacture

Little attempt was made to integrate and rationalise primary manufacture within Glaxo's various UK sites until 1972 when Austin Bide as deputy chairman introduced a series of organisational reforms. Until then each of the factory managers tended to act independently in operational matters and were known as the 'northern barons'.[22] The distance from Greenford gave the barons considerable freedom of action, and they often took advantage of their detached situation. Appointed northern director in 1949, Dr Wilkins based himself at Ulverston where he developed a distinctive management style, akin in many ways to a general leading his troops. On his arrival, he hung a signed photograph of Field Marshal Montgomery behind his desk and on the side wall a large map of the Northern Hemisphere, showing the relative positions of the USA and USSR.[23] From his headquarters, he built up an intensely loyal inner staff, entrusted with the execution of his strategic plans. In addition, Wilkins gathered a group of young and ambitious managers and scientists to whom he looked for innovative ideas.[24] When Wilkins moved to Greenford to take up broader executive responsibilities within Glaxo Laboratories, the northern factory managers had greater freedom of action. Arthur Lockwood, who succeeded Campbell as factory manager at Barnard Castle in 1950, commented that 'you would bloody get on with it in the way that you thought Glaxo wanted it', while the main board to whom he reported did not expect to be bothered 'with trivialities, only with important things'.[25] Hugh Gurney, who followed Lockwood in 1963, communicated directly with his managing director at Greenford only once or twice every two weeks. Otherwise contact was by letter or telex; financial and output data were sent to Greenford monthly. As a result, as Gurney recalled, 'you were very much master in your own house'.[26] On his own authority, he was able to build up substantial stocks so that the factory could meet unconfirmed orders at short notice, and head office made no demand that he reduce this costly overhead so long as output targets were achieved and no appreciable delays arose in serving customers.

In November 1972, Bide initiated a programme of structural reform designed to gather power to the centre and to improve communications with the more distant elements of the group. A 'technical directorate' was established by W. J. Hurran, together with a Group Technical Policy Committee to debate production issues and implement the Holdings board's strategic decisions. A Technical Development and Planning Unit under Dr Alan Raper, until then factory manager at Barnard Castle, was also set up to provide detailed input on the manufacture of pharmaceuticals.[27] The creation of the Primary Product Division in 1974 provided a forum in which managers from the group's plant at Ulverston, Montrose, Cambois and Edinburgh could meet on a regular basis to discuss practical matters of production and labour and, in particular, resolve any difficulties that might have arisen in the chain of supply. The Division was not constituted as a subsidiary company and had no legal entity but represented an important stage in a gradual process of unification. In July 1978, when a new overarching subsidiary, Glaxo Operations UK Limited was formed (see p. 202), the primary-process factories at Ulverston, Montrose and Cambois fell under its control, together with the secondary production facilities at Barnard Castle, Ware and Speke.

In view of the group's commitment to antibiotics, and in particular to the development of new cephalosporins (see p. 310), in 1977 the board considered various strategies to raise output, including the closure of Ulverston and the transfer of its production to the modern factory at Cambois. Ulverston then had fifty-seven fermenters, ranging in size from 6,000 to 25,000 gallons. Eight installed in 1948 and a further seventeen between 1950 and 1953 were close to the end of their productive lives.[28] The majority were of mild steel construction, in contrast to the eighteen stainless steel 25,000 gallon units installed at Cambois, each with powerful agitator motors and computer controls.[29] In addition Ulverston, which had suffered from the economies imposed during the 1950s and 1960s, had a high burden of infection due in part to the age and design of the plant.[30] It seemed sensible to close Ulverston in favour of greater production at Cambois. However, the latter had been designed specifically for the manufacture of penicillin G and modifications, estimated at £4.6 million, were needed to make cephalosporin C and streptomycin,[31] while an extraction plant with a capacity of 200 tons per annum would add a further £9 million.[32] In the meantime, a sustained effort had been made to improve output at Ulverston. Under Dr Joe Blaker, deputy fermentation works manager, the twenty-eight 25,000 gallon fermenters installed in 1965–67 (of which eight were of stainless steel, together with a further four stainless steel fermenters, installed in 1971), became, in effect, a pilot plant as his team experimented to raise yields. Their determination led to significant efficiencies enabling the factory to match the performance of Cambois,[33] and these results persuaded the Glaxo board that the Ulverston site should remain the focus for continued investment in cephalosporin manufacture.

In the autumn of 1975, when it had become clear that labetalol, or AH 5158 as it was then known, was likely to develop into a potent and commercially viable anti-hypertensive medicine, plans were laid to build a new factory for its manufacture. From a short list of locations, Annan, Dumfriesshire, situated on the north bank of the Solway Firth, was chosen on land re-zoned for industrial use by the Scottish Development Council.[34] It had plentiful supplies of water while effluent, after treatment, could be disposed on the ebb tide into the Solway Firth. Annan had good road links with Barnard Castle, where granulation and packaging would be undertaken. Initial plans drawn up in March 1976 provided for plant with a capacity of 150 tons per annum at a cost of £11.6 million.[35] An extended commissioning period (fourteen months rather than the usual six) delayed its operation until 1980 and raised the final cost to £17.3 million.[36] Because Annan was designed to manufacture large runs of one or two chemicals, an automated plant with a high level of computerisation had been installed. In the event, this proved problematical and, when the specifications were being drawn up for a major primary factory to make ranitidine in Singapore, these teething troubles influenced the choice of a manually operated system that would be more flexible and could also be brought to full operation more quickly (see p. 433). While Annan was being commissioned, Montrose supplied labetalol from a specially commissioned plant that was subsequently diverted to make ranitidine (see p. 273). Output from Annan rose to a peak of 141,012kg in 1986 and fell to a ten-year low in 1992. Being, in essence, a one-product factory, its fortunes were tied to sales of Trandate, which traded in a highly competitive therapeutic field.

In 1978, when the group had three primary process factories (Ulverston, Montrose and Cambois) with a fourth (Annan) under construction, it was decided to set up a subsidiary to manage the growing volume of chemical sales to customers outside Glaxo. Sefton Bulk Pharmaceuticals was established as a trading organisation based at Greenford and it rapidly became the fourth-largest subsidiary in the group.[37] During the 1950s, Ulverston had sold surplus supplies of penicillin G and non-sterile potassium penicillin to other pharmaceutical companies, notably Beecham, which converted the latter into semi-synthetic variants. The trade expanded during the 1960s and, when penicillin production transferred to Cambois in the following decade, it became an important part of the factory's business. By the end of the 1980s, Cambois had become one of the world's largest suppliers of penicillin for human and veterinary use, 90 per cent of its output ultimately being destined for export. Also in great demand were the cephalosporin intermediates (7-ACA for injectables and 7-ADCA for the oral form) made at Ulverston, but which could readily be converted into a final product. These were also sold on the bulk market by Sefton AG and its successor companies. In 1972, the Sefton subsidiary was moved to Zug, Switzerland, where it sat at the centre of a global network. Its chief executive was John Morris, formerly the marketing director of Murphy Chemical, whose considerable linguistic skills had encouraged his appointment. In July 1991, as part of the general strategy of focusing Glaxo's activities on novel prescription medicines, it was decided to withdraw from the bulk chemical market.[38] At the time, Cambois was trading at a loss, being solely reliant upon sales of penicillin G, a business characterised by cyclical fluctuations, and the factory was subsequently sold to Synpac.

Restructuring primary production: Glaxochem

As part of a more general process of reviewing the group's structure, in January 1982 the Technical Directorate was dismantled in favour of a functional subsidiary, and Glaxochem was established under Dr Hugh McCorquodale as a company to manage the group's primary process companies in Britain. The secondary plants were gathered together and placed under the remit of another new subsidiary, Glaxo Pharmaceuticals. With its headquarters at Greenford, Glaxochem was responsible for four factories (Ulverston, Montrose, Cambois and Annan) and also for the Sefton Division.

By the late 1970s the future of Montrose had again become clouded by uncertainty. Although the factory had an expertise in steroid chemistry and diversified into the production of cephalexin and salbutamol, the manufacture of labetalol was due to be transferred to Annan. To secure its future it needed a new and successful product. With the impending launch of ranitidine in mind, Glaxo considered various production options including the general purpose plant, constructed in 1975–77 at a cost of £1.9 million to make labetalol.[39] It was agreed in July 1979 to spend £1.8 million redesigning the facility, though the decision was taken 'without prejudice to any future … location of production facilities for this drug'.[40] Using a four-stage process, the plant had an annual capacity of 15 tons. Over the next five years outputs were increased by almost ten times with negligible capital expenditure following improvements to the process and the optimum use of plant. Subsequently, the rapid growth in the demand for Zantac led to a £22 million investment in 1984[41] together with further major spending in July 1986, outputs eventually rising to over 300 tons three years later.[42]

Ulverston continued to be the group's principal producer of cephalosporins, making cefuroxime from 1977 and the initial stages of ceftazidime from 1981. Demand for the latter was such that in April 1984 the Holdings board authorised the expenditure of £48.7 million on a new plant to raise output as this third-generation cephalosporin was launched in new overseas markets (see p. 316).[43] The first plans were drawn up by Foster Wheeler, in conjunction with Ulverston's own engineers, though the original ten-stage manufacturing process was later reduced to six. The use of resin technology, costing only £250,000, increased extraction rates by 10 per cent, saving £1.3 million in the first six months of operation.[44] The development of an oral version of cefuroxime led to the expenditure of £13.9 million on manufacturing facilities at Ulverston in 1986.[45] Unlike most of the earlier capital projects at Ulverston, the cefuroxime axetil programme was managed in-house by staff assisted by a small number of specialist sub-contractors.

Set up in the late 1940s and early 1950s, Glaxo's primary process factories, such as Ulverston and Montrose, used advanced technologies licensed from the United States. Although expertise was recruited from outside (notably in the cases of Dr A. H. Campbell and Dr F. J. Wilkins), Glaxo generally sought to redeploy existing members of staff. Working with novel equipment and processes, they often learned by trial and error. The factory locations, far from industrial conurbations and with no tradition of pharmaceutical manufacture, fostered a spirit of self-reliance and placed a premium on problem solving. In later years, the need to compete in international rather than local markets increased the pressure to remain efficient. Ulverston, for example, may be Glaxo's only primary producer of cephalosporins and the largest of its kind in the UK, but it has to measure itself against European and US rivals if the group is to survive in such a fiercely contested therapeutic area.

Environmental issues assumed increasing importance during the 1980s and have had their greatest impact on Glaxo at its primary process factories. From the outset great efforts were made to recover the solvents used at Ulverston, not only because of fears about their potential as pollutants but simply because of their cost; the factory could not compete without their reuse. Continuous spending on more efficient methods has led to a recovery rate of over 95 per cent, while at Montrose, where operations are characterised by larger number of processes on a smaller scale, the corresponding figure is 70 per cent. During the 1950s and 1960s, effluent from Ulverston was discharged into the sea without being treated. With revenues flowing from Zantac, Glaxo spent £3.2 million at Ulverston in 1988 on a storage, filtration and discharge system constructed in conjunction with North West Water.[46] At Montrose, £2 million was invested on plant for the recovery of isopropyl alcohol from ranitidine production.[47] In addition to solvent recovery, environmental controls take two forms: abatement (the use of scrubbers to remove pollutants or odours from emission gases), and incineration equipment to destroy waste products. The factories at Ulverston, near to the southern borders of the Lake District, Montrose close to wetlands of international importance and at Annan in a site of special scientific interest, have to be particularly sensitive to environmental issues.

In spring 1988, Dr Hugh McCorquodale, the group technical director, was asked to investigate whether Glaxo should continue in the business of primary production or simply purchase active ingredients from outside suppliers. His report concluded that it was important for the group to remain vertically integrated for several pressing reasons:

> the need for certainty of supply (notably when undertaking the initial investment in manufacturing capacity prior to launching a new product); the need to ensure manufacture to Glaxo's standards; and the close relationship between development and production, particularly in the early stages, and the interface therefore with the protection of Glaxo's intellectual property. Primary production costs are less than 10 per cent of total sales and primary manufacture by Glaxo companies proved to be as cheap as using outside operators ...[48]

The imperative question of quality proved to be the overriding consideration. The importance of dual sourcing for the group's leading products was discussed and this ultimately led to continued investment in the Singapore factory (see p. 433).

Secondary manufacture

A significant characteristic of Glaxo's secondary manufacture during the 1960s and 1970s was the proliferation of products, with an even greater number of specifications for overseas markets. Whilst the primary factories made no more than sixteen to twenty individual chemicals, the various secondary plants turned out many hundreds of generic and prescription products. At Speke alone in 1971 over 400 types of medicine were manufactured, many of which were standard preparations such as paracetamol or cough syrups.[49] At Barnard Castle the situation was scarcely less complex as the factory made topical creams and ointments, tablets and injectables (filled as vials, ampoules and syringes).[50] Because the factory supplied four marketing organisations (Allen & Hanburys, Duncan Flockhart, Glaxo Laboratories and Evans Medical), a bewildering variety of formulations were needed, varying from generics in short runs to significant ethical preparations such as betamethasone and, from 1981, Zantac.[51] Among the former were tubocararine, suxamethonium and triiodothyronine, while other portfolio oddities included Oterna ear drops, sulphacetamide eye drops and Sea Legs tablets.[52] The different packaging requirements of national markets increased this diversity still further and the group as a whole was responsible for about 11,000 different presentations of its products. In this period, before the advent of exceptionally rigorous safety standards and the high levels of automation permitted by advances in computer science, plant was not particularly capital intensive. Many filling and packing operations were still semi-automated, while those for small batches, which did not merit the setting up of machinery, were sometimes completed by hand. As a result, the group's secondary factories were not operated intensively and during the 1970s most ran on a single shift. Only rapidly burgeoning sales of Zantac led to the introduction of a second shift, and on occasion twenty-four-hour working, at Barnard Castle. At first, the commercial pressure behind these changes was rising demand set against the capital cost of modern plant, to which was added a third factor, uncertainty of demand. In the 1990s as profit margins tightened and competition became more intense, manufacturers were forced to be more responsive to changes in the market-place. No longer could they afford to have expensive plant standing idle for several days a week and sought to run it as close to its capacity for as long as possible in order to maximise returns.

Because Glaxo had grown, in part, through acquisition, it found itself with a considerable number of secondary manufacturing operations whose products related to the historical specialisms of their former owners. So, in March 1968, Bide set up a study group under the chairmanship of E. K. Samways, production director of Allen & Hanburys, to investigate the strategic organisation of these factories. Reporting in December, Samways confirmed that there was an imbalance in favour of the south-east and recommended the transfer of some production capacity north where it would be closer to the group's primary factories.[53] In addition, a measure of rationalisation was proposed: that the number of sites making and packaging tablets should be reduced; that Barnard Castle be developed as a secondary plant, taking over the tablet work currently undertaken at Greenford, that ampoule filling for all subsidiaries be concentrated there and that it become a centre for making speciality creams and ointments. The Samways team also suggested that liquid and powder filling then carried out at Ware and Greenford be transferred to Speke, to use the space created by the transfer of Evans ampoule filling to Barnard Castle. The net result would be that Greenford would focus on research and development and serve as the administrative headquarters for Glaxo Laboratories, while its function as a food filling and packing factory was reconsidered.

In September 1968 it was formally agreed that, with the transfer of its antibiotic production to Ulverston and Cambois, Barnard Castle would operate solely as a secondary process factory.[54] A new building was commissioned in May 1969 at a cost of £2.5 million.[55] Although some staff were transferred from fermentation to secondary process tasks, these changes created a new demand for labour. Employees at Greenford, who were to be made redundant because of the rationalisation, were encouraged to apply for the 600 vacancies at Barnard Castle. Although many visited the plant and town, only a small proportion chose to move to County Durham. Dr Alan Raper, the factory manager, had the task of recruiting over 500 employees from the surrounding area, which had no tradition of industrial work. Many came from farms or had been in service and were sent to Greenford for training before they were assigned to production lines, filling ampoules, or making tablets and creams.[56] During the 1970s, Barnard Castle made an increasing number of medicines not only for Glaxo Laboratories but also for Evans Medical, Allen & Hanburys and the group's veterinary subsidiaries. Volumes grew as the factory agreed to undertake small runs and an increasingly diverse range of pharmaceuticals. By 1983 Barnard Castle was responsible for over 3,000 different packs, of which a third were specially prepared variants of the general export presentation. These commonly required a distinctive print run and sometimes a modification of the manufacturing process, such as the requirement that topical creams for Scandinavia be produced in sterile conditions.[57] The situation with regard to ampoule filling was even more complex. Some seventy-two products were prepared in this way in as many as seven different fill volumes, three strengths and a variety of pack collations in response to particular market requirements.[58]

Despite the Samways' recommendations and the transfer of operations from Greenford, Glaxo's secondary manufacture continued at three principal sites: Barnard Castle, Ware and Speke. In 1983, however, as part of a general strategy of focusing the group's activities on prescription pharmaceuticals, Dr Joe Blaker, newly appointed as technical director of Glaxo Pharmaceuticals, was asked to review the secondary factories and suggest ways of rationalising manufacture among them. In a report presented to Paul Girolami, the chief executive, Blaker outlined the need to restructure secondary production in the UK.[59] The group's factories had limited space and ageing buildings, poor communications between sites, an over-complex product range with varying standards of manufacture, together with uncertain long-term demand.[60] However,

Blaker also identified a number of strengths: relatively modern plant (the result of consistent investment), a depth of production expertise, a number of major products and an established source (Evans Medical) for speciality or low-volume medicines.[61]

Ware and Barnard Castle

Blaker proposed that Glaxo concentrate on 'the production of research-based ethical products, together with the best available technical expertise at Barnard Castle and Ware to derive the benefits of economies of scale', and the high profit that followed from scientific innovation.[62] In practice, this involved a projected expenditure of £93 million, spread over five years, to expand and update manufacture at the two sites to meet higher safety and output targets. Low-profit penicillin work at Barnard Castle was to be ended, while its prescription medicine production was to be increased to find employment for the 220 displaced staff. This included a new aerosol and Rotacap plant for respiratory medicines to take up the slack created by the running down of Speke, and the construction of a cephalosporin building at an estimated cost of £18 million for the manufacture, filling and packaging of injectable and oral forms.[63]

These ambitious plans involved fundamental changes to the pattern of secondary manufacture. These changes were driven not only by the need to rationalise but also by developments in the United States. Although Ware, Barnard Castle and Speke were responsible for 40 per cent of the group's finished ethical products in 1985, this figure was set to halve when Zebulon in North Carolina reached its planned capacity.[64] The scale of the US market generated long production runs, which left the UK plants increasingly dependent upon smaller orders, contracts, and first-production runs of new medicines. Greater flexibility and the more efficient use of capital intensive machinery were therefore required. To this end, double-day shift working was introduced in order to meet the target of 70 per cent plant utilisation and the need to change runs at regular intervals. Although Glaxo continued to run down the former Evans Medical factory at Speke (and indeed Bernard Taylor prepared plans for its complete closure[65]), a concerted campaign led by Graham Vitty, the factory manager, ultimately persuaded the board of its value and prompted a reinvestment in plant and buildings (see p. 281).

Having identified Ware and Barnard Castle as the two key sites for secondary manufacture in the UK, Glaxo embarked on a programme of intensive capital expenditure at both factories. Although Barnard Castle had established a reputation for technical competence under John Brennand,

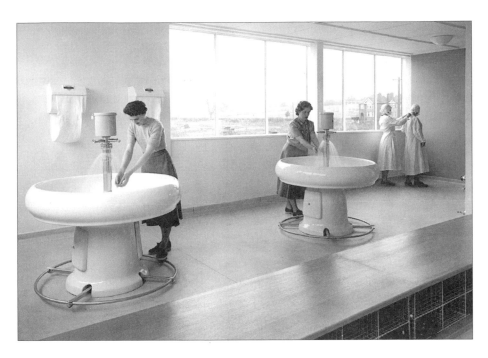

89. Women scrubbing up and robing at Ware in the late 1950s.

the factory manager, and had built up export sales to 75 per cent of output, it was not regarded as commercially alert and much of the plant had become outdated. 'A' block, built in 1945, and 'B' block, built two years later, were close to the end of their productive lives, while 'C' block, opened in 1971 and still regarded as advanced, was in need of modernisation.[66] With funds beginning to flow from burgeoning sales of Zantac, important capital projects were implemented. An automated warehouse was completed in March 1984, followed in 1986 at a cost of £25 million by a new cephalosporin building, which provided aseptic conditions for the filling and sealing of vials.[67] To raise standards of production and ensure uniformity, 'L' block, a quality assurance building, was completed in June 1988 at a cost of £8.9 million.[68]

Substantial rebuilding was also envisaged at Ware on a site that still had operational buildings dating from 1903 to 1914 and a number of World War Two Nissen huts. A bewildering range of products had been made during the 1970s in a variety of formulations, including Ventolin (an inhaled bronchodilator), Piriton (an antihistamine), DF118 (a dihydrocodeine analgesic), Beta-Cardone (a beta-blocker) and Fentazin (a neuroleptic), together with the OTC preparations Dequadin and Haliborange. Furthermore, the factory produced intravenous fluids, packed blackcurrant pastilles and until the early 1970s also made malt extract. A gradual process of rationalisation proceeded during the decade as generic and OTC medicines were discontinued, such that by 1983–84 half of the expected sales revenue of £110 million came from aerosols and Rotacaps. Yet, it was not until the mid 1980s and the decision to focus on novel prescription products that Ware concentrated on the manufacture of tablets and respiratory drugs. As income from Zantac flowed into Glaxo, so any impediments to capital projects were removed. In February 1985, for example, £2.8 million was spent upgrading 'U' building at Ware,[69] while later in the year an equivalent sum was allocated for the manufacture of Rotadisks on the site.[70] The most important capital project at the factory was the tablet production and packaging facility authorised in March 1986 at a cost of £17.3 million.[71] Opened in June 1990, with a capacity of 4 billion tablets per annum, it was designed for long runs of the group's leading prescription medicines including Zantac, Volmax, Zofran and Imigran.

Evans Medical at Speke

In 1986, Glaxo decided to withdraw from the market for generic pharmaceuticals. As a result, it was decided to review the future of Evans Medical, a company that had developed as a supplier of medicines whose patents had expired, vaccines and a wide range of OTC preparations. If these products were to be sold or discontinued, the future of the factory as a contract supplier looked bleak. The original buildings occupied by Evans, Sons, Lescher and Webb in central Liverpool had been severely damaged by enemy bombs in 1941. A replacement factory, located at a thirty-acre greenfield site in the suburbs of Speke and leased from the Liverpool Corporation, was completed in 1943 and owed much to the exigencies of modern warfare. Fire regulations dictated that it be designed as three distinct units, and the corridors were built of reinforced concrete to provide protection during air raids. The design and poor quality of some construction materials combined to limit the possibilities for redevelopment and led to Speke being identified as the least favourable site in the UK.[72]

In 1968 a new vaccine producing unit had been commissioned and completed two years later adjacent to the existing plant, operating under the style Evans Biologicals. Although technically more advanced than the main factory, rising costs increasingly undermined the profitability of its main products (Mevilin, a measles vaccine, together with Admune and Fluvirin, influenza vaccines).[73] While a review conducted in the summer of 1981 recommended reducing the range of its activities (abandoning the output of human bacterialogicals, such as tuberculin, tetanus, diphtheria and pertussis, and the manufacture of ear and eye drops),[74] the plant continued to record a loss. In 1983, it was calculated that the Speke factories manufactured over 2,000 different types of pack, many of which were in small volumes. Although sales for that year were expected to realise £70 million, two-thirds of the income derived from aerosols.[75] In 1986, Evans Biologicals was subject to a management buy-out and took the Evans Medical name. This called into question the future of the main Speke factory, which had been losing around £4 million a year during the mid 1980s. Although greater volumes of generics were produced, unit costs never fell to a level at which they could compete with small specialist manufacturers. The Speke factory remained a substantial employer with a total of 1,117 staff (including Evans Biological) in June 1981 at a time when Ware had 907 and Barnard Castle 1,312.[76] A review conducted by Graham Vitty revealed a lack of investment and outdated working practices, though the staff remained highly motivated. His survival strategy identified the need for capital spending on plant in return for substantial redundancies and retraining for many of those who remained. The workforce was cut from 800 to 362 and the Holdings board agreed to a £4 million investment in a liquid and tablet production facility, while a further £6 million was spent to increase the output of aerosols and Rotacaps to compensate for the loss of older unprofitable medicines. The drawing up of the Speke Charter in 1990 led to greater flexibility in working practices and retraining designed to broaden the skill base. In May 1992, £17 million was authorised for the construction of a new inhalations centre for the production of Rotacaps and aerosols, completed in the following year.

Dual sourcing: the international dimension

Having suffered from a series of industrial disputes in its northern factories during the late 1960s and early 1970s (see p. 290), Glaxo became acutely aware of the need to have a second source of supply should output be curtailed from any cause. As a result, it was planned to build a primary process plant in Indonesia on land that had been acquired in 1969. However, Sir Alan Wilson was persuaded that limited resources would be invested more profitably in Australia and the scheme was abruptly abandoned in 1971 (see p. 432). It was not until 1979 that the idea of primary manufacturing overseas was again considered seriously. With the prospect of a major new product on the horizon, a pilot plant for ranitidine was built in Singapore. Given financial encouragement by the authorities, Glaxo invested heavily in the factory that came on stream in June 1982 and developed as the group's principal source of ranitidine (see p. 433). Further expenditure

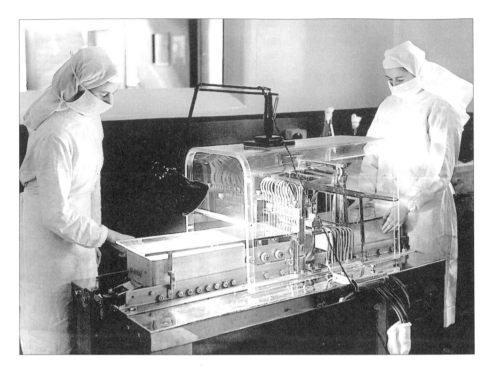

90. Two women operating a multiple ampoule filling machine at Barnard Castle in the early 1950s.

enabled the plant to make the active ingredients for salmeterol, ondansetron and sumatriptan. In this way Glaxo safeguarded its essential supplies and introduced an element of internal competition. Thus, Ulverston and Singapore became the group's largest primary factories, supported by Annan, a specialist labetalol plant, and Montrose, which with its development expertise, was employed to make products newly launched on to the market.

Secondary production was more complicated, though the principle of dual sourcing was also adopted. During the 1960s and 1970s, the main source of supply was the UK factories with few alternatives in an emergency. Although Glaxo had constructed a number of small-scale secondary-process plants around the world, largely to package products for local requirements, it was not until March 1984 that a major factory came on stream – at Zebulon in North Carolina (see p. 397). Initially, it focused on Zantac, Ventolin and Beclovent, though the completion of a cephalosporin building in the summer of 1991 widened its portfolio and resulted in Glaxo Inc. achieving a degree of self-sufficiency with the capacity to supply other countries if they had production problems. With its wealth of experience in development, the UK has remained the proving ground for new medicines: Ulverston or Montrose undertaking their primary manufacture and Barnard Castle or Ware their secondary processes. Once the medicine is established, its production is commonly transferred to other factories located closer to national markets.

The apparent imbalance between the number of primary and secondary plants has arisen for a variety of reasons. First, the group made it a rule that if a national subsidiary generates sales beyond a certain level then it is obliged to establish a second source of supply to ensure reliability. Secondly, the cost of installing a local secondary plant to produce simple formulations and package them for distribution within that territory is relatively low in contrast to regional or strategic factories (the latter being capable of introducing any products and supplying all markets with the highest level of technology). Thirdly, some national regulators make it a requirement that multinational pharmaceutical companies open manufacturing as well as sales and marketing facilities to avoid being wholly dependent on imported medicines and to provide employment. Fourthly, commercial advantages accrue from siting packaging operations as close to the market as possible. In the past, for example, when Barnard Castle attempted to supply virtually all of the group's overseas markets, it was forced to process short runs and hold extensive stocks in order to respond to orders quickly. By siting packaging operations locally in a host of small-scale plants, response times have been accelerated. Although the group built up surplus capacity in some of its secondary operations, their relatively low cost in a time of buoyant profits prevented this from becoming a significant issue.

Finally, the fact that Glaxo now operated on a global stage had implications for quality standards in its factories wherever they were. During the 1960s and 1970s, there had been considerable variation in the regulations imposed by particular national authorities. Once Glaxo sold its products directly in the United States, FDA inspectors claimed the right to monitor plant elsewhere in the world because the original active ingredients were produced either at Ulverston, Montrose or Singapore. Equally, the regulatory authorities in the UK exercised the right to inspect plant in New Zealand or Australia if their medicines or chemicals were ultimately consumed in Britain. Hence the internationalisation of both supply and demand have indirectly led to the standardisation of quality controls and manufacturing procedures. Regulators hold the key to market access; they can, for example, demand stringent checks for a new product and thereby delay its launch, or close a facility once in operation. Multinational pharmaceutical companies such as Glaxo cannot afford to fall foul of the increasingly rigorous regulatory demands.

Food manufacture

By the early 1960s pharmaceuticals were established as Glaxo Group's core activity and its traditional foods business, though still significant in terms of turnover, had to fight hard to obtain finance for capital projects. Although a modern spray-drying factory had been built at Kendal in 1962, Greenford remained the principal factory and the introduction of new products created considerable congestion as filling and packing processes remained semi-automated.

In 1962, a Job Day packing machine was purchased for £22,500 and run on an experimental basis at Greenford to evaluate its performance.[77] It dramatically improved productivity as before a line of eight to ten women could finish 8–9,000 packs a day, whereas the new technology achieved 30,000. It was calculated that two machines, together with an improved layout, would save Glaxo £40,000 a year, and in June 1963 the board agreed to spend £150,000 on modernisation at Greenford.[78] A Job Day packing machine had already been installed at Kendal to pack Farex and this was transferred to Greenford in exchange for older equipment to speed up the rationalisation.[79] In April 1965, a further machine was purchased, together with a continuous blending unit for Complan manufacture at a total cost of £60,000.[80]

Because the Driffield roller-drying plant had experienced supply difficulties and it was considered risky to rely on the Kendal factory alone, in 1965 it was decided to build a second spray-drying factory in Ireland. Opened at Loch Egish, Monaghan, in June 1966 by Charles Haughey, then Minister of Agriculture and Fisheries, it was situated in a dairy farm region near to a co-operative creamery.[81] The project was supported by a capital grant from the Industrial Development Authority, though the entire output of skimmed milk powder was exported to the UK for Ostermilk and Complan. In the event, the decision to rationalise the group's food business resulted in the factory having a relatively short life (see p. 201). Earlier in 1954, Glaxo had set up a small secondary process and packing plant at Grand Canal Street, Dublin, and a subsidiary, Glaxo Laboratories (Ireland), was formed in the following year. Having outgrown its original premises, the offices, warehouse and pharmaceutical factory moved to modern buildings at Rathfarnham, in the southern outskirts, of Dublin in 1971.[82]

In 1968, to gain economies of scale in a business characterised by modest profit margins, Glaxo approached Farley's Infant Food, their principal rival in the UK, with proposals for a merger. Their offer was accepted in March[83] and the Farley factory in Plymouth became part of Glaxo Group (see p. 162). The production of Farex and Farex Fingers (introduced in 1965 to meet the challenge of Farley's Rusks) was transferred to Devon, so that

Greenford could concentrate on the manufacture of milk-based foods such as Ostermilk, Complan and Casilan.[84] Later in the year Glaxo spent £134,000 on the reorganisation of Farley's distribution system and transport fleet, while a further £67,000 was authorised for factory extensions at Plymouth.[85] As part of the general improvements, £50,000 was invested in a product development unit at Kendal.[86] A year earlier it had been announced that the Driffield factory would close in 1969 because of difficulties in obtaining adequate quantities of milk from the surrounding dairy farms, such that plant had to be diverted to other activities when supplies were at their lowest.[87]

91. Ostermilk packaging at Greenford after the replacement of tins by cartons in 1962.

The food products made by Glaxo Laboratories were also influenced by developments in nutritional science. In March 1964, following recommendations from the Ministry of Health, Glaxo spent £12,000 on equipment to add vitamin C to Ostermilk packed at Greenford.[88] However, sales in the UK grew only gradually during the 1960s (Table 19, p. 454), the final limiting factor being the birth rate, which fell from 1967 onwards.[89] This market contraction, together with a fierce price war with their main rivals Cow & Gate and SMA, saw Glaxo surrender valuable ground. In 1970, for example, the company lost 18 per cent of the hospital post-natal market, reducing its overall share to only 3 per cent.[90] In an attempt to reverse this trend, in October 1970 Glaxo Laboratories launched Golden Ostermilk.[91] Made from spray-dried milk, it was a freer-flowing powder which contrasted with the flakey appearance of the roller-dried version. In addition it was easier to reconstitute, though the shelf-life was shorter. Golden Ostermilk, a full-cream powder, had been introduced with the intention that it would supplant Ostermilk No. 2 as the company's leading brand (a blend of the Kendal product and imports of roller-dried powder from Bunnythorpe), provided that the price of the latter could be gradually increased to the pre-mium charged for the former.[92] In the event, the strategy failed, largely be-cause market forces turned against Glaxo. Milk costs rose by 33 per cent in the year to August 1972, discouraging consumers from switching to Golden Ostermilk.[93] Retailers, led by Boots, introduced discounts on the brand leaders whilst continuing to sell Golden Ostermilk at its full retail price. As a result, turnover fell short of expectations, reaching only 2.1 million lb in 1971–72 against a target of 6.9 million. Because spray-drying was more costly than the roller process, it was not possible to cut the price of Golden Ostermilk and, in these circumstances, it seemed unlikely that it would capture more than 20 per cent of Glaxo's entire milk sales. Managers feared that they would be left with two minor products, while their main com-petitor, Cow & Gate, became the brand leader.

By April 1973, the situation had become critical as sales of Golden Oster-milk levelled off, while the share formerly held by Ostermilk No. 2 was being eroded by Cow & Gate.[94] Glaxo decided to abandon Ostermilk No. 2 to its fate and divert all promotional activity to Golden Ostermilk in the hope that its superior quality and the brand name would combine to make it a market leader. The plan was impeded, however, by the introduction of Formula V designed by Cow & Gate as a direct competitor.[95] In May 1973, when it had become clear that sales of Golden Ostermilk had peaked, Peter Scruton, marketing director of Glaxo Laboratories, concluded that the product had failed and the company should expect its market share to de-cline.[96] Henceforth, promotional drives were directed towards the tradi-tional Ostermilks in an effort to re-establish their position, and by February 1974 it looked as though the fall in their consumer appeal had been halted.[97] Golden Ostermilk was discontinued in the following month and all stocks were destroyed.[98] Its withdrawal clarified what had become a complex marketing strategy and sales of the Ostermilks began to improve for the first time in two years,[99] continuing to move upwards with the launch of Ostermilk Complete Formula in August 1973. In part, this was a response to medical criticism of full-cream milk powder (used for both Os-termilk No. 2 and Golden Ostermilk)[100] and the compelling case that it should be modified to approximate as closely as possible to breast milk.[101] It was predicted that Ostermilk Complete Formula would immediately supplant Ostermilk No. 1 and, as mothers were educated to abandon the full-cream versions, would also gradually displace No. 2. Although Oster-milk Complete Formula was well received in hospitals, it encountered con-sumer resistance and Glaxo's success in regaining a further 2 per cent of the retail market for infant milks (bringing its total share to 42 per cent)[102] by the end of May 1974 relied on its two traditional Ostermilks.[103]

In January 1975 Glaxo was forced to make a radical change to its distribution policy. In the past Ostermilk, and its other infant foods, had been sold exclusively through retail chemists and welfare centres, where they were promoted by the pharmaceutical sales force.[104] Because pharmacy shops were in decline, their numbers falling from 15,302 in 1955 to 11,673 in 1973, it became difficult for mothers in certain parts of England to buy infant foods. The Monopolies Commission had agreed in 1967 that Glaxo could sell its milk through grocery stores in those places where no retail chemist was situated within half a mile of a post office. In 1979, the rising cost of milk forced Glaxo to increase the price of Ostermilk No. 2 by 41 per cent over fifteen months. In turn, mothers began to switch to unmodified cows' milk earlier in a baby's life as National Dried Milk remained at 20p and the doorstep price of bottled milk was heavily subsidised at 5p. The fact that Ostermilk was not routinely stocked in grocers encouraged this trend. Wyeth had recently fostered the promotion of SMA in the grocery trade and seemed to be the only company experiencing genuine growth. When trial runs of Ostermilk and Complan in twenty branches of Asda did not provoke an adverse reaction from retail pharmacies, it was decided that all products sold by Glaxo Farley Foods (with the exception of Adexolin liquid and capsules) would be supplied to grocery wholesalers. The marketing division of Glaxo Farley Foods, set up in October 1973, was better equipped to promote these foods than the sales force of Glaxo Laboratories, which was increasingly orientated towards pharmaceuticals.

To safeguard the future of Farex as a weaning food, Glaxo developed a rice cereal variant with a higher protein content (14 per cent), double that of its competitors. At a cost of £30,000 in new machinery, the investment was justified by a projected turnover of £60,000 after two years and estimated to generate profits of £27,000.[105] Nevertheless Farex, like Complan and Glucodin, earned a significantly lower turnover than Ostermilk (Table 19) and because the latter was the company's brand leader most of the promotional effort went into boosting its sales. When Glaxo sold its food business in 1985, Boots, the purchaser, continued to use the Farley name because of its established reputation. While Farex and Complan continued to be marketed as such, the Ostermilk trademark was abandoned in favour of 'Farley's Infant Feeding First and Second Milks'.

Although turnover from the foods business continued to rise in the early 1970s, its profitability fell, and in 1973–74 recorded a small loss.[106] In his annual statement, Austin Bide announced the creation of a Glaxo-Farley-Foods Division based at Plymouth to rationalise the sales and administrative functions.[107] Privately, Bide admitted to the board that these reorganisational and cost-cutting measures would not be sufficient to pull the foods business back into a profit, so great had been the inflationary rise in costs, which the company was unable to pass on to the consumer because of price sensitivity.[108] It was decided to gather together the group's food operations into a newly incorporated company, in part to improve its commercial performance but also as a preliminary to a possible sale. Douglas Back was asked to consider a plan to end food production at Greenford and its transfer to Plymouth and Kendal. He calculated that the relocation, costed at £349,000, would generate annual savings of £206,000.[109]

In addition a new company, Glaxo-Farley Infant Food, was set up as a subsidiary of Glaxo Holdings. The reorganisation, which also involved closing the group's Irish factory at Loch Egish, together with the heightened emphasis on quality control, turned the business round and it returned to profitability in 1975–76. Much of the detailed analysis and restructuring was undertaken by E. R. C. Farmer, who had joined Glaxo in 1974 as the Foods Division product manager. Following the success of this operation, Farmer became managing director of Glaxo-Farley Infant Food in 1975.[110] Although the company continued to record a surplus during the late 1970s and early 1980s (when it was renamed Farley Health Products), it became increasingly peripheral to the group's interests, though plans for its disposal were postponed because of the subsidiary's continuing profitability. Whilst no longer central, the business continued to demand investment and in November 1983, for example, £5.7 million was spent at Kendal on a replacement spray dryer.[111] Following the decision to focus its activities on prescription medicines, Glaxo sold Farleys to Boots in 1986, though the price was ultimately demolished by an outbreak of salmonella at the Kendal factory (see p. 215).[112]

Industrial relations

By the early 1960s two systems of industrial relations had grown up within Glaxo Group. The first, which prevailed at Greenford, Barnard Castle and Ulverston, relied on direct negotiation between managers and employees in joint advisory committees in place of union representation. Formed of delegates elected from all sections of the workforce, each was autonomous, acting independently of agreements reached by other joint advisory committees. They could only make recommendations, so that final decisions on pay and conditions remained with the company boards. Elsewhere within Glaxo, employees were represented by the established unions through formal negotiating procedures. One feature common to all subsidiaries, except Murphy Chemical and Vestric, was the existence of staff associations and other types of formal gathering. Allen & Hanburys, for example, had both a staff liaison committee chaired by the managing director, Cyril Maplethorpe, and works committees at their Bethnal Green and Ware factories. Staff associations worked alongside the union officials or the joint advisory committees but were considered by management as helpful in resolving difficulties in an informal way before attitudes had hardened.[113] Jephcott, who believed in a federal system, allowed subsidiaries to devise their own industrial relations policy and to settle disputes themselves so far as possible without reference to other companies in the group.

The growth in the size and complexity of Glaxo Group and the increasingly problematic nature of British industrial relations led Sir Alan Wilson in 1963 to set up a Personnel and Pension Policy Committee, to make general policy recommendations to the main board.[114] Chaired by Wilson himself, its membership comprised Herbert Palmer, the general manager, together with the chief executives of Glaxo Laboratories, Allen & Hanburys and Evans Medical – Dr F. J. Wilkins, Cyril Maplethorpe and Dr F. S. Gorril, respectively. Its terms of reference were broad, governing

> industrial and human relations and terms and conditions of employment throughout the Glaxo Group of companies and in particular ... conditions of service, salaries/wages, hours of work, holidays, incentive schemes, insurances, safety, health and welfare, recruitment selection, education and training and promotion of staff, transfer of labour, communications and joint consultation in the factory, voluntary negotiation and consultation, conciliation and arbitration between management and staff.[115]

This remit was over ambitious and in July 1966 it was replaced by the Group Personnel Committee under the chairmanship of Austin Bide.[116] To make its task more manageable subsidiaries were grouped into 'assemblies' in which personnel matters were dealt in common. Four assemblies were identified, Glaxo Laboratories (which included Macfarlan Smith and Glaxo Research), Allen & Hanburys, Evans Medical and Murphy Chemical.

Although its terms of reference encompassed wages and salaries, together with employment protection (redundancy) policy, the Group Personnel Committee did not supplant the two systems of industrial relations within the group and these remained the way workplace grievances were resolved. The committee advised and informed the various assemblies in the factories and laboratories on policy issues without seeking to resolve specific issues.

The late sixties and early seventies witnessed a gradual deterioration in labour relations throughout the UK as progressive governments sought to limit wage rises. The advent of the Prices and Incomes Board in 1965, and the prospect of restrictive legislation (which was to manifest itself in the prices and incomes freeze of July 1966), naturally led some union representatives, as Bide remarked, to 'make as much hay as possible, while the sun still shines'.[117] In June 1966, the group was besieged by 'last gasp' demands for pay increases, of which that submitted to the board of Allen & Hanburys appeared the most questionable. The engineers at its factories and laboratories threatened to ban overtime without a generous increase. The management feared that they would not settle for less than 7 per cent, which conflicted with the National Guiding Light's recommendation of 3 to 3.5 per cent. The Ministry of Labour did not attempt to enforce these restrictions, informing the company that it would be 'happy and even surprised' if rises were limited to 5 per cent in 1966.[118] Protracted discussions resulted in an increase of 6 per cent throughout the group, which averted the threatened overtime ban.

Senior management at Glaxo were becoming aware of a growing threat from militant union leaders. Bide, chairman of Glaxo Laboratories following the death of Wilkins, decided as a priority that customers should not suffer. It was also thought, in view of its importance to the group (Table 13), that Glaxo Laboratories would be a target for industrial action. His first concern was to safeguard output. John Farrant, the factory manager at Ulverston, and Arthur Lockwood at Barnard Castle were encouraged to build up stocks in the free port of Rotterdam, which could be drawn upon in the event of short-time working or a shutdown. Bide was also concerned that a fully manned plant could be brought to a halt if its electricity supply were cut off as all of the group's factories drew power from the National Grid. A considerable sum, around £12 million, was spent installing standby generators so that factories could continue to operate independently. These actions passed unnoticed by the unions who may, as a result, have underestimated the strength of Glaxo's resolve.

Despite the successful negotiation of wage demands in 1966, a group of 145 craftsmen at the Ulverston factory pressed their demands for special recognition, while the production staff continued to work normally. Many of them had worked for shipbuilders before joining Glaxo and so brought to pharmaceuticals a tough and uncompromising culture forged in countless battles in a relatively poor and declining industry; the suffering and adversity endured by earlier generations gave them a particular motivation. As a result of sustained pressure, the Ulverston craftsmen, unlike any other employees of Glaxo Laboratories, negotiated pay and conditions through the Barrow Confederation of Shipbuilding and Engineering Unions. Labour in the Barrow peninsula and near by had a reputation for bellicosity and the Confederation, led by Eric Montgomery, formerly of Vickers Shipbuilding, was renowned for militant behaviour. The issue at Ulverston

92. *Workers at a Joint Advisory Committee meeting held at Greenford in 1961 and chaired by Dr Fred Wilkins, who leans back in his seat* (right hand side).

centred on the engineers' claim for an increase of £2 a week based on a measure of co-operation they had afforded, while the Barrow Confederation argued that this be backdated to 1 October 1965. This claim far exceeded the 6 per cent accepted by Glaxo Laboratories staff elsewhere. At a meeting with the Confederation on 3 June 1966, W. J. Hurran offered a rise of £1 a week, representing 6 per cent, which was rejected.

The unresolved dispute was of concern to the Glaxo management for two reasons: first, a major expansion programme at Ulverston, budgeted at £2.5 million, would be jeopardised by the continuing overtime ban: secondly, if Glaxo acceded to the craftsmen's demands it would have implications for other wage earners and, in turn, for salaried staff.[119] These worries caused Glaxo to standardise the review procedure in their major subsidiaries. Hitherto the date and timescale of these varied considerably. From 1 July 1967 it was agreed that changes to pay and conditions would all take effect on that day, thereby reducing the likelihood of one company being played off against another in negotiations between unions and staff.[120]

Whilst managerial fears over manipulation of its industrial relations system remained, the main threat came not from organised labour but from the government's implementation of a prices and incomes policy. Aubrey Jones, chairman of the National Board for Prices and Incomes, outlined the Labour government's determination to try to restrict increases:

> Without any doubt we are moving historically towards intervention by the state in collective bargaining. At the turn of the century … the law intervened to prevent wages falling below a certain level, now we are evolving towards a situation in which the law has to prevent wages rising above a certain level.[121]

In a surprising judgement, the Ministry of Labour refused to allow Glaxo to implement the general 6 per cent increment it had negotiated, but agreed that the Ulverston craftsmen could be paid an additional £2.30 to take account of commitments made prior to the pay freeze. This represented a gain of 11.1 per cent at a time when the rest of the workforce were denied any form of wage award. Management recognised that this settlement was likely to generate further disputes as the anomaly created resentments elsewhere.[122] Their fears proved well grounded as in March 1967 the craftsmen at the Kendal foods factory withdrew from the works committee, announcing their intention to identify with the Barrow Confederation. At Ulverston the chargehand craftsmen, some of whom were to receive lower wages than those they supervised, contacted their MP in order to take their case of 'relative injustice' to the House of Commons.[123] R. S. Stokes, the personnel director of Glaxo Laboratories, was sympathetic to the union's position (subsequently standing as a Labour parliamentary candidate) and, on occasion, took initiatives which were thought too conciliatory by Bide and other members of the board. At Barnard Castle, employees enrolled in unions in the hope that representation would act as a safeguard against further disadvantageous treatment. It was not just weekly paid factory workers who felt aggrieved. Scientific staff, particularly at Sefton Park, voiced their criticisms of the joint advisory committee system of consultation, which were increasingly viewed as ineffectual 'talking shops'. Members of these groups bemoaned the new regulated economy, harking back to the past when 'Sir Harry or Dr Wilkins could deliver the goods on the spot'.[124] The concern was that amicable negotiation within individual works had come to an end and that power was being concentrated in the hands of a group chairman too remote to appreciate their problems and who would, in their view, arbitrarily determine the overall level of pay settlements.

However, the Group Personnel Committee had little room for manoeuvre and was forced to wait for the government's forthcoming White Paper on prices and incomes policy. It had become clear that productivity deals were impractical as the Prices and Incomes Board had introduced seven new tests which would require several years of negotiation before a deal could be reached. Although Glaxo were a long way from resolving these inherent problems, the pay freeze had made it clear to management that the joint advisory committee system could not survive much longer and that its flaws had been concealed in the past because the company had generally paid above the prevailing industry rates. In the event, the severe restraint was relaxed by the government in a new White Paper published in June 1967. The upshot was that the 6 per cent increase and the introduction of incremental pay scales in its factories were approved. Despite this 'unfreezing' of wages and salaries within Glaxo, the company continued to encounter problems at its Ulverston factory, particularly from the pipefitters, who were accused by the management of leading 'guerrilla activities'.[125] A dispute over the training of a semi-skilled pipefitter's mate in welding techniques, for example, led to a week-long stoppage by nineteen employees in July 1967. Troubles also developed at the Kendal food factory where the craftsmen refused to accept the 6 per cent general increase despite being a party to the agreement submitted to the Ministry of Labour through the early warning system. The Kendal craftsman, who were few in number, continued to demand the special conditions granted to their counterparts in Ulverston, though their lack of industrial muscle enabled Glaxo to resolve the dispute without concessions. Nevertheless, relations continued to deteriorate at Ulverston, culminating in a strike in August 1968 when 150 maintenance staff walked out in support of twenty-three Electrical Trades Union members who had been suspended following their imposition of a work to rule.

The ongoing and apparently intractable nature of the dispute between the company and the Ulverston craftsmen led management to believe that the time had arrived when they had to shoulder the inevitable consequences of industrial action.[126] Thus, when the maintenance staff chose to strike, the outcome of what was to develop into a long-running battle was viewed by the Glaxo board as crucial to the group's industrial relations. A defeat would establish the strength of the militant craftsmen and encourage other unions elsewhere to push for extravagant claims. On the other hand, it was thought that victory would diminish the risk of further disruption by showing that hard-line union support did not automatically lead to better pay and conditions. Throughout September and October talks continued, but stumbled over the issue of victimisation. Glaxo insisted that the unions should not discipline those members who had continued to work but the AEU representatives argued that such proposals were 'completely unacceptable' and would 'create a blackleg charter and undermine the whole basis of trade unionism in Glaxo'.[127] In the event, negotiations brought a return to work on 28 October despite the failure to agree on questions of pay structures and the victimisation of those who had not joined the strike.

As 1968 drew to a close, pressure from staff throughout Glaxo mounted for a further pay increase. This demand intensified following press reports of national pay agreements that did not comply with the provisions of the government's prices and incomes policy, together with the publicity given to the group's successful trading figures. Glaxo decided to take the initiative and proposed a productivity-based submission to the Department of Employment to justify a general increase of 3.5 per cent. It was also hoped that this strategy would bring the Ulverston craftsmen within the overall Glaxo pay structure. Management were encouraged by reports from the factory that after fifteen months of continuous disputes the craftsmen were becoming disillusioned with the Barrow Confederation.[128] The lack of progress in negotiations had been compounded by the realisation that, by refusing to accept incremental pay scales, they were now earning less than their counterparts elsewhere and that their wages had fallen below those of some process workers. The aggressive line taken by the Barrow Confederation, resisted by management, had resulted in the Ulverston craftsmen being more poorly paid than their fellow engineers elsewhere in the group. Glaxo proposed balloting the craftsmen to find out whether they were now prepared to abandon the union position and join the company's incremental pay structure. Between 28 February and 7 March 1969, 152 ballot papers were sent to the craftsmen and, of seventy valid votes, sixty were cast in favour of the Glaxo scheme. Moreover, of the forty-seven votes returned from the 'hard line group', forty-three supported the new system.[129] From these results the management concluded that there were, in essence, two groups among the craftsmen: those in the civil trades and boiler operations were generally in favour of the incremental scales, while those in the traditional craft trades wished to remain represented by unions and were on balance opposed to the scheme. Aware that a conciliatory gesture to one faction might antagonise the other, Glaxo proceeded cautiously. Austin Bide, as chairman of the Group Personnel Committee, decided in May 1969 to send a letter offering incremental scales to those who had indicated their approval. This course of action had initially been resisted by Hugh Gurney, who had succeeded Farrant as factory manager in 1967, and John Brennand, the chief engineer, who argued it would create two unmanageable groups and that it would antagonise the Barrow Confederation. Bide and

Stokes, however, sent the letter, since to do nothing could alienate those in favour of the new pay scales. In the event, its despatch ended the dispute as the terms were accepted unanimously. By August, even the minority who continued to oppose the reforms showed signs of capitulation and at a meeting with the Confederation the incremental system was formally adopted for the entire Ulverston workforce.

However, the calm that fell upon Glaxo's industrial relations was soon to be disturbed by the return of a Conservative government in 1970 and an attempt to implement a new policy described in their manifesto as 'A Fair Deal at Work'. In introducing their Industrial Relations Act, they encountered vigorous opposition from the TUC and a determination by unions to submit pay claims before the legislation became effective. It was in this atmosphere that Bide, as deputy chairman of Glaxo Group, drew up a blueprint for the company's industrial relations policy. He argued that the existing system of factory based negotiations required reform if wholesale and rapid unionisation were to be avoided.[130] Bide considered that Glaxo Laboratories could avoid direct contacts with the unions for some time 'if the company conducted its industrial relations skilfully'.[131] This view was supported by findings from meetings held with Glaxo Laboratories staff from all regions and the response that they wished to 'KEEP THE UNIONS OUT'.[132] The management favoured this option as it was argued that their presence led to restrictive practices and to complex negotiations over pay and conditions. To secure these advantages Bide advocated reforms to the Joint Advisory Committees. 'The process of change', he observed,

> has been somewhat hastened by inflation's rapid erosion of real income and by the frustration of a pay freeze. That frustration has been exacerbated by our diminishing ability and willingness to buy peace and popularity in recent years, as in the fifties and early sixties by keeping wages in Glaxo Laboratories considerably above the normal going levels. This change has been considerably due to the enlargement of the UK group to include companies whose profitability and economic attractions generally are much less than those of Glaxo Laboratories, but whose workers, spurred on by the Glaxo Laboratories example and by more general wage adjustments, aspire to equivalent treatment. The result is costly.[133]

Two three-day sessions were held in February 1971 with representatives of the three joint advisory committees to discuss proposed changes. The key innovation was to grant them negotiating status over wages and salaries, premium payments, shift allowances, working hours, holidays and sick pay. To reflect this fundamental reform, they were renamed joint consultative and negotiating committees (JCNC). The evolutionary nature of this approach was a Bide hallmark and, as he observed, 'we may alienate staff goodwill if we fail to take sufficient account of their opinions and fears and push too far too fast'.[134]

Despite these reforms, three unions continued to campaign for formal recognition within Glaxo Laboratories. The Association of Professional Scientists and Technologists claimed substantial support at Ulverston and at Greenford amongst laboratory staff, the National Union of General and Municipal Workers argued that the process workers at Cambois were eager to join, while the Association of Scientific, Technical and Managerial Staffs pressed to represent scientists and supervisors at Ulverston.[135] The management's fear that the JCNC system would be eroded by union involvement was heightened in May 1973 when 115 ASTMS members staged a walkout at Ulverston in response to what they considered was the unfair dismissal of one member of staff. In July, 300 craftsmen at the factory staged an overtime ban. To prevent further escalation the management agreed that all employees of Glaxo Laboratories should be balloted on the question of union representation. In what was called the 'recognition ballot', 64 per cent of the 425 engineering technicians, works supervisors and draughtsmen at eight Glaxo plants who voted were in favour of the ASTMS being granted bargaining rights on their behalf.[136]

Glaxo Laboratories also found itself lobbied by other unions during 1973, notably the NUGMW and TGWU for the right to represent manual workers. In October the company commissioned the Department of Employment to undertake a membership audit of factory grades, excluding craftsmen and apprentices, at its primary production sites at Montrose, Cambois and Ulverston. The results (Table 20, p. 454) revealed that 54.2 per cent of employees favoured union representation.[137] These figures encouraged Glaxo to recognise both the TGWU and the GMWU at the three factories. The year proved, therefore, to be an important one in the development of a coherent and effective industrial relations policy, albeit one that had been shaped by powerful forces from outside. By revitalising the joint advisory committees and introducing union negotiators within this framework, Glaxo had been able to preserve much of the goodwill and flexibility that had existed when Jephcott was chairman.

The comparative calm that had fallen over Glaxo's industrial relations was shattered in April 1974 when the Amalgamated Union of Engineering Workers called a one-day strike at Barnard Castle, where they believed that the management had prevaricated over their claim to represent engineers and craftsmen.[138] This was the first stoppage in the history of the factory and it is doubtful whether the union really had mass support; of the 300 engineering workers at the site, only eighty agreed with the action. On 4 September 1974, the AUEW organised a further strike at Cambois over Glaxo's refusal to hold local negotiations over pay and conditions and sent a 'blacking' request to their counterparts at Montrose, Ulverston and Barnard Castle for similar stoppages there. The call was subsequently taken up by maintenance engineers in these factories, together with their counterparts at Kendal two days later. With 500 key staff refusing to work, production at Barnard Castle was disrupted, so that some process workers were transferred to Greenford to fill vials and temporary employees were laid off. Cambois ceased manufacturing for almost three weeks in September, and Ulverston's output was also severely curtailed. Despite these operational pressures, Bide and the Glaxo board stood firm, refusing to negotiate until the engineers returned to work. When the AUEW strengthened its picket lines, the management assumed that this would prove to be a lengthy dispute and drew up contingency plans.

In October, the union called for the nationalisation of the company. However, the board knew that such demands would not be favourably received because in July the group had surveyed its staff on this question, following statements made by Tony Benn that the Labour government was considering taking the pharmaceutical industry into state control. From verbal reports, the overwhelming consensus amongst Glaxo Laboratories employees was that they wished to remain in the private sector, believing that nationalisation was a 'road to failure'.[139] At this point, Bide chose to take the initiative and wrote to all 16,000 group employees in the UK to warn them of the dangers of nationalisation. While it may have served to reinforce the views of the majority who were already opposed to this proposed action, it fuelled the hostility of the militants in the AUEW and precipitated similar disagreements at some southern factories, notably Farley's plant in Plymouth. In the meantime, negotiations with other unions, notably the TGWU, GMWU and APST, over annual pay increases proceeded smoothly as agreements were reached. In October, Glaxo approached Hugh Scanlon, general secretary of the AUEW, requesting a meeting to discuss wage claims on a national basis. This followed on 14 November when the management resisted pressure to increase its original offer of £44.50 to £48 per week, but agreed to renegotiate if the strikers returned to work. This solution was presented to the engineers at a number of mass meetings at which they voted in favour, with the sole exception of Cambois, where the dispute continued into 1975. The firmness and resolve exhibited by the Glaxo board undoubtedly played a major part in the resolution of the dispute, though it had not been without costs in terms of production schedules and a loss of goodwill on both sides.

Since there seemed to be little sign of the strike at Cambois being resolved, in January 1975 Glaxo referred the matter to the Conciliation and

Arbitration Service, though the two meetings it convened brought no further progress. The dispute had now passed its 200th day and Glaxo again contacted Scanlon to arrange a meeting. On 16 April John Farrant, the company's production controller, and John Beal, its personnel manager, met George Arnold, divisional officer of the AUEW. After a week of negotiations, Arnold emerged to speak of a 'quite reasonable compromise',[140] though his claim that the strikers had won a 'big' pay increase,[141] appeared exaggerated when it emerged that the Cambois workers had accepted the same deal offered to other Glaxo Laboratories factories and could have reached the same settlement six months earlier.[142] The dispute, which had lasted for 233 days, was the longest in the history of Glaxo. It appeared to have resolved the immediate question of union militancy and the annual negotiations for 1976 between employees' representatives and management proceeded without rancour.

In the later part of the seventies the influence of the JCNCs continued to decline in favour of direct bargaining with union officials. Nevertheless, Glaxo remained committed to the principle of employee involvement. In 1977, for example, following publication of the *Report of the Committee of Inquiry on Industrial Democracy* chaired by Lord Bullock, Bide addressed the issue of 'industrial democracy' in the *Annual Report*:

> Much has been said in recent times of the need for more worker participation, for 'industrial democracy' and for better communications. We are anxious to encourage progress on all these fronts, but not in a rigid form imposed by legislation. What is needed is voluntary evolution towards such greater employee involvement as will lead to fuller job-satisfaction.[143]

Glaxo opposed many of the Bullock Report's recommendations, in particular the call for worker directors, but did foster schemes at its sites to encourage employee participation and consultative arrangements. In later years, this commitment led to the introduction of quality circles, in which production teams would have regular meetings to consider ways of improving work practices, and the Glaxo Group share option scheme, which was unusual for the time in allowing all employees of three years' service to benefit from the company's commercial success.

In July 1977 the limits which the Labour administration had imposed on pay settlements threatened to cause a major dispute and, as Napier Drewitt informed the board, considerable risk existed 'of serious industrial relations problems in all parts of the group … arising from the very confused and explosive situation over the government's pay policy, or its lack thereof'.[144] The threat of strike action at Barnard Castle was alleviated by the introduction of a bonus payment scheme, suggested by Girolami, which fell within the guidelines stipulated by the Department of Employment. However, trouble flared there in 1978 when Glaxo attempted to enforce the government's Stage III Pay Restraint Policy which recommended a target figure of 10 per cent of gross earnings. In September, GMWU members at Barnard Castle introduced a work to rule and overtime ban which led to the matter being referred to both the Advisory, Conciliation and Arbitration Service and to the Department of Employment. Although these organisations endorsed Glaxo's decision, the matter was not finally resolved in the management's favour until March 1979.

Industrial relations for Glaxo in the seventies had been a relatively turbulent period in which its traditional methods for resolving disputes were reformed. From a position of having no unions within Glaxo Laboratories, the group now found itself negotiating with a number of representative bodies, while the paternalistic system of joint consultation that Jephcott had initiated almost forty years earlier and had operated successfully until the mid 1960s was now in decline. None the less, the group emerged from a decade of troubled industrial relations relatively unscathed and, more importantly, with the goodwill of its workforce largely intact. The eighties and nineties proved to be trouble free years, partly because of these changes but also because falling inflation together with sustained and rapid growth within Glaxo enabled the company to pass on real increments to the workforce at regular intervals, while rising levels of unemployment also served to discourage strikes. In addition, the character of the group's factories, both primary and secondary, had changed considerably. The introduction of computer-guided manufacturing processes demanded a workforce both highly trained and flexible, within which the traditional distinctions between managers and men have become diluted. The introduction of 'quality circles' was designed to encourage a unity of purpose as all team members are invited to consider ways of increasing efficiency and raising safety standards.

RESEARCH AND DEVELOPMENT,
1962–1985

---

§

THE CRUCIAL areas of activity by which pharmaceutical businesses stand or fall take place at either side of manufacture, namely the discovery and development of novel and effective drugs, and their subsequent marketing and sale in a highly competitive, international environment. Without a regular flow of new products, no major pharmaceutical company can survive; they are its life blood.

Glaxo Laboratories had not begun its commercial existence with the intention of finding novel medicines. Wishing to improve the competitiveness and range of its infant foods, the company entered the manufacture of vitamins. It became skilled in fine chemical development, an expertise reinforced by its work on penicillin during the Second World War and the refinement of other antibiotics afterwards. Seeking to develop new compounds, Glaxo was then drawn into two expanding therapeutic areas, steroids and cephalosporins, which were to remain an important source of medicines for the next forty years. Allen & Hanburys, by comparison, had begun by supplying apothecaries and grew as a supplier of traditional drugs, galenicals and over-the-counter preparations, building up an important business in surgical instruments and hospital furniture. During the 1950s it had become clear to Maplethorpe that Allen & Hanburys could survive only if it shifted its focus to research-based synthetic medicines. He concluded agreements with some of the larger US pharmaceutical companies, including Nepera Chemical Co. (later part of Warner-Lambert) and the Schering Corporation, to obtain access to new products. By such diverse and indirect routes the scientists at Greenford and Ware found themselves competing at the highest level of pharmaceutical endeavour.

Although research and development are today regarded as two separate albeit interdependent activities, with different philosophies and a requirement for different competencies, the distinction was not clear cut in the early part of the twentieth century. At a time when the various scientific disciplines were less well defined and when many researchers were as pre-occupied with the search for novel manufacturing methods as they were with the discovery of new compounds, it was more difficult to categorise these forms of experiment. Today, research in the pharmaceutical industry may be defined as the search for new medicines which take the form of original molecules or preparations, either through the discovery of natu-rally occurring substances or the transformation of existing chemical enti-ties. It involves imagination, breadth of vision and, to some extent, serendipity. Development, which typically employs double the number of scientific staff and is usually a protracted process, commonly concerns the study of how a new molecule is absorbed, metabolised and excreted in vol-unteers and patients. Alternatively, experiments may be designed to seek new applications for existing compounds or to improve their efficacy by al-tering the formulation or the way that it is taken by the patient. Further-more, development addresses the crucial question whether the production of a novel molecule can be scaled up from the laboratory bench to an effi-cient and reliable industrial process. Although this work also requires cre-ativity, it demands scrupulous attention to detail to meet increasingly complex regulations. Of paramount importance in running a research and development programme is the judgement required to abandon projects which are unlikely to yield useful products as soon as possible to minimise the waste of human and financial resources.

Five major scientific disciplines – chemistry, biology, pharmacology, pharmacy and medicine – characterised pharmaceutical research and de-velopment in the post-war period. Chemists probably regarded themselves as undertaking the purest science, given that they worked with a defined and rigorous theoretical model in their search for new molecules and were engaged as much in abstract reasoning as in practical experiment. Biolo-gists were more prominent in research at Allen & Hanburys than at Glaxo Laboratories because of their different strategic directives, though microbi-ologists played an important part in the discovery of new antibiotics at the latter. At Ware, through their growing understanding of the physiological processes at work in the human body, biologists were able to suggest ways in which these might be modified by drugs which mimic or inhibit the actions of messenger chemicals (neurotransmitters or hormones) or are substrates or inhibitors of enzymes.

Within the field of development, pharmacologists investigate the inter-action of drugs within a functioning biological system. This work, in turn, is sub-divided into 'pharmacokinetics' and 'pharmacodynamics'. Pharma-cokinetics studies the time course of absorption, distribution, metabolism and excretion of drugs and the corresponding pharmacological responses.[1] It attempts to measure the movement of a drug into and out of the body so that predictions can be made about concentration levels in particular parts and the design of dosage regimens. Pharmacodynamics examines the action of drugs on cells, tissues or organs and is concerned with the changes that they bring about to the body.[2] Emerging from the discipline of pharmacology and given an imperative demand by the thalidomide disaster was toxicology, designed to test in animals the safety of new medicines. Toxicologists are the one group that can kill a project at a stroke if they discover that a compound has toxic potential. Finally, pharmacists are required to investigate the formulation of a drug: how should it be prepared, delivered (by injection, as a syrup, in tablet form, by an inhaler and so forth) and to ensure its stability. It is also important to undertake drug interaction studies to identify potentially dangerous complications with other drugs.

Greenford: research and development

The scope and nature of scientific endeavour at Greenford had originally been defined by Sir Harry Jephcott. Having been the first chemist employed by Joseph Nathan & Co. and responsible for the company's laboratory, he continued to take a close interest in research and development until his retirement in 1963. Because of his training as a pharmacist, work on vitamin products and the commercial success Glaxo had enjoyed from importing deep fermentation techniques for the manufacture of antibiotics, Jephcott favoured development projects often at the expense of novel research. This created tension between Jephcott and Glaxo's post-war director of research, Dr Tom Macrae, who was regularly presented with innovative and exciting ideas by his growing team of scientists.

Prominent among these was Dr B. A. Hems, whom Macrae had appointed head of chemical research. With a double-first in physiological and organic chemistry from Glasgow University, Hems joined Glaxo in 1937. During the war, Hems spent much laboratory time on projects to increase the yield of penicillin G, working on amino acids for use in synthetic culture media and improved processes for extracting the antibiotic. However, his first major contribution came in 1950, when his team succeeded in designing a ten-stage process for synthesising L-thyroxine that was commercially viable. Used to treat myxoedema and other symptoms of an under-active thyroid gland, it represented a significant therapeutic advance and this research, together with later work on antibiotics and steroids, was instrumental in Hems' election as an FRS in 1969. His ability and dedication won him steady promotion, though a predisposition to depression led

him to remain somewhat detached from his colleagues.
Yet, the complementary nature of the personalities of
the two Scottish scientists
proved significant for research at Greenford. In a
typically acrid observation,
Hems likened their partnership to a salad dressing in
which Macrae provided the
oil while he added the vine-
gar.[3] A benign father figure
to many of the staff, Macrae
mitigated the sharper ap-
proach of Hems. The former
also shielded the latter from
Jephcott's negative view of
certain projects, notably
those on prednisone and
prednisolone, but it is
doubtful that Hems ever
fully appreciated what a

*93. Dr Arthur Hems in his office at Greenford. He is
pictured here as a communicator though, in reality,
Hems was a taciturn man who measured his words
carefully and could intimidate those of lesser intellect.*

friend and protector he had in Macrae. Hems had an unusual management
style in that he ran every project in detail, and this involved regular interviews with individual chemists to interrogate them on progress. The best of
them found these encounters enjoyable though others felt intimidated or
even bullied. Indeed, Hems himself believed that staff worked to their full
potential only when under pressure, and also applied this dictum to himself, undertaking a punishing schedule.[4] In 1962 Hems was appointed to the
board of the newly formed Glaxo Research as director of chemical research
and when Macrae retired five years later he became its deputy chairman
and managing director. From the late 1940s, these two scientists were responsible for the selection and execution of projects at Greenford, though
at times this brought them into conflict with Jephcott, who as chief executive had legitimate concerns about costs but who also overestimated his
understanding of scientific matters and, in particular, of research.

Research and development at Greenford during the late 1940s and 1950s
did not proceed according to a strategic plan that had identified key therapeutic targets; rather, projects were considered simply on their merits and
within rigid budget constraints. Nevertheless, Glaxo Laboratories built up

four areas of specialist expertise: nutrition, vaccines, antibiotics and steroid chemistry. The first was based on the company's traditional expertise in vitamins and was boosted in 1947 by Dr Lester Smith's isolation of the curative factor for pernicious anaemia. Later termed vitamin B_{12}, it conferred on the Greenford laboratories an international status, though the product, Cytamen, was not of great commercial significance (see p. 121). Subsequently, work on vitamins continued, though in view of the limited pharmaceutical applications, on a reduced scale. The development of BCG and tetanus toxoid vaccines justified the construction of new biology laboratories at Greenford in 1956 and new facilities at Sefton Park (see p. 116). Scientists at the latter were responsible for developing the Salk vaccine against poliomyelitis (Polivirin). However, in terms of their commercial impact and the opportunities they created, vaccines remained a specialist area with defined limits in terms of revenue and medical applications.

In two therapeutic areas, however, Glaxo was able to find greater opportunities for growth: antibiotics and steroids. Although much scientific experiment was usefully directed towards improving the efficiency of fermentation techniques and broadening the range of penicillin products, significant pharmaceutical advance followed the request from the National Research Development Corporation in the late 1950s to assist with the manufacture of cephalosporin C. In July 1958, Glaxo Laboratories succeeded in supplying Abraham and Newton, the Oxford scientists, with the first 100g batch of high purity cephalosporin C, and this set the company on its own search for a new, broad-spectrum antibiotic (see p. 311). In 1952, the chemists at Sefton Park had begun work on griseofulvin as it seemed a promising horticultural antifungal. In the event, griseofulvin proved to be an effective treatment for ringworm when given orally to humans (see p. 118). At the request of the Medical Research Council, Glaxo had also become involved in steroid chemistry and in 1951 worked on a way of making cortisone from ergosterol, subsequently designing a process that began with hecogenin. Although the company's first corticosteroid products, cortisone and hydrocortisone, were launched in 1955, it was eight years before the Greenford chemists found a truly novel product – betamethasone-17-valerate (see p. 316). Thus, by the 1960s Glaxo had built up substantial research and development facilities with over 600 scientific staff based at a variety of laboratories, though the majority at Greenford worked on antibiotics and corticosteroids.

Early science at Allen & Hanburys

Although Allen & Hanburys could claim to be Britain's oldest pharmaceu-

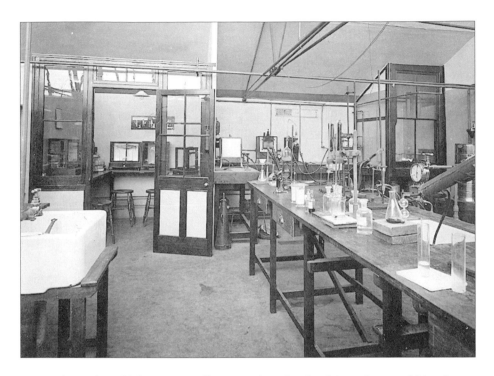

94. The analytical laboratory at Allen & Hanburys' Bethnal Green factory which, when opened, was regarded as state of the art.

tical company, it had not entered the field of ethical drug manufacture until 1923 when it pioneered the production of injectable insulin, a hormone treatment for diabetes.[5] It had already established an analytical laboratory at its Bethnal Green factory to test the purity of its varied product lines; this moved temporarily to nearby Hague Street following bomb damage by German aircraft in May 1918.[6] During the rebuilding, which occupied the company until 1922, the opportunity was taken to expand the laboratory facilities.[7] Whilst Allen & Hanburys' business was in traditional drugs and galenicals, the technical aspects of pharmacy were becoming more complex and legislation required higher levels of scientific expertise. The Dangerous Drugs Act of 1923, for example, that related to the manufacturing, wholesale and retail sides of pharmacy alike, necessitated the employment of qualified staff to carry out its provisions.[8] The Pharmacy and Poisons Act of 1933 tightened further the regulations concerning the sale and dispensing of listed poisons and controlled drugs, which could now be undertaken only by registered members of the Pharmaceutical Society.[9]

After the reconstruction, the laboratories occupied about half of the top floor of the new building at Bethnal Green, having an area of about 120ft by

40ft.[10] The director Norman Evers, whose staff included seven chemists and a number of assistants, could claim to have some of the finest facilities available to any 'wholesaling druggist' in Britain. The history of Allen & Hanburys recorded that 'in the place of the badly lit and smoke-tainted room we find airy and evenly lighted laboratories, spotlessly clean, with convenient supplies of gas, electricity, hot and cold water and high pressure water, with the beams so arranged that additional pipes and cables can be placed in position with the minimum of time and trouble'.[11] According to a report in *The Chemist and Druggist* for 1925, the laboratories functioned

> with an eye to the future: new preparations are made in small batches with the object of discovering how best they can be manufactured on a large scale; old methods of manufacture are examined in the light of recent knowledge: investigations are made upon vexed and troublesome problems in chemistry, pharmacy and pharmacology, and new manufacturing plant is tested.[12]

This was, therefore, classical developmental work, and Allen & Hanburys did not purport to challenge the mighty laboratories that were being assembled in America and Germany by the largest pharmaceutical firms for the discovery of new chemical entities.

However, the Bethnal Green laboratories were to play an important part in the development work needed to provide a British source of insulin. The hormone had been isolated and extracted in a pure form from the pancreas by Frederick Banting and Charles Best at the University of Toronto during the summer of 1921, and was initially manufactured by Eli Lilly in the United States, the British patent rights being offered as a free gift to the Medical Research Council in London. Early in 1923, Allen & Hanburys were among a small number of UK companies that signed an agreement to introduce and improve methods of insulin production. In the event, Allen & Hanburys joined forces with The British Drug Houses and set up a large-scale manufacturing plant in the latter's Graham Street premises. The work undertaken at Bethnal Green on the insulin project introduced the company's chemists to the slowly accelerating world of pharmaceutical innovation.

The next major turn taken by Allen & Hanburys' research and development department was largely the result of chance. On 20 September 1940 a parachute high-explosive bomb fell on the Bethnal Green factory, destroying the manufacturing laboratory; this was followed by an incendiary device which wrecked the analytical and research departments together with their large library.[13] Although heroic attempts were made to re-establish these functions, the initiative now passed to the company's Ware factory, where E. K. Samways had set up a laboratory to serve the Sterivac line, which filled bottles with intravenous fluids.[14]

In 1896 Allen & Hanburys had leased a mill on the River Lea close to Ware lock to make their dried milk products in air unpolluted by the factories and coal fires of east London.[15] Two years later more land was acquired and malted food production added to that of milk, and in 1900 the pastille and capsule departments transferred from Bethnal Green. In 1932, with the appointment of Cyril Maplethorpe as manager at Ware, much-needed scientific expertise was introduced. Only the second qualified pharmacist to be employed at the works, he became actively involved in product development once in a position of authority. During the 1930s, Maplethorpe was responsible for the introduction of Isogel, a bulk laxative made from the husk of the Indian *Isphagula* seed.[16] In 1944 he was appointed managing director of Allen & Hanburys and began to implement a strategy that would lead the company away from traditional and galenical products and towards research-based pharmaceuticals.

At Ware, Maplethorpe began to build up a team of scientists. In 1938, he had recruited E. K. Samways (the third qualified pharmacist to work at the site), and in 1945 appointed Dr Harry Collier who became head of pharmacology, having a particular expertise in neuromuscular blocking agents.[17] The first research chemist, Norman R. Campbell, was hired to work on sex hormones. In 1950, when Dr Norman Evers retired as chief chemist and director of research, Allen & Hanburys recruited Dr F. Arnold Robinson to co-ordinate the development of new medicines. Robinson had previously been employed by Glaxo Laboratories at Greenford, where as head of chemical research, he had worked on a range of drugs including stilboestrol, thiamine and other B vitamins.

Although none of the new products launched by Allen & Hanburys during the 1950s represented a radical new discovery, and some were based on licences from larger pharmaceutical firms, the company built up a range of scientific skills for the development of prescription medicines. In 1956, for example, choline theophyllinate (Choledyl), a bronchodilator for the treatment of asthma and chronic bronchitis, was launched under licence from Napera.[18] From Schering, a new range of medicines based on chlorpheniramine (Piriton), a potent antihistamine, was introduced. Also in conjunction with Schering, in 1957 Allen & Hanburys launched perphenazine (Fentazin), a phenothiazine neuroleptic, for the short-term management of schizophrenia and severe anxiety.[19] The new laboratories at Ware were principally housed in 'P' building, which had been constructed during the war for the production of penicillin by surface culture. With the completion of large-scale deep fermentation plants in the north of England in 1946, it never came into full operation.[20] Although the interior of the building was in semi-darkness for the cultivation of penicillin moulds, it proved possible to adapt the structure with artificial lighting and special ventilation.[21]

After the take-over of Allen & Hanburys by Glaxo in 1958, there was little change to the research and development function. A year earlier Maplethorpe had announced that the production of traditional drugs and galenicals would cease.[22] It had been a conservative family business and Jephcott had no wish to upset or disturb what he believed was a successful culture.

Glaxo Research Ltd: a new initiative

As part of the structural reorganisation that created Glaxo Group in 1962, a new subsidiary company, Glaxo Research, was formed.[23] As conceived by Jephcott, it was designed to oversee the research and development work undertaken at Greenford and Ware, together with the laboratory staff at Evans Medical (acquired the previous year) and Edinburgh Pharmaceuticals. Because the scale of activities was so much larger at Glaxo (with a research budget of nearly £1 million, five times that of Allen & Hanburys), Dr Tom Macrae, research director at Greenford, was appointed as the chief executive of the new organisation. At the time that Glaxo Research was set up, Greenford employed 600–700 scientific staff, Ware 120, Edinburgh Pharmaceuticals 100 and Evans Medical 100. In the event, because of resistance from Dr David Jack, head of research and development at Allen & Hanburys, Ware never came under the control of Glaxo Research (see p. 327), while scientific investigation at the other two subsidiaries was wound down or incorporated at Greenford. These changes also corresponded with a limited degree of rationalisation between the two principal laboratories. However, the major change resulted from Jack's determination to establish Ware in a complementary but distinct role. He chose to focus upon pharmacology-based research, rather than chemistry- or microbiology-led investigation, and to work in different therapeutical areas such as respiratory medicine and later the cardiac and gastrointestinal fields. Hence, Ware grew not as a subsidiary of Greenford but largely as a separate entity.

Dr Tom Macrae continued to serve as managing director of Glaxo Research until his retirement in December 1966.[24] Educated at Glasgow and Munich, where he had studied the biochemistry of enzymes, Macrae worked on pituitary hormones and later nutrition at the Lister Institute. Recruited by Jephcott after demobilisation from the RAF in March 1946, he was appointed director of research at Greenford and was a key member of the research and development committee throughout the 1950s. Described as 'an independent-minded and iconoclastic Scot',[25] Macrae was forced to use all his debating skill and ingenuity to obtain funding for original or imaginative projects which Jephcott would have considered risky. He was succeeded as managing director by Hems, then director of chemistry, in what was a straightforward hierarchy. This consisted of six divisions organised by scientific discipline: chemistry (under Dr T. Walker), biochemistry (Dr W. F. J. Cuthbertson), fermentation (Dr A. H. Campbell), pharmacology and toxicology (Dr J. P. Currie), biological research (Dr P. W. Muggleton) and pharmacy (K. A. Lees). Each divisional head was in turn responsible for a number of departments or groups. Chemistry, for example, was sub-divided into chemical research, physical chemistry and chemical development; pharmacology also included histopathology and toxicology, while biological research took responsibility for antibiotics, general microbiology and parasitology.[26]

However, two key events took place in the period 1961 to 1963 that were to transform the nature of Glaxo's research and development functions, and these, in turn, helped to transform the group itself. The first was the decision in 1961 to appoint Dr David Jack as research director at Ware, where he dramatically altered the focus of the search for new medicines (see p. 327). The second was Sir Harry Jephcott's recommendation to the Glaxo board that they appoint an eminent scientist, Sir Alan Wilson, as his successor as chairman.

Wilson had studied natural sciences at Emmanuel College, Cambridge, where a first together with the Smith's Prize in 1928 led to his election to a fellowship in the following year. In 1933, he became a fellow of Trinity College and a university lecturer in mathematics, holding both positions until 1945. He wrote two standard works on physics and undertook important research into semi-conductors.[27] During the Second World War, Wilson worked on radio communications and atomic energy, being elected a FRS in 1942. As the hostilities drew to a close, in February 1945 he accepted the post of director in charge of research and development at Courtaulds.[28] Samuel Courtauld, chairman since 1921, was concerned that technological advances were leaving the business behind and that a new laboratory headed by a scientist with a proven record of achievement was needed. Wilson revitalised the department and was responsible for the search for new fibres (the acrylic fibre 'Courtelle' and the polyethylene yarn 'Courlene') and the discovery of new qualities in existing fibres.[29] Such was his success as an industrial scientist that Wilson became managing director in 1954 and deputy chairman three years later. With his experience of pure and applied research, Wilson took a different strategic line from Jephcott. In a paper delivered to the Royal Society in 1953, he had outlined his philosophy at Courtaulds:

> the study of man-made fibres covers a very wide range of scientific knowledge. Further, the research programme must be on a large scale if significant results are to be achieved, and since the sums of money involved in carrying out the work and more particularly in utilising the results obtained are considerable, the formulation of a research programme depends as much upon economic considerations as upon scientific possibilities.[30]

Sir Alan Wilson recognised the speculative nature of research, the costs involved and the scale required if it were to prove effective. For example, in 1968, when salbutamol was close to being launched, Jack submitted a plan for expansion to Wilson. It included the construction of a new laboratory at Ware to house 200–300 staff and had involved much thought and detailed work. Wilson replied tersely by return of post, writing 'go ahead'.[31] This was the three-storey biological sciences building, which was opened at Ware by Lord Rosenheim, emeritus professor of medicine at University College Hospital, in October 1972.[32]

Under the chairmanship of Wilson expenditure on research and development was not subject to tight restrictions. There was a steady and progressive rise from £4 million in 1969 (when it represented 2.9 per cent of turnover) to £7 million in 1972 (3.8 per cent of turnover – see Table 21, p. 455). Sir Austin Bide also followed this policy as investment in research rose in real terms throughout the latter part of the 1970s and early 1980s. Thus, Wilson had effectively reversed Sir Harry Jephcott's policy of suppressing any tendency to increase spending and to mistrust any venture with an element of speculation.

Cephalosporins: cephaloridine, cefuroxime and ceftazidime

Although Glaxo launched its first cephalosporin antibiotic, cephaloridine (Ceporin), in November 1964, the medicine had a lengthy and complex history. The cephalosporium mould from which the cephalosporins was ultimately derived had been discovered in 1945 by an Italian scientist, Professor Giuseppe Brotzu, while working in Sardinia.[33] Observing a local outfall of sewage into the Gulf of Cagliari, he noticed an area where the water seemed to be unusually clear and hypothesised that it might contain something that killed the contaminating bacteria.[34] From a sample of seawater, Brotzu isolated a fungus, later named *Cephalosporium acremonium*, which produced antibiotic material active against both Gram-

95. *Professor Giuseppe Brotzu on a visit to Sefton Park accompanied by Dr Enrico Fezzi of Glaxo's Italian subsidiary* (left to right): *Beale, Fezzi, Brotzu, Campbell, not known, and Peter Gent, managing director of Laboratori Glaxo S.p.A.*

positive and Gram-negative bacteria. Apparently dispensing with toxicity experiments in animals, he then injected culture filtrates of the organism directly into staphylococcal and streptococcal lesions. He also made a crude extract containing active material and injected it intramuscularly and intravenously into patients with brucellosis and typhoid fever. Brotzu thought the results promising and, lacking the resources to continue the work, contacted a friend, Dr Blyth Brooke, who had been a British Public Health Officer in Sardinia at the end of the war. Brooke suggested that he contact Sir Howard Florey at the Sir William Dunn School of Pathology at Oxford.[35] Research proceeded there initially on cephalosporin P but it was soon realised that this could not have been responsible for the broad range of antibacterial activity described by Brotzu.[36] A second substance, cephalosporin N, was isolated and, in September 1953, Professor E. P. Abraham and Dr G. G. F. Newton succeeded in detecting a very small quantity of a substance, which they arbitrarily named cephalosporin C.[37] A preliminary study of cephalosporin C showed that it was a reasonably active broad-spectrum antibiotic, stable in dilute acid and resistant to hydrolysis by penicillinase. The latter was particularly important as strains of staphylococci had developed in hospitals that existing penicillins could no longer treat; this created a pressing need for an antibiotic with the therapeutic properties of penicillin but without its inherent weaknesses.

Both Glaxo and Eli Lilly in the United States had shown a serious interest in cephalosporins from an early stage. Sir Harry Jephcott had kept in contact with Florey because of the company's manufacture of penicillin and streptomycin, while Lilly's involvement followed from the research of Edwin H. Flynn. In 1956, however, the future of the cephalosporin project remained in doubt, partly because Abraham and Newton's efforts to determine the structure of cephalosporin C were impeded by difficulties in producing the compound in any quantity. The National Research Development Corporation (NRDC), which co-ordinated the work in the UK and took responsibility for patent protection, appealed to the pharmaceutical industry and particularly those expert in fermentation techniques, to assist in the development programme. Both Glaxo Laboratories and Eli Lilly volunteered, and were subsequently licensed by the NRDC to manufacture cephalosporin C commercially.

In order to aid the Oxford researchers in their quest to determine the chemical structure of cephalosporin C, Glaxo scientists experimented with fermentation techniques to raise yields and worked to improve isolation and purification procedures. In the event, Glaxo became the first company in the world to make 100g of pure cephalosporin C, supplied in two instalments. The first was handed to Dr Newton at Oxford on 31 July 1958 and the second on 1 April 1959.[38] This material enabled Abraham and Newton to propose that cephalosporin had a beta-lactam-dihydrothiazine structure, which was soon confirmed by X-ray crystallography.[39] After nearly 400g of highly pure chemical had been produced by Glaxo in the period April–June 1960, the main board authorised a new project to discover a cephalosporin analogue which would serve as a novel antibacterial agent.[40]

The early contributions of Glaxo and Lilly gave them a favoured position in their subsequent dealings with the NRDC. Apart from being licensed to manufacture cephalosporin C, they were founder members of the 'Cephalosporin Club', a formal gathering of scientists and manufacturers designed to facilitate the discovery and development of truly effective cephalosporin antibiotics. They were confronted with two major obstacles. First, pure cephalosporin C was very expensive, largely because of low yields from the fermentation broths and difficulties in isolating the substance. Secondly, methods for making analogues of cephalosporin C were inefficient and unsuitable for commercial product development. Higher yields were obtained by using mutant forms of the mould by exposing it to chemical mutagens of irradiation. This early work was undertaken by

Brendan Kelly and his staff at the Medical Research Council's Antibiotics Research Station at Clevedon.[41] Glaxo scientists at Sefton Park and Ulverston tested nearly 40,000 mutant strains and the best of them, together with improved extraction techniques, made the large-scale production of cephalosporin C feasible.[42]

Of crucial importance in taking the production of cephalosporins from the laboratory bench to a large-scale commercial process was the role of the pilot plant at Greenford run by Dr Peter Wilkinson, head of chemical development. He had joined Glaxo in 1940, having com-

96. *Assaying the potency of mutants of cephalosprin C at Sefton Park, Stoke Poges in 1964.*

pleted a doctorate at Imperial College, where he worked on the synthesis of vitamins including D_3, A and B_1.[43] Wilkinson saw the need for a general-purpose pilot plant to scale up processes in preparation for their transfer to the group's primary factory at Ulverston. In 1947 he presented the idea to Austin Bide, then head of technical research, with whom he shared an office. Bide presented the proposals to Herbert Palmer and they were authorised to build a pilot plant. Assisted by Victor Salvage, a mechanical engineer who had formerly worked for Taylor Woodrow, they designed a series of vessels for heating or freezing chemicals so that they could replicate a range of reactions. Glaxo was the first pharmaceutical company in the UK to have such a facility and it contributed greatly to the speed with which new medicines were brought to the market.

Three 'generations' of increasingly effective cephalosporin antibiotics were developed at Greenford. The first generation, which included Glaxo's cephaloridine and cephalexin, was especially active against Gram-positive bacteria such as staphylococci, though less active against Gram-negative organisms. The second generation, which includes cefuroxime from Glaxo, retained Gram-positive activity but with increased potency against Gram-negative organisms such as *Escherechia coli*. The third generation, of which

Glaxo's ceftazidime is a member, are especially active against Gram-negative bacteria such as *Pseudomonas* species which cause life-threatening infections in man.

Cephaloridine, the first Glaxo cephalosporin, was selected from 600 different combinations of the two side chains to 7APA on the basis of extensive *in vitro* and *in vivo* tests. The compound, designated 87/4, had a bactericidal action, which was unusual in a broad-spectrum antibiotic, and showed a resistance to staphylococcal penicillinase.[44] Sadly, it was later found to be toxic to the kidney in some susceptible patients and this limited its use. When it was launched in 1964, cephaloridine (Ceporin) was greeted with considerable enthusiasm by the medical press, as an 'effective alternative to penicillin in most Gram-positive infections'.[45] Cephaloridine was indicated for use against urinary and respiratory tract infections, meningitis, septicaemia and soft-tissue infections.[46] Unfortunately the antibiotic was inactive when given orally and was therefore delivered by intramuscular injection.[47] However, the *British Medical Journal* regretted the hype that had accompanied the launch:

> Publicity of this kind makes it difficult for the practising doctor to make a sober assessment of the qualities of a new drug, especially in the face of importunity from patients whose ideas about the new 'wonder drug' are bound to be confused by propaganda.[48]

Glaxo, however, had not been the first pharmaceutical company to market a cephalosporin. Eli Lilly, which had been working in tandem, launched cephalothin (Keflin), an injectable, a year earlier in 1963. Under the licences issued by NRDC, Glaxo and Lilly shared access and had the right to sell each other's products. Inevitably a dispute then arose over who had invented cephaloridine and a protracted legal battle began. Dr Cynthia O'Callaghan, who had been involved in the development of this drug and of cephalexin, made extensive visits to Indianapolis, the headquarters of Eli Lilly, during the dispute to represent Glaxo Laboratories.[49] In the event, the litigation proved inconclusive and both companies continued to develop their own rival cephalosporin products.

The next major advance after cephaloridine and cephalothin was cephalexin, an orally active, first-generation product, which was made by Glaxo and Lilly scientists independently at about the same time. Well absorbed from the gut, it was more convenient to use and likely to command a substantial market. However, one major problem had to be solved before it could be developed because the synthetic manufacture from cephalosporin C was grossly inefficient. The solution came from Lilly researchers who established that the five-membered ring of penicillin could be expanded to six and thus serve as a cephalosporin intermediate. It was Dr Tom Walker, recently appointed as head of chemistry, who recommended the investigation of this new route to cephalexin and supervised the development of an efficient manufacturing process. Cephalexin (Ceporex) was launched in December 1969 and, as forecast, became a substantial product.[50]

The medical profession's sustained and sometimes profligate use of antibiotics in the 1960s and 1970s in effect filtered resistant strains of bacteria which, in turn, mutated to protect themselves from attack. Increasingly, certain streptococcal and, more importantly, staphylococcal infections proved themselves immune to established drug therapies. It became imperative to find more potent versions of the early cephalosporins as gaps began to appear in their spectra of activity. Some Gram-negative bacteria, for example, produced beta-lactamase enzymes that destroyed the first-generation medicines. Glaxo chemists, under Elks, examined hundreds of molecules from which they selected a small number for microbiological research by O'Callaghan and Dr Richard Sykes to test the effectiveness of compounds against microbes.[51] The end product was cefuroxime (marketed in May 1978 as Zinacef), a second-generation cephalosporin, resistant to most beta-lactamoses and effective against many Gram-positive and Gram-negative bacteria.

Although several second-generation cephalosporins were introduced during the 1970s, none was orally active, so their therapeutic advantage was not readily available to general practitioners. This problem was solved in Glaxo by making a less polar, non-acidic derivative of cefuroxime which was similar in principle to some earlier orally active penicillins. Cefuroxime axetil is absorbed from the gut and then hydrolysed in the body to generate cefuxomine. However, only half of the axetil is absorbed, the remainder being converted to free cefuroxime in the gut. This is undesirable, because significant concentrations of the substance inhibit the growth of intestinal bacteria and cause diarrhoea. Fortunately, tolerated doses of cefuroxime axetil were found to generate clinically effective blood levels of the free drug. Cefuroxime axetil (Zinnat), marketed in November 1987 for recalcitrant chest and urinary tract infections, was the subject of a Queen's Award for Technical Achievement five years later.

Early in 1976 with cefuroxime in clinical trials, Dr Christopher Newall, a chemist recently appointed to head the antibiotic group, was asked to find a new cephalosporin with increased potency against *Pseudomonas* and a resistant to beta-lactamases. The breakthrough came in 1978 when Dr Alan Long's section made a compound that had a broad spectrum against Gram-negative pathogens and was exceptionally active against life-threatening *Pseudomonas*. Although David Livermore succeeded in making the molecule, much development work was to follow as the cephalosporins, being unstable, were notoriously difficult to manufacture in large quantities. Ceftazidime was launched in March 1983 as Fortum, having been five years in development, a short period by the standards of the time. A third-generation injectable cephalosporin, ceftazidime proved superior to many competitor antibiotics that were subsequently introduced. Dr Newall attributed its efficacy to Glaxo's fifteen years of accumulated expertise and the ability to compare new molecules with an archive of in-house compounds. Research on the cephalosporins continued for a further ten years in search of a fourth-generation compound, but it had become progressively harder to improve on what were already very advanced antibiotics.

Glucocorticoid steroids: betamethasone

Glaxo had first become involved in glucocorticoid steroid research in 1950 following a request from the British government that they devise a manufacturing process for cortisone that avoided paying royalties to the US. The Greenford scientists had made cortisone and hydrocortisone by a complex route from hecogenin (see p. 122). In the meantime, Schering had developed betamethasone, a more potent and highly selective steroid, but had no commercially viable manufacturing process. Both the Schering chemists led by E. B. Hershberg, a product of Harvard, and the Glaxo chemists led by Hems were aware that the hecogenin-based technology might provide a solution.[52] The outcome was a research agreement between Glaxo and Schering by which the former undertook to develop a practical route to betamethasone and to supply the drug in return for licences to sell prednisone, prednisolone and betamethasones when approved for sale. D. H. R. Birkbeck, later a Nobel Laureate, played a major catalytic role in Glaxo–Schering affairs as he was an expert consultant on steroid chemistry to both companies.[53] The agreement to develop betamethasone proved to be of great importance to Glaxo because it served as the starting point for several research projects in the 1960s which yielded highly effective treatments for skin diseases and bronchial asthma. Betamethasone (Betnelan) tablets were launched in the UK in 1961 and later as an aqueous solution of betamethasone sodium phosphate (Betnesol) to contain inflammation in the eye, ear and nose.

Earning significant revenues from ointments and creams containing cortisol acetate, Glaxo were concerned when the Syntex Corporation introduced a novel dermatological product containing fluocinolone acetonide

(Synalar). This new steroid was so much more effective than existing treatments for eczema and psoriasis that it began to dominate the topical steroid market. To defend its commercial position, Glaxo had to respond quickly. Since there was no reliable animal test for quantifying topical anti-inflammatory activity, it was difficult to identify product candidates. This problem was solved in a most unlikely way when the Glaxo chemists were introduced to a novel method for assessing topical activity simply by applying steroids to human skin. The test had been devised by a dermatologist, Dr A. W. McKenzie, who had developed a method of comparing the percutaneous absorption of steroids when holding an exchange fellowship at the Western Reserve University at Cleveland, Ohio. He applied dilutions to the forearms of volunteers and covered them with a plastic film protected by either a metal guard or Saran Wrap[54] – a method now known as the McKenzie skin blanching test. Initially he was interested only in the percutaneous absorption but it subsequently occurred to him that drug potency might be related to an ability to blanch the skin. His tests confirmed this hypothesis and McKenzie published the results with Dr R. B. Stoughton (who had provided the laboratory facilities) in the *American Archives of Dermatology* for 1962.

Returning to London, McKenzie was appointed to a senior registrar post at St John's Hospital for Diseases of the Skin, Lisle Street, near Leicester Square, where his research attracted considerable attention.[55] Professor Charles Calnan, a consultant dermatologist there, mentioned these findings in passing to Jack Hanson of Glaxo Laboratories. In the late summer of 1962, Hanson called on McKenzie at St John's where they discussed the potential of the test, though the former appeared doubtful about the ease and constancy of the assay. Within a few days McKenzie travelled to Greenford with his own Saran Wrap, metal arm shields and pipettes. Glaxo provided serial dilutions of fluocinolone acetonide (Synalar) and these he applied to the forearms of four technicians. Returning the next morning, McKenzie read the results, and thereafter made many visits to Greenford to help perfect the technique of the company's researchers and give guidance on the interpretation of true vasoconstriction.[56] The great advantage of the McKenzie patch test was that it accelerated and increased the predictability of the evaluation. The chemists could, for example, make a new compound on a Monday, which could then be investigated by the pharmacologists and be applied to the forearms of volunteers on the Wednesday. The results could be recorded the next day and be available for interpretation early the following week, enabling the Greenford scientists to explore hundreds of compounds quickly.

Armed with the new experimental technique, the steroid group under

97. *The McKenzie skin blanching test to assess the potency of dermatological preparations. Its speed and accuracy dramatically shortened the development time for betamethasone valerate (Betnovate).*

Joseph Elks (and including Drs Gordon Phillipps, Peter May and Gordon Gregory) focused their attention on the esters and ortho-esters of betamethasone as these had been found to be much more active than betamethasone itself. Activity peaked with the 17-valerate ester, which was selected for development.[57] Betamethasone 17-valerate was shown to be 3.6 times more active than fluocinolone acetonide (Synalar) in the McKenzie test.[58] Dr Michael Atkinson was responsible for *in vivo* testing and he gave McKenzie some samples of betamethasone 17-valerate in ointment form for uncontrolled trials in consenting patients. Full-scale clinical trials then followed under the supervision of Dr David Williams at King's College Hospital, who had previously assisted with the *in vivo* studies of griseofulvin. Sadly Dr McKenzie's reward for his crucial part in the research and development of betamethasone valerate was a gramophone and his effort was publicly acknowledged in nothing other than an insert to the veterinary product Vetsovate. Launched as Betnovate in 1963, only a few months after being made in the laboratory, betamethasone 17-valerate proved to be particularly effective and rapidly gained an important market share (see p. 246). Betnovate was perhaps the first novel compound that represented a distinct advance on existing medicines to be discovered by Glaxo Research as their earlier products were the result of development work.[59]

The therapeutic and commercial success of Betnovate encouraged a continuing programme of work on corticosteroids for dermatological conditions. The McKenzie test showed that clobetasol propionate was more than twice as active as betamethasone valerate and therefore more effective in treating difficult skin diseases such as severe psoriasis. It was launched as

Dermovate in 1973. Clobetasone butyrate (Eumovate), less active than betamethasone valerate, was introduced two years later. Beclomethasone
dipropionate, which was a little more active than betamethasone valerate,
was licensed to Allen & Hanburys and marketed as Propaderm, though it
was later used to pioneer the use of steroids by inhalation in asthma (see
p. 332).

Other steroid products

A further avenue for steroid chemistry explored by Glaxo was anaesthetics.
In 1966, Dr Gordon Phillipps directed a team under Niall Weir to investigate the use of steroids as an induction anaesthetic, to provide a rapid loss
of consciousness for dentistry or before the administration of a major
anaesthetic in surgery. It had been established that steroids had two major
advantages over barbiturates as anaesthetics: a greater therapeutic ratio
and thus a wider margin of safety, and secondly rapid elimination from the
bloodstream by the liver rather than by redistribution. However, there was
a significant practical difficulty in turning them into clinically useful drugs.
They are sparingly soluble in water but had to be administered by intravenous injection.[60] This problem was solved by using a mixture of two
steroids, alphaxolone and alphadolone acetate, which was more soluble
than either of the components and was sufficiently solubilised in water by
the surface active agent Cremaphor EL. Althesin entered clinical trials in
1971 and was launched in June the following year, having been the subject
of a two-day conference involving senior clinicians held at the Royal College of Physicians. The proceedings were published in a supplement to the
Postgraduate Medical Journal.[61] Althesin appeared to have many properties
of the ideal intravenous anaesthetic:

> It produced sleep in one arm–brain circulation time after a single dose, with
> minimal involuntary muscle movements and without pain on injection. Its car-
> diovascular effects were similar to other agents used for a comparable purpose
> … Furthermore, it was not antanalgesic and anaesthetists were impressed by the
> quality of recovery following its use, this being rapid with a low incidence of
> nausea and vomiting. Patient acceptance was also high.[62]

Early clinical studies, including a trial involving 153 patients in the Sal-
ford area[63] and a sample of 800 in Northern Ireland, did not reveal any unpleasant or dangerous side-effects.[64] An assessment of the drug published
in the *Proceedings of the Royal Society of Medicine* in 1973 concluded that 'it
is of shorter duration of action than thiopentone when used for minor

surgery and rapid and clear-headed recovery can be achieved; and it has a high safety margin'.[65]

However, it soon became clear that Althesin was associated with a significant incidence of allergic reactions. In November 1972, Dr Eric Snell reported to the Glaxo Laboratories board that there had been 'five or six severe reactions ... an incidence of one in 20,000 patients'.[66] These continued and it appeared that the true incidence was in the order of one in 750 to 1000. Anaphylaxis (an alarming and occasionally fatal reaction to a substance to which the individual has become unusually sensitive) was recorded following first exposure to the drug, though the majority of episodes were of a minor nature. Nevertheless, many anaesthetists considered that the considerable advantages of Althesin outweighed its occasional side-effects and continued to use it in hospitals. The solubilising agent, Cremaphor EL (polyoxyethylated castor oil), was found to release histamine in dogs and was thought to be the cause of the reactions.[67]

Although the number of reported adverse reactions remained relatively stable, medical perception of the anaesthetic had become tarnished and in April 1978 the board of Glaxo Laboratories recognised that 'the sales performance of Althesin continued to be adversely affected by papers and reports in journals concerned with reactions to the product'.[68] Finally, in March 1984 Glaxo withdrew the drug on the recommendation of the medical department, concerned about anaphylactic reactions. A decision by the Italian government to ban the use of preparations containing Cremaphor EL (notably propanidid and Althesin) precipitated this action. Research on a replacement steroid anaesthetic at Greenford was also curtailed as the candidate steroid was found to be weakly carcinogenic in rats. Further research on anaesthetics was not pursued as the company had by then built up a portfolio of important medicines and had begun a policy of discontinuing work on what were regarded as relatively minor products. Surprisingly, the rapid decision to withdraw Althesin proved an unpopular one with anaesthetists:

> Anaesthetists had no opportunity to put forward their views before the event, and although they would freely admit to the disadvantages of Althesin, it was considered by many to have several distinct advantages particularly in the practice of intensive care, and its abrupt withdrawal left a vacuum in available techniques.[69]

Gordon Phillipps believed that inhaled steroids might have an important part to play in respiratory therapy. He took the idea to Dr Eric Snell, medical director at Greenford, who assessed the likely clinical implications.

Snell was concerned that the tissue of the lungs might respond in the same fashion as skin and that collagen-forming cells would be inhibited, leading to dangerous thinning. Steroids might also lead to symptom suppression in lung infections and result in their undetected spread. Frustrated by these objections, Phillipps abandoned any plans to test the hypothesis. However, Dr Wilfred Simpson, medical director at Allen & Hanburys, had considered the idea quite independently of the Glaxo scientists. It was soon taken up by David Jack's teams at Ware, who, having worked on salbuta-

98. The chemistry laboratories at Greenford during the 1960s.

mol, had a fuller understanding of respiratory medicine and were able to take the idea through to a safe and efficacious product (see p. 331).

In 1968 Glaxo took over The British Drug Houses and thereby acquired their contraceptive Volidan, one of whose ingredients was megestrol acetate, a progestogen invented at their laboratories. However, the drug soon ran into serious difficulties when scientists at Mead Johnson, a licensee of BDH, discovered that megestrol acetate administered to female dogs induced malignant growths in their mammary ducts. This was subsequently shown to be a general characteristic of potent progestogens. Although Volidan also contained an oestrogen, these results gave Glaxo no option but to withdraw the contraceptive. Independent work at Greenford supervised by Phillipps designed to develop a progestogen-only 'mini-pill' was also abandoned, despite having identified some promising compounds.

In January 1967, Hems succeeded Macrae as managing director of Glaxo Research, having joined its board three years earlier. Hems found the transition from departmental head to chief executive of a large research group difficult because it necessitated the delegation of responsibility to experts in a variety of fields, many of which fell outside his own technical understanding.[70] This ran contrary to his detailed management of chemistry

99. The new biological building at Greenford opened in July 1956.

projects. Furthermore, the complexity of research now demanded the creation of multidisciplinary teams that Hems resisted, discouraging lateral communication between the chemists and their biologist colleagues. He never fully came to terms with the devolved management style required or with the inherent uncertainties of the biological sciences. Hems did, however, recognise the need to diversify beyond cephalosporins and corticosteroids and set up important projects on cancer and diseases of the central nervous system before his retirement in 1975. A taciturn man who chose his words carefully, Hems was highly organised and sought to solve scientific problems rationally. When questioning team leaders at monthly meetings, his focused memory often allowed him to continue talking at the point where he had finished on his last visit.

Hems was succeeded as managing director of Glaxo Research by Dr Tom Walker, like him formerly head of chemistry at Greenford. Walker had studied the action of analgesics for his doctoral thesis at Glasgow and had been recruited by Macrae, who regularly toured selected science departments looking for talented graduates.[71] He joined Glaxo Laboratories in 1948 but two years later won a scholarship to study chemical engineering in the United States at the University of Wisconsin. On returning to Greenford, Walker worked on the complicated task of converting ergosterol into cortisone.[72] After five years as production manager at Glaxo's Montrose factory, Walker returned to Greenford in 1958 and worked on the griseofulvin project. Dr Fred Wilkins then asked him to go to India in 1961, where his knowledge of chemical engineering was to prove useful in improving and extending production processes. In 1967, he became head of chemistry at Greenford with a seat on the board of Glaxo Research. Like Hems, Walker was a skilled organiser but, being of a gentlemanly disposition, was considered more approachable. It was thought by some of his colleagues that his time in India working on manufacturing processes for which reliability and safety are watchwords had inhibited a natural dynamism and made him cautious. After the formation of Glaxo Group Research, uniting the various interests in the company, Walker remained in charge of the Greenford laboratories until 1980, when he moved to Japan in an executive role primarily to establish links between Nippon Glaxo and indigenous pharmaceutical companies.

When Walker became managing director of Glaxo Research, Dr Jack Chapman was appointed director of chemistry and Dr Gordon Gregory took the post of head of physical chemistry. Although these departments were responsible for finding novel molecules with antibiotic properties, much of the development work needed to translate these into practical medicines was performed by the microbiologists under Dr Peter Muggleton. A key member of his department was Dr Cynthia O'Callaghan, who played a major role in the search for cefuroxime. Together with Ann Harris, a microbiologist who worked in the veterinary department, O'Callaghan was one of the few women scientists employed at Greenford in what was traditionally a male world. A further member of the microbiology division was Dr Richard Sykes who was later to become research and development director of Glaxo Holdings, and ultimately chairman of Glaxo Wellcome. He had joined Glaxo Laboratories in 1972 as head of the antibiotic research unit.[73] Sykes had completed a doctorate in microbiology at Bristol University under the supervision of Mark Richmond, professor of bacteriology.[74] In 1968, Glaxo Laboratories had agreed to supplement his award from the Science Research Council because of the clear connection between his post-graduate research and the company's work on antibiotics. He kept in regular contact with the staff at Greenford and in 1972 was offered a post there. Unsure whether to accept, Sykes discussed the offer with Professor Richmond, walking the country lanes near The Bull at Gerrards Cross, where they were staying for a meeting with Dr Muggleton.[75] In the event, Sykes accepted and worked at Greenford until 1977, when he left to become assistant director of microbiology for Squibb at Princeton, New Jersey. During these years he

100. The entrance hall and staircase of Glaxo's biological building.

had worked almost exclusively on cephalosporins, playing a significant part in the development of cefuroxime and later ceftazidime.

Veterinary medicines

In the early 1950s, cortisone products were shown to have an effect on metabolism in animals, which was especially important for cattle and horses. In addition, the anti-inflammatory action of cortisone created opportunities for its use in veterinary medicines. A department had been set up in 1953 following the recruitment of Olga Uvarov, a veterinary surgeon, with the brief to develop products for use in animals, train a new force of representatives, and offer guidance on packaging and publicity.[76] As she recalled, experimental testing was not without its difficulties

> The medical department agreed to let me have some of their precious cortisone but problems arose when I sought far bigger quantities than they had envisaged. Only tiny amounts were used in human clinical trials whereas my doses had to be ounces at least, for animal sizes and weights and for study in more than one species. The medical department yielded eventually, tests proceeded followed by trials at various institutes and Ministry of Agriculture laboratories ... By 1963 we had a proven veterinary range of betamethasone eye and skin ointments, eye and ear drops, tablets and injections.[77]

Throughout the 1960s the laboratories at Greenford produced new veterinary medicines, often drawing on the areas of established expertise in humans. In 1964 two vaccines were launched: Iblin to protect poultry from infectious bronchitis, and Clostrin to act against seven of the most common diseases in sheep. These were followed in 1965 by Myxilin, a vaccine against Newcastle Disease (fowl pest) in laying hens. In 1967, Glaxo introduced an injectable antibiotic, Propen, in the form of a sterile suspension containing procaine penicillin and benzathine penicillin for use in horses, cattle, pigs, sheep, goats, dogs and cats. During the early 1970s, a new poultry vaccine was launched (Bron-

101. Dr Tom Walker, photographed in 1967, who became head of chemistry at Greenford in succession to Dr Hems.

virin), a corticosteroid cream to treat animal skin infections (Vetsovate), a formulation of the induction anaesthetic Althesin for cats (Saffan), a long-acting steroid injection to alleviate sore joints in dogs, horses and cats (Betsovet) and ear drops to overcome otitis externa in cats and dogs (Oterna).[78] In 1976 the development work on the cephalosporins generated its first veterinary products in the form of Ceporin and Cepoxillin (containing cephoxazole and procaine penicillin G) for the treatment of mastitis in cows.[79] Cepravin Dry Cow (containing cephalonium, a broad spectrum bactericidal antibiotic) followed for the treatment of sub-clinical infections in cows, particularly those associated with bovine mastitis.[80] Olga Uvarov, who retired from Glaxo in 1970, subsequently became the first woman president of the Royal College of Veterinary Surgeons and was awarded a DBE in 1983.

Ware: strategic redirection

In 1961, Cyril Maplethorpe appointed Dr David Jack as head of research and development at Allen & Hanburys when Dr Arnold Robinson left to take charge of the Twyford laboratories of Arthur Guinness & Sons. Aware of the need to discover novel and commercially viable medicines if Allen & Hanburys were to preserve its independent identity, Maplethorpe turned to Jack, posting him a cutting of the job advertisement without an accompanying letter.[81] The two had recently met when Jack had been interviewed for the post of professor of pharmacy at Glasgow and Maplethorpe had sat on the panel. The latter had been impressed by Jack's experience and dynamic presence and decided to recruit him.

Before he joined Allen & Hanburys, Jack had pursued a varied career. After a pharmaceutical apprenticeship in his native Fife, he studied at Glasgow University and the Royal Technical College, graduating in 1948 with a first in pharmacy and pharmacology.[82] He then taught pharmacology at the former and physiology at the latter for brief periods. In 1951, recruited by Dr Tom Macrae, he joined Glaxo Laboratories as a research pharmacist and came south to Greenford. Set to work on antibiotics, Jack found experimental pharmacy insufficiently challenging and judged that the career opportunities then open to him at Greenford were limited. Two years later, he joined Menley & James, in Coldharbour Lane, Brixton, as their senior development chemist, responsible for pharmacy and chemistry. Although a small company, they were the UK agent for both Smith Kline & French and Eaton Laboratories, a subsidiary of Norwich Pharmacal Co. of New York. Thus, Jack was entrusted with the varied tasks of taking products discovered in the United States through the developmental process before they could be launched in Britain. In the event, Smith Kline & French soon acquired Menley & James and Jack was appointed head of laboratory services. Working in what initially was a small organisation, Jack gained a wide experience of pharmaceutical science; he had, for example, to do his own chemistry and, to broaden his technical knowledge in this area, completed a doctorate on a part-time basis at London University in 1960. His responsibilities grew as the department expanded to about a hundred staff drawn from pharmacy, pharmacology and chemistry. Yet he tired of a diet composed almost exclusively of development work and sought new opportunities. In 1961 at the age of 38, Jack moved to Ware with a broad knowledge of pharmaceutical development but little experience of drug research.

Having been given an undertaking by Jephcott and Maplethorpe that resources would be made available to run a research programme, Jack reviewed the department. Inheriting a staff of 120, Maplethorpe agreed that he could increase their number to 200 and he was given a period of at least five years to prove their innovative capacities.[83] However, these plans were jeopardised in 1962 when Jephcott established Glaxo Research, in part to co-ordinate research and development activities but also to tighten control over expenditure. Maplethorpe asked Jack to become a director of the new company but he declined because he found himself at odds with Jephcott's attitude to research and feared that his autonomy might be pruned at board meetings. 'Jephcott', recalled Jack, 'may have been the greatest man who worked for Glaxo, but he was suspicious of speculative research and was a champion of development activities, of products licensed from other companies, especially American ones, or government sponsored projects.'[84] Although this strategy had worked successfully during the 1940s and 1950s, Jack and Maplethorpe both realised that the supply of new chemical entities from overseas was drying up and that, if Glaxo wished to survive, the company would need to discover its own products. Jephcott honoured his agreement and Jack was appointed to the board of Allen & Hanburys in June 1962 on the understanding that he could run the Ware laboratories without direct reference to Glaxo Research.

The problems at Ware were twofold. First, because the company had made galenicals and products licensed from other pharmaceutical firms, its expertise was primarily in development rather than discovery. Secondly, about three-quarters of the experimental work was directed towards the control of bacterial and parasitic infections, which duplicated much of Glaxo's enterprise. As the Greenford laboratories were far larger and had an established reputation in antibiotic and steroid development, there was little reason to continue with this work and Jack transferred some parasitology projects to Glaxo, discontinuing much of the rest. It was essential, he believed, to make a fresh start in therapeutic areas not explored by the Greenford scientists. Jack was concerned to ensure that Ware made its own distinctive contribution. Since there was no pharmacology-based research at Glaxo and this was an area he knew well, Jack chose to specialise in the field.

'Taking a hammer to the crystalline organisation',[85] Jack recruited staff and moved others to new positions, causing a considerable stir in what had become a conservative culture. Key appointments included Dr Roy Brittain, who had joined Allen & Hanburys in 1955 from the School of Pharmacy at London University.[86] Although aged only 32, Brittain became head of the pharmacology department, Jack having been impressed by his 'irrepressible enthusiasm and optimism, and his receptivity to new ideas'.[87] Thus began a fruitful and important partnership as Brittain was increasingly entrusted with the practical execution of many projects. In 1973, to reflect his growing responsibilities and the significant managerial role he had

102. Sir David Jack, who joined Allen & Hanbury's in 1961, and later became the Glaxo Holdings' director responsible for research and development. Under his auspices the laboratories at Ware discovered both salbutamol (Ventolin) and ranitidine (Zantac).

performed in the discovery of salbutamol, Brittain became director of biology at Ware. Desmond Poynter, 'a naturally sensitive biologist',[88] agreed to forsake parasitology and set up a new department of pathology. Alec Ritchie joined from Glaxo and Norman Harper from Chelsea College to strengthen chemistry. Les Martin from Bengers Laboratories became head of biochemistry and Deryck Rhodes from Pfizer took pharmacy. Dr Ivor Mitchell, from Glaxo's factory at Ulverston, was appointed senior administrator and head of product registration. Having Jack's confidence, he was able to offer an objective and informed second opinion without having to qualify it out of trepidation. Dr Denis Cahal, later chief executive of the Committee on the Safety of Drugs, was briefly medical director but was succeeded in 1964 by Dr Wilfred Simpson and five years later by Dr David Harris.

At the same time as Jack was gathering together a team of scientists, he also planned a strategy for research and development. Maplethorpe allowed him considerable scope, commenting: 'I don't care what you do as long as you are successful'.[89] Jack began with an understanding of the body's underlying biological processes.[90] Of particular importance were enzymes and receptor proteins for physiological mediators (including nerve transmitters and hormones). Both are protein catalysts that accelerate chemical reactions without themselves being used up, and are involved in all the metabolic processes on which life depends. These discoveries encouraged researchers in the 1960s either to consider the inhibition of particular enzyme pathways by using natural or modified substrates, or to mimic or antagonise the actions of physiological mediators selectively by employing modified mediators. In essence, the designers of such medicines sought to find ways of controlling the switches that regulated the natural functions of the body as a means of suppressing pathological processes.

To apply these ideas, research needed to be organised on an interdisciplinary basis, and required close collaboration between chemists and biologists, gathered into project teams. In one respect, Jack was fortunate: the comparatively small scale of Ware made it easier to break down traditional divisions as new staff were assigned to specific projects. At Greenford, with six times the number of scientists and well-established demarcation lines between disciplines, it would have been more difficult to introduce these changes. Starting with only 120 staff, linked by short or informal lines of communication, it was possible to build a powerful internal culture. This, in turn, fostered the cross-fertilisation of ideas, and enabled Jack to keep in close personal contact with all his research teams. It was perhaps this friendly co-operation, professional intimacy and enthusiasm that created an atmosphere of innovation, which larger, more bureaucratic research organisations struggled to repeat. Looking back on this pioneering phase, Sir David Jack wrote:

> research management is mainly about focusing and encouraging informed enthusiasm. Personal initiative should be welcomed and inertia minimised, particularly by assigning problems to specialised multi-disciplinary project teams with the tactical freedom and resources needed to solve them. The R & D director must also be patient and create a secure overall environment for his staff to contain the inherent uncertainties of research work. They are unlikely to perform well under pressure or if they are worried about their jobs.[91]

Having decided that the overall strategy for research and development at Ware would take the form of modifying or inhibiting the body's own chemical messengers, activity focused on the modification of the action on non-peptide physiological mediators. This work, in turn, spawned projects on the central nervous system aimed at producing medicines for the control of pain, anxiety, depression and schizophrenia, in the cardiovascular field for the better control of high blood pressure and in respiratory medicine to treat bronchial asthma.[92] Jack believed that the diseases targeted should be common ones, not only because of the obvious commercial advantage but also because of the greater improvement that would result to the nation's health. The early projects had a straightforward plan and were largely based on analogues of known drugs with a view to eliminating side-effects, or the screening of compounds to discover new applications. One of the most successful projects began in 1963, designed to find a bronchodilator with a more persistent relaxant effect than isoprenaline on the bronchial muscle. The outcome of this research, the discovery of salbuta-mol (Ventolin) in 1966, was to revitalise the commercial fortunes of Allen & Hanburys. It also advanced Jack's understanding of how to look for drugs and led to further projects for the treatment of asthma, peptic ulcers and high blood pressure.

New treatments for asthma

Asthma is classified as a set of allergic symptoms, a form of atopy, that can have a variety of causes. It is characterised by breathlessness and wheezing which result from inflammation in the lungs. The inflammation is initiated and maintained by the inhalation of allergic foreign proteins or by their lo-calised generation during bacterial or viral infections.[93] The most common cause of airway constriction in mild asthma results from contraction of the bronchial muscle, which can be relieved by adrenaline, while the most dan-gerous cause of airway constriction is physical occlusion of the bronchi fol-lowing damage to their lining and excessive formation of mucus. This obstruction is not cleared by bronchodilators and treatment with inhaled steroids is essential to prevent or reverse this life-threatening condition. When the asthma project started at Ware in 1963, the most effective bron-chodilator was isoprenaline ('Medihaler'). Isoprenaline, a simple analogue of adrenaline, had been shown by Raymond Ahlquist in 1948 to act selec-tively on what are now called beta-adrenoceptors. The advantages of iso-prenaline was its intense and rapid onset of action. It had the disadvantage of only lasting for one or two hours, while its stimulation of the heart in chronic asthma patients produced a potentially dangerous combination of effects. Indeed, it was estimated that as many as 3,000 young people died in the UK during the early 1960s because of intensive use of isoprenaline in-halers in the absence of appropriate steroid treatment to control damage to the bronchial mucosa.

The objective that Jack set his scientists in 1963 was the discovery of an analogue of adrenaline that would be relatively stable in the body and therefore intrinsically longer acting by inhalation and probably active by mouth as well.[94] Initially, the chemists had difficulty providing the com-pounds that the biologists requested. Dr Roy Brittain discussed the prob-lem with Dr Larry Lunts, who suggested that they work on non-catechol analogues of adrenaline (catechols being short acting and unstable). 'Some of them did not look particularly exciting', recalled Brittain, but that was 'one of our first important lessons'.[95] They were learning that compara-tively small changes to a molecule could sometimes produce dispropor-tionate changes to its properties. One of the first compounds to be investigated was the saligenin analogue of isoprenaline (AH 3021), which in June 1966 was sent for testing. Brittain recalled how Valerie Cullum, a junior pharmacologist,

> came into my office … and said that there was something funny about this beta-stimulant: it relaxed the bronchial smooth muscle, but it wouldn't stimulate the heart. The result was in front of us and all I did was to send her back to the laboratory to do the experiment again. She came the next day and said exactly the same thing. I still didn't exactly believe it, so I sent her back again. On the third day she came back yet again and I went and did an experiment for myself. Then we realised that there was something uniquely different in that molecule. But when everything suddenly lands almost in your lap, you don't actually believe it.[96]

The properties of AH 3021 suggested that there might be two types of beta-adrenoceptors: one which stimulated the heart and the other which relaxed bronchial muscles.[97] Soon afterwards a related compound AH 3365 (later called salbutamol) was found to be even more selectively active on the bronchi and more potent.[98] Salbutamol was immediately subjected to intensive investigations in animals and then in man, the findings being published in two papers to *Nature* in 1968.[99]

Allen & Hanburys launched salbutamol as the Ventolin inhaler in 1969, and in tablet form the following year. If inhaled, it rapidly induced intense bronchodilation without significant side-effects and was active for about four hours.[100] Chronic asthmatics did not become tolerant to its therapeutic action and it proved an effective treatment in long-term use as well as for acute attacks. Salbutamol was, therefore, the first clinical product to emerge from the new research and development strategy and was to prove one of the most commercially successful, receiving a Queen's Award for Technological Achievement in 1973. The selective action of salbutamol also led Jack to believe that the receptor proteins for many physiological mediators were more varied than was commonly supposed and nearly all the subsequent projects at Ware involved the identification of sub-types of receptors and their manipulation to achieve selective drug action.

After the discovery of salbutamol in 1966, the Ware scientists explored the use of anti-inflammatory steroids in the lungs to aid the treatment of severe cases of asthma.[101] Dr Wilfrid Simpson, medical director of Allen & Hanburys (and independently Drs Phillipps and Snell at Greenford) proposed that a topical corticosteroid of the type that had been prepared for skin disorders could be developed for inhalation. However, such medicines in regular use inhibited collagen formation and led to thinning of the skin, and such an action in the lung would be potentially catastrophic. Another concern was the possibility of significant systemic activity as 80 to 90 per cent of an inhaled dose of a drug is swallowed and available for absorption. The steroid would, therefore, have to be highly active in the lungs but weakly active in the mouth. Beclomethasone dipropionate, licensed from Glaxo for use in Propaderm skin preparations, was a suitable candidate because tests on volunteers at Ware showed that it was poorly absorbed from the gut. Marketed in 1972 as the Becotide Inhaler it became an established treatment for chronic asthma and received a Queen's Award for Technological Innovation in 1975. The Ware scientists also explored the use of beclomethasone dipropionate as a nasal spray to combat the symptoms of allergic rhinitis or hay fever and in 1974 launched a product called Beconase.

Research into asthma at Ware continued. An early objective was an orally active $beta_2$-adrenergic bronchodilator without the systemic side-effects of salbutamol. No evidence of sub-types of these receptors was found and the programme was abandoned in 1976. Other projects, including the modification of prostaglandin E, failed to lead to safe and effective medicines. In view of the short patent life left to salbutamol, in 1981 Jack reconsidered the $beta_2$-adrenergic problem. The one serious defect of salbutamol was that its limited duration of action could not prevent an asthma attack while the sufferer enjoyed a full night's sleep. Initially this was achieved not by creating a molecule with a long half life but by providing an osmotic coating to the tablet which prevented it from being broken down in the stomach while allowing liquid to permeate through so that the drug could emerge from a small laser-drilled hole in the form of a solution. Volmax was launched in 1987 as a Glaxo product, though it later transferred to the Allen & Hanburys trademark.

In addition to a controlled-release tablet, David Jack wished to find a long-acting analogue of salbutamol. To create interest in the launch of Ventolin by Glaxo Inc., a closed symposium was held at Boston in 1981 at which leading physicians and scientists were asked to present their latest findings on salbutamol. For his presentation, Jack explored the possibility of finding more efficient $beta_2$-adrenaceptor stimulant as a bronchodilator and concluded that a drug which binds firmly at its site of action in the receptor protein could remain efficacious for at least eight hours.[102] On returning from Boston, Jack set up a project team led by Dr Ian Skidmore, under the overall direction of Dr Roy Brittain, and they began the painstaking programme of testing analogues of salbutamol in the face of some scepticism from their scientific colleagues. The outcome of this research was salmeterol, which was shown to be similar to salbutamol in $beta_2$-adrenoceptor selectivity but about ten times more potent. Although it was slower to act

103. The biological research building at Ware opened in 1972

on the smooth muscle of the airways, salmeterol has a remarkably long duration of action, between ten and twelve hours.[103] Launched in 1990 as Serevent, its clinical effectiveness has been translated into significant world-wide sales.

Although inhaled beclomethasone dipropionate (Becotide) proved to be well tolerated, the greater daily doses used to control severe asthma had modest but significant systemic glucocorticoid effects. A market existed, therefore, for a potent topical steroid that was inactive by mouth. Accordingly, in 1982 Jack surveyed the Glaxo library of steroids, selecting fluticasone propionate for investigation because it had been shown to be twice as active as beclomethasone in the McKenzie test and was virtually inactive after oral administration in the mouse. Further trials showed that the drug was inactivated in the liver and could be developed as a selective anti-inflammatory for the treatment of chronic asthma, being launched as Flixotide in 1992.

Cardiovascular research: labetalol (Trandate)

The strategy at Ware of taking the body's own chemical messengers and modifying or inhibiting them was applied to cardiology and, in particular, to the control of high blood pressure and angina pectoris. This was an important and extensive therapeutic market. Much work had already been undertaken, notably by James Black at ICI Pharmaceuticals where the first beta-blockers had been developed. These medicines antagonise the actions of adrenaline at Ahlquist's beta-receptors, which, amongst other things, control the rate and force of cardiac contraction. Black had hypothesised that a specific beta-blocker could diminish the physiological effects of the sympathetic nervous system on the heart, making it beat more slowly and less forcibly becoming, as a result, a more efficient pump and consuming less oxygen. It could, therefore, benefit patients with angina pectoris, whose pain is caused by deficient oxygen supply to the heart due to a narrowing of the coronary blood vessels. Propranolol, launched by ICI in 1964 as Inderal, proved a great medicinal and commercial success.

The Ware researchers looked for a beta-blocker of longer duration that acted on the heart and not bronchial receptors. Propranolol and similar beta-blockers were contra-indicated for asthmatic patients because they induce bronchospasm by blocking these receptors. The Ware programme was largely based on the finding that AH 3474, the salicylamide analogue of salbutamol, is a beta-blocker of modest potency and short acting. Chemical modification yielded an unusually long-acting beta-blocker which was chosen for development, though this proved to be toxic in animals and was never tested in man.[104] The void was filled by the serendipitous discovery that AH 4077, another salicylamide derivative, unlike simple beta-blockers reduced blood pressure immediately after intravenous injection in dogs. Modification of its structure led to AH 5158, labetalol, which was shown to be more potent and longer acting. Larry Lunts was responsible for the chemistry in this programme. Labetalol was found to have a rapid action in animals and man (whereas propranolol took effect gradually over seven to ten days) because it not only blocked beta-receptors but also alpha-receptors in the arterioles of the skin and abdominal viscera, which then become dilated and aid the flow of blood, thereby reducing its pressure.[105] The result is that resting cardiac output is normal in patients treated with labetalol because their peripheral blood vessels are dilated, whereas in patients receiving propanolol the cardiac output is reduced and peripheral vessels remain relatively contracted. Dr David Richards played a key role in the medical development of labetalol, which was launched in 1977 as Trandate. As a specific anti-hypertensive drug used in cardiac emergencies, it has been modestly successful, but Trandate failed to achieve a major place in the UK beta-blocker market (see p. 254).

Ranitidine (Zantac)

The Ware scientists achieved their greatest commercial success with the design of a medicine to inhibit gastric acid secretion for the treatment of duodenal and stomach ulcers. Because peptic ulcers are a common complaint and were poorly controlled by existing treatments, a large unmet therapeutic opportunity existed. Maintenance was effected by antacids, which had to be taken in large doses and did nothing to tackle the underlying causes of the disease, being merely symptom relief. Surgery was painful, not always successful, and carried significant morbidity and mortality.

A small project team was set up in 1970 to find a selective inhibitor of gastric acid secretion. They were aware of the work being undertaken by James Black then at Smith Kline & French in Welwyn Garden City and of others at Pfizer and Eli Lilly in America to inhibit the stimulant action of histamine on the production of concentrated hydrochloric acid in the stomach. Parietal cells in the lining of the stomach were known to be responsible for the secretion and it had been shown that the anti-allergic anti-histamine drugs pioneered in 1940 by Daniel Bovet, a Swiss pharmacologist, had no inhibitory effect.[106] The physiological role of histamine in acid secretion was, therefore, open to some doubt so Jack and his researchers started by investigating other physiological mediators, notably gastrin, a peptide hormone. Then, in April 1972, Black published a paper in *Nature*, which was ultimately to transform the treatment of ulcers. He described his research into burimamide, a synthetic histamine analogue, which showed that it could specifically inhibit gastric acid secretion.[107] However, before these results had appeared in print, Black gave a lecture at Hatfield Polytechnic, attended by both Jack and Brittain, at which he discussed the role of burimamide. Jack immediately switched the focus of the work on ulcers in response to Black's findings. In retrospect, Jack described 1972 as the 'annus mirabilis' of the Ware research organisation and even of Glaxo Group itself. In that year, the new pharmacology building at Ware was opened, in which the serotonin project was set up and ultimately led to several novel medicines, including ondansetron and sumatriptan (see p. 336). It was the year when Becotide was launched and became a major therapeutic agent in the treatment of asthma and when research to find an effective anti-ulcer compound took a significant step forward. The same year witnessed the addition of one important drug to the group's portfolio and significant developments in the discovery of three more, one of which was to become the highest selling prescription medicine.

Despite the insights achieved by Black, the research to discover an anti-ulcer drug proved more problematic than anticipated because it was difficult to find a compound that fulfilled the structural requirements for this new kind of antagonist. Burimamide was not itself of practical value because of low potency and inactivity by mouth.[108] However, Smith Kline & French, who had a lead over Allen & Hanburys, solved these problems and in 1976 launched cimetidine (Tagamet), twelve years after the Welwyn project had begun. Cimetidine transformed the treatment of peptic ulcers and greatly reduced the need for surgery. It was an unbounded commercial success and by 1981 had become the highest selling prescription drug of all time with a turnover in that year of $620 million. The only significant disadvantage of cimetidine was that it was not totally selective at therapeutic doses, inhibiting enzymes in the liver which are normally involved in oxidative processes. In 1976, the year that Tagamet was marketed, the Ware team were given six months in which to find an effective and safe compound. 'We were ready for one last throw', Jack later recalled,[109] and fortunately a proposal by Dr John Clitheroe, the senior medicinal chemist in the team, led to a new class of histamine H_2-antagonists that were not covered by Smith Kline & French patents and intrinsically more potent and selective than the corresponding cimetidine series. Ranitidine, for example, proved to be almost five times more active in blocking gastric acid secretion than cimetidine and was found to have no significant inhibitory effect on the liver enzymes responsible for inactivating many medicines, so reducing the potential for drug interactions.[110]

Given the size of the anti-ulcer market and the need to catch up with Smith Kline & French, Glaxo put every effort into taking ranitidine through the development process as quickly as possible. Dr David Hartley, head of the new department of Chemical Development at Ware, recalled the frenetic activity that led to the design of an efficient manufacturing process in less than three and a half years. It was also decided to accelerate clinical trials and the traditional sequential approach was abandoned in favour of a parallel, simultaneous process. Dr David Richards, medical director at Ware, led the medical development team and clinical trials began in November 1978 in over twenty countries.[111] These trials established a treatment dosage of two 150mg tablets a day over a period of four to eight weeks, with a single tablet to prevent relapse.[112] This regimen and fewer side-effects distinguished ranitidine from cimetidine, which required patients to take a 200mg tablet four times daily. The UK and Italian health authorities were the first to authorise ranitidine for acute and maintenance treatment of peptic ulcers and for reflux oesophagitis. Meanwhile, the name Zantac had been chosen and the product was launched in October 1981; four years later it received a Queen's Award for Technological Achievement.

Serotonin projects: sumatriptan and ondansetron

In 1972, Brittain and Jack asked Patrick Humphrey to consider migraine as a therapeutic objective.[113] He chose to work on serotonin or 5-hydroxytryptamine (5HT), a hormone that is present in the gut, the brain and blood platelets, serving as a physiological mediator with a variety of roles including haemostasis, gastric secretion and neurotransmission.[114] A possible role for serotonin in migraine was indicated because of high concentrations of its metabolites in urine excreted during migraine attacks and the relief provided by an intravenous infusion of serotonin. Jack approved the project because the hormone, like adrenaline, had many pharmacological functions that were likely to be mediated by a range of cellular receptors whose activation or blockade might yield new medicines for various ailments.

Humphrey and his team hypothesised that serotonin reversed the painful engorgement of blood vessels in the head and searched for a drug that could selectively reverse the distention without affecting other parts of the body.[115] They began by investigating the action of methysergide (Deseril), a Sandoz product, effective in the prevention of migraine attacks but requiring a daily dosage and having undesirable side-effects. His team found that in anaesthetised dogs methysergide could selectively reduce blood flow in the region of the head supplied by the carotid artery. They also discovered that the saphenous vein taken from a dog's leg reacted in the same way to methysergide as did the carotid circulation in the unconscious animal. Humphrey was then assigned a group of Glaxo chemists to make analogues of serotonin to find whether they would behave as an agonist in the dog's vein and, therefore, inhibit the dilation. A promising compound, synthesised in 1978 and coded AH 21467, had the surprising effect of increasing rather than decreasing carotid blood flow but also led to a fall in blood pressure. After a further year of research, they hypothesised that AH 21467 stimulated not one serotonin receptor in the vasculature but two: at one it promoted vasoconstriction and at the other vasodilation, which therefore masked the effect of the former. The search continued for a more selective compound that would stimulate only the vasoconstrictor receptor, and resulted in the discovery of AH 25086 late in 1980.[116] The drug was well tolerated in healthy human volunteers, and then began trials in hospital migraine clinics.

Although AH 25086 proved efficacious in treating the symptoms of migraine attacks, it could only be administered by injection. Since most sufferers are not hospitalised, it was necessary to find a compound which could be taken by mouth. Early in 1984, Humphrey and his team identified GR 43175 (later termed sumatriptan), which possessed the selectivity of AH 25086 and which was shown to be well tolerated in humans.[117] It is hypothesised, therefore, that during a migrainous headache, intracranial blood vessels become distended, activating the Vth cranial nerve. Sumatriptan alleviates the ensuing pain by selectively constricting these vessels through its action upon 5-HT_1 receptors, without exercising an effect on cerebral blood flow.[118] Further experiments showed that it could be given orally, by subcutaneous injection and by instillation into the nose. The results of clinical trials were presented at a meeting of the Migraine Trust in September 1988. In 1991 it was launched as Imigran in the Netherlands, New Zealand and UK, and as Imitrex in the United States in 1992. An editorial in *The Lancet* written shortly after the launch of sumatriptan acknowledged its therapeutic value, given the absence of efficacious alternatives. Whilst recognising Glaxo's need to recoup nineteen years research and development expenditure, the journal questioned whether the cost of the medicine (at close to £20 per syringe) would deter some general practitioners from prescribing it for a relatively common but non-life-threatening complaint.[119] In 1996 sumatriptan won a Queen's Award for Technological Achievement.

The important research that Humphrey and his colleagues (notably Dr Wasyl Feniuk, E. Apperley and G. P. Levy) had undertaken in finding a selective serotonin agonist also contributed to the classification of cellular receptors for 5-hydroxytryptamine (5-HT). As early as 1957 J. H. Gaddum and Z. P. Picarelli had hypothesised that there were two receptors: 'D' that mediate contraction of intestinal muscle and 'M' receptors that activate nerves in the gut.[120] By the late 1970s it had become clear that there were at least two specific binding sites in the brain, leading to the suggestion that they be termed 5-HT_1 and 5-HT_2. This terminology was modified in 1986 to take account of the novel serotonin agonist identified by Humphrey and his team.[121] The new classification suggested that the 'M' receptor be called 5-HT_3, the 'D' become 5-HT_2, and the novel receptor for which sumatriptan has an affinity be termed 5-HT_1.[122] However, as research into serotonin has continued to advance, in part because of the perceived need for ever more selective medication, at least four groups of 5-HT receptor have been proposed.[123]

In the search for a selective, anti-migraine drug, the chemists at Ware had manufactured several hundred serotonin analogues, building up an extensive archive of compounds. It was speculated, given the ubiquitous role of 5-HT and the identification of a growing number of receptors, that some of these could be turned into valuable medicines. When Dr Mike Tyers was appointed head of pharmacology in 1980, he had been given the brief of rationalising the number of drug targets and of focusing research within the field of the central nervous system.[124] Work then proceeded in earnest to find a compound that could inhibit what was later classified as the 5-HT_3 receptor and thus treat a variety of disorders related to the central nervous system. The phenothiazines (notably chlorpromazine hydrochloride) as dopamine antagonists had, for example, been used to treat nausea and vomiting, while in higher doses they had become a standard medication for schizophrenia and other psychoses. Tyers and his fellow researchers hypothesised that a serotonin antagonist could be employed on a more selective basis to combat these disorders with fewer side effects.

In 1983 Tyers, and Dr Donald Straughan, accompanied by about two-thirds of the Greenford pharmacology department, moved back to Ware to head a neuropharmacology team. Their research led to the discovery of GR 38032, subsequently called ondansetron, which entered clinical trials for the prevention of severe and unpleasant vomiting induced by anti-cancer drugs and radiotherapy. One study of thirty-three myeloma patients receiving chemotherapy in the form of high-dose melphalan (Alkeran) demonstrated that in 42 per cent of cases vomiting was either abolished or reduced to a maximum of two episodes.[125] Ondansetron was shown to be an effective, non-sedative anti-emetic. In December 1991, this achievement was formally recognised by the grant of the Prix Galien, Europe's most prestigious award for pharmaceutical innovation, to Glaxo for its work on the discovery of ondansetron. Dr Patrick Humphrey, Mike Tyers and Alex Oxford, the senior medicinal chemist in the serotonin project, jointly received the 1997 Mullard Award of the Royal Society for innovative science of commercial importance for the UK.

Glaxo Group Research

In September 1975, Hems retired as managing director of Glaxo Research, and was succeeded by his deputy Dr Tom Walker. The Greenford and Ware divisions of Glaxo Research continued to operate as largely autonomous organisations until March 1978, when David Jack was appointed to the newly created post of research and development director on the Glaxo Holdings board.[126] This event heralded a strategy designed to bring the two laboratories closer together with a unified structure. In July the two UK research companies (Glaxo Research and A & H Research) were renamed as Glaxo-Allenburys Research (Greenford) and Glaxo-Allenburys Research (Ware) to indicate that they were no longer to be regarded as separate and independent bodies.[127] Henceforth, the managing directors of these subsidiaries were to report to Jack.[128] In addition to drug discovery, Glaxo Group Research was given responsibility for the development of new medicines across the world, a function previously carried out by the International Product Development Group set up to co-ordinate the introduction of Zantac world-wide.

Further organisational change took place in 1979 when Glaxo Group Research was set up. It resulted in a more complex divisional structure. Glaxo Research and A & H Research, as Jack observed, were 'complete research companies', so that the multi-site operation had become expensive and inefficient mainly because of the cost of services rather than over-lapping research activities. There was, however, obvious duplication of toxico-logical activities at Harefield and Ware, and some of the laboratories, especially those at Sefton Park and the pharmacology laboratories at Greenford, were frankly out of date for their intended purposes. Pharmaceutical chemistry was undesirably fragmented.[129]

The laboratories at Sefton Park closed in 1980 and new microbiology and biotechnology facilities were commissioned at Greenford. Toxicology was centralised at Ware so that Harefield could concentrate solely on veterinary research, augmented by the transfer of sixty-two staff from Greenford in 1981 to create Glaxo Animal Health. Vaccine research at Speke ended in 1982 (see p. 281). Although these changes did not greatly influence total numbers (Table 22, p. 455), they did represent an important redeployment of staff with significant recruitment in medicine, cell biology and computer sci-ence. The existing subsidiary companies were replaced by four divisions: Greenford, Ware, Medical & Development and Administration. Walker and Brittain became research directors at Greenford and Ware respectively. As a result of these changes the overall pattern of research expenditure was mod-ified rather than subject to dramatic change (Table 23, p. 456). The principal areas of spending remained antibiotics (which in 1982 included £3 million for the development of ceftazidime), the alimentary tract (including £2.7 million for the further development of ranitidine) and the cardiovascular system which in 1981–82 accounted for 16 per cent of total costs.

Aware of the strong company loyalties, Jack also sought to rationalise re-search by scientific discipline, taking advantage of existing specialist exper-tise.[130] Biochemical projects were concentrated at Greenford, which worked on antibacterial agents, cancer, immunology and animal health. In addition, research into metabolic diseases, such as diabetes, was transferred there from Ware. Henceforth, Ware undertook pharmacological research and projects set up by Hems into the central nervous system, employing former BDH scientists, were transferred to Hertfordshire. Jack estimated that restructuring required a further 200 scientific staff, bringing the total number to 1,800 (of whom 1,000 would be located at Greenford and the re-mainder at Ware). The strategic decision to broaden research on cancer, immunology, metabolic disease and skin biology also demanded capital in-vestment. Jack believed that 'expansion and diversification' were essential if the company were to discover novel products even though these changes would, of necessity, upset traditional loyalties and work practices.

Although Jack, as group research and development director continued to serve as chief executive of Glaxo Group Research until his retirement in

1987, there were a number of important changes to the senior management and organisation. In 1982, following the departure of Walker to Japan two years earlier, Dr Alan Williamson was recruited as research director of the Greenford division.[131] Williamson was then Gardiner professor of biochemistry at Glasgow and had built up an international reputation in the field of immunochemistry. While the laboratories continued to work upon cephalosporin and steroid chemistry, Jack sought to broaden their therapeutic base and to introduce new scientific disciplines, notably cell biology. To change established methods, it was important to bring in an outsider who had not become steeped in the organisation's culture. Williamson's record of academic research was beyond question, but he found the scale and rigidities of Greenford a considerable challenge. In 1987, Dr Richard Sykes appointed Williamson research director of the mammalian biology division based in Geneva, where he remained until leaving to head Merck's immunology programme.

With important strategic decisions to be made about the direction and organisation of Glaxo Group Research, Jack was concerned to find a successor well before his retirement. In October 1984, he recruited Dr W. I. H. Shedden as managing director on the understanding that he would become the new chief executive.[132] However, the appointment was to prove short lived. Shedden had qualified in medicine at Edinburgh, completing a doctorate at Birmingham, before joining Eli Lilly as their UK medical director. Jack had formed a high opinion of his abilities, which were confirmed when Lilly promoted him to vice president and gave him worldwide responsibilities as medical director at their Indianapolis headquarters. Shedden had an established record in product development and direct experience of the US market and methods, but was willing to return to Britain. Before Shedden had left Lilly, concerns had arisen about benoxaprofen (Opren), a non-steroidal anti-inflammatory drug for the treatment of arthritis, which was later shown to have been the cause of death in several elderly patients from renal failure.[133] The drug was withdrawn by Lilly but the US authorities decided to press charges and selected Shedden, who had by now moved to Glaxo in the UK, as their target rather than the company which had discovered and marketed the product. Pleading 'no contest', Shedden was fined for his role as medical director. The verdict, in what had become an emotive case, created difficulties for Glaxo's fast-growing but potentially vulnerable American subsidiary and when pressure was brought by a US government procurement agency, Shedden was asked to resign at the behest of the non-executive directors. Thus ended a tortuous and distressing episode, which ultimately deprived the company of a manager and scientist of considerable ability.

As a result, Jack was forced to postpone his retirement and begin the search for a successor for a second time. He identified Dr Richard Sykes who, having worked for Glaxo as a microbiologist in the mid 1970s, had emigrated to America and was currently vice president of biological sciences at Squibb in New Jersey. In 1977, in order to broaden his experience, Sykes had accepted the post of assistant director of microbiology in their Princeton laboratories, becoming the director two years later.[134] He had no immediate plans to return to the UK but on being approached during 1986 was attracted by Glaxo's achievements and the opportunity to move to Britain. In September he took up the post of deputy chief executive of Glaxo Group Research, assuming full responsibility in January 1987.[135] When Jack retired from the board of Glaxo Holdings in June, Sykes was elected group research and development director.[136]

Although some have argued that increases in company size are not associated with equivalent increases in research spending, this finding was not true of Glaxo.[137] Not only did the annual total rise in real terms but expenditure as a proportion of turnover also increased from 5.2 per cent in 1980 to 8.6 per cent in 1987, when Jack retired, rising thereafter to 15.2 per cent in 1994 (Table 24, p. 456). In fact, Jack had resisted any pressure to raise the proportion beyond 10 per cent as he believed that the natural fluctuations in a company's commercial fortunes could make it difficult to sustain such levels, leading to cuts and an atmosphere of uncertainty. In the event, Glaxo was able to maintain its research and development spend at around 15 per cent for most of the 1990s. This was in common with the rest of the UK pharmaceutical industry, with expenditure rising in real terms from a total of £30 million in 1970 (when it represented 6.6 per cent of gross output), £79 million (7.5 per cent) in 1975, £251 million (10.3 per cent) in 1980 to £977 million (15.4 per cent) in 1989.[138] This trend stood in stark contrast to the rest of British industry. Spending on research and development by all UK manufacturers at constant prices rose by only 122 per cent between 1966 and 1989, while that on pharmaceuticals rose by 769 per cent.[139] Within Europe, British companies were among the leading investors in pharmaceutical research, accounting for about 18 per cent of the total in 1990, and 8 per cent of global spending.[140]

To a large extent the great increase in research and development spending, particularly after 1980, was a function of the rising costs of discovering and developing new medicines. The pace of product development in the industry as a whole had been frantic until the 1970s: on average the world's pharmaceutical companies introduced eighty-three new chemical entities every year between 1961 and 1974. Subsequently the rate fell and by the late 1980s had stabilised at around fifty per annum.[141] The high levels of expen-

104. The research laboratories built for Glaxo at Stevenage and opened in April 1995.

diture recorded by Glaxo and its UK competitors were also evident in France, Japan, Germany and the US where, as early as 1975, 15 per cent of revenue was diverted to research and development.[142] Why had drug discovery become such a costly business? More rigorous government controls for the testing of medicines raised the standards of development programmes. In the aftermath of the thalidomide disaster, the range and number of these investigations for dangerous side-effects increased from the mid 1960s onwards. By 1987, for example, the pathology division at Ware totalled 225 scientific staff and by 1995 topped 300.[143] An important innovation was the design of reproductive tests to prevent a repetition of the teratogenic effects of thalidomide. In 1966, under the direction of Dr Lehmann, the United States Food and Drug Administration published guidelines for a three-part study to detect adverse effects on fertility and pregnancy, this being adopted in its essentials throughout the world.[144] A more recent change has been the advent of genetic toxicology to assess the potential impact that unidentified but widely disseminated mutagens could have on cancer frequencies and other heritable diseases. From the mid-1970s onwards various countries began to issue guidelines for mutagenicity testing, including Italy (Comma, 1977), the US (EPA, 1978) and the UK (DHSS, 1981).[145]

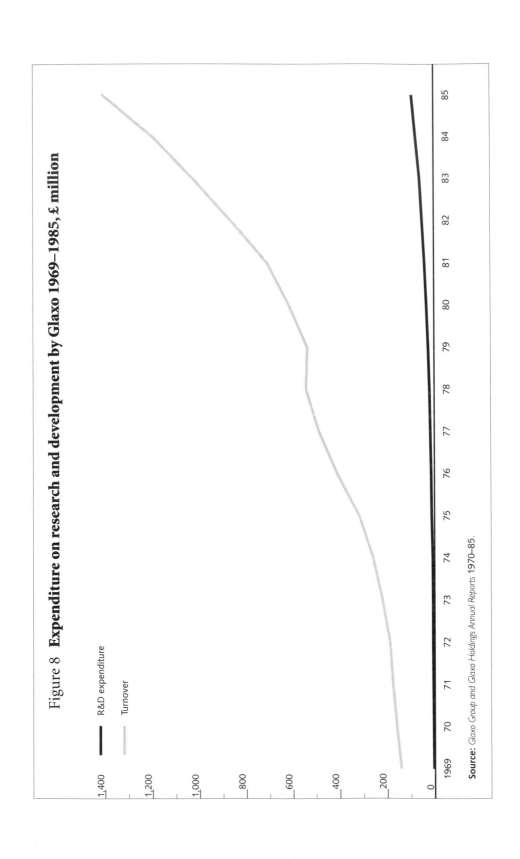

Figure 8 Expenditure on research and development by Glaxo 1969–1985, £ million

R&D expenditure

Turnover

Source: *Glaxo Group and Glaxo Holdings Annual Reports 1970–85.*

The progressive advance of science was the second cause of increased expenditure. In the field of antibiotics, for example, Glaxo succeeded in discovering second- and third-generation cephalosporins, each being more potent and less susceptible to attack than its predecessor. A search for a fourth-generation product continued for over a decade, but the complexity of the problem and the exhaustion of so many options have to date conspired to prevent the discovery of a superior drug. It is possible that the rapidly developing sciences of genetics and cell biology may liberate established methods of discovery and generate a tranche of new medicines, thereby reducing costs, but to date pharmaceutical companies have spent considerable sums in these areas with as yet few tangible rewards.

In 1909, Paul Ehrlich (1854–1915) published a monograph in which he outlined his discovery of salvarsan, a dye derivative that attacked the spirochaete of syphilis in the body without harming the host.[146] Many hailed this as the beginning of a chemotherapy revolution and Ehrlich himself in the same paper provided a theoretical basis for the nascent pharmaceutical industry. 'The discovery of specific (i.e. truly curative) drugs', he argued, 'must be the supreme objective of medical ingenuity.'[147] He reasoned that the therapeutic action of salvarsan could serve as a model for other drugs:

> The outstanding feature of *serum therapy* is that the protecting agents are products of the body, which exert a selective *parasitotropic* action and are devoid of an organotropic action. In this case, we deal with what could be called magic bullets which are aimed at the noxious organism which is foreign to the body, but have no effect on the body itself and its cells … We want to hit the parasites as selectively as possible. In other words, we must *learn to aim and to aim in a chemical sense.*[148]

The goals that Ehrlich laid down at the beginning of the twentieth century continued to dominate strategy, though the tactics of finding these 'magic bullets' may have changed.

GLAXO IN ITALY

DURING THE early 1980s before the rise of Glaxo Inc. in the
United States, the Italian subsidiary, prospering from the sale of
Zantac, recorded a higher turnover than the UK and was the leading national company. This commercial success dated back to March 1923
when Joseph Nathan & Co. had appointed the Verona firm of merchants
and distributors, Carattoni & Monti, as their sole agents. It is not known
why the Nathans chose to trade in Italy. Not only did the Italian market
generate significant sales for foods and pharmaceuticals, it also provided
the company with experience of how to manage a major trading, manufacturing and later research subsidiary.

The distribution agreement with Carattoni & Monti was renewed in July
1926 and again in June 1929. In October 1929, Frederick Randall, a London
director of Nathans, met Count Bompiani, Monti's son-in-law and the executive responsible for the Glaxo business.[1] They discussed the possibility
of setting up a jointly owned company in Verona and, on his return to the
UK, Randall enthusiastically recommended the flotation:

> the basis of this company should be the purchase of Ostelin [vitamin D in sus-
> pension] from London and the packing of the product here ... The idea behind
> this new company would be to build slowly and as required an organisation
> capable of giving the complete service of marketing, advertising, selling and –
> if desirable – distributing proprietary articles. This could be done on the back
> of the savings which ... can be effected by packing Ostelin here.[2]

However, the scheme was dismissed by the London directors, who
thought it risky and uneconomic. Randall revised his plans and concluded
that

the best way to provide for the undoubted need of our own established organisation in Italy is to have a young and active London-trained man living in the
territory, gradually over a period of two to three years becoming acquainted
with every agent and sub-agent who handles our goods ...[3]

Following this recommendation, early in 1930, the Nathans recruited
H. A. 'Peter' Gent, a Cambridge graduate in law and modern languages, as
their resident representative in Verona. Later in the year, concerned to gain
greater control over their emerging business, they set up a joint company
that appointed Carattoni & Monti as its distributors. Gent and Bompiani
were managing directors of Società Anonima Italiana Nathan Bompiani,
which came into being on 30 March 1932.[4] From the outset, Gent showed
skill when handling staff and customers. As a young man he regarded Jephcott as a mentor, though in later years was frustrated by his unwillingness
to invest in the Verona factory. Gent had charm and style[5] but was not without a touch of hubris.[6] It was reported, for example, that when in the UK to
lobby Jephcott as chairman of Glaxo Laboratories, Gent remarked forcibly
'there's your company and there's my company', implying an arrangement
of equals. As if to emphasise this point, Gent commissioned a bronze bust
of Sir Harry, based on photographs, from the Rome sculptor, Vittorio di
Colbertaldo, to mark Jephcott's retirement, and presented it to Glaxo
Group in May 1964.

In the first year of trading, S.A. Italiana Nathan Bompiani, had sales of
1.2 million lire (£13,333) and profits of 35,900 lire (£400), representing a 3
per cent return on the investment. In 1932 a two-storey factory was rented
at the junction of Via Settembrini and Via Quirico Filopanti, in an industrial suburb of Verona. Late in 1936, however, Gent proposed that the company move its operations westwards to Milan, where he had found an
empty building formerly occupied by Coty.[7] The board of Glaxo Laboratories accepted his recommendation and, to finance the transfer internally,
agreed to limit any dividend payments to a maximum of 8 per cent. This
scheme had become attractive because the Italian government had 'closed
all avenues for the export of currency' so that profits could no longer be returned to the UK.[8] The London board subsequently vetoed the move, perhaps because Milan then had a reputation for strikes. Verona, by
comparison, was the centre of an agricultural area and could guarantee
plentiful labour at lower cost. Initially, the factory packed Glaxo powder
into tins and filled Ostelin and Adexolin. Ampoules of Colloidal Calcium
with Ostelin imported from Greenford, were also packed in Verona. The
lower cost of exporting in bulk from the UK led to local manufacture being
abandoned, but the introduction of higher import duties in 1933 made this

a viable proposition again, though low annual sales discouraged further investment. In November 1935, Mussolini introduced a policy of autarky, reinforced by severe import barriers and restrictions on the transfer of profits to parent companies overseas.[9] As a result, the Italian company developed into 'a self-contained manufacturing and distributing unit'[10] and a small laboratory, under an English chemist, was installed for the local production of Colloidal Calcium and Ostelin, registered in 1938 under the tradename 'Calci-Ostelin'. To reflect the diminished role of Count Bompiani (he finally resigned as a director in November 1938, having set up a perfume business) and to be 'more in keeping with its trading activities', the name of the company was changed to S.A. Italiana Laboratori Glaxo in May 1936.[11] The subsidiary enjoyed success protected behind national tariff walls and, in January 1938, Gent obtained permission from the board of Glaxo Laboratories to extend the Verona factory to ease 'the congestion that was steadily becoming acute'.[12]

When Italy entered the war in 1940, Gent and the other English staff of Glaxo's subsidiary were forced to leave and in October the company was placed under a sequestrator, Baron Mario Ostini, managing director of the Instituto Nazionale Opoterapico of Pisa. The company's assets were valued at 5.7 million lire in January 1941 and the auditor's report delivered later in the year concluded that 'it is a very sound business, excellently directed, and one which, under the prudent administration of the sequestrator, is continuing in production with complete self-sufficiency'.[13] At about this time, the company acquired the freehold of the Via Filopanti factory, and operations continued throughout the war, though handicapped by shortages of basic materials. Ostini showed a remarkable fairness in his administration of the business, abiding by an agreement to pay Glaxo Laboratories a royalty of 10 per cent on sales, so that by August 1945 the UK parent had been credited with 4.16 million lire in backdated income. When, in the summer of 1944, the Allied advance neared Verona, the station marshalling yards and the surrounding industrial suburb were subject to intense aerial bombardment. Ampoule filling machines were moved from the Via Filopanti factory to deep caves at Avesa Grotto, about six miles north of Verona, in the foothills of the Dolomites. Having been quarried for the pink marble that characterised much of the city's architecture, they provided secure shelter for a temporary pharmaceutical plant. When Ostini was cut off by the Allied advance on Verona, a new sequestrator, Dr Ugo Noceti of Genoa, was appointed and the transfer supervised by the company's accountant Azzino Azzini.

In May 1945, Peter Gent, then on the staff of the Allied Commission in Rome, travelled to Greenford to lobby for the re-acquisition of the Italian-owned shares, which had been sold to a number of local nationals. Glaxo decided 'not only to rehabilitate the Italian subsidiary company, but to take every advantage of the opportunity which the circumstances afford for expanding its activities'.[14] In December the entire holding was purchased by Glaxo for 6 million lire, met out of accumulated profits held in Italy.

Laboratori Glaxo S.p.A.: post-war recovery

Gent returned in February 1946 with ambitious plans to reap commercial advantage from the reconstruction of the pharmaceutical market in Italy. He sought to re-establish the import business in Colloidal Calcium and Ostelin, which before the war had 'contributed in a

105. Caves at Avesa Grotto used for pharmaceutical production in 1943–44 when the Allies were bombing Verona. The car used by Dr Enrico Fezzi is parked at their entrance.

spectacular and, perhaps, disproportionate manner to the company's financial success'.[15] Gent relaunched Ostelin Forte, a fortified dried milk, and Minadex, a vitamin preparation, while in July 1947 the company sold penicillin in Italy for the first time. This proved to be of great significance as it established Glaxo in the strong antibiotic market. For a short time in 1949–50, when it was difficult to get sufficient supplies of penicillin to Italy by road, Gent resorted to shipping the medicine by flying boat, which touched down on Lake Garda, generating much useful publicity. Herbert Palmer visited the Via Filopanti factory in July 1947 and reported that the 35,000sq.ft. premises had become 'extremely congested and needed additional space if they are to continue to expand in the relatively restricted pharmaceutical field in which their present sales volume lies'.[16] In 1948 the company was renamed Laboratori Glaxo S.p.A. and its capital increased to 50 million lire, partly to fund the new manufacturing block. This was officially opened in 1949 by Sir Alexander Fleming, who was attending an international medical congress in Verona.

106. Peter Gent collecting deliveries of penicillin flown to Lake Garda from the UK by flying boat in 1949.

By 1950 annual sales had reached almost 100 million lire, driven by an unrelenting demand for penicillin. Yet in 1952, as supply caught up with demand, the price of penicillin tumbled. Gent attempted to maintain profits by setting up an incentive scheme for the sales force. As the price of penicillin continued to fall, Palmer argued that the subsidiary's food business could be built up to replace lost antibiotic sales, suggesting that Farex and Casilan might find a niche market. Gent believed that neither food would appeal to Italian tastes, and pressed Jephcott for permission to launch new pharmaceuticals, notably Calciferol. By the mid 1950s it had become clear that Laboratori Glaxo was precariously reliant on a small number of well-established products, notably Colloidal Calcium and Ostelin. Profits before tax in 1956 were estimated at 28 million lire and when they rose in the following year to 37 million lire, Jephcott commented that the Italian company was 'making its way out of the doldrums of the last few years, though the process was laboriously slow'.[17]

In November 1962, Jephcott agreed to visit Verona. Sales for the previous year were up by 40 per cent and profits before tax up by 102 per cent.[18] Jephcott agreed that 'a very real need' existed for greater working space as the Via Filopanti factory was already congested. Jephcott authorised the 'preparation of a detailed scheme',[19] and in January 1964 Palmer presented

*107. The new factory and offices of Laboratori Glaxo at Via Filopanti opened by Sir
Alexander Fleming in 1949.*

plans to spend £400,000 (715 million lire) on a fermentation factory in
Verona.[20] A site, between the Via Alessandro Fleming and the Milan–Venice
autostrada, five kilometres south of the city, had been found to
accommodate the foods business, pharmaceutical packing and the
production of penicillin and griseofulvin. With reserves of 800 million lire,
the Italian subsidiary was expected to finance the project without
assistance from the UK.[21]

The factory was constructed against a background of rising sales (increasing from £1.6 million in 1963 to £3.2 million in 1966) with a corresponding growth in profits from £330,000 to £620,000.[22] By 1966
Laboratori Glaxo had moved up to seventh place in the Italian league
table of pharmaceutical companies, with a turnover of £4.2 million and
a market share of 1.9 per cent.[23] Bentelan was its principal product with
sales of £1.1 million and a dominant 22.1 per cent of the market for plain
corticosteroids.[24]

An administration block, secondary production facility and warehouse
were opened at the Via A. Fleming site in March 1967.[25] The plan to build a
fermentation plant to make penicillin was abandoned, though the board
did agree to the construction of a small primary plant for the final manufacturing stages of griseofulvin and certain corticosteroids. Gent also pur-

sued a programme of diversification and, in April 1965, at a cost of £140,000 acquired a mill at S. Giovanni in Croce for the production of animal feed-stuffs,[26] and in the following year purchased a retail pharmacy, Farmacia Martini S.p.A., for £33,000.[27]

Gent retired as managing director in 1970, when he was appointed president as a mark of his contribution to Laboratori Glaxo. His departure created something of an executive hiatus as his long-serving deputy, Dr U. Rinaldi, was due to retire six months later. At one stage it appeared that D. T. Manton, the production director, would take Gent's place.[28] In the event, Gordon Thomas, who had been transferred from Greenford as financial director, was appointed. Despite some resistance from the senior Italian management (including Remo Rossi, the marketing director who subsequently resigned), Thomas remained as managing director until October 1975. He was succeeded in the following year by Dr Enrico Fezzi, a chemist by training who had worked as an explosives expert during the war. He had joined Glaxo in February 1948, having answered an anonymous advertisement. Interviewed by Gent, Fezzi was appointed to provide the sales force with technical information and to find new pharmaceutical products. Making regular visits to Greenford, he built up a network of contacts among scientists and managers which helped him to advance the cause of the Italian subsidiary. Against much scepticism in 1949, for example, he persuaded Glaxo to manufacture a Calci-Ostelin suppository for the Italian market and later successfully argued for the adoption of a heat-stable form of cephaloridine (see p. 354).[29] Fezzi did not, however, have equal success in 1970 when he attempted to launch a new formula milk for infants up to three months. He believed that this would introduce mothers to Glaxo products before their babies were old enough to have other foods such as Farex. Having discussed the idea with Dr Cuthbertson at Greenford, a new formulation was prepared and entered clinical trials in a number of paediatric hospitals in Italy. Despite early signs of success, Gent called the project to a halt. Infant foods had made little profit for the company in the post-war period and Gent believed that the sales effort would detract from pharmaceutical products. Fezzi was succeeded as managing director by Dr Mario Fertonani in December 1979.

Innovations in marketing

The injectable antibiotic cephaloridine (Ceporin) was not only to prove of enormous commercial importance to the Italian company but the marketing lessons that were learned subsequently had major implications for the group as a whole. Ceporin was launched in Italy in November 1966, two

108. The offices of the new headquarters of Laboratori Glaxo in Via Alessandro Fleming, Verona, opened in March 1967.

years later than in the UK. Such was the success of the sales strategy that by 1969 it had become the leading injectable antibiotic in Italy and three years later was the country's highest selling prescription product.[30] Nowhere else in the world did Ceporin achieve such a dominance of its therapeutic field – a reflection of the particular characteristics of the national market. First, Italian patients, and hence their doctors, often chose symptomatic rather than prophylactic medicines. They liked drugs that had a rapid effect, and so chose injectables and suppositories rather than tablets, which can take longer to be absorbed. Italians also showed a preference for home rather than hospital treatment. Patients wished to be nursed by their relatives and the regulations surrounding the administration of intramuscular drugs were looser than in many other European countries. While injections are traditionally given in the UK by a doctor or nurse, in Italy any member of the public can perform the procedure. As a result, the market for injectable antibiotics developed substantially in Italy since such medication could be taken at home, while in the UK it was limited to hospital use or administration by a GP or district nurse.

Eager to find new pharmaceutical products and aware of the potential size of the market for injectable antibiotics, the Italian company put considerable effort into the sale of cephaloridine. The commercial director, Remo Rossi, devised an inspirational plan that translated the drug's disadvantages into selling points. First, it was an expensive drug and secondly, before a heat-stable version was manufactured, Ceporin had to be stored in a refrigerator, at a time when few pharmacists possessed such equipment.[31] This inconvenience was used to stress the potency of the drug. Instead of reducing their profit margin to a bare minimum, Rossi in discussions with Gent and Fezzi, decided to stress the life-saving qualities of the drug and sell it at a high price (about 4,800 lire, equivalent to £3.00, a vial). A daily dose was commonly 2g, costing 10,000 lire, when the leading competitor antibiotic, ampicillin, sold at 500 lire per vial.[32] Ceporin, therefore, cost ten times more than established therapeutic equivalents. Such a strategy was made possible only by the liberal nature of the Italian regulatory system. Had Glaxo launched Ceporin with a similar margin in the UK, it would have come under scrutiny from the VPRS and had the price been authorised any medicines subsequently launched by the company would have been subject to severe financial constraints. The marketing campaign also drew on the drug's Italian pedigree: the original antibiotic effect in a fungus had been observed by Professor Brotzu working in Sardinia, which he named *Cephalosporium acremonium*.

The success of Ceporin in Italy also relied on the efforts of a determined sales force led by Remo Rossi. A pharmacist by training, he had joined Laboratori Glaxo as a representative, working in central Italy, and subsequently as an area manager based in Rome. Rossi, a dynamic and inspirational leader, placed particular emphasis on training. The first opportunity he had to demonstrate the effectiveness of his reforms came in January 1962 when betamethasone (Bentelan), a corticosteroid, was launched in injectable and oral forms for the treatment of inflammatory and allergic disorders. The Italian company had pioneered a small change in the formulation of the oral form, developing a soluble effervescent tablet which increased gastric tolerance to the drug. Within a year Bentelan became the leading product in its therapeutic class. At first there were worries that the medicine might cause an anaphylactic reaction, even though clinical trials had not revealed any adverse side-effects. A picture of a small child who had been treated with the antibiotic was used in an advertising campaign to emphasise its safety.[33] Soon afterwards, Laboratori Glaxo launched betamethasone valerate (Ecoval, known as Betnovate in the UK) as a topical preparation for inflammatory skin disorders and within eighteen months it, too, had become the highest selling drug in its therapeutic class. By 1966, Ecoval was the company's leading product by sales, followed by Bentelan.[34] The commercial success of the corticosteroids established the pharmaceutical credentials of the Italian company and advanced its claim for greater control over manufacturing processes. In 1971, Sir Alan Wilson agreed to spend £170,000 on plant at Verona for the final chemical stages required in the production of betamethasone valerate.[35]

Between 1962 and 1976 the Italian subsidiary relied on four key medicines for its income (Ceporin, Bentelan, Ecoval and Ventolin). Largely as a result of sales of Ceporin, Laboratori Glaxo became the leading pharmaceutical company in Italy by turnover. Its commercial success was based on a small number of efficacious products discovered in the UK but marketed with skill and enthusiasm by a proficient and growing sales force. In 1961 it had just fifty-six representatives but by the end of the 1970s the numbers had increased to about 200. By growing gradually, Rossi and Dr Mario Fertonani, commercial director from 1972, could offer the sales force comparatively high levels of training.

Whilst a number of cultural factors worked in favour of Laboratori Glaxo, one aspect of the legal system proved to be a major drawback. Until 1979 pharmaceutical companies were denied patent protection. Article 6 of the Law on Industrial Patents, passed in 1859, decreed that medicaments could not be safeguarded in this way. As a result, many of Glaxo's innovative products were copied and sold at a lower price. Ceporin, in particular, was subject to pirate versions against which the company was powerless to act. Furthermore, the refusal to grant intellectual property rights for novel medicines led to the establishment of large numbers of small or medium-sized domestic pharmaceutical companies, which could neither afford, nor particularly needed, research and development departments, so long as they could copy the products of foreign multinationals. In 1962, for example, it was estimated that there were 1,200 such businesses in existence, of which only eighty were noteworthy.[36] This fragmentation of the Italian pharmaceutical industry was to have unforeseen consequences for Glaxo during the 1980s (see p. 357). In 1978 the Italian constitutional court ruled that the prohibition of pharmaceutical patents was unlawful and in the following year intellectual property rights were instituted. Had the court not made this ruling, Italy as a signatory of the Munich treaty on patents would, in any case, have been forced to make these changes. The imposition of these basic rights was a contributory factor in Glaxo's decision to launch ranitidine (Zantac) simultaneously in Italy and the UK.

Marketing was the acknowledged strength of the Italian company. Dr Mario Fertonani, who succeeded Fezzi as its managing director in 1979, was a marketing specialist. He had joined the company in January 1961 as a representative, becoming sales manager seven years later and then commercial director. When, in 1972, Bide created a system of 'Parent Board Counsellors' to advise overseas subsidiaries, Italy fell initially to Smart, though later to Girolami, who had been born there and was fluent in Italian. Girolami often visited Verona and built up a considerable rapport with Fertonani, leading to the regular exchange of ideas.[37] When considering a strategy for Zantac, Girolami consulted his Italian advisors. Fertonani and his marketing director, Dr F. Fantini, recommended that the drug should be priced at a premium over cimetidine (Tagamet), its principal competitor, as this would emphasise its superiority and efficacy.[38] The Italian economy was then subject to inflation, so that any new medicine sold at a discount was doomed to make at best marginal profits. Fertonani had registered Zantac with the Italian authorities at a 30 per cent premium over Tagamet. In July 1981, Fertonani and his team told Girolami, then chief executive of Glaxo Holdings, of their view. This stood in sharp contrast to the group's proposals to launch Zantac at a discount, which Girolami fiercely opposed at a meeting on 21 July 1981, and forced a reconsideration (see p. 251). Ultimately, as a result of this debate, the group adopted the Italian marketing position. Dr Fantini recalled that the strategy adopted by the UK team had been pragmatic and that there was something inspirational in the Italian approach which, though more risky, held out far greater rewards, and was supported by Laboratori Glaxo's experience with Ceporin.[39]

Zantac was launched in Italy in September 1981, a week before being introduced in the UK. It recorded spectacular sales in Italy, which led to an unprecedented period of rapid and sustained growth. Turnover increased from £90 million in 1981–82 to £220 million in 1985–86, when the company secured over 4 per cent of the Italian pharmaceutical market.[40] Sales of Zantac, reinforced from 1984 by ceftazidime (Glazidim), resulted in Laboratori Glaxo recording higher volumes than the UK so that it became the largest of the operating companies by turnover. However, the sustained expansion of Glaxo Inc. in the United States was soon to eclipse even the Italian performance.

In 1984 the Italian company launched the third-generation cephalosporin, ceftazidime (Glazidim), with high hopes that this would match the performance of Ceporin introduced eighteen years earlier. Despite meeting fierce competition, Glazidim rapidly established a significant share, which by the mid 1990s stood at 40 per cent. Whilst it never achieved the same turnover as Zantac, the two products sold at a significantly higher level than the remainder of the subsidiary's drug portfolio and during the early 1990s they represented over 70 per cent of total sales. Laboratori Glaxo had, in fact, played an important role in the development of ceftazidime. In 1983 fears had been raised by the Greenford scientists that the antibiotic might carry a significant risk of anaphylactic shock and the Group Management Committee considered halting clinical trials. Aware of the potential importance of the drug for his company, Dr Fertonani agreed to take responsibility for further trials and 10,000 hospital cases were tested in Italy, which showed that ceftazidime was safe.

Having repeatedly demonstrated their ability to promote new medicines, executives from the Italian

109. Dr Mario Fertonani, chief executive of Glaxo's Italian subsidiary.

company were given marketing responsibilities elsewhere in the group. From 1983, for example, Dr Fertonani supervised sales strategies and product launches in Spain, Portugal, Switzerland, Austria, Greece and Turkey, being assisted two years later by Dr Fantini, the marketing director of Laboratori Glaxo.[41] When it was decided to introduce Zantac in Spain, the two played a major advisory role, visiting the country every two weeks to help local management recruit and train an effective sales force. In this fashion, expertise built up over several generations of management was transferred to younger subsidiaries in Southern and Eastern Europe, the Middle East and Africa.

Co-marketing and government regulation

The success of Zantac was partly due to the negotiation of co-marketing arrangements that enabled the drug to gain a dominant share of its therapeutic class within a relatively short period of time. This was not a wholly original approach as in 1980 Hoeschst and Roussel had joined forces to launch the injectable cephalosporin, cefotaxime (Claforan), on a global basis.[42] The principal alliance concluded by Glaxo for Zantac was with the Italian company Menarini, which in effect doubled the number of representatives promoting the new medicine. Menarini sold ranitidine under the trade name Ranidil and the success of this operation encouraged Glaxo to repeat the arrangement with other smaller companies, so that by 1986 it had around 1,000 salesmen operating within Italy. Although it had no established tradition of researching novel products, Menarini had grown under the leadership of Dr Alberto Aleotti to be the largest indigenous pharmaceutical company in Italy. For medicines, it relied on licences from the major multinationals and had, for example, many products from Squibb and Pfizer. As president of the Italian Pharmaceutical Association, Dr Aleotti had considerable influence with the regulators and was able to facilitate the registration process and ensure a price that would yield a reasonable rate of return. The system of domestic alliances was encouraged by the Ministry of Health in order to give the Italian pharmaceutical industry time to establish its own research and development facilities. The introduction of patent law in 1979 resulted in Italian companies having no immediate access to new medicines unless they were able to negotiate co-marketing agreements. It was decided to allow the status quo to continue for a further five years in the expectation that these domestic businesses would establish their own research laboratories and no longer depend on novel medicines discovered abroad.[43]

Production

In March 1967 Laboratori Glaxo moved to its new headquarters at Via Alessandro Fleming, where a secondary production factory and small primary plant were opened. Originally the warehouse and factory were within a single structure, though the rise in orders led to the construction of purpose-built storage facilities, creating additional space for manufacture. In May 1971 the Holdings board authorised the expenditure of £1.4 million at the site but, in view of higher projected growth rates, it was decided to add a wing for the production of sterile medicines (such as injectable cephalosporins) and for a pharmacy unit;[44] approval of the scheme entailed the expenditure of a further £1.1 million.[45] The success of the Italian company in selling cephalosporins encouraged the construction of a dedicated antibiotic unit, completed in 1980.[46]

With income flowing from Zantac, in January 1984, Glaxo bought and equipped a pharmaceutical factory at Parma for £16.9 million.[47] The opportunity to purchase a factory from Italchemi S.p.A., then in liquidation, had arisen during negotiations to buy one of its products, Citrosil, a popular branded disinfectant based on benzalkonium chloride. Among the advantages they identified was the fact that the factory 'is conveniently situated at Parma and can go into operation as required without delay'.[48] The total cost of the project included the rights to manufacture and market Citrosil, which at the time had sales of £2 million a year, generating a profit of £700,000.[49] During 1985 the Parma factory was re-equipped for vial filling and packaging injectable cephalosporins, together with a tableting department for cefuroxime axetil (Zinnat).[50] In July 1986, £4.6 million was spent on installing plant for the production of Ventolin controlled release tablets, the long-acting form of salbutamol.[51] The only manufacture to remain at Verona was for injectable and oral cephalosporins, so that the site could be rationalised as the administrative and sales headquarters, together with the research and development laboratories.

Research and development

When Laboratori Glaxo moved to the Via A. Fleming site in 1967, the plans included a modest development laboratory for products discovered in the UK. Three years later, under Professor Del Campo, an immunologist, a research and development division was established in Verona. Much of its activity related to the registration of new drugs for sale in Italy, extending or repeating tests or clinical trials already conducted in other countries in order to meet domestic requirements for approval. In 1976, when the research and development division numbered about 100 staff, work began on the discovery of novel medicines, concentrating on three therapeutic areas: non-steroidal anti-inflammatories, anti-infectives and gastro-intestinal pharmaceuticals. Much of this research was led by Professor Coppi, a biochemist, who had succeeded Del Campo as head of department in 1979. With the relatively small number of scientists involved at Verona, targets proved more elusive than anticipated and in 1980 Dr David Jack, research and development director of Glaxo Group, decided that the laboratory required a new focus. In February of the following year, he recruited Professor Carlo Carpi, who had trained in both pharmacy and medicine and worked in the pharmaceutical industry at Milan. Political and regulatory pressures on Laboratori Glaxo encouraged the company to reduce its reliance on new products imported from abroad.

Professor Carpi began to build up an effective and experienced research team. In September 1981, he appointed Dr Giovanni Gaviraghi, then working at I.S.F. in Milan, as a medicinal chemist. Dr Gaviraghi had originally been a lecturer in organic chemistry and qualified in medicine while working for Glaxo. He was initially appointed as 'Assistant for Co-ordination of Primary Research' and was given the role of setting up small research teams with defined goals. In October 1981, Dr Gaviraghi spent six weeks at Glaxo's Ware laboratories to find out which topics might be free for the Verona scientists to tackle.[52] It was agreed with Jack that the Italian company would undertake microbiological research into five projects: two on antibacterial agents and three with a pharmacological basis. Although the overarching

110. The entrance to the research centre completed at Verona in 1990 and designed by Romualdo Cambruzzi and constructed by Foster Wheeler Italiana.

strategy and the specific therapeutic areas were agreed with Glaxo Group Research, the precise targets and the methods of investigating them were devolved to the local scientists. Professor Carpi recalled a meeting with Dr Jack at which the latter commented

> You have to use me as a consultant. If I give you advice, however, you have to re-member you are responsible for what is done … The research unit in Verona – and what is done there – is your responsibility, not mine.

Both Carpi and Gaviraghi had experience in cardiovascular research, Carpi having studied anti-hypertensive compounds when at I.S.F., while Gaviraghi had investigated peripheral vasodilatation as a chemist there. They were attracted to the cardiovascular field for both commercial and scientific reasons. First, it was the largest therapeutic market with a turnover of £13.3 billion in 1989.[53] Although it was fiercely fought territory, Glaxo needed to capture only 1 per cent in order to earn a substantial in-come. Secondly, the group had just one product in the field, allowing space for the Italian company to stake a claim. Thirdly, anti-hypertensive medi-cines are relatively straightforward to evaluate in humans, clinical trials involving a review process every four weeks. Carpi and Gaviraghi believed that if they could find a long-acting calcium antagonist with a single dose regimen, it would offer considerable therapeutic and commercial advantages over the existing drug, nifedipidine (Adalat), which had to be taken three times a day. High blood pressure does not generally express itself in symptoms, so patients are often reluctant to take prophylactic medication, so that a drug with a simple dosage regimen and minimal side-effects is more likely to foster adherence.

In 1982 Carpi and Gaviraghi decided that

> it was wise to start to establish research in the cardiovascular area … and we selectively discussed different approaches: calcium antagonists, ACE [angiotensin-converting enzyme] inhibitors and renin inhibitors. One problem was that we had no cardiovascular pharmacologist … We knew Dr Claudio Semeraro (who had worked at I.S.F. between 1976 and 1981) … and he joined us in September 1982 to set up a cardiovascular pharmacology laboratory.[54]

They excluded ACE inhibitors because one compound, captopril (Capoten), was already well established as an anti-hypertensive, while a second, enalapril maleate (Innovace), was in advanced development by Merck, and there seemed little chance of improving on these medicines. Although Jack supported the idea of working on renin inhibitors, Carpi and Gaviraghi thought that the Verona scientists lacked the experience to tackle such innovative science. A research programme into calcium antagonists, by contrast, was more straightforward and could draw on Dr Semeraro's expertise in the field.

Research into an improved calcium antagonist began in 1982 under Dr Semeraro. On 25 February 1984, Dr Duro Micheli performed a number of key experiments, which suggested that compound GX 1048, subsequently called lacidipine, was a potent calcium channel blocker with a long duration of action.[55] Further research proved promising and it moved into development, entering Phase III trials in mid 1989. Lacidipine (Lacipil) was launched in Italy in September 1991 with a once daily dose regimen. The project had been carried through to completion in less than nine years. The Verona scientists had been helped in getting lacidipine from laboratory bench to market with such speed by the uncomplicated nature of the molecule which, in turn, aided investigation and facilitated manufacture. Unfortunately lacidipine did not find a place in the Glaxo international development programme and was licensed to Boehringer Ingleheim for sale in many major countries.

Early in 1985, because of the clear progress made with lacidipine and other new molecules, Glaxo approved a recruitment programme to increase the number of scientific staff at Verona from 120 to 200–300. Such an expansion required more laboratory space and in the spring of 1985 preliminary plans were drawn up for a new research centre to be built at the Via A. Fleming site. This, when authorised in November 1986, was to be the largest single capital project at Verona with a budget of £61.7 million.[56] By this time staff numbers had grown to 227 and it was expected that they would rise further to 350. The preliminary designs had been drawn up in 1985 by Steril, a pharmaceutical engineering subsidiary of Foster Wheeler Italiana based in Milan, and Studio Architetto Romualdo Cambruzzi of Verona.[57] The team was instructed to prepare plans for a laboratory block, which would house the following departments: pathology and biochemical pharmacology, pharmacology, pharmacy, microbiology and chemistry research. There was also to be an office block for the administrative functions together with a scientific library and conference hall, seating 450.[58] At first, fifteen models were prepared to find the most efficient arrangement which, in turn, were reduced to two, one being based on a horizontal layout, while the other was predominantly vertical. In the successful design, all the laboratories were gathered together in a single block of five storeys with a mezzanine for service ducts between each floor. The chemical development laboratories were in a single building for safety reasons, while a third block, connected to the laboratories by a glazed hallway and reception area, contained auxiliary services and the auditorium.[59] Construction of the centre began in December 1986, supervised by Foster Wheeler Italiana of Milan.[60] Opened in October 1990, it finally cost £10.7 million more than budgeted, in part because of the need to respond to higher safety standards imposed by FDA inspections and rapid technological advance in instrumentation.

THE GREAT LEAP:
THE UNITED STATES
1977–1985

Entry to the US market can never be easy for a foreign company ...
However, the profits which could be obtained by a successful
operation are very substantial indeed, provided always that the
parent company is able to supply a continuing succession of
significant new products.

H. W. Palmer and R. D. Smart, 29 January 1971.[1]

T HE USA is the largest national market for pharmaceuticals in the
world, with 31 per cent of global sales in 1994. Although this dominance has been, in part, the product of recent growth (rising from 19
per cent of both consumption and production in 1975),[2] it has always been a
leading player. Sales of ethical medicines to pharmacies and hospitals, for
example, amounted to over £1,500 million per annum in 1970, and that year
thirteen of the top twenty pharmaceutical companies, ranked by turnover,
were American.[3] No business could hope to compete at the highest level in
the industry without having established a significant market share in the US.

From its foundation in 1935, Glaxo Laboratories under the leadership of
Sir Harry Jephcott deliberately avoided direct involvement in America.
Aware of the size and resources of its domestic producers, he established
working relationships with US companies on the basis of licences. Initially,
Glaxo acquired new products from America but, in time, as the group discovered its own medicines, Jephcott negotiated arrangements for their sale
with payment in royalties. Having encountered difficulties at Courtaulds
with anti-trust legislation, Sir Alan Wilson never attempted to challenge
this strategy. Although there were periodic discussions on the wisdom of
establishing a trading organisation in America, the plan never advanced
beyond the creation of an inactive subsidiary, Glaxo Inc., in 1972.

Preoccupied with internal reorganisation and European priorities, it was not until 1977 that Glaxo was able to act resolutely on America. That year, they acquired the entire assets of Meyer Laboratories, a small-scale pharmaceutical company with a sales force of 168 representatives based at Fort Lauderdale, Florida. This was to form the vehicle for the group to launch its own products under the Glaxo name throughout the American market. Acutely aware of the risks of attempting to enter this highly competitive territory and of the significant cost implications, the board had debated the question extensively before taking such a dramatic step. It was increasingly recognised, however, that the group's very autonomy rested on commercial success in the US. If it failed to achieve representation there, it would remain vulnerable to takeover, while a strong presence would confer true global status on Glaxo. The reasons behind this radical change of direction and the events which followed are the subject of this chapter.

Part I: Strategy, plans & attempts to enter the US market

Early links with America

Allen & Hanburys had, in fact, come close to setting up an American subsidiary at the turn of the century. Ralph Dodd, a director, travelled to the US in 1897 and returned 'much impressed with the belief that there was a large opening for some of the goods manufactured by our company'.[4] While on a visit to North America during 1898, F. J. Hanbury set up an agency in Canada and a branch office in New York. But despite the distribution of many free samples, sales remained low and, after writing off a loss of £4,634, it was decided to run North American operations from Canada, a subsidiary being established for that purpose in 1902. What had possibly been a great opportunity was surrendered.

Glaxo Laboratories had no formal representation in the US until after the Second World War. Sir Harry Jephcott travelled regularly across the Atlantic by aeroplane or liner between 1943 and 1948 in order to negotiate technical aid and licences to use the new deep fermentation techniques for making penicillin and, from 1947, for streptomycin. The original agreement of April 1945 had been concluded with a consortium composed of Merck, Pfizer and Squibb. While on a visit to New York in January 1950, Jephcott arranged to meet James J. Kerrigan, president of Merck. Because heightened competition had forced US pharmaceutical companies to reduce their profit margins, Kerrigan floated the idea of a merger between Glaxo and

Merck. Jephcott was unimpressed by the proposal, recording in his diary that he could not 'see the advantage which would accrue to ourselves, although I can see the advantage from Merck's point of view. I expressed a wish to consider the matter.'[5]

In July 1951 a second penicillin arrangement was signed with Merck alone, where they agreed to provide Glaxo with information on production processes, the equipment to be used, cultures, raw materials and intermediates for which Glaxo paid a royalty on output. In this way Jephcott acquired the most advanced methods of manufacturing antibiotics without incurring the heavy development costs associated with improving the existing small-scale fermentation methods. Merck had only a modest sales force in the US and virtually no representation elsewhere, being primarily manufacturers of pharmaceuticals with a powerful research and development department at Rahway, New Jersey. It was of great benefit to them to enter into trading agreements with companies in territories where they could not sell directly themselves.[6] Jephcott formed close personal ties with Merck executives and was on occasion indiscreet about Glaxo's own research, believing that a 'free exchange' of information should exist between the two groups.[7]

Although the US had an established lead in the discovery of new medicines, the flow of products was not exclusively from west to east. In 1949 Dr Hems and his team had succeeded in devising a commercial synthesis of L-thyroxine, marketed the following year as Eltroxin for the treatment of hypothyroidism (myxoedema).[8] During the early 1950s, these processes were licensed to Smith Kline & French in America. However, later in the decade circumstances and Jephcott's attitude both changed. American companies with their greater size and access to large research budgets were increasingly viewed as a threat rather than as potential collaborators. Intimacies, which had been based on Jephcott's personal relations with key executives, cooled when he retired, or as younger colleagues, such as Dr Fred Wilkins, began to visit the US on Glaxo's behalf. Furthermore, the merger between Merck and Sharp & Dohme in 1953 was to have important implications. Sharpe & Dohme had substantial sales and distribution networks not only in America but also in the UK and had been taken over in order to provide Merck with a vertically integrated business. As Jephcott recalled in 1962,

> the then President of Merck [James J. Kerrigan] immediately informed me the situation had, consequent upon this merger, fundamentally changed, and our association could not continue in the manner to which we had become accustomed. That has proved to be the case and today the intimate association has virtually ceased.[9]

Following its merger, Merck no longer needed to license new products to competitors or to sell them in bulk to other pharmaceutical companies, but was able to market them as its own branded medicines.

Nevertheless, Jephcott continued to look for collaborative arrangements with Merck and other leading US manufacturers. Their size and resources for research gave them a significant technical lead and there appeared no other way of minimising its commercial consequences. Much of the negotiation now fell to Wilkins and in 1954 he reported that there was scope for joint work on antibiotics. Merck executives had become concerned by the costs of penicillin and streptomycin projects (to widen their spectrum of activity or, in the case of penicillin, to overcome growing resistances) for which margins had been squeezed. As Wilkins reported, Merck recognised the need to maintain their research and development commitment

> to remain in the market but the profits are so small that they don't justify their present expenditure. They would very willingly agree to collaborate on research programmes so as to reduce duplication and make our R&D budgets go further.
>   There are three main difficulties:
>   (1) the impact of Anti-Trust Laws.
>   (2) the cross-licensing of Merck's other licensees for discoveries of Glaxo.
>   (3) Merck's lack of confidence in some of our R&D work.[10]

Although an informal, non-mandatory arrangement would have circumvented the problems created by anti-trust laws, and Glaxo was prepared to compromise on the question of cross-licensing, there seemed to be no answer to the lack of confidence in the group's research capacities. 'They say that, so far, Glaxo has put very little into the kitty', wrote Wilkins, adding, 'I could only accept this and say that we had recently made a start, so that there were a number of things coming along which I thought might be of value.'[11] In the event, no further agreements were concluded with Merck, partly because Glaxo was able to form trading alliances with another American pharmaceutical company, the Schering Corporation.

Again, it was possible to conclude an arrangement based on complementary needs. Schering in the 1950s had a sound research record, particularly in the field of steroids,[12] and a well-established sales force in the United States but no representation in the UK. Nor did it have the manufacturing and process development expertise that Glaxo could command. In 1956, Schering had licensed Allen & Hanburys to make a range of products based on chlorpheniramine maleate (Piriton), a potent antihistamine, used to treat a wide range of allergic disorders in the form of an injection, tablet or linctus. It proved commercially successful in the UK. Mutual needs and a measure of business trust led to Schering becoming Glaxo's 'most important single customer', while Schering benefited from Glaxo's 'ability to devise economic methods of manufacture and indeed to manufacture more economically than they could themselves'.[13] The agreements with Schering were also driven by fear of take-over. When Smith Kline & French took over the British company A. J. White in 1955, Palmer had written 'now … all our American friends have arrived and settled in the UK and we may expect even severer competition than we are now experiencing'.[14]

In November 1958 when it appeared clear that griseofulvin (Grisovin) would prove to be an important antifungal antibiotic, Austin Bide, then joint company secretary of Glaxo Laboratories, travelled to America to explore the possibility of establishing sales agreements with the major pharmaceutical firms.[15] Responses were mixed. Schering immediately wanted to promote griseofulvin in the human and veterinary fields, while Johnson & Johnson, a company with considerable experience of dermatologicals, also expressed an interest. By contrast, DuPont and Merck, Sharp & Dohme were cool. As a result of these meetings, Bide negotiated agreements by which each company would undertake the promotional work and submit applications to the government's Food and Drug Administration (FDA) for the medicine's approval. Glaxo would then supply them with the packaged product in return for a royalty of 7.5 per cent on net sales, or 2.5 per cent if they purchased the bulk ingredient and undertook secondary processes themselves. Both Schering and Johnson & Johnson displayed griseofulvin at the spring meeting of the American Medical Association in 1959, before receiving approval from the FDA.[16] Johnson & Johnson embarked on an ambitious promotional campaign and in October one of their subsidiaries, McNeil Laboratories, funded an international symposium on griseofulvin and dermatomycosis at the University of Miami, which attracted over 200 physicians from eleven countries; the global press coverage that followed helped to publicise griseofulvin's therapeutic value.

By 1957 the Glaxo board had become sufficiently concerned about the disparities in scale between themselves and their US counterparts to request a formal statistical comparison.[17] The following year the analysis was extended to a further five businesses. The results showed that Eli Lilly, Merck, Pfizer and Parke Davis had more than double the capital resources of Glaxo Laboratories.[18] The differences of turnover were equally dramatic, with some US companies achieving pharmaceutical sales four times greater than those of Glaxo. While two-thirds of Glaxo's total turnover (including foods) originated overseas, their American counterparts relied far less on exports (between 14 and 33 per cent), showing the size and prosperity of the US market. So concerned was Jephcott by these findings that the exercise was repeated annually until 1961.[19]

The comparative analysis based on the financial results for 1960 revealed that the gap was as wide as ever: Glaxo had a capitalisation of £27.6 million and a turnover of £34.9 million, while the figures for Merck were £67.0 million and £77.9 million respectively. Yet, the analysis indicated that growth rates in the US were slowing and that increments to their profits were proportionately smaller. These findings led to the premature conclusion that

> the pharmaceutical industry as a whole [in America] is beginning to operate on a pattern that more closely resembles those already established by older, mature industries. An industry-wide band-wagon, surging forward every year with almost everybody aboard has passed out of the picture. Companies are now mounting their individual tractors geared for long, hard upward climbs.[20]

This interpretation heightened fears of an American bid for Glaxo. If US companies found that greater competition at home impeded growth, one way to boost their fortunes was to acquire overseas subsidiaries and sell directly in more favourable markets.

By 1960 a pattern had emerged in Glaxo's commercial dealings with the American market. It was not the result of long-term strategic planning but had evolved in a practical fashion based on the personal negotiations of Sir Harry Jephcott and Dr Fred Wilkins. Crucially, it relied on Glaxo remaining 'effectively out of the US market' and finding an American collaborator who had no wish to sell directly in the UK. There were considerable difficulties. First, the major pharmaceutical firms in the US were ambitious and exhibited increasing reluctance to refrain from trading in Britain. Secondly, there were different philosophies on the question of pricing. For shared products the price was 'substantially greater' in America than the UK and there was an understandable desire on the part of Schering that the higher level should prevail in countries where both companies operated. Aware of these tensions, Gerald Smith, a director of American Home Products (AHP), approached Sir Harry Jephcott in 1960 to propose a joint arrangement in the US. He demonstrated that the returns available to Glaxo by licensing their products to American companies were much smaller than would result from a share of profits from a jointly owned sales organisation. Accordingly, he proposed that Wyeth, a subsidiary of AHP and ranked seventh amongst American pharmaceutical companies, should be entrusted with the sale of Glaxo's products in the US and that the net profit would then be shared equally between the two groups. This state of affairs would continue

> until the sale of those products was adequate to sustain a separate manufactur-

ing and marketing organisation (which point he estimates to be reached when the turnover is 15 million dollars annually), and that from there on it should be constituted as a separate organisation with the stock held equally by the Glaxo Group and American Home Products, with the right resting with the Glaxo Group after a period of say ten years to purchase from American Home their interest in the joint company at valuation.[21]

Fearing, perhaps, that this might lead to a take-over, Jephcott was reluctant to enter into such a close business relationship with a larger American competitor, and turned down this option two years later when he was presented with a similar proposal.

Proposed merger with Schering

In January 1963 Francis Brown, president of Schering, made a formal approach to Jephcott, proposing that two groups be amalgamated in one of four ways: first, through a holding company based in Panama, secondly an exchange of shares between the two holding companies, thirdly, through a holding company set up in America or in the UK, or fourthly, an exchange of new issues of B ordinary capital, representing 50 per cent of the equity of both companies.[22] These suggestions arose from research collaboration after 1958 for the development of betamethasone, product licensing arrangements and two years of trade negotiations. The outcome of these merger talks was to have profound implications for the future of Glaxo Group.

In November 1961 Francis Brown and Mortimer Fox, a vice president of Schering, had discussed the possibility of broadening the 'existing research collaboration' with Glaxo and working towards 'closer co-operation in other respects, particularly in connection with the European Common Market'.[23] Given that Glaxo Laboratories had poor representation on the Continent and that Jephcott was anxious to preserve the integrity of Glaxo in the face of growing competitiveness from America, it was agreed that he should enter into talks. Herbert Palmer, the general manager and a board member, was asked in spring 1962 to survey the strategic options available to Glaxo and to make recommendations on 'future policy'. Presenting his findings in June, Palmer acknowledged the important contribution of the research and development departments of Glaxo Laboratories but concluded that this would not have been sufficient without input from, in the first instance, Merck and 'during the last five years or so a developing contact with the Schering Corporation ... in the steroid field, not to mention their antihistamine and tranquilliser which A&H have successfully exploited'.[24] Without supplies of the intermediate 'EAX' from Merck, Montrose would not have been able to make cortisone or hydrocortisone until 1955 when the company perfected a route from hecogenin. Equally Glaxo had been able to take advantage of Schering's research into corticosteroids in 1958 only when the latter suggested a collaborative arrangement. The Greenford chemists then set about discovering a way of making betamethasone from hecogenin on the understanding that the two companies would share exclusive rights over any medicines that resulted. In the same year Schering licensed to Glaxo the corticosteroids prednisone and prednisolone, which the latter successfully marketed as Predsol, Prednelan and Prednesol.

The major change detected by Palmer was the increasingly ambitious territorial strategies of American pharmaceutical houses. Before and immediately after the Second World War, the only foreign companies to establish significant representation in the UK were Parke Davis & Co. of Detroit, Bayer, Meister & Lucius of Germany, Sharp & Dohme of Philadelphia and the French company Rhône-Poulenc through their subsidiary May & Baker. By 1962 the only firms in the top twenty American manufacturers not to be actively involved in the UK market were Schering, Robins and Wallace. Glaxo could no longer rely on the major American groups for a supply of novel medicines as a supplement to their own research efforts. Palmer also expressed concern over the interest that these companies were beginning to show in the Continent. 'The dangers', he wrote, 'particularly for the smaller firms are great and increasingly threatening.'[25] Although Glaxo had little involvement in Europe, preferring an Imperial and Commonwealth bias, managers feared that these markets could be denied to them and worse still that French and German companies linked to, or merged with, US groups could then assault the UK market.

Having presented this 'gloomy view', Palmer suggested that four courses of action were open to Glaxo. First, 'long-term co-operative agreements or even merger' (to exchange novel products and for sales agreements) could be negotiated with companies not yet established in the UK.[26] 'These contacts', Palmer wrote, 'are likely to be made in the USA, France, Germany and Japan', though from his earlier observations there were few choices for the first and time appeared to be limited for the remainder. His second option was defensive in nature and entailed taking over or amalgamating with other UK companies whose operations 'need not necessarily be limited to the field of pharmaceutical, medical speciality trade. Any worthwhile investment', Palmer argued

which served to broaden the base and increase the profitability of our interest in foods, veterinary products, surgical equipment, proprietary medicines, and agricultural chemicals or could usefully be associated with them, would stabilise the group's profitability and improve its staying power particularly during periods of poor return from our continuing major research expenditure.[27]

The third recommendation scarcely represented a strategic change of direction but was really a subset of the second. This involved strengthening the wholesaling organisation of Evans Medical to 'develop an effective national distributive network capable of handling other products'. The final strategy proposed by Palmer was to merge with, or take over, companies in Glaxo's principal overseas markets such as India, Pakistan or Australia and to build on such limited representation as the group had established on the Continent.[28]

The first of Palmer's four options held the greatest promise of reward for Jephcott and in autumn 1962 he travelled to Schering's headquarters in Bloomfield, New Jersey, for discussions about a closer association. On his return, Jephcott reported to the Glaxo board and it was agreed 'to incur the substantial expenditure necessary to investigate the financial and legal implications of various forms of union'.[29] Schering favoured the formation of a single holding company with a cross shareholding arrangement on a '50/50 basis'.[30] This suggestion appeared too radical for Sir Harry, who proposed as a first step that

> the association might more desirably be based on a commercial and technical contract supported by an exchange of minority shareholdings (say 35 per cent), without prejudice to the possible later enlargement of the cross shareholdings.[31]

It was at this point that Schering proposed a formal union in one of four ways. These were investigated on Glaxo's behalf by Lazards, the group's merchant bankers, who, having consulted the Bank of England on the question of exchange control regulations, advised that a merger through a Panamanian holding company would be considered 'unacceptable'.[32] An exchange of parent company shares or an amalgamation through a UK holding company were both considered legally possible. However, Lazards concluded that both of these courses of action were impractical. They considered that no American investor would agree to exchanging their shares in a US corporation for those in a UK company, while the restrictions in Schering's articles of association concerning the foreign ownership of shares, and registration complications under Securities Exchange Commission regulations led Lazards to observe that 'the idea of a UK holding company presents so many difficulties that it is hardly worth pursuing'.[33]

THE BUSINESS OF MEDICINE

The fourth scheme involved Schering and Glaxo in a mutual exchange of new issues of B ordinary capital, representing 50 per cent of the two companies' combined equity, Lazards envisaged so many complications that this arrangement seemed almost unworkable:

> (a) a large international organisation of this kind could not remain static and it would certainly be found necessary ... to acquire new businesses ... In order to preserve equality it would be necessary that such acquisitions should be made jointly by the two companies and this could only be done for cash. Share issues by one side or the other as a consideration for an acquisition would inevitably upset the balance ... (b) It would probably prove virtually impossible to withdraw from an arrangement of this kind. Whereas X [Schering] could under US law repurchase its own shares, Y [Glaxo] could only do so by a reduction of capital and there would be no certainty that this step would be authorised either by its shareholders or by the courts.[34]

Faced with these difficulties, Lazards recommended a limited association on the lines of the Unilever agreement between their UK and Dutch companies with an exchange of shares up to 15 or 20 per cent of the voting and quoted equity. They acknowledged that this scheme really did no more than postpone the problems that would emerge if the exchange of stocks were to be increased. It would, they believed, at best serve 'as a tangible indication of an association between the two groups, although it has the disadvantage that through changes in relative earnings, earning yields and market prices between London and New York there is no certainty that an exchange of shares which starts as apparently of equivalent value will remain so'.[35]

Schering, in turn, took advice from Merrill Lynch, Pierce, Fenner & Smith, the New York merchant bankers, and received equally unenthusiastic advice but for different reasons. They were strongly of the opinion that

> a working arrangement between the companies, similar to that now in effect between Royal Dutch or Unilever, would have a detrimental effect upon the market price of Schering Corporation common stock. The investing public in this country is not accustomed and, as a result, does not look with favor on this kind of a profit-pooling arrangement.[36]

They were also unimpressed by the formation of a holding company in a third country. Although this was technically feasible, Merrill Lynch believed that this scheme would not inspire market analysts as 'the number of American investors interested in owning foreign securities is limited'.

Because stock in Schering was 'highly regarded' by shareholders and was 'considered a good long-term holding of the institutional type', Merrill Lynch argued that 'the only feasible method of preserving this important asset would be a merger of the foreign company [Glaxo] into Schering'.[37] They considered that the 'size of the combined enterprises and the increased market scope would more than offset the fact that a relatively small percentage of the new company's sales volume would be domestic'. Merrill Lynch took a rather optimistic view of Glaxo's response, suggesting that 'such a combination should not be considered as a sell-out, but rather a partnership'.[38]

Given the legal and organisational difficulties, and the understandable reluctance of either company to surrender its autonomy, it was not surprising that negotiations foundered and no merger took place. A union between the two companies could only have made business sense if one of the parties was, in effect, prepared to be taken over such that either Glaxo or Schering became the holding company, the other continuing as a subsidiary. Schering with its sound record of research and development and a significant share of the vast American market, saw no reason to make this sacrifice, while Jephcott did not feel so threatened by US competition that he saw no alternative to submission.

The merger scheme with Schering having become moribund, Jephcott was left with the problem of how to improve the flow of new medicines. He called a special meeting of the executive directors of Glaxo Group on 7 May 1963 to discuss the possibility of research collaboration with a major pharmaceutical company.[39] Recognising that the discovery of novel medicines demanded 'large and powerful blocks of industrial endeavour' making it 'increasingly more difficult to adopt successfully an isolationist policy', Jephcott concluded that partnerships had an important part to play, with the caveat that exchanges of information should be in 'selected fields' rather than the totality of the company's interests.[40] As regards specific collaborations, the board agreed that the

> Schering Corporation did, in fact, appear to be the most suitable partner, having regard to our past associations with them, that there is a parity between the two companies with regard to research effort, and that Schering's research activities are, in some measure, complementary to ours.[41]

Despite the failed attempt at merger, it was decided to approach Schering and propose such an arrangement.

On 12 May Francis Brown, chairman and president of Schering, arrived in London with Dr Maurice Pechet, the head of research and development, for discussions with members of the Glaxo board. Several days of talks followed in which current research projects and product development plans were reviewed in order to identify areas of mutual interest that might justify collaboration and 'result in greater effectiveness and economy'.[42] Although it had become 'abundantly clear' that an agreement on the exchange of technical information was practical and could be worthwhile, Brown believed that 'a fundamental difference of philosophy' on the pricing of new medicines would prevent the signing of a comprehensive partnership agreement. Difficulties had already arisen over the betamethasone project. 'The American attitude', Jephcott summarised,

> is that for any medical product the price should be the maximum that competition will permit, and in that regard a best wholesale price of three times the factory door cost is looked upon as the minimum. It is significant that in the last 12 months Smith Kline & French received for the whole of their business (including a substantial wholesaling business) four times the factory door cost of the goods, i.e. they had a gross profit of 75 per cent. The corresponding figure for Scherings was 76.8 per cent.[43]

Glaxo generally sought a gross profit of 50–55 per cent, though for medicines with limited applications this figure was increased to 60–65 per cent.

Francis Brown argued that the UK market would have borne a higher price for betamethasone valerate (Betnovate), launched in 1963. He believed that Glaxo had undercharged with the result that Schering had been embarrassed by the differentials between their respective corticosteroid products in countries where both companies operated independently, such as the Bahamas and elsewhere in the West Indies. Jephcott concluded from these discussions that the existing research collaboration would be widened only if the question of pricing was resolved. In view of strong opinions on both sides, this appeared to be unlikely and hence Jephcott considered that

> the association with Scherings ... would tend to be restricted to granting to the Glaxo Group licences in respect of patented products, such licences being strictly limited to markets such as the UK and Ireland in which Scherings were not themselves operating.[44]

These predictions proved to be well founded and in the months following the visit of Brown and Pechet Schering made no attempt to communicate further.[45] In June 1963, Sir Harry Jephcott announced his intention to resign as chairman and responsibility for US policy passed to Sir Alan Wilson.[46]

By the time of Sir Harry Jephcott's retirement, something of an inferiority complex had developed at Glaxo in relation to America, which was not without foundation. The group's own investigations had shown that the leading pharmaceutical companies in the US were far larger than Glaxo in terms of capital assets and turnover, and with a vast and prosperous home market they seemed impervious to any challenge from Britain. Furthermore, they exhibited a growing ambition to sell direct to foreign territories, no longer content to license competitors overseas. Jephcott was concerned not only that Glaxo could lose export business but that these American groups might harbour designs on his company. Having failed to conclude a partnership of equals with Schering, his strategy was to continue to strengthen Glaxo's base in the UK by further take-overs and to build up its representation in the Commonwealth. He steadfastly refused to establish a subsidiary in the US in order to avoid any possible threat to rival producers and to leave the way open for collaborative deals on new products and research initiatives.

Towards an American venture

Initially Sir Alan Wilson was content to follow the American policy that had emerged under Jephcott. His experiences at Courtaulds had taught him to be wary of the US. During the early 1960s, Wilson had supported plans to expand Courtaulds North America Inc. (which he had described as 'a small struggling company in a country of giants') by linking it with an indigenous firm.[47] Courtaulds, together with Koppers, attempted to acquire the fibre and Cellophane interests of the American Viscose Corporation but in attempting to steer clear of anti-trust legislation a series of bids and misunderstandings led to the deal falling through. The episode left Wilson so disillusioned with US business that he refused to consider taking Glaxo directly into this market. He directed the group's priorities elsewhere (notably in building up Glaxo's research and development functions and in extending its representation in Europe). The collaborative agreement with Schering for corticosteroids continued, together with the product licences. Relations between the two companies remained cordial and respectful despite their inability to conclude a formal union. In December 1965, for example, Francis Brown wrote to Sir Alan to tell him that they were 'considering entering the proprietary and patent medicine business in the UK'.[48] Schering were at pains to stress that 'there was no question of extending to the ethical pharmaceutical or animal feed business' and that they would welcome a partnership in this enterprise. The Glaxo board, for their part, agreed that the group's 'investigation of the patent medicine field that had been conducted last year be made available to Schering'.[49]

The matter that was to have greatest impact on Glaxo's attitude to the United States and to influence its policy towards American pharmaceutical companies was the development of a broad-spectrum oral cephalosporin. Increasingly organisms showed resistance to penicillin and the drug was not active against Gram-negative bacteria. Although other antibiotics had been developed (notably streptomycin in 1945 and the semi-synthetic penicillins from 1959), there was considerable demand for a drug with a wide spectrum of activity. In 1964 Glaxo had launched cephaloridine (Ceporin), an injectable cephalosporin which was effective against a number of Gram-positive and Gram-negative pathogens. The development teams at Greenford had now turned their attention to producing a tablet which could be administered by patients themselves. In a culture which still described antibiotics as 'wonder drugs' and for which there was a genuine and pressing need, Glaxo believed that the cephalosporins were of great commercial value. Given Schering's criticisms of their licensing arrangements for griseofulvin in America, the board considered their strategy carefully.

The situation was not straightforward. Glaxo had not been responsible for the discovery or even the early development work on the cephalosporins but had become involved under a licensing arrangement when the National Research and Development Corporation (NRDC) had appealed for help. Eli Lilly, then one of the largest American pharmaceutical companies, had also been licensed by the NRDC and had made considerable advances launching their injectable product, cephalothin (Keflin), in 1963, a year before Glaxo introduced cephaloridine. Under the terms of the NRDC agreements Glaxo were granted automatic access to the Lilly research material after an interval of six to twelve months. The group had also been granted a 'reserved territory', namely the UK and the Commonwealth including South Africa, where they alone could sell cephalosporin products whether they had discovered them or not.[50] However, Herbert Palmer thought it unlikely that this highly favourable situation could continue 'particularly perhaps where Lilly discovers an important oral cephalosporin that we might fail to make available with sufficient speed'. Lilly had an undoubted expertise in the field and, with far greater resources at its command, seemed likely to beat Glaxo in a race for new forms of the antibiotic.

As a result, Palmer thought it prudent to try to negotiate a collaborative research deal with Lilly rather than having them 'forced upon us' by the NRDC under the pressure of events.[51] He also considered that a trade arrangement might be possible by which Glaxo bought cephalosporins from Lilly's fermentation plant at Speke, recently acquired from Distillers. This was in the Glaxo 'reserved territory'; that is the UK and Commonwealth where Distillers and Glaxo had been granted licences by the NRDC but which had not been transferred to Lilly when they purchased the former's plant. In return for this trading concession, Palmer believed that Lilly might agree to research collaboration with Glaxo to find new cephalosporins and might provide them with 'as yet unidentified facilities … In the States in aid of our possible first-hand exploitation' of antibiotics there. Glaxo already had the right to sell cephaloridine in America and had encouraged Schering to begin clinical trials as the necessary preliminary to gaining FDA approval. Palmer now favoured a major partnership with Lilly as the least risky route to establish Glaxo in the United States:

> a collaborative research arrangement with Messrs. Eli Lilly coupled with the fruits of the bargain identified above may for the future put us in a position of profitability to make an entry into the USA market on our behalf. We should be sharing with Eli Lilly the substantial turnover that might well be available for an orally active cephalosporin, but it must be remembered that Eli Lilly are the leading US manufacturer of ethical pharmaceuticals.[52]

This strategy, he acknowledged, assumed that Glaxo would need to set up its 'own American agency' and that 'our share of the US market [for cephalosporins] … would inevitably be less than that of Eli Lilly'.[53]

Because of the uncertainties surrounding Lilly's position, it was agreed that Wilkins, who was to travel to the United States in February 1965, would visit Lilly's Indianapolis headquarters. The report and strategy outlined by Wilkins on his return showed considerable vision and ambition.[54] However, by the time that it was discussed by the board on 12 April, the preliminary negotiations with Lilly had broken down, though, as Wilkins observed, entry into the US market 'was not necessarily dependent on their successful conclusion'.[55] Wilkins considered that there were two options: 'the simplest and least complicated way … is to set up there a new company' and secondly to enter into some form of union with an established US enterprise. The first, he thought, offered 'the greatest risks and the greatest rewards'. Such a strategy had been adopted by Pfizer, who according to Wilkins, were

> legendary in being the only company to break into the ethical pharmaceutical market in the US in this century. The parallel would be obvious and it would provide an irresistible story to the American commercial and medical journalist. Assuming we have a good oral compound, we should have no problem in establishing the name of Glaxo in the US market. This publicity would do it for us.[56]

In fact, Wilkins was misled as Pfizer had been set up in New York in 1849 by two German immigrants and was therefore an American company in origin, though it had used its tetracycline products to achieve a smooth transition from bulk chemical manufacture to prescription medicines, setting up a sales and marketing organisation from scratch. Nevertheless, his assessment of the risks in setting up a business from scratch in the US remained valid. Circumstances had changed since Pfizer launched the first broad-spectrum antibiotic, oxytetracycline (Terramycin), and such medicines, though still valuable, had lost some of their magical appeal. Furthermore, Glaxo did not have exclusive rights over any new cephalosporin that they developed, Lilly also having a claim to novel compounds under the NRDC agreements. Wilkins warned that Lilly were regarded as 'among the first, if not the first, of American pharmaceutical houses in marketing and selling to the American doctor'. Alternatively, Glaxo could spread the risks of trading in the US by joining a domestic enterprise but, despite the size of the market and the number of manufacturers, he could identify only two possible companies suitable for merger. Rörer of Philadelphia was one choice, selected because an American analyst had identified them as the fastest growing US pharmaceutical house. With a high reputation for marketing, they sold OTC lines through general practitioners with considerable skill and advertised their preparations only in the medical press. Rörer were really chemical manufacturers that had developed a successful pharmaceutical product, 'Maalox', an antacid, which was reported as grossing $12 million per annum. As a company with no new scientific products and having a proven and sophisticated marketing and sales department, they were the ideal foil for Glaxo if it could provide new products. This strategy therefore bore a remarkable resemblance to the one which the group followed in 1977 when it acquired Meyer Laboratories (see p. 385). Although Rörer appeared to be interested in a trading arrangement, press reports indicated that they would resist a take-over.

As an alternative Wilkins considered an 'association with a larger company' and, given Glaxo's research collaboration and licensing arrangements with Schering, they seemed the obvious choice, though talks had failed comprehensively only two years before.[57] Wilkins had spoken to Francis Brown and still found him very receptive to a 'world-wide association'. Furthermore, one major obstacle to a union had recently been removed: 'a new ruling had been given by the Justice Department which made it possible for Schering stock to be held other than by US domiciled shareholders. All Schering directors needed now is the consent of their shareholders.'[58] Although Brown favoured 'the construction of a joint world-wide enterprise' he was prepared, in the face of Glaxo's reservations, to compromise on 'a limited association with us which would be of such a character that at some time of our choosing we could take over the whole operation as a Glaxo company provided that Schering had some part of the equity'. More precisely he and Wilkins had discussed the idea that they would set up a new joint company, which had the advantage of introducing 'a considerable hedge on the financial risk and with the clear expectation' that Glaxo would finally have an enterprise, if not wholly owned, at least securely under its operational control.

Wilkins also considered two other American companies with whom a joint company might be established: Kodak and Miles Laboratories.[59] Kodak was known to be interested in entering the pharmaceutical business. However, Kodak had

> no sales force for ethical proprietories and ... their sales and marketing organisation for radiologicials and X-ray film was unsuited to the purpose ... Kodak's contribution would be essentially money, together with their knowledge of the American scene ... A major drawback to a joint venture with Kodak is that it is unlikely to lead to an independent Glaxo company. It is known that Kodak likes wholly-owned subsidiaries.[60]

An association with Miles Laboratories was explored because of their established reputation in the OTC market, as the manufacturer of Alka Seltzer and a range of multivitamin preparations. Of greater potential interest to Glaxo were their two subsidiaries, Ames Laboratories and Dome Chemicals. Ames was a market leader in diagnostics, and with an active sales force targeted at practitioners and hospitals that could provide a vehicle for Glaxo products. Dome, which specialised in ethical dermatological medicines, was considered a possible outlet for topical steroids developed at Greenford. On his visit to the United States, Wilkins had discussed such an association with Walter Beardsley, chairman of Miles, and Walter Compton, its president, both of whom had expressed interest in such a strategy.[61]

Considering all of these options, Wilkins favoured an association with an American company and concluded that the setting up of 'a joint company ... for the marketing of a new broad spectrum oral antibiotic' was the best way of entering the US market. Because of their existing links with Schering and the enthusiasm of Brown, their chairman, he thought that they would be co-operative and the most likely to grant Glaxo ultimate control of the new enterprise.[62] In the event, he and the group were over optimistic about the ability of the development team at Greenford to produce an oral cephalosporin, and it was not until December 1969, some four years later, that Glaxo was able to launch cephalexin (Ceporex). Sir Alan Wilson did not believe that Glaxo could enter the US without a novel medicine because its leading prescription drugs were already subject to licensing agreements, notably griseofulvin with Schering and Johnson & Johnson, betamethasone with Schering, and the cephalosporins with Eli Lilly. As a result, Wilson shelved these strategies until such time as a new product was developed.

As subsequent events were to confirm, the launch of salbutamol (Ventolin) in 1969 could have provided the ideal product for entry to America. It was a truly novel medicine designed to treat a common and sometimes life-threatening condition. Salbutamol, or albuterol as it was known in the US, became one of the world's largest selling drugs with an exceptionally long product life and the capacity for a wide variety of line developments. However, Wilson had lost any enthusiasm for an American adventure, perhaps because the group's territorial expansion was directed towards Europe. Consequently, salbutamol was licensed to Schering and for many years sales, and therefore profits, were unspectacular.

Glaxo Inc.

The question of direct entry into the United States remained a low priority until the summer of 1970, when Glaxo explored the possibility of acquiring fourteen pharmaceutical products, together with their attendant customer lists and marketing records, from the newly established Ciba-Geigy Corporation (USA).[63] The Swiss chemical and pharmaceutical companies, CIBA Ltd. and J. R. Geigy S.A., both based in Basle, had decided to amalgamate all of their undertakings on a world-wide basis. In America, where both had subsidiaries, they encountered objections to the union from the government. These were resolved by a consent judgment entered by the US District Court of New York on 8 September 1970 whereby the merged US enterprise undertook within two years to sell certain unspecified assets of their pharmaceutical business. Having heard of this, on 27 August 1970 Glaxo contacted the president of CIBA to express an interest in the potential sale. Later in the year, they received a full description of the designated assets: fourteen pharmaceutical products, including chlorthalidone (Hygroton) and Regroton, two anti-hypertensive medicines, together with the option to purchase the Geigy factory at Cranston, Rhode Island, where the active ingredients were manufactured, and the right to select and employ half of the personnel engaged on the marketing of these drugs.[64]

A policy recommendation was prepared by Herbert Palmer and David Smart, the commercial director, who concluded that there were two significant advantages to an acquisition of the Ciba-Geigy assets. First, it would provide Glaxo with an instant portfolio of products, circumventing the need to make lengthy and costly submissions to the FDA. Secondly, they would be able to set up an effective marketing organisation recruited from the existing Geigy sales force, which at the time numbered 554 detailers (the American term for representatives). 'This organisation', they commented,

> is large enough to cover even the low population density areas of the United States moderately effectively. The minimum number of representatives necessary to provide national cover of the main centres of population is about 200. A sales force of this magnitude would enable about 50,000 of the country's 170,000 doctors to be visited four times a year or about 90,000 to be seen twice annually.[65]

However, Palmer and Smart calculated that the cost of 200 detailmen, together with advertising, would amount to $4.75 million a year, which was expensive for just two major products. They believed that the stringencies of FDA regulations would delay the introduction of Glaxo products by two to three years, and in the case of significant new medicines could cost over $1 million.

So, Palmer and Smart concluded that the Ciba-Geigy offer was of insufficient commercial advantage and recommended terminating negotiations. Nevertheless, the debate had provided the opportunity to move the American issue up the ladder of Glaxo's priorities. 'The US ethical market', they observed,

> is easily the largest in the world; purchases made by pharmacies and hospitals amount to more than £1,500,000,000 annually. Even a one per cent share of this market would provide the basis of a substantial business.[66]

Although it presented an immensely attractive opportunity, Palmer and Smart identified three major difficulties. First, competition was 'intense' and was based on product differentiation rather than price. It was not sufficient, therefore, to undercut a rival as 'substantial promotional expenditure' was needed to establish a new medicine. Secondly, operating costs were significant, given that advertising fees and representatives' salaries were both high. However, these were offset by larger gross profits than in the UK, Geigy quoting 87 per cent for 1970.[67] Finally, they were concerned by the expensive and time-consuming procedures required to obtain FDA approval for novel medicines.

Palmer and Smart considered that there were three ways of entering the

United States. The obvious route was simply to acquire an existing company or, as in the Ciba-Geigy case, to purchase a portfolio of established products. Opportunities were limited partly because the major US firms were all considerably larger than Glaxo and very few of those of medium or small size would welcome a take-over. Secondly, there was the option of forming 'a jointly owned enterprise with an established pharmaceutical company'. This had the advantages of reducing the financial risks and providing direct access to market intelligence but carried the potential for disagreements over policy or commercial interests. The experience of trying to negotiate such an arrangement with Scherings had shown that this was not straightforward. Thirdly, they explored the possibility of establishing a wholly owned subsidiary without external assistance. Once set up, this could operate in one of three ways: to sell a full range of the group's prescription products throughout the United States; to hold a full portfolio of medicines but targeting sales within a specific market sector or in selected cities; or thirdly, to concentrate on a specialised therapeutic area but 'seeking to provide effective national cover'.[68] The first strategy was considered too costly, and likely to produce a negative cash flow for some years, while the second approach had the inherent weakness of limited promotional campaign. As a result, Palmer and Smart favoured a strategy to create a 'beach-head', 'covering costs as far as possible by concentrating sales effort in a limited market while building up the product portfolio and the marketing organisation'.[69] Given that Glaxo Research had Althesin, an induction agent, in development and Allen & Hanburys were working on a short-acting curarising agent (AH 7060), they thought that anaesthetics might prove a suitable vehicle for their plans. Their report, which was considered by the Glaxo board in February 1971,[70] ended on a note of caution:

> Entry to the US market can never be easy for a foreign company and it is almost inevitable that losses will be sustained for some years. However, the profits which could be obtained by a successful operation are very substantial indeed, provided always that the parent company is able to supply a continuing succession of significant new products.[71]

Although Ventolin had been launched in 1969 and important research work was in hand, particularly in the Ware laboratories of Allen & Hanburys, the Glaxo board could not guarantee a flow of novel medicines. The collective will and self-confidence did not then exist for a radical, capital intensive and risky enterprise. Discouraged by his experiences at Courtaulds, Wilson abandoned any plans to establish a company in the United States in favour of further consideration of a collaborative venture in a focused market sector, such as anaesthetics.[72] Yet fresh talks with Ciba-Geigy came to nothing and by the end of 1971 Glaxo found itself fighting for its very existence when Beecham mounted its take-over bid.

Following the sudden death of Francis Brown in a road traffic accident, Sir Alan Wilson visited his successor as chairman of Schering, W. H. Conzen, early in 1972 to establish whether he would renew the research and trading links between the two companies.[73] Although Conzen agreed to continue, the change in executive authority and the weakening links between the two companies encouraged Glaxo to act positively.

In June 1972, Paul Girolami, the finance director, reported that

> a wholly-owned subsidiary had been incorporated in the state of Delaware, USA, having the name Glaxo Inc. and with a nominal share capital of $10,000. The subsidiary, whose first directors are Mr. A. E. Bide, Mr. P. Girolami and Mr. R. D. Smart, is now in a position to activate itself into a viable operating subsidiary as and when circumstances require.[74]

Although Glaxo Inc. was now formed, it was to remain little more than a legal entity for four years. The group, in fighting off the Beecham bid, had been forced to submit its own defensive alliance with Boots to the Monopolies Commission. So there was little enthusiasm for an enterprise fraught with risk and requiring considerable capital investment. The priorities identified by Austin Bide, who succeeded Wilson as chairman in 1972, were internal organisation and structure together with the development of the group's territorial representation in Europe. Given the significance of these objectives and the need to rebuild the group's confidence, it was not surprising that any American initiative was postponed.

It was, therefore, not until the beginning of 1976 that Glaxo began to plan in earnest to enter the American market on its own account. Taking over a US pharmaceutical company was now considered to be the best strategy. David Smart visited New Jersey to sound out the Purepac Corporation, a generic manufacturer, but on his return, the board decided against purchasing an equity interest.[75] Smart argued that entry should not be delayed by the 'search for acquisition opportunities among existing US manufacturing/distribution companies', and that Glaxo Inc. should be activated as soon as possible, The subsidiary could then organise clinical trials and set in train the often lengthy applications required to obtain FDA approval for the introduction of new products. Secondly, he suggested that Glaxo Inc. should begin to trade, initially promoting a narrow group of specialist medicines such as anaesthetics, but have as its long-term objective the sale of 'bronchodilators and bronchial steroid products and thence products of other therapeutic classes'.[76] Although the strategy of expansion into America had the committed support of other board members, including Girolami, these were radical proposals and Bide asked for detailed plans for further discussion.

Once again a great deal of work was done outlining the options for the board. This time the commercial directorate under Smart was entrusted with the task of drawing up recommendations for the timing and method of entering America. Dr I. L. S. Mitchell and J. P. Scott were the authors of a plan which suggested that the first step should be the creation of

> an United States Co-ordination Unit, which will be charged with the responsibility for progressing through the Federal Food & Drug Administration the submissions necessary to obtain approval for us to sell certain of our products directly in the US market. It will also initiate and co-ordinate such local clinical pharmacology and clinical trials as may be necessary to complete those submissions.[77]

It was proposed that a team of three be appointed (a medical advisor, office manager and a secretary) and that Mitchell would take responsibility for the unit until the subsidiary company in the US became operational. This also required Glaxo Inc. be brought to life and Girolami and Smart sought approval from the main board to raise its share capital from $10,000 to $100,000. A. E. Bide (president), R. D. Smart, Dr I. L. S. Mitchell and J. P. Scott were formally appointed directors.[78]

To accommodate the Co-ordination Unit, an office was rented close to Washington (for access to the FDA) in Maryland. Its first objectives were defined as securing 'the earliest possible registration' of alfathesin (an anaesthetic), cefuroxime (Zinacef, a second-generation cephalosporin), and two drugs in development: AH 15777 (a short-acting curarising agent) and AH 16111 (a bronchodilator).[79] Because Glaxo had licensed most of its new products to Schering, it was important to explain the change in policy. In 1976 Schering was in the process of registering three Glaxo products (Ventolin, Becotide and Trandate) with the FDA and it was agreed that the new Co-ordination Unit should be given access to their submissions in order to accelerate their progress through clinical trials to approval.[80] From now onwards the 'special relationship' between the two companies dissipated as existing licensing and collaborative arrangements expired and no new agreements were introduced in their place.

Part II: Glaxo arrives in the US

Meyer Laboratories

Smart and Girolami, the principal proponents of the American enterprise, believed that Glaxo Inc. needed an indigenous ally in the US.[81] So, they searched for an enterprise with a vigorous sales and marketing organisation that was also short of new products. In 1977 it seemed they had found the company they sought. J. C. Barnett and John Warren reported on a visit to the Fort Lauderdale headquarters of a small pharmaceutical business, Meyer Laboratories Inc. Barnett concluded that

> Meyer Laboratories was a very attractive proposition to enable Glaxo to move into the USA at an early date. Their lack of research and manufacturing activities means that we would not be paying for unwanted facilities; and at the same time we could expand in any direction we wished ... What we would obtain is surely what we need – an established and well-run sales force, and wholesaler distribution, with a national coverage.[82]

W. J. Hasey, the chairman, president and also majority shareholder of Meyer, together with W. H. O'Brien, vice chairman and treasurer, were reported as wanting an 'early decision' on Glaxo's intentions. They had been approached by several companies, including Fisons in 1973, but believed that Glaxo offered the 'best fit' of products. Aware that Hasey wished to sell the business, O'Brien, a former president of Shulton Industries, New Jersey (the manufacturers of Old Spice aftershave), took on the role of negotiator between the two parties.[83] The willingness of both Hasey and O'Brien to continue in office after a take-over was considered important given their experience and to impart 'a feeling of stability amongst members of staff'.[84] The findings of Barnett and Warren were reported to the board of Glaxo Holdings on 25 July and arrangements made to act swiftly.[85]

Meyer Laboratories, with its headquarters at 1900 W. Commercial Boulevard, Fort Lauderdale, was a comparatively small enterprise. The company had its origins in a retail pharmacy in Detroit owned by Al Meyer who, in 1946, had set up a laboratory to manufacture injectable medicines. Meyer Laboratories was recapitalised in 1960 when William J. Hasey became both majority stockholder and the operational manager. He had previously been marketing manager with A. H. Robins Co. in the USA and Canada.[86] In the early seventies Hasey moved the Michigan-based company to Florida, and in September 1976 took over Bluline Laboratories Inc. That year Meyer's turnover totalled $7,068,840 and net profits amounted to

$900,073.[87] Almost all of the company's medicines had to be obtained on prescription and Meyer had built up a specialisation in vitamins. 'Vicon C' capsules were their leading product with sales in 1976 of $1,984,000 of which $1,541,000 was gross profit. In fact, their Vicon range generated 40 per cent of sales. Cardiovascular products, Athemol, Athemol-N (with sales of $755,000 in 1976) and Ethatab tablets ($1,019,000), accounted for 20 per cent of turnover, while Theobid Duracap capsules ($338,000), for the relief of chronic asthma attacks, were also an important product. Apart from vitamins and vasodilators, Meyer's portfolio also included a urinary antiseptic (Renalgin) and an antihistamine (Histabid). From its beginnings until the early 1960s, Meyer mainly sold its products to doctors who also dispensed their own medicines, though as their numbers declined, detailers were forced to widen the focus of their promotional efforts.[88]

It was a lean, family-owned business.[89] Although bottling and packaging were undertaken at Fort Lauderdale, manufacture was contracted out. In essence, therefore, Meyer was a sales and marketing company. In January 1977, for example, there were 150 employees, of whom 128 were detailers or sales managers, while at Bluline nineteen of the forty-one staff were in sales.[90] The combined sales force numbered 151 at the time that Barnett completed his report in July 1977.[91] When Coopers & Lybrand undertook a valuation of Meyer in June 1979, they calculated a sales force of 168,[92] spread across the United States but with concentrations in Florida and Miami and in the north around Michigan. There were offices in Detroit, San Paulo, Windsor, Ontario and at Hata Rey, Puerto Rico.

In September 1976, Meyer had taken over Bluline Laboratories Inc. of St. Louis, Missouri, whose principal prescription product was Corticaine, a cream containing hydrocortisone and dibucaine for the treatment of haemorrhoids. It had been developed by a microbiologist, Hazel Rummer, who had joined the company in 1949 having graduated from the University of Illinois.[93] Rummer was responsible for production and packaging at the Bluline factory in St. Louis. Meyer had taken over Bluline to get Corticaine but found themselves with an ageing six-storey factory (built in 1915) with outdated processes. Meyer renovated one floor but were reluctant to spend more capital on the plant given that their own products were manufactured by contract by ICN of Cincinnati and KV of St. Louis.[94]

During autumn 1977, the senior management of Glaxo debated the wisdom of acquiring Meyer Laboratories. For the scheme to be 'justified', David Smart argued,

it should be demonstrable that purchase would effect a saving in expense, or in opportunity cost, or both. Since the only alternative to acquisition, if our

defined aims are to be achieved, is the establishment of a Glaxo company from a
'cold start', it is with the latter possibility that a comparison will be made.[95]

To calculate the cost of a 'cold start', Smart made the following assumptions: that products would either be imported or manufactured locally on
contract; a sales force of at least 100 detailers would be needed; office and
warehouse accommodation be purchased; and that about eight Glaxo
medicines would be introduced over five years. The acquisition of Meyer
created an annual charge of $7.5 million over the same period, or a total of
$37.5 million. This figure compared unfavourably with the projected crude
negative balance of $8.47 million at the end of five years based on a 'cold
start'. The question, therefore, that the board was asked to consider was
whether the take-over of Meyer would enable Glaxo Inc. to generate substantially larger sales to compensate for the annual loss of $7.5 million
incurred over five years.

Austin Bide consulted his non-executive directors, notably Sir David
Barran, a former managing director of the Shell Group and then deputy
chairman of the Midland Bank, first about the wisdom of entering the US
by take-over and secondly whether Meyer Laboratories was a company
suited to this strategy.[96] Barran was 'wholly in favour' of the acquisition as,
unlike the cold start, it provided Glaxo with the nucleus of an experienced
sales force with an established reputation.[97] The new subsidiary could
begin to trade from its birth without having to pause to set up a basic commercial organisation. When detailed proposals were presented at the November board meeting, the take-over was approved.[98] Smart and Girolami
were both convinced that Glaxo must seek to establish itself directly in the
US, the world's largest pharmaceutical market. If it did not, and continued
to sell its products there under licence, Glaxo would remain a target for acquisition itself by one of the leading American groups. The Beecham experience had taught the board that Glaxo was valuable but vulnerable. In
Girolami's judgement, the ruling of the Monopolies Commission had
given the company an eight-year period of grace to strengthen themselves
against any future predator.[99]

At this stage, Bide and Smart concluded that the relatively modest sales
force of 150 representatives allowed them two possible marketing strategies.
The first involved concentrating on specific areas of high population, such
as Illinois, and Chicago in particular, where the small force of Meyer detailmen were well known, in order to promote a portfolio of the group's
medicines. The alternative was to spread the representatives more widely
but reduce the number of products to be marketed, focusing on one or two
therapeutic classes. Anaesthetics were a favoured field as the number of

specialist doctors was relatively small, the administration of anaesthetics being commonly entrusted to trained nurses. Having established themselves in this way, Smart believed that Glaxo Inc. could then direct its sales effort towards respiratory medicine, a far larger and more profitable area.

Although Glaxo Inc. agreed to acquire all the issued shares of Meyer Laboratories, payment for these was deferred until February 1978 by which time the latter's audited accounts (year ended 31 December) would be available to calculate the final purchase price.[100] Of Meyer's issued capital, 88 per cent was held by four shareholders: William J. Hasey, the chairman and president (71.2 per cent), William H. O'Brien, treasurer (6.8 per cent), Roy M. Greenwell, vice president sales and training (5.9 per cent) and Philip A. Priola, secretary (3.7 per cent). The remaining stockholders were largely individuals involved with the business or relatives of William Hasey and there would be no difficulty in purchasing their shares.

When the take-over was finalised in February 1978, Glaxo had the seed for its US expansion, including a small sales and marketing organisation in the United States. For the group this was to prove as momentous an event as the landing of the Pilgrim Fathers in 1620 had been in the history of America. When Glaxo arrived in the US, it was a medium-sized company with strong roots in the Commonwealth. Twenty years later it had become a world leader and had achieved this pre-eminence in large measure because of the success of its new American subsidiary.

Glaxo paid £18 million for Meyer and the announcement was greeted in the UK financial press with 'a sigh of disappointment'.[101] Because it was widely known that the group had been planning a US acquisition, analysts expected that a major deal would follow. Austin Bide defended the strategy in *The Times*:

> We thought it sensible to start with a business that was viable *ab initio*. We did not have the right to be over-venturesome. The US market can be a dangerous place for the unwary.[102]

Bide explained that the advantage of a take-over was that it established a beach-head 'without subjecting shareholders to unwarrantable risk'. Predicting that Glaxo Inc. would soon have a secondary-process factory, he declared that the group had ambitious plans for its embryonic company. Whilst the take-over was formally completed on 30 June 1979, the name of Glaxo did not immediately make an impact on the US market. For legal reasons and in order to provide a transitional space, Glaxo Inc. (Maryland) changed its name to Meyer Laboratories Inc. (Maryland) on 1 July.[103] However, in view of 'rapidly changing events and especially considering the possibility of FDA approval of new products', it was decided to re-adopt the name Glaxo Inc. before a deadline of 1 January 1980 to provide sufficient time to prepare new labels, packaging, stationery and corporate signs.[104]

Glaxo fulfils its promise

The period from 1978 until 1983 when Glaxo Inc. moved its headquarters to Research Triangle Park in North Carolina was one of transition as a small-scale business with circumscribed goals expanded to take on the role that Glaxo had ambitiously defined for its future. The management was slowly transformed as either junior Meyer staff of promise were promoted or experienced managers from larger pharmaceutical companies were recruited. From the outset it was decided to entrust the daily running of the business to US nationals and that the company should act in a typically American manner. As Bide stressed at a board meeting of Glaxo Inc. in February 1978

> in no way was it intended for the day-to-day trade and business of Meyer to be other than in the hands of the present management with Mr Hasey in full control. However, there would be need from time to time for strategic matters to be considered and this could be done either through the formal mechanism of Glaxo Inc. board of directors meetings or by informal meetings.[105]

In March 1979, Douglas Back, a board member of Glaxo Holdings, was appointed a director of Glaxo Inc. to help communication with its parent company, while William Hasey became president and Charles E. Hart was recruited as executive vice president.[106] Hart had worked for a number of pharmaceutical companies in Germany, Switzerland, Italy and France in various sales and marketing roles, becoming vice president and director of European operations for A. H. Robins Co. in 1963.[107] Hasey had met Hart when they had both been working for Robins and formed a 'high regard' for his business abilities. In July 1980 both Hasey and O'Brien resigned and Hart was appointed president.[108] Roy Greenwell, vice president of sales for Meyer Laboratories, became vice president of marketing in Glaxo Inc., though he, too, resigned in November 1980.[109] Continuity was preserved by the persons of Philip Priola, who continued to serve as company secretary until 1985 when he was appointed a senior vice president,[110] and Mike Gallucci, who had joined Meyer Laboratories in 1973 from their auditors, Arthur Andersen. Gallucci became financial controller of Glaxo Inc. and in July 1980, on the resignation of O'Brien, was promoted to treasurer. In addition, James Butler, a sales representative with Meyer from 1969, became a vice president and general manager of the US division, Glaxo Pharmaceuticals, in 1987.

Because of the need to grow rapidly, executive posts were also filled from outside. In June 1979, for example, Dr Peter Wise was elected vice president of new product development. One of the few Englishmen in the company, he had been medical director of Beecham in the US from 1969 and was looking for a new challenge but wanted to continue working in America.[111] He knew both Dr David Harris, medical director of Allen & Hanburys, and Dr Roy Foord, who held the equivalent post at Glaxo Laboratories. He had considerable experience of submitting new products to the FDA for approval, having worked on Beecham's semi-synthetic penicillins, notably amoxycillin (Amoxil), and knew the problems of being a subsidiary of a British parent company. Alan Steigrod was another recruit. Hired from Eli Lilly, he became vice president of sales and marketing in succession to Greenwell. When the appointment of Charles Hart as president proved short lived, Steigrod assumed further executive authority until a permanent successor was in office.

The key appointment to Glaxo Inc. was made in October 1981 when Joseph J. Ruvane became president. Born in 1925, he graduated from the University of Virginia in 1947 with a degree in biological science, and had begun post-graduate studies in economics before joining Hoffmann-La Roche the following year as an administrative assistant and purchasing clerk. Promotion brought him to Roche-Organon in 1949 and two years later when Organon, a Dutch company, bought out Roche's share of the business, Ruvane continued to work for Organon Inc. in a variety of sales and marketing roles. In 1968 he was appointed executive vice president and three years later became president.[112] Ruvane had been told of the vacancy at Glaxo Inc. by the chairman of Schering. Several meetings followed in New York with Girolami. Ruvane appealed to Glaxo because he had worked for the overseas subsidiary of a European multinational and built up a medium-sized company (with an annual turnover of $40 million) from modest beginnings, gaining broad experience from a sales and marketing base in the process.

At the outset, Glaxo decided to introduce a small number of key products to the Meyer portfolio: albuterol (the American term for salbutamol), which was marketed as Ventolin, and beclomethasone dipropionate (Beclovent and Beconase). However, because of the existing licensing and research agreements with Schering, Glaxo could not simply launch these medicines under their own brand names. Schering were already selling albuterol as Proventil and beclomethasone as Vanceril and Vancenase and were in the process of submitting labetalol to the FDA for approval. The agreements were renegotiated to allow Glaxo Inc. to co-market these products and to bring to an end the collaboration over new medicines, so that labetalol would be the last product that they promoted simultaneously. Henceforth, all new medicines discovered at Greenford or Ware would be marketed exclusively in the United States by Glaxo Inc.

Having cleared the legal and regulatory obstacles preventing Glaxo Inc. from marketing its own respiratory medicines, it was important to expand and re-educate the Meyer sales force. There were areas of poor coverage, notably the Midwest where detailmen were recruited to fill the gaps. In addition, Meyer's product range was aimed primarily at family doctors, and the hospital sales force comprised a mere three representatives. A small number of detailmen with hospital experience were recruited from Eli Lilly, Bristol-Myers and the other major pharmaceutical companies. Ruvane was careful not to lure away too many staff from a single company so as to minimise any annoyance that might be caused. This policy also enabled him to build a new culture and prevent Glaxo Inc. from becoming a clone of an existing organisation.[113] Ruvane, assisted by Steigrod and Butler, doubled the existing Meyer sales force to around 300 by 1983.

As successful as this policy had been, the expanded sales force could not cope with the entire portfolio of Glaxo medicines. With several cephalosporins in the product pipeline, detailmen with expertise in antibiotics were needed. In addition, ranitidine (Zantac) had been launched with great success in the UK and Italy, and it had become imperative to introduce the product to the American market as soon as the FDA would permit. When Girolami met Ruvane in New York in the autumn of 1982, he expressed his concern over the promotion of Zantac. Its chief rival cimetidine (Tagamet) was a Smith Kline & French product and their US sales force numbered around 800.[114] Because Glaxo Inc. could not trade on anything like equal terms with its main competitors, the Holdings board had been planning to licence Merck, Sharp & Dohme. There also seemed a possibility that research collaboration would follow.[115] However, no agreement had been signed and, in November 1980, as negotiations entered their final stages Girolami was appointed as chief executive. A determined supporter of Glaxo Inc., he countered the policy. As chairman Sir Austin Bide gave Girolami the authority he sought and discussions with Merck were closed.

In order to market Zantac effectively in the US, Glaxo needed to hire the services of a major sales force. Initially Girolami approached Bristol-Myers, who expressed an interest in an arrangement if Glaxo were also prepared to license their new third-generation cephalosporin, ceftazidime (Fortum). He was reluctant to surrender an important medicine which could be marketed more profitably by Glaxo Inc. and Bristol-Myers eventually turned down the proposal. Girolami discussed the matter with Ruvane and he suggested that Hoffmann-La Roche, a Swiss company with a

111. Joe Ruvane, chief executive of Glaxo Inc. and a key mover in the joint marketing plan to sell Zantac in partnership with Roche.

major American subsidiary, might agree to an arrangement. Ruvane had been on friendly terms with their US chief executive, Erwin Lerner, and he telephoned him to ask whether they could 'rent his sales force'.[116] The suggestion was greeted with incredulity but a meeting was then arranged between Lerner, Ruvane and Girolami at the 21 Club in New York. Roche had enjoyed great commercial success in the 1960s following the launch of diazepam (Valium) and chlordiazepoxide (Librium), both benzodiazepine anxiolytics. However, Ruvane knew that the patents on these medicines were drawing to an end and Roche, with a sales force of 700, were looking for new products to market. At five meetings over six weeks a deal was negotiated. Roche and Glaxo Inc. agreed to promote and sell Zantac jointly, though the product would carry only the Glaxo name; Roche was granted a return of 40 per cent of sales revenue on a rising scale over five years.[117]

In November 1982 when the marketing arrangement was announced, *Business Week* commented that this, together with Zantac itself, 'could give executives at SmithKline Beecham Beckman Corp. more than a slight twinge in the stomach'.[118] The success of the arrangement relied on two factors. First, it was generous to Roche so that there could be no misgivings in carrying out its terms or resentment about the distribution of profits. Secondly, it crucially relied on the two companies co-operating and forming a close working relationship. Ruvane and Lerner both made a concerted effort to achieve a combined strategy. Each addressed the other's sales forces to encourage a business partnership and a joint promotion committee was established. The arrangement gave Glaxo over 1,000 representatives to market Zantac, more than their major competitor, SmithKline, and

13. The Glaxo Volume *first published in 1948 and issued almost annually thereafter. It had scholarly papers on medical science and helped to foster Glaxo's reputation for scientific probity.*

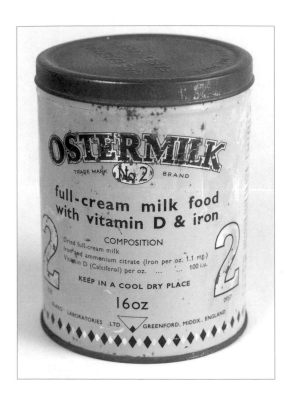

14. A tin of Ostermilk No. 2 filled at Greenford and dating from the late 1940s (above), together with a later variant (right).

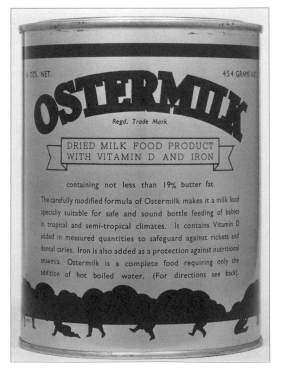

15. *An advertisement for Cytamen, an injectable form of vitamin B$_{12}$ to treat pernicious anaemia. Never a high volume product, nevertheless it did much to establish Glaxo Laboratories as an innovative pharmaceutical company.*

16. Sir Alan Wilson (1906–1997), chairman of Glaxo Group from 1963 to 1973, portrayed by Edward Halliday in 1969. He is holding a copy of his seminal work The Theory of Metals *(1936).*

17. *Copies of Glaxo Group News from 1972 when Beecham mounted a predatory bid for Glaxo, which in turn formed a defensive alliance with Boots. Both schemes were rejected by the Monopolies Commission.*

*18. Sir Austin Bide,
chairman of Glaxo
Holdings from 1973 to 1985.*

*19. Sir Paul Girolami,
chairman of Glaxo
Holdings from 1985 to 1994.*

20. *The distinctive five-sided tablet designed for ranitidine (Zantac) and first launched in Italy and the UK in 1981.*

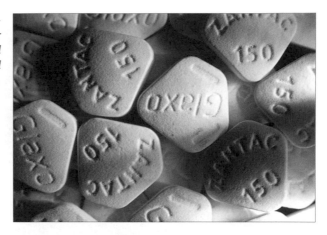

21. *Offices and decorative sculptures at Research Triangle Park, North Carolina, the headquarters of Glaxo Inc.*

22. *The new research laboratories constructed for Glaxo at Stevenage and opened in 1995, showing the main administrative block entered across an ornamental lake.*

23. Sir Richard Sykes, chairman of Glaxo Holdings from 1994 and architect of the takeover of Wellcome plc in 1995 and merger with SmithKlineBeecham in 2000.

Glaxo Inc. continued to build up its own sales force. The great commercial success of Zantac in the US proved to be of immense importance to both companies and inspired a number of similar co-promotion agreements in the pharmaceutical industry.

Research Triangle Park

In addition to building up the size of the sales force Glaxo Inc. also had to expedite new drug applications to the FDA so that they could be launched in America under the company's name. The process of gaining approval was costly and time consuming so it was essential that the clinical trials were undertaken rapidly. Responsibility fell to Dr Peter Wise, who moved to Fort Lauderdale in June 1979. Meyer as a sales and marketing company had no existing resources to draw on and it was imperative to recruit a team of pharmacologists and clinical pharmacists.[119] Dr Wise's first priorities were to secure approval for ranitidine, followed by ceftazidime and then to undertake the further work needed on labetalol and albuterol. In August 1981, Wise moved his department of twelve to rented accommodation in Research Triangle Park in North Carolina. There were no laboratories at Fort Lauderdale and he needed to recruit a range of experts from an industry based largely in New Jersey and New York. Since it was envisaged that the entire Glaxo Inc. organisation would also move from Fort Lauderdale, it was important to choose the new location carefully. A consultancy was commissioned to look at sites which would attract professional staff, key criteria being educational facilities, communications, the quality of life and tax rates. They identified four possibilities, Dallas, Texas, Atlanta, Georgia, an unspecified site in New Jersey, and Research Triangle Park in North Carolina. They recommended the last.

Almost equidistant between the three towns of Chapel Hill, Durham and Raleigh, Research Triangle Park had its origins in a series of proposals put forward in 1936 by Howard Odum, then chairman of the Institute for Research in Social Science at the University of North Carolina, for a public research institute near Raleigh-Durham airport where scholars from the major state universities could meet to exchange ideas.[120] By the early 1950s, it had become clear that North Carolina, a state with one of the lowest per capita incomes, could not generate appreciable growth from its traditional industries of tobacco, textiles and furniture.[121] In 1952 a Greensboro builder, Romeo Guest, had proposed setting up an industrial park for the discovery of new products as a solution to the problem of attracting new business and retaining the best university graduates. Guest coined the term 'Research Triangle' to denote the area defined by the area's three main universities: the University of North Carolina at Chapel Hill, Duke University in Durham and North Carolina State University in Raleigh. In the spring of 1955, Governor Luther Hodges appointed a committee of business and university leaders under the chairmanship of Robert Haines to consider strategies for economic development in the region. From this group, the Research Triangle Foundation was established in 1959 with a former student of Odum, George Simpson, as its first president. A team of salesmen drawn from the university staff then toured the country to lure executives in pharmaceuticals, chemicals and electronics to the advantages of locating their businesses in the Triangle. Although Chemstrand opened a laboratory in 1959, the project foundered and was in danger of collapse. But in 1965, IBM and the National Institute of Environmental Health Sciences were persuaded to build facilities in the Park and other organisations followed at a steady rate including, in 1972, the British-owned pharmaceutical subsidiary, Burroughs Wellcome. Because Research Triangle Park consisted of 6,800 acres of mixed forest, it was made a strict condition of entry that companies could not engage in manufacture and that activities be limited to research, development and their attendant administrative, sales and marketing functions.[122] In order to preserve the character of the woodlands, businesses could build on only 15 per cent of their land and build no higher than 60 feet so that structures remained below the tree-line. New freeways were laid through the park to provide rapid transport to the three major towns and to Raleigh-Durham airport.

North Carolina was one of the original thirteen colonies and was formerly known as the Old North State, following the division of the Carolinas in 1710. Established at Chapel Hill in October 1793, the University of North Carolina (UNC) had closed during the Civil War but re-opened in 1875 and grew rapidly in the twentieth century to a population of 24,000 students. It developed important specialisations in public health, medical research, business and computer technology. Neighbouring Durham, granted the epithet, 'the City of Medicine' during the 1980s, had grown up around the North Carolina Railroad in the mid nineteenth century as a tobacco processing town. Prominent in the business in the latter part of the century was W. Duke & Sons, founded by Washington Duke (1820–1906), who subsequently funded the transfer of Trinity College from Randolph County to its present location in Durham. In 1924 James Buchanan 'Buck' Duke, the most powerful entrepreneur in the cigarette industry, donated $6 million to the college and later named it as the principal beneficiary of the $40 million Duke endowment. Trinity College was renamed Duke University and a well-funded recruitment campaign helped the medical school to establish a high reputation, its hospital being ranked among the top ten in the United States.[123] By locating its headquarters at Research Triangle Park, Glaxo entered an area of recognised excellence in higher education with a particular emphasis in the areas of science and health. Not only could Glaxo draw on graduates from these institutions, it could also use their departments for clinical trials and other development projects.

When Dr Peter Wise moved Glaxo Inc.'s small product development department to North Carolina, plans for the transfer of Glaxo Inc. were still in an embryonic state. Because of the uncertainties,[124] he rented half of the first floor in the Pamlico Building, an office block in the Triangle opposite the Governor's Inn, a hotel and sciences complex for Park tenants. Recruitment then began in earnest as it was imperative to complete the clinical and submissions trials for ranitidine as soon as possible. By 1983 the department had grown to around fifty, including Pam Jones, who had been a clinical research pharmacist at the Duke Medical Center. She recalled how their small numbers, relative inexperience and youth, together with a family atmosphere, created a powerful amalgam of enthusiasm and self confidence.[125] Organised into two teams, one on ranitidine led by Dr Fred Eshelman and another on ceftazidime under James Chubb, they worked long hours. Based in large part on scientific information provided by a UK Glaxo team led by Dr David Richards, the ranitidine submission to the FDA comprised 229 volumes, each of around 400 pages, most of which had to be typewritten. Authorisation was obtained for ranitidine in just over three years, studies having begun in December 1979 and approval being granted in 1983. This was a remarkable achievement, in which the usual schedule was cut by over a year. The ceftazidime project was completed in around forty months, being approved in the same year.

The new headquarters

Having transferred the new product development department to Research Triangle, plans were laid to move the headquarters of Glaxo Inc. from Fort Lauderdale. In June 1982 Girolami, as chief executive, proposed that larger premises be leased in the Triangle to house the forty product development personnel together with the executive and administrative staff from Fort Lauderdale.[126] With the transfer scheduled for the summer of 1983, he calculated an office would be needed to accommodate 150, predicting that growth over five years would increase the total by 27 per cent to 190.[127] It was important, Girolami argued,

> for Glaxo to establish and maintain a prestigious image as a relative newcomer in the US pharmaceutical marketplace. This image should convey to the

industry and the general public that Glaxo is a solid, well-funded, research-orientated pharmaceutical firm. A well designed, dignified, corporate headquarters produces a tangible and visible representation of the Glaxo desired image.[128]

The expenditure, estimated at $5.25 million of which $1.5 million would be recouped by the sale of the Florida headquarters, was ratified by the main board in June 1982.[129]

Just over a year later, in September 1983, Glaxo Inc. moved its US headquarters to Research Triangle Park to a newly completed three-storey building (57,000sq.ft.) leased from Teer Enterprises Inc. The company also acquired twenty-two acres of land in the Park and had the option to purchase the offices. Situated at 5 Moore Drive, off Alexander Drive, the building was designed to accommodate 200 staff, though when opened it had 140: 50 from the product development department, 30 from Florida and 60 recruited locally.[130] Nobody, however, had anticipated the speed at which Glaxo Inc. would grow and the medium-term plans for expansion were to prove hopelessly inadequate as a major programme of construction was to get underway at Research Triangle Park.

By May 1984 it had become clear that the original building leased from Teer Enterprises was too small as Glaxo Inc. had already expanded to 235 staff, and temporary accommodation had to be leased elsewhere in the Park. Girolami presented a forecast that numbers could rise to 645 by 1988–89 and that a further 165,000sq.ft. of office space was needed.[131] It was decided to build anew and competitive tenders were submitted by three firms of architects and civil engineers. O'Brien/Atkins of Chapel Hill won the contract. The cost of the building and additional land required under the Research Triangle Park rules was estimated at $13.5 million (£9.8 million). The 170,000sq.ft. building, entered through a glazed, three-storey atrium, was completed on schedule in October 1985 and dedicated at a ceremony attended by Governor James Martin and Sir Austin Bide, after whom the offices were named.

Yet the sustained and rapid expansion of Glaxo Inc. resulted in even the Bide building becoming overcrowded. In July 1986, when numbers at the Park site had reached 500, the Holdings board authorised spending $10 million (£6.6 million) to construct an information centre and central power plant to house management information and distribution services together with records retention departments.[132] It became clear that if Glaxo Inc. continued to grow at the same rate even more office space was needed and another administration building was required. So another three-storey office building was designed by O'Brien/Atkins and constructed to the north of the Bide and Headquarters buildings. Occupied in

January 1988, Administration I was followed by a second structure, executed in a similar style, which was to house the company's senior executives and the board room, together with office accommodation for their executive staffs. Construction was finished late in 1988 and Administration 2, as it was originally called, was renamed the Ruvane Building. In essence, this completed the South Campus at the Park, while the North Campus consisted of the research and development laboratories, sales training centre, central utility plant and the Charles A. Sanders Center, housing information technology and technical services.

Manufacturing: Zebulon

In 1980 Glaxo debated the merits of secondary manufacture in the US and a plant location agency was commissioned to make recommendations. Having decided that the south-east quadrant of the country was the most suitable, they prepared a shortlist of five towns of which two (Dallas/Fort Worth in Texas and Nashville in Tennessee) were eliminated. This left three possibilities: Smithfield, ten miles south-east of Raleigh, the community of Oconee County, near Clemson, South Carolina, and Peach Tree City, south of Atlanta, Georgia.[133] Balancing everything (proximity to a major airport, good labour relations, quality of life and cost of land), Smithfield was considered the most favourable. In February 1982, L. J. Wyman and D. W. Murray visited the Smithfield area of North Carolina at a time when the Holdings board envisaged that both 'the factory and a new office building would be accommodated on one site'.[134] They estimated that the production facility and its warehouse would occupy between 120,000 and 200,000sq.ft., while the administration headquarters would need 100,000sq.ft., adding that 'it is difficult to envisage it getting much larger than this'. They calculated that the new enterprise would require about sixty acres, though a further forty acres would provide space for 'a prestigious development with buffer zones maintained between our activity and others'.

Two sites in the Smithfield area were examined: the Industrial Park, and an area of farmland near by, both of which had access from Highway 95. Although Wyman and Murray were convinced that either would prove 'very satisfactory' as locations for a factory with relatively low labour costs, they were 'less than certain that it is the ideal place for a Head Office development'.[135] As a result, they explored the north-west outskirts of Raleigh, which had been recommended as an attractive geographical area and the site of a number of science-based enterprises. The land was more costly and wage rates were reported to be a dollar an hour higher. They also

112. The lake at the Zebulon secondary pharmaceutical factory in North Carolina.

considered Research Triangle Park and visited Ned Huffman, executive vice president of the Triangle Foundation. Although Park regulations prevented the factory from being sited there, they discovered that sales and marketing staff could be accommodated 'provided that about 25 per cent of the people employed in the building were engaged in work that could be described as directly related to the NDA [New Drug Application] activity or other scientific work'.[136] The cost of land in the Park was expensive ($25,000 an acre) increased by the rules that building was limited to 15 per cent of the total site.[137]

In the event, Glaxo decided that the advantages of Research Triangle outweighed the additional costs and it was selected as the location for the head office together with any research and development laboratories that might be constructed. As a result, Smithfield was not a suitable site for a factory, being too distant from the new headquarters. In July 1981 the management committee recorded the intention of Glaxo Inc. to build a factory and warehouse in North Carolina, and in November a contract for the preliminary designs was awarded to Lockwood Greene & Co. of New York for $600,000. The entire project was costed at $42 million with a two-year timetable.[138] Having also investigated the possibility of purchasing two relatively modern pharmaceutical factories in the state and finding that they fell short of Glaxo's technical needs, it was decided to proceed with the project and, in February 1982, the company acquired eighty-three acres of land north of Zebulon in Wake County. Twenty-seven miles from Raleigh and forty-five miles from the proposed new headquarters in Research Triangle Park, the site offered ample space for expansion and proximity to a large local labour pool.

In June 1982 the board of Glaxo Holdings, at Girolami's request, approved the expenditure of $1.2 million for the levelling of the site and a further $500,000 for design work.[139] Designed on a modular plan to allow for future expansion, the plant specification provided for the production of 12 million aerosol cans (for Ventolin, Becotide and Beconase), 500 million tablets (Zantac, Ventolin and Trandate), 200 million capsules (Ventolin and Beclovent Rotacaps) and 200 tubes of ointments and creams (Temovate, Eumovate and Corticaine) in a single-shift operation. Supplying the American market either from manufacturing facilities in the UK and Europe or of sub-contracting to US producers had both been rejected. Girolami argued that these were 'impracticable' and 'would lead to occasional logistical problems and a disruption of supplies to the market'.[140] Domestic manufacture, he concluded,

> is more likely to respond quickly to market requirements. It should improve liaison with the FDA and speed up approval of product and manufacturing changes. It will also avoid the duplication of quality assurance facilities, which would otherwise have to be provided both by the manufacturing company and by Glaxo Inc.[141]

Local production would also enable the company to keep stock levels low through efficient production schedules and a reduction in the value of shipments. Finally, the lease on Meyer's ageing factory at St. Louis expired in October 1986, making it essential that an alternative site be found for the production of Corticaine.

Supervising the construction and commissioning of the plant fell to Bernard Remmelts. A chemistry graduate from the University of Groningen, he had joined Evans Medical at Liverpool in 1955, and took a degree in chemical engineering from Manchester College of Science and Technology in 1960. The following year Evans Medical were taken over by Glaxo and Remmelts found himself employed in Nigeria and then in Pakistan and Japan, where he helped with the installation of new production facilities or the updating of existing plant.[142] Construction at Zebulon began in the summer of 1982 and the secondary-process factory was completed on schedule at a cost of $42 million in March 1984. It was dedicated by Sir

Austin Bide in November. The two-storey administration building housed the offices, training facilities, computers, quality-control laboratories, library and cafeteria, and was separated from the factory and warehouse by a landscaped 855ft. waterway. The two are linked by an enclosed bridge. The design by the architects, Lockwood Green, was intended to be innovative while yet respecting the quality of the site's natural surroundings. The plant, layout and techincal specifications came from the UK, and most of the equipment was purchased from European suppliers. When Zebulon was occupied in March 1984, there were fifty staff but in January 1985 numbers had risen to 193 and by the end of the year were 295. The factory manufactured and packaged Ventolin and Beclovent inhalers and from 10 January 1985 also made Zantac tablets, which formed the bulk of its output (Table 25, p. 457). Zantac tablets were particularly important with annual output passing one billion in 1989, the year that Zebulon celebrated the production of over three billion in total.

When Zebulon was planned Glaxo Inc. intended it to be largely self sufficient in terms of secondary manufacture, importing only active ingredients in bulk from Singapore or the UK. As Table 25 (p. 457) hows, this has largely been achieved, with the exception of some cephalosporins, which are filled into vials in the UK before being despatched to Zebulon for labelling and packaging. As the output of Zantac and Ventolin together with the dermatological products increased, pressure grew on the manufacturing capacity at Zebulon. Also, under new rules antibiotics had to be made in a separate building to remove any possibility of cross-contamination. Accordingly, in July 1985 Girolami presented a proposal to the Holdings board for the construction of a cephalosporins building, and an initial expenditure of $4 million (£3.2 million) was approved.[143] By making Glaxo Inc. self-sufficient in the secondary production of cephalosporins, there would be annual savings on duty, freight, brokerage and insurance costs of $3 to $5 million. The entire project was estimated at $34.17 million (£26.16 million) and the building itself was to be completed by June 1988, and came on stream in the following year.[144] Shortly afterwards, the board also agreed to spend $3.2 million (£2.6 million) at Zebulon on additional aerosol filling and packaging lines and to incur a further $2.33 million (£1.85 million) on an extra tablet packaging line.[145] The rapidly growing output of manufactured and packaged medicines in turn put great pressure on existing storage facilities at Zebulon and in June 1987 Ruvane presented plans for the construction of a new high-density warehouse on the site.[146] Construction work on the 71,000sq.ft structure began in January 1988 and was completed by the end of the year at a final cost of $11 million (£7.24 million).

However, the implementation of the plan for a cephalosporin building was not straightforward. In July 1988 it was decided to locate the facility not at Zebulon, as originally planned, but in Durham itself. The rationale for the change was explained by Dr Ernest Mario, then CEO of Glaxo Inc., in a board paper:

> Building in this location will give Glaxo a visible presence in Durham which has an international reputation as the 'City of Medicine'. This project will also give Glaxo the opportunity to strengthen its ties with Duke University, a major medical teaching university. Duke is one of the primary participants behind the redevelopment of this part of Durham, which has been hurt by the closing of a large tobacco facility. The overall positive impact on the local economy and the benefits associated with being in Durham are considered important enough to justify the additional cost of this location.[147]

A 11.5 acre site, once the property of the American Tobacco Co. and adjacent to Dillard and Blackwell Street had been acquired in an area designated for urban renewal at a cost of $39.6 million (£23.3 million) and the existing structures demolished.[148] In February 1989, at an estimated $8.6 million (£5.1 million), it was decided to add offices to the factory project to provide overspill accommodation for staff from Research Triangle.

In January 1990 it was decided to abandon the Durham site and to construct the cephalosporin building as originally planned at Zebulon.[149] Not only was this less expensive, but it also provided operational and administrative savings. In May 1989 the purchase of seventy-five acres at Zebulon for $3.1 million had been approved to maximise site security and flexibility for long-term development.[150] In December 1989 it had been agreed to spend $26.7 million on renovating and enlarging the administration building at Zebulon, providing a further 88,300sq.ft. of offices and a 3,500sq.ft. lobby. In particular, the quality assurance laboratories were to be upgraded and extended and conference facilities added. Given that the construction of the new administration building would begin during the summer of 1990, it made engineering sense to complete the 16,300sq.ft. cephalosporin facility at the same time. Under the project director, Tim Tyson, work on the latter began in October 1990 and the construction team reached a peak of 200 workers the following February before completion in the summer.

Zantac: transformation of the business

Zantac was launched in the United States in June 1983 at a 20 per cent premium above the daily treatment cost of Tagamet. Promotional material and advertisements in the medical press stressed that it was more potent,

safer and more convenient (with a prolonged action) than existing therapies.[151] Tagamet was then the world's largest selling drug and it seemed that
executives at SmithKline initially underestimated the potential competition from the combined Glaxo and Roche sales forces. When SmithKline
responded, their marketing team chose to emphasise the seven-year safety
record of Tagamet, its product director arguing that

> Tagamet's side effects are generally low in incidence, well defined, mild in nature,
> and reversible. Zantac is a new drug in the US and it hasn't been on the market
> that long. Its clinical profile is still evolving.[152]

This defence was too cautious and did little to dent the commercial advance of Zantac. During its first week in the United States 7,000 prescriptions were written, 19,000 in the second and 40,000 in the third. On this
evidence the stockbrokers, Paine Webber, issued a report predicting that
sales of Zantac would reach $150 million by 1984 and rise to over $300 million in 1986.[153] In fact, even these ambitious estimates proved pessimistic.
In 1984 the total turnover of Glaxo Inc., boosted by the exploding demand
for Zantac, increased almost five times to $198,405,000, and doubled the
company's market share. In the twelve months from its launch Zantac
earned $134 million in sales, a record for any prescription product in the US
in its first year.[154]

Having captured 8.9 per cent of the market for the treatment of peptic
ulcers in 1983, Zantac rapidly gained ground and by 1986 occupied 44.1 per
cent. Its commercial success increased the turnover of Glaxo Inc. by 76 per
cent from $198 million in 1984 to $349 million in 1985 and by a further 75
per cent to $610 million by 1986. This had the effect of lifting Glaxo from
twentieth place to ninth in a ranking of US pharmaceutical companies
based on sales.[155] In 1987 Zantac took 50 per cent of the anti-ulcer market
and became the largest-selling prescription medicine in the United States.
Its share peaked in 1989 with 52.7 per cent, and then began a gradual decline
as it came under increasing competition from the introduction of a number of rival products, notably omeprazole (Losec). Nevertheless, the
turnover of Zantac continued to rise as it was licensed for other uses, in
particular, as part of a maintenance regimen.

To what, then, did Zantac owe its unparalleled commercial success in the
United States, regarded by many as the toughest but most valuable market
in the world? Both Zantac and Tagamet were H_2-receptor antagonists,
though Zantac with a longer duration of action had a simpler dose regimen, twice daily in comparison with four times for Tagamet. Equally, a variety of clinical trials undertaken in Europe and Australia had shown that

Zantac was more potent with an ulcer healing rate 6 per cent higher than that of Tagamet.[156] On the issue of safety, in human trials Zantac was shown to have remarkably low toxicity levels at therapeutic doses, while Tagamet, which had been on the market since 1976, had revealed a number of side-effects, including gynaecomastia, reversible liver damage, mental confusion in the elderly and very ill, together with adverse interactions with warfarin, phenytoin and theophylline. Nevertheless, Tagamet as the *New England Journal of Medicine* observed, had been demonstrated after 'extensive clinical experience' to be both an efficacious and a safe medicine.[157] Physicians, however, were keen to have an alternative to Tagamet, which at the time was the only H_2-antagonist available for the treatment of peptic ulcers, and so there was a market waiting for a product.

The sustained commercial success of Zantac owed as much to its acceptance as a prophylaxis against relapse as it did for the acute treatment of ulcers. Shortly after the launches in the UK and Italy, Glaxo scientists at Ware had the idea of extending its use to the prevention of peptic ulcer recurrence, since this was a common presentation, occurring in two-thirds of patients within twelve months. If it could be shown that Zantac had superior preventative properties, it would greatly enhance sales as the medicine would be taken on a regular and continuing basis rather than for short and intermittent periods. Glaxo helped to set up and fund two double-blind, randomised studies to compare the efficacy of ranitidine and cimetidine at maintenance doses (150mg and 400mg respectively) to prevent relapse in patients with recently healed duodenal ulcers. The clinical trial in America was managed by Dr Fred Eshelman at Research Triangle Park and undertaken by Dr Stephen Silvis of the Veterans Administration Medical Center, University of Minnesota, while in the UK it was led by Dr K. R. Gough of the Royal United Hospital Bath, and supervised by Dr R. N. Smith of Glaxo Group Research at Greenford.

The results of the British study were published first and appeared in *The Lancet* for September 1984.[158] A total of 484 patients were tested over twelve months and an analysis of the results, performed by Glaxo Inc. at Research Triangle, showed that the annual relapse rate was 23 per cent with ranitidine and 37 per cent with cimetidine. The American trial, which involved 125 patients, gave relapse rates of 15 per cent for ranitidine and 44 per cent for cimetidine.[159] These findings were published in a supplement to the *American Journal of Medicine* following a symposium held at Innisbrook, Florida, on the 'Management of the Ulcer Patient', funded by Glaxo Inc. The authors of both papers were unable to explain the clear pattern of their results because, as Silvis noted, 'the two drugs appear very similar in their ability to heal acute duodenal ulcers when given in recommended doses'.[160]

Although SmithKline had obtained FDA approval for long-term maintenance treatment in 1980, it had not promoted this concept strongly,[161] while Glaxo seized on the two studies as evidence of Zantac's superior effectiveness. The effect was probably the result of differences in approved dosages rather than an inherent pharmacological property of ranitidine. Because ranitidine is five times more potent than cimetidine, the equivalent maintainance dosage would have been 750mg a day rather than the 400mg chosen by SmithKline. These findings encouraged Glaxo Inc. to add a new dimension to their marketing strategy and in 1984 they launched a campaign to persuade physicians that Zantac should be used for long-term maintenance with one 150mg tablet to be taken at bedtime.[162] Further development work was undertaken to simplify the dosage regimen for acute treatment, and in September 1984 a single 300mg tablet was launched in the UK, and introduced to the United States in March 1986.[163] SmithKline responded with an 800mg tablet and a once-a-day regimen.

In 1986, ahead of Tagamet, Glaxo Inc. won approval from the FDA for Zantac as a treatment for reflux oesophagitis (in which excessive stomach acid flows up the oesophagus causing inflammation and superficial ulceration of the oesophageal mucosa).[164] It was in this year that Zantac overtook Tagamet, first in global sales and then in terms of prescriptions. It became the largest selling ethical product world-wide and the first to achieve sales of $1 billion, a landmark that earned it an entry in the *Guinness Book of World Records*. The contribution of Glaxo Inc. was becoming ever more important and in 1987 the company generated 33 per cent of the group's entire sales, and was ranked ninth in the US based on prescription sales.[165]

Inevitably, competitors soon appreciated the scale and value of the US anti-ulcer market and rival medicines began to be introduced with increasing regularity. In July 1986 a third H_2-receptor antagonist, famotidine, was launched in Japan by Yamanouchi and marketed in America by Merck under the brand name Pepcid.[166] The following year, Eli Lilly introduced another H_2-receptor antagonist, nizatidine, with the proprietary name Axid. Both drugs had a similar pharmacological action and to give them a competitive advantage, they were priced about 10 per cent below ranitidine. In addition, SmithKline obtained FDA approval for a wider range of uses for Tagamet and stepped up the number of line extensions, including a 200mg effervescent tablet. In 1988 a co-promotion agreement with Du Pont led to a 10 per cent increase in the available sales force. Of potentially greater threat to Zantac's dominance of the anti-ulcer market was the introduction of omeprazole (Losec) by the Swedish company Astra in March 1988. Unlike other recent competitors, it had a novel means of action: a proton pump inhibitor with a more powerful and lasting ability to inhibit gastric acid secretion. In order to cover the US effectively, Astra concluded a marketing agreement with Merck, which had a sales force of 1,500, and omeprazole was launched in 1989 under the brand name Losec (now Prilosec). As a result of such intense competition, Zantac's market share in the US peaked in 1989 and began a slow but progressive decline. Despite this, sales of Zantac continued to grow, showing that the gastro-intestinal market had not yet reached its limits.

The United States, being the largest and most profitable national market for pharmaceuticals, has been subject to the closest scrutiny by the major manufacturers. Sometimes a fine line has to be drawn between legitimate promotion and unacceptable aggression. During the 1960s and 1970s, Glaxo had been criticised for failing to exploit commercial opportunities, and this was perhaps followed by some overenthusiasm in the 1980s. In May 1986, for example, the FDA complained to Glaxo Inc. about a promotional letter which they had sent to the Hawaii and the California Medical Therapeutics and Drug Advisory Committees, which contained unsubstantiated claims for the superior efficacy of Zantac over Tagamet.[167] The *Washington Post* and other newspapers carried stories that Glaxo Inc. had made 'false and misleading claims for Zantac'.[168] In a legitimate attempt to pursuade the Hawaii and California state formularies to include Zantac, Glaxo had argued that ranitidine had a 'greater efficacy in both acute ulcer healing and prevention of ulcer relapse than cimetidine'. The FDA questioned this assertion and argued that there was 'no adequate or substantial data of which we are aware that shows Zantac is superior in overall effectiveness and/or safety'.[169] Although Glaxo pointed to marginally faster healing rates and fewer hazardous drug interactions, they withdrew the claims from future promotional letters.[170]

Commercial record

In the early years, Glaxo Inc. did not generate any profits as the heavy initial expenditure on land, buildings and staff recruitment exceeded rising sales figures. Operating losses of $2.7 million and $1.9 million were incurred in 1979 and 1980 respectively.[171] However, sales in the US rose from $4.9 million to $13.1 million by 1980 and in 1983, the year that Zantac was launched, achieved $13.6 million, giving the company a 0.62 per cent share of the country's prescription market. This dramatic growth was achieved by the success of a small number of ethical products. The Glaxo representatives worked hard to sell Ventolin and income from this medicine rose to $1,296,000 in 1981, while Beclovent earned $2,136,000, more than doubling its previous annual total of $975,000. In the year 1983–84, further gains accrued and the following figures were recorded for the company's respiratory medicines: Ventolin $23,272,000, Beclovent $3,422,000 and Beconase $7,912,000.[172] Glaxo had also licensed salbutamol, or albuterol as it was known in the US, to Schering, who sold it under the name Proventil. Sales of salbutamol grew progressively during the 1980s so that by the end of the decade Glaxo and Schering together had captured 77 per cent of the medicine's therapeutic class.

Antibiotics were also to play an important part in the commercial success of Glaxo Inc. Given the group's expertise in cephalosporins, great efforts were made by the product development department to accelerate the passage of cefuroxime, a second-generation injectable, through the FDA's regulatory procedures. Sold as Zinacef, it was launched by Glaxo Inc. in 1983 and, though never achieving spectacular sales figures, the product prepared the ground for a more advanced antibiotic. In August 1985, ceftazidime (Fortaz), a third-generation cephalosporin, was introduced in America. Within two years it had claimed 12 per cent of the $565 million cephalosporin market and had surpassed sales of Zinacef. Although one of the most advanced antibiotics available, Fortaz could never hope to achieve the commercial success of Zantac, largely because other pharmaceutical companies, notably Eli Lilly, had developed considerable expertise in the area and had discovered equivalent compounds. Having made their first application in July 1985, Glaxo Inc. were granted FDA approval to market an oral form of their second-generation cephalosporin, cefuroxime axetil. Introduced the following year as Ceftin (known as Zinnat in the UK), it was Glaxo's first oral antibiotic sold in the United States. Ceftin rapidly became the company's leading antibiotic with sales of £141,251,000 in 1992, considerably more than those for Fortaz (£45,681,000) and Zinacef (£35,958,000). By 1992 Glaxo Inc. had established itself in the US as an important distributor of antibiotics, having achieved an 11.5 per cent share of the market for injectable cephalosporins and 12.1 per cent of that for their oral counterparts.

Cardiovascular medicine has assumed great importance in the US, with one in four Americans reportedly suffering from hypertension. This has, of course, attracted a large number of medicines designed to reduce blood pressure. In September 1984, when labetalol hydrochloride (Trandate) was introduced by Glaxo Inc. in a co-marketing arrangement with Schering, there were already over fifty related products available. At the end of its first year, Trandate had earned £14,384,000, which represented 2.7 per cent of the beta-blocker market (or 0.8 percent of the cardiovascular market. Its growth, as might be expected in a highly competitive field was gradual but by 1992 sales totalled £44,340,000, or 6.9 per cent of the total market. Being both an alpha- and beta-antagonist (acting as a vasodilator as well as a cardiac blocker), it was targeted at those patients who had historically responded poorly to existing medication, notably blacks and, in low doses, the elderly.[173]

Given Glaxo's expertise in the UK for the treatment of dermatological disorders, it was also decided to focus on them. Headed by Robert Zeiger, the company established Glaxo Dermatology Products in 1985 with a national sales force of thirty-four and support staff at Research Triangle Park. Its first task was to launch clobetasol propionate, a synthetic corticosteriod for the short-term treatment of severe inflammatory skin conditions such as recalcitrant eczema and psoriasis. Although it had been sold in the UK under the name Dermovate, it was decided to market the product as Temovate. It proved a considerable success with sales of £2,933,000 in 1986, rising to £17,094,000 six years later. In 1988, Glaxo Inc. concluded a co-promotion agreement with Schering-Plough for the sale of alclometasone dipropionate (Aclovate), a mild potency steroid for eczema and similar disorders. Launched in 1991, fluticasone propionate (Cutivate), developed at Greenford as a potent but specific treatment for eczema and psoriasis, soon established itself in the United States as an important specialist product. In 1989 Glaxo Inc. had obtained approval to market oxiconazole nitrate (Oxistat), an anti-fungal cream for body ringworm (tinea corporis), jock itch (tinea cruris) and athlete's foot (tinea pedis). The product had been licensed from the Swiss company, Siegfried Pharmaceuticals, but was manufactured at Zebulon. With three dermatological medicines, Glaxo Inc's share of the market rose to 6.3 per cent in 1990 and by 1993 was 7.5 per cent.

During the 1970s the pharmaceutical industry had been criticised for focusing its research on common diseases and neglecting those with a relatively low or localised incidence even though their impact on a region or small population might be highly significant. In response to this and some government pressure, the Pharmaceutical Manufacturers' Association set up a Commission on Drugs for Rare Diseases to facilitate the provision of medicines for 'orphan' diseases. [174] In 1983 the Orphan Drug Act was passed to grant pharmaceutical companies a seven-year period of market exclusivity to cover medicines which could no longer be patented in order to encourage them to undertake costly development work. In 1989 Glaxo Inc. introduced its first orphan drug, ethanolamine oleate, which had earlier been sold in Canada and the UK by Evans Medical as a scleroscant in the treatment of varicose veins. Glaxo Inc. developed its use to prevent bleeding from oesophageal varices, a potentially life-threatening condition, arising from cirrhosis of the liver. It was estimated that 50,000 people suffered from oesophageal varices in the United States, of whom around 17,500 would experience fatal bleeds in a year. [175]

In November 1983 addressing the Pharmaceutical Advertising Council at its meeting in Secaucus, New Jersey, Ruvane took the opportunity to assess the achievements of Glaxo Inc. over the previous five years. With sales of $200.5 million, an increment of 294 per cent, it was the 'fastest-growing pharmaceutical company' in the country.[176] He quoted the judgement of the *New York Times*, which had observed of the acquisition of Meyer Laboratories that 'Glaxo is entering the American market with too little too late'[177] – a view echoed by financial commentators in the UK. Describing the embryonic business as a 'new kid on the block', Ruvane recalled their success in marketing Ventolin and Becotide, both in competition with their former ally, Schering. These two products had given Glaxo Inc. recognition from the medical profession and established a base in market share. From these foundations, they had been able to challenge SmithKline's dominance of the anti-ulcer market and in 1983 launched Zantac throughout the United States.[178] Ruvane remarked with a little hyperbole that the company had taken on

> a whole new personality. The old Meyers' reps were hard-sell, low-tech. For Glaxo's ethical line, we needed professional-sell, high-tech. But, we wanted to retain a certain amiable flintiness that the Meyers' reps had. I think we are developing a staff with the best of these qualities. We now have 450 professional field reps. Seventy of these are hospital detailers. The average age is 30. They are dynamos … souped-up professionals who give up their vacations to get a new compound to market. We call them the 'foreign legion', because we hired them wherever we could find reps with top qualifications.[179]

In fact, the Meyer representatives were better quality than Ruvane suggested and many were held in high regard by the physicians they regularly visited; their experience and reliability had been regarded by Bide and Smart as key reasons for acquiring the company.[180]

The objective set for Glaxo Inc. at the time of Ruvane's appointment was to rank in the top fifteen pharmaceutical companies in the United States by 1988. In fact, so rapid was the growth in its turnover, that it had achieved the goal three years earlier (Table 26) and moved into fourth place in 1987. Glaxo Inc. expanded so fast because of its ability to capture market share from competitors, though as the rising number of employees showed this was not achieved without substantial costs in recruitment and capital spending in office buildings, production facilities and laboratories.

Organisational and managerial change

By 1982 a rudimentary structure was in place at Glaxo Inc. Ruvane deliberately avoided constructing a highly defined organisational hierarchy as he believed that it would inhibit growth in a period when flexibility was at a premium. His philosophy was that 'any structure will work, if you put the right people in the right places'.[181] Individual managers found themselves with considerable freedom and responsibility. With only 140 staff in the first headquarters at Research Triangle, the business could not afford specialists to cover all functions in detail. Executive authority was vested with Joseph Ruvane as president and five vice presidents: Philip Priola (administration and corporate secretary), Dr Peter Wise (new product development), Bernard Remmelts (technical affairs), Alan Steigrod (sales and marketing) and J. Bryan Williams, succeeded in 1983 by Tom Haber (finance), while Tom D'Alonzo (general counsel) was appointed in the same year. It was essential to maintain flexibility as complicated or rigid reporting lines would have impeded decision-making and enterprise. As a result, the hierarchy was straightforward and based on function. Growth was frenetic: in 1984, for example, 454 staff joined Glaxo Inc.

The largest of the departments was sales and marketing, which by the end of 1985, numbered 864.[182] There were seven regional managers, sixty-six district managers and 627 representatives organised from North Carolina and five regional offices in Atlanta, Chicago, Dallas, Los Angeles and Danbury, reporting to James Butler director of sales. In addition, there were 164 hospital representatives, under Jerry Ennis, who had succeeded Richard A. Gurley, also organised on a territorial basis. As the number of products that Glaxo Inc. was authorised to market by the FDA grew and as its sales forces continued to expand, this structure became unwieldy. In July 1988 five operating divisions were created, comprising three sales groups (Glaxo Pharmaceuticals, Allen & Hanburys, Glaxo Dermatological Products) together with two support groups (Sales and Marketing Services, and Strategic Development and Corporate Sales). The sales groups were structured about common therapeutic areas and reflected their progenitors in the UK. Glaxo Pharmaceuticals, led by James Butler, marketed ranitidine (Zantac), ceftazidime (Fortaz), cefuroxime (Zinacef), cefuroxime axetil (Ceftin) and cepthalothin sodium (Seffin), while the Allen & Hanburys division, under Bob Zeiger, had a respiratory focus including betamethasone dipropionate (Beclovent and Beconase), albuterol (Ventolin and Volmax), labetalol (Trandate) and isradipine (Dynacirc) licensed from Sandoz. Jon McGarity led the Glaxo Dermatological Products division and had responsibility for Corticaine, clobetasol propionate (Temovate) and in the following year oxiconazole nitrate (Oxistat). In December 1989 as part of the strategy of focusing on novel prescription medicines Glaxo Inc. sold its general products line, including Corticaine and the Vicon vitamin preparations, to Whitby Pharmaceuticals of Richmond, Virginia, thereby severing the final pharmaceutical link with Meyer Laboratories.

Rapid growth and the continuous recruitment of staff enabled Ruvane to appoint increasing numbers of specialists and the number of departments and vice presidents increased. The reputation of the company and the recognition that North Carolina offered a high quality of life meant that Glaxo Inc. could hire direct through advertisements in the national press and professional journals. Much of this work fell to the human resource department under Ronald McCord. When he joined the company in September 1984, from Mallinckrodt Inc., the personnel department, as it was then called, had five staff but by the end of the following year had grown to twenty-six.[183] In 1985 alone, 383 appointments were made: 156 appointments to professional and managerial posts, 158 to office and laboratory support and 69 to operational positions. Traditionally the US pharmaceutical industry has been characterised by a low turnover of staff with departure rates of about 8 per cent a year compared to 12 per cent for manufacturing in general. Because Glaxo Inc. was able to sustain rapid growth and therefore provide a continuous stream of new opportunities, the company recorded low figures of 3 to 4 per cent during the 1980s and early 1990s. One-third of employees were promoted every year in this period.

In July 1986 Ruvane was appointed to the board of Glaxo Holdings and also given responsibility for its subsidiaries in Central and South America.[184] In order to free him from daily management responsibilities, Dr Ernest Mario was recruited from the Squibb Corporation to be president and chief operating officer, Ruvane becoming chairman of Glaxo Inc. At the time of his appointment, Mario was group vice president and chief executive officer of the Squibb medical products group but, following a restructuring programme, had decided to seek fresh opportunities elsewhere.[185] He knew Richard Sykes from the latter's time at the Princeton research institute and a formal introduction to Paul Girolami was arranged. The two met in New York in June 1986 at Glaxo's Park Avenue offices. They struck an immediate rapport and Mario flew to London by Concorde on a Sunday to meet Bernard Taylor and other board members.

A native of Clifton, New Jersey, Mario had qualified as a pharmacist at Rutgers University and earned his doctorate in physical sciences from the University of Rhode Island at Kingston. He worked for SmithKline in Philadelphia, becoming vice president of manufacturing operations, and joined Squibb in 1977 in a similar capacity. In 1983 he was appointed president and chief executive officer of Squibb medical products and was elected to the parent board in the following year. Having a broad range of experience of the US pharmaceutical industry, Mario was given responsibility for all management matters in Glaxo Inc. except research and licensing, which were retained by Ruvane.

The next two years were a period of uninterrupted and rapid growth. Mario believed in driving the company's products to higher levels of sales and committed large resources to the recruitment of additional salesmen and staff. He was a high-profile and inspirational leader who generated affection among employees and in March 1988, in recognition of these achievements, Mario was appointed to the board of Glaxo Holdings.[186]

In June 1988 Ruvane retired from the board of Glaxo Holdings and took the post of vice chairman of Glaxo Inc. in order that Mario could become chairman and chief executive officer.[187] Ruvane with his orderly and determined style had succeeded in taking the company from 65th place in 1981 to fourth in the ranking of US pharmaceutical companies. It was a remarkable achievement. In 1988 a new administration building was named after Ruvane, a tribute to his leadership in which he had campaigned the cause of Glaxo Inc. within the group and succeeded in establishing a major research and development function in the US.

With Mario's appointment as chairman, a vacancy was created for the office of president, with responsibility for the daily management of the company. In October 1988 Tom D'Alonzo, the executive vice president, having been vice president of manufacturing and engineering, was given the job. A lawyer by training, he had joined Glaxo Inc. in 1983, having been general counsel for Adria Laboratories in Columbus, Ohio.[188] When interviewed by Ruvane, D'Alonzo commented that he doubted whether a company of around 450 employees would generate enough work to keep him busy.[189] He was one of the six vice presidents reporting to Ruvane, responsible for corporate affairs as well as legal matters, and headed the administration division following the retirement of Philip Priola in 1986. After eight months in charge of the Glaxo Inc.'s Zebulon factory, he became executive president in October 1987.

Research and development

Interviewed in July 1982 as president of Glaxo Inc., Joseph Ruvane declared that 'it would be unthinkable for a major pharmaceutical company to not have an R&D presence in the United States'.[190] Yet, the establishment of such a facility was not part of the first five-year plan for the company and the proposal met some resistance in the UK. The group already had major laboratories in Greenford, Ware and Verona and to some it seemed that a fourth site would simply dilute or duplicate activities. Ruvane, however, continued to lobby for a research role on the grounds that Glaxo Inc. could not take its place among the leading pharmaceutical companies in the United States so long as its activities were limited to sales and secondary manufacture. It needed its own research and development to counter the view among its competitors that the subsidiary was simply the outpost of a UK parent. In 1984 Ruvane persuaded Girolami of his case and in July the Holdings board approved the expenditure of $9 million (£6.8 million) for the construction of a 40,000sq.ft. Science Building adjacent to the administrative headquarters at Research Triangle Park.[191] Girolami told the board that the US pharmaceutical market

> has its own particular requirements for the form in which products are packed, the dose to be prescribed and the various methods of giving the medicine to the patient ... Glaxo Inc. has plans to introduce new products at a rapid rate and our pharmaceutical development facilities in the UK, are operating at full stretch, and to relieve the situation ... it is proposed that Glaxo Inc. should establish its own facilities.[192]

In the short term, Glaxo Inc. planned to lease laboratory space at the University of North Carolina, Chapel Hill, until such time as the new Science Building was completed. The nature of the research had yet to be decided and the costings did not include an allocation for equipment which could only be determined when its purpose was defined. Dr David Jack recommended virology as it had important possibilities for pharmaceutical research and did not duplicate the group's current initiatives. During the summer of 1985 a ground-breaking ceremony was performed and foundations were dug in the expectation that the structure would be completed the following year.[193] In the event, the project never came to fruition and the site subsequently became part of a new administration block, which ironically was called the Ruvane Building.

However, the plan to rent laboratories at the University of North Carolina (UNC) proceeded apace and in 1986 Glaxo Inc. renovated the basement of the chemistry building, installing modern analytical equipment.[194] A chemistry team remained there for four years, leaving in 1991. In addition, the company constructed a cell biology building on the UNC campus which undertook research into cancer and virology. When the Glaxo scientists transferred to new premises at Research Triangle Park (see p. 397), their former laboratories were given to the university. Although it proved to have been a mutually rewarding partnership between an institution of higher education and industry, at the time it had encouraged a lively debate about the propriety of a publicly funded state university allowing its facilities to be used by a private, profit-making organisation and raised fears that a mission to seek knowledge for its own sake might become tainted by commercial motives.

An American culture

Although the subsidiary of a British holding company, Glaxo Inc. was consciously designed to derive its ethos and managerial methods from the indigenous business culture. In the winter of 1977–78, Bide had decided that the company should be managed by US nationals and should act in a typically American manner. Great efforts were made to encourage the staff of Meyer Laboratories to remain and recruitment focused on other US pharmaceutical companies rather than encouraging existing Glaxo employees in the UK and elsewhere to cross the Atlantic to work in Florida. The only Englishman to occupy a senior executive post in the early years, Dr Peter Wise, had already worked in America from October 1969. The appointment of Ruvane as president of Glaxo Inc. in October 1981 emphasised this strategy. In turn, he recruited managers and representatives from a range of pharmaceutical companies to prevent thinking at Glaxo Inc. from becoming dominated by a single philosophy and to foster the emergence of a fresh culture. Differences arose when the experimental and entrepreneurial approach taken by the US subsidiary came into conflict with the established methods employed in Glaxo's major operating companies. An early debate concerned the type of information technology that Glaxo Inc. should adopt. Peter Dobson, who had overall responsibility within the group, advocated a network of personal computers purchased from Hewlett Packard, having recently introduced such a system to Glaxo Australia. Ruvane favoured an IBM mainframe system and set up a small committee comprising Bryan Williams and Mike Gallucci, the treasurer, who in turn commissioned Arthur Young to provide technical advice. The information technology experts recommended IBM and Ruvane bought a mainframe rather than the mini-computers adopted by Glaxo.

It was perhaps a reflection not only of the growing importance of Glaxo Inc. within the group's world-wide operations but also its wish to be considered a truly American enterprise that in February 1987 the Holdings board took the decision to list its shares on the New York Stock Exchange.[195] The Bank of New York was appointed to issue Glaxo American Depositary Receipts.[196] Formal listing followed in April and henceforth Glaxo stock could be traded in America.[197] Large numbers of physicians who had been prescribing the company's products were encouraged by the listing to purchase Glaxo shares, and as sales continued to rise, they prospered from their investments. This, no doubt, served to reinforce the impression of Glaxo Inc. as a truly American enterprise.

George Bernard Shaw is reported to have described Britain and America as 'two countries divided by a common language', implying that linguistic similarity conceals significant cultural differences. As Glaxo Inc. has grown in importance (in 1993–94, for example, it contributed 43 per cent to the group's turnover, greater than any other territorial grouping, Europe as a whole totalling 35 per cent),[198] so there has been a need for closer co-operation between the holding company based in London and its largest subsidiary. This process has been encouraged by an exchange of staff at senior levels. For example, Dr Ian Skidmore, who became head of development at the Research Park laboratories, had been based at Ware, while Mario transferred from North Carolina to London as chief executive of Glaxo Holdings. In recent years, teaching programmes and seminars have been organised for managers to draw attention to the cultural differences to prevent misunderstandings and encourage effective communication. An outward example of how US business methods have influenced behaviour in the UK was provided in 1995 when the option of wearing 'smart casual' clothes was introduced for head office staff, this being a well-established practice in America.

This has been the story of an outstanding business success. It began with a carefully planned strategy to minimise what was an inherently risky operation – to take on the leading American pharmaceutical companies in their home territory. The choice of Meyer as a vehicle for the assault gave Glaxo a small but well-trained team of representatives on which it could build sales of its own products. Because this was an American business and because Glaxo continued to recruit US nationals, the company avoided the impression of being a foreign interloper and arrived as a UK company that wished to invest in domestic enterprise. Zantac was vital in generating income for investment in both staff and a modern headquarters, and the co-marketing arrangement negotiated with Roche was a masterstroke. This partnership gave the youthful Glaxo Inc. a national sales force of the size and financial resources to challenge SmithKline. The combination of a world-beating product and the careful construction of a dynamic organisation took Glaxo Inc. from sixty-fourth place to number one in only fifteen years – an almost unbelievable achievement.

EUROPE,
THE COMMONWEALTH
AND THE FAR EAST

§

A FUNDAMENTAL SHIFT in the pattern of Glaxo's trade across the world took place in the thirty years from 1962. Originally, most of the group's business was in the UK, together with the Commonwealth where India and Pakistan were of greatest importance (Table 27, p. 458). Subsidiaries on the Continent also earned significant sales, though these were dominated by the Italian company, which had its own secondary manufacturing facilities. This geographical distribution was conditioned by the fact that around 40 per cent of turnover was generated by food products, which sold widely in Asia and had an established market in Britain. As an increasing proportion of Glaxo's turnover arose from pharmaceuticals, so the relative significance of both regions declined. During the late sixties and seventies considerable investment was channelled into Europe, subsidiaries being set up in Portugal, Spain, Sweden, Austria and Switzerland, while existing sales organisations in France and Germany diversified into secondary manufacture. With the relative decline of Commonwealth markets, the Continent assumed a particular importance during the mid seventies, accounting for 35 per cent of sales. Although the group's European subsidiaries continued to grow during the eighties and nineties, phenomenal expansion in the US saw their contribution to turnover fall. As late as 1980 North and Latin America together earned only 12 per cent of sales, but ten years later generated 47 per cent. The Far East, including Japan, did not prove a particularly fruitful area for the group, its contribution amounting to only three per cent in 1994, though the region remains, in view of its size and wealth, a market of great potential.

France

Although the Nathans had set up a roller-drying factory at Le Breuil-en-

Ange in the dairy region of Calvados in 1913 (see p. 18), little interest was subsequently shown in the Continent. Only in Italy did Glaxo Laboratories establish a European subsidiary in the interwar period and this, once the Second World War had ended, remained a focus for continental investment. Until the early sixties, Jephcott's interest in overseas markets continued to be oriented towards the Commonwealth and in particular India, Pakistan and Australia. In 1961, when Britain applied to join the European Common Market for the first time, Glaxo reviewed its policy towards the Continent, aware that it had been neglected.[1] Outside Italy, Glaxo had made very little headway: in Belgium, a joint company (Glaxo/Union Chimique Belge) had been established in 1960 but progress had been 'slow and difficult', compounded by local tax increases and tight controls over prices.[2] The group had inherited representation in France through the acquisition of Evans Medical, which had set up a 51 per cent owned subsidiary, Evans S.A. (France). A comparatively low turnover of £300,000 per annum resulted in losses[3] and it was concluded that the only solution was to purchase the 49 per cent share held by Laboratoires Delagrange S.A. so that the business could be managed as a direct subsidiary of Glaxo.[4] This having been done, the turnover of the French subsidiary, renamed Laboratoires Glaxo-Evans,[5] rose steadily from 5.8 million francs in 1961 to 14.2 million francs (of which 9.5 million derived from milk and farinaceous foods and 4.6 million francs from medicines) in 1963, though even this rise was not enough to avoid a loss of 0.13 million francs.[6]

In June 1965, the subsidiary at last earned a profit, 489,200 francs, but it had become apparent that growth could not continue without investment in secondary production. In 1967 a site at Evreux, about 100 kilometres northwest of Paris, was acquired for a factory.[7] Profits had increased steadily, rising from £12,750 in 1964–65 to £204,700 in 1966–67,[8] and to protect this valuable business in a nation that was sometimes hostile to overseas competitors it was proposed to invest in the manufacture of the pharmaceuticals contracted to Delagrange and to IBF, which made Ceporin. A growing proportion of Laboratoires Glaxo's total turnover was earned by pharmaceuticals rather than foods, the former contributing 42 per cent in 1964–65 and 52 per cent in 1966–67. The cost of the factory was estimated at 4.4 million francs, which was just over three times the annual bill paid to outside manufacturers.[9] Although Glaxo's French business was not large compared with that in the Commonwealth, it was significant in relation to its competitors. In 1967 Glaxo was the seventh largest foreign pharmaceutical company with a market share of 1.2 per cent on a turnover of 44 million francs, only Sandoz (3.2 per cent), Roche (2.1), Pfizer-Clin (1.7), Geigy (1.6), Guigoz (1.6) and Labaz (1.4) were larger. In authorising expenditure on a new factory, the Glaxo board believed they could develop a substantial presence in a market dominated by indigenous producers.[10] In 1967, for example, UK manufacturers accounted for only 10 per cent of sales in Britain (49 per cent falling to US companies), while in France 78 per cent of sales derived from local drugs companies.[11]

Laboratoires Glaxo prospered in the early eighties, encouraging further investment in its Evreux factory. After ranitidine (marketed as Azantac), Ventolin and Becotide became two of its leading products. Azantac, launched in 1984 by Laboratoires Glaxo and licensed to Laboratoires Fournier as Raniplex, rapidly established a powerful presence in the anti-ulcer market. Sales of ranitidine lifted the French company from thirty-fifth to twenty-fourth place in only nine months,[12] and when turnover rose by 30 per cent in 1987, Glaxo improved its ranking in France to sixteenth.[13]

Germany

In the immediate post-war years Glaxo ignored Germany, but as enmities weakened the board recognised that they could not afford to reject this crucial market. In August 1962, discussions with Dr H. Harms, the chairman of E. Merck A.G. of Darmstadt, were opened.[14] Agreement was ratified in June 1963, whereby Glaxo would market the German company's speciality products in the UK under the name E. Merck A.G. while Merck would sell Glaxo's medicines in Germany, a royalty of 10 per cent being paid in each case. In February 1964, Wilson decided to establish a wholly owned organisation because 'of the immediate or imminent availability of a number of products with a substantial potential market in West Germany'.[15] A turnover of £250,000 was set as the target for the first year of trading, to be trebled over three years, at which time the subsidiary was to break even.[16]

Having established a sales organisation (Glaxo Pharmazeutika GmbH) in 1969, W. F. H. Robinson, the managing director of the German subsidiary, drew up plans for the construction of a small secondary production unit[17] and administrative offices.[18] Glaxo agreed to the expenditure of £670,000 in May 1971 and the factory was constructed in an industrial zone to the west of Bad Oldesloe[19] during the following year.[20] Because 80 per cent of the subsidiary's turnover derived from sales of Betnovate and Betnesol creams, ointments and lotions, it was decided to manufacture these dermatologicals from bulk ingredients supplied from Montrose.

In 1969 the German market for prescription medicines was ranked fifth in the world by sales and was double the size of the UK. However, Glaxo Pharmazeutika was a relatively minor participant with a share of 0.14 per cent and sales of 3.9 million marks. Despite its potential rewards, Germany was 'difficult because of the fairly conservative attitudes of the medical profession, the less welcoming attitude of foreign companies, and the competitive atmosphere of the industry'.[21] Nevertheless, by 1970 the embryonic subsidiary had made progress and its eighty staff recorded a turnover of 5.5 million marks and profits of 627,000 marks. Managers forecast that sales would increase by 250 per cent over six years with profits rising in step, maintaining the margin of 65 per cent.[22]

To launch a range of cephalosporins while lacking the manpower to do it, Glaxo concluded two agreements with Hoechst in January 1973.[23] Under the terms of the first, Glaxo Pharmazeutika contracted the secondary production of cephalothin (Ceporacin) and cephaloridine (Ceporin) to Hoechst, the active ingredients being supplied in bulk from the UK. The products were to be marketed jointly in West Germany under Glaxo trademarks, though both companies' names appeared on the labelling and Hoechst retained 75 per cent of the margin on sales.[24] The second agreement on cephalexin (Ceporex) granted Hoechst agency rights with similar terms. The nature of these arrangements was determined by German cartel law, which required 'vertical' agreements; that is between enterprises on at least two economic levels. As a result, Glaxo had to contract out the secondary manufacture of two of the three antibiotics.[25] The introduction of the cephalosporins and a range of corticosteroid products (notably Becotide in April 1975)[26] led to progressive growth in both turnover and profits, which rose to £9.2 million and £1.1 million respectively in 1976. The following year when total sales increased by 21 per cent to £10.1 million, cephalosporin antibiotics contributed 39.6 per cent of the total, corticosteroid products 49.9 per cent and Ventolin 9.3 per cent. In view of this progress and a longer-term goal to assume complete control over the manufacture and distribution of Glaxo's cephalosporins, in December 1977 the main board authorised the expenditure of £2.5 million at Bad Oldesloe on the construction of additional offices and secondary production facilities.[27] In 1978, when sales totalled £14.1 million, Glaxo Pharmazeutika was deemed a 'mature company', having become Glaxo's fourth largest operating subsidiary outside the UK, exceeded in size only by India, Italy and Japan.[28]

By the early 1980s, the German pharmaceutical market was the third largest in the world with a value of £2.6 billion.[29] Glaxo recognised the difficulty of challenging German companies on their home territory and, in view of Glaxo Pharmazeutika's ranking at thirty-second place,[30] decided that a co-marketing arrangement with an established domestic producer (Merck A.G. in twelfth place with a turnover of £51.3 million) represented the most effective strategy. In October 1981 Glaxo agreed to purchase a 50 per cent holding in Cascan GmbH, then a wholly owned subsidiary of

E. Merck of Darmstadt. The jointly owned company, renamed Cascan-Glaxo, served as a co-marketing vehicle for either parent's products.[31]

Throughout the 1980s Glaxo Pharmazeutika prospered with rising turnover and profits. Turnover increased from £15.7 million in 1982 to £29.8 million by 1987, doubling the company's share of the prescription market to over 2 per cent.[32] The principal areas of commercial success were ranitidine (marketed in Germany as Zantic) which accounted for 44 per cent of sales in 1987, the cephalosporins Zinacef and Ceporex (12 per cent), respiratory products (Ventolin, 13 per cent, and Becotide, 6 per cent) while the corticosteroids, Betnovate and Dermovate, contributed a further 14 per cent.[33]

Other European subsidiaries

Most overseas subsidiaries set up by Glaxo in the post-war era, including those in Switzerland (1963), Sweden (1967), Denmark (1968) and Austria (1975), were sales and marketing organisations that demanded relatively little capital investment. This was not the case in Spain. The decision in 1976 to build a secondary production plant at Alca la de Henares, near Madrid, was determined by the national regulations for the establishment of wholly owned companies.[34] Hitherto, Glaxo's products had been manufactured and sold by Inibsa, a Spanish pharmaceutical business based in Barcelona. In 1969, turnover reached £0.5 million, or 0.4 per cent of the national market, which was then growing at 11 per cent a year. In view of this potential it was decided to set up a subsidiary,[35] though negotiations with both Inibsa and the state authorities were protracted. To prevent the company from being solely an import and sales business, the government had insisted that any enterprise also engage in primary manufacture and research. The project to build a plant, originally conceived in February 1974, was costed at £4.4 million, and the new subsidiary named Safesa Iberica S.A. The expenditure was justified by the importance of the Spanish pharmaceutical market, valued at £464 million and ranked sixth in the world.[36] Furthermore, prices to wholesalers had been growing at an annual rate of 15 to 20 per cent largely because of the dominance of prescription medicines, which led the group to conclude that Spain offered 'great potential for Glaxo products'.[37] This prediction proved well founded despite the absence of patent protection for novel medicines. Under John Cuthbert, the subsidiary's first managing director, sales of respiratory products and later ranitidine, which had to compete against pirate copies, grew impressively so that by 1988 Glaxo S.A. had captured almost 3 per cent of the Spanish prescription market.[38]

Although most of Glaxo's overseas business was conducted through sub-sidiaries, agencies had sometimes played a key role in establishing the company's name and products. Nowhere was this truer than in Greece, where the Harvalias family had been Glaxo's representatives. On the death of their father in 1954, the patriarch's two daughters took over the agency. Euphrosyne Patiniotis became the chief executive and Margaret the production director. In September 1975, when Stam. Harvalias S.A. (renamed Glaxo AEBE three years later) was acquired as a wholly owned subsidiary, Mrs Patiniotis became the first woman chief executive within Glaxo Holdings.

During the 1970s and early 1980s subsidiary companies within Europe largely operated independently, reporting to Douglas Back, the Holdings director responsible for the Developing Trade Areas Directorate, though each had access to a parent board counsellor as well. In the early 1980s John Farrant, who had succeeded Back as the board member responsible for the region, set up two confederations, Glaxo North Europe and Glaxo South Europe, each with an area controller in order to effect a measure of co-ordination. The former brought together the sales and marketing subsidiaries in Belgium, Denmark, Finland, Holland, Ireland, Norway and Sweden, while the latter included Austria, Greece, Portugal, Switzerland and Turkey. The larger companies in Germany, Spain, Italy and France, with their own manufacturing facilities, were excluded from these confederations. Because the demand for Zantac gave Glaxo's European subsidiaries the potential to grow quickly, Farrant devoted much time to the careful recruitment of senior executives.[39] However, the need to co-ordinate both sales and production operations across the EEC, encouraged the group to set up a formal framework.[40] Called Glaxo Europe, it had no subsidiaries of its own. Dr Mario Fertonani was appointed its chairman and chief executive, while the board was drawn from the managing directors, general managers and area controllers of the group's continental companies. Although marketing tactics were devolved under Girolami, Glaxo Europe was one of the executive instruments employed to ensure that local policies remained within the overall strategy defined by the Holdings company.

India

By 1962, when Glaxo Group was formed, the Indian subsidiary was the largest operating company in terms of capital employed and profits.[41] Glaxo Laboratories (India) was assured of its lead by the opening of the fine chemicals plant at Thana that year. Indeed, its completion marked a zenith in the subsidiary's relative importance as henceforth the focus of the group's international strategy switched first to Europe and then to the United States and Japan. Although both turnover and profits continued to rise the contribution of the Indian company to group earnings declined. The company duplicated many of the activities undertaken by its UK parent: the Thana factory manufactured vitamin A, corticosteroids and other medicines, the roller-drying plant at Aligarh dried buffalo milk for Glaxo and Ostermilk, while the Worli factory, also the administrative headquarters, made both foods (Complan and Farex) and pharmaceuticals.

Reporting on his visit to India in 1962, Palmer concluded that the subsidiary was 'an effective organisation competently administered' and added that his only concern was 'how in the years to come we can secure top management of the quality necessary for ... this very large organisation'.[42] Experienced executives were relatively elderly: R. A. Haryott had just retired as managing director after thirty years' service in the country, while his successor, J. G. Kidd, had only a further four years in office. The management of the company remained largely in the hands of expatriates on lengthy contracts. John Reece, for example, latterly sales director and deputy general manager of Glaxo Laboratories (India), had originally joined the pharmacy unit at Greenford in 1950. Two years later, when Jephcott had asked for volunteers to work overseas, he became a sales promotion manager in Bombay, remaining in India for a further seventeen years.[43] Because of the company's commercial importance to the group, a period in India was considered valuable training for middle-ranking executives and refusal could end a promising managerial career. In 1968, for instance, having been general manager at Ulverston, John Farrant was encouraged to go to India as commercial director on the understanding that he would ultimately become its chief executive.[44] When he left in 1973, the process of recruiting and training local managers was so well advanced that he handed over to the last Briton employed by Glaxo in the country.

Although turnover rose throughout the sixties, the profitability of Glaxo Laboratories (India) fell, declining from 14.4 million rupees to 11.9 million rupees between 1965 and 1968, despite the fact that sales rose from 133.1 to 182.8 million rupees.[45] This was the result of inflationary wage and material costs when prices were subject to rigid government controls. However, an upturn in 1969 saw profits climb to 19.3 million rupees, restoring confidence to the company. The improvement followed the spectacular progress of the Animal Health Division, set up in 1968. Nevertheless, the pharmaceutical business continued to be hampered by state controls, heightened in August 1970 by the implementation of the Drug (Price Control) Order.[46] Glaxo found that the prices of ninety-three of its medicines had been compulsorily reduced and that an application for increases had been granted for only twenty of seventy-one products.[47] As a result, profits in 1971 fell to

15.4 million rupees even though turnover had risen by 10 per cent. Having taken over as managing director in 1970, Farrant realised that considerable efficiencies could be achieved in the running of what had become a large and diverse business if it were divided into self-contained units. Four divisions (Pharmaceuticals, Animal Health, Family Products and Laboratory Chemicals) were created, each having sole responsibility for production and commercial operations.[48] Having weathered the economic storm caused by the 1970 Drug Order, the pharmaceutical division returned a 9 per cent increase in sales during 1971–72, the year of the launch of Ceporan and Ventolin. However, the progress that followed the structural changes was counteracted in 1973 by a downturn in the Indian economy, accentuated by a widespread drought. For the first time in two decades the steady upward trend in turnover was reversed as sales fell by 4.6 per cent. Supplies of buffalo milk became scarce, driving prices to record levels so that sales of the infant products collapsed by almost 40 per cent.[49]

To combat the increasing pressure on margins, S. Bhoothalingam, the chairman of Glaxo Laboratories (India), introduced further structural reforms in January 1974. The company's operations were streamlined by the merger of the pharmaceutical and animal health divisions and setting up three service divisions: finance and secretarial, administration and technical, to support their commercial activities.[50] This reorganisation, together with the introduction of a 'Management by Objectives' programme to define targets for the company as a whole and for its operating divisions, was designed to focus executive effort.[51] Although the changes led to an increase in turnover of 18 per cent, they were not reflected in profits, which fell by 11 per cent to 15.5 million rupees. At this level, profit was 9.5 cent of equity and reserves and, being unacceptably low, threatened the implementation of any plans for capital projects. At a time when Glaxo had just fought off a predatory bid from Beecham and had become aware how perilous its survival was, the board was increasingly reluctant to invest in projects without the prospect of substantial returns.

A measure of recovery in 1976 followed an improvement in the supply of agro-based raw materials and consequent fall in their price.[52] Profits grew well into the eighties despite high inflation. Glaxo continued to experience difficulties with the regulatory authorities. From 1961 increments to the pharmaceutical price index authorised by the government had failed to keep pace with inflation and during the late seventies the company had remained in surplus by cutting costs. By the end of the decade, Bhoothalingam concluded that the company had reached the limit of this process and that permission to raise prices had become critical.[53] In 1979, twenty-seven applications were subject to review, most of which had been pending for eighteen months. The fears expressed by Bhoothalingam were realised in both 1980 and 1981 when profits lagged behind growth in turnover, falling by 22 per cent in 1981. It was not until 1983 that the Indian authorities granted increases to the company's pharmaceutical products, many of which remained at 1977 prices despite inflation.[54]

The most notable feature of 1983 occurred when Glaxo was forced to reduce its equity and share capital to 40 per cent by the Reserve Bank of India under section 29 of the Foreign Exchange Regulation Act of 1973.[55] Glaxo sold 2.8 million equity shares and made a public issue in June of a further 5.6 million equity shares and repaid a preference capital of 8 million rupees to each stockholder.[56] As a result of these dealings, Glaxo, though still the largest single shareholder, no longer had absolute control of its Indian subsidiary. Nevertheless, the planned expansion of the business continued, and work on the secondary production plant in the Ambad Industrial Estate at Nashik, Maharashtra, and the primary production factory at Ankleshwar in Gujarat both pressed ahead. Despite the government's statement that companies with a foreign equity of no more than 40 per cent would be treated as if they were domestic businesses, the delays and difficulties in negotiating increments continued. In 1985, for example, an upturn of 21 per cent in turnover did not translate into higher profits, which rose by only 2.6 per cent. The following year the situation worsened, even though the new bulk chemical factory at Ankleshwar and the formulations plant at Nashik had become fully operational. Manufacturing savings were no longer sufficient to offset rising costs and prices that fell in real terms. In December 1986, the government announced a new policy 'Measures for Rationalisation, Quality Control and Growth of Drugs and the Pharmaceuticals Industry in India' which was followed in August 1987 by an updated Drugs (Prices Control) Order.[57] These reversed the tough market conditions in which the pharmaceutical division had attempted to operate over the previous decade, introducing shorter periods of price controls, higher percentage increases and rewards for good manufacturing practice. In 1985–86 Glaxo launched ranitidine (sold as Zinetac), while industrial licences were granted for the manufacture of cephalexin and griseofulvin. In 1989, turnover of the associated company rose by 14 per cent, largely as a result of rising demand for Zinetac and cephalexin (Ceporex). In 1994, after lengthy negotiations and the adoption of a more liberal attitude by the regulatory authorities, the group was granted permission to re-acquire its majority interest in Glaxo India and it again became a subsidiary.[58]

New Zealand

New Zealand had, of course, been the birthplace of Glaxo's parent, Joseph

Nathan & Co., and though operations remained relatively small scale after 1945, the country continued to hold a special place in the affections of the London headquarters. A new secondary process factory and offices had been constructed at Palmerston North in 1947, the year that John Hurran succeeded Norman Ratcliffe as managing director of Glaxo Laboratories (N.Z.). Hurran, a chemist by training, had been posted overseas to broaden his experience.[59] In April 1954 he was recalled to the UK to be replaced by Roy Stagg, an ebullient pharmacist who had joined the company before the war.[60] Stagg appears to have fallen foul of Jephcott and to have been sent to New Zealand almost as a punishment. He continued to incur the displeasure of Jephcott, who after a visit in 1960 described him as a 'very complete individualist'. He considered that Stagg had failed 'to knot our New Zealand staff together into a team' and relished being surrounded by a 'weird mob'.[61] Griff Hunt, managing director of the Australian subsidiary, supported this view, adding 'his executives are an odd assortment, but in the main … capable. The younger ones are enthusiastic and ambitious, and being so, probably get in one another's hair occasionally.'[62] Among those whom Stagg identified as talented and encouraged were Ken Huse, Tony Hewett and Bernard Taylor.[63] Depending on food products for the bulk of its business, the New Zealand company was characterised by static turnover and falling profits during the 1950s. The unpredictability of the weather bedevilled supplies of milk and the UK's Milk Marketing Board resisted attempts by the subsidiary to increase its exports.

In 1962 the New Zealand subsidiary was capitalised at £754,000 and earned gross profits of £167,000.[64] Despite attempts to build a business in vitamins and veterinary vaccines, the company made the bulk of its turnover from food products and pharmaceuticals imported from the UK and packaged in its factory at Palmerston North.[65] Commercial pressures increased in 1963 when the New Zealand government enforced price reductions on all prescription medicines for which the profit margin was greater than 38 per cent of the production cost.[66] The sixties were a period of modest growth for the New Zealand subsidiary, net profits rising from £53,066 in 1961 to £63,098 in 1967. Betnovate was the New Zealand company's most successful pharmaceutical product, followed by Ceporan. When Betnovate suffered from increasing competition from Synalar and Ultralan, the introduction of Ventolin proved commercially important and by 1972 had secured 38 per cent of its therapeutic class. That year Glaxo ranked third in the national sales league with 8.3 per cent of the prescription market. With the introduction of Becotide, the subsidiary moved to second and then first place in August 1975.[67] The relatively small scale of the New Zealand market enabled Glaxo to achieve a remarkably high share (in 1991, based largely

113. The offices and factory at Palmerston North.

on the success of Zantac, it rose to 17.8 per cent) but it also discouraged the Holdings board from committing major capital resources.

Australia

By 1962 Glaxo Laboratories (Australia) had become the group's third most important company in terms of capital employed. Although many of the problems surrounding antibiotic production at Port Fairy had been resolved, the relatively small scale of its operations threatened its existence should the protective tariff walls ever be lowered. The situation was exacerbated by the mergers with Allen & Hanburys, Evans Medical and later BDH, each of which had Australian subsidiaries. In 1967 the local board expressed their concerns over the administrative and production problems and proposed the concentration of manufacture at Boronia, twenty miles east of Melbourne.[68] Construction began in 1968 and though costs rose to $A3,284,000,[69] the project was completed the following year.

Commercially, the 1960s were a decade of consolidation for the Australian subsidiary marked by modest increases in turnover, which rose consistently from £1.48 million in 1961 to £2.06 million in 1966, and reached $A4.81 million in 1970.[70] Pharmaceuticals contributed the lion's share, while food products declined progressively. This pattern of gradual expansion was reflected in sales figures for the 1970s: $A10.45 million in 1970, $A13.46 million in 1975 and $A24.77 million in 1978. However, in the context of the Australian market the period 1970 to 1978 was one of significant success, with growth rates considerably in excess of the domestic industry. In May 1973, Glaxo subsidiaries achieved an increase of 7.7 per cent on sales against a general rise of 4.0 per cent, margins that were sustained later in the decade.[71] This commercial achievement was the result of a broadening product portfolio, following the launch of Ventolin in 1972 and Becotide in 1974, while Glaxo's traditional strength in antibiotics was reinforced by the introduction of the cephalosporins Ceporex and Ceporacin. By 1975, Ventolin had secured a 72 per cent share of its therapeutic class, so that by 1977 the A & H Division contributed 35 per cent of the subsidiary's total turnover,[72] figures that helped to lift Glaxo Australia Pty up the league table of pharmaceutical companies, rising from eleventh place in 1971, to fifth in 1977 and first in 1989.[73]

Bernard Taylor, as managing director of Glaxo Australia Pty from 1972 to 1982, presided over much of this period of sustained growth. He had joined the group in 1963, working initially as a sales manager in New Zealand before returning to the UK as new products manager for Glaxo Pharmaceuticals. Taylor improved the organisation and training of the representative teams so that subsidiary's share of the prescription market rose from less than 1 to over 4 per cent,[74] while after the launch of Zantac it rose to 10.5 per cent by 1991.[75] Until the early 1980s sales in Australia were greater than in the United States, and it was an indication of the importance attached to the subsidiary that in 1983 Taylor was recalled to Britain to serve as chairman and managing director of Glaxo Pharmaceuticals (UK). Taylor was subsequently succeeded as managing director of Glaxo Australia by Ken Windle, a New Zealand national who had joined the group in his home country as a product development pharmacist.[76] Talent-spotted by Ken Huse, chief executive of the New Zealand subsidiary, Windle was seconded to the UK for two years, and was the first member of staff to be drawn into the centre from abroad, against the current of expatriates seconded to overseas postings. He held a number of sales and marketing positions before being appointed managing director of Glaxo Australia in 1986.

Japan: Shin Nihon and Glaxo-Fuji

After North America, Japan has consistently been the second most important pharmaceutical market of the last thirty years. A population of 124 million and a culture that regards medicines highly combined to generate a powerful and sustained growth in per-capita consumption. In 1975, for example, on average each person consumed medicines worth $92, a figure that rose to $276.7 by 1990 (the corresponding expenditure in America was $124 and that in the European Community was $103).[77] As a result, total spending on pharmaceuticals in Japan has surpassed that of far larger nations, accelerating from $5.72 billion in 1975 to $14.4 billion in 1980.[78] However, the Japanese system of reimbursement (by which the government sets a price to repay hospitals and GPs that have purchased medicines) may exaggerate these figures. Glaxo, for example, sold cephalexin at less than half the sanctioned rate suggesting that the true market value is lower than the official returns. Japan has remained remarkably self-sufficient until recently. Only 3.6 per cent of all drugs prescribed in 1975 were imported, a percentage which fell to 2.1 in 1989, in contrast to 11.1 and 17.5 per cent respectively for the European Community.[79] The Ministry of Health and Welfare had set itself the goal of achieving a stable supply of modern drugs. The most cost-effective way of achieving this objective was to license medicines from foreign producers, so that Japanese industry manufactured domestic formulations of products discovered overseas. Protective tariffs were introduced to give indigenous companies a secure market and they grew almost exclusively on home sales. The leading Western pharmaceutical companies rely on exports, deriving at least one-third of their turnover from foreign markets, while their counterparts in Japan rarely sell more than 6 to 8 per cent of their output abroad.[80]

In recent years the escalating cost of medicines has compelled the Japanese Ministry of Health to weaken the protective wall surrounding its domestic manufacturers. It has reduced reimbursement levels by over 30 per cent since 1985 and producers of innovative medicines have been allowed higher charges. A number of multinationals, including Glaxo, have gained the right to manufacture and distribute their medicines, so that by 1990 21 per cent of pharmaceutical sales in Japan had been captured by overseas producers.[81] Glaxo had not been as successful as some of its leading international competitors, in 1985 being ranked fifty-fourth by sales, having gained a market share of only 0.4 per cent.[82]

Glaxo had taken its first tentative steps into the Japanese market in November 1954 when Shin Nihon was granted the exclusive right to market and distribute propyliodone (Dionosil),[83] a radiological medium developed by Glaxo in 1952 for the investigation of bronchial carcinoma and other tumours of the lung.[84] Shin Nihon had its origins in a business founded in 1950 by Toshio Konishi, a graduate of Meiji University who had worked in the public health bureau of the Ministry of Health before setting up an agency for the import of raw cotton. In 1951, having named the company Shin Nihon Jitsugyo (which translates as 'New Japan Trading Co.'), he diversified into medical instruments, opened a drug store, and signed an agreement with Connaught Medical Research Laboratories of the University of Toronto to market their insulin in Japan. With the collapse of the

114. Bernard Taylor in February 1986 shortly after being appointed chief executive of Glaxo Holdings in succession to Sir Paul Girolami.

textile boom following the end of the Korean War, Shin Nihon Jitsugyo went into liquidation. In the same year, Konishi re-established the company solely for the import of pharmaceutical products and medical instruments. Because of the damage caused by the Pacific War, the Japanese drugs industry remained constrained by shortages of capital and equipment. Konishi proved himself adept at selling Dionosil and other prescription products so that in 1955 he was appointed as Glaxo's sole agent in Japan. Ambitious to enter secondary manufacture and undertake development work, in November 1954 Konishi set up Fuji Pharmaceutical Laboratories, and two years later the plant came into operation producing Dionosil under licence. Although still a relatively small company employing eighteen staff in 1960, its turnover had risen to ¥285 million. Two years later a new factory and laboratories, principally for the manufacture of insulin, were completed for Fuji at Yahara, Nerima-ku, in the suburbs of Tokyo.

Although sales of Glaxo medicines (chiefly Ceporin and Betnovate) reached £1.5 million in 1966–67 with a net profit of 62 per cent,[85] the group was concerned by its general lack of progress. Maurice Williams, who had been assigned from Glaxo-Allenburys (Export) to Japan, concluded that the nature of the relationship with Shin Nihon prevented the emergence of anything like 'a company image … other than that arising from … trade names on the sales packs'.[86] Recognising the difficulties encountered by foreign pharmaceutical companies seeking to establish themselves there, Williams suggested the formation of a joint venture to handle sales and distribution like their competitors Japan Lederle and Japan Merck Banyu. As a result, Williams was authorised to open discussions with Shin Nihon on

ways of setting up a collaborative enterprise. Whilst Toshio Konishi declared himself 'favourably inclined' towards a joint enterprise, he argued
that product application, import licences and negotiations with the health
authorities should remain under his exclusive authority.[87] This led to Glaxo
acquiring 40 per cent of Fuji Pharmaceutical Laboratories in October 1968
at a cost of around £80,000.[88] The latter was, in effect, a wholly owned subsidiary of Shin Nihon, 70 per cent of its shares being held by Toshio Konishi.[89] Williams observed that the acquisition represented 'a small step
within the heavily entrenched local industry', surrendered in part because
98 per cent of Shin Nihon's turnover was in Glaxo products.[90]

It rapidly became clear that the existing plant at Nerima-ku could not
cope with the rising volume of business. In 1967–68, for example, Glaxo
had sold pharmaceuticals worth £1.7 million in Japan (generating profits
of £1.2 million) through Shin Nihon, figures that rose to £4.1 million and
£2.5 million respectively in 1970–71.[91] Construction of a new factory at
Imaichi, north of Tokyo, began in March 1971 supervised by Bernard
Remmelts and was completed two years later when manufacture
transferred from the older Nerima-ku site.[92] Remmelts then remained in
Japan as production director, playing a key role in the operational
development of the factory. Despite this important investment, Shin
Nihon continued to market and distribute Glaxo products. Because Shin
Nihon had successfully guided a number of products through the complex
registration procedures, Wilson moved carefully but believed it was
imperative that Glaxo acquire a holding in the company and its
distribution subsidiary, International Drug House.[93]

Konishi agreed to Glaxo's acquisition of 20 per cent of Shin Nihon Jitsugyo for £1.65 million, and a 50 per cent interest in the equity of International Drug House for £21,000.[94] The joint company, called Nihon-Glaxo,
was composed of ten directors, five drawn from Glaxo and five from Shin
Nihon.[95] It was agreed to change the name of International Drug House
(which was already jointly owned) to Nippon Glaxo and to develop it as a
marketing and wholesaling business. Under this scheme therefore there
were three companies: Shin Nihon Jitsugyo (80 per cent owned by the Konishi family and 20 per cent by Glaxo), Glaxo-Fuji Pharmaceutical Laboratories (which was responsible for secondary manufacture and whose
proprietorship was divided between Glaxo with 40 per cent and Shin
Nihon with 60 per cent), and Nippon Glaxo, a trading company, owned
equally by Glaxo and Shin Nihon.

After a visit to Japan in May 1973, Back expressed concern over the future
of Nippon Glaxo. The company appeared to have few medicines to sell and
its executives appeared to be intimidated by the board of Shin Nihon,

115. The entrance to Glaxo Nippon's administration building at the Imaichi factory, north of Tokyo.

which appeared reluctant 'to channel new products into this company'.[96] He summarised the difficulties encountered by Glaxo but believed that regulatory changes would ease the situation:

> a large part of the local profits still go to Shin Nihon, although this company will in the future increasingly be only a middle man between Glaxo Holdings and Nippon Glaxo. I can envisage a time ... when we may wish to merge Nippon Glaxo and Glaxo Fuji and transfer the Japanese agency to the newly merged company in which we would have a 50 per cent stake.[97]

To improve relationships with Shin Nihon and the domestic management of Nippon Glaxo, it was decided to offer opportunities to 'Hiroshi Konishi and other young Japanese executives to visit the UK for training and to gain closer acquaintance with the company's products and business philosophy'. [98] In 1975, following the relaxation of domestic regulations, Glaxo increased its holdings in both Shin Nihon (raised to 30 per cent at a cost of £1.3 million)[99] and Glaxo-Fuji (increased from 40 to 50 per cent).[100] In addition, Toshio Konishi agreed that Glaxo would be allowed to acquire a 50 per cent holding in Shin Nihon by June 1977, and that if he, or his family, sold any shares in the business that the group would be given first refusal.[101] In 1976 Austin Bide became a director of Shin Nihon and Glaxo's holding was raised to 44 per cent before reaching parity in May of the following year.[102] To simplify and rationalise the group's holdings, in July 1979 it was arranged with Shin Nihon that Nippon Glaxo and Glaxo-Fuji would merge as Nippon Glaxo, responsible for secondary manufacture and sales and marketing.[103] Nevertheless, the ownership and practical operation of Glaxo's Japanese subsidiary remained complex and confused. The group had only 50 per cent of Nippon Glaxo and, although it had a similar stake in Shin Nihon, this left the Japanese executive team led by Toshio Konishi with considerable authority. Little could be achieved without their agreement.

At the beginning of 1980, Dr Tom Walker, formerly head of research and development at Greenford, was appointed a director of Nippon Glaxo. He immediately set up Glaxo KK, a wholly owned subsidiary to finance the major development planned in Singapore (see p. 433). Remaining in Japan until the middle of 1983, Walker concentrated on establishing links between Nippon Glaxo and other Japanese pharmaceutical companies, as these relationships had been handled almost exclusively by Shin Nihon.[104] Shortly before his arrival, it had been decided to abandon co-marketing arrangements and to promote all new products in-house. But, this resulted in falling orders and Glaxo decided to return to co-promotion. In the past, the choice of partner and the terms had been negotiated by Shin Nihon and Toshio Konishi wished to re-introduce this principle. Bide refused and lengthy discussions between Girolami and the Konishi family led to Nippon Glaxo being granted the right to negotiate such deals with Japanese pharmaceutical companies in return for an undertaking that Glaxo would not attempt to increase its 50 per cent holding in the business.

Nippon Glaxo made uneven progress through the 1980s as sales rose from ¥14,860 in 1980 to ¥41,493 in 1990, having fallen back in the middle years of the decade (Table 28, p. 459). New medicines marketed by Nippon Glaxo, either independently or in conjunction with a domestic company, included: Zinacef (with Tanabe) and Beconase, both in 1982, Trandate (with Takeda) in 1983, and Zantac (with Sankyo) in 1984. The launch of Zantac was considered particularly important. It had generated huge commercial success for Glaxo Inc. in the United States and it was hoped that it would transform Nippon Glaxo into one of the leading pharmaceutical businesses in Japan. In July 1983 a co-marketing arrangement was concluded with Sankyo, one of the largest Japanese pharmaceutical companies, and a jointly owned company, Glaxo-Sankyo, was set up. Tom Walker had recommended a partnership with Takeda, to whom Glaxo had licensed griseofulvin, but was overruled by Girolami, who believed that with Sankyo they could reproduce something of the promotional drive that had followed from the combination of the Roche and Glaxo Inc. sales forces in America. Although sales rapidly achieved a market share of 10 per cent, they never moved significantly beyond that point and these figures compared poorly with Glaxo's results in western Europe and the United States.

In February 1987 the board decided to float Glaxo Holdings on the Tokyo Stock Exchange at the same time as a listing was obtained in New York.[105] Ordinary shares of 50p each were to be traded and the Toyo Trust Co. was appointed as the company's agents. This was designed to root Glaxo more deeply in the Japanese economy, and to enable physicians and others who had dealings with the company to purchase its shares without having to resort to overseas exchanges. In July 1988 Shin Nihon and Nippon Glaxo merged to form a single company, with almost 500 employees and sales of ¥40,000 million, under the Nippon Glaxo name. Despite the determined efforts of the group and a succession of managers sent from the UK, sales in Japan never took off as they did in the United States. Although internal regulations undoubtedly presented a barrier to foreign pharmaceutical manufacturers, some of Glaxo's international competitors made greater progress in this potentially rich market. The complex network of associated companies through which the group conducted its business probably played a major part in this comparative failure.

Indonesia and Singapore

In July 1979, as Glaxo laid plans for the introduction of ranitidine, it was decided to set up a pilot plant for its manufacture in Singapore at a cost of £1.8 million.[106] This was a preliminary to establishing a second major primary production facility outside the UK (Thana, near Bombay, was the first). At the beginning of the decade Glaxo had planned to open a secondary-process factory in Indonesia and a substantial plot of land was acquired.[107] By January 1970 negotiations with the authorities in Djakarta were well advanced and the group had allocated a capital investment of $1.6 million.[108] The area manager, Cliff Hammond, had worked hard to build up a team of representatives and sales were growing substantially. However, Sir Alan Wilson was persuaded that investment prospects were brighter in Australia, and in March 1971 he cancelled the Indonesian development.[109] Rival pharmaceutical companies were not deterred so that when Glaxo attempted to revive its trade in the early 1980s, the group encountered considerable competition. Eventually Glaxo set up a new Indonesian subsidiary but many executives believed that an important commercial opportunity had been lost by the decision not to build a plant in 1971.

Early forecasts of global demand for ranitidine ranged from forty to sixty-eight tons per annum by 1986, five years after the initial launch.[110] Given that Montrose, which had produced early samples of the drug for clinical trials, had a maximum projected capacity of only twenty tons per annum, it became imperative to find a second site for its manufacture. For strategic reasons, Glaxo decided to seek a location abroad and the Economic Development Board in Singapore offered the group pioneer status, exempting the company from corporate taxation for ten years.[111] An efficient port, modern airport at Changi and a stable government under Lee Kuan Yu that sought to encourage science-based industries added to the attractions of Singapore. A subsidiary company, Glaxochem (Private), was incorporated in Singapore in September 1979 to run the plant. It was decided, after some debate on the volume of future demand, to authorise expenditure of £19.8 million for a factory with an annual capacity of forty tons.[112] An eighteen-acre site had been identified at Jurong and construction began in September 1980.[113] The plant was designed by Glaxo engineers and was completed in February 1982. Because Montrose might not be able to cope with a rapid rise in demand, it was essential that Singapore be fully operational by the summer and from the end of July it worked three shifts a day seven days a week.[114] Orders exceeded forecasts and there were times when Montrose and Singapore only narrowly succeeded in meeting demand.

Because of low wage costs in Singapore and the problems experienced in commissioning the computerised control plant at Annan, the idea of a fully automated factory was rejected in favour of manual operation. At first, all the key managerial and technical staff were transferred from the UK. John Brennand, the first factory manager, and Malcolm Copley, the production manager, came from Ulverston and Montrose respectively,[115] while the first chemists were Joe Caldwell and Mike Hope. The technical laboratory was run by Russell Smith and quality control by Gordon Monro from Ware. Four supervisors and eight key operators were recruited locally and sent to Montrose for training six months before the plant opened, others following in their footsteps. In time, all the managerial posts passed to Singapore nationals, with the exception of Dr Alan Catterall who became factory manager in 1990. By the mid 1980s staff numbers had risen from an initial intake of 120 to over 200, while output topped 200 tons per annum.

China

By the early 1930s, Glaxo was selling a limited quantity of dried milk and a few pharmaceuticals to China through their agents, ICI (China). In view of the potential size of the market and the barriers to entry, Jephcott recommended the opening of a regional office.[116] Accordingly, in 1934 Arthur Scrimgeour, a representative with H. J. Foster & Co., Glaxo's Indian

subsidiary, was transferred from Calcutta to Shanghai.[117] He had been recruited by the company four years earlier on graduating in Spanish from
Aberdeen University. Scrimgeour had answered a characteristically blunt
advertisement placed in *The Scotsman*: 'Wanted: Scottish graduate with a
knowledge of Spanish to work for expanding pharmaceuticals company.
Contact Glaxo Laboratories'.[118] Jephcott had specified a Scotsman because
he believed they worked harder than the English. (This conviction appears
to have influenced the appointment of scientists at Greenford, notable examples being Macrae, Hector Walker, Hems and Tom Walker). Jephcott
sought a Spanish speaker because he intended to send the recruit to work
in South America and the Caribbean, though after a period of practical
training in the UK, Scrimgeour was sent to Calcutta to cover for a representative who was taking six months' leave. Described by Jephcott as 'one of
our very bright men', he was chosen to manage the China operation.

Jephcott himself visited Shanghai in April 1934 to devise an operating
strategy. He proposed concentrating the sales effort on Ostermilk, targeting
doctors and offering a special introductory discount to dealers, while also
running a limited advertising campaign to raise public awareness. If this
initiative were successful, then a small number of pharmaceuticals, such as
Glucose-D and Adexolin, could be promoted. Jephcott was pleased to
discover

> an English woman doctor – Dr D. Galbraith – at the Margaret Williamson
> Hospital, the largest lying-in hospital in Shanghai, using Adexolin as rou-
> tine hospital treatment for in-patients and out-patients, and purchasing
> 4oz bottles. Their use could be substantially increased with more
> favourable prices.[119]

Whilst occupying a room in ICI's offices,[120] Scrimgeour visited all the
English doctors and hospitals in Shanghai to introduce them to Glaxo's
food and vitamin products, gradually extending his contacts by trips to
Hankow, Peking, Tientsin and Nanking. Having appointed and trained a
small number of Chinese representatives, he transferred Glaxo's business
from ICI to Dodwells, a much smaller organisation, which Scrimgeour believed would be more efficient.[121] In 1937, Jephcott gave him responsibility
for the entire Far East with a brief to build up the company's business in
Singapore, Hong Kong, Siam and Indonesia. When war was declared in
September 1939, Glaxo's Far Eastern organisation had five Chinese representatives, two based in Shanghai, two in Hong Kong and one in Malaya.
Based in Singapore, Scrimgeour kept trading until the Japanese invaded at
the beginning of 1942, when he enlisted in the Straits Settlements Volunteer

Force. He was captured and remained a prisoner-of-war until his release in
August 1945.

After recuperating in the UK, in March 1946 Scrimgeour persuaded
Jephcott to let him return to Singapore to reconstruct the business. Renting
an office in the Mercantile Bank building as his base,[122] he travelled
through Malaya, Thailand, Hong Kong and Indonesia to re-establish business contacts, helped by having a range of new medicines to sell. Agreements with US companies and research at Greenford gave him antibiotics
(penicillin and streptomycin in particular) and vitamin B_{12}. Wartime damage to Singapore's infrastructure made conditions particularly arduous and
Scrimgeour had to work from a cramped partition office. Nevertheless,
business boomed and further staff were recruited, including Robin
McAdam, who became manager of the Hong Kong office.

Opportunities for trade with China remained limited during the 1950s
and 1960s, confined to antibiotics and corticosteroids, and was conducted
from Glaxo's Hong Kong office, which had gradually become an important
sales and distribution centre.[123] Originally much of its business was contracted out to agents, but in 1970 Neil Maidment, the resident manager, established Glaxo Hong Kong and brought the trading in house. He had
joined A & H (Surgical Engineering) in 1965 as their Far East representative
based in Singapore and had built up extensive contacts in the region. In
1971 Maidment began to visit China, attending trade fairs in Canton every
six months to sell penicillins. He and his small sales force were not permitted to visit hospital physicians until the end of the Cultural Revolution in
1980.[124] In October 1981 the China National Technical Import Corporation
visited Glaxo's Ulverston factory and the following year approached the
company for technical information on the cephalosporins, and in particular cephalothin and cephaloridine.[125] Glaxo was interested in the proposal
as it appeared to provide an entrée to a large and unexploited pharmaceutical market. Alan Raper, the group technical director, outlined the conun-
drum facing the group:

> Given that our main motive is to increase sales to the Peoples' Republic of China,
> in the interests of good relations it is considered desirable that an offer of
> cephalosporin technology be made, as a refusal would be likely to offend the
> Chinese. The difficulty is in setting a price; there is no good reason for setting a
> low price for this technology.[126]

Although the State Pharmaceutical Administration favoured a simple
cash sale, Raper believed this was not in the group's long-term interest.
He proposed a package of £2 million, payable in cash, and a balance of

the £4 million to be retained in China as an investment in a new business, such as an aerosol factory.[127] The Chinese, who were making aerosols for respiratory products in a converted apartment block in Shanghai, wanted a modern plant to raise annual output to 6 million items. Opportunities to develop trade with China looked enticing and Glaxo held further discussions with officials in Peking and Shanghai about the sale of packed products and bulk chemicals, together with the prospect of clinical trials of Zantac and Zinacef. Despite these hopeful signs, negotiations failed because a price could not be agreed for the transfer of cephalosporin technology.

Because trade with China had continued to grow (rising from £0.3 million in 1983 to £0.8 million in 1985 and reaching £1.6 million in 1987), Glaxo opened negotiations with the State Pharmaceutical Administration of China in Beijing at the beginning of 1987. They offered to contribute half of the £3 million cost of the aerosol factory to be built in Chongqing, Sichuan Province. The finance was channelled through a new holding company, Glaxo China Enterprises (set up in 1988),[128] of which Glaxo Hong Kong, Glaxo China and the joint-venture business would each be subsidiaries. Construction started at Chongqing early in 1989 and the factory produced its first aerosols in October 1991. Set up by Maidment as the main trading vehicle, Glaxo China Enterprises had its headquarters in Hong Kong, though branches were soon opened in Beijing, Shanghai and two other locations.[129] Over a hundred resident sales staff were recruited in South China, together with a further fifty based in Hong Kong, who covered the Chinese market. The main demand was for medicines to treat acute rather than chronic conditions so that antibiotics, and Fortum in particular, generated significant sales.[130]

CONCLUSIONS:
CONTINUITY AND CHANGE

§

Organic growth is no longer an option on its own. Pharmaceuticals is no longer a protected market. We are selling to governments, insurance companies, and pharmacy benefit managers. It's a competitive market, and we have to have the lowest costs just to compete. We are not trying to downsize; we are trying to make ourselves better.

Sir Richard Sykes, January 1995[1]

GLAXO LABORATORIES did not begin life as a pharmaceutical company. Established by Alec Nathan and Harry Jephcott in 1935, the business was built on the manufacture of milk-based foods, fortified with vitamins and minerals. In a sense, the style, Glaxo Laboratories, was misleading because the Greenford site was constructed as a factory, warehouse and offices. The word 'Laboratories' had been chosen to emphasise the scientific origins of some of the ingredients in 'Glaxo', the trade name for the company's dried milk powder. Unlike Wellcome or May & Baker, Glaxo Laboratories had no tradition of scientific research but employed experimental techniques to ensure quality control and later to enhance the value of its food products. Although Glaxo had begun to manufacture vitamins in 1924, it was not until the Second World War that the company became a fully fledged pharmaceutical business. With the return of peace, the Glaxo board thought less about managing a food business and began to regard themselves as manufacturers of medicines. Nevertheless, Jephcott had no innate enthusiasm for serendipitous research. A paternalistic leader with a sense of moral justice, he had a patriotic concern for the prosperity of the British pharmaceutical industry. With a deep personal commitment to Glaxo, Jephcott worried about the group's profitability and became somewhat pessimistic about its future prospects. He abhorred risk-taking and, operating with comparatively restricted funds, decided that there was little alternative to licensing novel products and processes from Glaxo's larger US competitors. As a result, the group built up a considerable reputation in steroid and cephalosporin chemistry and its Greenford pilot plant became expert at translating laboratory processes into mass-production techniques.

The scientific endeavour that came to play an increasingly important role in the group's activities contributed to the meritocratic atmosphere in which few were recruited from the major public schools or Oxbridge. However, the dominance exerted by scientists in management was not without its drawbacks and to outsiders the business seemed to lack a cutting edge, leading to the epithets 'the university of Greenford', and 'the only quoted university on the Stock Exchange'. These descriptions implied that Glaxo was more interested in solving complex pharmaceutical problems than in exploiting commercial opportunities. Yet genuine camaraderie existed at Glaxo and many who had joined the company from university continued to work there until retirement. During the 1980s, when the group's management became increasingly international in character and the pharmaceutical industry became ever more competitive, the culture began to change. A greater emphasis on marketing skills and the need to respond swiftly to the business environment led to a less certain but more highly rewarded executive world.

Although Glaxo had become a recognised pharmaceutical company by 1960, its expertise lay in the development of existing products. When Sir Alan Wilson succeeded Jephcott as chairman in July 1963 a higher priority was given to the research of innovative medicines. As a scientist of international stature, he authorised expenditure for the progressive expansion of Dr David Jack's pharmacology-based laboratories at Ware. Whilst thoroughly at home with both theoretical and applied science and possessed of a quick and decisive mind, Wilson never really settled in the world of corporate business. Remote and uncommunicative to those he did not know, he failed to inspire managers and remained implacably opposed to any venture into the United States. His parting gift to Glaxo was to convince the Monopolies Commission of the importance of maintaining a number of competing pharmaceutical research centres so as not to diminish scientific enterprise in the UK. This, in turn, led the Commission to turn down both the proposal by Beecham to acquire Glaxo and the group's own defensive alliance with Boots. Ironically, it was this very notion that Glaxo sought to dispel when mounting its take-over bid for Wellcome, arguing that the costs of research and development had risen to the point where only large-scale organisations could afford to research novel medicines and market them internationally.

The decision by the Monopolies Commission to turn down both the Beecham and Boots merger plans proved to be a turning point in the history of Glaxo. The group's confidence had been disturbed by the bid and senior management forced to consider strategies for its future prosperity. Unless Glaxo strengthened its defences, the company would be subject to further assault. This required growth, particularly in the United States where the group had no direct representation. No major pharmaceutical company could afford to ignore the world's largest and most profitable national market.

When Wilson retired in March 1973, he was succeeded by Austin Bide, who had played a key role in the defence of Glaxo and, as deputy chairman, initiated a programme of structural reorganisation. Like Jephcott, Bide had trained as a scientist and worked for the greater part of his life in Glaxo. He knew the business as a research chemist, factory manager and company secretary. Bide, with the help of David Smart, chairman of Allen & Hanburys, drew up plans for a centrally managed and integrated group. The various subsidiaries, which had been rescued from take-over by foreign competitors by Jephcott and which retained a high degree of autonomy, were dismantled, though their names and trademarks were kept. A programme of personnel exchanges and joint committees created a unifying level of loyalty to Glaxo Holdings as well as to the former companies. Under Bide, managerial confidence was painstakingly rebuilt as the group redefined itself and prepared to go on to the offensive.

On the premise that 'you can't join the club without paying the subscription', Bide committed the group to ever higher levels of expenditure to research.[2] Spending increased in both real terms and as a proportion of turnover, rising from 3.8 per cent in 1972 to 5.8 per cent by 1982. During the seventies, Glaxo's research enterprise was divided between two sites, Ware and Greenford, each with its own distinctive culture and expertise. Ware was pharmacology based and generated three important medicines over this period: salbutamol, labetalol and ranitidine. Greenford specialised in the chemistry of steroids and antibiotics. Although its laboratories never discovered a blockbuster medicine, the achievements of its scientists led to a range of cephalosporins, culminating in the third-generation ceftazidime. They also developed a portfolio of topical corticosteroids for the treatment of inflammatory skin conditions, including betamethasone valerate, launched in 1963, and beclomethasone dipropionate, later developed at Ware as an inhaled treatment for asthma. These products established the international reputation of Glaxo Laboratories in two therapeutic areas and led to steady and valuable sales. However, the real gains to the group's profitability came from Ventolin and Zantac, though in quite different ways.

As chief executive from 1981, Paul Girolami was instrumental in defining the marketing strategy for Zantac. Not a revolutionary drug, it had clinical advantages over Tagamet, the first H_2-receptor antagonist for the treatment of ulcers, and these were exploited with consummate skill. In setting the price higher than that of Tagamet, and in negotiating a co-promotional agreement with Roche in the United States, he created the necessary commercial opportunities for the medicine. Income from Zantac exceeded all expectations and allowed Glaxo to expand geographically and to increase its investment in research and development. Ventolin, by comparison, was a truly novel compound and represented a major advance in the treatment of asthma. Launched in 1969, sales of the product, together with the many line extensions that followed, grew progressively into the nineties, and demonstrated that medicines can enjoy a remarkable longevity even when the original formulation has long lost patent protection.

Recognising the great importance of the North American market, Girolami was also a consistent proponent of the strategy to establish a wholly owned subsidiary in the United States. The decision in 1977 to acquire Meyer Laboratories, a small pharmaceutical business based at Fort Lauderdale, proved to have momentous consequences. Meyer provided a beach-head for a concerted assault on the US market as Glaxo sought, for the first time, to establish itself as an autonomous trading force in America. If Meyer Laboratories were to serve as the vehicle for the invasion, Zantac, supported by Betnovate, Ventolin and Zinacef, comprised the strike force. The rapid and sustained growth of Glaxo Inc. at its headquarters in Research Triangle Park was as remarkable a phenomenon as the mushrooming global sales of Zantac. Indeed, the two events were inextricably linked, for without a blockbuster drug, Glaxo Inc. could never have developed as it did.

In December 1985, the chairmanship of Glaxo Holdings passed to Girolami, who continued to channel profits from Zantac into research and development together with capital projects for the US subsidiary. He also introduced a new style of devolved management, particularly to sales and marketing companies. Research remained centrally co-ordinated, as did manufacture and certain head-office functions, notably patent protection, while the group's operations were increasingly diversified across the world. Girolami believed that managers of national subsidiaries with their specialised knowledge could achieve better results if they had autonomy within defined boundaries. Whilst Glaxo was being strengthened internationally, Girolami strategically focused the group's activities, divesting those companies not related to the core business of prescription medicines. In 1985 Vestric, the UK wholesaling subsidiary, was sold, followed by the food company, generic medicines and then veterinary products. Glaxo Holdings remained, as its mission statement proclaimed,

> an integrated research-based group of companies whose corporate purpose is to create, discover, develop, manufacture and market throughout the world safe, effective medicines of the highest quality ...[3]

Ultimately, pharmaceutical companies stand or fall by the quality of their products. No amount of marketing skill or promotional drive can turn a drug with minimal therapeutic advantage into a world beater. Equally, a truly innovative compound can fail to achieve its due rewards if sold in an unimaginative and unenthusiastic manner.

The years from 1985 to the present have continued to see events move at a pace in Glaxo. Considerable investment continued to be directed into Glaxo Inc., the US subsidiary, and a major research and development laboratory was completed in the autumn of 1991 at a cost of $337 million. However, the largest capital project undertaken by the group, and indeed the most costly in Europe after the Channel Tunnel, was the construction of the research laboratories at Stevenage, originally costed at £464.5 million and opened April 1995. Glaxo grew strongly during the remainder of the 1980s and, though the rate of expansion fell in the late 1990s, the group continued to earn significant profits.

In March 1993, Sir Richard Sykes, formerly head of Glaxo Group Research, was appointed deputy chairman and chief executive, and in May 1997 he became chairman. Sykes had joined Glaxo Laboratories in 1972 as head of the antibiotic research unit. A microbiologist, he had been partly funded by the company as a research student at Bristol. However, career opportunities then drew him to Squibb in Princeton, where he remained until September 1986 when Sykes returned to Greenford as Dr David Jack's successor. With his experience acquired in both the UK and US, Sykes was the natural choice to succeed Girolami in what was becoming an increasingly competitive scientific environment.

The first challenge facing Sykes was the group's commercial reliance on Zantac. In 1994, it still generated 43 per cent of turnover and many commentators argued that Glaxo would have difficulty maintaining sales and profit growth when the medicine's basic patent expired in July 1997.[4] Given the size of Zantac's contribution, the only way to offset the anticipated sudden loss of revenue was the acquisition of a medium-sized company with innovative products. With an expertise in antiviral medicines and UK origins, Wellcome was an obvious choice, particularly as shareholders had become concerned by its recent performance. Once it had become clear that the Wellcome Trust could sell its 39.5 per cent holding in the company, Glaxo pressed ahead with the take-over. Effected in March 1995, the merger significantly broadened the group's therapeutic range and the combined business had a turnover of £8,341 million and profits of £3,132 million.[6] The Wellcome medicines introduced an element of balance to the group's portfolio of products. In 1996, for example, sales of antiviral medicines by Glaxo Wellcome totalled £1,360 million, almost equivalent to the £1,931 million earned by Zantac and, as a result, its contribution fell to 23 per cent. Three years later it was only 9 per cent, though this, in part, reflected the extraordinary growth in sales of Flixotide (fluticasone propionate).[7] In this way, Sykes successfully avoided a potential short-term financial crisis for Glaxo.

Announced in January 2000 by Sir Richard Sykes and J. P. Garnier, the merger of Glaxo Wellcome and SmithKline Beecham was a union of equals. With first-half sales of £4.6 billion and £4.1 billion respectively, the new merged group had an estimated annual turnover of £18.1 billion and pre-tax profits of £5.4 billion.[8] In comparison with other technological industries, pharmaceuticals have been fragmented and even the largest companies have held relatively small market shares. As late as 1988, for example, the largest twenty-five businesses had only 44 per cent of the global pharmaceutical market – an average of 1.8 per cent.[9] The aim of the amalgamation was to achieve, in Sykes' words, 'critical mass'.[10] GlaxoSmithKline has a 7 per cent share of the prescription market together with a research and development budget of £2.4 billion.

Why, then, was this strategic increase in scale considered so important? During the 1990s important paradigm changes were taking place in the discovery of innovative medicines. In June 2000, it was announced that the sequencing of the Human Genome Project was almost complete, a project that at one time had seemed unfeasibly ambitious. This information provides an important tool that can be used to understand better the causes of disease and thereby discover medicines that address underlying aetiologies. Human genome information can help doctors identify patients at risk from specific diseases and to tailor medication accordingly. It may also be possible to engineer cells to carry genes to destroy cancer cells or stimulate the immune system's defences.[11] In the recent past, genes had been identified for rare, inherited conditions, but modern therapies will increasingly target common disorders such as diabetes, Alzheimer's and heart disease. At a time when medicines introduced to the market are scrutinised by regulatory bodies to assess both their therapeutic and economic impact, advances of this nature can claim to be truly innovative. Both Glaxo Wellcome, with its strengths in genetics (having already found genes associated with migraine, psoriasis, diabetes and Parkinson's disease) and combinatorial chemistry, and SmithKline Beecham, with its genomic research into disease targets, have made significant investments in this scientific and technological revolution. Because the advances have been so rapid and operate across a number of disciplines, it requires considerable resources to exploit the many opportunities that will arise.

In increasingly competitive global markets, leading pharmaceutical companies not only have to discover a stream of novel products but also manage sales organisations on a truly international scale. In the years between the two mergers, Sir Richard Sykes had concentrated considerable efforts into building up marketing capacity, particularly in the United States where the total number of representatives had reached 4,900 by 2000. As a result, group sales increased by 12 per cent in the six months to July 2000, returning to the double figures achieved when Zantac was driving the business forward. The combination of Glaxo and SmithKline generated a sales and marketing force of 43,000, including 8,000 representatives in the US.

Founded in 1873, Joseph Nathan & Co. evolved from a general merchandise business based in Wellington, New Zealand, to a limited liability corporation with interests in the production and sale of dried milk powder marketed as 'Glaxo' and later 'Ostermilk'. Manufacture became more important than merchanting and in 1935 the newly created Glaxo Laboratories moved to purpose-built premises at Greenford. There followed three pivotal events. First, the traditional foods business was transformed into a pharmaceutical company. This took place over an extended period, arguably between 1924, when Ostelin was launched, and the mid 1940s, when Glaxo became the UK's largest producer of penicillin. The second paradigm shift resulted from the discovery and marketing of Zantac. Once the world's largest selling prescription medicine, the revenue it earned enabled what was a UK- and Commonwealth-based company of middling size to become a truly multinational group of the front rank. By allowing Glaxo to expand rapidly in the US, it irrevocably altered the aspect and culture of the business. The third fundamental change occurred between 1995 and 2000 when the company merged first with Wellcome and then with SmithKline Beecham. This strategy dramatically increased the scale of the organisation and provided the new business with the resources needed to participate fully in the genetic revolution. As a result, GlaxoSmithKline continues to be a significant and dynamic agent for change in an industry at the leading edge of scientific discovery.

APPENDIX:
TABLES

Table 1 **The profit and loss account of the Glaxo Department 1908–1915** (£)

		Gross profit	Adjusted
To Sept.	1908	(2,930)	(4,014)
	1909	(5,166)	(6,981)
	1910	(2,191)	(2,809)
To June	1911*	(225)	(281)
	1912	2,028	2,386
To Sept.	1913†	4,603	5,414
	1914	6,441	7,578
	1915	7,919	7,332

Notes: Figures in brackets indicate a loss; * 9 months †15 months; figures adjusted by the Sauerbeck Statist index, 1866–77 = 100.
Source: Alec Nathan 'The Story of Glaxo' (typescript, 19 March 1917).

Table 2 **Turnover of Glaxo and expenditure on advertising 1913–1916** (£)

		Turnover	Adjusted	Expenditure per £1 of sales
To Sept.	1913*	56,539	66,516	4s.1d. (20p)
	1914	77,254	90,887	6s.9d. (34p)
	1915	120,697	111,756	3s.3d. (16p)
	1916	194,911	143,317	1s.9d. (9p)

Notes: *15 months; figures adjusted by Sauerbeck *Statist* index 1867–77 = 100
Source: Noble Scott, 'The advertising of Glaxo' (typescript, *c.* 1917), p. 4.

Table 3 **The profits of Joseph Nathan & Co. 1915–1946** (£)

	Net profit	Adjusted		Net profit	Adjusted
1915	9,570	54,375	1931	52,311	249,100
1916	12,400	59,615	1932	28,789	140,434
1917	25,272	100,685	1933	39,522	198,603
1918	321,70	111,315	1934	55,563	276,433
1919	50,481	164,971	1935	74,432	364,862
1920	70,850	199,577	1936	85,166	407,493
1921	63,671	197,736	1937	91,398	417,342
1922	20,176	77,302	1938	90,647	408,312
1923	11,486	45,761	1939	88,510	393,378
1924	32,118	128,988	1940	87,600	334,357
1925	50,694	201,968	1941	72,849	256,511
1926	27,167	110,886	1942	82,942	291,025
1927	55,474	232,109	1943	84,298	296,824
1928	61,216	259,390	1944	77,563	271,199
1929	65,377	279,389	1945	87,988	304,457
1930	68,066	302,516	1946	97,298	335,510

Note: Figures adjusted by the Bank of England's index of consumer prices, January 1974 = 100
Source: Joseph Nathan & Co. Annual Accounts.

Table 4 **Glaxo Laboratories: sales and profits 1936–1946** (£)

	Sales	Adjusted	Profits	Adjusted
1936	683,585	3,270,741	143,569	686,933
1937	789,971	3,607,173	143,525	655,365
1938	985,440	4,438,918	175,660	791,261
1939	1,182,841	5,257,071	230,761	1,025,604
1940	1,391,738	5,311,977	261,586	998,419
1941	1,774,560	6,248,451	345,878	1,217,880
1942	2,077,204	7,288,435	397,645	1,395,245
1943	2,499,928	8,802,563	565,627	1,991,644
1944	2,521,292	8,815,706	503,383	1,760,080
1945	2,528,907	8,750,533	512,277	1,772,584
1946	3,598,000	12,406,896	563,857	1,944,334

Note: Figures adjusted by the Bank of England's index of consumer prices, 1974 = 100.
Source: Glaxo Laboratories Annual Report and Accounts (1936–1946).

Table 5 **Glaxo Laboratories UK Sales 1936–1945** (£)

	Foods		Pharmaceuticals	
	Sales	Adjusted	Sales	Adjusted
1936	253,602	1,213,406	221,155	1,058,157
1937	296,832	1,355,397	280,400	1,280,365
1938	382,982	1,725,144	345,317	1,555,481
1939	496,699	2,207,551	417,934	1,857,484
1940	583,641	2,227,637	474,007	1,809,187
1941	764,445	2,691,707	629,441	2,216,341
1942	984,138	3,453,116	650,447	2,282,270
1943	1,273,724	4,484,943	758,757	2,671,679
1944	1,173,642	4,103,643	836,484	2,924,769
1945	1,204,879	4,169,131	811,805	2,809,013

Note: Figures adjusted by the Bank of England's index of consumer prices, January 1974 = 100
Source: Glaxo Laboratories Annual Report and Accounts (1936–1945).

Table 6 **Research output of UK pharmaceutical companies 1936–1941**

Company	Patents	Papers	Doctorates
British Drug Houses	7	32	5
Boots	12	10	24
Glaxo Laboratories	13	34	8
May & Baker	40	11	15
Burroughs Wellcome	6	220	24

Source: Davenport-Hines and Slinn, *Glaxo: A History to 1962*, p. 139.

Table 7 **Glaxo Laboratories consolidated sales and profits 1947–1962** (£000)

	Sales	Adjusted	Net profit	Adjusted
1947	4,548	15,575	1,191	4,080
1948†	4,276	13,749	976	3,139
1949	6,688	20,900	930	2,907
1950	5,928	17,964	1,237	3,749
1951	7,538	20,940	1,333	3,702
1952	7,632	19,420	1,580	4,021
1953	8,069	19,923	1,581	3,903
1954	7,149	17,310	1,484	3,594
1955	na	–	1,557	3,611
1956	9,517	21,009	1,765	3,897
1957	11,970	25,522	1,838	3,918
1958*	14,069	29,128	2,611	5,405
1959	18,740	38,560	3,018	6,209
1960	20,338	41,422	3,760	7,659
1961	27,703	53,792	3,718	7,219
1962	29,037	54,788	3,343	6,307

Notes: †6 months only; *9 months only; na = not available.
From 1959 figures include sales and profits earned by Allen & Hanburys; figures adjusted by the Bank of England's index of consumer prices, January 1974 = 100.
Source: Glaxo Laboratories Annual Accounts.

Table 8 **Trading profits of the overseas subsidiaries of Glaxo Laboratories 1951–1961** (£)

	1951	1956	1961
Argentina	23,700	62,100	170,000
Australia	65,100	33,000	123,000
Brazil	91,700	7,500	(9,400)
Canada	(9,700)	10,500	7,000
Ceylon	–	–	31,000
Columbia	–	–	27,000
Cuba	–	–	6,900
Ghana	–	–	(2,600)
India	468,700	704,500	1,986,000
Italy	264,000	29,200	156,000
Malaya	–	–	60,000
New Zealand	82,000	94,400	134,000
Pakistan	130,000	214,000	517,200
South Africa	28,500	21,200	99,000
Uruguay	5,300	4,300	3,000

Note: Figures in brackets indicate losses.
Source: Davenport-Hines and Slinn, *Glaxo, A History to 1962*, p. 374.

Table 9 **Glaxo Group–Glaxo Holdings turnover and trading profits 1962–1985**
(£million)

	Turnover	Adjusted	Profits	Adjusted
1962	42.7	318.2	6.8	50.7
1963	46.8	341.9	7.6	55.5
1964	53.3	377.0	9.3	65.8
1965	59.3	400.1	11.2	75.6
1966	63.6	413.0	11.9	77.3
1967	69.8	442.3	13.1	83.0
1968	131.0	793.0	19.3	116.8
1969	143.1	821.0	21.9	125.7
1970	160.7	867.2	24.0	129.5
1971	176.5	870.3	24.3	119.8
1972	189.3	871.9	27.4	126.2
1973	219.5	925.8	37.2	156.9
1974	258.6	940.0	45.6	165.8
1975	317.8	930.1	46.0	134.6
1976	411.1	1,032.1	76.0	190.8
1977	488.0	1,057.7	85.9	186.2
1978	543.5	1,087.9	83.2	104.1
1979	539.1	951.5	73.9	130.4
1980	618.1	924.7	68.6	102.6
1981	710.5	950.0	90.5	121.0
1982	865.8	1,066.1	132.6	145.4
1983	1,027.5	1,210.0	182.0	214.2
1984	1,199.9	1,345.6	248.9	279.1
1985	1,412.1	1,492.9	363.5	384.3

Note: Figures adjusted by the RPI, January 1987 = 100; the figures for 1979, 1983 and 1985 have each been
adjusted for the changes in accounting policy which occurred in the following year.

Source: Glaxo Group and Glaxo Holdings Annual Reports.

Table 10 **Glaxo Group–Glaxo Holdings capitalisation 1963–1985**

	Net assets (£ million)	Adjusted	Capital expenditure (£ million)	Adjusted	Return on capital employed (%)
1963	34	248	na	–	23.8
1964	22	262	na	–	43.6
1965	41	277	na	–	28.3
1966	45	292	na	–	28.0
1967	49	311	na	–	28.4
1968	55	333	5	30	34.5
1969	72	413	9	52	30.7
1970	81	437	20	108	30.0
1971	88	434	18	89	27.0
1972	53	244	12	55	50.8
1973	70	295	11	46	47.9
1974	90	327	14	51	47.9
1975	103	301	18	53	39.8
1976	164	412	19	48	45.1
1977	199	432	29	63	43.7
1978	214	428	38	76	40.2
1979	319	563	41	72	22.6
1980	342	511	47	70	19.3
1981	387	518	55	74	22.5
1982	434	534	65	80	30.9
1983	546	643	70	82	34.1
1984	683	766	98	110	37.5
1985	836	884	126	133	46.7

Notes: na = not available; figures adjusted by RPI, January 1987 = 100.
Source: Glaxo Group and Glaxo Holdings Annual Reports.

Table 11 **Glaxo Group – Glaxo Holdings earnings and dividends per share**
          1963–1985

	Earnings per share (p)	Increase %	Dividends per share (p)	Increase %	Number of shares (million)
1963	0.2	–	–	–	–
1964	0.2	–	–	–	–
1965	0.3	50	–	–	–
1966	0.3	–	–	–	–
1967	0.4	33	–	–	–
1968	0.4	–	0.1	–	1,762
1969	0.5	25	0.1	–	1,762
1970	0.5	–	0.1	–	2,203
1971	0.5	–	0.1	–	2,203
1972	0.6	20	0.2	100	2,203
1973	0.8	33	0.2	–	2,203
1974	0.9	13	0.2	–	2,203
1975	0.8	(11)	0.2	–	2,203
1976	1.3	62	0.3	50	2,699
1977	1.5	15	0.3	–	2,700
1978	1.5	–	0.3	–	2,704
1979	1.7	13	0.5	67	2,705
1980	1.5	(12)	0.6	20	2,707
1981	2.2	47	0.7	17	2,709
1982	2.9	32	0.8	14	2,751
1983	3.7	28	1.1	38	2,928
1984	5.7	54	1.6	45	2,945
1985	8.9	56	2.5	56	2,961

Source: Glaxo Group and Glaxo Holdings Annual Reports.

Table 12 **Glaxo Holdings turnover by region 1972–1985** (£million)

	Europe	North America	Rest of the world	Total
1972	80(55)	7(5)	59(40)	146
1973	97(57)	8(5)	66(33)	171
1974	113(57)	9(4)	81(39	203
1975	140(57)	9(4)	97(39)	246
1976	171(54)	18(5)	130(41)	319
1977	203(54)	24(6)	148(40)	375
1978	219(53)	24(6)	167(41)	410
1979	230(58)	23(6)	144(36)	397
1980	252(58)	22(5)	160(37)	434
1981	298(56)	28(5)	211(39)	537
1982	361(54)	45(7)	257(39)	663
1983	447(57)	66(9)	266(34)	779
1984	514(56)	193(21)	208(23)	915
1985	611(52)	333(28)	242(20)	1,186

Notes: Figures in brackets are percentages; figures exclude wholesaling.
Source: Glaxo Holdings Annual Reports.

Table 13 **The trading profits of Glaxo Laboratories and its major subsidiaries 1959–1961** (£)

	1959	1960	1961
Glaxo UK	2,836,852	2,887,532	2,239,108
India	1,563,187	1,924,036	1,971,400
Pakistan	422,695	540,277	460,969
New Zealand	134,225	135,930	153,946
Italy	128,059	122,755	210,684
Canada	1,851	970	966
Cuba	6,939	3,397	10,272
Ireland	6,265	12,931	23,157
Glaxo/Allenburys:			
Ceylon	49,419	27,729	45,762
Malaya	3,240	36,436	67,468
Australia	207,414	106,831	113,846
South Africa	20,913	58,439	93,787
Nigeria	38,856	58,912	15,409
Ghana	na	9,979	34,418
Allen & Hanburys	691,130	682,429	805,619
Evans Medical	na	na	504,929

Note: na = not available.
Source: Glaxo Laboratories Group Trading Position board papers, 1960–1961.

Table 14 **Glaxo Group – Glaxo Holdings: staff numbers 1962–1985**

	Total	UK	Overseas	Sales per employee (£)	Adjusted
1962	na	na	na	na	na
1963	16,250	9,700	6,550	2,814	20,555
1964	16,850	9,800	7,050	3,118	22,051
1965	17,400	9,850	7,550	3,315	22,368
1966	18,200	10,150	8,050	3,441	22,344
1967	18,950	10,450	8,500	3,627	22,985
1968	26,940	16,870	10,070	4,735	28,662
1969	28,557	17,120	11,437	5,008	28,748
1970	30,087	17,356	12,731	5,318	28,699
1971	31,243	17,784	13,459	5,665	27,934
1972	30,107	17,000	13,107	6,278	28,918
1973	29,765	16,568	13,197	7,358	31,033
1974	30,079	16,344	13,735	8,611	31,301
1975	31,520	17,084	14,436	10,089	29,526
1976	30,683	16,132	14,551	13,395	33,630
1977	30,540	15,944	14,596	15,979	34,632
1978	30,901	15,881	15,020	17,572	35,173
1979	29,781	15,602	14,179	18,099	31,943
1980	29,187	14,816	14,371	21,174	31,679
1981	28,218	13,725	14,493	25,161	33,647
1982	28,106	13,188	14,918	30,812	37,941
1983	27,768	13,605	14,163	36,985	43,537
1984	25,053	13,685	11,368	47,898	53,715
1985	25,634	13,463	12,171	55,083	58,233

Notes: na = not available; figures adjusted by RPI January 1987 = 100.
Source: Glaxo Group and Glaxo Holdings Annual Reports.

Table 15 **Gross cost of prescription medicines to the NHS 1950–1958**

	Gross cost (£million)	Adjusted (£million)	Change (%)
1949–50	31.7	96.1	–
1950–51	36.9	102.5	6.7
1951–52	42.4	108.0	5.4
1952–53	44.7	110.4	2.2
1953–54	43.5	105.3	4.6
1954–55	47.5	110.2	4.7
1955–56	52.1	115.0	4.4
1956–57	56.4	120.3	4.6
1957–58	62.8	130.0	8.1

Note: Figures adjusted by Bank of England's index of consumer prices 1974 = 100.
Source: Final Report of the [Hinchcliffe] Committee ..., London: HMSO (1959), p. 24.

Table 16 **Output of the UK pharmaceutical industry and sales to the NHS 1960–1990**

	Gross output (£million)	Sales to NHS (£million)	Sales to NHS (%)	Medicines as % of NHS total cost
1960	199	54	27	na
1970	525	154	29	7.6
1980	2442	905	37	7.6
1985	4030	1543	38	8.4
1990	6735	2524	38	8.9

Notes: All figures refer to manufacturers' prices; na = not available.
Source: ABPI, *Pharma Facts and Figures* (1992), pp. 12–42.

Table 17 **Sales of Betnovate 1964–1967** (£)

	UK sales	Exports	Total	Adjusted total
1963–64	408,986	132,339	541,325	970,116
1964–65	1,177,127	824,066	2,001,193	3,426,700
1965–66	1,776,573	1,315,886	3,092,459	5,094,660
1966–67	2,074,723	1,715,030	3,789,753	6,083,070

Note: Figures adjusted by the Bank of England's index of consumer prices, January 1974 = 100.
Source: Glaxo Laboratories BP 167/67, 'Betnovate'.

Table 18 **Worldwide sales of Zantac 1982–1995** (£million)

	Sales	Adjusted
1982	37	46
1983	97	114
1984	248	278
1985	432	457
1986	606	620
1987	829	814
1988	989	925
1989	1,291	1,121
1990	1,551	1,230
1991	1,606	1,203
1992	1,807	1,305
1993	2,172	1,544
1994	2,442	1,694
1995	2,255	1,513

Note: Wholesale purchase figures adjusted by RPI January 1987 = 100.
Source: Glaxo Holdings Annual Report and Accounts.

Table 19 **Sales of Glaxo food products 1967–1975** (£000)

| | — Ostermilk — | | — Complan — | | — Glucodin — | | — Casilan — | | — Farex — | |
	Home	Export	Home	Export	Home	Export	Home	Export	Home	Export
1967	3,359	243	925	176	136	95	na	69	228	231
1968	3,385	258	817	221	112	109	22	267	57	83
1969	3,607	285	874	231	114	24	na	na	na	275
1970	3,838	309	909	168	105	175	24	45	na	274
1971	4,716	396	1,003	192	107	196	32	57	na	253
1972	4,028	na	1,164	na	120	na	44	na	na	na
1973	4,324	na	1,577	na	151	na	34	na	na	na
1974	5,375	na	2,120	na	201	na	42	na	na	na
1975	3,794	na	1,398	na	138	na	31	na	na	na

Note: na = not available
Source: Glaxo Laboratories Minute Books.

Table 20 **Union membership at Glaxo Laboratories primary production centres in 1973**

Factory	Staff totals	TGWU and GMWU membership	%
Cambois			
Process	69	55	80
Ancillary	52	7	13
Total	121	62	51
Montrose			
Process	202	152	75
Ancillary	49	22	45
Total	251	174	69
Ulverston			
Process	486	287	59
Ancillary	258	82	32
Total	744	369	50
Grand total	**1116**	**605**	**54.2**

Notes: TGWU = Transport and General Workers Union; GMWU = General and Municipal Workers Union.
Source: Group Management Committee Paper 73/194.

Table 21 **Expenditure on research and development by Glaxo 1969–1985** (£million)

	R & D expenditure	Turnover	Expenditure as % of turnover
1969	4	143	2.9
1970	5	161	3.2
1971	6	177	3.5
1972	7	189	3.8
1973	7	220	3.3
1974	8	259	3.1
1975	12	318	3.8
1976	14	411	3.4
1977	17	488	3.5
1978	20	544	3.7
1979	25	539	4.6
1980	32	618	5.2
1981	40	711	5.6
1982	50	866	5.8
1983	60	1,028	5.8
1984	77	1,200	6.4
1985	93	1,412	6.6

Source: Glaxo Annual Report and Accounts (1970–1985).

Table 22 **Staff numbers in Glaxo Group research, 1979–1982**

1978–79		1981–82	
Glaxo Research	951	Greenford Division	515
A & H Research	506	Ware Division	423
Evans Biological Research	40	Pharmacy Division	192
		Medical Division	109
		Regulatory Affairs and	
Planning Division	69		
		Central Services Division	256
		Animal Health Division	55
Total	1,566	Total	1,550

Source: Glaxo Holdings BP 87/29.

Table 23 **Distribution of research and development expenditure for Glaxo Group research 1979–1982**

Therapeutic area	—— 1979–80 ——		—— 1981–82 ——	
	£million	%	£million	%
Anti-infective agents	7.4	32.0	9.5	27.7
Alimentary tract	2.6	11.3	5.6	16.3
Cardiovascular system	2.2	9.6	5.4	15.7
Central nervous system	2.1	9.0	2.0	5.8
Immunology/inflammation	1.9	8.3	1.5	4.4
Respiratory system and allergy	0.9	3.8	1.6	4.7
Animal health	0.7	2.9	1.2	3.5
Prostanoids	0.6	2.7	(included in other projects)	
Metabolic disorders	0.5	2.2	0.5	1.5
Oncology	0.38	1.6	0.9	2.6
Skin biology	–	–	0.3	0.9
Miscellaneous development work	3.8	16.5	5.8	16.9
Total	23.1	100.0	34.3	100.0

Source: Glaxo Holdings BP 87/29.

Table 24 **Expenditure on research and development by Glaxo 1980–1994** (£million)

	R&D expenditure	Adjusted	Turnover	Expenditure as % of turnover
1980	32	48	618	5.2
1981	40	54	711	5.6
1982	50	62	866	5.8
1983	60	71	1,028	5.8
1984	77	86	1,200	6.4
1985	93	98	1,412	6.6
1986	113	116	1,429	7.9
1987	149	146	1,741	8.6
1988	230	215	2,059	11.2
1989	323	280	2,570	12.6
1990	420	333	3,179	13.2
1991	475	356	3,397	14.0
1992	595	430	4,096	14.5
1993	739	526	4,930	15.0
1994	858	5,956	5,656	15.2

Note: Figures adjusted by RPI, January 1987 = 100.
Source: Glaxo Annual Report and Accounts (1981–95).

Table 25 **Medicines manufactured by Glaxo Inc. at Zebulon 1988–94**

	1988	1989	1990	1991	1992	1993	1994
Dermatologicals(kg)							
Aclovate							600
Corticaine	23,400	12,500	5,500	500	2,300	3,400	
Cutivate				9,600	19,500	16,500	15,300
Oxistat		6,800	8,100	14,400	12,000	15,500	12,000
Temovate	35,800	25,400	43,300	48,300	51,800	47,400	64,300
CNS							
Imitrex tablets					1,140,300	2,680,000	5,023,400
Respiratory							
Beclovent inhaler	4,566,100	4,172,100	1,743,000	93,300	3,144,200	9,431,800	3,905,200
Serevent inhaler						451,600	11,182,462
Ventolin inhaler	12,791,900	11,547,200	17,108,300	16,979,100	19,984,500	19,237,900	21,512,300
Ventolin tablets						17,083,300	11,171,100
Cardiovascular							
Trandate tablets							133,399,800
Gastrointestinal							
Zantac tablets	943,015,900	1,198,958,200	1,215,975,500	1,458,781,300	1,514,273,000	1,687,455,900	1,950,485,200

Note: Some of the proprietory names are exclusive to the United States, and their equivalents in the UK are as follows: Temovate = Dermovate; Imitrex = Imigran.

Table 26 **Share of the US prescription market of Glaxo Inc. 1978–1995**

	Market share (%)	Total sales* ($000)	Adjusted ($000)	Company ranking in US	Total number of employees
1978	–	4,905	7,523	na	na
1979	0.14	11,082	15,264	na	250
1980	0.13	13,047	15,834	65	280
1981	0.16	15,435	16,980	59	310
1982	0.26	31,575	32,720	53	310
1983	0.62	44,137	44,314	36	410
1984	1.35	198,405	190,958	20	560
1985	1.79	348,555	324,237	13	1120
1986	3.15	610,331	556,364	9	na
1987	3.66	937,249	824,318	4	2,245
1988	4.29	1,284,158	1,085,510	4	3,149
1989	3.57	1,669,522	1,346,389	4	3,867
1990	3.54	1,956,889	1,497,237	4	4,304
1991	5.23	2,292,920	1,683,495	2	na
1992	5.41	2,786,878	1,986,371	2	5,411
1993	6.5	3,176,400	2,198,201	2	6,440
1994	6.9	3,681,500	2,482,468	2	6,500
1995	7.0	3,883,700	2,548,360	1	6,240

Notes: *These totals include domestic sales for Meyer Laboratory products up to 1990 when they were discontinued, and exclude bulk products; na = not available; figures adjusted by Consumer Price Index, 1982–84 = 100.
Source: Glaxo Inc.

Table 27 **Worldwide distribution of Glaxo sales 1965–1994** (%)

	1965	1975	1980	1985	1990	1994
United Kingdom	38	21	25	19	12	9
Europe excluding UK	20	35	33	32	30	26
North America	4	4	}12	28	45	43
Latin America	3	7		3	2	4
Africa and Middle East	7	7	5	6	2	2
Southern Asia and Far East	24	21	21	9	6	3
Australasia	4	5	4	3	3	2

Source: 1965 and 1975 from Girolami, *The Development of Glaxo*, p. 13; 1980, 1985, 1990 and 1994 from *Glaxo Holdings Annual Report and Accounts*.

Table 28 **Sales of Nippon Glaxo (formerly Shin Nihon) 1972–1993** (¥ million)

1972	8,431	1983	27,633
1973	9,813	1984	17,391
1974	12,363	1985	24,452
1975	14,786	1986	25,055
1976	16,325	1987	35,402
1977	15,543	1988	39,946
1978	18,352	1989	39,522
1979	5,626	1990	41,493
1980	14,860	1991	43,287
1981	17,861	1992	43,700
1982	26,910	1993	44,953

GLOSSARY OF SCIENTIFIC TERMS

§

Agonist/Antagonist In pharmacy, an agonist is a specific chemical substance or ligand with an affinity for a specific cell receptor, which produces an effect resembling that caused by a naturally occurring endogenous substance, such as a hormone or neuro-transmitter. An antagonist, by contrast, is a ligand which binds to its receptor without producing a biological response.

Alpha- and beta-blockers Drugs that achieve their effects by adrenergic blockade, that is, the stimulation of the sympathetic nervous system or of the circulating catecholamines, adrenaline and noradrenaline. Alpha-blockers selectively block effects at a class of adrenergic receptor known as alphareceptors, which mediate contraction of vascular smooth muscle and hence cause vasoconstriction. Beta-blockers selectively inhibit sympathetic beta-effects, which include cardiac stimulation and bronchodilatation. Beta-blockers relieve anxiety and reduce blood pressure; they are often prescribed in heart disease.

Calciferol One of two vitamin D compounds: ergocalciferol (vitamin D_2) or cholecalciferol (vitamin D_3) used in the treatment of rickets.

Cephalosporins Antibiotics related to the penicillins but relatively penicillanse-resistant. The newer cephalosporins are mainly used against Gram-negative organisms.

Co-marketing More than one company marketing products with the same active ingredient but under their own distinctive brand names.

Co-promotion More than one company marketing the same product under the same brand name.

Corticosteroids Steroids secreted by the adrenal cortex and their synthetic analogues. They are of two main groups: (1) glucocorticoids (cortisone, cortisol, hydrocortisone, prednisone, prednisolone), which act predominantly on carbohydrate, fat, and protein metabolism, have many medical uses and are widely employed as anti-inflammatory and immunosuppressant agents, and (2) mineralocorticoids, which have as their main function the maintenance of fluid and electrolyte balance.

Diathermy The process of heating tissues by passing an electric current of high-frequency electromagnetic radiation through them. It can be used to warm muscles and joints beneath the skin or in surgery to cause heat coagulation and necrosis by localised intense application.

Ethical A term describing prescription drugs as distinct from over-the-counter (OTC) medicines which can be freely purchased by the public.

Generic A term denoting the non-proprietory, unbranded name of a drug or pharmaceutical preparation. For example, ranitidine is the generic name of the proprietory medicine Zantac.

Penicillin The first of the antibiotics. The original penicillin G was from *Pencillium notatum.* Collectively they have a wide spectrum of activity against Gram-positive micro-organisms (staphylococci, streptococci and pneumococci) but also some which are Gram-negative (meningococci, gonococci) and some spirochaetes, clostridia and fungi.

Pharmacogenetics The study of genetically determined variation in individual responses to drugs.

Pharmacokinetics The dynamics of drug distribution in biological systems.

Serotonin (also known as 5-hydroxytryptamine) Substance widely distributed in the body and found with high concentrations in the pineal gland and central nervous system. It has a number of physiological roles, including haemostasis, inhibition of gastric secretion and neurotransmission in the brain. It is derived from the amino acid trytophan.

Staphylococcus Gram-positive bacteria widely distributed in the environment and often present on the skin and in the nasal cavity of healthy subjects. They vary in their capacity to produce infection, and most that do so belong to the species called *Staphyloccus aureus.* They are responsible for many types of superficial infection (boils, carbuncles, impetigo) and more serious, deep infections including septicaemia, osteomyelitis, enteritis, pneumonia and abcesses. Many staphylococci have acquired resistance to particular antibiotics.

Streptococcus One of a large and heterogeneous group of Gram-positive bacteria named for their tendency to grow in chains. *Streptococcus pyogenes* cause over 90 per cent of human infections, particularly of the upper respiratory tract (tonsillitis and scarlet fever), skin and subcutaneous tissues and blood (septicaemia), and are also indirectly responsible for rheumatic fever.

NOTES

§

Preface

1. Sir William Osler, *Science*, 17 (1891), 170.
2. *Glaxo Wellcome Annual Report and Accounts* (1998), 3.
3. Ibid., 87.
4. Sir Harry Jephcott, *The First Fifty Years, An account of the early life of Joseph Edward Nathan and the first fifty years of his merchandise business that eventually became the Glaxo Group*, Ipswich: Privately printed (1969).
5. *Glaxo Holdings Annual Report and Accounts* (1987), frontispiece.
6. Quoted from 'Glaxo Laboratories in Britain' (colour film *c.* 1955), directed by Stanley Schofield.
7. Alec Nathan, 'It can be done', 14 September 1923.
8. Judy Slinn, *A History of May & Baker 1834–1984*, Cambridge: Hobsons (1984).
9. James Foreman-Peck, *Smith & Nephew in the Health Care Industry*, Cheltenham (1995).
10. Geoffrey Tweedale, *At the Sign of the Plough, Allen & Hanburys and the British Pharmaceutical Industry 1715–1990*, London: John Murray (1990).
11. Rolv Petter Amdam, *Nycomed* (1996).
12. R. P. T. Davenport-Hines and Judy Slinn, *Glaxo, A History to 1962*, Cambridge: Cambridge University Press (1992).

1 The Nathans and the origins of Glaxo

1. James Taggart, *The World Pharmaceutical Industry*, London: Routledge (1993), 206.
2. *Values and Visions, A Merck Century*, Rahway (1991), 13.
3. Taggart, *The World Pharmaceutical Industry*, 340, 356.
4. Hans Conrad Peyer, *Roche, A Company History 1896–1996*, Basel: Editiones Roche (1996), 27–29.
5. Tweedale, *At the Sign of the Plough*, 14, 34, 56.
6. Taggart, *The World Pharmaceutical Industry*, 322.
7. Letter, M. J. Nathan to Alec Nathan (*c.* 1946), 1–2.
8. Jephcott, *First Fifty Years*, 13.
9. L. M. Goldman, *The History of the Jews in New Zealand*, Wellington: A. H. & A. W. Reid (1958), 51; *New Zealand Mail*, 'Special Wellington Number', 12 June 1907.
10. Jephcott, *First Fifty Years*, 26; *The Cyclopaedia of New Zealand* (n.d.), 714–15.
11. Jephcott, *First Fifty Years*, 37; S. Jacobs, 'Some notes, probably not in chronological order, of the history of Joseph Nathan & Co Ltd' (typescript, 3 February 1953), 2.
12. *New Zealand Mail*, May 1874, quoted from Julia Millen, *Glaxo, From Bonnie Babies to Better Medicines, The People who Made Glaxo*, Palmerston North (1991), 12; *Wellington Independent*, 26 June 1873.
13. Letter, M. J. Nathan to Alec Nathan (*c.* 1946), 2.
14. Davenport-Hines and Slinn, *Glaxo*, 29.
15. Ibid., 33.
16. Letter, J. E. Nathan (23 Pembridge Gardens) to his sons, David, Louis and Maurice Nathan, 8 November 1899.
17. 'Premises in the UK' (typescript *c.* 1958); Davenport-Hines and Slinn, *Glaxo*, 39.

18. Letter, L. J. Nathan to Alec Nathan, 4 February 1930, 6; T. Lindsay Buick, *Old Manuwatu*, Palmerston North: Buick & Young (1903), 389–91.
19. *New Zealand Mail*, 12 June 1907.
20. Quoted from Jephcott, *First Fifty Years*, 45.
21. Letter, J. E. Nathan to David, Louis and Maurice Nathan, 8 November 1899.
22. Davenport-Hines and Slinn, *Glaxo*, 15.
23. Joseph Nathan & Co. Board Minutes, vol. I, 24 October 1899.
24. Ibid., 16 February 1902, 27 October 1904, 17 May 1908.
25. Jephcott, *First Fifty Years*, 65–66.
26. Will and Codicil of Joseph Edward Nathan, 22 October 1911.
27. Jephcott, *First Fifty Years*, 114–15.
28. Letter, L. J. Nathan to Alec Nathan, 4 February 1930, 7.
29. Ibid.; Davenport-Hines and Slinn, *Glaxo*, 11.
30. Ibid., 62; Jacobs, 'History of Joseph Nathan & Co.', 3–4.
31. Davenport-Hines and Slinn, *Glaxo*, 19.
32. Letter, M. J. Nathan to Alec Nathan, 4 February 1930, 3; Jephcott, *First Fifty Years*, 68–69.
33. Alec Nathan, 'The story of Glaxo' (typescript, 19 March 1917), 1–2.
34. Ibid., 1–2.
35. Quoted in R. E. Clevely, *Bunnythorpe and District 1872–1952*, Wellington (1953), 57.
36. *Glaxogram*, August 1921; Fred Nathan, 'The genesis of Glaxo', ibid., December 1921, 9; Alec Nathan 'The story of Glaxo', 2.
37. 'Specification for building Dried Milk Factory at Bunnythorpe' (typescript, n.d.).
38. Alec Nathan, 'Memorandum', 29 March 1917.
39. 'The organisation of a pure milk supply', *The Lancet*, 1 (29 June 1901), 1841–42.
40. 'Municipal Authorities and the Feeding of Infants', *Lancet* 2 (31 August 1901), 608.
41. Nathan 'Memorandum'.
42. Report by Richard Woosnam, Analytical Laboratory, Brentwood, Essex, 9 May 1905.
43. Davenport-Hines and Slinn, *Glaxo*, 27; W. H. Beable, *Romance of Great Businesses*, London: Heath Cranton (1926), 212.
44. Clifford Turner, 'From where we all began', *Glaxo World*, 17, December 1991, 22.
45. Jephcott, *First Fifty Years*, 76.
46. Nathan, 'The story of Glaxo', it. 2.
47. Noble Scott, 'The advertising of Glaxo' (typescript, *c.* 1917), 6.
48. *Daily Mail*, 27 May 1908, 1.
49. Nathan, 'The story of Glaxo', it. 7.
50. Noble Scott, 'The advertising of Glaxo', 7.
51. Nathan, 'The story of Glaxo', it. 7.
52. Alec Nathan, 'Business as a career' (typescript, 9 April 1943), 2.
53. Nathan, 'The story of Glaxo', it. 8.
54. Ibid., it. 11.
55. Noble Scott, 'The advertising of Glaxo', 11.
56. *Notable Personalities* (1927), 'Alec Nathan'.
57. Nathan, 'Memorandum'.
58. Noble Scott, 'The Advertising of Glaxo', 8.
59. Quoted ibid.
60. Joseph Nathan Board Minutes, 3 February 1913.
61. Noble Scott, 'The advertising of Glaxo', 1.
62. Quoted ibid., 4.
63. Virginia Woolf, *Mrs Dalloway*, [1925], Harmondsworth: Penguin (1964), 23–24.
64. Joseph Nathan & Co. Minute Book, vol. I, 5 November 1912.
65. Joseph Nathan & Co. Minute Book, vol. II, 27 January 1914, 20.
66. Ibid., 15 September 1914, 40–41.
67. Ibid., 12 July 1916, 104.
68. Ibid., 31 January 1919, 212.
69. Ibid., 20 May 1919, 234.
70. Ibid., 31 October 1919, 285.
71. Joseph Nathan & Co. Minute Book, vol. III, 15 December 1921, 153.
72. Ibid., 3 March 1922, 182.
73. Nathan, 'The story of Glaxo', it. 44, 60.
74. Ibid., it. 40.
75. *Souvenir of Dinner … to the London Office Staffs of Joseph Nathan & Co.* (1920).
76. Joseph Nathan & Co. Board Minutes, vol. II, 15 September 1914, 42.
77. 'Confidential Reports', municipal sales 1915–1917.
78. Quoted from Jephcott, *First Fifty Years*, 106.
79. Davenport-Hines and Slinn, *Glaxo*, 44–45; Glaxo Medical Department, *Dried Milk: Its Medical Aspect* (n.d.), 4.
80. *The Times*, 13 April 1918, 'Joseph Nathan & Company … Continued Growth of the Business'.
81. *The Times*, 29 April 1919, 'Joseph Nathan & Company, the principles of economical advertising'.
82. Joseph Nathan & Co. Board Minutes, vol. I, 18 March 1913.
83. Joseph Nathan & Co. Board Minutes, vol. II, 7 November 1919, 2.

84. Davenport-Hines and Slinn, *Glaxo*, 46; *Who's Who*, London (1947), 2379.

85. Souvenir of Dinner and Dance ...to the London Office Staffs of Joseph Nathan & Co. (1920).

86. *Glaxo House, Osnaburgh Street* (n.d.).

87. 'Executive Officers' (typescript plan).

88. Jephcott, *First Fifty Years*, 85–86; Joseph Nathan & Co. Board Minutes, vol. II, 11 March 1919, 220.

89. *Glaxo House, Osnaburgh Street.*

90. Jephcott, *First Fifty Years*, 115–16; 'Stepping stones in the affairs of Joseph Nathan & Co.' (typescript, 1950).

91. Davenport-Hines and Slinn, *Glaxo*, 53.

92. Circular from Sir Harry Jephcott, 5 January 1956.

93. 'Stepping stones in the affairs of J. N. & Co.'

94. Alec Nathan, 'To the "It can be done" Letters', 1 January 1923.

95. Alec Nathan, Letter 10; 'Courtesy', 2 March 1923.

96. Alec Nathan, Letter, No. 37, 'Is business a profession?', 7 September 1923.

97. Alec Nathan, 'Business as a Career' (typescript, 9 April 1943), 4.

98. *Staff Bulletin in tribute to Alec Nathan*, December 1954, 3.

99. 'The romance of business, no. 4, Glaxo', *John Bull*, 17 February 1923.

100. *Newspaper Advertising*, 1 (November 1925), 'Personalities in advertising, Alec Nathan', 6.

101. *In Tribute to Alec Nathan*, 10.

102. Joseph Nathan & Co. Board Minutes, vol. III, 10 March 1921, 100.

103. Jephcott, *First Fifty Years*, 89.

104. R. P. T. Davenport-Hines, 'Sir Harry Jephcott', *DBB*, 3 (1985), 491; Davenport-Hines and Slinn, *Glaxo*, 47.

105. *The Bulletin*, 260 (February 1961), 4.

106. Ibid., 'My Brother Charles', 6–7.

107. Ibid., 5.

108. Jephcott, *First Fifty Years*, 91.

109. Ibid., 91–92.

110. W. F. J. Cuthbertson, 'Alfred Louis Bacharach', *Proceedings of the Society of Analytical Chemistry*, 4 (1967), 67–69; Harry Jephcott, 'Alfred Louis Bacharach', *Chemistry and Industry* (1966), 1651–53.

111. Quoted in Millen, *Glaxo, from Bonnie Babes*, 63.

112. *The Manufacture of Glaxo*, London (n.d.), 5.

113. Ibid.

114. Glaxo Medical Department, *Dried Milk*, 9.

115. 'The etiology of rickets', *BMJ*, 2 (12 October 1918), 411.

116. 'Environment and diet in the causation of rickets', *BMJ*, 2 (23 December 1922), 1231.

117. E. V. McCollum, N. Simonds, J. E. Becker *et al.*, *Journal of Biological Chemistry*, 53 (1922), 293.

118. E. V. McCollum, N. Simonds J. E. Becker, *et al.*, *Bulletin Johns Hopkins Hospital*, 33 (1922), 229; see also Maurice E. Shils and Vernon R. Young (eds), *Modern Nutrition in Health and Disease*, Philadelphia: Lea & Febiger (1988), 313.

119. H. Jephcott, 'Ostelin' (typescript, 26 August 1926), 7.

120. Joseph Nathan & Co. Board Minutes, vol. IV, 15 February 1924, 62.

121. Joseph Nathan & Co. Board Minutes, vol. V, 8 September 1927, 55.

122. H. Jephcott, 'Ostelin sales and propaganda' (typescript, 26 November 1926).

123. Jephcott, 'Ostelin', op.cit., 8.

124. Ibid., 12.

125. 'Concentrated preparations of vitamins', *BMJ*, 2 (12 December 1925), 1133.

126. Jephcott, 'Ostelin', 1.

127. Ibid., 13.

128. Ibid., 2.

129. Ibid., 14.

130. Ibid., 18.

131. Ibid., 19.

132. *Glaxo Laboratories, A Decade of Vitamin D 1924–1934*, 10.

133. Ibid., 5.

134. Elmer V. McCollum, *A History of Nutrition, the Sequence of Ideas in Nutrition Investigations*, Boston (1957), 284–85.

135. Shils and Young (eds), *Modern Nutrition*, James A. Orson, 'Vitamin A, retinoids and carotenoids', 292.

136. Davenport-Hines and Slinn, *Glaxo*, 81.

137. Glaxo Laboratories Board Minutes, vol. I, 30 October 1935, 11.

138. Joseph Nathan & Co. Board Minutes, vol. V, 17 April 1928, 97.

139. Ibid., 28 August 1928, 128; 4 October 1928, 135.

140. Joseph Nathan & Co. Board Minutes, vol. VI, 25 February 1930, 1.

141. A. R. Lewis, 'Fifty years' continuous service with Glaxo Laboratories 1920–1970' (typescript 31 July 1970), 3.

142. Joseph Nathan & Co. Board Minutes, vol. VI, 22 October 1931, 116.

143. Memorandum, E. W. Pates to Col. Rose, 'Temporary labour at Hayes', 4 June 1935.

144. Lewis, 'Fifty years', 4.

145. 'Ostelin and Ostermilk' (typescript, 1957).

146. Hugo Wolff, 'The history of Ostermilk' (typescript, 25 August 1938), 1, 8.

147. Ibid., 3.

148. Ibid., 5.

149. Ibid.

150. Ibid., 7.

151. Ibid., 8.

152. Harry Jephcott, 'Cereal food' (typescript, 24 July 1934), 1.

153. Davenport-Hines and Slinn, *Glaxo*, 82.

154. Jephcott, 'Cereal food', 2.

155. Memorandum, Mr Preston to Mr H. Jephcott, 'Farex', 9 March 1935.

156. Davenport-Hines and Slinn, *Glaxo*, 83.

157. Preston, 'Farex'.

158. Davenport-Hines and Slinn, *Glaxo*, 84.

159. Glaxo Laboratories board memorandum, March 1935.

160. Mr Dodds, 'Manufacture of Minadex' (typescript, n.d.).

161. Joseph Nathan & Co. Board Minutes, vol. VI, 26 February 1931, 71.

162. Ibid., 20 March 1931, 75; 22 March 1932, 146.

2 Glaxo comes of age 1935–1939

1. Sir John Betjeman, *Collected Poems*, London: John Murray (1958), 164.

2. 'Directors' Report to be submitted at the first AGM of Glaxo Laboratories'; Davenport-Hines and Slinn, *Glaxo*, 85–86.

3. Glaxo Laboratories Board Minutes, vol. I, 21 October 1935, 4.

4. *Victoria County History of Middlesex*, vol. IV, London (1971), 124.

5. Charles E. Lee, *The District Line, A Brief History*, London: London Transport Executive (1973), 29.

6. M. A. C. Horne, *The Central Line, A Short History*, London: Douglas Rose (1987), 43.

7. *Victoria County History of Middlesex*, vol. III, London (1962), 214.

8. John Stevenson, *British Society 1914–45*, Harmondsworth: Penguin Books (1984), 130.

9. Alastair Forsyth, *Buildings for the Age, New Building Types 1900–1939*, London: HMSO (1982).

10. J. B. Priestley, *English Journey* [1934], Harmondsworth: Penguin Books (1977), 10.

11. Joan Skinner, *Form and Fancy, Factories and Factory Buildings by Wallis Gilbert & Partners 1916–1939*, Liverpool: Liverpool University Press (1997), 16–23.

12. Ibid., 114–18, 147–57; Edgar Jones, *Industrial Architecture in Britain 1750–1939*, London: B. T. Batsford (1985), 213–14.

13. Forsyth, *Buildings for the Age*, 20.

14. Quoted in Skinner, *Wallis Gilbert & Partners*, 282.

15. Davenport-Hines and Slinn, *Glaxo*, 85.

16. Quoted in Skinner, *Wallis Gilbert & Partners*, 282.

17. Ibid., 284.

18. Ibid., 285.

19. C. Turner, *Gold on the Green, Fifty Glaxo Years at Greenford*, London: Glaxo Pharmaceuticals Ltd (1986), 32–33.

20. Glaxo Laboratories Board Minutes, vol. I, 28 November 1935, 17.

21. Quoted in Skinner, *Wallis Gilbert*, 177.

22. Glaxo Laboratories Board Minutes, vol. I, 10 October 1939, 254.

23. Quoted in Davenport-Hines and Slinn, *Glaxo*, 90.

24. Turner, *Gold on the Green*, 37.

25. Fuller, Horsey, Sons and Cassell, 'Schedule of Fixed and Loose Plant and Machinery … at Greenford Road, September 1942', 2.

26. Ibid., 20–21; Turner, *Gold on the Green*, 40.

27. *The New Glaxo Laboratories, Greenford, Middlesex* (1935), plans 1–3.

28. *The New Home of Glaxo Laboratories Ltd* (n.d.), 2.

29. Turner, *Gold on the Green*, 95.

30. 'A review of the year ending September 1938' (typescript, 9 December 1938), it. 152.

31. Ibid.

32. Glaxo Laboratories Board Minutes, vol. I, 30 October 1935, 12.

33. Ibid.

34. 'A review of the year ending September 1938' (typescript, 9 December 1938), it. 17.

35. Ibid., it. 6, table 1.

36. Ibid., it. 3.

37. Glaxo Laboratories Board Minutes, vol. I, 30 October 1935, 14.

38. Ibid.

39. Ibid., 1 January 1936, 25.

40. Ibid.

41. [Alec Nathan], 'Representatives' working instructions', Greenford, October 1936.

42. Ibid., para (e).

43. 'A review of the year ending September 1938', it. 65.
44. Ibid., it. 66.
45. Ibid., it. 72.
46. Ibid., it. 73.
47. Ibid., it. 76, 75.
48. Ibid., it. 100.
49. Ibid., it. 149.
50. Glaxo Laboratories Board Minutes, vol. I, 16 June 1936, 56.
51. Ibid., 21 March 1939, 218–19.
52. Ibid., 18 April 1939, 223.
53. Ibid., 27 June 1939, 238.
54. Ibid., 22 September 1936, 71.
55. Ibid., 72.
56. Ibid., 24 November 1936, 88.
57. Ibid., 11 December 1936, 91; Letter, Milk Marketing Board to Glaxo Laboratories, 10 December 1936.
58. Ibid., 19 January 1937, 101.
59. Ibid., 9 February 1937, 103–104.
60. Ibid., 27 April 1937, 119; Report, E. H. Farmer to H. Jephcott, 'Visit to Driffield' (19 March 1937).
61. 'Driffield, siding for Glaxo Laboratories Ltd'.
62. Glaxo Laboratories Board Minutes, vol. I, 25 May 1937, 122.
63. Ibid., 5 October 1937, 135; Skinner, *Wallis Gilbert & Partners*, 182–83.
64. Quoted in Davenport-Hines and Slinn, *Glaxo*, 94.
65. Ibid., 3 March 1936, 32.
66. Ibid., 27 November 1936, 90.
67. Turner, *Gold on the Green*, 104.

3 Glaxo at war

1. Glaxo Laboratories Board Minutes, vol. I, 6 December 1938, 185.
2. Ibid., 26 November 1940, 320.
3. Davenport-Hines, 'Sir Harry Jephcott', 492; F. H. K. Green and Sir Gordon Covell, *Medical History of the Second World War, Medical Research*, London: HMSO (1953), 361.
4. Glaxo Laboratories Board Minutes, vol. II, 13 November 1944, 150–51.
5. Ibid., 151.
6. Ibid., 11 January 1945, 166.
7. Ibid., 25 September 1945, 207.
8. Ibid.
9. Ibid., 27 November 1945, 214.
10. Glaxo Laboratories Board Minutes, vol. I, 27 June 1939, 237.
11. Ibid., 30 April 1940, 291.
12. Ibid., 14 November 1939, 257.
13. Ibid., 30 April 1940, 291.
14. Ibid., 3 September 1940, 310.
15. Ibid., 311.
16. Ibid., 28 January 1941, 325.
17. Ibid.
18. Ibid., 13 May 1941, 350.
19. Ibid., 25 February 1941, 340.
20. Ibid., 339.
21. Ibid., 340.
22. Ibid., 13 May 1941, 347.
23. Glaxo Laboratories Board Minutes, vol. II, 17 March 1942, 47.
24. Ibid., 47–48.
25. Ibid., 48.
26. Ibid., 5 October 1942, 62.
27. Ibid., 64.
28. Ibid., 3 May 1943, 89.
29. Ibid., 24 August 1944, 140.
30. Ibid., 4 September 1944, 143.
31. Ibid.
32. Ibid., 13 November 1944, 150.
33. Editorial, 'The National Loaf', *The Lancet*, 1 (31 May 1941), 698.
34. Glaxo Laboratories Board Minutes, vol. I, 29 January 1941, 333–34.
35. Interview with Dr Peter Wilkinson, 27 October 1995.
36. Glaxo Laboratories Board Minutes, vol. II, 16 September 1941, 6.
37. Ibid., 4 November 1941, 18.
38. Ibid., 3 March 1942, 41.
39. Ibid., 7 July 1942, 54.
40. *The Lancet*, 1 (31 May 1941), 699.
41. Sir H. W. Florey, 'Penicillin: a survey', *BMJ*, 2 (1944), 169.
42. John Hunt, 'Pioneering penicillin production in Britain', *Pharmaceutical Journal*, 21–28 December 1991, 807–08.
43. R. V. Christie and L. P. Garrod, 'An investigation of the therapeutic properties of penicillin, a report of the Medical Research Council', *BMJ*, 1 (1944), 513.
44. Editorial, 'Penicillin: an antiseptic of microbic origin', *BMJ*, 1 (1941), 310.
45. See also G. L. Hobby, *Penicillin: Meeting the Challenge*, New Haven: Yale University Press (1985).
46. E. Chain, H. W. Florey, A. D. Gardner *et al.*, 'Penicillin as an antibacterial agent', *The Lancet*, 2 (1940), 226.
47. Mr Treves Brown, 'Notes on the history of

penicillin in Glaxo Laboratories' (typescript, October 1946), 1.

48. Memorandum, F. A. Robinson to H. Jephcott, 'Penicillin', 31 October 1941.

49. Ibid., 2.

50. Treves Brown, 'History of penicillin', 2.

51. Memorandum, Col. E. A. Rose to H. Jephcott, 'Penicillin production' (typescript, 12 October 1942), Appendix.

52. Ibid., 1–2.

53. Glaxo Laboratories Board Minutes, vol. II, 7 October 1941, 11.

54. Davenport-Hines and Slinn, *Glaxo*, 140.

55. Ibid., 141.

56. Glaxo Laboratories Board Minutes, vol. II, 17 November 1941, 26.

57. Ibid., 27.

58. W. F. J. Cuthbertson and J. E. Page, 'Ernest Lester Smith', *Biographical Memoirs of Fellows of the Royal Society*, 40 (1994), 356.

59. Memorandum, F. A. Robinson to H. Jephcott, 'Penicillin', 31 October 1941, 1.

60. J. E. Page, *Biochemist*, 13 (1991), 2.

61. Hunt, 'Pioneering penicillin production', 809.

62. E. Lester Smith, 'British Penicillin Production', *Journal of the Society of Chemical Industry*, 65 (1946), 309.

63. Letter, R. Barrington Brock of Townson & Mercer to H. W. Palmer, 16 June 1943.

64. Cuthbertson and Page, 'Ernest Lester Smith', 357.

65. Lester Smith, 'British penicillin production', 311.

66. Ibid.

67. Ibid., 2.

68. Ibid., 5, 7.

69. L. H. Robinson to Col. Rose, 'Annual Report on Penicillin Production at Aylesbury Factory for year 1943 to 1944', 1 November 1944, 2.

70. Christie and Garrod, 'Therapeutic properties of penicillin', 513.

71. Editorial, 'Penicillin', *BMJ*, 1 (1943), 481.

72. Editorial, 'The penicillin position', *BMJ*, 2 (1943), 269.

73. Editorial, 'Penicillin in battle wounds', *BMJ*, 2 (1944), 750; 'Reports of societies, discussion on penicillin', ibid., 654.

74. Glaxo Laboratories Board Minutes, vol. II, 12 July 1943, 95.

75. Ibid., 6 September 1943, 97.

76. Ibid., 4 October 1943, 99.

77. Treves Brown, 'History of penicillin', op.cit., 9.

78. H. Jephcott, 'Penicillin' (typescript, 11 November 1943), 1.

79. Ibid., 2.

80. Hunt, 'Pioneering penicillin production', 809.

81. Quoted ibid., 809.

82. Treves Brown, 'History of penicillin', 12.

83. Glaxo Laboratories Board Minutes, vol. II, 22 February 1944, 121; 1 ibid., May 1944, 128.

84. Treves Brown, 'History of penicillin', 13.

85. 'Penicillin points' (typescript, May 1947).

86. Glaxo Laboratories Board Minutes, vol. II, 3 April 1944, 126.

87. Ibid., 5 June 1944, 132.

88. Ibid., 153.

89. Ibid., 13 November 1944, 152.

90. Letter, Control of Factory & Storage Premises, Board of Trade to H. Jephcott, 29 July 1944.

91. Nigel Watson, *Glaxo at Barnard Castle, A Celebration* (1994), 12.

92. Glaxo Laboratories Board Minutes, vol. II, 4 September 1944, 145.

93. Ibid., 13 November 1944, 153.

94. Ibid., 4 December 1944, 156.

95. Letter, Sir Cecil Weir to H. Jephcott, 4 September 1944.

96. Glaxo Laboratories Board Minutes, vol. II, 2 January 1945, 162.

97. Ibid.

98. Ibid., 23 January 1945, 169.

99. Ibid., 15 February 1945, 170.

100. Ibid., 27 March 1945, 176; letter, F. C. Everett of the Penicillin Production Control, Ministry of Supply, to H. Jephcott, 2 February 1945.

101. Glaxo Laboratories Board Minutes, vol. II, 177.

102. Ibid., 11 May 1945, 182.

103. Ibid., 28 August 1945, 200.

104. A. H. Campbell, 'Fermentation Division–Barnard Castle, first quarterly report' (typescript 30 April 1946), 1; Watson, *Glaxo at Barnard Castle*, 16.

105. Quoted ibid., 17.

106. Campbell, 'First quarterly report', 6.

107. 'Notes on a discussion … proposed production of penicillin by Distillers' (typescript, 4 June 1944), 1.

108. 'What is deep culture?' (typescript, May 1947).

109. Campbell, 'First quarterly report', 24 July 1945, 195.

110. Watson, *Glaxo at Barnard Castle*, 17.

111. Glaxo Laboratories Board Minutes, vol. II, 20 September 1945, 202.
112. Ibid., 24 October 1945, 209.
113. Turner, *Gold on the Green*, 45.
114. Glaxo Laboratories Board Minutes, vol. I, 14 November 1939, 259.
115. Ibid., 11 June 1940, 301.
116. Ibid., 302.
117. Glaxo Laboratories Board Minutes, vol. II, 16 September 1941, 8.
118. Ibid., 1 December 1944, 32.
119. Ibid., 22 December 1944, 34.
120. Ibid.
121. Glaxo Laboratories Board Minutes, vol. I, 17 September 1940, 313.
122. Interview with Sir Austin Bide, 10 February 1997.
123. Glaxo Laboratories Board Minutes, vol. I, 29 January 1941, 333.
124. Turner, *Gold on the Green*, 44, 47.
125. Glaxo Laboratories Board Minutes, vol. II, 4 September 1944, 143.
126. Ibid., 144.
127. Chief Accountant's Report on the Accounts for the year ended 30 September 1946 (typescript), 2.

4 The Jephcott Era 1946–1961

1. *The Man in the White Suit*, Ealing Studios (1951), based on a play by Roger MacDougall, produced by Michael Balcon.
2. *GL Staff Bulletin*, special edition, January 1947.
3. Interview with Clifford Turner, 25 June 1997.
4. Glaxo Laboratories Board Minutes, vol. II, 25 September 1945, 207.
5. *Joseph Nathan & Co. Ltd., Annual Report and Accounts for year ended 30 September 1946*, 'Statement by the chairman'.
6. Interview with Clifford Turner, 25 June 1997.
7. *Nathan Annual Report 1946*, 'Statement by the chairman'.
8. Glaxo Laboratories was recapitalised by £1.5 million; this involved issuing 500,000 7 per cent preference shares, 400,000 8 per cent preferred ordinary shares, 1,592,000 ordinary shares of 1s each and 720,365 unclassified shares of £1 each. Glaxo Laboratories Board Minutes, vol. II, 3 January 1947, 299–300.
9. Ibid., 31 January 1947, 307.
10. Ibid., 29 January 1946, 231.
11. E. F. Laidlaw, *The Story of the Royal National Hospital, Ventnor*, Newport, IOW (1990), 94.
12. Ibid., 69.
13. Glaxo Laboratories Board Minutes, vol. II, 29 January 1946, 231.
14. Ibid., 30 April 1946, 245.
15. H. W. Palmer, 'Site requirements' (typescript, January 1946).
16. Letter, A. Turner, Board of Trade, to Glaxo Laboratories, 25 February 1946.
17. Letter, A. Turner, Board of Trade, to Glaxo Laboratories, 4 March 1946.
18. Glaxo Laboratories Board Minutes, vol. II, 30 April 1946, 245.
19. Letter, F. C. Everett, Ministry of Supply, to Glaxo Laboratories, 23 April 1946.
20. Glaxo Laboratories Board Minutes, vol. II, 16 May 1946, 252.
21. Ibid., 30 April 1946, 245.
22. Ibid., 23 July 1946, 269.
23. Ibid., 4 June 1946, 259.
24. Letter, A. Turner, Board of Trade, Manchester, to H. Jephcott, 11 June 1946.
25. Glaxo Laboratories Board Minutes, vol. II, 25 June 1946, 261.
26. Ibid., 23 July 1946, 267.
27. Glaxo Laboratories Board Minutes, vol. II, 4 November 1946, 290.
28. Information provided by Dr Joan Skinner, 21 October 1996.
29. Glaxo Laboratories Board Minutes, vol. II, 4 July 1947, 329.
30. Glaxo Laboratories BP 4/47, H. Jephcott, 'Extension of production and other facilities', 23 January 1947.
31. Glaxo Laboratories Board Minutes, vol. II, 25 July 1947, 332.
32. Glaxo Laboratories Board Minutes, vol. III, 30 April 1948, 20.
33. 'Press release: Glaxo development in the North, the Ulverston enterprise' (typescript, c. 1953), 2.
34. Glaxo Laboratories Board Minutes, vol. III, 26 November 1948, 37.
35. Memorandum, Sir Harry Jephcott to Dr F. J. Wilkins, 13 December 1951.
36. 'The Harry Lee story of 50 years at Ulverston' (typescript, 11 March 1996), 6.
37. A. J. Mitchell, 'Ulverston technical improvements' (typescript, 22 October 1996), 1.
38. Glaxo Laboratories Annual Accounts for year ended 30 September 1945, Schedules 1.C. and 1.D.

39. Glaxo Laboratories Board Minutes, vol. II, 4 June 1946, 256.
40. Glaxo Laboratories Executive Board Minutes, vol. I, 5 May 1948, 4.
41. Glaxo Executive Board Minutes, 16 December 1948, 5.
42. Ibid., 23 September 1948, 3.
43. Ibid., 7 October 1948, 5.
44. Ibid., 4.
45. Glaxo Laboratories BP 57/43, 'Notes on cash forecast to 31 October 1957'.
46. Glaxo Laboratories BP 58/34, 'Group sales to 31 March 1958'.
47. Glaxo Laboratories BP 59/50, 'Group trading position to 31 March 1959'; BP 59/84, 'Group trading position year to 30 June 1959'.
48. Glaxo Laboratories Executive Board Minutes, 60/1, 21 January 1960, 4.
49. Ibid., 62/1, 5 January 1962, 3.
50. Ibid., 63/18, 19 September 1963, 5.
51. Ibid., 61/7a, 26 July 1961, 2.
52. Ibid., 61/8, 21 September 1961, 3–4.
53. Ibid.
54. Ibid., 63/15, 8 August 1963, 3.
55. Ibid., 63/7, 5 April 1963, 3.
56. Macrae sat on the Accessory Food Factors' Committee of the Medical Research Council, while Jephcott served on the Vitamin Claims' Sub-committee. Green and Covell, *Medical Research*, 360–61; Davenport–Hines and Slinn, *Glaxo*, 175.
57. T. K. Lyle, T. F. Macrae and P. A. Gardiner, 'Corneal vascularisation in nutritional deficiency', *The Lancet* 1 (1944), 393–95; E. M. Glaser, 'Lack of vitamins on the war-time army diet', *Journal of the Royal Army Medical Corps*, 99 (1952–53), 29–33.
58. Interview with George Childs, 20 May 1997.
59. Glaxo Laboratories Executive Board Minutes, 23 September 1948, 4.
60. Glaxo Laboratories BP 57/45, F. J. Wilkins, 'Farex manufacture', 27 May 1957.
61. Ibid.
62. Glaxo Laboratories BM 59/109, Group trading position to 31 March 1959.
63. Glaxo Laboratories Executive Board Minutes, 60/1, 21 January 1960, 4.
64. Interview with George Childs, 20 May 1997.
65. Glaxo Laboratories BP 59/30, 'Notes on a talk with Mr W. F. Spencer of the Milk Marketing Board on 24 February 1959'.
66. Ibid., 2.
67. Glaxo Laboratories Executive Board

Minutes, 59/2, 19 March 1959, 6.
68. Glaxo Laboratories BP 59/113, H. W. Palmer, 'Milk powder supplies', 27 October 1959.
69. Ibid.
70. *Glaxo Bulletin*, October 1961, 4–5.
71. Glaxo Laboratories BP 58/59, 'Glaxo Group sales to 30 June 1959'.
72. *Glaxo Laboratories Statement of Accounts for the year ended 30 June 1949*, 12–13.
73. Glaxo Laboratories Board Minutes, 31 December 1952, 203.
74. Ibid., 23 January 1953, 205.
75. Ibid., 31 May 1954, 248; 6 September 1954, 256.
76. *Report of the [Sainsbury] Committee into the relationship of the Pharmaceutical Industry with the National Health Service*, London: HMSO (1967), 21.
77. *Final Report of the [Hinchliffe] Committee on the Cost of Prescribing*, London: HMSO (1959), 29.
78. Glaxo Laboratories BP 58/98, H. Jephcott, 'Index numbers of parent company costs and selling prices', 25 November 1958.
79. Ibid., 2.
80. 'British penicillin mass produced', *Manufacturing Chemist and Manufacturing Perfumer*, 17 (1946), 230–31.
81. 'Introductory dates of Glaxo preparations' (typescript, February 1956).
82. Glaxo Laboratories Executive Board, 60/1, 21 January 1960, 5.
83. Ibid.
84. Ibid., 60/10, 20 October 1960, 3.
85. Ibid., 62/8, 3 May 1962, 3.
86. *Glaxo Today* (*c.* 1953), 23.
87. Glaxo Laboratories BP 58/9, 'Group sales six months to 30 June 1958', 1.
88. Glaxo Laboratories Executive Board, 59/1, 22 January 1959, 5.
89. Ibid., 60/1, 21 January 1960, 4.
90. Glaxo Laboratories BP 57/16, H. W. Palmer, 'Commercial background to proposals for poliomyelitis virus research' (25 February 1957), 1.
91. Glaxo Laboratories BP 58/34, 'Group sales nine months to 31 March 1958'.
92. Glaxo Laboratories BP 58/59, 'Group sales year to 30 June 1958'.
93. Glaxo Laboratories BP 59/14, 'Combined group sales to 31 December 1958'.
94. Glaxo Laboratories Board Minutes, 10 January 1946, 225.
95. Ibid., 5 September 1947, 335; Sir Harry

Jephcott, 'Miss Townsend to retire' (typescript, December 1955).

96. Ibid., 3 January 1947, 294.
97. *Who's Who 1947*, 432, 858–59.
98. Glaxo Laboratories Board Minutes, 31 December 1948, 41.
99. *Who's Who 1947*, 1394.
100. Ibid., 31 December 1948, 41.
101. Ibid., 24 March 1948, 16.
102. Ibid., 29 October 1948, 33.
103. Ibid., 7 November 1956, 309.
104. *Who's Who 1947*, 2268.
105. Davenport-Hines and Slinn, *Glaxo*, 157.
106. *Who's Who 1947*, 1400.
107. Davenport-Hines and Slinn, *Glaxo*, 157.
108. Glaxo Laboratories Board Minutes, 1 November 1954, 266.
109. Ibid., 28 April 1952, 176.
110. Interview with Sir David Jack, 18 January 1994.
111. Glaxo Laboratories Executive Board, 6 March 1949, 1.
112. Glaxo Laboratories Board Minutes, 31 December 1948, 41.
113. Ibid., 29 July 1949, 59.
114. *Glaxo Laboratories Report and Accounts* (1950), 12.
115. Ibid., 29 June 1951, 143.
116. Ibid., 31 May 1954, 247.
117. Ibid., 5 November 1954, 344.
118. Interview with Clifford Turner, 25 June 1997.
119. Ibid., 30 January 1950, 85.
120. Ibid., 29 December 1950, 124.
121. Glaxo Laboratories Board Minutes, 7 November 1955, 309.
122. Ibid., 11 December 1961, it. 4.
123. Ibid.
124. Ibid., 5 November 1956, 344.
125. Ibid., 6 November 1961, it. 196.
126. Glaxo Laboratories Board Minutes, 3 January 1947, 294.
127. Ibid., 30 March 1951, 135; 29 February 1952, 168.
128. Glaxo Laboratories BP, H. Jephcott, 'Company organisation', September 1961, 3; 'Settling down at Park Street', *The Bulletin*, 271 (February 1962), 33–34.
129. Ibid., 29 December 1950, 124.
130. Ibid., 30 March 1951, 135.
131. Ibid., 27 June 1952, 183.
132. *Glaxo Laboratories Report and Accounts* (1952), 17.
133. Davenport-Hines and Slinn, *Glaxo*, 165.

134. Glaxo Laboratories Board Minutes, 25 July 1952, 184; 29 August 1952, 188.
135. Ibid., 1 February 1954, 237.
136. 'The Murphy story', *Nurseryman, Seedsman and Glasshouse Grower*, 6 April 1961; *The Murphy Story* (1970), 5.
137. Glaxo Laboratories Board Minutes, 7 November 1955, 306.
138. Ibid., 5 December 1955, 311.
139. Memorandum, Sir John Hanbury to M. J. Smith, 22 February 1979.
140. Sir Harry Jephcott, draft notes, (n.d.).
141. Ibid.
142. Glaxo Laboratories Board Minutes, 31 March 1958, it. 50.
143. Davenport-Hines and Slinn, *Glaxo*, 171.
144. Glaxo Laboratories Board Minutes, 30 June 1958, it. 107.
145. Ibid.
146. Interview of Cyril Maplethorpe by B. E. Baker, August 1974.
147. Interview with E. K. Samways, 2 September 1994.
148. Glaxo Laboratories Board Minutes, 13 January 1961, it. 16.
149. A. E. Smeeton, 'Chronological history of Evans Medical Supplies Ltd' (typescript, 1 January 1960), 1.
150. Ibid., 3.
151. Davenport-Hines and Slinn, *Glaxo*, 173.
152. I. V. L. Fergusson, notes of a meeting held on 5 January 1961.
153. I. Fergusson to Evans managers, 9 January 1961.
154. Glaxo Laboratories Board Minutes, 6 March 1961, it. 38.
155. H. Jephcott to Rupert Pearce, 21 November 1939.
156. *Glaxo Laboratories in Britain*, (c. 1954), directed by Stanley Schofield.

5 Research in crisis

1. Sir Harry Jephcott, 'How much research?', *Research, Science and its Application to Industry*, 5 (1952), 3.
2. Sir Harry Jephcott, 'The Glaxo research organisation', in Sir John Cockroft [Editor], *The Organisation of Research Establishments*, Cambridge (1965), 48–67.
3. Ibid., 163.
4. *Glaxo Laboratories Report and Accounts for year ended 30 June 1958*, 18.

5. Jephcott, 'The Glaxo research organisation', 158.

6. Ibid., 159.

7. Sir Harry Jephcott, 'Diary', 30 January 1950, 6.

8. Jephcott, 'How much research?', 2; 'Glaxo research organisation', 159.

9. Ibid., 166–67.

10. Jephcott, 'How much research?', 4.

11. Minutes of the Research and Development Committee, 13 December 1957, it. 28.

12. Ibid.

13. Glaxo Laboratories Board Minutes, 30 June 1958, it. 108.

14. Glaxo Laboratories BP 58/72, A. E. Bide, 'Glaxo/Schering research collaboration', 26 September 1958, 1.

15. Ibid.

16. Glaxo Laboratories Executive Board Minutes, vol. VI, 58/9, 16 October 1958, 4.

17. Glaxo Laboratories Board Minutes, 5 January 1959, it. 6.

18. Ibid.

19. Glaxo Laboratories BP 59/77, H. Jephcott, 'Research and development budget 1959–60', 2 July 1959.

20. 'Chairman's review, draft' (typescript, 28 October 1959), 6.

21. Glaxo Laboratories Executive Board Minutes, 61/5, 18 May 1961, it. 37.

22. At numbers 2, 2a and 42a; Glaxo Laboratories Board Minutes, 26 January 1951, 125; photograph of 2 Bravington Road, 'Headquarters of Development Division January 1947'.

23. Glaxo Laboratories Board Minutes, 28 February 1949, 47.

24. Ibid., 29 April 1949, 51; 28 February 1949, 47.

25. Glaxo Today (c. 1953), 'Organisation of Glaxo research'.

26. 'Introductory dates of Glaxo preparations'.

27. Davenport-Hines and Slinn, Glaxo, 136.

28. Ibid., 190.

29. Glaxo Laboratories Press Department, '£400,000 biological department for Glaxo'.

30. Souvenir Programme for Open Day at the New Biological Department, 5 December 1956.

31. Ibid., 192.

32. Glaxo Laboratories Board Minutes, 5 December 1953, 228.

33. Davenport-Hines and Slinn, Glaxo, 193.

34. Glaxo Laboratories Board Minutes, 4 March 1957.

35. Glaxo Laboratories BP 57/16, H. W. Palmer,

'Commercial background to proposals for poliomyelitis virus research', 25 February 1957, 2.

36. Glaxo Laboratories BP 57/17, F. J. Wilkins, 'Development of virus research laboratory facilities, Sefton Park'.

37. Glaxo Laboratories BP 59/51, F. J. Wilkins, 'Virus vaccine facilities, Sefton Park', 1 May 1959.

38. Davenport-Hines and Slinn, Glaxo, 202–203.

39. 'Griseofulvin, notes on its development' (typescript, 19 August 1959), 2.

40. Ibid., 3.

41. Ibid., 8, 9.

42. Ibid., 5.

43. J. C. Gentles, 'Experimental ringworm in guinea-pigs; oral treatment with griseofulvin', Nature, 182 (August 1958), 476.

44. 'Griseofulvin, notes on its development', 11.

45. D. I. Williams, R. H. Marten and I. Sarkany, 'Oral treatment of ringworm with Griseofulvin', The Lancet, 2 (6 December 1958), 1212.

46. Davenport-Hines and Slinn, Glaxo, 212.

47. Glaxo Laboratories BP 59/18, F. J. Wilkins, 'Griseofulvin', 28 January 1959.

48. W. F. J. Cuthbertson and J. E. Page, 'Ernest Lester Smith', Biographical Memoirs of Fellows of the Royal Society, 40 (1994), 358.

49. Memorandum from Dr H. M. Walker to H. Jephcott, 'Liver extract research', 29 July 1938.

50. 'Isolation of the anti-anaemic factor', Glaxo Volume, 1 (1948), 46.

51. E. Lester Smith, 'Crystalline Anti-Pernicious Anaemia Factor', BMJ, 2 (1949), 1367.

52. Memorandum, Dr E. Lester Smith to Sir H. Jephcott, 'Isolation of pernicious anaemia factor progress report', 9 August 1946, 7.

53. Cuthbertson and Page, 'Lester Smith', 359.

54. Memorandum from S. F. Woodward to C. Turner et al, 'Vitamin B_{12} 1948: the facts', 8 January 1960.

55. E. Lester Smith, 'Recent work on vitamin B_{12}', Proceedings of the Royal Society of Medicine, 43 (1950), 535.

56. 'Cytamen, minutes of a meeting held on 14 October 1949', it. 1.

57. Glaxo Laboratories Executive Board Minutes, 60/1, 21 January 1960, 4.

58. Glaxo Laboratories Board Minutes, 1 March 1954, 238.

59. Glaxo Laboratories Board Minutes, 30 March 1951, 135.

60. H. Jephcott, 'Hecogenin from sisal waste' (typescript, 10 July 1951); Turner, *Gold on the Green*, 79.
61. Memorandum, Sir Harry Jephcott to H. W. Palmer, 2 November 1951.
62. H. Jephcott, 'Notice to staff' (typescript 2 July 1952).
63. Glaxo Laboratories Board Minutes, 29 May 1953, 214.
64. Ibid., 215.
65. Glaxo Laboratories Board Minutes, 3 January 1952, 163; 25 January 1952, 167.
66. Ibid., 28 March 1952, 173.
67. Ibid., 27 June 1952, 183.
68. Ibid., 28 April 1952, 177; Dr P. A. Wilkinson, 'Minutes of a meeting held at Montrose on 23 June 1954', it. 27.
69. Interview with Albert Hall, Dr Ian McEwan and Donald McInnes, 28 January 1997.
70. Glaxo Laboratories BP 59/20, 'Six months to 31 July 1959', 1.
71. Glaxo Laboratories BP 59/84, 'Group Grading Position', 1.
72. Glaxo Laboratories Executive Board, 60/1, 21 January 1960, 4; 60/11, 17 November 1961, 6.
73. Ibid., 63/19, 3 October 1963, 2.

6 Imperial Glaxo

1. 'The Waikato factories, résumé of the history' (typescript n.d.), 1.
2. Ibid., 2.
3. J. A. Nathan, 'Notes taken at Bunnythorpe factory, season 1920–21', 42.
4. Deed between Joseph Nathan & Co. and the New Zealand Dairy Association Co., 18 December 1919; Millen, *Glaxo*, 62.
5. 'The Waikato factories', 6.
6. 'Closing of the Matamata factory' (typescript 5 March 1925).
7. 'The Waikato factories', 7.
8. J. Nathan & Co. Minute Book February 1923–December 1945, 22 September 1927, 89.
9. Ibid., 11 February 1932, 243–44.
10. Ibid., 16 May 1933, 280; 18 December 1934, 323.
11. Ibid., 114.
12. John Garside, *A History of Glaxo in Port Fairy* (1995), 5.
13. Ibid., 6.
14. Ibid., 9; A. Nathan, 'Report on Australian business historical' (typescript, n.d.).
15. Letter, Joseph Nathan & Co., Wellington, to

London Office, 16 St Helens Place, 9 August 1922.
16. Garside, *History of Glaxo in Port Fairy*, 11.
17. Ibid., 116.
18. Ibid., 28.
19. Letter, Joseph Nathan & Co. to London Office, 9 August 1922; Davenport-Hines and Slinn, *Glaxo*, 298.
20. Ibid., 300.
21. Memorandum, R. C. Pearce to H. Jephcott, 28 March 1955.
22. Davenport-Hines and Slinn, *Glaxo*, 301.
23. Glaxo Laboratories, BP 51/63, H. Jephcott, 'Memorandum on Australian project', 21 November 1951.
24. Quoted in Davenport-Hines and Slinn, *Glaxo*, 303.
25. Ibid., 305–306.
26. Memorandum, R. C. Pearce to H. Jephcott, 4 January 1955.
27. Ibid., it. 37.
28. Memorandum, R. C. Pearce to H. Jephcott, 27 July 1955, it. 8.
29. Ibid., it. 15.
30. Brian Jones, 'An Ulverstonian's visit to Australia' (typescript, 16 October 1996).
31. Davenport-Hines and Slinn, *Glaxo*, 307.
32. Ibid., 308.
33. Memorandum, Pearce to Jephcott, 5 January 1955, it. 37.
34. Jephcott, *First Fifty Years*, 98.
35. Joseph Nathan & Co. Board Minutes, vol. II, 18 March 1919, 221.
36. Ibid., 13 June 1919, 238.
37. Ibid., 239.
38. Ibid., 1 November 1921, 141.
39. Glaxo Laboratories BP 6/47, 'H. J. Foster & Co. Ltd., capital reconstruction'; Joseph Nathan & Co. Ltd, Board Minutes, vol. III, 6 May 1924, 73.
40. Ibid., 7 January 1926, 172; 22 April 1926, 205.
41. Davenport-Hines and Slinn, *Glaxo*, 117.
42. Ibid., 119.
43. Quoted ibid., 119–20.
44. H. Jephcott, 'India' (typescript, February 1934), 15.
45. Ibid., 17–18.
46. Ibid., 20–21.
47. Davenport-Hines and Slinn, *Glaxo*, 122.
48. Joseph Nathan & Co. Board Minutes, vol. VI, 20 April 1933, 220.
49. 'H. J. Foster, capital reconstruction'.
50. Davenport-Hines and Slinn, *Glaxo*, 274.

51. Quoted ibid., 278.
52. L. B. D. Bryceson, 'History of Glaxo (Pakistan) Ltd.' (typescript, n.d.), 2–3.
53. Davenport-Hines and Slinn, *Glaxo*, 294.
54. Ibid., 296.
55. Joseph Nathan & Co. Board Minutes, vol. III, 21 June 1921, 120.
56. Davenport-Hines and Slinn, *Glaxo*, 100.
57. Joseph Nathan & Co. Board Minutes, vol. III, 1 November 1921, 138.
58. 'Glaxo in Argentina' (typescript, Buenos Aires, March 1965), 1; Davenport-Hines and Slinn, *Glaxo*, 103.
59. 'Glaxo in Argentina', 3.
60. 'Glaxo in South America, Uruguay, Chile and Paraguay' (typescript, Buenos Aires, October 1965), 1.
61. Ibid., 3.
62. 'Overseas Subsidiary Companies' (typescript, 1957).
63. 'Glaxo in Argentina', 5–6.
64. Ibid., 6–7.
65. Davenport-Hines and Slinn, *Glaxo*, 265.
66. 'Glaxo in Argentina', 10.
67. Quoted in Davenport-Hines, 'Glaxo as a multinational', 154.
68. Sir Robert Hutchings, 'Recommendations for the staffing of overseas units', 14 March 1961.
69. Glaxo Laboratories BP 58/43, 'Financial results: US pharmaceutical companies', statistical appendix.
70. Ibid., 1.

7 Glaxo Group: structure and management 1962–1971

1. Sir Harry Jephcott, 'Company organisation', Glaxo Laboratories BP, 27 April 1961, 1.
2. Ibid.
3. Ibid.
4. *Glaxo Laboratories Ltd, Report and Accounts* (1961), 14.
5. Ibid., 2–3.
6. Jephcott, 'Company organisation'.
7. Ibid., 1.
8. Ibid., 2.
9. Joseph Nathan Board Minutes, vol. V, March 1931, 75.
10. Jephcott, 'Company organisation', 3.
11. Ibid.
12. Sir Alan Wilson. 'Company structure', Glaxo Group BP 63/109, 1.
13. Ibid.

14. Ibid.
15. Ibid., 2.
16. Sir Alan Wilson, 'The Glaxo Group', paper presented to the Society of Investment Analysts, 19 February 1970, 2.
17. Glaxo Group BP 65/148, H. W. Palmer, 'New Group Headquarters'.
18. Glaxo Group Board Minutes, 8 November 1965, it. 179.
19. Glaxo Group BP 70/50, Sir A. H. Wilson, 'Central London office accommodation', 17 March 1970, 2.
20. Stephanie Blackden, *A Tradition of Excellence, A Brief History of Medicine in Edinburgh*, Duncan Flockhart & Co. (n.d.), 9, 21.
21. Ibid., 25, 27; 'Genealogy of Duncan Flockhart & Co.' (typescript, *c.* 1930).
22. Deric Bolton, 'The Development of alkaloid manufacture in Edinburgh 1832–1939', *Chemistry and Industry*, 4 September 1976, 702.
23. Ibid., 702, 706.
24. Blackden, *Medicine in Edinburgh*, 28–29.
25. Glaxo Group Board Minutes, 7 January 1963, it. 4.
26. *Glaxo Group Board Report* (1964).
27. *Glaxo Group Annual Report* (1965), 8.
28. 'Evans Wholesaling' (typescript, n.d.), 1.
29. Glaxo Group BP 65/84, H. W. Palmer and A. E. Bide, 'Wholesaling', 8 July 1965, 3.
30. Glaxo Group Board Minutes, 14 June 1965, it. 91.
31. Glaxo Group BP 65/94, A. H. Wilson, 'Wholesaling', 8 July 1965, 3.
32. Glaxo Group Board Minutes, 11 October 1965, it. 164.
33. Glaxo Group BP 76/56, P. Girolami, 'Vestric Ltd – accounts year ended 31 December 1966', 1.
34. Glaxo Group BP 68/19, A. E. Bide, 'Vestric Limited', 6 February 1968.
35. 'London wholesale houses amalgamate', *Pharmaceutical Journal*, 21 November 1908.
36. Michael Bliss, *The Discovery of Insulin*, London (1988), 167.
37. Tweedale, *At the Sign of the Plough*, 128–29.
38. *BDH Group Annual Report* (1966), 11.
39. Glaxo Group BP 67/120, Sir A. H. Wilson, 'B.D.H. Group Limited', 7 November 1967, 4.
40. Glaxo Group Board Minutes, 13 November 1967, it. 139.

41. Ibid., 8 January 1968, it. 1.

42. Glaxo Group BP 68/19, A. E. Bide, 'Vestric Limited', 6 February 1968.

43. Tweedale, *At the Sign of the Plough*, 83.

44. Ibid., 132–33.

45. Ibid., 198.

46. Glaxo Group Board Minutes, 8 April 1963, it. 62.

47. Glaxo Group BP 63/56, C. W. Maplethorpe, 'Allen & Hanburys Ltd – Surgical Division', 2 April 1963, 1.

48. Glaxo Group: Managing Director's Report to the Board, Surgical Division.

49. Glaxo Group BP 68/56, A. E. Bide, 'Allen & Hanburys Ltd. – Surgicals', 8 April 1968.

50. Glaxo Group Board Minutes, 13 February 1967, it. 18.

51. Bide, 'Surgicals', 1.

52. Memorandum, Sir Alan Wilson to J. G. Beevor, H. W. Palmer et al., 'A & H Surgical Engineering Ltd', 11 April 1968.

53. Glaxo Group BP 68/104, R. D. Smart, 'Surgical activities'.

54. Ibid., 2.

55. *Glaxo Group Annual Report* (1968), 4.

56. *Glaxo Group Annual Report* (1965), 7.

57. Glaxo Group BP 68/22, Sir Alan Wilson, 'Farley's', 18 January 1968, 1.

58. Ibid.

59. Glaxo Group BP 68/24, M. R. Camp, 'Farley's Infant Food Limited', 8 February 1968, 1.

60. 'Edwin Farley, Baker, and establishment of the company' (typescript, *c.* 1980).

61. IMS data: total sales to chemists in the UK for 1962.

62. *The Times Review of Industry and Technology* (1965), v.

63. *Scrip League Tables* (1983–84), 2.

64. IMS data: total chemists' purchases in the UK for 1982.

65. *The Times 1000 1981–92*, 32–33.

66. *Glaxo Group Annual Report and Accounts* (1968), 4–5.

67. Glaxo Group BP BM 62/80, H. W. Palmer, 'Future policy', 22 June 1962.

68. Ibid., 1.

69. Ibid.

70. Ibid., 2.

71. Ibid., 3.

72. Ibid.

73. Ibid.

74. Ibid.

75. *Glaxo Group Annual Report and Accounts*

(1970), 6.

76. Ibid.

77. Glaxo Group Board Minutes, 1 January 1962, it. 4(5).

78. Glaxo Group Board Minutes, 5 November 1962, it. 147.

79. D. C. Coleman, *Courtaulds, and Economic and Social History*, vol. III, *Crisis and Change 1940–1965*, Oxford (1980), 242.

80. Glaxo Group Board Minutes, 7 January 1963, it. 3(a).

81. Ibid., 8 April 1963, it. 77.

82. Memorandum, Clifford Turner to R. A. M. Henson, 4 January 1960.

83. 'The pharmacist who reshaped DSIR', *New Scientist*, 18 June 1959, 1345.

84. Interview with Mrs. F. J. Wilkins, 15 November 1993.

85. Sir Alan Wilson, 'Obituary', *Nature*, 209 (5023), 558.

86. A. R. Lockwood, Obituary, *Chemistry and Industry*, 12 February 1966, 284–5; *The Times*, Obituaries, 28 and 30 November 1965.

87. Interview with Mr. D. J. R. Farrant.

88. *The Bulletin*, 313 (November 1965), front cover, southern edition.

89. Ibid., 3–4.

90. Wilson, 'Obituary', 559.

91. Glaxo Group Board Minutes, 13 May 1963, it. 106.

92. Interview with Sir Austin Bide, 21 July 1995.

93. *The Bide Years* (1985), 8.

94. Turner, *Gold on the Green*, 106.

95. Davenport-Hines and Slinn, *Glaxo*, 182.

96. Judi Bevan, 'The impish alchemist kicks his Glaxo habit', *Sunday Telegraph*, 13 November 1994.

97. *The Accountant*, 130 (4128) (30 January 1954), 127.

98. Interview with Monica Hayes, 16 May 1995.

99. Glaxo Group Board Minutes, 13 May 1968, it. 67.

100. Glaxo Group Board Minutes, 8 November 1965, it. 174.

101. Letter, Sir Edward Playfair to Sir Alan Wilson, 9 June 1970.

102. Glaxo Group Board Minutes, 8 June 1970, it. 104.

103. Letter, Sir Alan Wilson to Sir Edward W. Playfair, 6 July 1970.

104. Glaxo Group Board Minutes, 10 May 1971, it. 69; 13 March 1972, it. 63.

105. Ibid., 12 March 1973, it. 10.

8 The Beecham bid

1. Glaxo Group Board Minutes, vol. II, 2 December 1971, it. 168.
2. Ibid.
3. *The Monopolies Commission, Beecham Group Ltd. and Glaxo Group Ltd.*
4. Centre for the Study of Industrial Innovation, *Reaching World Markets*, National Economic Development Office, London (1971).
5. Ibid., 31.
6. Ibid., 33.
7. Ibid., 34.
8. Ibid., 35.
9. Ibid., 3.
10. Ibid., 3; *Beecham Group Annual Report* (1970), Chairman's Statement.
11. Interview with Sir Paul Girolami, 15 March 1994.
12. *Beecham and Glaxo, A Report on the Proposed Mergers*, 66.
13. Coleman, *Courtaulds*, vol. III, 18–19.
14. Quoted ibid., 319.
15. Interview with Sir David Jack, 18 January 1994.
16. *Independent*, 9 October 1995, Paul Girolami, 'Obituary Sir Alan Wilson'.
17. Letter, Sir James Taylor to Sir Alan Wilson, 7 January 1971.
18. Letter, Sir James Taylor to Sir Alan Wilson, 12 January 1971.
19. Ibid.
20. Ibid.
21. Letter, Sir James Taylor to Sir Alan Wilson, 13 January 1971.
22. Letter, Sir James Taylor to Sir Alan Wilson, 15 January 1971.
23. Letter, Sir James Taylor to Sir Alan Wilson, 18 January 1971.
24. Letter, Sir James Taylor to Sir Alan Wilson, 8 February 1971.
25. Glaxo Group Minutes, 13 December 1971, it. 175.
26. *Daily Telegraph*, 15 November 1971.
27. Letter from Sir Paul Girolami to the author, 28 February 1996.
28. *A Report on the Proposed Mergers*, 7, 14–15.
29. Ibid., 15.
30. *Glaxo Group Annual Report and Accounts* (1971), 9.
31. *A Report of the Proposed Mergers*, 7, 14–15.
32. T. A. B. Corley, 'The Beecham Group in the world's pharmaceutical industry' (unpublished paper), 6.
33. Ibid., 7.
34. H. G. Lazell, 'Development and organisation of Beecham Group Ltd.', (LSE Seminar on Problems in Industrial Administration, Paper No. 252, 23 February 1960), 2.
35. Corley, 'The Beecham Group', 11.
36. William Breckon, *The Drug Makers* (1972), 25.
37. Corley, 'The Beecham Group', 12.
38. Ibid., 13.
39. Margaret Ackrill, 'Sir Ronald Edwards', *DBB*, 2 (1984), 238–41.
40. Lazell, 'Development and Organisation of Beecham Group Ltd', it. 20.
41. Interview with Sir Paul Girolami, 15 March 1994.
42. *A Report on the Proposed Mergers*, 33.
43. Glaxo Group Minutes, 2 December 1971.
44. *The Bide Years*, 27.
45. Coleman, *Courtaulds*, vol. III, 242.
46. Ibid., 244.
47. Interview with Sir Arthur Knight, 13 January 1994.
48. Letter, Sir Paul Girolami to the author, 28 February 1996.
49. Glaxo Group Minutes, 6 December 1971, it. 170.
50. *The Bide Years*, 27.
51. Glaxo Group Minutes, 9 December 1971, it. 172.
52. Ibid., it. 173.
53. Glaxo Group Minutes, 13 December 1971, it. 175.
54. *Financial Times*, 3 December 1971.
55. *Chemical Age*, 10 December 1971, 'Perspective', 19.
56. Quoted ibid.
57. *The Times*, 16 December 1971, Richard Spiegelberg, 'Why Glaxo is resolved to fly solo'.
58. Ibid.
59. Quoted ibid.
60. Glaxo Group Ltd, *Beecham Takeover Bid*, 21 January 1972, 1.
61. *The Times*, 14 January 1972, R. Spiegelberg, 'Making up the pharmaceutical compact'.
62. *Proposed Merger of Beecham and Glaxo* (10 January 1972), 3.
63. Glaxo newspaper advertisement, 11 January 1972.
64. Glaxo Group Minutes, 10 January 1972, it. 26; 12 January 1972, it. 27.

65. *Investors Chronicle*, January 1972, Stuart Mansell, 'Glaxo's defensive merger' 26.
66. *Glaxo Group Limited, Merger with the Boots Company*, 14 January 1972.
67. *Sunday Times*, 16 January 1972, James Poole, 'What Boots' bid is really worth'.
68. *Glaxo Group News*, 59 (13 January 1972), 3.
69. *Pharmaceutical Journal*, 22 January 1972, 67.
70. *A Report on the Proposed Mergers*, 21–22; Stanley Chapman, *Jesse Boot of Boots the Chemists, A Study in Business History*, London (1968) 201–202.
71. *Investors Chronicle*, 21 January 1972, 27.
72. *Chemist & Druggist*, 22 January 1972, 'Bigger and bigger'.
73. *A Report on the Proposed Mergers*, 21.
74. *Observer*, 16 January 1972, Michael Braham, 'Glaxo Boots Beecham'.
75. Glaxo Group Minutes, 24 January 1972, it. 32.
76. Ibid., 27 January 1972, it. 40.
77. Ibid., 28 January 1972, it. 42.
78. *Boots and Glaxo Recommended Merger*, 31 January 1972, 4.
79. *Boots and Glaxo Recommended Merger*, 14 January 1972.
80. *Hansard, House of Common Reports*, 17 January 1972.
81. *Glaxo Group News*, 60 (February 1972), 1.
82. Glaxo Group Minutes, 14 February 1972, it. 44.
83. Glaxo Group Minutes, 15 March 1972, it. 68.
84. Letter, Sir Paul Girolami to the author, 28 February 1996.
85. *The Bide Years*, 28.
86. *Glaxo Holdings, Annual Report and Accounts* (1972) 8.
87. Letter, Sir Alan Wilson to Sir Harry Jephcott, 20 March 1972.
88. 'Glaxo Group Limited, the scheme of arrangement – an explanation' (typescript, 2 May 1972), it. 1.
89. Ibid., it. 2.
90. *Guardian*, 21 March 1972, 'Glaxo building up defences'.
91. Glaxo Group Minutes, 24 April 1972.
92. *Daily Telegraph*, 21 March 1972, Peter Welham and Peter Duffy, 'Gearing up Glaxo could increase its bid price'.
93. Monopolies and Mergers Act *c.* 50 (1965).
94. *Glaxo Group News*, 61 (March 1972), 3.
95. *Glaxo Group Limited, Reference to the Monopolies Commission Submission* (18 February 1972).
96. Ibid., 32.
97. Ibid.
98. Ibid., 33.
99. Ibid.
100. Ibid., 39.
101. Ibid., 39.
102. 'Monopolies Commission Note of the Hearing on 3 March 1972' (typescript).
103. Ibid., 1–6.
104. Ibid., 18, 30, 46.
105. Ibid., 42, 48.
106. Ibid., 34.
107. Ibid., 35.
108. Ibid., 37.
109. Ibid., 39.
110. Ibid., 38.
111. 'Replies to "Note of possible weaknesses in the organisation and activities" of the Glaxo Group attached to the Monopolies Commission's letter of 25 April 1972' (typescript, n.d.).
112. Press Notice, Department of Trade and Industry, 13 July 1972.
113. *The Bide Years*, 27.
114. Ibid.
115. *Financial Times*, 14 July 1972, 'Monopolies Commission Report on Glaxo's bids'.
116. Interview with Sir Paul Girolami, 15 March 1994.
117. Interview with D. J. R. Farrant, 14 December 1993.
118. Letter, Sir Edward Playfair to Sir Alan Wilson, 9 June 1970.
119. Letter, Sir Edward Playfair to Sir Alan Wilson, 6 July 1970.
120. Glaxo Group Minutes, Letter 13 March 1972 signed by A. H. Wilson, E. W. Playfair, P. Girolami, R. D. Smart and H. Lintott.
121. Ibid., 12 March 1973, it. 10.
122. 'Sir Ronald Edwards', *DBB*, 241.
123. Price Waterhouse, *The Reporter*, 70 (1989), 1.
124. *Scrip League Tables* (1989), 49.
125. Ibid., 2.
126. *The Reporter*, 70 (1989), 1.
127. *Scrip League Tables* (1990), 2.
128. *Scrip League Tables* (1991), 47.
129. *Independent*, 2 June 1993, Patrick Hosking, 'Doctors play safe on Manoplax'.
130. *The Boots Company Report and Accounts* (1995), 25.

9 *Restructuring and managerial change 1972–1985*

1. Glaxo Holdings Board Minutes, 31 July 1972,

it. 56.

2. Interview with Sir Austin Bide and David Smart, 11 October 1995.
3. *Glaxo Holdings Limited Reorganisation* (n.d.).
4. Ibid., p. 2.
5. Interview with Michael Allan, 23 August 1995.
6. *Glaxo Holdings Annual Report* (1973), 'Statement by the chairman', 4.
7. *Glaxo Holdings Limited Reorganisation*, Appendix 1.
8. Ibid., Appendix 14, 12.
9. Ibid., 3.
10. Interview with Sir Austin Bide and David Smart, 11 October 1995.
11. *Glaxo Holdings Limited Reorganisation*, p. 4.
12. *Glaxo World*, 1 (Winter 1986), Paul Girolami, 'The next five years', 3.
13. Interview with Sir Austin Bide and David Smart, 11 October 1995.
14. Interview with Sir Austin Bide, 24 October 1995.
15. Glaxo Holdings Board Minutes, 13 February 1978, it. 29.
16. Interview with E. R. C. Farmer, 8 February 1994.
17. Glaxo Holdings Board Minutes, 10 February 1975, it. 18.
18. Glaxo Holdings BP 75/16, F. C. D. Back, 'Foods rationalisation', 6 February 1975.
19. Interview with E. R. C. Farmer, 8 February 1994.
20. Glaxo Holdings Board Minutes, 13 October 1980, it. 108(2).
21. Glaxo Holdings BP 86/63, 'Glaxo animal health – policy recommendation', 6 May 1986, 1.
22. Glaxo Holdings BP 73/69, A. E. Bide, 'Research and development', 3 October 1973, 3.
23. *Glaxo Holdings Annual Report and Accounts* (1979), 5.
24. Letter, Michael Ball to the author, 11 January 1994.
25. *Glaxo Holdings Annual Report and Accounts* (1980), 5.
26. *Glaxo Holdings Annual Report and Accounts* (1985), 4.
27. *Glaxo Holdings Annual Report and Accounts* (1983), 4.
28. *Glaxo Holdings Annual Report and Accounts* (1984), 4.
29. *Glaxo Holdings Annual Report and Accounts* (1985), 4.

30. Glaxo Group BP 65/111, F. J. Wilkins, 'Replacement of data processing computer', 21 July 1965.
31. Turner, *Gold on the Green*, 101–102.
32. Glaxo Group BP 68/123, P. Girolami, 'Data processing developments – UK', 1.
33. Ibid., 2.
34. Ibid., 3.
35. Interview with Colin Jack, 28 January 1997.
36. Glaxo Holdings Board Minutes, 12 March 1973, it. 28.
37. Interview with Sir Austin Bide, 24 October 1995.
38. Glaxo Holdings Board Minutes, 12 March 1973, it. 28.
39. Ibid., 10 December 1973, it. 136.
40. Ibid., 14 September 1977, it. 105.
41. Ibid., 14 November 1977, it. 132; 30 November 1977.
42. Ibid., 13 December 1976, it. 160.
43. Interview with Dr A. H. Raper, 10 January 1994.
44. Glaxo Holdings Board Minutes, 25 September 1972, it. 64(2); *Glaxo Holdings Annual Report* (1972), p. 7.
45. Coleman, *Courtaulds*, vol. III, 326.
46. Ibid., pp. 244–45.
47. Glaxo Holdings Board Minutes, 13 March 1978, it. 41.
48. Interview with D. J. R. Farrant, 14 December 1993.
49. Glaxo Holdings Board Minutes, 14 April 1980, it. 46.
50. *Glaxo Annual Report and Accounts* (1985), 4.
51. Interview with Monica Hayes, 16 May 1995.
52. Glaxo Holdings Board Minutes, 13 October 1980, it. 108.
53. Glaxo Holdings Board Minutes, 13 June 1983, it. 69.
54. Interview with C. B. Newcomb, 15 March 1993. Jackson, Pixley & Co. became Clark Pixley following a merger.
55. Glaxo Holdings Board Minutes, 9 February 1976, it. 12.
56. *Glaxo Holdings Annual Report and Accounts* (1984), 4.
57. Glaxo Holdings Board Minutes, 15 April 1985, it. 33.
58. *Glaxo Holdings Annual Report and Accounts* (1985), 10.
59. Glaxo Holdings Board Minutes, 13 December 1976, it. 161, 162; Interview with M. D. Allan, 13 August 1995.

60. Glaxo Holdings BP, E. R. C. Farmer, 'Disposal of Vestric', 30 January 1985, 1.
61. Ibid.
62. Ibid., p. 2; Glaxo Holdings Board Minutes, 11 February 1985, it. 18.
63. Ibid., 10 June 1985, it. 56.
64. *Glaxo Holdings Annual Report* (1985), 8.
65. Glaxo Holdings Board Minutes, 11 November 1985, it. 146.
66. Glaxo Holdings Board Paper, 'Farley Health Products Limited, disposal', Appendix 1.
67. Ibid., 1.
68. Glaxo Holdings Board Minutes, 11 November 1985, it. 146.
69. Ibid., 20 January 1986, it. 1.
70. Interview with E. R. C. Farmer, 8 February 1994.
71. Glaxo Holdings BP 86/64, B. D. Taylor, 'Generics policy', 6 May 1986, 1.
72. Ibid.
73. Ibid., 2.
74. Ibid.
75. Glaxo Holdings Board Minutes, 28 July 1986, it. 93(c).
76. Girolami, 'The next five years', 3.
77. Ibid.
78. Glaxo Holdings BP 89/60, P. Girolami, 'Group organisation', 1 June 1989, 1.

10 Government regulation and the market

1. *Report of the Committee of Enquiry into the Relationship of the Pharmaceutical Industry with the National Health Service 1965–1967* [Sainsbury Report], London: HMSO (1967), 5, it. 2.
2. K. Hartley, R. J. Lavers and A. K. Maynard, 'Regulation and development times in the UK pharmaceutical industry', *Scottish Journal of Political Economy*, 33 (1986), 355.
3. William Breckon, *The Drug Makers*, London (1972), 123.
4. Sir Derrick Dunlop, 'Legislation on medicines', *BMJ*, 2 (26 September 1970), 760.
5. *Final Report of the [Hinchliffe] Committee on Cost of Prescribing*, London: HMSO (1959), 69.
6. Breckon, *The Drug Makers*, 176.
7. PRO, MH 104/25, Committee on Pharmaceutical Industry: CDI Evidence (65) 3, 22 July 1965, 7.
8. *Hinchcliffe Report*, 70.
9. Ibid., 5.
10. Ibid., 24, 27.
11. Ibid., 9.
12. *Study of Administered Prices in the Drug Industry, Report of the Subcommittee on Antitrust and Monopoly of the Senate Judiciary Committee, Pursuant to Senate Resolution 52, Eighty-Seventh Congress, First Session*, Washington, DC: Government Printing Office (1961); Henry Steele, 'Patent restrictions and price competition in the ethical drugs industry', *Journal of Industrial Economics*, 12 (1964), 198.
13. Breckon, *The Drug Makers*, 178; W. Duncan Reekie, *The Economics of the Pharmaceutical Industry*, London (1975), 101.
14. Breckon, *The Drug Makers*, 126.
15. Glaxo Group Board Minutes, 5 November 1962, it. 144(i).
16. Ibid., 3 December 1962, it. 165(i).
17. Dunlop 'Legislation on medicines', 760.
18. T. B. Binns and W. J. H. Butterfield, 'Clinical trials, some constructive suggestions', *The Lancet*, 1 (23 May 1964), 1150.
19. *Hinchcliffe* Report, 10.
20. 'Trials and tribulations', *The Lancet*, 1 (21 January 1967), 152.
21. Quoted in Brian Inglis, *Drugs, Doctors and Disease*, London (1965), 96.
22. Quoted ibid., 97.
23. Quoted ibid., 98.
24. 'Cephaloridine', *BMJ*, 2 (14 November 1964), 1212.
25. *Drug and Therapeutic Bulletin*, 22 January 1965.
26. Ibid.
27. Inglis, *Drugs, Doctors and Disease*, 217–18.
28. 'New laws on control of drugs', *The Lancet*, 2 (16 September 1967), 601.
29. Ibid., 602.
30. Dunlop, 'Legislation on medicines', 760.
31. Ibid., 761; Olga Uvarov, 'The Medicines Act, 1968: some implications in the veterinary field', *Veterinary Record*, 11 March 1972, 294.
32. O. M. Bakke, W. M. Wardell and L. Lasagna, 'Drug discontinuations in the United Kingdom and the United States, 1964 to 1983: issues of safety', *Clinical Pharmacology and Therapeutics*, 35 (1984), 562.
33. Quoted in Breckon, *The Drug Makers*, 179–180.
34. Ibid., 181.
35. *Glaxo Laboratories Report and Accounts* (1958), 17.

36. PRO, MH 104/25, 'Committee on Pharmaceutical Industry: CDI Evidence (65) 3', 22 July 1965, 5.

37. Glaxo Group Board Minutes, 12 April 1965, it. 66.

38. Ibid., 25 July 1966, it. 126.

39. Glaxo Group Limited BP 66/133, 'Memorandum of evidence' (typescript), 2.

40. Ibid., 3.

41. Ibid., 4.

42. *Sainsbury Report*, it. 124, 38.

43. Ibid.; 'Sainsbury Report', *BMJ*, 2 (7 October 1967), 2.

44. Sainsbury Report, 49.

45. Ibid., it. 287, 81.

46. Ibid., it. 310, 86; it. 314, 87.

47. Ibid., it. 315, 87.

48. Hans Conrad Peyer, *Roche, A Company History 1896–1996*, Basel: Roche (1996), 240.

49. Ibid., 243.

50. Quoted from W. Duncan Reekie, *The Economics of the Pharmaceutical Industry*, London (1975), 103.

51. Robert H. Jones, 'The Pharmaceutical Price Regulation Scheme in the United Kingdom', *Drug Information Journal*, 29 (1995), 1182.

52. Quoted from W. Duncan Reekie and Michael H. Weber, *Profits, Politics and Drugs*, London (1979), 70.

53. Horst-Manfred Schellhaass and Ulrich Stumpf, 'Price regulation in the European pharmaceutical industry', in J. Finsinger (ed.), *Economic Analysis of Regulated Markets*, London (1981), 154.

54. Sanjaya Lall, 'Price competition and the international pharmaceutical industry', *Oxford Bulletin of Economics and Statistics*, 40 (1978), 11.

55. 'The British pharmaceutical industry: 1961–1991', George Teeling-Smith (ed.), *Innovative Competition in Medicine*, London: OHE (1992), 69.

56. Ibid., 70.

57. W. Duncan Reekie, 'Price comparisons of identical products in Japan, the United States and Europe', in Finsinger (ed.), *Economic Analysis*, 168–81.

58. Ibid., 175.

59. Ibid., 176.

60. Ibid., 180.

61. *Glaxo Laboratories Report and Accounts* (1960), 15.

62. Interview with David Smart, 17 July 1995.

63. Glaxo Holdings Board Minutes, 14 October 1974, it. 118.

64. Quoted in Matthew Lynn, *The Billion-Dollar Battle, Merck v. Glaxo*, London: Mandarin (1991), 233.

65. Robert H. Jones, 'The approach to pricing innovative research-based medicine', *Pharmaceutical Medicine*, 8 (1994), 35.

66. Ibid., 30.

67. M. J. Buxton and B. J. O'Brien, 'Economic evaluation of ondansetron: preliminary analysis using clinical trial data prior to price setting', *British Journal of Cancer*, 66 (1992), supplement XIX, 564.

68. *British National Formulary* (March 1997), 187–89.

69. Editorial, 'Sumatriptan, serotonin, migraine and money', *The Lancet*, 339 (18 January 1992), 151.

70. Adrian Towse, 'The UK pharmaceutical market, an overview', *Pharmaco Economics*, 10, supplement 2 (1996), 14.

71. Heinz Redwood, 'Public policy trends in drug pricing and reimbursement in the European Community', *Pharmaco Economics*, 6, supplement 1 (1994), 5.

72. *Scrips Yearbook 1994*, 1, 56.

73. Ibid., 50.

74. Pamela K. Geyer, *Healthcare Scenarios in the Year 2000*, Frost & Sullivan Market Intelligence (1993), 1–3.

75. Ibid., 1–6.

76. US Office of Technology Assessment, *Pharmaceutical R & D: Costs, Risks and Rewards*, Washington (1993); F.M. Scherer, 'US industrial policy and the pharmaceutical industry', in Adrian Towse (ed.), *Industrial Policy and the Pharmaceutical Industry*, London: OHE (1995), 34–35.

77. Scherer, 'US industrial policy', 26.

78. Redwood, 'Public policy trends', 5–6.

79. Henry Steele, 'Monopoly and competition in the ethical drugs market', *Journal of Law and Economics*, 5 (1962), 161.

80. Sainsbury Report, it. 279, 79.

81. Ibid., it. 271, 78.

82. 'Brand names', *BMJ*, 1 (30 March 1968), 781.

83. Bernard S. Bloom et al., 'Cost and price of comparable branded and generic pharmaceuticals', *Journal of the American Medical Association*, 256 (1986), 2523.

84. Ashok K. Gumbhir and Christopher A. Rodowskas, 'Consumer price differentials

between generic and brand name prescriptions', *American Journal of Public Health*, 64 (1974), 982.

85. Bernard A. Kemp and Paul R. Moyer, 'Equivalent therapy at lower cost', *Journal of the American Medical Association*, 228 (1974), 1013–14.
86. Bloom et al., 'Cost and price', 2526.
87. Ibid., 2529.
88. *The National Enterprise Board, Report of a Labour Party Study Group*, London (1973), 9.
89. *The Labour Party Manifesto 1974*, 11.
90. Glaxo Holdings Board Minutes, 29 July 1974, it. 91(i).
91. Ibid., it. 91(2).
92. *The Labour Party Manifesto, October 1974*.
93. Glaxo Holdings Board Minutes, 12 June 1978, it. 82.
94. Glaxo Holdings Board Minutes, 9 June 1986, it. 77.
95. Glaxo Holdings Board Minutes, 11 May 1987, it. 45.
96. *Glaxo Annual Report and Accounts* (1987), 23.
97. *Glaxo Annual Report and Accounts* (1993), 23.
98. Interview with Lord Fraser, 23 August 1994.
99. R. A. Prentis and S. R. Walker, 'Innovation and development of new chemical entities by the UK owned pharmaceutical companies (1964–1980)', *Proceedings of the British Pharmaceutical Society*, 11–13 April 1984, 303p–304p.
100. Ibid., 304p.
101. J. P. Griffin and G. E. Diggle, 'A survey of products licensed in the United Kingdom from 1971–1981', *British Journal of Clinical Pharmacology*, 12 (1981), 462.
102. Ibid., 463.
103. A. H. Sheppard, 'Product innovation – a cause for concern', *Medical Marketing and Media*, 14 (1979), 30–38.
104. Editorial, 'After Sainsbury', *The Lancet*, 2 (7 October 1967), 759–60.
105. Michael D. Rawlins and David B. Jefferys, 'Study of United Kingdom product licence applications containing new active substances, 1987–9', *BMJ*, 302 (1991), 223–25.
106. Ibid., 225.
107. K. I. Kaitin, P. A. DiCerbo and L. Lasagna, 'The new drug approvals of 1987, 1988 and 1989: trends in drug development', *Journal of Clinical Pharmacology*, 31 (1991), 116.
108. Ibid., 117.
109. Ibid., 120; see K. I. Kaitin, B. W. Richard and

L. Lasagna, 'The new drug approvals of 1987, 1988 and 1989: trends in drug development', *Journal of Clinical Pharmacology*, 27 (1987), 542–48.
110. P. Temin, *Taking Your Medicine: Drug Regulation in the United States*, Cambridge, Mass.: Harvard University Press (1980); William Comanor, 'The political economy of the pharmaceutical industry', *Journal of Economic Literature*, 24 (1986), 1202–1205.
111. Comanor, 'Political economy', 1202.

11 *Sales and marketing*

1. *Glaxo Laboratories Ltd., Representatives' Working Instructions* (October 1936), it. (c).
2. Ibid., it. (d).
3. Ibid., it. (e).
4. *G. L. Monthly Bulletin*, 11 (August 1938).
5. *Representatives' Working Instructions* (1936), it. 4.
6. *Glaxo Laboratories Representatives' Working Instructions* (c. 1950).
7. Glaxo Laboratories Board Minutes, vol. I, 18 April 1939, 222.
8. 'Schedule of the … motor vehicles at Greenford' (typescript, 1942), 493–94.
9. Glaxo Laboratories Board Minutes, vol. II, 8 February 1944, 118.
10. Glaxo Laboratories Board Minutes, vol. I, 6 December 1938, 185.
11. Davenport-Hines and Slinn, *Glaxo*, 109.
12. Interview, R. Davenport-Hines with Reg Harryot, 4 October 1984.
13. Glaxo Laboratories Board Minutes, vol. III, 29 June 1951, 143.
14. Interview with John Hunt, 22 October 1997.
15. Glaxo Laboratories BP 167/67, F. C. D. Back, 'Betnovate – price reduction', 12 September 1967, 1.
16. Ibid., 2, Appendix A.
17. Ibid., 1.
18. V. H. T. James, D. D. Munro and M. Feiwel, 'Pituitary-adrenal function after occlusive topical therapy with betamethasone-17-valerate', *The Lancet*, 2 (1967), 1059–61.
19. D. Czarny and J. Brostoff, 'Effect of intranasal betamethasone-17-valerate on perennial rhinitis and adrenal function', *The Lancet*, 2 (1968), 188–90.
20. Allen & Hanburys Board Report by B. E. Baker, July 1967, 1–4.
21. 'Steroid anaesthesia', *Postgraduate Medical*

Journal, 48 (June supplement, 1972), 9–111.

22. *The Clinical Use of Ranitidine, A Glaxo International Symposium, Abstracts* (1981); A. J. Riley and P. R. Salmon (eds), *Ranitidine, Proceedings of an International Symposium*, Amsterdam (1982).

23. *Glaxo Holdings Annual Report and Accounts* (1978), 6.

24. 'Proceedings of the second symposium on labetalol', *British Journal of Clinical Pharmacology*, 8 (Supplement 2, 1979), 89S–183S.

25. 'Combined alpha-and beta- adrenoceptor blockade with labetalol', *Postgraduate Medical Journal*, 56 (Supplement 2, 1980).

26. 'The UK ethical prescription market, report prepared for Glaxo Operations UK Limited'.

27. Ibid., Table A.

28. Ibid., Table B.

29. Glaxo Holdings Board Minutes, 9 March 1981, it. 22.

30. GMC 81/52, J. Reece, 'Corporate plan, Zantac, decisions and follow up', 30 March 1981, it. 2.1.

31. Ibid., it. 2.2(a)–(c).

32. Ibid., it. 2.3(a).

33. Ibid., it. 2.4(a).

34. GMC 81/34, 'Zantac corporate plan', 26 February 1981; Reece, 'Corporate Plan', 5.4(b).

35. Ibid., 5.4(a).

36. GMC 81/71, John Reece, 'Corporate Plan' (April 1981), it. 5.2.

37. Ibid., it. 5.2.1.

38. Interview with John Reece, 19 July 1994.

39. GMC 81/138, Paul Girolami, 'Zantac – UK pricing', 22 July 1981.

40. Interview with E. R. C. Farmer, 8 February 1994.

41. Girolami, 'UK pricing', op. cit., it. 5.

42. Ibid., it. 6.

43. Ibid., it. 3.

44. Ibid., it. 4.

45. Ibid., it. 13.

46. GMC 81/142, John Reece, 'Summary paper' 28 August 1981, it. 1.2.

47. Ibid., it. 2.1.

48. Reinhard Angelmar and Christian Pinson, *Zantac*, Fontainebleau: INSEAD (1991), 9.

49. Glaxo Holdings Board Paper, 82/144, P. Girolami, 'Monthly report', 5 November 1982.

50. Girolami, 'Zantac – UK pricing', it. 13.

51. *British National Formulary*, 9 (1985), 217.

52. Interview with David Smart, 17 July 1995.

53. *Glaxo Wellcome Annual Report* (1995), 73; ibid. (1996), 85.

54. Allen & Hanburys Board Report by B. E. Baker, July 1970, 1–3.

55. Ibid., July 1971, 1–6.

56. Ibid., August 1973, 1–6.

57. Ibid.

58. Ibid., August 1977, 1–4.

59. *Glaxo Holdings Annual Report* (1981), 7.

60. Glaxo Holdings BP 86/86, 'Group forecast', 3.

61. Glaxo Holdings BP 88/126, 'Group forecast', 4, 5.

62. Glaxo Marketing Development, *Commercial Intelligence Review, Glaxo and the Global Pharmaceutical Market 1986*.

63. Allen & Hanburys Board Reports by B. E. Baker, August 1973 and August 1977.

64. *British National Formulary*, 33 (March 1997), 120.

65. *Glaxo Holdings Annual Report* (1988), 15.

66. Joel Lexchin, 'Doctors and detailers: therapeutic education or pharmaceutical promotion', *International Journal of Health Services*, 19 (1989), 663.

67. Sainsbury Report, it. 216, 63.

68. Ibid., it. 243, 70–71.

69. Ibid., it. 231, 67.

70. Ibid., it. 246, 71; see also Comanor, 'Political economy', 1199.

71. G. Eaton and P. Parish, 'Sources of drug information used by general practitioners', *Journal of the Royal College of General Practitioners*, 26, supplement 1 (1976), 58–64.

72. D. Woods, 'PMAC to spend almost $1 million to reach "stakeholders"', *Canadian Medical Association Journal*, 134 (1986), 1387–89.

73. R. W. Martin, 'Drug costs', *New Zealand Medical Journal*, 86 (1977), 202.

74. J. D. McCue, C. J. Hansen and P. Gal, 'Physicians' opinions of the accuracy, accessibility and frequency of use of ten sources of new drug information', *Southern Medical Journal*, 79 (1986), 441–43.

75. Lexchin, 'Doctors and detailers', 676.

76. Richard Smith, 'Doctors and the drug industry: too close for comfort', *BMJ*, 239 (11 October 1986), 906.

77. William A. Gouveia, 'Hospital pharmacy and industry – conflict and collaboration', *American Journal of Hospital Pharmacy*, 41 (July 1984), 1392.

78. Ibid.

79. Ibid.

80. *IFPMA Code of Pharmaceutical Marketing Practices* (1994), 1.
81. Ibid., 2.
82. Ibid., 6.
83. Ibid., 10.
84. Ibid., 16.
85. Interview with J. A. W. Strachan, 25 April 1994.
86. P. W. Grubb, 'Patents in medicinal chemistry', *Annual Reports in Medicinal Chemistry*, 22 (198/), 333.
87. The Patent Office, *Patent Protection*, Cardiff (1992), 7–8.
88. *Statute of Monopolies* (21 Ja. I c. 3).
89. *Patents and Designs* (9 & 10 GeoV c.80).
90. E. Zucker, *Patents and Pharmaceuticals*, Basle (1980), 53; Comanor, 'Political economy', 1201–1202.
91. Ibid., 331.
92. Ibid., 332.
93. Group Management Committee, 88/228, Corporate Policy Unit, 'Parallel trading of group products', 2 December 1988, it. 3.
94. Ibid., it. 5 (Articles 30–36, 85 and 86).
95. Ibid., it. 2.
96. Ibid.
97. Ibid., it. 25.

12 Manufacture: foods to pharmaceuticals

1. Davenport-Hines and Slinn, *Glaxo*, 148.
2. Interview with George Kay, 15 August 1996.
3. *Glaxo Bulletin*, November 1965, 22; *Glaxo Bulletin*, March 1965, 11.
4. Glaxo Group Board Minutes, 14 December 1964, it. 155; Glaxo Group BP, 65/39, F. J. Wilkins, 'Expansion of production facilities for Ceporin', 25 March 1965.
5. Glaxo Group Board Minutes, 12 April 1965, it. 58.
6. Glaxo Group Board Minutes, 26 July 1965, it. 135.
7. Interview with Dr A. H. Raper, 10 January 1994.
8. Glaxo Group BP, 67/24, A. E. Bide, 'Ceporin', 7 February 1967.
9. Glaxo Group Board Minutes, 8 July 1968, it. 116.
10. Glaxo Group Board Minutes, 14 October 1968, it. 158.
11. Glaxo Group BP 68/133, A. E. Bide, 'The manufacture of cephalosporins', 7 October 1968, 2.
12. Glaxo Group BP 69/17, A. E. Bide, 'Selection of site for fermenter operations', 8 January 1969, 1.
13. Glaxo Group Board Minutes, 9 June 1969, it. 99; 9 March 1970, it. 41.
14. Glaxo Group BP 70/165, A. E. Bide, 'Cambois factory – phase II', 9 December 1970.
15. Glaxo Group Board Minutes, 14 July 1969, it. 133.
16. Ibid., 9 March 1970, it. 43(b).
17. Interview with Dr J. C. Hamlet, 1 February 1994.
18. Ibid.
19. Glaxo Holdings Board Minutes, 10 March 1975, it. 28.
20. Interview with Dr Alan Bell, 28 January 1997.
21. Interview with Albert Hall, Dr Ian McEwan and Donald McInnes, 27 January 1997.
22. Watson, *Glaxo at Barnard Castle*, 77–78.
23. 'The Harry Lee story of 50 years at Ulverston' (typescript, 11 March 1996), 4.
24. Interview with Dr J. C. Hamlet, 1 February 1994.
25. Quoted in Watson, *Glaxo at Barnard Castle*, 81.
26. Quoted, ibid.
27. *Glaxo Holdings Limited, Reorganization* (n.d.), Appendix 1, 12; Glaxo Holdings Limited, Reorganization (1973), Appendix 6, 'Technical directorate', 17–18.
28. Dr J. C. Hamlet and A. N. Boyd, 'Fermentation strategy' (typescript, 1 March 1978), B.9.
29. Ibid., B.2.
30. Interview with Dr G. J. Blaker, 5 August 1996.
31. Hamlet and Boyd, 'Fermentation strategy', B.3, D.5.
32. Ibid., D.6.
33. Ibid., D.5.
34. Glaxo Holdings Board Minutes, 13 October 1975, it. 128.
35. Glaxo Holdings BP 76/30, W. J. Hurran, 'New factory site – Annan', 9 April 1976, 3.
36. Glaxo Holdings Board Minutes, 9 April 1979, it. 42.
37. GMC Paper, Peter Scruton, 'Progress report concerning Sefton Bulk Pharmaceuticals', 10 May 1978.
38. *Glaxo Holdings Annual Report and Accounts for 1991*, 18.
39. Glaxo Holdings Board Minutes, 10 March 1975, it. 27.

40. Ibid., 30 July 1979, it. 84.

41. Ibid., 30 July 1984, it. 92; 12 November 1984, it. 138.

42. Ibid., 28 July 1986, it. 104.

43. Ibid., 9 April 1984, it. 39.

44. Mitchell, 'Ulverston technical improvements', op.cit., 3.

45. Glaxo Holdings Board Minutes, 10 November 1986, it. 148(a); 6 February 1989, it. 2(a); Jim Walton, *Glaxo Wellcome at Ulverston, The First Fifty Years*, Ulverston (1998), 65–66.

46. Glaxo Holdings Board Minutes, 9 May 1988, it. 44(a)(ii).

47. Ibid., it. 44(a)(i).

48. Ibid., 11 April 1988, it. 36.

49. Interview with George Kay, 15 August 1996.

50. Interview with Douglas Rutherford, 15 August 1996.

51. Dr G. J. Blaker, 'Glaxo Pharmaceuticals Ltd., production investment strategy', vol. I, (1983), 20.

52. A. P. Swaddle, 'Glaxo Pharmaceuticals, UK secondary production trends 1978–88', 25 November 1983, 1.

53. Glaxo Group BP 68/168.

54. Glaxo Group Board Minutes, 12 May 1969, it. 80.

55. Ibid., 13 July 1970, it. 128.

56. Interview with Dr A. H. Raper, 10 January 1994.

57. A. P. Swaddle, 'Glaxo Pharmaceuticals Limited, proposals for development of UK secondary factories' (typescript, 24 November 1983), 23.

58. Ibid., p. 24, Appendix 1A.

59. Dr G. J. Blaker, 'Glaxo Pharmaceuticals Ltd., production investment strategy', 2 vols (14 July 1983).

60. Dr G. J. Blaker, 'Glaxo Pharmaceuticals Ltd., production investment strategy … to the Group Management Committee' (8 November 1983), 18.

61. Ibid., 19.

62. Ibid., 4.

63. Ibid., 43.

64. GMC Paper 85/83, B. D. Taylor, 'Glaxo Pharmaceuticals, UK secondary manufacturing facilities', 30 April 1985, 1.

65. Glaxo Holdings Board Minutes, 11 February 1985, it. 19.

66. Watson, *Glaxo at Barnard Castle*, 44–45.

67. Ibid., 10 June 1985, it. 63.

68. Ibid., 14 October 1985, it. 128.

69. Ibid., 11 February 1985, it. 20.

70. Ibid., 14 October 1985, it. 132.

71. Ibid., 10 March 1986, it. 35.

72. Blaker, 'Production investment strategy', 80.

73. 'Secondary production' (typescript 1981), Appendix G16.

74. Ibid., Appendix G21.

75. A. P. Swaddle, 'Glaxo Pharmaceuticals Limited, proposals for development', (typescript, 24 November 1983), 49–50.

76. Ibid., Appendix B12.

77. Glaxo Group Board Minutes, 2 June 1962, it. 77.

78. Glaxo Group BP 63/75, F. J. Wilkins, 'Modernisation of food packing, Greenford', 7 May 1963.

79. Glaxo Group Board Minutes, 13 May 1963, it. 90.

80. Ibid., 12 April 1965, it. 76, 77.

81. Ibid., 12 April 1965, it. 57; *Glaxo in Ireland* (May 1967), 11–12.

82. Glaxo Group Board Minutes, 13 July 1970, it. 136; 14 December 1970, it. 211.

83. Glaxo Group Board Minutes, 7 March 1968, it. 32.

84. Ibid., 8 July 1968, it. 118.

85. Ibid., 11 November 1968, it. 186.

86. Ibid., 29 July 1968, it. 135.

87. *Glaxo Group News*, September 1967.

88. Glaxo Group BP 64/41, F. J. Wilkins, 'Vitamin C fortification of Ostermilk', 27 March 1964.

89. Glaxo Laboratories BP 201/70, 18 November 1970.

90. Ibid., 212/70, 23 December 1970.

91. Ibid., 173/70, 29 September 1970.

92. Ibid., 27/72, 25 January 1972.

93. Glaxo Information Sheet, 'Why milk prices have gone up' (n.d.).

94. Glaxo Laboratories Board Minutes, 4 April 1973, it. 61.

95. Ibid., it. 77.

96. Ibid., 4 May 1973, it. 97.

97. Ibid., 1 March 1974, it. 24.

98. Ibid., it. 60; Glaxo Laboratories BP 39/74, 14 March 1974.

99. Ibid., 24 April 1974, it. 74(2).

100. *The Ostermilk Story*, Greenford (1972).

101. Glaxo Laboratories Board Minutes, 31 May 1974, it. 116(2).

102. Ibid.

103. Glaxo Laboratories BP 54/74, 17 April 1974.

104. Glaxo Laboratories BP 167/74, 12 December 1974.
105. Glaxo Group BP 64/71, F. J. Wilkins, 'Farex rice cereal', 8 May 1964.
106. Glaxo Holdings Board Minutes, 13 January 1975, it. 4.
107. *Glaxo Holdings Annual Report and Accounts* (1974), 'Chairman's statement', 6.
108. Glaxo Holdings Board Minutes, 13 January 1975, it. 4.
109. Glaxo Holdings BP, F. C. D. Back, 'Foods rationalisation', 6 February 1975; Glaxo Holdings Board Minutes, 10 February 1975, it. 18.
110. Interview with E. R. C. Farmer, 8 February 1994.
111. Glaxo Holdings Board Minutes, 14 November 1983, it. 142.
112. Ibid., 11 November 1985, it. 146.
113. Group Management Committee, 73/25, J. G. N. Drewitt and P. Scruton, 'Industrial relations: Glaxo companies in the UK and their relationships with employee representative bodies', 12 February 1973, 5.
114. Glaxo Group BP 63/123, A. H. Wilson, 'Administration relating to personnel and pensions', 29 July 1963, 1–2.
115. Ibid., 2.
116. Glaxo Group BP 66/97, A. E. Bide, 'Personnel matters: Group Personnel Committee', 8 June 1966, 1.
117. Ibid., 3.
118. Ibid., 4.
119. Glaxo Group BP 66/97, Bide, 'Personnel matters', 4–5.
120. Glaxo Group BP 67/74, A. E. Bide, 'Personnel matters', 7 June 1967, 2.
121. Quoted in Glaxo Group BP, R. S. Stokes, 'Early warning submission by Glaxo Laboratories Ltd. to Ministry of Labour', 14 March 1967, 1.
122. Ibid., 1–2.
123. Ibid., 2.
124. Ibid., 3.
125. Glaxo Group BP 147/67, R. S. Stokes, 'Craftsmen – Ulverston and Kendal', 2.
126. Stokes, 'Early warning submission', op.cit., 4.
127. *North Western Evening Mail*, 11 October 1968.
128. Glaxo Group BP, 6/69, '1969 revision of pay scales', 6.
129. Glaxo Laboratories BP 78/69, R. S. Stokes, 'Ulverston craftsmen', 14 May 1969, 2.
130. Glaxo Group BP 71/12, A. E. Bide, 'Glaxo Laboratories industrial relations', 8 February 1971, 2–3.
131. Ibid., 2.
132. Ibid.
133. Ibid., 3.
134. Ibid., 2.
135. Glaxo Laboratories Board Minutes, 26 February 1973, 'JCNCs', it. 51.
136. Group Management Committee 73/25, J. G. N. Drewitt and P. Scruton, 'Industrial relations: Glaxo companies in the UK', 12 February 1973, 4.
137. Group Management Committee 73/194, 'Industrial Relations – TGWU/GMWU', 2 November 1973.
138. *Darlington Evening Despatch*, 5 April 1974.
139. Group Management Committee 74/176, A. E. Bide, 'Government intrusion and related matters', 15 July 1974, 1.
140. *The Journal*, 19 April 1975.
141. *Northern Echo*, 19 April 1975.
142. *Evening Chronicle*, 22 April 1975.
143. *Glaxo Holdings, Annual Report and Accounts 1977*, 6.
144. Group Management Committee Minutes, 14 July 1977, it. 2642(a).

13 *Research and development, 1962–1985*

1. H. F. Grundy, *Lecture Notes in Pharmacology*, Oxford (1985), 1.
2. John L. Read et al., *Lecture Notes on Clinical Pharmacology*, Oxford (1985), 7.
3. Quoted in David Jack and Tom Walker, 'Benjamin Arthur Hems', *Biographical Memoirs of Fellows of the Royal Society*, 43 (1998), 221.
4. Ibid.
5. Tweedale, *At the Sign of the Plough*, 128.
6. Ibid., 124.
7. Ibid., 126.
8. 13 & 14 Geo V c. 5, *Dangerous Drugs and Poisons Act* (1923).
9. 23 & 24 Geo V c. 25, *Pharmacy and Poisons Act* (1933).
10. Ernest C. Cripps, *Plough Court, The Story of a Notable Pharmacy 1715–1927*, London: Allen & Hanburys (1927), 125.
11. Ibid.
12. 'A & H Laboratories for Analysis and Research', *The Chemist and Druggist*, 179 (1963), 920–21.

13 Desmond Chapman-Huston and Ernest C. Cripps, *Through a City Archway, the Story of Allen and Hanburys 1715–1954*, London: John Murray (1954), 222–23.

14. Tweedale, *At the Sign of the Plough*, 170.

15. Ibid., 87–89.

16. Ibid., 174.

17. Ibid., 182.

18. Ibid., 183–84.

19. Davenport-Hines and Slinn, *Glaxo*, 197.

20. Chapman-Huston and Cripps, *Through a City Archway*, 232–33.

21. Ibid., 236.

22. Tweedale, *At the Sign of the Plough*, 187.

23. Davenport-Hines and Slinn, *Glaxo*, 198.

24. Glaxo Group Board Minutes, 12 December, 1966, it. 185.

25. Davenport-Hines and Slinn, *Glaxo*, 182.

26. Glaxo Research Ltd, Executive Committee papers 1968, 2C/3/RI.

27. Coleman, *Courtaulds*, vol. III, 18–19.

28. Ibid., 19.

29. Ibid., 174.

30. A. H. Wilson, 'The Research Department of Courtaulds Limited', *Proceedings of the Royal Society*, Series B 142 (1954), 305.

31. Interview with Sir David Jack, 18 January, 1994.

32. *Bulletin International: The Glaxo Group Quarterly*, 22 (Autumn 1972), 6–7.

33. *Glaxo Group News*, February 1973, 'Decade of cephalosporins', 10.

34. E. P. Abraham, 'A glimpse of the early history of the cephalosporins', *Review of Infectious Diseases*, 1 (1979), 99; G. R. Donowitz and G. L. Mandell, 'Cephalosporins', in Mandell et al. (eds), *Principles and Practice of Infectious Diseases*, New York (1990), 246.

35. Abraham, 'Early history of the cephalosporins', 99–100.

36. E. P. Abraham, 'Cephaloridine: historical remarks', *Postgraduate Medical Journal*, 43, supplement (1967), 9.

37. National Research Development Corporation, 'Cephalosporin project' (typescript, 28 October 1964), 1.

38. *International Conference on Cefuroxine, 27–28 September 1977*, A. E. Bide, 'Opening address'.

39. Abraham, 'Early history of the cephalosporins', 102.

40. Editorial, 'Cephaloridine', *BMJ*, 2 (1964), 1211–12.

41. Glaxo Laboratories, 'Ceporin – Britain's new major antibiotic' (typescript, 6 November 1964).

42. Glaxo Laboratories, 'Sefton Park's part in the Ceporin project' (typescript, 6 November 1964).

43. Interview with Dr Peter Wilkinson, 27 October 1995.

44. *Ceporin*, Glaxo Laboratories (September 1963), 3.

45. *BMJ*, 2 (1964), 1212; P. W. Muggleton, C. H. O'Callaghan and W. K. Stevens, 'Laboratory evaluation of a new antibiotic-cephaloridine (Ceporin)', *BMJ* 2 (1964), 1234–37.

46. 'Preliminary report on "Ceporin" cephaloridine' (typescript, 12 October 1964), 2.

47. Glaxo Research Ltd, 'Cephaloridine, biological properties' (typescript, July 1965).

48. *BMJ*, 2 (1964), 1212.

49. Interview with Sir Mark Richmond, 9 May 1994.

50. Glaxo Research Ltd, 'Cephalexin, biological properties' (March 1968).

51. C. H. O'Callaghan, R. B. Sykes, A. Griffiths and J. E. Thornton, 'Cefuroxime, a new cephalosporin antibiotic: activity in vitro', *Antimicrobial Agents and Chemotherapy*, 9 (1976), 511–19; C. H. O'Callaghan, R. B. Sykes and S. E. Staniforth, 'A new cephalosporin with a dual mode of action', *Antimicrobial Agents and Chemotherapy*, 10 (1976), 247–48.

52. Hershel Herzog and Eugene P. Oliveto, 'A history of significant steroid discoveries and developments originating at the Schering Corporation (USA) since 1948', *Steroids*, 57 (1992), 619.

53. Ibid., 621.

54. A. W. McKenzie and R. B. Stoughton, 'Method for comparing percutaneous absorption of steroids', *Archives of Dermatology*, 86 (1962), 608–10.

55. A. W. McKenzie, 'Percutaneous absorption of steroids', *Archives of Dermatology*, 86 (1962), 611–14.

56. Correspondence with Dr A. W. McKenzie, 10 March 1995.

57. A. W. McKenzie and R. M. Atkinson, 'Topical activities of betamethasone esters in man', *Archives of Dermatology*, 89 (1964), 744.

58. Ibid.

59. Interview with Sir David Jack, 18 October 1994.

60. J. A. Sutton, 'A brief history of steroid

anaesthesia before Althesin (CT 1341)',
Postgraduate Medical Journal, 48
(Supplement, June 1972), 9.

61. 'Steroid anaesthesia', *Postgraduate Medical
Journal* 48 (Supplement, June 1972).

62. M. Morgan and J. G. Whitwam, 'Editorial –
Althesin', *Anaesthesia*, 40 (1985), 121.

63. M. Swerdlow, 'Studies with Althesin – a new
steroid anaesthetic', *Postgraduate Medical
Journal*, 48 (Supplement, June 1972), 105–108.

64. W. Carson, 'Group trial of Althesin as an
intravenous anaesthetic', *Postgraduate
Medical Journal*, 48 (Supplement, June 1972),
108–11.

65. R. S. J. Clarke, J. W. Dundee and I. W.
Carson, 'A new steroid anaesthetic –
Althesin', *Proceedings of the Royal Society of
Medicine*, 66 (1973), 1029.

66. Glaxo Laboratories Board Minutes, 29
November 1972, it. 173; Research Report BP
72/121.

67. P. J. Simpson, S. G. Radford, J. A. Lockyer and
J. W. Sear, 'Some predisposing factors to
hypersensitivity reactions following first
exposure to Althesin', *Anaesthesia*, 40 (1985),
422–23.

68. Glaxo Laboratories Board Minutes, 5 April
1978.

69. Morgan and Whitwam, 'Editorial – Althesin',
122.

70. Jack and Walker, 'Benjamin Arthur Hems', 22.

71. Interview with Dr Tom Walker, 7 February
1994.

72. Turner, *Gold on the Green*, 79.

73. Interview with Sir Richard Sykes, 7 April
1994.

74. Interview with Sir Mark Richmond, 9 May
1994.

75. Ibid.

76. Turner, *Gold on the Green*, 76–77, 85.

77. Quoted ibid., 94.

78. *A Glaxo Guide to Otitis Externa* (1974).

79. Glaxo, *Cepoxillin, Some Important Facts*
(1976).

80. Glaxo, *Cepravin Dry Cow* (1976).

81. Interview with Sir David Jack, 18 January
1994.

82. Tweedale, *At the Sign of the Plough*, 206.

83. Interview with Sir David Jack, 18 January
1994.

84. Quoted in Tweedale, *At the Sign of the
Plough*, 208.

85. Ibid.

86. Interview with Dr R. T. Brittain, 8 March
1994.

87. Quoted from Tweedale, *At the Sign of the
Plough*, 208.

88. Ibid.

89. Interview with Sir David Jack, 18 January
1994.

90. David Jack, 'The challenge of drug discovery',
Drug Design and Delivery, 4 (1989), 167–69.

91. David Jack, 'Research and development in
the pharmaceutical industry', *Science in
Parliament*, 49 (1992), 5.

92. Tweedale, *At the Sign of the Plough*, 210.

93. Jack, 'Research and development', 6.

94. Jack, 'Challenge of drug discovery', 171.

95. Quoted in Tweedale, *At the Sign of the
Plough*, 213.

96. Quoted ibid.

97. R. T. Brittain, 'A comparison of the
pharmacology of salbutamol with that of
isoprenaline', *Post Graduate Medical Journal*,
47, Supplement (1971), 11.

98. Ibid.

99. D. Hartley, D. Jack, L. H. C. Lunts and A. C.
Ritchie, 'New class of selective stimulants of
B-adrenergic receptors', *Nature*, 219 (24
August 1968), 861–62; R. T. Brittain, J. B.
Farmer, D. Jack, L. E. Martin and W. T.
Simpson, '(AH 3365): a selective B-adrenergic
stimulant', *Nature*, 219 (24 August 1968), 862–63.

100. Valerie A. Cullum, J. B. Farmer, D. Jack and
G. P. Levy, 'Salbutamol: a new selective B-
adrenoceptive receptor stimulant', *British
Journal of Pharmacology*, 35 (1969), 149.

101. Ivor Mitchell, 'A & H research continues to
expand', *Bulletin International: The Glaxo
Group Quarterly*, 13 (1970), 5.

102. David Jack, 'A way of looking at agonism and
antagonism: lessons from salbutamol,
salmeterol and other B-adrenoceptor
agonists', *British Journal of Clinical
Pharmacology*, 31 (1991), 504–505.

103. D. I. Ball, R. T. Brittain, R. A. Coleman et al.,
'Salmeterol, a novel, long-acting B_2
adrenoceptor agonist: characterisation of
pharmacological activity *in vitro* and *in vivo*',
British Journal of Pharmacology, 104 (1991),
670.

104. Tweedale, *At the Sign of the Plough*, 216.

105. R. T. Brittain, G. M. Drew and G. P. Levy,
'The X-and-B-adrenoceptor blocking
potencies of labetalol', *British Journal of
Pharmacology*, 77 (1982), 105–14.

106. Tweedale, *At the Sign of the Plough*, 220.
107. J. W. Black, W. A. M. Duncan, C. J. Durrant, C. R. Ganellin and E. M. Parsons, 'Definition and antagonism of histamine H_2-receptors', *Nature*, 236 (1972), 385–90.
108. R. T. Brittain and David Jack, 'Histamine H_2-antagonists – past, present and future', *Journal of Clinical Gastroenterology*, 5, Supplement (1983), 71.
109. Quoted in Lynn, 193.
110. L. Tillman, 'Landmarks in the history of Zantac' (n.d.), 1.
111. E. P. Woodings, G. T. Dixon, C. Harrison, P. Cary and D. A. Richards, 'Ranitidine – a new H_2-receptor antagonist', *Gut*, 21 (1980), 187–91.
112. J. Bradshaw, R. T. Brittain, J. W. Clitherow, M. J. Daly, D. Jack, B. J. Price and R. Stables, 'Ranitidine (AH 19065): a new potent, selective histamine H_2-receptor antagonist', *British Journal of Pharmacology*, 66 (1979), 464P.
113. Interview with Professor P. P. A. Humphrey, 13 May 1994.
114. Patrick Humphrey 'The challenge of drug discovery', in Andrew Scott (ed.), *Frontiers of Science*, Oxford (1990), 5–7.
115. Humphrey, 'The challenge of drug discovery', 5–7.
116. Ibid., 9.
117. P. P. A. Humphrey et al., 'A rational approach to identifying a fundamentally new drug for the treatment of migraine', in P. R. Saxena et al., *Cardiovascular Pharmacology of 5-Hydroxytryptamine*, Dordrecht (1990), 426–27.
118. P. P. A. Humphrey and W. Feniuk, 'Mode of action of the anti-migraine drug sumatriptan', *Trends in Pharmacological Sciences*, 12 (1991), 444–45; W. Feniuk et al., 'Rationale for the use of 5-HT_1-like agonists in the treatment of migraine', *Journal of Neurology*, 238 (1991), 557–61.
119. Editorial, 'Sumatriptan, serotonin, migraine and money', *The Lancet*, 339 (18 January 1992), 151–52.
120. P. P. A. Humphrey, 'Peripheral 5-hydroxytryptamine receptors and their classification', *Neuropharmacology*, 23 (1984), 1503.
121. P. B. Bradley et al., *Neuropharmacology*, 25 (1986), 563–76.
122. P. P. A. Humphrey, P. Hartig and D. Hoyer, 'A proposed new nomenclature for 5-HT receptors', *Trends in Pharmacological Sciences*, 14 (1993), 233.
123. Ibid., 236.
124. Interview with Dr Mike Tyers, 28 April 1994.
125. C. V. Viner, P. J. Selby, G. B. Zulian, M. E. Gore, M. E. Butcher, C. M. Wootton and T. J. McElwain, 'Ondansetron – a new safe and effective antiemetic in patients receiving high-dose melphalan', *Cancer, Chemotherapy and Pharmacology*, 25 (1990), 449–53.
126. Glaxo Holdings Board Minutes, 13 March 1978, it. 41(4).
127. *Glaxo Group Organization* (1978), Appendix 7, The Research and Development Directorate, 22.
128. Ibid., 24.
129. Glaxo Holdings BP 82/57, David Jack, 'The development and future of Glaxo Group Research Ltd.', 20 April 1982, 1.
130. Ibid.
131. *Glaxo Holdings Annual Report and Accounts* (1982), 9.
132. Box 398, GGR Board Minutes, 3 October 1984, it. 48.
133. 'Opren Scandal', *The Lancet*, 1 (29 January 1983), 219–20; 'Opren case arbitration'; *The Lancet*, 1 (13 February 1988), 370.
134. Interview with Sir Richard Sykes, 7 April 1994.
135. Glaxo Holdings Board Minutes, 8 December 1986, it. 159(a).
136. *Glaxo Holdings Annual Report and Accounts* (1987), 4.
137. Comanor, 'Political economy', 1190.
138. Association of the British Pharmaceutical Industry, *Pharma Facts and Figures*, London (1992), 27.
139. Ibid.
140. Ibid., 4.
141. R. Balance, J. Pogany and H. Forstner, *The World's Pharmaceutical Industries*, Aldershot (1992), 85–86.
142. Ibid., 90.
143. Interview with Dr David Tweats, 28 April 1994.
144. J. M. Ratcliffe, P. R. McElhatton and F. M. Sullivan, 'Reproductive toxicity', in B. Ballantyne et al., *General and Applied Toxicology*, London (1993), 989.
145. D. J. Tweats, 'Mutagenicity', in Ballantyne et al., *General and Applied Toxicology*, 893–94.
146. Office of Health Economics, *Medicines: 50 Years of Progress 1930–1980*, London (1980), 7.

147. Quoted in B. Holmstedt and G. Liljestrand, *Readings in Pharmacology*, Oxford (1963), 284.
148. Quoted ibid., 285–86.

14 Glaxo in Italy

1. Davenport-Hines and Slinn, *Glaxo*, 123.
2. GA 19/4/5, letter, F. Randall to M. J. Nathan, 2 October 1929.
3. GA 19/4/5, F. Randall, memorandum, 11 November 1929.
4. *Glaxo, le origini e il suo sviluppo in Italia*, Verona (1982), 16.
5. Davenport-Hines and Slinn, *Glaxo*, 124.
6. Interview with Dr Enrico Fezzi, 10 September 1996.
7. Ibid.
8. Glaxo Laboratories Board Minutes, vol. I, 24 November 1936, 87.
9. Ibid., 28 November 1935, 16–17.
10. Ibid., 24 November 1936, 87.
11. Ibid., 26 May 1936, 52; 25 May 1937, 123.
12. Ibid., 12 January 1938, 153.
13. Quoted in Davenport-Hines and Slinn, *Glaxo*, 151.
14. Glaxo Laboratories Board Minutes, vol. II, 29 May 1945, 185–86.
15. H. A. Gent, 'Report of September 1946'.
16. Herbert Palmer to Sir Harry Jephcott, 'Italian factory' (typescript, 22 July 1947), 1; Glaxo Laboratories Board Minutes, vol. II, 25 July 1947, 330.
17. Ibid., 24 June 1957, 1; 14 June 1956, 1.
18. Glaxo Group BP 62/124, H. Jephcott, 'Italy', 29 November 1962.
19. Ibid.
20. Glaxo Group BP 64/10, H. W. Palmer 'Italy', 7 January 1964, 1.
21. Ibid., 2.
22. Glaxo Group BP 66/79, 'Major overseas subsidiaries', figures derived from bar charts 'Italy'.
23. Marketing Services Division, Glaxo International, 'The Italian pharmaceutical market 1966' (typescript, October 1966), 2.
24. Ibid., 11.
25. *Glaxo, le origini e il suo sviluppo in Italia*, 20.
26. Glaxo Group Board Minutes, 12 April 1965, it. 63.
27. Ibid., 4 April 1966, it. 56.
28. Glaxo Group BP 69/32, 'Laboratori Glaxo S.p.A., Italy'.
29. Interview with Dr Enrico Fezzi, 10 September 1996.
30. Interview with Dr Mario Fertonani, 9 September 1996.
31. Interview with Dr Enrico Fezzi, 10 September 1996.
32. Interview with Dr F. Fantini, 10 September 1996.
33. Interview with Dr Enrico Fezzi, 10 September 1966.
34. Glaxo Group BP 66/79, 'Major overseas subsidiaries', 2.
35. Glaxo Group Board Minutes, 8 February 1971, it. 31.
36. Davenport-Hines and Slinn, *Glaxo*, 340.
37. Interview with Dr Mario Fertonani, 9 September 1996.
38. Interview with Dr F. Fantini, 10 September 1996.
39. Ibid.
40. *Glaxo Holdings Annual Report and Accounts* (1986), 10.
41. Glaxo Group Management Committee (1983).
42. Taggart, *The World Pharmaceutical Industry*, 357, 365.
43. Interview with Dr G. Sciacchero, 10 September 1996.
44. Glaxo Holdings BP 73/58, W. J. Hurran, 'Laboratori Glaxo S.p.A., building investment programme', 27 July 1973, 2.
45. Glaxo Holdings Board Minutes, 30 July 1973, it. 79.
46. Ibid., 9 April 1979, it. 45.
47. Ibid., 9 January 1984, it. 8.
48. Glaxo Holdings BP 84/9, P. Girolami, 'Glaxo S.p.A., expansion of secondary manufacturing facilities', 5 January 1984, 3.
49. Ibid., 4.
50. Glaxo Holdings BP 85/100, P. Girolami, 'Glaxo S.p.A., re-equipping the Parma factory', 8 October 1985, 1–2.
51. Glaxo Holdings Board Minutes, 28 July 1986, it. 105.
52. Interview with Dr G. Gaviraghi, 9 September 1996.
53. Paul Girolami, *The Development of Glaxo*, London, Glaxo Holdings plc, 12.
54. Interview with Dr G. Gaviraghi, 9 September 1996.
55. *Glaxo World*, 18 (May 1992), 16.
56. Glaxo Holdings Board Minutes, 10 November 1986, it. 148(c).

57. *The Glaxo Research Center, Case History of a Project Verona 1987–1990*, Milan (1991), 15.
58. Glaxo Holdings BP 86/152, M. Fertonani, 'Glaxo S.p.A., new research centre, Verona, Italy', 30 October 1986, 1.
59. *Glaxo Research Center*, 26–27.
60. Ibid., 15.

15 The great leap: The United States 1977–1985

1. Glaxo Group BP 71/20, H. W. Palmer and R. D. Smart, 'The U.S.A. market', 29 January, 1971, 5.
2. Balance et al., *World's Pharmaceutical Industries*, p. 226; *Glaxo Annual Report and Accounts* (1994), 8.
3. *Monopolies Commission, A Report on the Proposed Mergers*, 66.
4. Tweedale, *At the Sign of the Plough*, 108–10.
5. Sir Harry Jephcott, Diary (typescript, February 1950), 29 January 1950, 4.
6. H. Jephcott, 'American associations' (typescript, 25 June 1962), 1; *Values and Visions, A Merck Century* (1991), 72–78.
7. Davenport-Hines and Slinn, *Glaxo*, 244.
8. Stanley Schofield (director), *Glaxo Laboratories in Britain* (colour film, *c.* 1965).
9. Jephcott, 'American associations', 1.
10. F. J. Wilkins, 'Report on visit to Merck of 30 November to 2 December 1954', D1/1/31.
11. Ibid.
12. Hershel Herzog and Eugene P. Oliveto, 'A history of significant steroid discoveries and developments originating at the Schering Corporation (USA) since 1948', *Steroids*, 57 (1992), 617–23.
13. Jephcott, 'American associations', 1.
14. Memorandum, Herbert Palmer to Sir Harry Jephcott, 11 March 1955.
15. Davenport-Hines and Slinn, *Glaxo*, 214–16.
16. Ibid., 220.
17. Glaxo Laboratories, BM 58/43; Davenport-Hines and Slinn, *Glaxo*, 169.
18. Ibid., 168.
19. Glaxo Laboratories BP 58/43.
20. Glaxo Laboratories BP 61/65, 1.
21. Ibid.
22. Glaxo Group BM 63/46, 21 March 1963, 1.
23. Glaxo Laboratories Board Minutes, 6 November 1961, it. 185.
24. Glaxo Group BM 62/80 'Future policy', 1.
25. Ibid., 2.
26. Ibid., 3.
27. Ibid., 3.
28. Ibid., 4.
29. Glaxo Group Minutes, 5 November 1962, it. 153.
30. Ibid., 16 January 1963, it. 20.
31. Ibid.
32. Glaxo Group BM 63/46, 21 March 1963, 1.
33. Ibid., 'X and Y', 14 March 1963, 1.
34. Ibid., 3.
35. Ibid.
36. Glaxo Group BM 63/46, copy of letter to Francis C. Brown, Chairman and President, Schering Corporation, Bloomfield, New Jersey, from Merrill, Lynch, Pierce, Fenner & Smith, 27 February 1963, 1.
37. Ibid.
38. Ibid., 2.
39. Glaxo Group BM 63/82, meeting held at 47 Park Street, London, on 7 May 1963.
40. Ibid., 1.
41. Ibid., 2.
42. Glaxo Group BM 63/91, 'Collaboration with Schering' 29 May 1963.
43. Ibid.
44. Ibid.
45. Glaxo Group Minutes, 10 June 1963, it. 118.
46. Ibid., 8 April 1963, it. 77.
47. Coleman, *Courtaulds*, vol.III, 262.
48. Glaxo Group Board Minutes, 13 December 1965, it. 210.
49. Ibid.
50. Glaxo Group BM 65/21, H. W. Palmer, 'The cephalosporins', 2 February 1965.
51. Ibid.
52. Ibid., 2.
53. Ibid.
54. Glaxo Group BM 65/41, F. J. Wilkins, 'Glaxo Group and the U.S.A.', 31 March 1965.
55. Ibid., 1.
56. Ibid.
57. Ibid., 2.
58. Ibid.
59. Ibid., 3.
60. Ibid.
61. Ibid., 4.
62. Ibid.
63. Glaxo Group BM 71/20, H. W. Palmer and R. D. Smart, 'The U.S.A. Market' 29 January 1971, 1.
64. Ibid., 2.
65. Ibid., 3.
66. Ibid., 4.

67. Ibid.
68. Ibid., 5.
69. Ibid.
70. Glaxo Group Board Minutes, 8 February 1971, it. 37.
71. Palmer and Smart, 'The U.S.A. Market', 5.
72. Glaxo Group Board Minutes, 8 February 1971, it. 37.
73. Ibid., 10 April 1972, it. 78.
74. Glaxo Holdings Board Minutes, 12 June 1972, it. 22(i).
75. Ibid., 8 March 1976, it. 38.
76. Ibid., it. 38(iii) and (iv).
77. R. D. Smart, 'Commercial policy directive, the United States', 8 April 1976.
78. Glaxo Holdings Board Minutes, 12 April 1976.
79. R. D. Smart, 'The United States', 2.
80. Glaxo Holdings Board Minutes, 14 June 1976, it. 87.
81. Girolami, The Development of Glaxo, 17.
82. J. C. Barnett to A. E. Bide and R. D. Smart, 'Meyer Laboratories Inc.', 18 July 1977, 6.
83. Letter, J. C. Barnett to A. E. Bide and R. D. Smart, 18 July 1977.
84. Barnett, 'Meyer Laboratories', 6.
85. Glaxo Holdings Board Minutes, 25 July 1977, it. 100.
86. Letter, J. C. Barnett to A. E. Bide and R. D. Smart, 18 July 1977.
87. Meyer Laboratories Inc. Combined Internal Profit and Loss Statement to 31 December 1976.
88. Coopers & Lybrand, 'Meyer Laboratories Inc., valuation and determination of tax bases' (30 June 1976), 2.
89. Interview with Mike Gallucci, 10 June 1994.
90. Meyer Laboratories Inc., List of Employees, 11 January 1977.
91. Barnett, 'Meyer Laboratories', 3.
92. Coopers & Lybrand, 'Meyer Laboratories Inc.'
93. Interview with Hazel Rummer, 9 June 1994.
94. Letter, J. C. Barnett to A. E. Bide and R. D. Smart, 18 July 1977
95. R. D. Smart, 'Glaxo in the United States', 8 September 1977, 1.
96. Glaxo Holdings Board Minutes, 14 September 1977, it. 103.
97. Ibid., it. 103(a).
98. Glaxo Holdings Board Minutes, 14 November 1977, it. 127.
99. Interview with Sir Paul Girolami, 15 March 1994.
100. Glaxo Holdings BP 77/102, 'Proposed acquisition of Meyer Laboratories', 10 November 1977.
101. The Times, 17 February 1978, Michael Rothwell, 'Mr. Glaxo talks about that move into the U.S. market', Money News, 2.
102. Ibid.
103. Meyer Laboratories Inc. Board Meeting, 2 August 1979, it. I, II.
104. Ibid., it. II.
105. Glaxo Inc. Board Meeting, 27 February 1978, it. 7.
106. Glaxo Inc. Board Minutes, 15 March 1979.
107. Meyer Laboratories Inc., W. J. Hasey, 'Special announcement', 2 April 1979.
108. Glaxo Inc. Board Minutes, 8 July 1980.
109. Ibid., 21 November 1980.
110. Ibid., 20 November 1985.
111. Interview with Dr Peter Wise, 7 June 1994.
112. Pharmaceutical Executive, July 1982, Suzanne Harvey, 'Joe Ruvane helps Glaxo go American'.
113. Interview with J. J. Ruvane, 8 June 1994.
114. Ibid.
115. Interview with Sir Paul Girolami, 12 May 1994.
116. Interview with J. J. Ruvane, 8 June 1994.
117. Interview with Sir Paul Girolami, 12 May 1994.
118. Business Week, 22 November 1982, 'Executive suite'.
119. Interview with Dr Peter Wise, 7 June 1994.
120. Newcomer's Guide, Chapel Hill ... Research Triangle Park (1993–94), 21.
121. S. D. Williams, 'Introduction', Park Guide, The 1994 Guide to Research Triangle Park, 8 (1994), 15.
122. Ibid., 16.
123. Newcomer's Guide (1993–94), 15.
124. Interview with Dr Peter Wise, 7 June 1994.
125. Interview with Pam Jones, 10 June 1994.
126. Glaxo Holdings, GMC 82/79, P. Girolami, 'Glaxo Inc., new administration headquarters', 2 June 1982.
127. Ibid.
128. Ibid.
129. Glaxo Holdings Board Minutes, 14 June 1982, it. 77.
130. Durham Morning Herald, 4 September 1983, 'Glaxo Inc.'.
131. Glaxo Holdings BP 84/74, Paul Girolami, 'Glaxo Inc., expansion of administrative headquarters building', 25 July 1984.

132. Glaxo Holdings Board Minutes, 28 July 1986, it. 107.

133. 'American secondary production factory, site search', (typescript, n.d.).

134. L. J. Wyman and D. W. Murray, 'American factory site search', 24 March 1981, 1.

135. Ibid., 3.

136. Ibid., 4.

137. Ibid., 5.

138. Glaxo Holdings, Group Management Committee 82/91, P. Girolami, 'Glaxo Inc., construction of warehouse and factory', 7 June 1982.

139. Glaxo Holdings Board Minutes, 14 June 1982, it. 78.

140. Girolami, 'Glaxo Inc.'.

141. Ibid.

142. *Durham Morning Herald*, 21 November 1985, supplement 'Glaxo Inc. headquarters to be dedicated', 3.

143. Glaxo Holdings Board Minutes, 8 July 1985, it. 75.

144. Glaxo Inc. BP GB 85/563, 'Cephalosporin facility'.

145. Glaxo Holdings Board Minutes, 29 July 1985, it. 91, 92.

146. Ibid., 8 June 1987, it. 54(c)ii.

147. Glaxo Holdings BP 89/14, E. Mario, 'Cephalosporin facility – site purchase'.

148. Glaxo Holdings Board Minutes, 6 February 1989, it. 2(b).

149. Glaxo Inc. Executive Committee Minutes, 17 January 1990, (v).

150. Ibid., 12 May 1989.

151. Angelmar and Pinson, 'Zantac', 10.

152. Quoted ibid.

153. Joseph J. Ruvane Jr, *Glaxo Inc., New Kid Competing in an Established Industry* (1983), 10.

154. *Durham Morning Herald*, 25 November 1984, 'Glaxo's sales'.

155. Ibid., 17 April 1986, 'Glaxo reports record earnings'.

156. A. J. Riley and P. R. Salmon (eds), *Ranitidine*, Amsterdam (1982), D. G. Colin-Jones, 'Ranitidine in the treatment of peptic ulceration', 16–17, 20.

157. J. B. Zeldis, L. S. Friedman and K. J. Isselbacher, 'Ranitidine: a new H_2-receptor antagonist', *New England Journal of Medicine*, 309 (1983), 1372.

158. K. R. Gough et al. 'Ranitidine and cimetidine in prevention of duodenal ulcer relapse', *The Lancet*, 2 (1984), 659–62.

159. Stephen E. Silvis, 'Results of the United States ranitidine maintenance trials', *American Journal of Medicine*, 77 (Supplement 5B, November 1984), 35–36.

160. Ibid., 36.

161. Angelmar and Pinson, 'Zantac', 5.

162. Ibid., Exhibit 22.

163. *Durham Sun*, 1 March 1986, Laura Woody, 'Glaxo markets new medication for ulcers'.

164. *Durham Morning Herald*, 25 June 1986, 'Glaxo ulcer drug'.

165. Ibid., 13 October 1987, 'Glaxo Inc. reports sales up 51%'.

166. Angelmar and Pinson, 'Zantac', 12.

167. *FDC Reports*, 5 (23) (4 June 1986), 'Glaxo claims of Zantac superiority to Tagamet criticised by FDA'.

168. *Washington Post*, 5 July 1986, 'Business', G1; *Raleigh Times*, 5 July 1986, 10-A.

169. *FDC Reports*, 5 (23).

170. *Raleigh News and Observer*, 30 October 1986, 'Glaxo settles one dispute'.

171. Glaxo Inc. Board Minutes, 3 August 1981; *Durham Morning Herald*, 25 November 1984, 'Glaxo's sales almost four times 1983's figures'.

172. Glaxo Inc., Profit Statement 1983–84.

173. *Glaxo Ink*, October 1985, 'Focus on Trandate', 4.

174. George S. Goldstein, 'Orphan-drugs – a pharmaceutical industry viewpoint', *Progress in Clinical and Biological Research*, 127 (1983), 197–98.

175. *Zebulon Record*, 9 March 1989, 'Glaxo markets first orphan drug'.

176. *Durham Morning Herald*, 25 November 1984.

177. Ruvane, *A New Kid*, 2.

178. Ibid., 5.

179. Ibid., 6.

180. Interview with Sir Austin Bide and David Smart, 17 July 1995.

181. Ruvane, *A New Kid*, 7.

182. Glaxo Inc. 1985, Report to Employees, 5.

183. Interview with Ronald J. McCord, 7 June 1994.

184. Glaxo Holdings Board Minutes, 28 July 1986.

185. Interview with Dr Ernest Mario, 8 June 1994.

186. Glaxo Holdings Board Minutes, 14 March 1988, it. 14(b).

187. Ibid., 30 June 1988, it. 70(b).

188. Interview with Tom D'Alonzo, 8 June 1994.

189. Wayne Koberstein, 'Tom D'Alonzo', *Pharmaceutical Executive*, 9 (October 1989).

190. Suzanne Harvey, 'Joe Ruvane helps Glaxo go American', *Pharmaceutical Executive*, July 1982.

191. Glaxo Holdings Board Minutes, 30 July 1984, it. 95.

192. Glaxo Holdings BP 84/75, P. Girolami, 'Glaxo Inc., USA, construction of a science building', 25 July 1984.

193. Interview with J. J. Ruvane, 8 June 1994.

194. Interview with Dr James Niedel, 9 June 1994.

195. Glaxo Holdings Board Minutes, 9 February 1987, it. 3(a).

196. Glaxo Holdings BP 87/27, 'New York Stock Exchange listing'.

197. Glaxo Holdings Board Minutes, 13 April 1987, it. 30.

198. *Glaxo Holdings plc Annual Report and Accounts 1994*, 13.

16 Europe, the Commonwealth and the Far East

1. Glaxo Group BP 61/108, H. W. Palmer, 'Europe', 26 September 1961, 1.

2. Ibid.

3. Ibid.

4. Glaxo Group Board Minutes, 4 June 1962, it. 83.

5. Glaxo Group Board Minutes, 29 July 1963, it. 158; Glaxo Group BP 63/120, H. W. Palmer, 'Evans S.A. (France)', 22 July 1963, 1.

6. Glaxo Group BP 64/92, H.W. Palmer, 'France', 8 July 1964, 1.

7. Glaxo Group Board Minutes, 9 October 1967, it. 130.

8. Glaxo Group BP 67/117, 'Laboratoires Glaxo S.A., France, factory project', 1.

9. Ibid., 2–3.

10. Dr G. B. Shirlaw, 'Foreign pharmaceutical firms in France' (typescript, 12 April 1968).

11. Ibid., 1.

12. *Glaxo Holdings Annual Report and Accounts* (1986), 9.

13. *Glaxo Holdings Annual Report and Accounts* (1987), 17.

14. Glaxo Group BP 63/92, H. W. Palmer and A. E. Bide, 'Germany', 5 June 1963, 1.

15. Glaxo Group BP 64/19, H. W. Palmer, 'Western Germany', 5 February 1964, 1.

16. Ibid., 2.

17. Glaxo Group Board Minutes, 8 December 1969, it. 235.

18. Glaxo Group BP 70/23, W. J. Hurran, 'Germany', 5 February 1970.

19. Glaxo Group BP 70/161, W. J. Hurran, 'Germany', 1.

20. Glaxo Group Board Minutes, 10 May 1971, it. 81; 11 October 1971, it. 143; BP 71/113, W. J. Hurran, 'Germany – Development Project'.

21. Glaxo Group BP 71/61, W. J. Hurran and P. Girolami, 'Germany – Development Project', 6 May 1971, 1.

22. Ibid., 3–4.

23. GMC 72/9, F. C. D. Back, 'Farbwerke Hoechst A.G', 13 November 1972; memorandum, Miss C. A. Marx to F. C. D. Back, 'Hoechst – Cephalosporins', 17 January 1973, 1.

24. Ibid.

25. GMC 74/24, 'Germany – Hoechst agreements'.

26. Group Management Committee, 1 July 1975, it. 1555 (a)(ii).

27. Letter from M. D. Allan to W. F. H. Robinson, 21 December 1977; GMC 77/148, F. C. D. Back 'Glaxo Pharmazeutika G.m.b.H., extension of factory', 8 December 1977.

28. GMC 79/33, F. C. D. Back, 'West Germany'.

29. Glaxo Market Economics Section, 'West Germany' (typescript, July 1982), 8.

30. Ibid., 22.

31. Glaxo Group, letter of intent, 15 October 1981, P. Girolami; Glaxo Holdings, P. Girolami, 'Notice to staff', 5 November 1981.

32. 'West Germany financial plant 1980/81–1986/87', 2.

33. Ibid., 3.

34. Glaxo Holdings BP 76/43, F. C. D. Back, 'Spanish factory project', 7 May 1976, 1–2.

35. Glaxo Group BP 70/12, W. J. Hurran, 'Spain', 2 February 1970.

36. Ibid., it. F(i).

37. Glaxo Holdings BP 76/43, 'Spanish factory project'.

38. *Glaxo Holdings Annual Report and Accounts* (1988), 18.

39. Interview with D. J. R. Farrant, 14 December 1993.

40. Glaxo Holdings BP 89/3, Mario Fertonani, 'Formation of Glaxo Europe Limited', 17 January 1989.

41. Glaxo Group BP 62/39, H. W. Palmer, 'Report on visit to overseas companies', 22 June 1962, 1.

42. Ibid., 2.

43. Interview with John Reece, 19 July 1994.

44. Interview with D. J. R. Farrant, 14 December 1993.

45. *Glaxo Laboratories (India) Ltd., Annual Report and Accounts* (1970), 16–17.

46. Ibid., 18.

47. *Glaxo Laboratories (India) Ltd., Annual Report and Accounts* (1971), 4.

48. Ibid., 20.

49. *Glaxo Laboratories (India) Ltd., Annual Report and Accounts* (1973), 2.

50. *Glaxo Laboratories (India) Ltd., Annual Report and Accounts* (1974), 4–5.

51. Ibid., 5.

52. *Glaxo Laboratories (India) Ltd., Annual Report and Accounts* (1976), 2.

53. *Glaxo Laboratories (India Ltd)., Annual Report and Accounts* (1979), Statement by chairman, 2.

54. *Glaxo Laboratories (India) Ltd., Annual Report and Accounts* (1983), 5.

55. Ibid., 4.

56. Ibid.

57. *Glindia Ltd. Annual Report and Accounts* (1987), 2.

58. *Glaxo Holdings Annual Report* (1994), 13.

59. Millen, *Glaxo, from Bonnie Babies*, 98.

60. Ibid., 97, 112.

61. Quoted in Davenport-Hines and Slinn, *Glaxo*, 309.

62. Ibid.

63. Millen, *Glaxo, from Bonnie Babies*, 130–31.

64. Davenport Hines and Slinn, *Glaxo*, 374, 376.

65. Ibid., 309.

66. Glaxo Group Board Minutes, it. 63/21, 1.

67. Ibid., 13 June 1975, 1.

68. Glaxo International Board Minutes, 26 January 1966.

69. Glaxo Group Board Minutes, 20 December 1968.

70. Glaxo-Allenburys Turnover Reports, 1961–1970.

71. Glaxo Australia Pty, Board Minutes, 30 May 1973; 28 July 1976, 2.

72. Ibid., 25 July 1977.

73. Ibid., 2 December 1975.

74. Interview with Bernard Taylor, 17 January 1994.

75. *Glaxo Holdings Annual Report and Accounts* (1991), 15.

76. Interview with Ken Windle, 6 April 1994.

77. Ballance, Pogany and Forstner, *World's Pharmaceutical Industries*, 30–31.

78. Ibid., 32.

79. Ibid., 52.

80. Ibid., 189.

81. Glaxo Holdings BP 86/86, 'Group Forecasts', 5.

82. *Synergy*, 6, 8–9.

83. 'History of Nippon Glaxo' (typescript, n.d.), 2.

84. *Glaxo Radiologicals*, April 1963, 'Dionosil'.

85. Glaxo International BP 68/6, M. J. Williams, 'Japan', 12 February 1968, 1.

86. Glaxo Allenburys (Export) BP 67/1, M. J. Williams, 'Japan', 16 January 1967, 1.

87. Glaxo-Allenburys (Export) BP 67/6, M. J. Williams, 'Japan', 11 May 1967, 1.

88. Glaxo Group BM 68/84, M. R. Camp, 'Japan', 5 June 1968, 1.

89. Glaxo International BP 68/6, M. J. Williams, 'Japan', 12 February 1968, 1.

90. Ibid., 3.

91. Glaxo Group BP 70/44, H. W. Palmer and P. Girolami, 'Japan site for expansion', 5 March 1970, 1; ibid., 72/10, W. J. Hurran, 'Japan', 6 January 1972, 2.

92. Glaxo Holdings Board Minutes, 9 April 1973, it. 46.

93. BP 72/10, Hurran, 'Japan', it. 12.

94. Glaxo Holdings BP 72/57, Paul Girolami, 'Japan, acquisition of interest in Shin Nihon and IDH', 9 November 1972.

95. GMC 73/8, F. C. D. Back and P. Girolami, 'Japan', 24 January 1973, 1.

96. Ibid., it. 4.

97. Ibid., it. 6.

98. Glaxo Holdings Board Minutes, 8 July 1974, it. 79.

99. Ibid., 6 May 1975, it. 44(2), 44(4); BP 75/41, P. Girolami, 'Shin Nihon Jitsugyo Co.', 5 May 1975.

100. Glaxo Holdings Board Minutes, 10 November 1975, it. 142.

101. Ibid., 13 October 1975, it. 125.

102. Ibid., 9 May 1977, it. 56.

103. Ibid., 9 July 1977, it. 76.

104. Interview with Dr T. Walker, 7 February 1994.

105. Glaxo Holdings Board Minutes, 9 February 1987, it. 3(b).

106. Glaxo Holdings Board Minutes, 30 July 1979.

107. Glaxo Group Board Minutes, 9 February 1970, it. 27.

108. Glaxo Group Board Minutes, 12 January 1970, it. 9.

109. Glaxo Group Board Minutes, 15 March 1971, it. 50.

110. GMC 79/155, D. J. R. Farrant, 'A new primary factory in Singapore', 3 January 1980,

Appendix A.

111. Ibid., 2; interview with Dr Alan Catterall, 10 February 1997.

112. Glaxo Holdings, BP 80/6, D. J. R. Farrant, 'A new primary factory', 10 January 1980, 1; Glaxo Holdings Board Minutes, 14 January 1980, it. 7.

113. *Glaxochem Singapore* (*c.* 1983), 2.

114. Ibid., Appendix A, it. 3.

115. Interview with Dr Mike Hope, 15 October 1996.

116. Letter, H. Jephcott to Messrs ICI (China), 4 April 1934.

117. Hilary Williams, *Arthur Scrimgeour, the Beginnings of Glaxo in China*, Hong Kong (1990), 11.

118. Ibid., 2.

119. H. Jephcott, 'China' (typescript, 30 April 1934), 15.

120. Williams, *Scrimgeour*, 12.

121. Ibid., 21.

122. Ibid., 93, 96.

123. GMC 85/72, A. H. Raper, 'China strategy', 26 April 1985, 1.

124. Interview with Neil Maidment, 14 March 1994.

125. GMC 82/81, A. H. Raper, 'China', 1 June 1982, 1.

126. Ibid.

127. Ibid., 2.

128. Glaxo Holdings Board Minutes, 13 June 1988, it. 56(b).

129. GMC 88/50, 'Strategy in China', 2–3.

130. Interview with Neil Maidment, 14 March 1994.

Conclusions: continuity and change

1. Quoted in the *Independent on Sunday*, 29 January 1995, William Kay, 'A bid to finish independence', 3.

2. Interview with Sir Austin Bide, 21 July 1995.

3. Quoted in *Glaxo Holdings Annual Report and Accounts* (1994), 2.

4. *Glaxo Wellcome Annual Review* (1996), 4.

5. *Glaxo Wellcome Annual Report and Accounts* (1996), 25.

6. Ibid., 42.

7. *Glaxo Wellcome Annual Report and Accounts* (1999), 37.

8. *Emerge*, 1 March 2000, 8–9.

9. Balance, Pogány and Forstner, *World's Pharmaceutical Industries*, 110.

10. *Daily Mail*, 28 July 2000, 'Glaxo chief says pressure is on for more megadeals'.

11. Steve Jones, *The Language of the Genes, Biology, History and the Evolutionary Future*, London: HarperCollins (1993), 218–19.

SOURCES

§

Manuscript sources

The notes to individual chapters should be consulted for details of the original sources employed. GlaxoSmithKline have records centres in the UK and US and these were the principal repositories for this investigation. Those who wish to study any of these sources should apply to the Archivist, Records Centre, GlaxoSmithKline, Greenford, Middlesex UB6 0NN. The following record offices, libraries and institutions were also of particular value: British Library, Business Archives Council, Business History Unit, London School of Economics, Office of Health Economics, the Public Record Office at Kew, and Guy's, King's and St Thomas' Medical School.

Journals

A number of journals were consulted for this study, including:
American Journal of Hospital Pharmacy
American Journal of Medicine
British Journal of Clinical Pharmacology
British Medical Journal
Clinical Pharmacology and Therapeutics
Journal of Clinical Pharmacology
Journal of Pharmaceutical Pharmacology
The Lancet
Nature
New England Journal of Medicine
Postgraduate Medical Journal

Personal recollections

The following is a list of retired directors and staff of Glaxo who generously agreed to be interviewed or who commented on the text:

Michael Allan
John Barr
Sir Austin Bide
Dr Joe Blaker
Dr Roy Brittain
John Burke
James Butler
Ray Camp
George Childs
Sandy Costa
Lord Cuckney
Tom D'Alonzo
Lord Dahrendorf
Ted Farmer
John Farrant
Dr Mario Fertonani
Lord Fraser of Kilmorack
Sir Paul Girolami
Albert Hall
Dr Chris Hamlet
Dr David Hartley
Monica Hayes
Lord Howe
Dr Franz Humer
Professor Patrick Humphrey
Dr John Hunt

Sir David Jack
Sir Arthur Knight
Neil Maidment
Dr Ernie Mario
Ronald McCord
Dr Hugh McCorquodale
Dr Ian McEwan
Donald McInnes
Charles Newcomb
Terry Norman
John Raisman
Dr Alan Raper
John Reece
Sir Mark Richmond
Hazel Rummer
Joseph Ruvane
E.K. Samways
Dr Charles Sanders
David Smart
Sir Richard Southwood
Bernard Taylor
Clifford Turner
Dr Tom Walker
Mrs F.J. Wilkins
Dr Peter Wilkinson
Dr Peter Wise

SELECT BIBLIOGRAPHY

Abraham, E. P. (1967), 'Cephaloridine: historical remarks'. *Postgraduate Medical Journal* 43 (Supplement): 9–10.

— (1979), 'A glimpse of the early history of the cephalosporins'. *Reviews of Infectious Diseases* 1, 99–105.

Alberto, L., Rodriguez, G., and Jick, H. (1994), 'Risk of gynaecomastia associated with cimetidine, omeprazole, and other antiulcer drugs'. *British Medical Journal* 308, 503–506.

Anon. (1967), 'Trials and Tribulations'. *The Lancet* 1, 152–154.

Anon. (1980), *Medicines: 50 Years of Progress 1930–1980*, London: Office of Health Economics.

Anon. (1993), 'Market for antimicrobials expected to double by 1997'. *American Journal of Hospital Pharmacy* 50, 32.

Asbury, C. H. (1981), 'Medical drugs of limited commercial interest: profit alone is a bitter pill'. *International Journal of Health Services* 11, 451–62.

Bakke, O. M., Wardell, W. M., and Lasagna, L. (1984), 'Drug discontinuations in the United Kingdom and the United States, 1964 to 1983: issues of safety'. *Clinical Pharmacology and Therapeutics* 35, 559–67.

Ball, D. I., Brittain, R. T., Coleman, R. A., Denyer, L. H., Jack, D., Johnson, M., Lunts, L. H. C., Nials, A. T., Sheldrick, K. E., and Skidmore, I. F. (1991), 'Salmeterol, a novel, long-acting β_2-adrenoceptor agonist: characterisation of pharmacological activity in vitro and in vivo'. *British Journal of Pharmacology* 104, 665–71.

Ballance, R., Pogany, J., and Forstner, H. (1992), *The World's Pharmaceutical Industries, An International Perspective on Innovation, Competition and Policy*, Aldershot: Edward Elgar.

Beadle, W. H. (1926), *Romance of Great Businesses*, London: Heath Cranton.

Bearn, A. G. (1981), 'The pharmaceutical industry and academe: partners in progress'. *American Journal of Medicine* 71, 81–8.

Binns, T. B. and Butterfield, W. J. H. (1964), 'Clinical trials, some constructive suggestions'. *The Lancet* 1 (7343), 1150–52.

Black, J. W., Duncan, W. A. M., Durant, C. J., Ganellin, C. R., and Parsons, E. M. (1972), 'Definition and antagonism of histamine H_2-receptors'. *Nature* 236, 385–90.

Black, S. J. (1986), 'Basic drug research in universities and industry'. *British Journal of Clinical Pharmacology* 22, 5S–7S.

Blackden, S. (1994), *A Tradition of Excellence, A Brief History of Medicine in Edinburgh*, London: Duncan Flockhart & Co.

Bloom, B. S., Wierz, D. J., and Pauly, M. V. (1986), 'Cost and price of comparable branded and generic pharmaceuticals'. *Journal of the American Medical Association* 256, 2523–30.

Boden, I. M. (1980), 'Fifty years of pharmaceutical development'. *Practitioner* 224, 513–15.

Bradley, P. B., Engel, G., Feniuk, W., Fozard, J. R., Humphrey, P. P. A., Middlemiss, D. N., Mylecharane, E. J., Richardson, B. P., and Saxena, P. R. (1986), 'Proposals for the classification and nomenclature of the functional receptors for 5-Hydroxytryptamine'. *Neuropharmacology* 25, 563–76.

Bradshaw, J., Brittain, R. T., Clitherow, J. W., Daly, M. J., Jack, D., Price, B. J., and Stables, R. (1979), 'Ranitidine (AH 19065): a new potent, selective histamine H_2-receptor antagonist'. *British Journal of*

Pharmacology 66, 464P

Brahams, D. (1991), 'Drug-company data and the public interest'. *The Lancet* 338, 502–3.

Breckon, W. (1972), *The Drug Makers*, London: Eyre Methuen.

Brittain, R. T. (1971), 'A comparison of the pharmacology of salbutamol with that of isoprenaline, orciprenaline and trimetoquinol'. *Postgraduate Medical Journal* 47 (Supplement), 11–16.

— (1972), 'Selective beta-adrenergic receptor active drugs [Abridged]'. *Proceedings of the Royal Society of Medicine* 65, 759–61.

Brittain, R. T., Drew, G. M., and Levy, G. P. (1982), 'The x and b-adrenoceptor blocking potencies of labetalol and its individual stereoisomers in anaethetized dogs and in isolated tissues'. *British Journal of Pharmacology* 77, 105–14.

Brittain, R. T., Farmer, J. B., Jack, D., Martin, L. E., and Simpson, W. T. (1968), 'x-[(t-Butylamino)methyl]-4-hydroxy-m-xylene-x1,x3-diol (AH. 3365): a selective β-adrenergic stimulant'. *Nature* 219, 862–3.

Brittain, R. T., Harris, D. M., Martin, L. E., Poynter, D., and Price, B. J. (1981), 'Safety of Ranitidine'. *The Lancet* 2, 1119.

Brittain, R. T. and Jack, D. (1983), 'Histamine H$_2$-antagonists – past, present and future'. *Journal of Clinical Gastroenterology* 5 (Supplement 1), 71–9.

Brogden, R. N., Carmine, A. A., Heel, R. C., Speight, T. M., and Avery, G. S. (1982), 'Ranitidine: a review of its pharmacology and therapeutic use in peptic ulcer disease and other allied diseases'. *Drugs* 24, 267–303.

Buick, T. L. (1903), *Old Manawatu*, Palmerston North: Buick & Young.

Burke, J. (1989), *The Management of Luck, An Original Guide to Business Success*, London: Macdonald & Co.

Busse, M. J., Hunt, P., Lees, K. A., Maggs, P. N. D., and McCarthy, T. M. (1969), 'Release of betamethasone derivatives from ointments – in vivo and in vitro studies'. *British Journal of Dermatology* 81 (Supplement 4), 103–12.

Buxton, M. J. and O'Brien, B. J. (1992), 'Economic evaluation of ondansetron: preliminary analysis using clinical trial data prior to price setting'. *British Journal of Cancer* 66 Supplement XIX, S64-S67.

Bynum, W. F. and Porter, Roy (1993), *Companion Encyclopaedia of the History of Medicine*, London: Routledge.

Carson, I. W. (1972), 'Group trial of althesin as an intravenous anaesthetic'. *Postgraduate Medical Journal* 48 (June Supplement), 108–11.

Centre for the Study of Industrial Innovation. (1971), *Reaching World Markets, A Report on International Marketing in the Pharmaceuticals Industry*, London: National Economic Development Office.

Chandler, A. D. (1977), *The Visible Hand, The Managerial Revolution in American Business*, Cambridge, Massachusetts: Harvard University Press.

Chapman, S. (1973), *Jesse Boot of Boots the Chemists, A Study in Business History*, London: Hodder and Stoughton.

Chapman-Huston, D. and Cripps, E. C. (1954), *Through a City Archway, The Story of Allen and Hanburys 1715–1954*, London: John Murray.

Clarke, R. J. S., Dundee, J. W., and Carson, I. W. (1973), 'A new steroid anaesthetic – althesin'. *Proceedings of the Royal Society of Medicine* 66, 1027–30.

Coe, F. A. (1980), *Burroughs Wellcome & Co., 1880–1980*, New York: Newcomen Society.

Comanor, W. S. (1965), 'Research and technical change in the pharmaceutical industry'. *Review of Economics and Statistics* 47, 182–90.

Comanor, W. S. (1986), 'The political economy of the pharmaceutical industry'. *Journal of Economic Literature* 24, 1178–1217.

Cooper, M. H. (1966), *Prices and Profits in the Pharmaceutical Industry*, Oxford: Pergamon.

Cooper, M. H. and Cooper, A. J. (1972), *International Price Comparison, A Study of the Prices of Pharmaceuticals in the UK and eight other countries in 1970*, London: National Economic Development Office.

Cooter, R., Harrison, M. and Sturdy S. [Editors] (1998), *War, Medicine and Modernity*, Thrupp, Stroud: Sutton Publishing.

Corley, T. A. B. (1994), 'The Beecham Group in the World's Pharmaceutical Industry 1914–70'. *Zeitschrift für Unternehmensgeschichte* 39, 18–30.

Cripps, E. C. (1927), *Plough Court, The Story of a Notable Pharmacy 1715–1927*, London: Allen & Hanburys.

Cromie, B. W. (1986), 'Drug research and development in the pharmaceutical industry'. *British Journal of Clinical Pharmacology* 22, 9S-14S.

Cuatrecasas, P. (1992), 'Industry – university alliances in biomedical research'. *Journal of Clinical Pharmacology* 32, 100–106.

Cullum, V. A., Farmer, J. B., Jack, D., and Levy, G. P. (1969), 'Salbutamol: a new, selective β-adrenoceptive receptor stimulant'. *British Journal of Pharmacology* 35, 141–51.

Currie, W. J. C. (1993), 'Drug development and registration in Japan: threshold of transition'. *Journal of Clinical Pharmacology* 33, 100–108.

Cuthbertson, W. F. J. and Page, J. E. (1994), 'Ernest Lester Smith, 7 August 1904–6 November 1992'. *Biographical Memoirs of Fellows of the Royal Society* 40, 349–65.

Davenport-Hines, R. P. T. (1985), 'Sir Harry Jephcott'. *Dictionary of Business Biography* 3, 491–7.

— (1986), *Markets and Bagmen, Studies in the History of Marketing and British Industrial Performance 1830–1939*, Aldershot: Gower.

— (1986), 'Glaxo as a Multinational before 1963', in Jones, G.G. [Ed.], *British Multinationals*, Aldershot: Gower, 137–63.

Davenport-Hines, R. P. T. and Slinn, J. (1992), *Glaxo: A History to 1962*, Cambridge: Cambridge University Press.

Davidow, W. H. (1986), *Marketing High Technology, An Insider's View*, New York: The Free Press.

Davies, J. (2000), 'It's all good practice – scientific archives and information management'. *Business Archives Principles and Practice* 79: 23–8.

DeVeaugh-Geiss, J. (1991), 'Academic medical center/industry collaboration'. *Archives of General Psychiatry* 48, 754–56.

Dixon, B. (1993), *Genetics and the Understanding of Life*, Seventeenth International Congress of Genetics, Reading: National Centre for Biotechnology Education.

Dunlop, Sir Derrick (1970), 'Legislation on Medicines'. *British Medical Journal* 3 (5725), 760–62.

Dziewanowska, Z. E. (1990), 'Globalisation of the pharmaceutical industry: opportunities for physicians in clinical rescarch'. *Journal of Clinical Pharmacology* 30, 890–92.

Editorial (1964), 'Cephaloridine'. *British Medical Journal* 2 (5419), 1211–12.

Editorial (1967), 'Sainsbury Report'. *British Medical Journal* 4 (5570), 1–2.

Editorial (1967), 'After Sainsbury'. *The Lancet* 2 (7519), 759–60.

Editorial (1967), 'New Laws on Control of Drugs?' *The Lancet* 2 (7516), 601–602.

Editorial (1968), 'Brand Names'. *British Medical Journal* 1 (5595), 781–2.

Editorial (1982), 'Cimetidine and Ranitidine'. *The Lancet* 1 (8272), 601–602.

Editorial (1983), 'Ranitidine or Cimeditine'. *Annals of Internal Medicine* 99, 551–3.

Editorial (1992), 'Sumatriptan, serotonin, migraine and money'. *The Lancet* 339, 151–2.

Ehmann, C. W. (1988), 'Dermatological Drug Development'. *Archives of Dermatology* 124, 950–51.

Fantes, K. H., Page, J. E., Parker, L. F. J., and Lester Smith, E. (1949), 'Crystalline anti-pernicious anaemia factor from liver'. *Proceedings of the Royal Society* B (136), 595–613.

Feniuk, W., Humphrey, P. P. A., Perren, M. J., Connor, H. E., and Whalley, E. T. (1991), 'Rationale for the use of 5-HT$_1$ – like agonists in the treatment of migraine'. *Journal of Neurology* 238, S57–S61.

Finsinger, J. E. (1983), *Economic Analysis of Regulated Markets*, London: Macmillan.

Flind, A. C. and Rowley-Jones, D. (1982), 'Cimetidine and Ranitidine'. *The Lancet* 1, 749.

Foreman-Peck, J. (1995), *Smith & Nephew in the Health Care Industry*, Cheltenham: Edward Elgar.

Galambos, L., Brown, M. S., and Goldstein, J. L. (1991), *Values & Visions, A Merck Century*, Rahway: Merck & Co., Inc.

Galambos, L. and Sewell, J. E. (1995), *Network in Innovations: vaccine development at Merck, Sharpe & Dohme, and Mulford, 1895–1995*, Cambridge: Cambridge University Press.

Garside, J. (1995), *A History of Glaxo in Port Fairy*, Boronia, Victoria: Glaxo Wellcome Australia.

Girolami, Sir Paul (1990), *The Development of Glaxo*, London: Glaxo Holdings plc.

Goldberger, F. (1991), *Pharmaceutical Manufacturing, Quality Management in the Industry*, Evreux: Ebur.

Goldman, L. M. (1958), *The History of the Jews in New Zealand*, Wellington: A. H. & A. W. Reid.

Goldstein, G. S. (1983), 'Orphan drugs – a pharmaceutical industry viewpoint'. *Progress in Clinical and Biological Research* 127, 197–205.

Gough, K. R., Bardhan, K. D., Crowe, J. P., Korman, M. G., Lee, F. I., Reed, P. I., and Smith, R. N. (1984), 'Rantidine and cimetidine in prevention of duodenal ulcer relapse'. *The Lancet* 2, 659–62.

Gouveia, W. A. (1984), 'Hospital pharmacy and industry – conflict and collaboration'. *American Journal of Hospital Pharmacy* 41, 1391–4.

Green, F. H. K. and Covell, S. G. (1953), *Medical History of the Second World War, Medical Research*, London: HMSO.

Griffin, J. P. and Diggle, G. E. (1981), 'A survey of products licensed in the United Kingdom from 1971–1981'. *British Journal of Clinical Pharmacology* 12, 453–63.

Grubb, P. W. (1987), 'Patents in medicinal chemistry'. *Annual Reports in Medicinal Chemistry* 22, 331–52.

Grundy, H. F. (1985), *Lecture Notes in Pharmacology*, Oxford: Blackwell Scientific Publications.

Guillebaud, C. W. (1956), *Report of the Committee of Enquiry into the Cost of the National Health Service*, London: HMSO.

Gumbhir, A. K. and Rodowskas, C. A. (1974), 'Consumer price differentials between generic and brand name prescriptions'. *American Journal of Public Health* 64, 977–82.

Hall, A. R. and Bembridge, B. A. (1986), *Physic and Philanthropy, A History of the Wellcome Trust 1936–1986*, Cambridge, Cambridge University Press.

Harding, S. M. (1990), 'The human pharmacology of fluticasone propionate'. *Respiratory Medicine* 84 (Supplement A), 25–9.

Hartley, D., Jack, D., Lunts, L. H. C., and Ritchie, A. C. (1968), 'New class of selective stimulants of β-adrenergic receptors'. *Nature* 219, 861–2.

Hartley, K., Lavers, R. J., and Maynard, A. K. (1986), 'Regulation and development times in the UK pharmaceutical industry'. *Scottish Journal of Political Economy* 33 (4), 355–70.

Hems, B. A. (1950), 'The chemistry of thyroxine'. *Chemistry and Industry*, 663–6.

— (1953), 'Chemistry of cortisone'. *Journal of Pharmaceutical Pharmacology* 5, 409–39.

— (1959), 'Cortisone from hecogenin'. *Chemistry and Industry*, 442–8.

Herzog, H. and Oliveto, E. P. (1992), 'A history of significant steroid discoveries and developments originating at the Schering Corporation (USA) since 1948'. *Steroids* 57, 617–23.

Hinchliffe, Sir Henry. (1959), *Final Report of the Committee on Cost of Prescribing*, London: HMSO.

Hirschmann, R. (1992), 'The cortisone era: aspects of its impact. Some contributions of the Merck Laboratories'. *Steroids* 57, 579–92.

Hogg, J. A. (1992), 'Steroids, the steroid community, and Upjohn in perspective: a profile of innovation'. *Steroids* 57, 593–616.

Holmstedt, B. and Liljestrand, G. (1963), *Readings in Pharmacology*, Oxford: Pergamon Press.

Howells, J. and Neary, I. (1996), *Intervention and Technological Innovation, Government and the Pharmaceutical Industry in the UK and Japan*, London: Macmillan.

Humphrey, P. P. A. (1984), 'Peripheral 5-hydroxytryptamine receptors and their classification'. *Neuropharmacology* 23, 1503–10.

Humphrey, P. P. A. and Feniuk, W. (1991), 'Mode of action of the anti-migraine drug sumatriptan'. *Trends in Pharmacological Sciences* 12, 444–6.

Humphrey, P. P. A., Hartig, P., and Hoyer, D. (1993), 'A proposed new nomenclature for 5-HT receptors'. *Trends in Pharmacological Sciences* 14, 233–6.

Hunt, John A. (1991), 'Pioneering penicillin production in Britain'. *The Pharmaceutical Journal* 247 (6667), 807–10.

Inglis, B. (1965) *Drugs, Doctors and Disease*, London: Andre Deutsch.

Jack, D. (1971), 'Sniffing Syndrome'. *British Medical Journal* 2 (763), 708–9.

— (1977), 'Developpement et pharmacologie du dipropionate de beclomethasone'. *La Nouvelle Presse médicale* 6 (15), 1273–76.

— (1988), 'Pharmacological control of gastric acid secretion'. *South African Medical Journal* 74, Supplement, 8–10.

— (1989), 'The challenge of drug discovery'. *Drug Design and Delivery* 4, 167–86.

— (1991), 'A way of looking at agonism and antagonism: lessons from salbutamol, salmeterol and other β-adrenoceptor agonists'. *British Journal of Clinical Pharmacology* 31, 501–14.

— (1992), 'Research and development in the pharmaceutical industry'. *Science in Parliament* 49, 4–10.

Jack, D., Poynter, D., and Smith, R. N. (1985), 'Antisecretory drugs and gastric cancer'. *British Medical Journal* 291, 675

Jack, D. and Richards, D. A. (1982), 'Cimetidine and ranitidine'. *The Lancet* 1, 914.

Jack, D., Richards, D. A., and Granata, F. (1982), 'Side-effects of ranitidine'. *The Lancet* 2, 264–5.

Jack, D., Smith, R. N., and Wise, P. J. (1984), 'Ranitidine and cimetidine'. *Annals of Internal Medicine* 100, 768–9.

Jack, D., Thomas, M., and Skidmore, I. F. (1985), 'Ranitidine and paracetamol metabolism'. *The Lancet* 2, 1067.

Jack, D. and Walker, T. (1997), 'Benjamin Arthur Hems, 29 June 1912 – 2 July 1995'. *Biographical Memoirs of Fellows of the Royal Society* 43, 215–33.

James, R. R. (1994), *Henry Wellcome*, London: Hodder and Stoughton.

Jephcott, Sir Harry (1965), 'The Glaxo Research Organisation'. In Cockroft, S. J. (ed.), *The Organization of Research Establishments*. Cambridge: Cambridge University Press, 148–67.

—— (1952), 'How much Research?' *Research, Science and its Application in Industry* 5, 1–4.

—— (1969), *The First Fifty Years, An Account of the early life of Joseph Edward Nathan and the first fifty years of his merchandise business that eventually became the Glaxo Group*, Ipswich: Privately Printed.

Jones, G. E. (1986), *British Multinationals: Origins, Management and Performance*, Aldershot: Gower.

Jones, R. H. (1994), 'The approach to pricing of innovative research-based medicines'. *Pharmaceutical Medicine* 8, 29–8.

Kaitin, K. I., Bryant, N. R., and Lasagna, L. (1993), 'The role of the research-based pharmaceutical industry in medical progress in the United States'. *Journal of Clinical Pharmacology* 33, 412–17.

Kaitin, K. I., DiCerbo, P. A., and Lasagna, L. (1991), 'The new drug approvals of 1987, 1988 and 1989: trends in drug development'. *Journal of Clinical Pharmacology* 31, 116–22.

Kefauver, E. (1961), 'Administered Prices: Drugs'. *Report of the Committee on the Judiciary, United States Senate made by its Sub Committee on Antitrust and Monopoly pursuant to S.Res 52 Eighty seventh Congress, First Session*, Washington.

Kemp, B. A. and Moyer, P. R. (1974), 'Equivalent therapy at lower cost'. *Journal of the American Medical Association* 228, 1009–14.

Kilgour, A. (1982), 'What ever happened to Glaxo's Shares?' *The Lancet* 2, 868–9.

Lall, S. (1978), 'Price competition and the international pharmaceutical industry'. *Oxford Bulletin of Economics and Statistics* 40 (1), 9–23.

Laurence, D. R. (1963), *Clinical Pharmacology*, London: J. & A. Churchill.

Lazell, H. G. (1975), 'From pills to penicillin: the Beecham story'. In *Anonymous London*, Heinemann.

Lexchin, J. (1989), 'Doctors and detailers: therapeutic education or pharmaceutical promotion?' *International Journal of Health Services* 19, 663–79.

Liebenau, J. (1986), 'Marketing high technology: educating physicians to use innovative medicines'. In Davenport-Hines, R. T. P. (ed.), *Markets and Bagmen*, Aldershot: Gower, 82–101.

—— (1988), *The Challenge of New Technology, Innovation in British Business since 1850*, Aldershot: Gower.

—— (1990), 'The rise of the British pharmaceutical industry'. *British Medical Journal* 301, 724–33.

Liss, R. H. and Batchelor, F. R. (1987), 'Economic evaluations of antibiotic use and resistance – a perspective: report of Task Force 6.' *Reviews of Infectious Diseases* 9 (Supplement 3), S297–S312

Lynn, M. (1991), *The Billion Dollar Battle: Merck v Glaxo*, London: William Heinemann.

Macdonald, G. (1980), *One Hundred Years, Wellcome 1880–1980, In Pursuit of Excellence*, London: Wellcome Foundation.

Macrae, T. F. and Hems, B. A. (1950), 'Modern developments in the synthesis and use of thyroxine'. *British Science News* 3, 128–30.

Mandell, G. L., Douglas, R. G., and Bennett, J. E. E. (1990), *Principles and Practice of Infectious Diseases*, New York: Churchill-Livingstone.

McKenzie, A. W. (1962), 'Percutaneous absorption of steroids'. *Archives of Dermatology* 86, 611–14.

McKenzie, A. W. and Atkinson, R. M. (1964), 'Topical activities of betamethasone esters in man'. *Archives of Dermatology* 89, 741–6.

McKenzie, A. W. and Stoughton, R. B. (1962), 'Method for comparing percutaneous absorption of steroids'. *Archives of Dermatology* 86, 608–10.

Millen, J. (1991), *Glaxo, From Bonnie Babies to Better Medicines, The People who made Glaxo*, Palmerston North: Glaxo New Zealand.

Milligan, R. C. E. (1986), 'Henry Wellcome'. Jeremy, D. J., (ed.) in *Dictionary of Business Biography, Volume 5*, London: Butterworths.

Monopolies Commission (1972), *Beecham Group Limited and Glaxo Group Limited ... A Report on the Proposed Mergers*, London: HMSO.

Morgan, M. and Whitwam, J. G. (1985), 'Editorial Althesin'. *Anaesthesia* 40, 121–3.

Muggleton, P. W., O'Callaghan, C. H., and Stevens, W. K. (1964), 'Laboratory evaluation of a new antibiotic – cephaloridine (Ceporin)'. *British Medical Journal* 2 (5419), 1234–7.

— (1967), 'The antibacterial activities of cephaloridine: laboratory investigation'. *Postgraduate Medical Journal* 43 (Supplement), 17–22.

Newton, G. G. F. and Hamilton-Miller, J. M. T. (1967), 'Cephaloridine: chemical and biochemical aspects'. *Postgraduate Medical Journal* 43 (Supplement), 10–17.

Nold, E. G. (1991), 'Hospital pharmacy in 1990: the year in review'. *American Journal of Hospital Pharmacy* 48, 720–30.

— (1992) 'Hospital pharmacy in 1991: the year in review'. *American Journal of Hospital Pharmacy* 49, 1143–51.

O'Callaghan, C. H., Sykes, R. B., Griffiths, A., and Thornton, J. E. (1976), 'Cefuroxime, a new cephalosporin antibiotic: activity in vitro'. *Antimicrobial Agents and Chemotherapy* 9, 511–19.

O'Callaghan, C. H., Sykes, R. B., and Staniforth, S. E. (1976), 'A new cephalosporin with a dual mode of action'. *Antimicrobial Agents and Chemotherapy* 10, 245–8.

Owen, Geoffrey (1999), *From Empire to Europe: the decline and revival of British industry since the Second World War,* London: HarperCollins.

Palumbo, F. B., Schondelmeyer, W., Miller, D. W., and Speedie, S. M. (1992), 'Battered bottom lines: the impact of eroding pharmaceutical discounts on health-care institutions'. *American Journal of Hospital Pharmacy* 49, 1177–85.

Peyer, H. C. (1996), *Roche, A Company History 1896–1996,* Basle: F. Hoffmann-La Roche.

Phillipps, G. H. (1990), 'Structure-activity relationships of topically active steroids: the selection of fluticasone propionate'. *Respiratory Medicine* 84 (Supplement A), 19–23.

Prentis, R. A. and Walker, S. R. (1984), 'Innovation and development of new chemical entities by the UK owned pharmaceutical companies (1964–1980)'. *British Journal of Clinical Pharmacology* 18, 303P–304P.

Prentis, R. A. and Walker, S. R. (1986), 'Trends in the development of new medicines by UK-owned pharmaceutical companies (1964–1980)'. *British Journal of Clinical Pharmacology* 21, 437–43.

Rawlins, M. D. (1990), 'Development of a rational practice of therapeutics'. *British Medical Journal* 301 (6754), 729–33.

Rawlins, M. D. and Jefferys, D. B. (1991), 'Study of United Kingdom product licence applications containing new active substances, 1987–9'. *British Medical Journal* 302, 223–5.

Read, J. L., Rubin, P. C., and Whiting, B. (1985), *Lecture Notes on Clinical Pharmacology,* Oxford: Blackwell Scientific Publications.

Reekie, W. D. (1975), *The Economics of the Pharmaceutical Industry,* London: Macmillan.

— (1983), 'Price comparisons of identical products in Japan, the United States and Europe'. *Economic Analysis of Regulated Markets* 168–81.

Reekie, W. D. and Weber, M. H. (1979), *Profits, Politics and Drugs,* London: Macmillan.

Reid, J. L., Rubin, P. C., and Whiting, B. (1985), *Lecture Notes on Clinical Pharmacology,* Oxford: Blackwell Scientific Publications.

Richards, D. A. (1983), 'Comparative pharmacodynamics and pharmacokinetics of cimetidine and ranitidine'. *Journal of Clinical Gastroenterology* 5 (Supplement 1), 81–90.

Riley, A. J. and Salmon, P. R. E. (1982), *Ranitidine, Proceedings of an International Symposium held in the context of the Seventh World Congress of Gastroenterology,* Amsterdam: Excerpta Medica.

Robson, M. (1988), 'The British pharmaceutical industry and the First World War'. Liebenau, J. (ed.), in *Challenge of New Technology,* Aldershot: Gower, 83–105.

Russo, J. B. (1978), 'Profitable and nonprofitable drugs'. *New England Journal of Medicine* 299, 156.

Sainsbury, Lord (1967), *Report of the Committee of Enquiry into the Relationship of the Pharmaceutical Industry with the National Health Service 1965–1967,* London: HMSO.

Saxena, P. R., Wallis, D. I., Wouters, W., and Bevan, P. E. (1990), *Cardiovascular Pharmacology of 5-Hydroxytryptamine,* Dordrecht: Kulwer Academic Publishers.

Schellhaass, H.-M. and Stumpf, U. (1983), 'Price regulation in the European pharmaceutical industry: benefits and costs'. In Fisinger, J., *Economic Analysis of Regulated Markets,* London: Macmillan, 151–67.

Schwartzman, D. (1976), *Innovation in the Pharmaceutical Industry,* Baltimore: Johns Hopkins Press.

Scott, A. E. (1990), *Frontiers of Science,* Oxford: Basil Blackwell.

Silvis, S. E. (1984), 'Results of the United States ranitidine maintenance trials'. *The American Journal of*

Medicine 77 (suppl 5B), 33–8.

Simpson, P. J., Radford, S. G., Lockyer, J. A., and Sear, J. W. (1985), 'Some predisposing factors to hypersensitivity reactions following first exposure to althesin'. *Anaesthesia* 40, 420–23.

Singer, C. and Underwood, E. A. (1962), *A Short History of Medicine*, Oxford: Clarendon Press.

Skinner, J. S. (1997), *Form and Fancy, Factories and Factory Buildings by Wallis Gilbert & Partners 1916–1939*, Liverpool: Liverpool University Press.

Slatter, S. (1977), *Competition and Marketing Strategies in the Pharmaceutical Industry*, London: Croom Helm.

Slinn, J. (1984), *A History of May & Baker 1834–1984*, Cambridge: Hobsons.

Slinn, J. (1999), *Pharmaceutical and Health Care: A History of Abbott Laboratories in the UK*, Cambridge: Granta Editions.

Smith, K. G. D. (1972), 'Profitability, risk and investment in research and development – the UK pharmaceutical industry'. *Pharmaceutical Industry and Society*, 59–87.

Smith, R. (1986), 'Doctors and the drug industry: too close for comfort'. *British Medical Journal* 293, 905–6.

Sneader, W. (1985), *Drug Discovery: The Evolution of Modern Medicines*, Chichester: John Wiley & Sons.

Snell, E. S. (1986), 'Profitability and improved patient care – industry's viewpoint'. *British Journal of Clinical Pharmacology* 22 (Supplement), 33S–39S.

Snell, L. A., Cowen, P. J., and Robson, P. J. (1995), 'Ondansetron and opiate craving, a novel pharmacological approach to addiction'. *British Journal of Psychiatry* 166, 511–14.

Somberg, J. C. (1992), 'Pharmaceutical costs'. *Journal of Clinical Pharmacology* 32, 1059

Somberg, J. C. (1993), 'Industry under siege'. *Journal of Clinical Pharmacology* 33, 295

Steele, H. (1962), 'Monopoly and competition in the ethical drugs market'. *Journal of Law and Economics* V, 131–65.

Steele, H. (1964), 'Patent restrictions and price competition in the ethical drugs industry'. *Journal of Industrial Economics* 12 (3), 198–224.

Steward, F. and Wibberley, G. (1980), 'Drug innovation – what's slowing it down?' *Nature* 284, 118–20.

Stockwell, C. (1988), *Nature's Pharmacy, A History of Plants and Healing*, London: Arrow Books.

Sutton, J. A. (1972), 'A brief history of steroid anaesthesia before althesin (CT1341)'. *Postgraduate Medical Journal* 48 (June Supplement), 9–13.

Swann, J. (1977), *Academic Scientists and the Pharmaceutical Industry*, Baltimore: John Hopkins University.

Swerdlow, M. (1972), 'Studies with althesin – a new steroid anaesthetic'. *Postgraduate Medical Journal* 48 (June Supplement), 105–8.

Sykes, R. B., Cimarusti, C. M., Bonner, D. P., Bush, K. et al (1981), 'Monocyclic β-lactum antibiotics produced by bacteria'. *Nature* 291, 489–91.

Sykes, R. B. and Richmond, M. H. (1970), 'Intergeneric transfer of a β-lactamase gene between *Ps. aeruginosa* and *E. coli*'. *Nature* 226, 952–4.

Taggart, J. (1993), *The World Pharmaceutical Industry*, London: Routledge.

Tansey, E. M. and Milligan, R. C. E. (1990), 'The early history of the Wellcome Research Laboratories 1894–1914'. In Liebenau, J. Higby, J. G. and Stroud, E. C. (ed.), *Pill Peddlers: Essays on the History of the Pharmaceutical Industry*, Wisconsin: American Institute of the History of Pharmacy, 91–106.

Teeling-Smith, G. E. (1972), *The Pharmaceutical Industry and Society, A Study of the Changing Environment and Economics of the International Industry*, London: Office of Health Economics.

— (1984), 'Drug profits'. *The Lancet* 1 (8386), 1126

— (1986), 'The economics of drug development and use'. *British Journal of Clinical Pharmacology* 22, 45S–48S.

— (1992), *Innovative Competition in Medicine, A Schumpetarian analysis of the pharmaceutical industry and the NHS*, London: Office of Health Economics.

Temin, P. (1980), *Taking your Medicine, Drug Regulation in the United States*, Cambridge, Massachusetts.

Tillman, L. (1993), 'Landmarks in the History of Zantac'.

Towse, A. (1993), '*Not What the Doctor Ordered*', *The Threat of Medicines' Substitution*, Belfast: The Queen's University of Belfast.

— (1995), *Industrial Policy and the Pharmaceutical Industry, The Proceedings of a Symposium held on 22 June 1994, London*, London: Office of Health Economics.

Turner, C. (1986), *Gold on the Green, Fifty Glaxo Years at Greenford*, London: Glaxo Pharmaceuticals Ltd.

Turner, H. (1980), *Henry Wellcome, The Man, His Collection and His Legacy*, London: The Wellcome Trust and Heinemann.

Tweedale, G. (1990), *At the Sign of the Plough, 275 Years of Allen & Hanburys and the British Pharmaceutical Industry 1715–1990*, London: John Murray.

Vagelos, P. R. (1991), 'Are prescription drug prices high?' *Science* 252, 1080–84.

Viner, C. V., Selby, P. J., Zulian, G. B., Gore, M. E., Butcher, M. E., Wootton, C. M., and McElwain, T. J. (1990), 'Ondansetron – a new safe and effective antiemetic in patients receiving high-dose melphalan'. *Cancer Chemotherapy and Pharmacology* 25, 449–53.

Wainwright, M. (1990), *Miracle Cure, The Story of Penicillin and the Golden Age of Antibiotics*, Oxford: Basil Blackwell.

Walton, J. (1998), *Glaxo Wellcome at Ulverston, The First Fifty Years*, Ulverston: Glaxo Wellcome Operations.

Wardell, W. M. (1973), 'Introduction of new therapeutic drugs in the United States and Great Britain: an international comparison'. *Clinical Pharmacology and Therapeutics* 14, 773–90.

—— (1978), 'The drug lag revisited: comparison by the therapeutic area of patterns of drugs marketed in the United States and Great Britain from 1972 through 1976'. *Clinical Pharmacology and Therapeutics* 24, 499–524.

Watson, N. (1994), *Glaxo at Barnard Castle, A Celebration*, Barnard Castle: Glaxo Manufacturing Services.

Weatherall, M. (1990), *In Search of a Cure, A History of Pharmaceutical Discovery*, Oxford: Oxford University Press.

Williams, H. (1990), *Arthur Scrimgeour, The Beginnings of Glaxo in China, A Life recollected by Helen Scrimgeour*, Hong Kong: Glaxo China Enterprises.

Williams, T. I. (1984), *Howard Florey, Penicillin and After*, Oxford: Oxford University Press.

Wilson, A. H. (1954), 'The research department of Courtaulds Limited'. *Proceedings of the Royal Society* B (142), 289–305.

Woodings, E. P., Dixon, G. T., Harrison, C., Carey, P., and Richards, D. A. (1980), 'Ranitidine – a new H_2-receptor antagonist'. *Gut* 21, 187–91.

Young, M. D. (1990), 'Globalisation of the pharmaceutical industry: the physician's role in optimising drug use'. *Journal of Clinical Pharmacology* 30, 990–93.

Zeldis, J. B., Friedman, L. S., and Isselbacher, K. J. (1983), 'Ranitidine: a new H_2-receptor antagonist'. *New England Journal of Medicine* 309, 1368–73.

INDEX

Page numbers in *italics* refer to photographs, tables and organograms in the text.